CIW™ Foundations
Certification Bible

CIW™ Foundations Certification Bible

Keith Olsen and Don Loughran

Hungry Minds™

Best-Selling Books • Digital Downloads • e-Books • Answer Networks • e-Newsletters • Branded Web Sites • e-Learning

New York, NY ✦ Cleveland, OH ✦ Indianapolis, IN

CIW™ Foundations Certification Bible

Published by
Hungry Minds, Inc.
909 Third Avenue
New York, NY 10022
www.hungryminds.com

ISBN: 0-7645-4908-1

Library of Congress Control Number: 2001094151

Printed in the United States of America

10 9 8 7 6 5 4 3 2 1

1P/SQ/QT/QS/IN

Distributed in the United States by Hungry Minds, Inc.

Distributed by CDG Books Canada Inc. for Canada; by Transworld Publishers Limited in the United Kingdom; by IDG Norge Books for Norway; by IDG Sweden Books for Sweden; by IDG Books Australia Publishing Corporation Pty. Ltd. for Australia and New Zealand; by TransQuest Publishers Pte Ltd. for Singapore, Malaysia, Thailand, Indonesia, and Hong Kong; by Gotop Information Inc. for Taiwan; by ICG Muse, Inc. for Japan; by Intersoft for South Africa; by Eyrolles for France; by International Thomson Publishing for Germany, Austria, and Switzerland; by Distribuidora Cuspide for Argentina; by LR International for Brazil; by Galileo Libros for Chile; by Ediciones ZETA S.C.R. Ltda. for Peru; by WS Computer Publishing Corporation, Inc., for the Philippines; by Contemporanea de Ediciones for Venezuela; by Express Computer Distributors for the Caribbean and West Indies; by Micronesia Media Distributor, Inc. for Micronesia; by Chips Computadoras S.A. de C.V. for Mexico; by Editorial Norma de Panama S.A. for Panama; by American Bookshops for Finland.

For general information on Hungry Minds' products and services please contact our Customer Care department within the U.S. at 800-762-2974, outside the U.S. at 317-572-3993 or fax 317-572-4002.

For sales inquiries and reseller information, including discounts, premium and bulk quantity sales, and foreign-language translations, please contact our Customer Care department at 800-434-3422, fax 317-572-4002 or write to Hungry Minds, Inc., Attn: Customer Care Department, 10475 Crosspoint Boulevard, Indianapolis, IN 46256.

For information on licensing foreign or domestic rights, please contact our Sub-Rights Customer Care department at 212-884-5000.

For information on using Hungry Minds' products and services in the classroom or for ordering examination copies, please contact our Educational Sales department at 800-434-2086 or fax 317-572-4005.

For press review copies, author interviews, or other publicity information, please contact our Public Relations department at 317-572-3168 or fax 317-572-4168.

For authorization to photocopy items for corporate, personal, or educational use, please contact Copyright Clearance Center, 222 Rosewood Drive, Danvers, MA 01923, or fax 978-750-4470.

Hungry Minds™ is a trademark of Hungry Minds, Inc.

About the Authors

Keith Olsen is an accomplished networking professional from Winnipeg Manitoba Canada. His many certifications include Microsoft Certified Systems Engineer (MCSE), Microsoft Certified Trainer (MCT), Certified Netware Engineer (CNE), Certified Netware Instructor (CNI), Certified Internet Webmaster Security Professional (CIWSP), and Certified Internet Webmaster-Certified Instructor (CIWCI). Keith currently works as a technical instructor for PBSC (a division of IBM), one of Canada's largest technical training centers, where he teaches Microsoft, Novell, and Certified Internet Webmaster certified courseware. When he's not working, Keith loves to spend quality time with his wife, Catherine, and his children, Kaleigh, Alexander, and Ashley. You can contact Keith at `ksolsen@hotmail.com`.

Don Loughran is a full-time technical instructor with Polar Bear Corporate Education Solutions and has been working in the microcomputer industry since 1980. His many certifications include CIW Certified Instructor, Certified Netware Engineer and Instructor, Microsoft Certified Systems Engineer and Developer, Microsoft Certified Trainer, Sun Certified Java Programmer, and Comptia A+ Certified Technician. Most of his time is spent in technical course delivery and custom course development, but he still finds time to develop software for Web-based and traditional applications.

Credits

Acquisitions Editor
Melody Layne

Project Editor
Marcia Brochin

Technical Editor
Robert J. Shimonski
Glen Clarke

Development Editor
Kevin Kent

Copy Editors
Rebekah Mancilla
Kala Schrager

Contributing Writer
Robert J. Shimonski

Editorial Manager
Ami Sullivan

Permissions Editor
Carmen Krikorian

Media Editor
Angela Denny

**Vice President and Executive
Group Publisher**
Richard Swadley

**Vice President and
Executive Publisher**
Bob Ipsen

Vice President and Publisher
Joseph B. Wikert

Editorial Director
Mary Bednarek

Project Coordinator
Jennifer Bingham

Graphics and Production Specialists
Joyce Haughey
Heather Pope
Betty Schulte

Quality Control Technicians
John Greenough
Marianne Santy
Charles Spencer

Proofreading
TECHBOOKS Production Services

Indexer
Liz Cunningham

Preface

The ever-changing face of the information technology field is a key challenge. It seems that as soon as you learn and become proficient in any aspect of technology, you must start the process anew for fear of becoming outdated. Most employers are well aware of this fact, and look for employees who can meet this challenge. They need employees who are willing to learn, adapt, and apply knowledge. Getting certified is your proof of knowledge.

About You, CIW Foundations, and This Book

The primary goal of this book is to prepare you for the Certified Internet Webmaster (CIW) Foundations exam (1D0-410) to earn you the Certified International Webmaster Associate designation. Throughout its 18 chapters, this book will present you with valuable information directly related to the CIW Foundations exam and its corresponding objectives. This book supplies this information in a format that is both easy to understand for the beginner and comprehensive enough to be useful as a resource beyond the scope of the exam for all networking professionals. This book serves as an excellent resource for those wishing to supplement an instructor-led training course or for those interested in an all-encompassing self-study guide.

The CIW Foundations curriculum is designed to give you a foundation of knowledge in the world of computer networking, the Internet, and Web page development. This knowledge and the corresponding CIW Foundations exam form the basic prerequisite for all of the Certified Internet Webmaster courses and certifications. Because the subject matter is truly meant to supply the basics, very little background in computers or networking is required. I recommend, however, that you be familiar with basic operations knowledge of one of Microsoft's Windows-based operating systems (Windows 95, 98, ME, XT, 2000, or XP).

Will you know all there is to know about networking after reading this book? No. Will you be considered among the elite of the high-tech professionals after reading this book and passing the exam? Not yet, but you will be well on your way.

What You Will Need

It is possible to read this book, memorize its contents, and pass the exam with out ever touching a computer. This approach, however, is not recommended. To truly benefit from the lab exercises and to access the many supplied resources, you should have access to a Windows 95, 98, ME, 2000, or XP-based computer with a CR-ROM and an Internet connection.

How This Book Is Organized

The organization of this book reflects the organization of the CIW Foundations exam. It has been broken up into the following four parts:

+ **Internet Fundamentals:** Chapters 1 through 7

+ **Fundamentals of Web Authoring:** Chapters 8 through 11

+ **Network Fundamentals:** Chapters 12 through 18

+ **Appendixes:** A through F

The following is a brief overview of the various parts of the book.

Part I: Internet Fundamentals

The goal of this section is to introduce you to the basic concepts required to effectively use and understand the Internet today. Forty percent of the CIW Foundations exam (24 of 60 scored questions) focuses on the concepts presented in these chapters.

Topics include the following:

+ **Introduction to the Internet (Chapter 1):** General overview of the Internet, Internet Service Providers, protocols, the Domain Name System, and Uniform Resource Locators (URLs).

+ **Viewing the Internet (Chapter 2):** An introduction to viewing the World Wide Web through the use of a Web browser client.

+ **Additional Internet Services (Chapter 3):** A look at additional Internet services, such as e-mail, mailing lists, newsgroups, File Transfer Protocol (FTP), and telnet.

+ **Understanding Internet Search Engines (Chapter 4):** The basics of locating information on the Internet through the use of Internet search engines.

✦ **Embedded Objects and Browser Plug-ins (Chapter 5):** A look at various technologies used to enhance and complement Web pages. Topics include ActiveX, Java, and a variety of Web browser plug-ins.

✦ **Internet Security Issues (Chapter 6):** An introduction to security-related issues concerning data transmission and privacy on the Internet.

✦ **Introduction to Electronic Commerce (Chapter 7):** Definitions, concepts, and issues concerning using the Internet to conduct business transactions.

Part II: Fundamentals of Web Authoring

This section presents essential information regarding the process of Web page authoring. Twenty percent (12 of 60 questions) of the CIW Foundations exam focuses on the following topics:

✦ **Web Page Authoring Basics (Chapter 8):** A general overview of Web page construction. This includes information on HTML editors, HTML history, HTML standards, XHTML, XML, and general Web page design considerations.

✦ **HTML Basics (Chapter 9):** A beginner's look at Hypertext Markup Language structure and syntax.

✦ **Intermediate HTML (Chapter 10):** A discussion on creating commonly used Web page elements, such as hyperlinks, tables and Web forms.

✦ **Advanced HTML (Chapter 11):** Advanced HTML concepts such as image maps, Animated GIFs, Frames, and HTML extensions.

Part III: Network Fundamentals

The focus of this section of the book is on basic networking concepts. Although there is some overlap with concepts presented in Part I, the thrust of these chapters is on general networking concepts and how they apply to all networks (not just the Internet). Forty percent (24 of 60 questions) of the CIW Foundations exam focuses on the following topics:

✦ **The Basics of Networking (Chapter 12):** An overview of the fundamental concepts found in networking today. These concepts include network models, network architectures, network topologies, and network operating systems.

✦ **Internetworking Concepts (Chapter 13):** This chapter presents topics related to the issues, technologies, and standards used to interconnect networks and networking systems.

✦ **Introduction to Local and Wide Area Networks (Chapter 14):** Building on the information presented in chapter 13, this chapter discusses technologies used to form Local and Wide Area networks.

✦ **Understanding TCP/IP (Chapter 15):** Introduction to the structure and inner workings of the "language of the Internet," the Transmission Control Protocol/Internet Protocol suite.

✦ **Servers in a TCP/IP Internetwork (Chapter 16):** An overview of server services offered in TCP/IP-based networks. This discussion Includes Web, proxy, caching, mirror, mail, FTP, news, media, certificate, directory, catalog, transaction, and DNS server services.

✦ **Extending Web Server Abilities (Chapter 17):** This chapter is a look at some of the technologies involved in enhancing the abilities of a Web server, including client- and server-side scripting, HTTP gateways, Common Gateway Interface (CGI), HTML form processing, server programming interfaces, Java servlets, and an overview of Web server database connectivity.

✦ **Introduction to Network Security (Chapter 18):** A discussion of general security issues with regards to networks. Topics include security auditing, security polices, threats, attacks, and methods and technologies used to protect against security violations.

Appendixes

Information presented in the appendixes provides additional resource information intended to supplement the concepts and topics presented throughout the book. The following appendixes are provided:

✦ **What's on the CD-ROM? (Appendix A):** Describes the content found on the CD-ROM that accompanies the book.

✦ **Objective Mapping Matrix (Appendix B):** A complete listing of the CIW Foundations exam objectives and the location in the book where they are addressed.

✦ **Sample Exam (Appendix C):** Test yourself with this sample exam that closely simulates the length, scope, and format of the real thing (answers and explanations included).

✦ **Exam-Taking Tips (Appendix D):** Essential tips and notes for the CIW Foundations exam.

✦ **HTML 4.01 Elements and Attributes (Appendix E):** This appendix is a table of common HTML elements and their associated attributes.

✦ **Overview of the CIW Certification Tracks (Appendix F):** This appendix discusses the various certification tracks for which the CIW Foundations exam is a prerequisite.

Chapter Structure

With the exception of the appendixes, each chapter has been laid out in a specific order to help assist you in preparing for the CIW Foundations Exam. The following bullet points describe the chapter structure:

✦ **Exam Objectives:** This section outlines the exam objectives covered in the chapter.

✦ **Chapter Pre-Test:** Presents a list of questions relating to the concepts presented within the chapter. These questions are provided as a measure of your existing understanding of the concepts presented within the chapter. Answers are provided in the Study Guide at the end of the chapter.

✦ **Main chapter body:** The actual topics of the chapter.

✦ **Key Point Summary:** This summary provides a review of the key points presented in the chapter. This can serve as an excellent last minute review prior to taking the exam.

✦ **Study Guide:** This guide presents practical lab exercises and questions to supplement and reinforce the information presented in the chapter. The study guide is further broken down into several sections as follows:

- **Assessment Questions:** Found in the Study Guide of all chapters, this section presents several questions covering the exam objectives. These questions are given in a format similar to the format found on the actual exam.

- **Scenarios:** This section presents critical-thinking questions designed to test your full understanding of key concepts presented within the chapter.

- **Lab Exercises:** These are hands-on exercises designed to reinforce many of the concepts presented within the chapter.

- **Answers:** Answers for all questions presented within the chapter, including the Chapter Pre-Test, Assessment Questions, and Scenario questions and Lab Exercise questions (when required).

✦ **Resources:** A listing of additional resources appears at the end of some of the chapters to supplement the information presented.

Icons Used In This Book

As you read through this book you will encounter several icons that provide you with additional information with respect to the concepts presented. The icons you will encounter appear as follows:

 A Caution icon advises you to take special care when performing a task or step, as damage to your hardware or software may result.

 A Cross Reference icon is used to indicate an additional location in the book that contains information relevant to the concept being discussed.

 This icon is used at the beginning of a chapter section that directly addresses concepts required to meet an exam objective.

 An Exam Tip icon alerts you to a concept or fact that has a high probability of being on the exam.

 This icon is used to present information that is relevant in the real world but doesn't directly apply to exam objectives.

 The Tip icon often presents short cuts for performing a particular task.

Contents at a Glance

Contents

· ·

Chapter 9: HTML Basics **301**

Chapter 10: Intermediate HTML **367**

Chapter 11: Advanced HTML **415**

Part III: Network Fundamentals 469

Chapter 12: The Basics of Networking 471

Chapter 17: Extending Web Server Abilities 681

Chapter 18: Introduction to Network Security 723

Internet Fundamentals

This part introduces you to the basic concepts required to effectively use and understand the Internet today.

Introduction to the Internet

EXAM OBJECTIVES

1. Trace the evolution of the Internet.

2. Explain the elements required to connect an Internet client to the Internet.

3. Describe how the client/server model functions on the Internet.

4. Describe push and pull technology.

5. Define TCP/IP and state how the Internet uses it.

6. Identify and describe major Internet protocols such as Hypertext Transfer Protocol (HTTP), e-mail, File Transfer Protocol (FTP), and newsgroups.

7. List several criteria for selecting an ISP.

8. Explain domain names and virtual domains.

9. Describe the functions of the ICANN and the InterNIC.

10. Identify the purpose and function of Uniform Resource Locators (URLs).

11. Describe the difference between the Internet, Intranets, and Extranets.

CHAPTER PRE-TEST

1. What was the name given to the first network to offer multiple connections between hosts?

2. What type of device determines the path that data will take over the Internet?

3. What three elements are required when the client/server model is used on a network?

4. True or False: Push technology refers to a client pushing requests for data to a server.

5. Name the six elements required to support an Internet client.

6. What is the common name for an organization that provides access to the Internet?

7. True or False: DSL is an example of a dial-up Internet connection.

8. What protocol is typically used to transfer files across the Internet?

9. What type of application is typically associated with SMTP, POP3, and IMAP?

10. What do the letters "fr" represent in the FQDN `www.poulet.fr`?

11. What does the "www" represent in the FQDN `www.poulet.fr`?

12. What organization is responsible for the domain name system management on the Internet?

13. What is the term used to refer to a domain name that is registered by one company but whose Web servers are maintained by another, such as a third party ISP?

14. Which prefix is typically used at the beginning of a Web page URL?

15. A Web site that limits access to select individuals, such as customers, is referred to as a _____.

✦ Answers to these questions can be found at the end of the chapter. ✦

Thishis chapter describes some of the most basic concepts and features of the Internet. After you have completed this chapter, you should have a basic understanding of the following Internet-related concepts:

✦ A history of the Internet

✦ Basic Internet functionality

✦ Client/server interactions

✦ TCP/IP

✦ Accessing the Internet

✦ The domain name system

✦ URLs

✦ Intranets

✦ Extranets

History of the Internet

 Trace the evolution of the Internet.

Although many people only became aware of the Internet within the past ten years or so, its roots can be traced back to the early 1960s. In 1962, at the height of the Cold War, the U.S. Air Force commissioned the RAND Corporation to do a study on how it could maintain command and control over its missiles and bombers after a nuclear attack. In other words, they desired a communication network that could continue to function—even if any single component in the network was lost.

After almost two years of study, RAND employee Paul Baran submitted what became known as the *RAND proposal*. In his proposal, Baran envisioned a network that would have no central authority, meaning that no one location or computer would serve as either the heart or the brain for the entire communications network. Baran's goal was to eliminate a single point of failure or weakness. To this end, Baran suggested that the network be designed with multiple data paths to provide fault tolerance should any one path suffer a failure. This redundancy would allow data to be redirected through a different route to successfully arrive at its final destination.

Crucial to Baran's network design was the concept of *packet switching*. Rather than sending data to another computer in one continuous stream, Baran's idea was to break the large stream of data into small chunks known as *packets*. Each packet contains a destination address, a source address, and reassembly information. When transmitting data, each packet is treated independently of all other packets. As each data packet travels through the network, decisions can be made automatically based on the best route for getting the packet to its destination. Route choices can change due to conditions such as network traffic or link availability. Essentially, each packet sent from one machine to another could travel a completely different path, as shown in Figure 1-1.

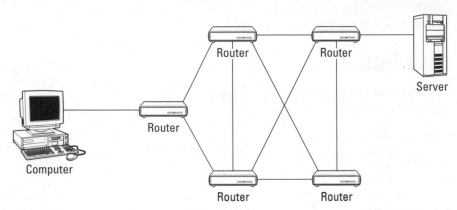

Figure 1-1: Data traveling in a packet-switching network

In his proposal, Rand cited several benefits to using packet-switching technology, including the following:

- ✦ **Error Recovery** — When a packet fails to arrive at a destination, the missing packet can be resent without resending the entire message.

- ✦ **Traffic optimization** — Data can be routed over the best route at a given moment, which can improve communication speeds.

- ✦ **No single point of failure** — Allows for the creation of a reliable network that can continue to function, regardless of host failure.

ARPANET

In 1968, the U.S. Department of Defense's Advanced Research Project Agency (ARPA, and later, DARPA) tested Rand's network principles and funded the first packet-switched based network: ARPANET. Originally, ARPANET was an interconnection of four main nodes. These nodes consisted of the University of California at Los Angeles, SRI in Stanford, the University of California at Santa Barbara, and the University of Utah. The primary function of this network was to provide access to research information for both university and government engineers.

NSFnet

ARPANET remained in existence until 1989 when the Department of Defense decommissioned it and transferred all of its sites to the National Science Foundation (NSF), forming a network called *NSFnet*. NSFnet became a network of other networks linking the government, the military, universities, and businesses. NSFnet was later interconnected with thousands of networks throughout the world, creating what is now known as the Internet.

Internet Functionality

 Explain the elements required to connect an Internet Client to the Internet.

The Internet, or the "Net" as it is commonly called, is a publicly accessible interconnected system of networks that spans the globe. This network of networks gives users and organizations throughout the world the ability to share and distribute information in a vast array of electronic formats, including electronic mail, Web pages, audio, and video. Six key elements are required to actively participate as a client on the Internet:

✦ **Internet-capable computer** — Most often, this is simply a personal computer (PC), but many additional devices can serve as Internet clients, including cellular phones and hand-held personal data assistants (PDAs). The device must include some way to connect to a network. For a PC, this connectivity requires devices such as a network adapter card (also known as a network Interface card) or a modem.

✦ **Operating system** — The client device requires some form of network-aware operating system (OS). Almost all modern operating systems have the ability to support Internet connectivity. The most common OSs include the following:

  • Microsoft Windows 95/98/ME/NT/2000 and XP

  • Linux

  • UNIX

  • Apple Macintosh OS X

  • Novell Netware

✦ **TCP/IP** — In simple terms, TCP/IP is software that supplies your computer with a language that it can use to communicate with other computers on the Internet. It defines communication rules that devices and Internet applications must follow to communicate with each other. All current versions of the operating systems mentioned in the previous point support the use of TCP/IP. With most systems, TCP/IP is installed by default when the operating system is configured with networking support.

✦ **Internet address** — Similar in concept to a mailing address for a house, all computers participating on the Internet require a valid, globally unique Internet address. When accessing a resource on the Internet, such as a Web server, the address of the resource must be known.

✦ **Client software** — Any software that can interact with network-available services is considered a *client*. On the Internet, typical client software includes Web browsers, e-mail programs, instant messaging clients, newsreaders, and so on.

✦ **Internet connection** — A connection to an Internet service provider (ISP) is required. This connection can be available either through a direct connection or dial-up.

The remainder of this chapter focuses on topics to help you better understand the remaining four critical elements.

Client/Server Computing on the Internet

 Describe how the client/server model functions on the Internet.

The Internet, for the most part, is based on the client/server model of networking. This model is comprised of three key elements: a client, a server, and a network connecting the two.

Client

A client application is software that typically runs on an end user's computer. Client software allows a computer to access server resources on a network. Client software allows Internet activities, such as Web browsing, file downloads, e-mail access, game playing, and so on. A single computer can run many client applications simultaneously. For example, a user can listen to an Internet radio broadcast while downloading music files and chatting online with friends; each of these activities will likely require a different client application. A good example of client software would be Microsoft's Internet Explorer, a commonly used Web browser client application.

Server

A server application is software that provides access to resources for clients. For example, Web server software stores and distributes Web pages for use by client software, such as a Web browser.

Many of the benefits offered by the client/server model of networking are due to its distributed processing nature. In a client/server network, the task of computing data is typically shared between both the client and server. The client software is generally responsible for providing a user interface (the display that you see on the monitor), for controlling how data is presented to the user, and for interpreting the user's interactions, such as keystrokes, mouse movements, etc. The server typically processes requests from the client software, but is not directly concerned with user interaction. This separation of duties allows you to use less powerful (and less expensive) computers to act as servers than were formerly required.

See Chapter 12 for more information regarding the benefits of Client/Server computing.

Using Web browser client software, such as Microsoft Internet Explorer, is an example of this distributed processing. When you visit a site on the Internet using your Web browser, your browser requests the page from the Web server. The Web server sends your browser a document describing how to display the required page. It is then up to your browser to actually interpret this document and display this information for you on the screen. As you view the document, you may scroll down the page or click a link. These actions are interpreted by your browser — and not by the server. If the browser determines that you are requesting additional information that it does not have, it will request that data from the server.

Using Web browser software is covered in detail in Chapter 2.

Client/server push and pull interactions

 Describe push and pull technology.

Client and server interactions typically use one of two types of communication technologies: pull or push.

Pull technology

Pull technology describes an interaction in which data is sent to a client only after it has been requested by that client, as shown in Figure 1-2. Client E-mail retrieval, for example, is often implemented by using a pull technology. Servers pass e-mail messages back to clients only when the clients have actually requested them. In other words, the client pulls the data from the server.

Send me my e-mail please!

Ok here it is

Figure 1-2: Pull technology is used when data is only received after it has been requested.

Push technology

Push technology describes an interaction in which a server sends data to a client without the client making a specific request for it. In other words, the server pushes data to the client. For example, many people have news information pushed to their computers. In this case, servers regularly send their computer stock price updates, weather information, sports scores, and breaking news stories. An illustration of this process is shown in Figure 1-3.

Figure 1-3: A server using push technology will send data to a client without a request.

Note   Microsoft Active Channels, which are found in Internet Explorer 4.0 and later versions, is an example of push technology.

TCP/IP

Objective   Define TCP/IP and state how the Internet uses it.

In any form of communication, both parties must follow certain rules to ensure that the communication is understandable. Various languages provide those rules for human beings. Each language defines words and a structure for combining those words. When two people want to communicate with each other, they must select a common language. These same concepts are also true for computers. Computers use protocols rather than languages to communicate with each other. These protocols define rules and the structure for network communication. As with human languages, a vast array of protocols is available, and as a result, computers and applications that want to communicate across a network must share a common suite of protocols. The suite of protocols chosen for communication across the Internet is Transmission Control Protocol/Internet Protocol (TCP/IP).

Typically implemented as software, TCP/IP provides the mechanisms that allow applications and computers to communicate over a distributed network, such as the Internet. All devices that need to communicate on the Internet must be configured with this suite of protocols.

Cross-Reference   This chapter presents only a brief overview of TCP/IP and its features. See Chapter 15 for more detailed information.

IP addresses

Remember that the Internet is a huge Internetwork of computers spread throughout the world. For communication to occur between any two computers across this Internetwork, they must be able to find each other quickly and efficiently. To aid in this task, each device that utilizes the Internet is assigned a unique Internet Protocol (IP) address. Much like your home address can identify where your house is located in the world, an IP address can identify where your computer is located on the Internet. When one computer needs to send data to another computer on the Internet, the sending computer's TCP/IP software divides the data into packets, labels each packet with both a source and destination address, and selects and sends the packets down an appropriate path (or route) to get them to their destination.

If the sending computer realizes that the destination happens to reside in the same network, it will deliver the packet directly to the destination. If the sending computer determines that the destination is not on the same network, it will send the data to a device known as a *router*. The router examines the destination IP address information, determines the appropriate path to the destination, and forwards the packet down that path.

 Cross-Reference See Chapter 14 for more information on routers and Chapter 15 for specific information regarding routing in a TCP/IP environment.

A device's IP address is typically represented by a *dotted quad notation*, which is a series of four numbers separated by dots (periods), such as the following:

```
192.168.220.45
```

 In the Real World The term "dotted quad" notation is used because it is in the official CIW foundations course material, most individuals refer to this notation however as "dotted decimal."

Each of the four numbers can range from 0 to 255. The significance of these numbers is that they each represent eight bits (binary digits) of a computer's complete 32-bit IP address.

 Note A *bit* is a binary (or base 2) digit and is the smallest unit of data in a computer. These binary digits can be either a one or a zero.

Roughly four billion dotted quad notation addresses are possible. This may seem like a large number but, in truth, relatively few are still available and the Internet is in serious danger of running out. This fact has led to the development of a new TCP/IP addressing scheme known as IPv6 (the current standard is IPv4). With IPv6, addresses are 128 bits in length, which allows for several trillion addresses. The following is an example of an IPv6 address written in hexadecimal format:

```
3A4A:0101:5F1E:11B1:C111:86E0:1CC2:EC12
```

Although not widely implemented yet, IPv6 is being used more and more. It is expected to be widely implemented somewhere between 2005 and 2015.

Common Internet protocols

Identify and describe major Internet protocols such as Hypertext Transfer Protocol (HTTP), e-mail, File Transfer Protocol, and newsgroups.

Recall that protocols define the rules that clients and servers use to communicate over a network. TCP/IP includes several protocols that provide connectivity between client and server applications. The following sections discuss some of the more common applications and their associated protocols currently being used on the Internet.

Hypertext Transfer Protocol

One of the most common protocols currently being used on the Internet is the Hypertext Transfer Protocol (HTTP). The role of HTTP is to allow HTTP clients, such as Web browsers, to request and receive hypertext-based documents (Web pages) from HTTP servers (also known as Web servers).

HTTP servers and clients form the basis for the World Wide Web (or "the Web" as it is more commonly called). Contrary to popular belief, the Internet and the Web are not the same thing. The Web is merely a set of programs that uses the Internet to communicate.

You can find further discussion on the World Wide Web in Chapter 2 and further information on HTTP in Chapter 15.

File Transfer Protocol

As its name suggests, File Transfer Protocol (FTP) is used to transfer files. More specifically, it is used to transfer files between FTP clients and FTP server applications. If you have ever had the opportunity to download software or other files from the Internet, you were probably using the FTP protocol. A considerable number of FTP sites on the Internet allow you to download files and programs, others allow you to upload files from your computer to the server, and still others allow both downloading and uploading of files.

Downloading typically refers to the transferring of files from a server to a client, whereas uploading refers to the transferring of files from a client to a server.

To access the services of an FTP site, you may be required to provide a valid user-name and password. These are required to prevent unauthorized access to the information stored on the server. A great many of these sites, however, do provide *anonymous access*, meaning that you are allowed to access all or part of the FTP site without having to provide an authorized name or password. If prompted for one, you typically enter the name "anonymous" and provide your e-mail address as your password.

In the Real World Although you are supposed to give your e-mail address as a password, most people prefer not to because it might lead to unwanted junk e-mail (often referred to as spam).

Anonymous access is generally used when an organization wants to provide an FTP service for anyone who wants to use it. Figure 1-4 shows the dialog box presented for anonymous login when you access an FTP site using Microsoft Internet Explorer.

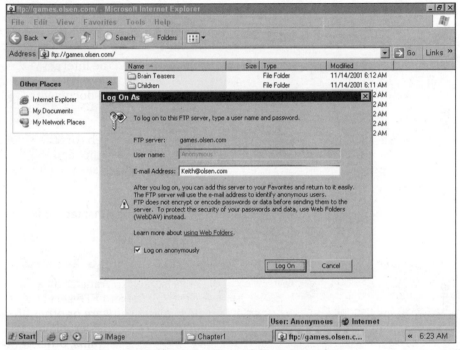

Figure 1-4: Anonymous FTP login in Microsoft Internet Explorer

Cross-Reference See Chapter 3 for more information about using FTP.

Electronic mail protocols

A very large portion of Internet traffic is dedicated to the sending and receiving of electronic mail (e-mail). Internet e-mail functionality is typically provided by the following three protocols:

✦ Post Office Protocol (POP)

✦ Internet Message Access Protocol (IMAP)

✦ Simple Mail Transfer Protocol (SMTP)

The first two, POP and the more feature-rich IMAP, allow clients to download mail from a mail server. Clients typically use SMTP to send mail. When setting up an e-mail client application, such as Microsoft Outlook Express, you must provide an address for both the POP or IMAP server and the SMTP server, as shown in Figure 1-5.

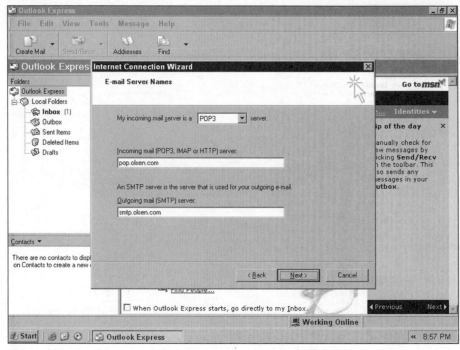

Figure 1-5: Configuring Outlook Express for Internet mail

Telnet

Telnet is a protocol used to support terminal emulation sessions from a client to a server. Through a telnet session, clients can log on to a remote telnet server computer and carry out commands as if they were sitting at the physical location of the server or at a terminal directly controlled by that server. Administrators also commonly use telnet to remotely manage network devices, such as routers and servers.

Figure 1-6 depicts a telnet client running on Windows 98 and being used to connect to a Linux server for remote administration purposes.

Network News Transfer Protocol

Network News Transfer Protocol (NNTP) is the protocol used to post, read, and distribute USENET news articles. USENET is a worldwide bulletin board system that was originally developed as an alternative to the Internet, but was eventually incorporated into it. USENET contains literally thousands of discussion-type bulletin boards, which are referred to as *newsgroups,* covering many topics from business to entertainment. Using an NNTP client application, users can read and contribute articles on the bulletin boards of their choosing.

Figure 1-6: Using a Telnet client for remote administration

Gopher

Gopher is a system and protocol developed by the University of Minnesota for organizing and displaying information in a text-based format over a network like the Internet. Using Gopher over the Internet allows people to search for and find information almost anywhere in the world in a fairly easy-to-use, hierarchical, menu-driven fashion. Although Gopher was one of the first Internet services to provide this sort of flexibility, its use in the past few years has greatly diminished due to the popularity and ease of use of the HTTP-based Web servers.

Accessing the Internet

The following sections give a brief overview of Internet Service Providers and the connection types available to access their services.

Internet Service Providers

List several criteria for selecting an ISP.

As previously stated, one of the key elements required to access the Internet is a connection to an Internet Service Provider or (ISP). An ISP is a company or organization that provides access to the Internet to individuals, other organizations, or both. Figure 1-7 shows the positioning of ISPs in relation to the Internet and its customers.

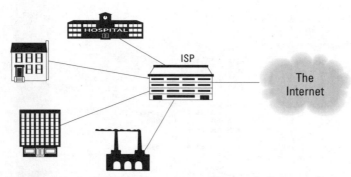

Figure 1-7: An ISP provides a connection to the Internet for its customers.

You have many ISPs to choose from; some ISPs, such as Microsoft Network (www.msn.com), Prodigy (www.prodigy.com), and America Online (www.aol.com), offer an extensive amount of online services. This type of ISP (often called an *online service*) provides not only access to the Internet, but also many other services, including the following:

- ✦ E-mail addresses
- ✦ Instant messaging
- ✦ Chat rooms
- ✦ Access to members-only feature pages
- ✦ Internet content search
- ✦ Content filtering

These online services typically charge a flat monthly or yearly rate, based on expected use and anticipated number of online hours per month. Additional charges will result if a user connects for more hours than are covered by the flat rate.

Many other regional and national ISPs offer Internet connectivity without the extensive features provided by the online services. These ISPs include most regional phone companies (such as AT&T, Sprint, and Bell), cable television companies, and dedicated Internet Service Providers. Similar to the online services, most of these companies charge a monthly flat rate for service; however, several services, such as NetZero (`www.netzero.com`) and Address.com (`www.address.com`), offer a free Internet connection.

In the Real World   Although these so-called free ISPs don't charge you money, they do come at a price. Most of them place a banner advertisement window into your Web browser. This banner window constantly displays advertisements that are paid for by the service's sponsors.

Internet connection types

Most ISPs now offer two main ways for customers to connect to the Internet: dial-up or direct. The type of connection depends on many factors, including cost, speed, and availability. Generally, however, the greater the speed and availability, the greater the cost.

Dial-up Internet connections

When using a dial-up connection, Internet access is provided through the use of a modem. A *modem* allows a computer to connect to the ISP through an ordinary analog phone line, or in some cases, through an Integrated Services Digital (ISDN) phone line.

Cross-Reference   Further explanations regarding dial-up connections and the associated hard technologies are included in Chapter 14.

Dial-up connections are generally considered "on-demand" connections because users connect to the Internet at the time they want to communicate. When they are finished, they disconnect. In other words, these users don't establish a permanent connection.

Connection speeds are a measure of the total bits of data that can flow through a connection over a given time—typically in seconds—so the measurement is bits per second (bps). Connections that transfer data in the thousands of bits per second are typically written as kilobits per second (Kbps); millions of bits per second is megabits per second (mbps); and billions of bits per second is written as gigabits per second (Gbps).

Exam Tip   Become familiar with these speed measurements and their abbreviations.

The speed of a dial-up connection is primarily dependent on the speed of the modem. Table 1-1 shows typical speeds available over a dial-up connection.

Table 1-1
Common Dial-up Connection Speeds

Speed	Description
28.8 Kbps	During the mid-1990s, this was considered fairly high speed. Many home users still use this speed today. Today, this speed is considered to be slow.
33.6 Kbps	Although still slow by today's standards, this connection speed does offer a moderate improvement over 28.8Kbps. Note that the official CIW curriculum lists this speed as moderately fast.
56 Kbps	For analog phone lines, this is the fastest dial-up speed available and represents the current standard found when purchasing a modem today.
64 Kbps	This is the speed generally obtained from a single channel ISDN connection across a digital phone line.
128 Kbps	This is a fairly common speed obtained by combining two 64-Kbps ISDN channels.

Two protocols are commonly used to transmit network data over a dial-up connection; they are Serial Line Internet Protocol (SLIP) and Point to Point Protocol (PPP). SLIP is an older protocol that lacks some of the more modern features that are supported by the now more popular PPP. The features that PPP supports that SLIP does not support include the following:

✦ **Multiple protocol suite support** — PPP supports many network protocols, such as TCP/IP, NetBEUI, and IPX/SPX; SLIP supports only TCP/IP.

✦ **User Authentication** — PPP supports the use of user IDs and passwords to identify and limit a user's ability to use the connection.

✦ **TCP/IP dynamic configuration** — With PPP, a client computer doesn't need to be manually assigned IP address information. This information can be dynamically obtained at dial-up.

✦ **Improved error control** — PPP supports much more extensive error checking and error recoverability.

 Exam Tip The CIW Foundations official curriculum only lists the first two of these PPP features. The remaining two are provided for your information only.

Direct Internet connections

Direct connections are typically characterized by two main features: they are continuous and high speed. Organizations that want to have an Internet presence or that require Internet connectivity for their employees will usually choose this type of connection.

Several types of direct connections are available, and of these, the CIW Foundations Exam focuses on the following:

✦ Local Area Network (LAN) connections

✦ Digital Subscriber Lines (DSL)

✦ Cable connection

LAN connections

In this type of connection, a local area network (LAN) is connected to the Internet through the use of a *router*. The router is connected both to the LAN and through a high-speed line to a router at the ISP. Figure 1-8 demonstrates this arrangement.

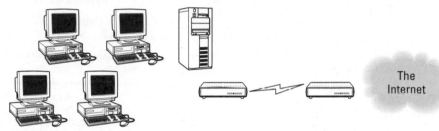

The
Internet

Figure 1-8: A router and a high-speed line connecting to an ISP

In the Real World Although the term "LAN connections" is used in the official CIW Foundations course material, the term most often used for this type of connection is "Dedicated Point to Point WAN Connections."

LAN connections typically charge on a monthly basis with prices ranging from a few hundred dollars a month to many thousands of dollars — depending on the needs of the organization. Speeds offered by this type of service typically range between 64Kbps and several hundred Mbps — again, depending on the type of connection desired.

Cross-Reference See Chapter 15 for a discussion of the various LAN connection types and their associated speeds.

Cable modem connections

This technology uses a *cable modem* to provide a computer with a high-speed Internet connection over cable TV lines. Many cable TV providers have now entered the ISP business by upgrading their infrastructure to support this type of connection. For those people who currently subscribe to cable TV, this method can be a very cost-effective way of getting a high-speed data connection because many providers bundle the two services together at fairly attractive prices. Cable modems can support speeds between 512Kbps and 52 Mbps; however, speeds may be slower than this range, depending on network conditions and service provider capabilities.

Digital Subscriber Lines

Digital Subscriber Lines (DSL) is a technology used to bring high-speed data transmission over copper-based digital telephone lines. DSL may require the installation of a digital telephone line, a DSL modem, and the installation of an Ethernet network card for the computer. This technology is typically offered through telecommunications companies and is expected to replace ISDN. With speeds ranging from 512 Kbps to 10 Mbps, many telecommunications companies are positioning DSL as an alternative to cable modems.

The Domain Name System

 Explain Domain names and virtual domains.

Recall that both your computer and the computers that you want to access on the Internet require unique IP addresses. For example, when you want to obtain information from a Web site, you must provide your Web browser with the IP address of the site. Considering that the Internet is comprised of millions of sites and has potentially billions of available addresses, finding these addresses and remembering them can be a challenging task. To ease this burden, the Domain Name System (DNS) has been developed to allow users to identify servers with easy-to-remember names instead of hard-to-remember IP addresses.

For example, if you want to access the homepage for Hungry Minds, Inc., you can open your Web browser and type `205.200.78.71` into its address bar.

Your browser should display the desired home page. To try another way to access this home page, type `www.hungryminds.com`.

If you need to access this Web page next week, which of these two addresses will you probably remember? If you are like most people, you're going to remember the name because meaningful names are much easier to recall than seemingly random sets of numbers.

DNS is both a TCP/IP protocol and a service whose primary job is to translate names into IP addresses and vice-versa. DNS enables you to use human-friendly names. To understand how DNS works, you must be familiar with how the names are constructed.

Fully qualified domain names

The names used to contact computers on the Internet are referred to as *fully qualified domain names* (FQDNs). FQDNs are written as three or more labels that consist of letters and numbers, separated by periods. The FQDN for the Hungry Minds, Inc. Web server, for example, is `www.hungryminds.com`. FQDNs are comprised of two component parts: The first is a host name and the second is a domain name.

Host name

The first part of any FQDN is its *host name*. The host name is simply the name given to the actual computer.

Organizations typically give meaningful host names to computers to indicate their role. For example, the host name `www` is often given to a Web server, `mail` is often used to indicate a mail server, and the host name `ftp` often indicates an FTP server.

Domain name

The second part of an FQDN is the *domain name*. The domain name is the remainder of the FQDN following the host name.

The domain name uniquely identifies an organization on the Internet. After a domain name has been assigned, no other organization may use it. The domains themselves are usually divided into two components: The registered domain name and the domain category (also referred to as a top-level domain).

Registered domain name

The registered domain name typically matches the owner's organization name, or — as is often the case — is simply a name meant to reflect the content of the Web site. For example, the Web site, `www.garden.com`, uses the name "garden" to tell the world that this site is dedicated to gardening.

An organization can also choose to subdivide a registered domain name. In fact, many companies subdivide a domain name by location, function, or department. For example, the customer support department of the ACME Anvil Company may use the registered domain name, `support.acme.com`, whereas its sales department may use `sales.acme.com`.

Top-Level domain

Top-level domains (TLDs) are used to organize domains into logical groupings. These groupings represent organizations within geographic locations (usually by country) or they represent organization type; for example, the .com TLD has been set aside for commercial organizations.

The geographic groupings are easily recognizable by their two-letter country codes. Table 1-2 shows examples of various country codes and the regions that they represent.

Table 1-2
Top Level Internet Domains Country Codes

Top Level Domain	Region
.au	Australia
.ca	Canada
.ch	Switzerland
.fr	France
.mx	Mexico
.uk	United Kingdom
.us	United States

Exam Tip   Although well over 200 country codes are in existence, memorizing the above chart should be sufficient for the exam.

Many regions support additional category groupings within their top-level domain. For example, Canadians often specify a province along with their country code. The Manitoba Theatre Centre in Winnipeg, Manitoba, Canada uses the FQDN, `www.mtc.mb.ca`. The `.mb` in this case is a second-level domain representing the province of Manitoba.

Note   In the previous example, the registered organization name "mtc" moves one position to the left.

Table 1-3 lists the original non-country code top-level domains and what they represent, categorized by purpose:

Table 1-3
Organization type Top Level Internet Domains

Top Level Domain	Purpose
.com	Commercial organization
.edu	U.S. educational institutions, such as universities
.gov	U.S. Government institution
.int	International organization (seldom used)
.mil	U.S. Military
.net	Internet Service Provider or network
.org	Nonprofit organizations

Memorize this list of TLDs and know their meanings.

To further organize the business of domain names, seven new TLDs have been selected for inclusion in the domain name system. These TLDs are described in Table 1-4.

Table 1-4 New Top Level Internet Domains	
Top Level Domain	**Purpose**
.aero	Air-transport industry
.biz*	Business
.coop	Cooperatives
.info*	Content and research
.museum	Museums
.name	Individuals
.pro	Professional

*.biz and .info became operational as of June 26, 2001

The Internet users of many countries commonly include an organization type along with the country code. In Australia, for example, names ending in .edu.au represent educational organizations within Australia; similarly, names ending in .org.au represent non-profit organizations within Australia. Additionally, some regions, such as the United Kingdom, have introduced their own codes for organization type, which again are combined with country codes. For example, commercial organizations often register their names under co.uk; co stands for *commercial*.

Registering domain names

Describe the functions of the ICANN and the InterNIC.

Originally the task of managing the domain name system for the Internet belonged to an organization called the Internet Network Information Center (InterNIC). InterNIC was a joint project between the U.S. government and a company called Network Solutions. In October 1998, however, the responsibility of managing the domain names of the Internet was assigned to an international non-profit organization called The Internet Corporation for Assigned Names and Numbers (ICAAN). One of ICAAN's chief responsibilities is to select and authorize those organizations that can serve as domain registrars. In order to have a presence on the Internet, an organization must make a formal request to a domain name registrar in order to have their domain name assigned.

Names can be registered long before they are actually used, and an organization can also register as many names as they want — as long as they pay the fees and meet all the requirements set by ICANN and the registrar. Organizations can also register a name even if they have no computers. A common practice is to register a name and have it actually hosted by another organization, such as a third-party ISP. This practice creates a *virtual domain*. These virtual domains can be quite handy for those organizations that don't have the staff, money, or the experience to maintain their own servers, but still want to have an Internet presence.

Each country is responsible for registrations into their own country code top-level domains. Canadian registrars are responsible for registering all domain names that end with `.ca`.

Prior to October 1998, InterNIC was the only registrar for .com, .org, and .net top-level domains. Currently, registrars throughout the world can register names as well as provide each of the following additional services:

✦ Domain name maintenance

✦ Access to resource links for policies and payment options

✦ WHOIS search capabilities for registered hostnames

Note   WHOIS is a search utility that can give you detailed information regarding who owns a particular domain name.

For a complete list of registrars and further information regarding name registration, visit the ICANN Web site at `www.icann.org`.

Uniform Resource Locators

As previously discussed, FQDNs are typically used to identify and locate an Internet server. The services and resources offered by these servers can be varied; for example, a server may offer Web content via HTTP, mail via SMTP, file downloads via FTP, and so on. You must use the appropriate client software for whichever service you choose.

At one time, services were only accessible through service-specific clients. For example, a user who needed to download files read Web pages, and access Gopher sites had to use three different client applications; an FTP client for downloads, an HTTP Web browser for Web access, and a Gopher client for Gopher access.

To reduce the number of individual applications required and to simplify Internet access, today's modern Web browsers act as clients for multiple services, including HTTP, FTP, and Gopher. Because of this, you must have a method of informing the browser which client you want it to use when accessing a particular resource on the Internet. You can accomplish this task through the use of a *Uniform Resource Locator* (URL). URLs are a form of addressing that supplies the location of a resource and the protocol or method that is used to access the resource. A URL typically consists of the following elements:

✦ A protocol followed by a colon (:) and two forward slashes (//); for example, http:// or ftp://. In the case of newsgroups and mail, the forward slashes may be excluded.

✦ An address of a server that contains the resource. This is typically an FQDN.

✦ A path to the document or file on the server. This is a file system path specified by using the forward slash (/) in a UNIX-style format — regardless of the real operating system being used on the server.

✦ The name of the actual resource preceded by a forward slash. This is typically the file name.

The following are examples of valid URLs for various Internet services:

✦ **Web page URLs:**

- `www.whitehouse.gov`
- `http://dailynews.yahoo.com/Full_coverage/`
- `www.icann.org/general/abouticann.htm`

✦ **FTP URLs:**

- `ftp://ftp.www.whitehouse.gov`
- `ftp://ftp.cecm.sfu.ca/pub/RMR/Ducati/`
- `ftp://tsx-11.mit.edu/pub/linux/docs/HOWTO/INDEX.html`

✦ **Gopher URLs:**

- `ftp://ftp.www.whitehouse.gov`
- `http://dailynews.yahoo.com/Full_coverage/`
- `www.icann.org/general/abouticann.htm`

✦ **Newsgroup URLs:**

- `news://news.vmware.com`
- `news:news.rdc1.mb.home.com`
- `news://partnerting2.microsoft.com/mct2001`

✦ **Mail URLs:**

- `mailto:bill@microsoft.com`
- `mailto:big_bad_wolf @threelittlepigs.org`

Note   Typing either newsgroup URLs or mail URLs in a browser address bar will typically cause your browser to automatically open your news reader application or default mail application.

Introduction to Intranets and Extranets

Many organizations have used the Internet's technology to build intranets and extranets.

Intranets

An *intranet* is an Internet-like Web site that an organization sets up for exclusive use by its employees. An intranet typically contains links to organization-specific data. The benefit of providing information in this format is that employees are able to access the information — regardless of the type of computer they are using by using standard Internet client software such as Web browsers and news readers. As long as the computers are capable of displaying Web content, employees can utilize the intranet.

Intranets can be self-contained networks with no external links to the Internet and with no access from the Internet. This is fairly common in high security networks.

Intranets often provide links to external Internet resources, but use some form of security, such as a firewall, to prevent access to the intranet from the Internet. This allows employees access to external information, yet still provides a secure environment for sensitive internal information.

 Cross-Reference   Security and firewalls are discussed in detail in Chapter 18.

Extranets

The term *extranet* refers to an Internet-accessible Web site that restricts who can access it. An organization, for example, may create an extranet by opening portions of their intranet for customers or business partners. In fact, companies often allow registered customers to access product support information. To restrict entry into the extranet, users are typically asked to provided user names and passwords; after their identity has been confirmed, they can access the site as they would any other Web site.

 Exam Tip   Be sure to understand the differences between the Internet, intranets, and extranets.

Key Point Summary

The following is a summary of the key points in this chapter:

✦ ARPANET was the predecessor to the Internet.

✦ The ARPANET's purpose was to provide a communication network that would continue to function, even if any one component in the network was lost.

✦ ARPANET was the first network to use the concepts of packets and packet switching.

✦ NSFnet replaced ARPANET in 1989 and later grew to be the Internet.

✦ To actively participate in the Internet, these six key elements are required:

- Internet-capable computer
- Operating system
- TCP/IP
- Client software
- Internet connection
- Internet address

✦ The Internet follows the Client/Server model of networking.

- Client software allows a computer to access server resources on a network.
- The role of the server is to provide access to resources for clients.
- Pull technology is a client/server interaction in which data is sent from a server after the client has requested it.
- Push technology is a client/server interaction in which a server will send data to a client without the client making a specific request for it.

✦ Protocols define rules and structure for network communication.

✦ TCP/IP is a set of protocols chosen for communication across the Internet.

✦ An IP address is a unique 32-bit number that identifies the location of a computer on a TCP/IP network, such as the Internet.

✦ IP addresses are represented in dotted quad notation.

✦ Common Internet-related protocols and services include:

- Hypertext Transfer protocol (HTTP)
- File Transfer Protocol (FTP)
- Post office Protocol (POP)
- Simple Mail Transfer Protocol (SMTP)
- Internet Message Access Protocol (IMAP)
- Telnet
- Network News Transfer Protocol (NNTP)
- Gopher

✦ An ISP is a company or organization that provides individuals and/or other organizations with access to the Internet.

✦ Dial-up connection Internet access is provided through the use of a modem. Comparatively speaking, dialup is slow and does not offer a permanent connection to the Internet.

✦ PPP and SLIP protocols transfer network data over a dial-up connection. SLIP is older and only offers TCP/IP protocol support and no user authentication.

✦ Direct Internet connections include the following:

  • Local Area Network (LAN) connections

  • Digital Subscriber Lines (DSL)

  • Cable connection

✦ DNS is both a TCP/IP protocol and a service whose primary job is to translate names into IP addresses and vice versa. It allows the use of human-friendly names to refer to computers on the Internet.

✦ FQDNs consist of a host name and a domain name.

  • A host name is the name given to the actual computer.

  • The domain name uniquely identifies an organization on the Internet.

✦ Top-level domains (TLDs) are used to organize domains into logical groupings. These TLDs either represent an organization's geographic location or its organization type.

✦ InterNIC was a joint project between the U.S. government and Network Solutions. One of its main responsibilities was to manage the domain name system for the Internet.

✦ In 1998, the responsibility of managing the domain names of the Internet was assigned to the Internet Corporation for Assigned Names and Numbers (ICAAN).

✦ One of ICAAN's chief responsibilities is to select and authorize organizations to serve as domain registrars.

✦ Virtual domains are formed when an organization registers a domain name that will be hosted by a third party, such as an ISP.

✦ URLs are a form of addressing that specifies the location of a resource and the protocol necessary to access that resource.

✦ An intranet is an Internet-like Web site that an organization sets up for the exclusive use of its employees.

✦ Extranets are Internet-accessible Web sites with restricted access.

✦   ✦   ✦

STUDY GUIDE

These assessment questions will test your memory on some of the key topics covered. The scenario questions will test you on your understanding of the concepts by presenting you with real-life scenarios for which you will have to answer chapter-related questions.

Assessment Questions

1. Which of the following best describes the design of the Internet?

   A. Centralized control, single point of failure

   B. Decentralized control, single point of failure

   C. Centralized control, no single point of failure

   D. Decentralized control, no single point of failure

2. Which network was the first to offer multiple data paths using packet-switching technology?

   A. Internet

   B. ARPANET

   C. DARPA

   D. NSFNET

3. Which of the following is not required to connect an Internet client to the Internet?

   A. Internet-capable computer

   B. Operating system

   C. Registered domain name

   C. TCP/IP

   D. Client software

   E. Internet connection

   F. Internet address

4. What type of device determines the path a data packet will take on the Internet?

    A. Server

    B. Network card

    C. Hub

    D. Directionometer

    E. Router

5. True or False: A computer can run multiple client applications at the same time.

6. True or False: Pull technology is a client/server interaction in which data is sent from a server only after the client has requested it.

7. What defines rules and structure for network communications?

    A. Languages

    B. Protocols

    C. Servers

    D. Client applications

    E. Network administrator

8. TCP/IP is responsible for breaking up data to be sent in small chunks. What is the name given to these small chunks of data?

    A. Segments

    B. Protocols

    C. Packages

    D. Parcels

    E. Packets

9. Which of the following protocols is used by Web browsers to request and receive hypertext-based document (Web) pages from Web servers?

    A. HTML

    B HTTP

    C. FTP

    D. Gopher

    E. NNTP

10. Which of the following protocols relate to e-mail? (Choose all that apply)

    A. SMTP

    B. SMNP

    C. POP

    D. IMAP

    E. NNTP

11. Which of the following protocols allows users to search for and find information almost anywhere in the world in a fairly easy-to-use, text-based, hierarchical, menu-driven fashion?

    A. HTML

    B HTTP

    C. FTP

    D. Gopher

    E. NNTP

12. Which of the following are considered direct Internet connections?

    A. ISDN

    B. DSL

    C. Modem

    D. Local Area Network connections

    E. Cable

13. Which of the following statements are true? (Choose all the apply)

    A. SLIP is an older protocol than PPP.

    B. PPP supports the use of TCP/IP but SLIP does not.

    C. PPP allows for dial-in authentication but SLIP does not.

    D. Given a choice, you should always choose SLIP over PPP.

    E. PPP supports multiple protocols in addition to TCP/IP.

14. Who should you contact when you want to connect your home computer to the Internet?

    A. An ISP

    B. ARPA

    C. InterNIC

    D. NSF

    E. ICANN

15. Which of the following are valid country codes? (Choose all that apply)

    A. .com

    B. .usa

    C. .ca

    D. .ch

    E. .org

16. Which of the following is an appropriate FQDN for a Web server owned by ACME Iron Works Corporation of Australia? (Choose all that apply)

    A. `acmeiron.www.au.com`

    B. `www.acmeiron.com.au`

    C. `au.com.acmeiron.www`

    D. `www.acmeiron.au.com`

    E. `www.acmeiron.au`

    F. `www.acmeiron.com`

17. Which of the following organizations is responsible for selecting domain name registrars?

    A. ISPA

    B. DARPA

    C. InterNIC

    D. NSF

    E. ICANN

18. What is created when a company registers a domain name but has a third-party ISP host the Web site?

    A. Virtual Web

    B. ISP Web

    C. Push Technology Web

    D. Pull Technology Web

    E. Virtual Domain

19. Which of the following are properly written URLs?

    A. `http:\\www.abc.com\members\login.asp`

    B. `mailto:kparnetta@hotmail.com`

    C. `http//www.disney.com`

    D. `ftp://ftp.smiles.org/bin/games/`

    E. `ftp://www.sandybeach.com/downloads`

20. Which of the following refers to an Internet-accessible Web site that restricts access to it?

    A. Intranet

    B. Extranet

    C. Internet

    D. Securenet

    E. Externet

Scenario 1

Ashley, a senior networking consultant has been hired to set up a network for Rub-a-Dub-Dub, Inc. — a cleaning supplies company in London, England. Following are the network design goals that Ashley must meet:

✦ Internet connectivity for all internal employees is required. It must be fast and available at all times.

✦ A Web site advertising Rub-A-Dub-Dub's products and services must be set up. This Web site must be easy for potential customers to find and will contain links to a set of Web pages protected by user IDs and passwords, which will provide technical support for current customers.

✦ Employees must have access to a Web-based information system that will supply them with company-related information. Because of the sensitive nature of the material, this Web based system must not be available through the Internet.

✦ Administrator must be able to use a terminal emulation client to allow remote administration of a series of Linux-based servers.

✦ Employees must be able to check their e-mail remotely through the Internet.

Based on the information provided and what you have learned in this chapter, answer the following questions regarding Rub-A-Dub-Dub's proposed network.

1. What type of Internet connection (dial-up or direct) should Ashley suggest for Rub-A-Dub-Dub? Why?

2. Assuming the host name for the Web server will be www and the registered domain name will be the company name written as rubadubdub, give three possible names that Ashley could suggest for FQDNs for Rub-A-Dub-Dub's Web server.

3. What is the common term used to describe the area of Rub-A-Dub-Dub's Web site that will be for customers only?

4. What term is used to describe the Web-based employee information system?

5. Based solely on the information given, what Internet protocols or services will be required for Rub-A-Dub-Dub's network? Why?

Scenario 2

Yin, a Rub-A-Dub-Dub employee, approaches Ashley and asks for her advice about getting connected to the Internet from home. Yin wants the connection so she can check e-mail from home, access newsgroups regarding her earthworm-collecting hobby, and periodically access various Web pages. Yin does not expect to use the connection every day. Yin tells Ashley that she currently has an older Windows 95-based computer that came with a 28.8 Kbps modem and does not want to spend a lot of money either for upgrading the computer or for the connection to the Internet.

Answer the following questions based on the information given.

1. What type of Internet connection will likely be best for Yin? Why?

2. Should Yin register a domain name? Why or why not?

3. What type of Internet client software will Yin likely require to meet her goals? What protocols will they involve?

4. What information will Yin require in order to set up her e-mail client software?

Answers to Chapter Questions

Chapter pre-test

1. **ARPANET** was the name given to the first network to offer multiple connections between hosts.

2. A **router** determines the path that data will take over the Internet.

3. The three elements required when the client/server model is used on a network are: **a client, a server, and a network connection between the two.**

4. **False**: Push technology does not refer to a client pushing requests for data to a server. Push technology refers to a technology in which servers push data to clients that have requested it.

5. The six elements required to support an Internet client are:

   - **Internet-capable Computer**
   - **Operating System**
   - **TCP/IP**
   - **Client Software**
   - **Internet Connection**
   - **Internet Address**

6. The common name for an organization that provides access to the Internet is an Internet Service Provider, or ISP.

7. **False**: DSL is not an example of a dial-up Internet connection; rather, it is a direct Internet connection.

8. **FTP** is the protocol typically used to transfer files across the Internet.

9. Mail applications are typically associated with SMTP, POP3, and IMAP.

10. The letters "fr" in `www.poulet.fr` represent the country of France.

11. Because `www.poulet.fr` is an FQDN, **www refers to the host name of a computer**. Note: the letters "www" are typically given to denote World Wide Web servers.

12. **ICANN** is responsible for the domain name system management on the Internet.

13. The term "**Virtual Domain**" refers to a domain that is registered by one company but whose Web servers are maintained by another, such as a third-party ISP.

14. The prefix "http://" is typically used at the beginning of a Web page URL.

Assessment Questions

1. Which of the following best describes the design of the Internet?

   D. Decentralized control, no single point of failure

2. Which network was the first to offer multiple data paths using packet-switching technology?

   B. ARPANET

3. Which of the following is not required to connect an Internet client to the Internet?

   C. Registered Domain name

4. What type of device determines the path a data packet will take on the Internet?

   E. Router

5. **True**: A computer can run multiple client applications at the same time.

6. **True**: Pull technology is a client/server interaction in which data is sent from a server only after the client has requested it.

7. What defines rules and structure for network communications?

   B. Protocols

8. TCP/IP is responsible for breaking up data to be sent in small chunks. What is the name given to these small chunks of data?

   E. Packets

9. Which of the following protocols is used by Web browsers to request and receive hypertext-based document (Web) pages from Web servers?

   B HTTP

10. Which of the following protocols relate to e-mail? (Choose all that apply)

    A. SMTP

    C. POP

    D. IMAP

11. Which of the following protocols allows users to search for and find information almost anywhere in the world in a fairly easy-to-use, text-based, hierarchical, menu-driven fashion?

    D. Gopher

12. Which of the following are considered direct Internet connections?

    B. DSL

    D. Local Area Network Connections

    E. Cable

13. Which of the following statements are true? (Choose all the apply)

    A. SLIP is an older protocol than PPP.

    C. PPP allows for dial-in authentication but SLIP does not.

    E. PPP supports multiple protocols in addition to TCP/IP.

14. Who should you contact when you want to connect your home computer to the Internet?

    A. An ISP

15. Which of the following are valid country codes? (Choose all that apply)

    C. .ca

    D. .ch

16. Which of the following is an appropriate FQDN for a Web server at ACME Iron Works Corporation of Australia? (Choose all that apply)

    B. `www.acmeiron.com.au`

    E. `www.acmeiron.au`

    F. `www.acmeiron.com`

17. Which of the following organizations is responsible for selecting domain names?

    E. ICANN

18. What is created when a company registers a domain name but has a third-party ISP host the Web site?

    E. Virtual Domain

19. Which of the following are properly written URLs?

    B. `mailto:kparnetta@hotmail.com`

    D. `ftp://ftp.smiles.org/bin/games/`

    E. `ftp://www.sandybeach.com/downloads`

20. Which of the following refers to an Internet-accessible Web site that restricts access to it.

    B. Extranet

Scenarios Questions

Scenario 1

1. Ashley should suggest a LAN-based direct connection to the Internet. It is appropriate because it offers high speed and a permanent connection, which meets the design goals for Rub-A-Dub-Dub's network.

2. Although many possibilities (as well as limitations) exist on available names, Ashley could suggest the following for FQDNs for Rub-A-Dub-Dub's Web server:

   • Because Rub-A-Dub-Dub is a commercial organization, Ashley could suggest `www.rubadubdub.com`.

   • Because Rub-A-Dub-Dub is in the United Kingdom, another suggestion is `www.rubadubdub.uk`.

   • Because Rub-A-Dub-Dub is both a commercial organization and is located in the UK, `www.rubadubdub.co.uk` may also work.

3. The common term used to describe the area of Rub-A-Dub-Dub's Web site that is for customers only is "**extranet**."

4. The term "**intranet**" describes the Web-based employee information system.

5. The Internet protocols and services required are the following:

   HTTP — Will be required for both internal and external Web access.

   SMTP — Will be required to send e-mail.

   Either POP or IMAP — Will be required to retrieve e-mail.

   Telnet — Will be required to allow administrators terminal emulations clients for administration of the Linux servers.

Scenario 2

1. A dial-up connection will be best for Yin because she does not want to spend a lot of money. She already has a modem, and she does not require a permanent connection.

2. Yin does not need to register a domain name because her computer will simply be a client, not a server.

3. Yin will require the following client software:

   - **An e-mail client application that uses SMTP for sending and either POP or IMAP for receiving e-mail**

   - **A newsgroup client that uses NNTP**

   - **A Web browser that uses HTTP**

4. Yin will require the FQDN of both her SMTP server and her POP or IMAP server in order to set up her e-mail client software.

Viewing the Internet

1. Describe the origins of the World Wide Web, and explain the difference between the Web and the Internet.

2. Define the term legacy application.

3. Access, view, and navigate Web pages using various Web browsers.

4. Enter Uniform Resource Locators (URLs).

5. View Web page source code.

6. Set Preferences to customize a Web Browser.

7. Configure browser home pages and manage History folders.

8. Configure and empty browser caches.

9. Save and organize frequently used Web page addresses in the Favorites and Bookmarks folders.

10. Control browser image loading.

11. Explain the function of the Wireless Application Protocol (WAP).

CHAPTER PRE-TEST

1. True or False: The terms Internet and World Wide Web are interchangeable.

2. The organization that controls standards and specifications for the World Wide Web is _____.

3. A Web browser that has become obsolete because it is unable to deal with common features found in most Web sites is referred to as a _____ browser.

4. Parts of Web pages that when selected can quickly transport you to another page or site are called _____.

5. The address of a Web page or site is called its _____.

6. One way of telling how recently a Web site has been updated is by looking at its _____ code.

7. The _____ folder keeps the URLs of recently visited Web sites.

8. The first Web page you see when you start your browser is your default _____.

9. The protocol used for wireless devices that browse the Web is _____.

10. People with slow modem connections may want to disable _____ to speed up their browsing experience.

11. Due to security and bandwidth issues, some system administrators require employees to disable _____ on their browsers.

✦ Answers to these questions can be found at the end of the chapter. ✦

You view, search, and investigate the World Wide Web using Web browser software. Web browsers guide you through the tremendous volume of information available on the World Wide Web. With the aid of your browsers, you can read text, view pictures, and more. Software designed to work with browsers allows you to watch or listen to film clips, streaming video, sound clips, music, and radio stations. Graphics and multimedia appeal to users and are at least partially responsible for the popularity of the World Wide Web.

Browser settings can be customized to suit the user. In this chapter you use and compare two browsers: Internet Explorer and Netscape Navigator. You learn how to do the following:

✦ View Web pages

✦ Navigate the Web using links

✦ Examine Web page source code

✦ Manage information with your browser

You also learn how to customize these browsers by adjusting preference options.

Web Browsers

 Describe the origins of the World Wide Web, and explain the differences between the Web and the Internet.

World Wide Web

Tim Berners-Lee is credited with creating the World Wide Web (WWW). As an employee of Conseil Européen pours la Recherché Nucléare (CERN), in Geneva Switzerland, his goal was to improve the dispersal and availability of information among scientists working on physics projects. Tim Berners-Lee achieved this goal, to manage large amounts of information, by developing a *hypertext system*. This system later became the World Wide Web. The hypertext system he developed is especially significant because it works across multiple platforms making it possible for computers with different operating systems, applications, and protocols to work together.

The hypertext system was fully implemented within CERN in March 1991. In August 1991, it was introduced to a Usenet newsgroup. The Web soon became a popular forum for business and personal use. Despite the many changes associated with the Web since its inception, many aspects remain unchanged.

The World Wide Web is not the Internet, but rather it is part of the Internet. The Internet is the largest computer network in the world and is also comprised of the following:

✦ Sharing files through File Transfer Protocol (FTP)

✦ Remote terminal connections (Telnet)

✦ Newsgroups (Usenet)

✦ E-mail through a point of presence (POP) and Simple Mail Transport Protocol (SMTP)

The World Wide Web is an organized structure for exchanging information and ideas through software, hypertext links, and protocols. Some liken the World Wide Web to a living organism that has been growing and changing at a furious rate since the day it was born.

Although Tim Berners-Lee developed the hypertext system that became the World Wide Web, Ted Nelson invented *hypertext* in the mid 1960s. Hypertext is a group of files that cross-reference each other. The cross references are links in the form of icons, text, or graphics that, when selected, transport you to a different location. Hypertext was originally used in large databases where information was organized according to relationship rather than in a set sequence.

Today, hypertext connects Web content within the same site and between different Web sites; you can link to virtually any site that is up and running on the Web. Hyperlinks and anchors attach Web pages to other pages' text, pictures, and multimedia. Text links are easy to recognize because they appear in a different color from the rest of the text and are usually underlined or highlighted. Hypertext pages are generally written in HyperText Markup Language (HTML).

Cross-Reference   HTML is covered in more detail in Chapters 8, 9, 10, and 11.

The World Wide Web Consortium (W3C), located at the Massachusetts Institute of Technology (MIT), is a global association. This organization was founded in 1994 to promote and uphold basic recommendations for hardware and software used for the Internet.

Cross-Reference   You can learn more about World Wide Web Consortium in Chapter 8.

Web browser basics

Access, view, and navigate Web pages using various Web browsers.

Web Browsers are applications that display Web pages. Modern browsers show pictures and text and, with the appropriate *plug-ins*, can play video and sound too. A plug-in is a module that allows a program to take on additional capabilities.

For more detailed information on plug-ins see Chapter 5.

Several browsers are on the market today. Microsoft's Internet Explorer and Netscape's Navigator remain the most popular. Internet Explorer 6.0 is shown in Figure 2-1, and Netscape Navigator is shown in Figure 2-2.

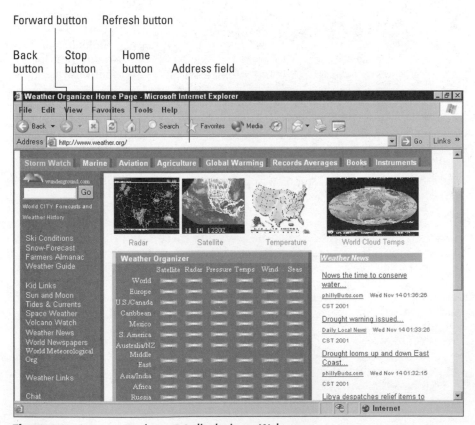

Figure 2-1: Internet Explorer 6.0 displaying a Web page

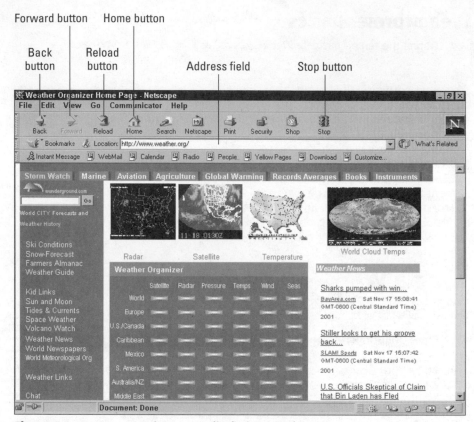

Figure 2-2: Netscape Navigator 6.1 displaying a Web page

In the preceding figures, both Internet Explorer and Netscape Navigator display the same Web site. The differences in the ways that these two programs display Web sites are often almost indistinguishable. Slight differences exist in the placement of graphics.

Depending on how the Web page was built, it may work better on one browser than the other. Companies often opt for one browser for consistency and ease of maintenance.

In the Real World

Cisco Corporation has released a device called a "Content Smart Switch," which can detect a whether a person is using Netscape Navigator or Internet Explorer. Using this information it can then direct the Web page requests to a server, which contains information formatted appropriately for browsers used by the viewer.

Legacy browsers

Define the term legacy application.

Like most software, different versions of browser programs have been released over the years. As of this writing, the latest browser from Netscape is Navigator 6.1, and the most recent version of Internet Explorer is Explorer 6.0. *Legacy browsers* are older versions of these and other browsers. Due to their age, legacy browsers may not support more recent technological developments and may limit the Internet content that they can display. Versions that are older than Internet Explorer 3.0 and Netscape Navigator 3.0 do not handle Web features such as frames and active content, which are now commonplace.

For information about frames and active content, refer to Chapters 5 and 11.

Viewing a Web Page

Access, view, and navigate Web pages using various Web browsers.

Enter Uniform Resource Locators (URLs).

Browser programs are designed to display Web pages. The page you see when you first open your browser is referred to as your default *home page*. To view another page within a Web browser, type its address (recall URL from Chapter 1) into the address field of your browser, and press the enter key.

URLs are discussed in more detail in Chapter 1.

When visiting a Web page, you may need to scroll down the page to read the information at the bottom of the page. The vertical scroll bar is located on the right hand side of your screen, and the horizontal scroll bar is at the bottom of your screen. By clicking the boxes with arrows on the ends of the scroll bars, you can easily change the view of your screen.

When visiting a Web page, don't just scroll up and down the page. Select links that look interesting. Links are easy to spot; when you hover your mouse pointer over a link, your mouse pointer changes into a hand. See Figure 2-3 for an example of a link.

Clicking a link transports you to another part of the same page, a different page of the Web site, or to an entirely different Web site. Links may take you to a page you don't want to see. To go back to the Web page you were at before you clicked the link; click the Back button on the browser's toolbar.

Figure 2-3: A link in a Web page

The Back buttons in Netscape Navigator and Internet Explorer can take you back more than one link. To go back several steps, click the Back button repeatedly. For a list of pages you have visited, click the arrow beside the Back button. You can select a page that you want to revisit from the list that appears, and your browser takes you there.

Clicking the Forward button moves you ahead to the Web sites that you most recently visited. You won't be able to use the Forward button until you've clicked the Back button at least once. Like the Back button it has an arrow that displays a list of Web sites.

The Home button on the browser's toolbar always takes you back to your default home page. This command can speed up your browsing and is especially useful if you need to refer back to your homepage frequently.

The Stop button on the browser's toolbar stops a page from loading. This command is useful when the page loads too slowly, and you decide not to wait for it to finish.

Both Netscape Navigator and Internet Explorer have Refresh buttons. These buttons are used to reload the content on a Web page when the Web page does not display properly initially. This button also updates your Web page assuring you view the most recent page rendering.

Source Code

When you view a Web page, you are actually looking at your Web browser's interpretation of the Web page's source code. This source code is a set of instructions that tell your browser how to display content. Source code is usually written in a special language called HyperText Markup Language (HTML). When you request a

Web page on the Internet, the source code is sent to your browser. Your Web browser interprets the code and displays the Web page.

 Cross-Reference For extensive information on HyperText Markup Language (HTML) and creating Web page source code see Chapters 8-11.

When viewing a Web page, it is sometimes difficult to determine if the information provided is current. Examining the source code of a Web page can help you establish when the Web page was actually created. If you want to develop your own Web pages, viewing another person's work can be very handy. You can view the source code of a Web page from inside your browser.

The following steps guide you through the process for both Internet Explorer and Netscape Navigator:

1. Use your Web browser to view any Web page whose source code you would like to see.
2. Choose the View menu, which is located in the menu bar near the top of the browser window.
3. If using Netscape Navigator, choose Page Source, as shown in Figure 2-4.

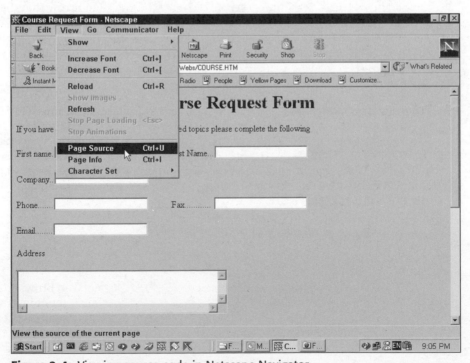

Figure 2-4: Viewing source code in Netscape Navigator

If using Internet Explorer, choose Source, as shown in Figure 2-5.

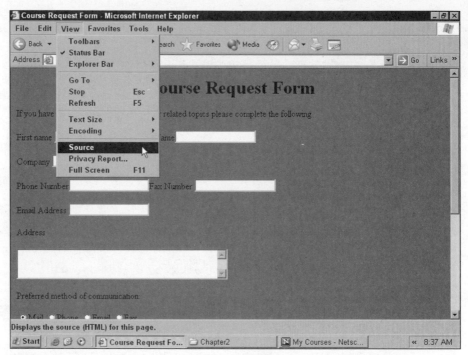

Figure 2-5: Viewing source code in Internet Explorer

The Web page source code appears in a separate window, as shown in Figure 2-6.

As you can see from the sample source code, the date information is often placed near the beginning of the Web page. Part II of this book shows you how easy it is to create a Web page and publish it for viewing. With this in mind, read Web pages you visit critically—just because a Web page is published does not mean the information that it contains is true.

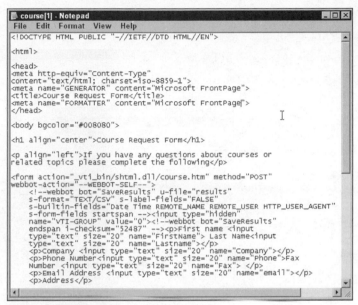

Figure 2-6: Example of source code

Managing Information

Save and organize frequently-used Web page addresses in the Favorites and Bookmarks folders.

Manage history folders.

As you move from one link to another, you can quickly lose track of an interesting Web site you want to revisit. Fortunately, browsers have a History folder that records where you've been during current and previous sessions. By accessing the History folder, you can obtain the address of a Web site that you would like to view again. Browsers also let you save URLs of sites that you plan to visit frequently, so that you can easily call them up without typing the URL every time you visit the site.

Favorites and bookmarks

In Internet Explorer, the folder that stores the URL of Web pages that you plan to visit frequently is called Favorites. In Netscape Navigator the analogous folder is called Bookmarks. Both folders serve the same function and work more or less the same way. The following steps walk you through how to save a URL in the Favorites or Bookmarks folder:

Adding favorites in Internet Explorer

1. Choose the Favorites menu.

2. Select Add to Favorites, as shown in Figure 2-7.

3. Click the OK button or press the Enter key on the keyboard.

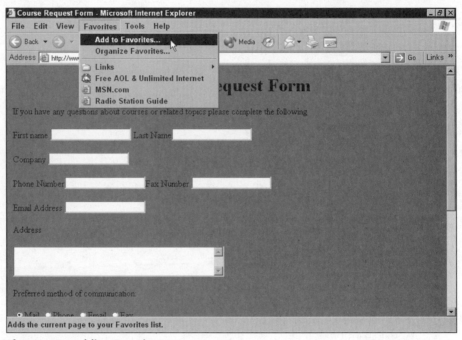

Figure 2-7: Adding Favorites

Adding bookmarks in Netscape Navigator

1. Choose the Bookmarks menu.

2. Select Add Bookmark, as shown in Figure 2-8.

Retrieving favorites in Internet Explorer

1. Choose the Favorites menu. A list of shortcuts to Web pages is displayed in the menu.

2. Select the name of the Web page that you want to view.

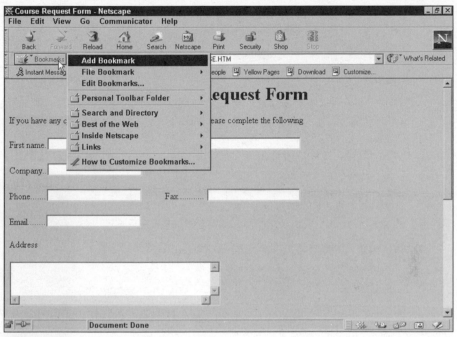

Figure 2-8: Adding bookmarks

Retrieving bookmarks in Netscape Navigator

1. Choose the Bookmarks menu. A list of shortcuts to Web pages is displayed in the menu.

2. Select the name of the Web page you that want to view.

It does not take long to accumulate many Web page addresses in your Favorites or Bookmarks folder. Both browsers allow you to create subfolders and to move, copy, and rename your saved URLs. The following sections describe how to manage these addresses.

Managing Favorites in Internet Explorer

1. Choose the Favorites menu.

2. Select Organize Favorites from the Favorites menu.

3. A dialog box as shown in Figure 2-9 appears with options to delete, move, or rename favorites.

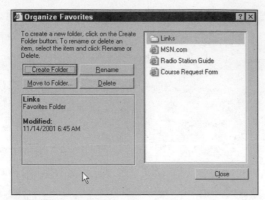

Figure 2-9: Managing favorites

Managing Bookmarks in Netscape Navigator

1. Choose the Bookmarks menu.

2. Select Manage Bookmarks from the Bookmarks menu.

3. A dialog box as appears with options to delete, move, or rename bookmarks. Refer to Figure 2-10.

Cross-Reference

Lab Exercise 2-2 walks you through marking, managing, and retrieving bookmarks in Netscape Navigator and favorites in Internet Explorer.

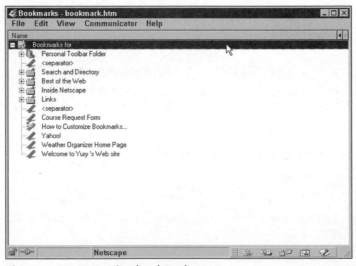

Figure 2-10: Managing bookmarks

Browser history

Both Netscape Navigator and Internet Explorer keep track of the name and associated URLs of the Web pages that you visit. How long these records remain within the `History` folder depends on your settings. To access the History list in Netscape Navigator 6.1, follow these steps:

1. Choose the Tasks menu.

2. Select Tools from the Tasks menu.

3. Select History from the Tools submenu.

A dialog box appears with a list of previously-visited sites, similar to the list shown in Figure 2-11.

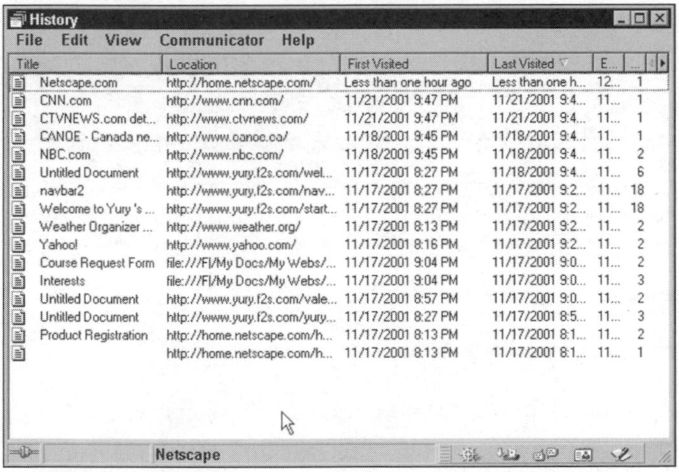

Figure 2-11: The History list in Netscape Navigator

To access the `History` folder in Internet Explorer, follow these steps:

1. Click the History button on the toolbar located at the top of the browser window.

2. A sidebar appears on the left side of your screen. Select from the icons in the sidebar to access a list of sites visited. Figure 2-12 shows this process.

When the History list is open you can click the time duration and choose from the list of sites that appears. The history is especially useful for locating sites that you neglected to mark as a favorite or bookmark, yet want to revisit.

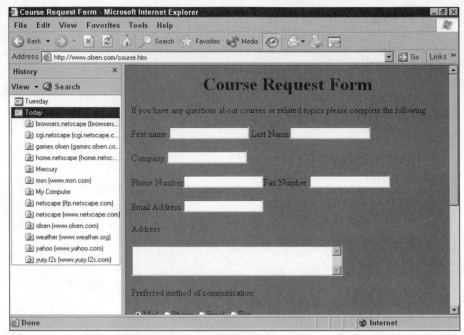

Figure 2-12: The History list in Internet Explorer

Changing browser default settings

Set Preferences to customize a Web browser.

Configure browser home pages and manage History folders.

Configure and empty browser caches.

Control browser image loading.

Several settings in Netscape Navigator and Internet Explorer can be configured to optimize your viewing experience. The following are some of the more commonly used settings:

✦ History settings

✦ Home page

✦ Font display

✦ Browser cache

✦ Image loading

✦ Disable active content

History settings

As previously stated, the History folder contains a list of the URLs visited. Most browsers, including Internet Explorer and Netscape Navigator, allow you to delete the history as well as adjust the length of time that URLs are kept.

Deleting entries from the History folder in Netscape Navigator

The following steps are required to delete entries from the History folder in Netscape navigator:

1. Choose the Edit menu.

2. Select Preferences. A dialog box opens.

3. Find the Navigator category on the left side of the dialog box. If there are no subcategories below it, select Navigator. A list of subcategories appears.

4. Select History. See Figure 2-13.

5. Click the Clear History button to remove URLs from the History folder, and click the Clear Location Bar button to remove the list of previously visited sites from the address bar.

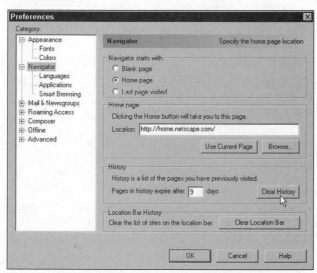

Figure 2-13: Deleting History list in Netscape Navigator

Deleting entries from the History folder in Internet Explorer

The following steps guide you through the process of deleting history entries in Internet Explorer:

1. Choose the Tools menu.

2. Select Internet Options. A dialog box opens.

3. Select the General tab in the dialog box.

4. Click the Clear History button to remove URLs from the `History` folder. See Figure 2-14.

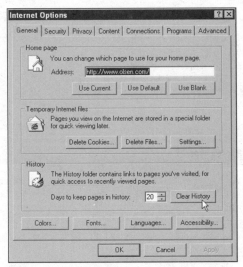

Figure 2-14: Deleting the History list in Internet Explorer

Specifying History folder size in Netscape Navigator

The following steps adjust the `History` folder size in Netscape Navigator:

1. Choose the Edit menu.

2. Select Preferences. A dialog box opens.

3. Find the Navigator category on the left side of the dialog box. If there are no subcategories below it, select Navigator. A list of subcategories appears.

4. Select History. See Figure 2-15.

5. In the `Session history size` field, enter a number to limit or extend the number of pages that can be saved in the `History` folder.

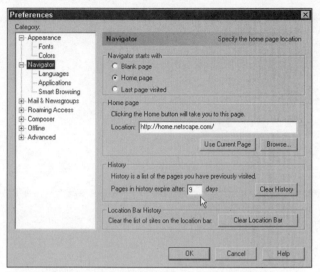

Figure 2-15: Changing the Session history size in Netscape Navigator

Specifying History folder size in Internet Explorer

Follow these steps to adjust the `History` folder size in Internet Explorer:

1. Choose the Tools menu.

2. Select Internet Options. A dialog box opens.

3. The General tab of the dialog box should be selected.

4. In the `Days to keep pages in history` field, enter a number to limit or extend the number of pages that can be saved in the `History` folder. See Figure 2-16.

Home page

A browser's default home page is the page shown when you first start the browser. The default home page for Internet Explorer is located at `www.msn.com` and Netscape Navigator's is at `www.netscape.com`. Although both of these Web sites provide a wealth of information and easy-to-use links and search engines that help locate information on the Internet, you may want to use a different home page. Both of these browsers allow you to specify a home page that is more to your liking than the default home page.

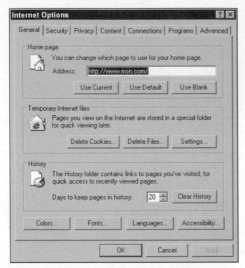

Figure 2-16: Changing History settings in Internet Explorer

Changing your default home page with Netscape Navigator

Follow these steps to change your home page in Netscape Navigator:

1. Choose the Edit menu.

2. Select Preferences. A dialog box opens.

3. Select the Navigator category on the left side of the dialog box.

4. In the Location field, type the URL of the page that you want to use as your home page. See Figure 2-17.

5. Click the OK button in the bottom, right-hand corner of the dialog box.

Changing your default home page with Microsoft Explorer

Follow these steps to change the home page in Microsoft Explorer:

1. Choose the Tools menu.

2. Select Internet Options. A dialog box opens.

3. The General tab of the dialog box should be selected.

4. In the Address field, type the URL of the page that you want to use as your home page. See Figure 2-18.

5. Click the OK button in the bottom, right-hand corner of the dialog box.

In the Real World

It is possible for a web site to automatically change your Home page for you, (whether you want it to or not); therefore knowing how to change it is a good skill to learn.

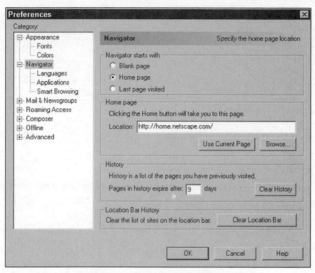

Figure 2-17: Changing the default homepage in Netscape Navigator

Figure 2-18: Changing the default homepage in Microsoft Explorer

Fonts

If you find that the text of most Web pages is too small (or perhaps too large) you can change the size by altering the browser default font size. People with vision limitations, or those who have set their monitor resolution to a very high setting (1024x768, 1280x1024, or larger), may find this to be a useful adjustment.

The font size can be adjusted in both Netscape Navigator and Internet Explorer with the following steps:

1. Choose the View menu.

2. Select Text Size.

3. Select the font size that you prefer from the Text Size menu.

You can also adjust the font type or style, which can also improve readability.

Changing the font type in Netscape Navigator

1. Choose the Edit menu.

2. Select Preferences. A dialog box opens.

3. Select the Appearance category on the left side of the dialog box.

4. In the submenu of the Appearance category, select Font. A dialog box appears, as shown in Figure 2-19.

5. Change the Font setting in the dialog box.

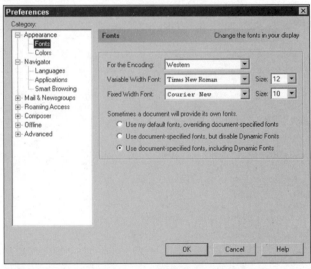

Figure 2-19: Changing the default font in Netscape Navigator

Changing the font type in Internet Explorer

1. Select the Tools menu.

2. Select Internet Options. A dialog box opens.

3. The General tab of the dialog box should be selected.

4. Click the Fonts button at the bottom of the dialog box. See Figure 2-20.

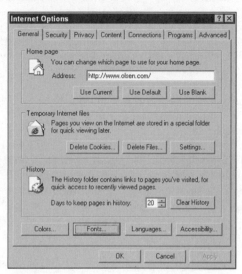

Figure 2-20: Changing the default font in
Internet Explorer

5. A second dialog box appears. In the fields provided, select the fonts that you
prefer to use as the default fonts. See Figure 2-21.

Figure 2-21: Fonts dialog box in
Internet Explorer

Lab Exercise 3, at the end of this chapter, provides an opportunity to practice configuring font size in Internet Explorer and Netscape Navigator.

Browser cache

Cache is a storage area on your hard drive. It holds Web files that contain text, graphics, and multimedia elements for the pages you visit with your browser. After a Web page is requested and downloaded, it is cached. If you request that same page again, the browser can pull up the cached version, rather than downloading the page across the Internet again. If you access the same Web pages frequently, you feel the benefits of cache, because cached Web pages are rendered to your browser more quickly than a page downloaded across the Internet. Conversely, if you rarely revisit the same site, or use the Back button on your browser, the benefits of cache are minimal.

The cached Web page may not be the most up-to-date version of the Web page. To see the most current version of a particular Web site you may need to activate the refresh or reload command. This is usually not a concern, because your browser automatically compares the cached version with the current Web site version of a page, and selects the most appropriate. You can configure settings to specify how frequently the cached version is compared to the live Web site. Settings are available to compliment almost any browsing style. See Figures 2-22 and 2-23.

You might also need to adjust your cache size from time to time. When making these adjustments, consider two issues: download speed and hard drive space. Increasing the size of your Web cache can decrease the time it takes for your browser to render Web pages. However, cache takes up space on your hard drive. If having enough space on your hard drive is a concern, set limits on the number of cache files that are stored.

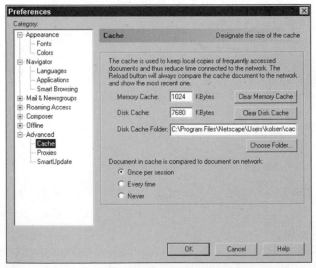

Figure 2-22: Changing the cache settings in Netscape Navigator

Figure 2-23: Changing the cache
settings in Internet Explorer

Adjusting cache settings in Netscape Navigator

1. Choose the Edit menu.

2. Select Preferences. A dialog box opens.

3. Find the Advanced category on the left side of the dialog box. If there are no subcategories below it, select Advanced. A list of subcategories appears.

4. Select Cache.

5. Make changes in this dialog box. See Figure 2-24.

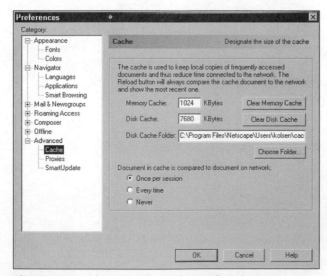

Figure 2-24: Changing the cache settings in Netscape
Navigator

Adjusting cache settings in Internet Explorer

1. Choose the Tools menu.

2. Select Internet Options. A dialog box opens.

3. The General tab of the dialog box should be selected.

4. Click the Settings button near the middle of the dialog box. See Figure 2-25.

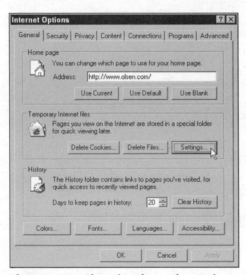

Figure 2-25: Changing the cache settings in Internet Explorer

5. The dialog box appears, as shown in Figure 2-26.

Figure 2-26: The Settings dialog box in Internet Explorer

Lab Exercise 2-3, at the end of this chapter, provides an opportunity to practice managing browser cache.

Image loading

The images that make many sites visually attractive can present problems for people with slow Internet connections. Image files tend to be large, take up more bandwidth, and take longer to load on your computer. When images are part of Web pages, they also load into cache, and their large file size takes up extra space.

Both Internet Explorer and Netscape Navigator allow you to disable image viewing. When you disable image viewing, the image files are not downloaded to your computer. Instead of seeing pictures, you see boxes with text descriptions of the picture, an X, or No Image Available. If you have a slow Internet connection, this setting results in Web pages loading much more quickly. If your Internet service provider (ISP) charges by the hour for connection service, disabling image viewing can also save you money.

Disable image viewing in Internet Explorer

1. Choose the Tools menu.

2. Select Internet Options. A dialog box opens.

3. The Advanced tab of the dialog box should be selected.

4. Scroll down the dialog box to the multimedia section, and deselect the Show pictures option. See Figure 2-27.

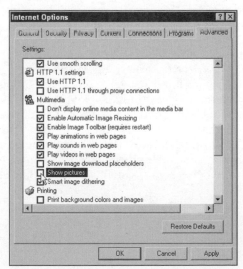

Figure 2-27: Disabling image viewing in Internet Explorer

Disable image viewing in Netscape Navigator

1. Choose the Edit menu.

2. Select Preferences. A dialog box opens.

3. Select the Privacy and Security category on the left side of the dialog box, and open its submenu.

4. Select the Images subcategory.

5. Select the Do not load any images radio button at the top of the dialog box.

6. Click OK.

Active content

Active content is a technology often used to create dynamic or changing objects within Web pages. This type of content can greatly increase the size of Web pages and the time that they take to download from the Web server. As well this Active content can be written in ways that may compromise the security of your computer and network. For these reasons, network administrators commonly insist that all client Web browsers have this functionality disabled.

Cross-Reference
For more detailed information about active content, see Chapter 5.

Wireless Application Protocol

You need a computer, a browser, and an Internet connection to use the Internet. These days your cell phone, Personal Digital Assistant (PDA), and other handheld devices can be used to access the Internet. However, these small handheld devices are limited in their capacity and cannot do everything that a PC can do.

Wireless devices use Wireless Application Protocol (WAP) to allow you to access the Internet. This protocol makes it possible to browse the World Wide Web, check e-mail, and access several other Internet-related services. When you browse with a wireless device, you are typically limited to a text only display. Most of these devices have tiny viewing screens that are not capable of showing multimedia and graphics. Wireless devices are also limited by the fact that they currently can only read Web pages written in Wireless Markup language (WML). A large part of the World Wide Web cannot be accessed with wireless devices at this time. E-mail is also limited because, although you can check your e-mail, you cannot access e-mail attachments.

Key Point Summary

The following is a summary of the key points covered in this chapter:

✦ Tim Berners-Lee is credited with creating the World Wide Web.

✦ The World Wide Web is not the Internet, but rather is part of the Internet.

✦ Hypertext was originally used in large databases where information was organized according to relationship rather than in a set sequence.

✦ Hyperlinks and anchors attach Web pages to other pages' text, pictures, and multimedia.

✦ Hypertext pages are generally written in HyperText Markup Language (HTML).

✦ The World Wide Web Consortium (W3C) was founded in 1994 to promote and uphold basic recommendations for hardware and software over the Internet.

✦ Web Browsers are applications that display Web pages.

✦ Outdated versions of Web browsers are often referred to as legacy browsers. These browsers are often limited in their ability to display recently developed Web pages.

✦ The page you see when you first open your browser is referred to as your home page.

✦ The Back button on a browser takes you to the previous Web page.

✦ If you want to return to a page that you used the Back button to leave, press the Forward Button.

✦ The Stop button stops the process of loading a Web page.

✦ The Refresh or Reload button forces the browser to redisplay the current window.

✦ A Web page's source code is the code — usually written in HTML — that produces the Web page.

✦ Creating favorites and bookmarks is a way of saving a reference to a Web page that you want to return to in the future.

✦ Web browsers keep track of the pages that you visit in their History folder. The size, age, and content of this history can be adjusted at any time.

✦ The default font settings of a Web browser can be adjusted to increase the readability of Web pages.

✦ Browser cache is a storage area on your hard drive where a browser places a copy of all the Web pages that you visit. The cache speeds up Internet access because you do not have to download Web sites that you have already visited.

✦ If you have a slow Internet connection, you can reduce the time it takes Web pages to download by disabling image loading. This also decreases the amount of space that your browser cache requires.

✦ Wireless devices use Wireless Application Protocol (WAP) to access the Internet.

✦ Web pages must be written in Wireless Markup Language in order to be accessible on a wireless device.

✦   ✦   ✦

STUDY GUIDE

Assessment Questions

1. Which of the following are related to the World Wide Web? (Choose all that apply.)

   A. Browsers, hypertext links, and HTML

   B. Remote Terminal connections

   C. Newsgroups

   D. E-mail

2. Choose all of the statements that are true about hypertext.

   A. Hypertext is only supported in non-legacy browsers.

   B. Hypertext is used to link Web content to local and remote sites.

   C. Hypertext links can be text, pictures, or icons.

   D. Hypertext organizes information according to relationship rather than in a set sequence.

3. Partial programs that work with larger programs to attach enhanced components or utilities are:

   A. Web browsers

   B. Legacy programs

   C. Plug-ins

   D. Illegal and pose security risks

4. The browsers Internet Explorer and Netscape Navigator are:

   A. Plug-ins that display Web pages

   B. The most popular browsers used on the Internet

   C. Expensive

   D. All of the above

5. Old browsers that cannot handle Web features such as frames and active content are referred to as what?

   A. Ancient browsers

   B. Legacy browsers

   C. Historic browsers

   D. WAP browsers

6. Which of the following settings can you adjust in Internet Explorer and Netscape Navigator?

   A. Default home page

   B Default font size

   C. Page length

   D. Cache settings

   E. Image loading

   F. Website's source code content

7. True or False: The latest versions of Explorer and Netscape Navigator interpret Web pages in exactly the same way.

8. Which of the following browser adjustments helps speed up Web page access over a slow Internet connection? (Choose all that apply)

   A. Disable image viewing

   B. Disable active content

   C. Install more RAM

   D. Increase your Web cache

   E. Delete your Web cache

9. Which of the following browser adjustments reduces the amount of hard drive space that your browser uses? (Choose all that apply)

   A. Disable image loading

   B. Disable active content

   C. Clear `History` folder

   D. All of the above

   E. None of the above

10. What language must Web page developers use if they want their pages to be available to handheld wireless devices? (Choose all that apply)

   A. WAP

   B. HTML

   C. WML

   D. SGML

Lab Exercise 2-1

To successfully complete this exercise you must

   ✦ Be connected to the Internet

   ✦ Have Internet Explorer installed on your computer

   ✦ Have Netscape Navigator installed on your computer

In this exercise you browse the World Wide Web using the two most popular browsers. At the time of this writing, Netscape Navigator 6.1 and Explorer 6.0 were the most current versions of these browsers.

1. Start Internet Explorer browser program by double-clicking the Internet Explorer icon or selecting Start ➪ Programs ➪ Internet Explorer. (If you are Using Netscape Navigator the process is similar: Start the Netscape Navigator browser program by double-clicking the Netscape icon or select Start ➪ Programs ➪ Netscape 6.1.) Your Web browser opens, and the default home page appears in the window.

2. Go to another place on the Web by clicking a hyperlink with your mouse. You can identify a link because your mouse pointer looks like a tiny hand when it hovers over a hyperlink. After clicking the link, you are be looking at a different location of the current Web page, another Web page within the same Web site, or a different Web site altogether.

3. Navigate back to your default home page, by clicking the Back button. You should be back where you started.

4. Go to a different Web site:

   a. Click in the address bar of your browser.

   b. Delete the existing address.

   c. Type the URL of a site you know or choose from the following:

   • www.weather.net

   • www.recipies.com

   • www.cnn.com

   d. After you have typed in the address, press the Enter key on your keyboard. A different Web site appears in your browser window.

5. Move to a new page or site by clicking a hyperlink with your mouse.

6. Use the Back button to take you back to the page that you were viewing at the end of Step 4.

7. Use the Forward button to return to the page that you linked to in Step 5.

8. Go to your home page by clicking the Home button on the toolbar at the top of the browser window.

9. If your default home page is www.microsoft.com, skip to Step 10. Otherwise type the URL www.microsoft.com into your address bar.

10. Some Web sites provide the option to view their site without graphics. This is useful if your Internet connection is slow.

    a. Scroll to the bottom of the Microsoft Web site.

    b. Click the Text Only link. Scroll up and down the new page to observe the differences.

11. View the source code of this page or another page that you have visited:

    a. Stay in the current Web page, or use the Forward and Back buttons to move to a different screen.

    b. Choose the View menu.

    c. Select Source. (If you are using Netscape Navigator, select Page Source.)

    d. A second window opens. It will be a text-editing program with the source code for the current Web page displayed within it.

    e. Examine the source code.

12. Close the source code window by selecting Exit from the File menu at the top of that window.

13. Close your browser program by selecting Close from the File menu the top of that window.

Lab Exercise 2-2

To successfully complete this exercise you must

✦ Be connected to the Internet

✦ Have Internet Explorer installed on your computer

✦ Have Netscape Navigator installed on your computer

In this exercise, you access Web pages stored in your History folder and change the default settings pertaining to your History folder. You also create Favorites and Bookmarks to save Web addresses, so that you can easily access them.

1. Start the Internet Explorer browser program by double-clicking the Internet Explorer icon or selecting Start ➪ Programs ➪ Internet Explorer. Your Web browser opens, and the default home page appears in the window.

2. View sites that you visited previously:

   a. Click the History button. A sidebar appears on the left side of your screen.

   b. Your screen looks similar to Figure 2-28.

Figure 2-28: Example of History sidebar in Internet Explorer

   c. This bar has different display settings. See Figure 2-29.

Figure 2-29: History bar display settings in Internet Explorer

   d. Choose the View menu on the History sidebar. Change the setting to By Site.

   e. Choose the View menu on the History sidebar. Change the setting to By Most Visited.

   f. Choose the View menu on the History sidebar. Change the setting to By Date.

   g. Choose the Today menu, and select a Website from the Today submenu.

   h. Select another Web site to view.

3. Close the History sidebar.

4. Make the Web site that you are visiting a favorite:

   a. Choose the Favorites menu.

   b. Select Add to Favorites.

   c. Click the OK button or press the Enter key on keyboard. The Web site is saved as a favorite.

5. Go to your default home page:

   a. Click the Home button on your toolbar.

6. Access the Web page that you saved as a favorite:

   a. Click the Favorites button on the toolbar. A sidebar opens on the left-hand side of the screen.

   b. Scroll through the list of favorites in the Favorites sidebar, and click the Web site that you saved as your favorite in Step 4. The Web page is displayed in your browser.

7. Make changes to your History settings.

   a. Choose the Tools menu.

   b. Select Internet Options. A dialog box opens.

   c. The General tab of the dialog box should be selected.

   d. In the `Days to keep pages in history` field, enter a number to limit or extend the number of pages that can be saved in the `History` folder.

   e. Click the OK button at the bottom of the dialog box.

8. Change font size of the Web site that you are viewing:

   a. Choose the View menu.

   b. Select Text Size from the View menu.

   c. Select Largest. Observe the Web page.

   d. Choose the View menu.

   e. Select Text Size from the View menu.

   f. Select Smallest. Observe the Web page.

   g. Choose the View menu.

   h. Select Text Size from the View menu.

   i. Select Medium. Observe the Web page.

9. Close Internet Explorer.

The process is similar in Netscape Navigator.

1. Start the Netscape Navigator browser program by double-clicking the Netscape icon or select Start ➪ Programs ➪ Netscape 6.1. Your Web browser opens, and the default home page appears in the window.

2. View sites that you visited previously:

   a. Click the arrow to the right of the address field. A list of the recently viewed Web sites appears. Click one of them. See Figure 2-30.

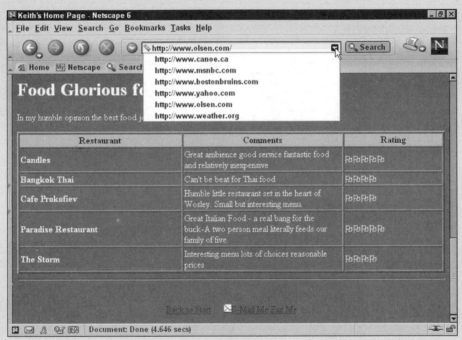

Figure 2-30: History list in Netscape Navigator

3. To bookmark a Web site, choose the Bookmark menu and select Add Bookmark.

4. Click the Home button on your toolbar to go to your default home page.

5. Access the Web page that you bookmarked:

   a. Choose the Bookmark menu. A list of shortcuts to pages is displayed in the menu.

   b. Select the name of the page you want to view.

6. Make changes to your History settings:

   a. Choose the Edit menu.

   b. Select Preferences. A dialog box opens.

   c. Find the Navigator category on the left side of the dialog box. If there are no subcategories below it, select Navigator. A list of subcategories appears.

   d. In the `Session history size` field, enter a number to limit or extend the number of pages to be saved in the `History` folder.

7. Change font size of the website you are viewing.

   a. Choose the View menu.

   b. Select Text Size from the View menu.

   c. Select 50%. Observe your web page.

   d. Choose the View menu.

   e. Select Text Size from the View menu.

   f. Select 200%. Observe your web page.

   g. Choose the View menu.

   h. Select Text Size from the View menu.

   i. Select 100% original. Observe your web page.

8. Close Netscape Navigator.

Scenario 2-1

You live in a rural community without ASDL (Asynchronous Digital Subscriber Line) or cable and use a 56K modem to access the Internet. You use the Internet for research and appreciate the wealth of information that can be found on the World Wide Web.

1. Waiting for pictures on Web pages to load is frustrating. You just need the information and usually couldn't care less about the pictures. It seems you spend most of your time waiting for the browser to load pictures so that you can view your web pages. What can you do to solve this problem?

2. You have so many websites in your `Bookmarks` folder that it is difficult to find the one that you want. What can you do to solve this problem?

3. You visited a Web site earlier in the day. You didn't bookmark the Web site and don't know the URL, but you would like to revisit the site. What steps could you take to return to this site?

4. The Web page you automatically see when you start your browser is not one that interests you. Is it possible to see a different page when you start your browser? How can you make this change?

5. You have recently had vision problems and find it difficult to read the small text on Web pages. What settings could you change to help adjust the font size to accommodate your sight limitations?

Answers to Chapter Questions

Chapter Pre-Test Answers

1. False. The World Wide Web is only one of several services offered over the Internet. Other services include e-mail, FTP, newsgroups, and Telnet.

2. The World Wide Web Consortium. (W3C)

3. Legacy

4. Links or hyperlinks

5. URL (Universal Resource Locator)

6. Source

7. History

8. Home page

9. WAP (Wireless Application Protocol)

10. Image viewing

11. Active content

Answers to Assessment Questions

1. **A.** Browsers, hypertext links, and HTML are related to the World Wide Web.

2. **B, C**, and **D.** Hypertext is used to link Web content to local and remote sites, hypertext links can be text, pictures, or icons, and hypertext organizes information according to relationship rather than in a set sequence.

3. **C.** Plug-ins are partial programs that work with larger programs to attach enhanced components or utilities.

4. **B.** Internet Explorer and Netscape Navigator are the most popular browsers used on the Internet.

5. **B.** Old browsers that cannot handle Web features such as frames and active content are referred to as legacy browsers.

6. **A**, **B**, **D**, and **E**. You can adjust the default home page, default font size, cache settings, and image loading.

7. **False.** The latest versions of Explorer and Netscape Navigator do not interpret Web pages in exactly the same way.

8. **A**, **B**, **C**, **D**, and **E**. Disabling image viewing and active content, installing more RAM, increasing your Web cache, and deleting your Web cache all help speed up Web page access over a slow Internet connection.

9. **D.** Disabling image loading, disabling active content, and clearing the `History` folder all reduce the amount of hard drive space that your browser uses.

10. **C.** Web page developers should use WML if they want their pages to be available to handheld wireless devices.

Answers to Scenario Questions

1. Increase cache, and disable image viewing.

2. Create subfolders in your `Bookmarks` folder, and move the Web pages from the `Bookmarks` folder to these subfolders.

3. Check the `History` folder.

4. Yes. You can change the home page. Choose the Edit menu, and then select Preferences. In the dialog box that opens, select the Navigator category. Type the URL of the page you would like as your new home page, and then click the OK button.

5. Select the View menu, select font size, and change the size of the font that the browser displays.

Resources

You may want to visit the following URL's for more information regarding the content of this chapter:

✦ `http://browserwatch.internet.com/browsers.html`

✦ `http://browserwatch.internet.com/`

✦ `www.zdnet.com/products/internetuser/browsers.html`

✦ `http://hotwired.lycos.com/webmonkey/reference/browser_chart/index.html` (This site contains a chart of what various browsers do and do not support.)

✦ `www.internet101.org/browser.html`

✦ `www.upsdell.com/BrowserNews/index.htm`

Additional Internet Services

✦   ✦   ✦   ✦

CHAPTER PRE-TEST

1. An e-mail application requires the address of the outgoing mail server. Which of the following is the outgoing server: POP, SMTP, or IMAP?

2. Which part of this e-mail address, k_olsen@olsen.mb.ca, is the domain name?

3. Which part of this e-mail address, k_olsen@olsen.mb.ca, is the POP3 account name?

4. What is the significance of typing an e-mail message in all capital letters?

5. What is the term for proper conduct on the Internet?

6. What is the name of the text that an e-mail client can place at the bottom of all e-mails automatically?

7. What is the name of a service in which you can subscribe to and any messages sent to that service are automatically sent to you?

8. What type of client software is required to access the messages sent in question 7?

9. What is an appropriate URL to connect to a FTP server named `ftp.someserver.ca` with the user name of *Leslie* and the password of *freelance*?

10. When you use a text-based FTP client, what command is issued to download a file named `game.exe`?

11. What FTP command is used to send the file called *report.txt* to an FTP server?

12. The messages in a newsgroup are referred to as _____.

13. Which newsgroup category is used for computer related topics?

14. What is the purpose of the asterisk (*) in the newsgroup rec.sport.golf*?

15. When you use a Telnet client to access a Telnet server which computer is performing the data processing?

✦ Answers to these questions can be found at the end of the chapter. ✦

Although the World Wide Web is often thought of when one thinks of the Internet, it is certainly not the only service offered. The Internet can and does provide many additional services as well. The focus in this chapter is to discuss client side issues regarding some of the more popular of these additional services including e-mail, mailing lists, FTP, Newsgroups, and telnet.

E-mail Basics

Electronic mail, or e-mail, remains one of the most critical services provided by the Internet. E-mail serves as the cornerstone service for user-to-user communication. To participate in e-mail, a user must have the following: an e-mail Address, an e-mail server, and an e-mail client.

E-mail addresses

In order to receive e-mail, a user must have an e-mail address. This address uniquely identifies an individual on the Internet. E-mail addresses always have the same syntax or format, which consists of a user name and a domain name separated by the "at" symbol (@), as shown in Figure 3-1.

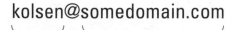

kolsen@somedomain.com

User Name   Domain Name

Figure 3-1: The composition of an e-mail address

The domain name in the e-mail address matches the registered domain name of the organization to which the user typically belongs. For example, suppose that the Great Falls Sewing Company registers the domain name greatfalls.mb.ca. Thus, all e-mail addresses issued by the company will end in @greatfalls.mb.ca.

Cross-Reference   For more information about registered domain names, see Chapter 1.

The user name portion of an address is used to identify a user's mail account within a domain. If you have ever exchanged e-mail address information with others, you know that the content of a user name can vary greatly — simply because a user name can include any of the following characters: numbers, letters, periods, and underscores. In most organizations, a user name is based on some form of naming convention. The following are some valid examples:

```
jpolowski@greatfalls.mb.ca
joanne_polowski@greatfalls.mb.ca
joannep@greatfalls.mb.ca
joanne.polowski@greatfalls.mb.ca
jp101@greatfalls.mb.ca
10122@greatfalls.mb.ca
designer@greatfalls.mb.ca
```

Exam Tip   Make sure you can recognize valid e-mail addresses.

Sending and receiving e-mail

Objective   Configure your browser to send e-mail.

The correct configuration of the mail client software enables users to send and receive e-mail. Although many mail client applications are available, they all require the same basic set of information in order to be properly configured. This information includes:

✦ User's Username

✦ User's e-mail address

✦ User's password

✦ SMTP server address

✦ POP3 or IMAP4 server address

Note   You can obtain this information from your e-mail server administrator or from your Internet service provider.

Although there are many applications that can function as e-mail clients, this chapter focuses on two of the most popular: Microsoft Outlook Express and Netscape Messenger.

Configuring Microsoft Outlook Express

Microsoft Outlook Express is the Internet mail client bundled with Microsoft's Internet Explorer. It can act as a client for mail, newsgroups, and directory access via LDAP.

The following steps outline the process involved in configuring Outlook Express as an e-mail client. (Obviously, for this to work, you must already have an e-mail account and have your computer configured for network and/or Internet access.)

1. Start Outlook Express by double-clicking the Outlook Express shortcut icon on your desktop, by clicking the Outlook Express Quick Launch button on your task bar, or by choosing the Outlook Express option in the Windows Start menu. These choices are shown in Figure 3-2.

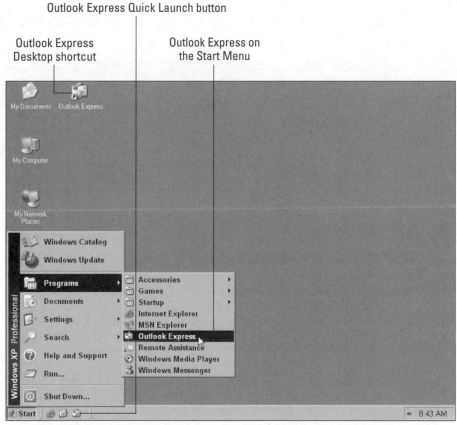

Figure 3-2: Starting Outlook Express

2. Upon startup, Outlook Express may ask you if you want to use this program as your default e-mail program. If you choose Yes, Outlook Express will start any time you click an e-mail hyperlink from within a Web page or when you use e-mail functions within other non-mail applications. For example, Microsoft Word offers an option that allows you to send the current document to an e-mail recipient.

3. When configuring Outlook Express on a computer that has an existing e-mail client, you may be asked if you want to import e-mail configuration information. If you are going to use Outlook Express to replace your existing e-mail client, then choose Yes; however, if are setting up Outlook Express to access an e-mail account different from the account used in your other e-mail client, then choose No.

Caution   You may want to avoid using two different e-mail applications or two different computers to access the same e-mail account. For example, If you use two different e-mail applications, mail downloaded into one will not be available when using the other and vice-versa. The same may occur when using two different computers; mail downloaded onto one of the two may not be available while using the other.

You are now presented with a screen similar to the screen shown in Figure 3-3.

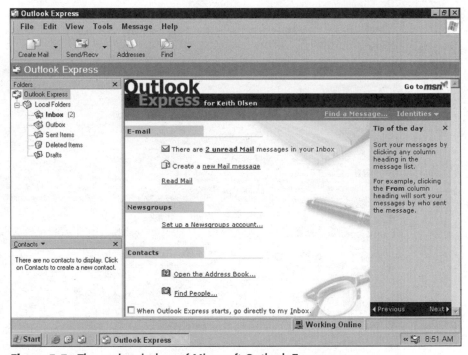

Figure 3-3: The main window of Microsoft Outlook Express

4. Choose the Tools menu at the top of the Outlook Express window and select the Accounts option. The Internet Accounts dialog box appears, as shown in Figure 3-4.

5. From the Internet Accounts dialog box, press the Add button and then choose the Mail option. The Internet Connection Wizard appears.

6. The first screen in the Internet Connection Wizard prompts you to input your name as you want it to appear in the From field of the messages that you will be sending. The name entered on this screen doesn't have to match the user name in your e-mail address, so choose any name that you believe is appropriate, as shown in Figure 3-5, then press the Next button.

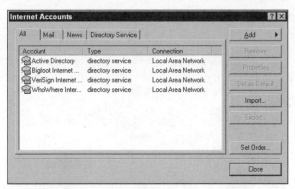

Figure 3-4: The Internet Accounts dialog box

Figure 3-5: Enter your name into the Internet Connection Wizard

7. The Internet Connection Wizard now prompts you for your e-mail address. Make sure that you have selected the "I have an e-mail address I would like to use" option and enter your e-mail address in the address area exactly as it appears from your e-mail administrator (or ISP), as shown in Figure 3-6. Press Next after you have completed this step.

8. Use the E-mail Server Name dialog box (as shown in Figure 3-7) to enter in the fully qualified domain names or the IP addresses of both your incoming and outgoing mail servers. (Most often, these are the same address.) Be sure to also select the appropriate incoming mail server type — POP3, IMAP, or HTTP. If you are unsure, contact your e-mail server administrator (or ISP). Press the Next button to continue.

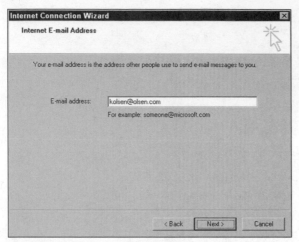

Figure 3-6: Enter your e-mail address into the Internet Connection Wizard

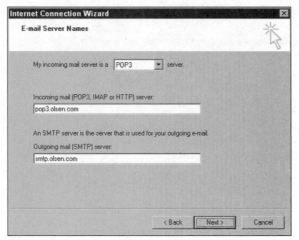

Figure 3-7: Enter in the addresses of the e-mail server(s)

9. Use the Internet mail logon screen (shown in Figure 3-8) to enter in your e-mail account name and associated password. (Most often, your e-mail account name matches the user name portion of your e-mail address.) After completing this dialog box, press Next.

Note   **Leave the** Log on using Secure Password Authentication **checkbox unchecked unless you are told to do otherwise by your e-mail administrator.**

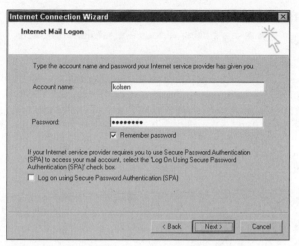

Figure 3-8: Enter in your e-mail user account name

If you turn on the `Remember password` option, you won't have to provide your user account and password information each time you use Outlook Express This option, however, poses a severe security risk because anybody else who starts Outlook Express from your computer may have full access to your e-mail account. This is especially true for users of Windows 95, 98, and Me because these operating systems have very little security built into them.

10. At the Internet Connection Wizard's Congratulations window, press the Finish button to bring up the Internet Accounts dialog box. Click on the Mail tab to see a screen similar to the screen shown in Figure 3-9; at this screen, you can see an entry for the e-mail account that you just added.

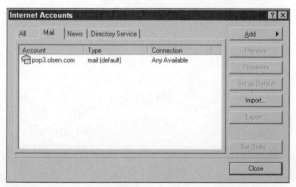

Figure 3-9: The configured Internet mail account list in Outlook Express

11. Press the Close button to exit the Internet Accounts dialog box.

Sending and receiving e-mail in Outlook Express

Objective ➡️ Send and receive e-mail messages using various e-mail client programs.

After you have completed the configuration of Outlook Express, you should be able to send and receive e-mails (as long as you have a valid account). You can test your e-mail configuration by sending an e-mail to a friend and ask that person to reply; or, you can simply send an e-mail to yourself. The following steps will guide you through this process.

To send e-mail in Outlook Express, follow these steps:

1. To begin an e-mail message, choose the New Mail icon located in the upper left of the main window, or open the Message menu and select New Mail Message. Figure 3-10 points out the major features of the New Mail message window that appears on your screen.

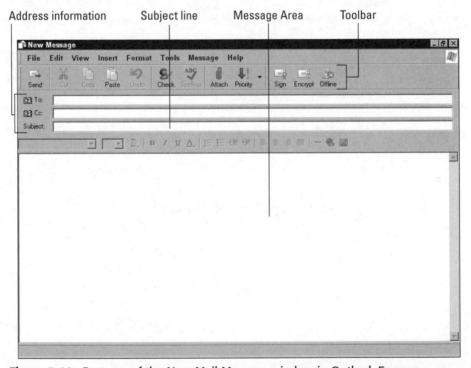

Figure 3-10: Features of the New Mail Message window in Outlook Express

2. Enter the e-mail address of the person to whom you want to send a message in the To: field. If you want to send the message to multiple recipients, type the addresses and separate them by commas, as shown in Figure 3-11.

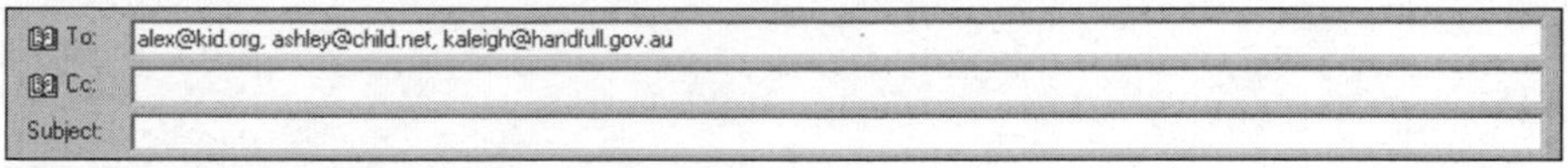

To:	alex@kid.org, ashley@child.net, kaleigh@handfull.gov.au
Cc:	
Subject:	

Figure 3-11: Entering multiple names

3. A *carbon copy*, or CC, recipient is a person or group of people to whom you want to send a copy of an e-mail—the text of which is really not directed at them. In many cases, the recipient simply needs to be aware of the message. If you want to add a CC to the message, simply type the person's e-mail address into the Cc: field.

4. A blind carbon copy, or BCC, is different from a carbon copy in that the individual's address is not listed anywhere in the e-mail in order to hide the different destinations of the message. To use a BCC, click the View menu and choose the All Headers option. The Bcc: field appears, allowing you to enter the addresses of your BCCs.

5. Click in the Subject line and type a short description of the content of the message.

6. Click your mouse in the text box and begin typing your e-mail message.

7. After you are satisfied with the content of your message, press the Send button, which is located in the upper left corner of your New Message window or select the Send Message option, which is located in the New Message window's File menu. Your message is sent to your e-mail server and you are returned to the Outlook Express main screen.

To receive e-mail in Outlook Express, follow these steps:

1. By default, Outlook Express checks for new e-mail at program startup and then at 30-minute intervals thereafter. If you don't want to wait, you can press the Send/Recv button, which is located on the toolbar.

2. New messages will appear in the inbox as unopened envelopes accompanied in bold letters by the name of the sender, the subject of the letter, and the date and time that the message was sent, as shown in Figure 3-12.

   To read the message, simply double-click it, and it should appear in a separate window, as shown in Figure 3-13.

3. After you have read the message, you can close it by clicking the Close Window button, which is located in the upper-right corner of the message window. The message now appears as an open envelope and is no longer bolded.

New Messages

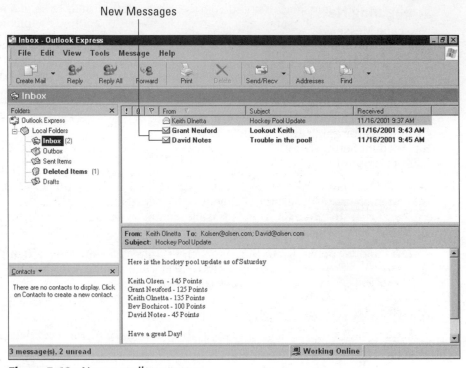

Figure 3-12: New e-mail messages

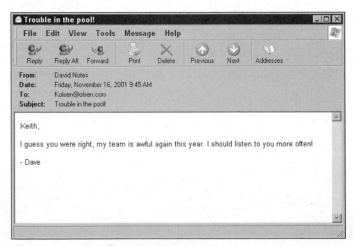

Figure 3-13: Reading a message

Configuring Netscape Messenger

Netscape Messenger is a mail client included with the popular Netscape Communicator suite of Internet client software. You can perform the configuration of Netscape Messenger either automatically or manually.

Perform the automated setup of Netscape Messenger by using Netscape Communicator's Profile Setup Wizard. (The first screen of this wizard is shown in Figure 3-14.) This wizard automatically appears the first time any of the Communicator applications is started. A series of screens, similar to the screens in the Account Setup Wizard in Outlook Express, guides the user through various configuration options.

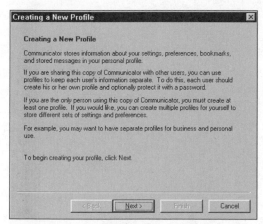

Figure 3-14: Netscape Communicator's Profile Setup Wizard

To manually configure Netscape Messenger, simply access the Preferences window, which is found in both Messenger and Navigator. The following steps guide you in performing a manual configuration of Messenger:

1. Start Netscape Messenger by accessing it through the Windows Start menu or by selecting it from the Quick Launch icon on the taskbar, as shown in Figure 3-15.

Figure 3-15: Starting Netscape Messenger

2. Upon startup, Messenger may ask you if you want to make Netscape Messenger your default mail application for Windows. Choose Yes if you want Netscape Messenger to start any time you click on an e-mail URL hyperlink from within a Web page or when using e-mail functions within other non-mail applications. If you intend to use Netscape Messenger as your primary e-mail application, choose Yes.

3. After Messenger appears on your screen, open the Edit menu and choose Preferences. The Preferences window appears, as shown in Figure 3-16.

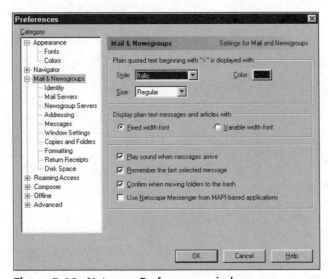

Figure 3-16: Netscape Preferences window

4. Click the Identity option within the Category pane. Enter your name into the Your Name field in the format that you want it to appear on all outgoing e-mails. This entry doesn't have to match the user name portion of your e-mail. Enter your e-mail address in exactly the format given to you from your system administrator. Your screen should be similar to the screen shown in Figure 3-17.

5. Click the Mail Servers option within the Category pane. The right side of the dialog box now shows the Mail Server settings.

6. If the Mail server is listed as an incoming server, click it and then click the Delete button. When asked to confirm the deletion, select Yes.

7. To configure an incoming mail server, click the Add button. The Mail Server Property dialog box appears on your screen.

8. Enter the Fully Qualified Domain Name or the IP address of either your POP3 or IMAP mail server into the Server name field. Be sure to select the appropriate server type. (If you are unsure, contact your e-mail administrator or ISP).

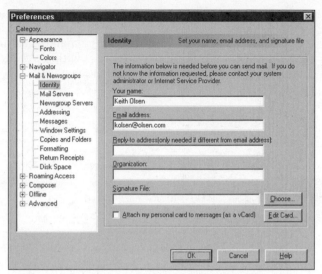

Figure 3-17: Identity settings in Netscape Messenger

9. Enter your e-mail user account name into the user name field (most often this name will match the user name portion of your e-mail address). The first time you send or receive e-mail in Netscape Messenger, you are prompted for your password. If you select the Remember Password option, this is the only time you are required to do so.

Caution

Turning this option on can pose a security risk because access to your e-mail will no longer require a password confirmation.

If you want Netscape Messenger to automatically check for incoming e-mails on a regular basis, click the `Check for mail every 15 minutes` check box. (Adjust the frequency as desired). The completed dialog box should look similar to the dialog box shown in Figure 3-18.

After you are satisfied that your server settings are complete, press the OK button.

10. To configure your Netscape Messenger for outgoing mail, enter your SMTP server FQDN or its IP address in the `Outgoing mail (SMTP) server` field and your SMTP server user account name into the `Outgoing mail server name` field. In most cases, the entries for these two fields will match those given in Steps 8 and 9.

Leave the `Use Secure Socket Layer (SSL) or TLS for outgoing messages` set to Never unless your e-mail administrator tells you otherwise.

Figure 3-18: Completed Mail Server
dialog box

Your completed Mail Server Preference screen should look similar to the
screen shown in Figure 3-19.

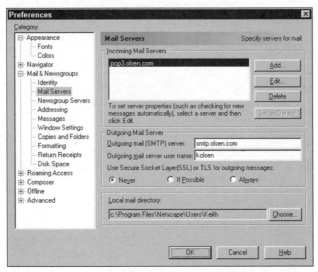

Figure 3-19: The completed Mail Server Preferences
screen

11. To finish your e-mail configuration, click the OK button.

Sending and receiving e-mail in Netscape Messenger

Objective
Send and receive e-mail messages using various e-mail client programs.

If you correctly completed all of the steps for setting up Netscape Messenger, you should now be able to send and receive e-mails. Test your setup by simply sending an e-mail message to yourself. If you receive it, you know that both functions are working correctly. The following steps guide you through sending an e-mail in Netscape Messenger.

To send e-mail in Netscape Messenger:

1. From the main Netscape Messenger window, press the New MSG button on the toolbar or choose the New Message option from within the Message menu. The New Message Composition window appears, as shown in Figure 3-20.

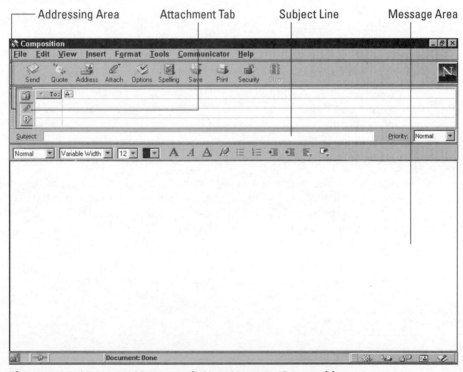

Figure 3-20: Netscape Messenger's New Message Composition screen

2. Use the To: field to enter in the intended recipient's e-mail address. If you want to add additional recipients, simply press Enter between each address. The result should look similar to that shown in Figure 3-21.

Note   You can Carbon Copy and Blind Carbon Copy recipients by clicking on the gray To: button beside each recipient's name and selecting the appropriate option.

3. Click your mouse in the Subject field and type an appropriate subject line for your message.

4. Hit Enter after typing your subject line to place your cursor into the message area of the composition form. Type your message.

5. To send your completed message, press the Send button on the Composition's toolbar or choose the Send Now option from the File menu. After your message is sent, you are returned to the main Netscape Messenger window.

To receive e-mail in Netscape Messenger, follow these steps:

1. If you want to force Netscape Messenger to check for new incoming mail, you may either press the Get Msg button on the Netscape Messenger toolbar or select the Get New Messages option from the File menu.

2. If prompted, type your password and press Enter.

3. New messages will now appear in the inbox. All unread messages appear bolded and new messages have a green down arrow attached to the accompanying envelope icon, as shown in Figure 3-21.

4. To read a message, double-click its subject and the message will appear in a window, as shown in Figure 3-22.

5. After you have read the message, you can close it by clicking the Close Window button located in the upper-right corner of the message window. The message you have just read is no longer bolded and the green arrow no longer appears on the envelope icon.

New Messages

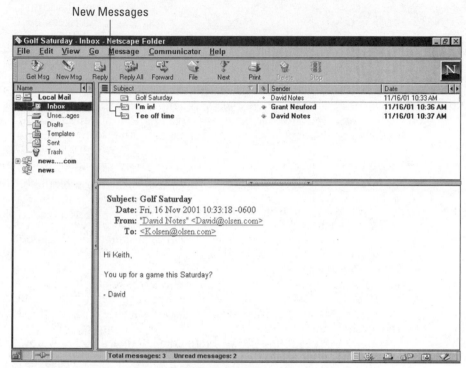

Figure 3-21: New messages in Netscape Messenger's inbox

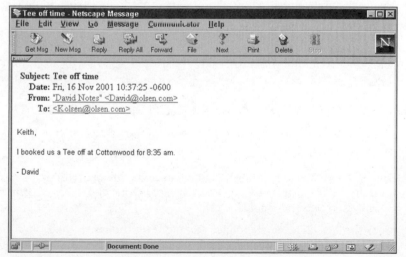

Figure 3-22: Reading a message in Netscape Messenger

Attachments

 Attach a file to e-mail messages.

Not only can you send text messages with e-mail, you can also exchange files by using e-mail attachments. An *attachment* is simply a file that is "attached" or sent along with a message. This can be an effective method for sending word processing documents, spreadsheets, images, and almost any other form of electronic file.

Here are a couple of simple suggestions that you should consider when sending an attachment:

✦ Make the attachment as small as possible. Consider using a data compression program, such as WINZIP or ZIPWIZ. This type of application can often compress a file up to 90 percent smaller than its original size. The smaller the file, the greater the likelihood that the file can be successfully sent. Many e-mail servers have administrator-controlled restrictions on the size of file attachments that a message may carry; therefore, the smaller the file, the greater the likelihood that the mail servers will pass the message on to the recipient. Recipients will appreciate a smaller file because it will speed the download of the message and the attachment to their client computers. You may want to talk to the recipient first, however, to confirm that they know how to deal with a compressed file. For example, if you use WINZIP to compress your file, then your recipient needs to use a program capable of uncompressing the file, such as WINZIP itself.

✦ Always mention the attachment in the text of the message. Some e-mail applications do a poor job of informing the user of an attachment (especially older e-mail applications), and the user may not realize that it exists. Also tell the user what type of file you are sending them; this information will aid them in dealing with the file when they actually receive it.

Attachments in Microsoft Outlook Express

The following instructions explain the steps required to attach an e-mail in Outlook Express:

1. Follow the steps for sending e-mail discussed previously in this chapter in the section, "Sending and receiving e-mail using Outlook Express." Stop prior to actually sending the e-mail.

2. Press the Attach icon (the paper clip icon) on the message toolbar or choose the File Attachment option in the Insert menu. Figure 3-23 shows the location of these options.

File attachment options

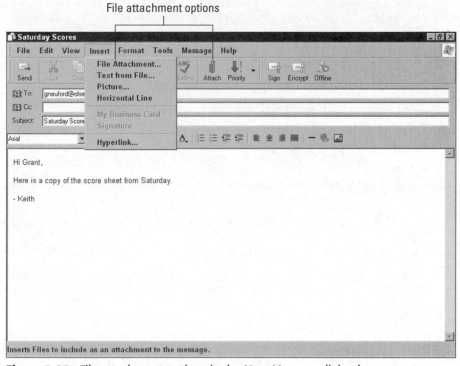

Figure 3-23: File attachment options in the New Message dialog box

3. In the Insert Attachment dialog box, locate and click the name of the file that you want to attach, and then press the Attach button.

4. Your file attachment appears directly beneath the subject bar of your message, as shown in Figure 3-24. If you need to add an additional attachment, repeat Steps 2 and 3.

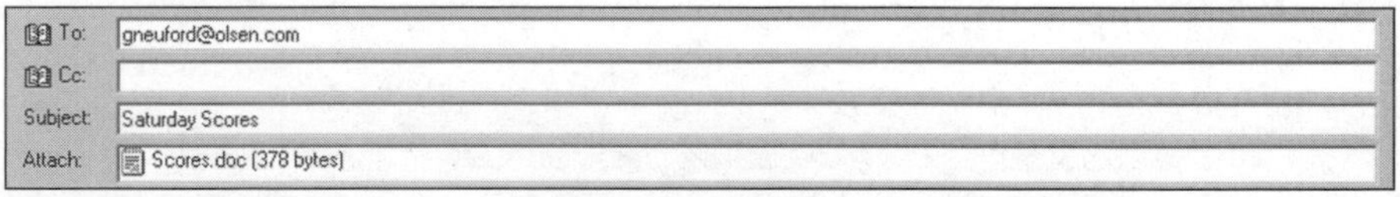

Figure 3-24: The Attachment indicator in the New Message dialog box

5. After you have completed attaching your files and are satisfied with the content of your message, press the Send button.

Outlook Express notifies you that an e-mail message contains an attachment by placing a small paper clip icon next to the message in the Outlook inbox, as shown in Figure 3-25.

Attachment Indicator

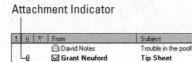

Figure 3-25: The Attachment indicator in the New Message dialog box in Outlook

To detach a file from an e-mail while using Outlook Express, follow these steps:

1. Locate and open the e-mail message containing the attachment.

2. Just beneath the subject line of the message, you can see the Attach line with an icon and the name of the file attached to the message, as shown in Figure 3-26.

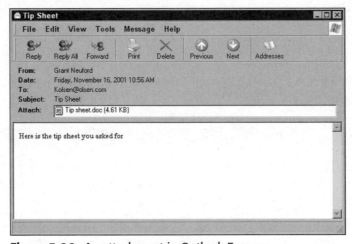

Figure 3-26: An attachment in Outlook Express

To extract the attachment, double-click its icon. You are presented with the Open Attachment Warning dialog box, as shown in Figure 3-27.

3. Read the warning screen. If you're sure that the file has come from a reliable source, and if you're running an up-to-date anti-virus application, then proceed to Step 4. Otherwise, press Cancel.

Figure 3-27: Open Attachment
Warning dialog box

4. If you want to view the attachment now, choose the Open it option. If you want to save the file for later use, then choose the Save it to disk option.

The Open it option tells Outlook Express to open the file in its associated application. For example, if you have been sent a Microsoft Word document as an attachment, this option will open Word and load the document. If you have been sent a document, and Outlook Express can't determine the appropriate application to use to open it, then you will be presented with a list of applications that are installed on your computer; you need to select the appropriate application in order to open the attachment.

The Save it to disk option allows you to extract the message from the e-mail message and save it to the disk location of your choosing.

5. After you have decided how to deal with the attachment, you can close the e-mail message.

Tip

Attachments can often be quite large; therefore, it's a good idea to delete the e-mail message from your inbox after you have obtained and saved the attachment.

Attachments in Netscape Messenger

The following instructions describe the process of attaching a file to an e-mail message in Netscape Messenger.

1. Follow the steps for sending e-mail as discussed previously in this chapter in the section, "Sending and receiving e-mail in Netscape Messenger." Don't actually send the e-mail, however.

2. Press the Attach icon (the paper clip) from the Composition toolbar or open the File menu and select Attach the File.

3. Use the Enter File to Attach dialog box to locate and select the file that you want to attach. After the file is highlighted, select Open. You are then returned to your e-mail. At the top of the window, you can now see your attachment on the Attachment Tab, as shown in Figure 3-28.

Attachment Tab   Attached File

Figure 3-28: An attached file in Netscape Messenger

4. After you are satisfied with both your attachment and the associated e-mail, press the Send button. Before you open a message with an attachment, Netscape Messenger doesn't indicate that the message contains an attachment. After you have opened and subsequently closed the message, however, Messenger indicates that the message contains an attachment by placing a small paper clip icon on top of the envelope icon next to the message in the inbox, as shown in Figure 3-29.

Attached File Indicator

Subject		Sender	Date
Golf Saturday	∘	David Notes	11/16/01 10:33 AM
I'm in!	∘	Grant Neuford	11/16/01 10:36 AM
It's Official	∘	Grant Pontman	9/8/01 6:52 AM
New Record!	∘	Grant Pontman	9/8/01 6:44 AM
Tee off time	∘	David Notes	11/16/01 10:37 AM

Figure 3-29: The Attachment indicator in the New Message dialog box in Netscape Messenger

The following steps describe the process of detaching and viewing an attachment in Netscape Messenger:

1. Locate and open the e-mail message that contains the attachment.

2. Attachments in Netscape Messenger appear as hyperlinks at the bottom of their corresponding e-mail messages, as shown in Figure 3-30.

Attachment Hyperlink

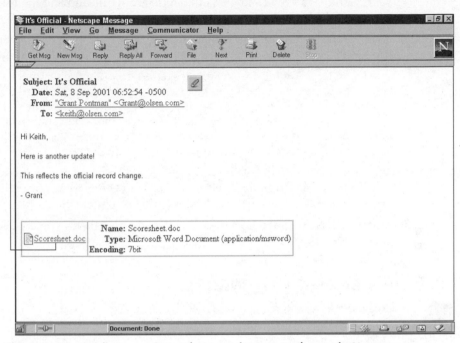

Figure 3-30: Reading a message that contains an attachment in Netscape Messenger

Click on the attachment hyperlink to begin the process of extracting the attachment. The warning shown in Figure 3-31 appears on your screen.

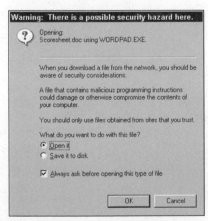

Figure 3-31: The Security Hazard Warning dialog box in Netscape Messenger

3. Read the warning screen. If you're sure that the file has come from a reliable source and if you're running an up-to-date anti-virus application, then proceed to Step 4. Otherwise, press Cancel.

4. If you want to view the attachment now, choose the Open it option; if you want to save the file for later use, then choose the Save it to disk option.

The Open it option tells Netscape Messenger to open the file in its associated application. For example, if you have been sent a Microsoft Word document as an attachment, this option will open Word and load the document. If you have been sent a document and Netscape Messenger can't determine the appropriate application to use to open it, then you will be presented with a list of applications that are installed on your computer. You need to select the appropriate application to open the attachment.

The Save it to disk option allows you to extract the message from the e-mail message and save it to the disk location of your choosing.

5. After you have decided how to deal with the attachment, you can close the e-mail message.

E-mail message signatures

Create e-mail signatures to e-mail messages.

An *e-mail signature* consists of a few lines of text that can be automatically added to the bottom of all outgoing messages. Signatures are commonly used to place the sender's name, address, and other contact information in a message. This information seldom changes and is usually desired on most outgoing correspondence, so rather than typing it manually at the bottom of all outgoing e-mails, you can simply create a signature.

Creating a signature in Outlook Express

The following steps describe the process of creating a signature in Microsoft Outlook Express.

1. From the main inbox window of Outlook Express, open the Tools menu and select Options. The Options dialog box appears on your screen.

2. Locate and click the Signatures tab located at the top of the Options dialog box. You should now see the Signature options, as shown in Figure 3-32.

3. Press the New button to activate the text entry area at the bottom of the Signature dialog box.

4. Turn on the checkbox labeled `Add signatures to all outgoing messages`.

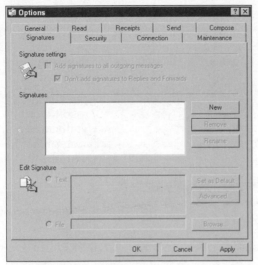

Figure 3-32: The Signature Option dialog box in Outlook Express

5. Type your signature text however you want it to appear at the bottom of your e-mail messages. See Figure 3-33 for an example of a signature text.

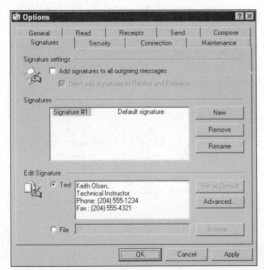

Figure 3-33: A sample e-mail signature

6. To test your e-mail signature, create a new message and send it to yourself. After it arrives, check its contents to see your signature as you created it.

Creating a signature in Netscape Messenger

Unlike Outlook Express, Netscape Messenger doesn't allow direct entry of a signature. You must first create a text document that contains the text of your signature, then set up Messenger to use this file. The following steps describe this process.

1. Start the Notepad text editor by clicking the Windows Start button, or by choosing Programs ⇨ Accessories ⇨ Notepad.

2. Type your signature text into Notepad the way you want it to appear at the bottom of all of your outgoing e-mails, as shown in Figure 3-34.

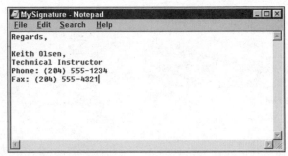

Figure 3-34: Creating a signature file in Notepad

3. After you have completed your signature, save your file by selecting the Save command from Notepad's File menu. Type in an appropriate name for your file (some users prefer "my signature") and press the Save button.

4. Exit Notepad.

5. Start up Netscape Messenger.

6. Locate the Preference Configuration dialog box by selecting the Edit menu and choosing the Preferences option.

7. In the Category list, select the Identity option located directly beneath the Mail & Newsgroup settings option.

8. To select your signature file, click the Choose button.

9. Locate and click the file that you saved in Step 3, and then press the Open button.

Note If you are having trouble locating your file, be sure to look in your "My Documents" folder because it is the default location that Notepad uses to save your files.

10. Close the Preferences dialog box by pressing the OK button.

11. Test your signature by starting a new e-mail; you should see your signature located at the bottom of the e-mail, as shown in Figure 3-35.

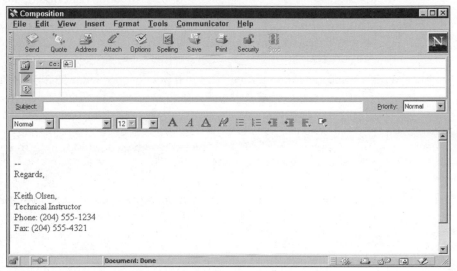

Figure 3-35: An e-mail signature added to a new message

Netiquette and Privacy

 Objective   Define and practice "netiquette:"

The *Encarta World English Dictionary* defines *etiquette* as follows: "The rules and conventions governing correct or polite behavior in society in general or in a particular social or professional group or situation."

Etiquette has been a necessary part of human communication for a long time, and communication over the Internet should be no exception. Whether using e-mail, newsgroups, chat rooms, or any other form of Internet communication, you should follow a set of rules and practices that encourage politeness and respect. These common-sense rules are collectively referred to as *netiquette*.

The following is a list of the most basic principles of netiquette:

✦ E-mail messages and newsgroup postings should always contain clear, concise subject lines that accurately reflect the content of the message or posting.

✦ Always check all communication for accuracy of grammar and spelling before sending.

✦ Always respond in a timely fashion to any message directed to you. Ensure that all responses have been carefully thought out and accurately address the content of the original message.

✦ Remember that date information is often automatically added to all outgoing messages. If you are tardy in responding to an e-mail, don't try to word your response to make it appear that it was typed and sent in a timely manner. The automatic date and time stamping will give you away because it accurately reflects the real date and time that the message was composed and sent.

✦ When communicating for work-related purposes, ensure that the tone and structure of the message reflects proper business language.

✦ Most face-to-face communication relies on voice tone, facial expression, and body language to convey meaning. This type of inflection can't be used when communicating over the Internet, so give careful thought to sentence structure and language to ensure that recipients properly understand your messages.

✦ Avoid the use of all capital letters in a message because it represents shouting or anger, which may offend the recipient.

Exam Tip   Remember these netiquette rules!

Related to netiquette is the issue of Internet and network privacy. Remember that your employer has legal ownership of all materials created by you while at work—this includes all material created for network communication, such as e-messages and newsgroup postings.

Organizations commonly monitor e-mails—some even read the contents of all outgoing and incoming correspondence. In some cases, individuals have been terminated and some even prosecuted for passing trade secrets, racist literature, pornography, and many other types of inappropriate content. You should always follow this general rule: Never put anything into an e-mail that may be deemed as inappropriate, offensive, or goes against an organization's non-disclosure agreement.

Mailing Lists

Objective   Describe the purpose of mailing lists.

E-mail is popularly used for *mailing lists* (also known as *list servs*). An electronic mailing list is a group of e-mail addresses that belong to individuals interested in a particular subject. Any e-mails sent to the mailing list are passed on to all those who belong to or subscribe to the list. These mailing lists can be a valuable resource for both personal and professional use. Thousands of mailing lists are available — covering virtually any subject you can imagine. Joining a mailing list is usually as simple as finding a newsgroup of interest and sending an e-mail to the newsgroup LISTSERV account specifying the fact that you want to subscribe. For example, if you are interested in acting, you can join the Professional Actor's and Director's list newsgroup by submitting an e-mail to `listserv@home.ease.lsoft.com` with the words: SUBSCRIBE ACTING-PRO either in the subject or body of the e-mail.

You can unsubscribe from most mailing lists by again sending a message to the LISTSERV account for the mailing list. Therefore, if you are a member of the Professional Actor's and Director's list, you can unsubscribe by sending an e-mail to `listserv@home.ease.lsoft.com` and include either in the subject or body of the message the following words: UNSUBSCRIBE ACTING-PRO.

Several sites on the Internet catalog and describe various mailing lists, including Neosoft's Publicly Available Mailing Lists Web site at `http://paml.net` and L-Soft's CataList at `http://www.lsoft.com/lists/listref.html`.

Cross-Reference For more information regarding mailing lists and mailing list servers, see Chapter 16.

Newsgroups and USENET

Objective Read and post messages to newsgroups.

Similar in concept to mailing lists, *newsgroups* are bulletin board-type discussion forums that interested parties can access to read messages (referred to as *postings*), share ideas, ask questions, submit answers, and generally discuss topics of common interest — all in a text-based format.

Newsgroups categories

On the Internet, the thousands of publicly accessible newsgroups are referred to collectively as *USENET*. USENET was originally developed at Duke University for open discussion within the university community. Since its inception, USENET has grown to well over 50,000 newsgroups — each of which is tightly focused on a particular subject matter. Like mailing lists, these newsgroups cover almost any topic imaginable and have grown well beyond the confines of universities. Newsgroups are now available to all who want to subscribe.

The content of the newsgroups vary greatly, and as a result, newsgroups have been organized by topic into various categories. The most popular, referred to as the "Big Eight," are shown in Table 3-1.

Table 3-1 Popular Newsgroup Categories	
Category	**Description**
alt	Alternative or controversial topics
comp	Computer topics
misc	Miscellaneous
news	USENET information
rec	Recreational topics, such as hobbies and the arts
sci	Sciences and scientific research topics
soc	Topics regarding socializing and social issues
talk	General discussion groups for topics such as religion, politics, and other issues

The newsgroup categories are divided into many subcategories, which in turn, may also be further divided into subcategories. The names of the newsgroups reflect these categories and subcategories in a "dotted" hierarchical format. For example, consider the following newsgroup:

```
rec.antiques.bottles
```

This newsgroup has been named to reflect the fact that it is focused on a recreation (rec), more particularly that of antique collecting (antiques), and even more specifically, the activity of collecting antique bottles (bottles).

The asterisk (*) character is commonly used to denote a newsgroup category that has been divided into several additional subcategories. For example, the newsgroup rec.arts.books* represents the fact that this topic has subdivisions, such as:

```
rec.arts.books.children
rec.arts.books.collecting
rec.arts.books.hist-fiction
rec.arts.books.reviews
```

Accessing newsgroups

Generally, you can access a newsgroup via a newsgroup client application using the Network News Transport Protocol (NNTP). Microsoft Outlook Express and Netscape Communicator can both serve as newsgroup clients. To access newsgroups by using these products, you will need to know the address of a newsgroup server. Most Internet service providers (ISPs) provide newsgroup access for their clients. If you need the address of your newsgroup server, contact your ISP.

Configuring newsgroup access in Outlook Express

The following instructions explain the basics on how to configure and use Outlook Express for newsgroup access:

1. Start Outlook Express.

2. Choose the Tools menu at the top of the Outlook Express window and select the Accounts option. The Internet Accounts dialog box appears.

3. From the Internet Accounts dialog box, press the Add button and choose the News option. The Internet Connection Wizard appears.

4. The first screen in the Internet Connection Wizard prompts you to enter your name in the style that you want it to appear in the From: field of all of the newsgroup postings. After you have entered your name, press the Next button.

5. You are now prompted to enter the e-mail address that others can use to contact you regarding any of the postings that you make to a newsgroup. If you have already configured Outlook for e-mail access, then this address should already appear. If you want to use a different e-mail address or have not previously configured Outlook Express for e-mail, enter your e-mail address. After you are finished, press the Next button.

6. If you are prompted, enter either the FQDN or the IP address of your newsgroup server. If your newsgroup server requires that you provide the FQDN or IP address along with a user name and password, then select the `My newsgroup server requires me to log on` dialog box. Press Next after you are finished.

7. If you are prompted, enter your user name and password as provided by your newsgroup server administrator. Press Next. If you aren't prompted, proceed to Step 8.

8. When you are presented with the Congratulations dialog box, press the Finish button. The Internet Account dialog box appears, in which you will now see an entry for the newsgroup server that you just configured.

9. Press Close to exit the Internet Accounts dialog box.

10. You will now receive a prompt asking if you want to download newsgroups from the newsgroup account that you just created. Choose Yes.

Note   Depending on the newsgroup server that you are using, you may have a substantial wait while it downloads the names of all the newsgroups available to your client computer.

After the newsgroup names have been downloaded to your computer, you are presented with the Newsgroup Subscription dialog box, in which you can now begin the task of selecting and subscribing to the newsgroups that interest you. This dialog box is shown in Figure 3-36.

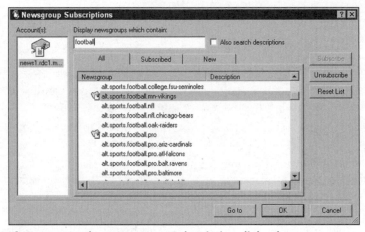

Figure 3-36: The Newsgroup Subscription dialog box

11. Click on any newsgroup that interests you and press the Subscribe button. A subscription icon appears next to that newsgroup. Repeat this step for all newsgroups that interest you.

12. After you have completed subscribing to your newsgroups, press the OK button. You are taken back to the Outlook Express main screen, where you will see the newsgroups that you subscribed to listed in its folder pane, similar to the folder pane shown in Figure 3-37.

13. To view the contents of any newsgroup, simply click its name in the folder list. The headers of recently posted articles appear.

14. Opening an article is similar to reading an e-mail message — you simply double-click its subject line.

15. To respond to an article, you may use the Reply to group option, which will allow you to create a reply and have it posted back to the newsgroup for all to see. If you would rather respond only to the individual who created the original posting, choose the Reply button from the Messages toolbar.

16. After you are finished reading a posting, simply close its window.

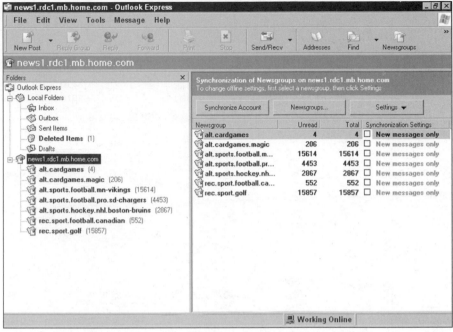

Figure 3-37: Newsgroup subscriptions in Outlook Express

17. To create your own posting for a newsgroup, press the New Post button from the main window toolbar, or open the File menu and choose New ➪ News Message.

18. Construct your News message just as you would construct an e-mail message and after you are finished, press the Send button.

Note Press the F5 key on your keyboard or choose the Refresh option from the View menu to update your newsgroup listing with the latest postings. Your own postings, however, may take several minutes to appear.

Configuring newsgroup access in Netscape Messenger

The following steps guide you through the process of configuring Netscape Messenger for newsgroup access. These steps also give you a brief introduction on how to subscribe, read, and post to newsgroups in Messenger.

1. Open Netscape Messenger.

2. Select the Edit menu and choose Preferences.

3. In the Category list, select the Newsgroup servers option located under the Mail & Newsgroup settings.

4. Select the Add button and type either the name or the IP address of your e-mail server. Unless told otherwise by your network administrator or ISP, leave the Port number at 119, don't select Supports encrypted connections

(SSL), and leave the `Always use name and password` option unchecked. After you have completed the Newsgroup Servers Properties dialog box, press the OK button.

5. The Newsgroup Servers preferences screen now lists the name of the newsgroup server that you just added, as shown in Figure 3-38.

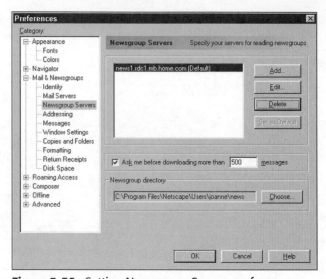

Figure 3-38: Setting Newsgroup Servers preferences

Verify that the name is entered correctly, and press the OK button.

6. After you have successfully configured your newsgroup client to connect to your newsgroup server, you must now subscribe to the newsgroups offered by your news server that interest you. To do so, right-click your newsgroup server name where it appears in the far left pane of the window. From the popup menu, select Subscribe to newsgroups. The communicator: Subscribe to Newsgroups dialog box appears.

7. The Subscribe to Newsgroups dialog box presents the newsgroups based on their first level newsgroup name, as shown in Figure 3-39.

To expand on the first level names, press the plus sign (+) located just to the right of the newsgroup folder icon. Repeat this step for any sub-newsgroups that interest you. The headings that appear without the plus sign are the actual newsgroups; if any spark your interest and you want to subscribe to them, click their names and press the Subscribe button. You will see a checkmark appear next to their names. After you have completed all of your selections, press the OK button.

8. All of the newsgroups to which you have subscribed now appear on the left pane of the main Netscape Messenger window. To see the posting for any of these newsgroups, click the newsgroup name.

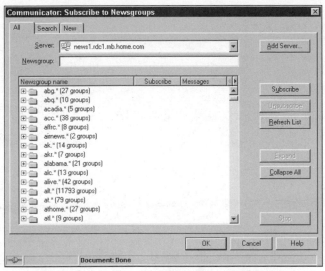

Figure 3-39: The Subscribe to Newsgroups dialog box

9. To read any posting, double-click its subject line.

10. To respond to an article, you may use either the Reply to sender only option or your may choose the Reply to newsgroup option. The Reply to sender option opens a new e-mail message, automatically addressed to the individual who posted the message that you are replying to. The Reply to newsgroup will create a newsgroup posting, which is posted back to the newsgroup, and is thus available to all subscribers to the newsgroup. You can access either option by clicking the Reply button located on the toolbar and choosing the appropriate type of reply from the resulting short menu.

11. After you are finished reading a posting, simply close the window that it appears in.

12. To create your own posting for a newsgroup, press the New MSG button from the Netscape Messenger toolbar or choose the New Message option from the Message menu. Enter your message just as you would enter an e-mail message, and then when you are satisfied, press the Send button.

Accessing newsgroups through HTTP

Web browser software is now commonly used to both search and access newsgroups through HTTP. The benefit of using Web browser software is that, unlike news client software, the Web browser doesn't need any special configuration. Simply connect to the Web site that hosts the newsgroups and use the hyperlinks and search capabilities provided through the Web page interface. Several sites now offer this service — the most popular is Google Groups (formerly Deja.com's Usenet Discussion Service). This site, located at http://groups.google.com, has an archive of some 650 million Usenet messages, dating back to 1995 and spread over thousands of readily accessible newsgroups.

For more information regarding newsgroups, see Chapter 16.

Access and download files using File Transfer Protocol (FTP).

FTP is a protocol that allows the transfer of files between FTP clients and FTP server applications. It is a hugely popular service due to its ease of use, reliability, and flexibility. The following section discusses client-side aspects of the FTP protocol and service.

FTP site contents

The content that a server provides is solely up to the owner of the FTP server. These files can be virtually any type, but generally consist of two main classifications: text files (plain documents with no formatting) or binary files (all non-plain text files such as programs, images, and program-specific file types). To save on FTP storage space and to speed transfer, these files are often stored on the FTP server in a compressed format. When you download these types of files, you will be required to uncompress them before you can use them. Generally, you can determine the type of file by its extension. Table 3-2 lists the common extensions often found on FTP sites.

Table 3-2 Common File Extensions	
Extension	**Description**
.txt	Plain text document with no form of compression. These are universally readable by any text editor or word processing program.
.asc	Plain ASCII text file. This format is a standard text format for use with all types of computers. Also readable in any text editor or word processing program.
.exe	Executable file. This can be a self-extracting compressed file or an application.
.zip	A very common file extension used by compression programs, such as WinZip, PKZIP, or ZipWiz.
.tar	A common extension indicating a UNIX compressed tape archive format file.
.sea	Indicates a self-extracting Macintosh compressed Stuffit file.
.sit	The standard extension for non-self-extracting compressed Macintosh Stuffit file.

Exam Tip   You are required to recognize these extensions on the exam.

The files provided by the FTP server are usually stored in directories (folders) within the FTP server file system. Sites will often divide these directories into several subdirectories to organize the content.

FTP site access

Access to an FTP server may also be subject to certain limitations. For example, some sites allow *anonymous access*. This type of access permits anyone to access the FTP server by simply using a common user name, such as "anonymous," "ftp," or "guest." Users, however, may be denied access if a limitation has been set to restrict the maximum number of clients at any one time. Other sites have been set up for exclusive use by particular individuals (referred to as *non-anonymous access*) and as such, any user desiring access to these sites must provide a valid user name and password.

After users are connected to the FTP, their actions may also be regulated. For example, an FTP server can be set up to allow only downloads (no uploads). In other words, users can retrieve files from the server but they can't send files to the server. Non-anonymous FTP sites may base this restriction on the actual user account; therefore, logging on with one user account may provide only download ability, whereas logging on with another account may provide access to both uploading and downloading.

Using an FTP client

In order to access an FTP site, you must use an FTP client. Clients generally come in two forms: Text-based and Windows or GUI- (graphical user interface) based.

Accessing FTP servers with a text-based client

Objective   Describe the FTP get and put commands.

Text-based clients are generally provided with your network operating system and are accessed through a command line interface.

Tip   Create a folder on your hard drive for files received from an FTP server. Prior to beginning your text-based FTP session, use the command prompt to switch to this directory.

With most operating systems, you start an FTP session by issuing the command `ftp` at the command prompt. The Windows-based FTP client responds with the following command prompt:

```
ftp>
```

To connect to an FTP server, issue the `open` command with the following syntax (*server* is the FQDN or IP address of the ftp server to which you want to connect):

```
open server
```

When using a text-based FTP client, you must always provide logon information. For FTP sites that provide anonymous access, you can usually just type the word **anonymous**. The ftp server will tell you that anonymous access is allowed and that you must provide your e-mail address as a password. This allows the server to track those who have accessed the system.

Figure 3-40 shows a typical text-based FTP client being used to connect to an anonymous FTP site (`ftp.olsen.com`).

Figure 3-40: Using a text-based client to connect to an FTP site

 Caution When accessing FTP sites on the Internet, you may not want to enter your real e-mail address because you may receive non-solicited e-mails, including spam (junk e-mail).

For non-anonymous FTP sites, enter in your user name and password as provided by the FTP site administrator.

After you are connected, you can issue several commands to interact with the FTP server. Table 3-3 describes some of the more commonly used commands:

Table 3-3
Commonly Used FTP Commands

Command	Description
open	Open a connection to a server.
dir	The directory command used to list the contents of an FTP directory.
ls	The list command used to list directory contents (same as dir).
ascii	Sets the file transfer type for the client to ASCII mode. (This is the default in most FTP clients.)
	FTP can download two file types (ASCII and binary). ASCII should be used for transferring text files.
binary	Sets the file transfer type to binary. This mode should be used when transferring executable files.
get	Used to download a file from an FTP server. For example, if you want to download a file called manual.doc, enter the command get manual.doc.
mget	Used to download multiple files from an FTP Server. For example if an FTP server had ten files all ending with a .doc extension and you wished to download them all you could type mget *.doc.
put	Used to upload a file to an FTP server. For example, if you want to upload a file called blaster.exe to the FTP server, enter the command put blaster.exe.
mput	Used to upload multiple files to an FTP server. For example if you want to upload all files that have an extension of .zip you could type mput *.zip.
cd	Used to change directory in an FTP hierarchical file system. Some command examples of this command are: cd \games — move to the directory called games. cd \ — move to the FTP root directory. cd .. — move one directory up in the FTP file system. (For example, if you are in a directory called \games\simulations\space, this command places you into the directory \games\simulations.)
disconnect	Disconnect from the server but remain in the FTP client. (Used if you want to issue the open command to connect to a different server.)
quit	Disconnect from server and the FTP client (returns you to the operating system command prompt).
bye	Same as quit.

Accessing FTP servers with a GUI-based client

GUI FTP-based clients allow you to browse, upload, and download in a graphical environment. For most, the benefit of this type of access is ease of use because you can perform most actions with a simple click of a mouse.

Many GUI FTP client utilities are available; ironically, many of them are available for download from Internet-based FTP servers. Some of the more popular utilities include: Ipswitch's WS_FTP Pro 7.0 (`www.ipswitch.com`), GlobalScape's CuteFTP (`www.cuteftp.com`), and FTPx's FTP explorer (`www.ftpx.com`). Web browser software, such as Microsoft Internet Explorer and Netscape Navigator, also provide FTP client access.

With a browser, accessing an FTP site is simply a matter of entering the FTP server's URL into the browser's address bar. Anonymous FTP access is generally provided without additional user input. Your Web browser will display a login dialog box when you access non-anonymous FTP servers. Or, you can include the non-anonymous name and password in the URL. A URL of this type looks like the following:

```
ftp://username:password@ftp.server.com
```

If a user has an FTP account named "dave" and a password of "music," he or she can use the following URL to gain access to a server named `ftp.server.com`:

```
ftp://dave:music@ftp.server.com
```

Caution   I don't recommend passing passwords through a URL like this because anyone looking over your shoulder can see both your user name and password.

Table 3-4 describes common FTP tasks and how they are accomplished in both Netscape Navigator and Microsoft Internet Explorer.

Table 3-4 FTP Tasks		
FTP Task	**Internet Explorer**	**Netscape Navigator**
Connect to an FTP server	Enter URL into browser's address bar and press Enter	Enter URL into browser's address bar and press Enter
Display directory listing	Automatic	Automatic
Change Directory	Double-click the directory that you want to change to	Click the name of the directory that you want to change to
Download a file (get)	Double-click the file	Click the file name

FTP Task	Internet Explorer	Netscape Navigator
Upload a file (put)	Drag and drop your files from any Windows Explorer window into the browser window	Drag and drop your files from any Windows Explorer window into the browser window (or choose the Upload file option from the File menu)
End FTP session	Close the browser or connect to another site	Close the browser or connect to another site

See Chapter 16 for more information regarding FTP servers.

Telnet Basics

Access resources usingTelnet.

Telnet is a protocol that is used to support terminal emulation sessions from a client to a server. Through a Telnet session, a client can log on to a remote telnet server computer and carry out commands as if the client were physically sitting at the server or at a terminal directly controlled by that server. As a result of this ability, Telnet sessions are often referred to as *remote host connections*.

The client computer does very little of the actual processing of information, which is similar to a dial-up shell account; in fact, even the keystrokes entered by a user are sent to the Telnet server where they are processed and then sent back for display on your screen.

Simple Telnet client software is generally provided with most network operating systems. For example, Windows NT comes with the Telnet client that you can access by typing **telnet *server*** (*server* is the name or IP address of the telnet server that you want to access).

Although most of the main stream Internet traffic has moved away from Telnet, network administrators still use it to remotely manage and access servers. These servers are, for the most part, UNIX-based servers; however, Windows 2000 now includes a Telnet server service that allows similar remote administration capabilities.

Key Point Summary

The following is a summary of the key points in this chapter:

✦ E-mail serves as the cornerstone service for providing user-to-user communication.

✦ An e-mail address uniquely identifies an individual on the Internet.

✦ E-mail addresses consist of a user name, an @ sign, and a domain name.

✦ Characters in a user name can include numbers, letters, periods, and underscores.

✦ All e-mail client applications require the following information in order to be properly configured:

- User's e-mail address

- User's password

- SMTP server address

- POP3 or IMAP4 server address

✦ Microsoft Outlook Express is the Internet mail client bundled with Microsoft Internet Explorer. It can act as a client for mail, newsgroups, and directory access via LDAP.

✦ Netscape Messenger is a mail client included with the Netscape Communicator suite of Internet client software.

✦ An attachment is simply a file that is "attached" or sent along with an e-mail message. This can be an effective method to send word processing documents, spreadsheets, images, and almost any other form of electronic file. The following are two general guidelines for attachments:

- Make attachments as small as possible.

- Always mention the attachment in the text of the e-mail.

✦ An e-mail signature consists of a few lines of text that can be automatically added to the bottom of all outgoing messages. It usually includes a closing salutation, the sender's name, and contact information.

✦ Netiquette is a set of rules and practices that encourage politeness and respect. These rules and practices include:

- Subject lines for e-mails and newsgroup postings should be clear and concise.

- Always ensure that grammar and spelling are correct before sending any message.

- Respond in a timely fashion to all correspondence.

- When communicating for work-related purposes, ensure that the tone and structure of the messages reflect proper business language.

- Give careful thought to the wording and structure of e-mails to ensure that the message is understood correctly.

- Avoid the use of all capital letters because it REPRESENTS SHOUTING!

✦ Remember that e-mail addresses supplied to you by your employer are the property of the employer; therefore, never put anything into an e-mail that may be deemed inappropriate, offensive, or goes against an organization's non-disclosure agreement.

✦ An electronic mailing list is a group of e-mail addresses belonging to individuals interested in a particular subject. E-mails sent to the mailing list are passed on to all those who belong to or subscribe to the list.

✦ Newsgroups are bulletin board-type discussion forums that interested users can access to read messages (referred to as *postings*), share ideas, ask questions, submit answers, and generally discuss topics of common interest — all in a text-based format.

✦ The thousands of publicly accessible newsgroups on the Internet are referred to collectively as USENET.

✦ Newsgroups are organized by topic into various categories; these categories are divided into subcategories, which may, in turn, be further subdivided and so on. A newsgroup's name reflects those categories and subcategories to which it belongs.

✦ FTP is a protocol that allows the transfer of files between FTP clients and FTP server applications.

✦ FTP files fall in two general categories: text and binary.

✦ A user accessing an anonymous FTP site doesn't need a unique user account or password.

✦ Common anonymous account names are "anonymous," "guest," or "ftp."

✦ Users accessing a non-anonymous FTP site require a user name and a password to gain access.

✦ Restrictions can be placed on what a user can do while connected to an FTP server.

✦ FTP client software is either text- or GUI-based.

✦ Using a `get` command allows you to download a file from an FTP server.

✦ Using a `put` command allows you to upload a file to an FTP server.

✦ GUI FTP based clients allow an individual to browse, upload, and download in a graphical environment.

✦ Telnet is a protocol used to support terminal emulation sessions from a client to a server.

✦ Telnet is similar to a dialup shell account in that the Telnet server provides the bulk of the data processing and the client computer simply acts as a terminal.

✦ Telnet is still commonly used by network administrators to remotely manage and access servers.

✦   ✦   ✦

STUDY GUIDE

The following assessment questions test your memory on some of the key topics covered in this chapter. The scenario questions test your understanding of the concepts by presenting you with real-life situations for which you must answer chapter-related questions.

Assessment Questions

1. Which of the following are examples of correctly formulated e-mail addresses? (Choose all that apply)

   A. keith@bruins.com

   B. keith_olsen@bruins.com

   C. keith olsen@bruins.com

   D. k123@bruins.com

   E. keith.bruin.com

2. Which of the following sets of protocols can be used to configure a client to both send and receive e-mails? (Choose only one answer)

   A. IMAP and POP

   B. IMAP and STMP

   C. POP and SNMP

   D. POP and SMTP

   E. None of the above because you need three protocols when setting up a client.

3. What suite of products includes an e-mail application called Messenger?

   A. Microsoft Internet Explorer

   B. Microsoft Office

   C. Microsoft Back Office suite

   D. Netscape Communicator

   E. Netscape Information Services

4. What two general rules should you follow when sending e-mail attachments?

   A. Try to keep the message as small as possible.

   B. Never send an attachment to someone that uses Internet Explorer.

   C. Always use the FTP protocol when transferring files as attachments.

   D. Always include some text in the e-mail that informs the user of the attachment.

   E. Limit the use of color in attachments, as many older e-mail clients can only display white text.

5. What name refers to a small amount of text that has been automatically added to the bottom of an e-mail?

   A. Closing

   B. Salutation

   C. Stamp

   D. Signature

   E. Attachment

6. Which two of the following practices are considered good netiquette?

   A. Never use any capital letters in an e-mail.

   B. Always call before sending an e-mail.

   C. Always check your spelling before sending a message.

   D. Always respond to e-mail queries in a timely fashion.

7. Which of the following terms are related to mailing lists? (Choose all that apply)

   A. LISTSERV

   B. USENET

   C. Subscribe

   D. Post

   E. None of the above because they are all related to newsgroups

8. True or False: To access mailing lists, you need to configure client software specifically designed for mailing list access.

9. Which of the following categories most likely contains newsgroup postings related to the sport of soccer?

   A. comp.*

   B. talk.*

   C. rec.*

    D. alt.*

    E. soc.*

10. Which of the following categories most likely contains newsgroup postings related to computer certification exams?

    A. comp.*

    B. talk.*

    C. rec.*

    D. alt.*

    E. soc.*

11. Which of the following is true regarding FTP?

    A. Anonymous FTP is allowed when you don't have a valid user name.

    B. The `put` command is used to put files onto the client from the server.

    C. The `get` command is used to send files from the server to the client.

    D. If you have the right to `get` you must have the right to `put`.

    E. Only text-based FTP allows uploading of compressed files.

12. Which of the following extensions usually indicate that a file is compressed? (Choose all that apply)

    A. .com

    B. .zip

    C. .tar

    D. .asc

    E. .sea

    F. .sit

13. Which of the following is similar to a dial-up shell account?

    A. Telnet

    B. USENET

    C. Bitnet

    D. FTP server account

    E. UNIX

14. True or False: The bulk of the processing occurs on the client computer during a Telnet session.

15. True or False: Telnet is strictly restricted to UNIX.

Scenarios

1. You have been asked by your boss to set up her home computer so that she can use it to access the corporate e-mail server for both sending and receiving e-mails. She also wants to be able to access USENET because several newsgroups greatly interest her. She has a Windows 2000 Professional computer with a copy of Internet Explorer 6.0 fully installed.

   It is extremely important that her computer be set up promptly and correctly.

   Based on this information and what you have learned in this chapter regarding providing access to Internet services, answer the following questions regarding this project.

   a. What information regarding her e-mail should you gather prior to going over to her home?

   b. What e-mail client will you configure for her?

   c. What protocols will require configuring for her to gain access to her mail?

   d. What newsgroup client should you configure on your boss's home computer?

   e. What information regarding her newsgroup access should you obtain prior to going to her house?

2. After configuring your boss's home computer, you receive an e-mail from her stating that she was thrilled with the job you did. In fact, she now wants you to configure her computer for access to mailing lists and anonymous FTP sites.

   Once again, based on the information provided here and in Scenario 1 and on what you have learned in this chapter regarding providing access to Internet services, answer the following questions regarding this project:

   a. Do these additional requests require a second trip to your boss's home? Why or why not?

   b. What will your boss need to do to join the mailing lists that she is interested in?

   c. What type of client FTP software can your boss use to access the FTP sites that she is interested in? If your answer includes two or more choices, which of your choices is most suitable for your boss because she is not very technically adept?

3. Your boss sends you another e-mail praising you on the excellent job you are doing in helping her out. She just has a few simple questions she needs answered. First, several people have responded oddly to her past e-mails asking her to stop yelling at them. Because she is simply corresponding with them using e-mail, she can't quite determine the problem. Because she does not want to offend anyone, she wants to know how she can avoid offending

people. She also wants an easy way to place all of her contact information at the bottom of outgoing e-mails.

> **a.** Why are people claiming she is yelling at them?
>
> **b.** What tips can you give your boss to help prevent her from offending anyone when sending electronic correspondence?
>
> **c.** How can your boss add her contact information to the bottom of all outgoing e-mails?

Answers to Chapter Questions

Chapter Pre-Test

1. Your outgoing e-mail server is an **SMTP** server.

2. The domain name portion of: k_olsen@olsen.mb.ca is **olsen.mb.ca**.

3. The POP3 account name for k_olsen@olsen.mb.ca is **k_olsen**.

4. Typing an e-mail message in all capital letters is considered shouting or yelling.

5. The term given to the practice of conducting yourself in a proper manner on the Internet is called **netiquette**.

6. The name for the text that an e-mail client can automatically place at the bottom of all e-mails is a **signature**.

7. A **mailing list** is a service to which you can subscribe and any messages sent to the mailing list are automatically sent to you.

8. Mailing lists require the use of an **e-mail client** to access the messages sent.

9. The appropriate URL to connect to an FTP server named `ftp.someserver.ca` with the user name of *Leslie*, and the password of *freelance* is `ftp://leslie:freelance@ftp.someserver.ca`.

10. The command to download a file named `game.exe` from an FTP server is `get game.exe`.

11. The command to upload a file called `report.txt` to an FTP server is `put report.txt`.

12. The messages in a newsgroup are referred to as **postings**.

13. The newsgroup category **comp** is used for computer-related topics.

14. The asterisk (*) in the newsgroup rec.sport.golf* specifies that there are further subcategories under this heading, such as rec.sport.golf.duffers, and rec.sport.golf.pro.

15. When you use a Telnet client to access a Telnet server, the server is performing the data processing.

Assessment Questions

1. Which of the following are examples of correctly formulated e-mail addresses? (Choose all that apply)

   A. keith@bruins.com

   B. keith_olsen@bruins.com

   D. k123@bruins.com

2. Which of the following sets of protocols can be used to configure a client so it can both send and receive e-mail? (Choose only one answer)

   D. POP and SMTP

3. What suite of products includes an e-mail application called Messenger?

   D. Netscape Communicator

4. What two general rules should you follow when sending e-mail attachments?

   A. Try to keep the message as small as possible.

   D. Always include some text in the e-mail that informs the user of the attachment.

5. What name is given to a small amount of text that has been automatically added to the bottom of an e-mail?

   D. Signature

6. Which two of the following are considered good netiquette?

   C. Always check your spelling before sending a message.

   D. Always respond to e-mail queries in a timely fashion.

7. Which of the following terms are related to mailing lists? (Choose all that apply)

   A. LISTSERV

   C. Subscribe

8. False: To access mailing lists all you need is an e-mail client.

9. Which of the following categories most likely contains newsgroup postings related to the sport of Soccer?

   C. rec.*

10. Which of the following categories would likely contain newsgroup postings related to the computer certification exams?

    A. comp.*

11. Which of the following is true regarding FTP?

    C. The `get` command is used to send files from the server to the client.

12. Which of the following extensions usually indicate that a file is compressed? (Choose all that apply)

    B. .zip

    C. .tar

    E. .sea

    F. .sit

13. Which of the following is similar to a dial-up shell account?

    A. Telnet

14. False. The bulk of the processing occurs on the server computer during a Telnet session.

15. False. Any operating system that supports TCP/IP can also support the use of Telnet. However, it is commonly used in a UNIX environment.

Scenarios

1. Following are the answers to Scenario 1:

    a. To set up your boss's e-mail, you should gather the following information: her e-mail address, her password, the SMTP server address, and the POP3 or IMAP4 server address.

    b. Because your boss has Internet Explorer, you should probably consider using Outlook Express because it will already be installed.

    c. The protocols that will require configuring for her to gain access to her mail are SMTP and either POP3 or IMAP.

    d. Again, you should use Outlook Express because she will be using it for mail and it is already installed.

    e. You should obtain the following information regarding her newsgroup access prior to going to her house: the newsgroup server address and your boss's newsgroup account and password (if required).

2. Following are the answers to Scenario 2:

a. The additional requests don't require a second trip to your boss's home because she can gain access to mailing lists by using her previously setup e-mail client; she can also gain access to the anonymous FTP sites by using her Internet Explorer browser, which includes a GUI FTP client.

b. Your boss will need to subscribe to the mailing lists she is interested in.

c. Because your boss is using Windows 2000 Professional, she can use either the text-based FTP client or the GUI-based Internet Explorer. Using the GUI-based Internet Explorer is probably a better choice for your boss because it offers a fairly easy-to-use, point-and-click style access while the text-based tends to be a little more confusing and difficult for less advanced users.

3. Following are the answers to Scenario 3:

a. The reason people may feel your boss is yelling at them is because she is typing her e-mail in all capital letters.

b. To help your boss avoid offending anyone when sending electronic correspondence, you may want to teach her about netiquette.

c. Your boss can have her contact information added to the bottom of all outgoing e-mails by configuring her e-mail client to add a signature.

Resources

The following resources can be used to further supplement the topics discussed in this chapter:

✦ *Webopedia: Online Computer Dictionary for Internet Terms and Technical Support*: www.webopedia.com

✦ Mary Houten-Kemp's *Everything E-mail*, an excellent guide to e-mail: http://everythingemail.net

Understanding Internet Search Engines

EXAM OBJECTIVES

1. Explain the function of search engines and their use of keywords.

2. Promote a Web site with enhanced search engines positioning.

3. Explain the functions of static, keyword, and full-text search indexes.

4. Use search engines to seek information.

5. Search for Internet data using AND, OR, AND NOT, NOT, NEAR, wildcards, and minus signs.

6. Use Boolean operators in an advanced Web search.

7. Search for graphics, people, and mailing lists on the Internet.

8. Describe the purposes of Archie, Gopher, and Veronica.

CHAPTER PRE-TEST

1. _____ are used to submit search requests for Web addresses stored in search engine indexes.

2. _____ are a class of software that find a list of Internet addresses containing information that match the search request that you provide.

3. Search engines use programs called *bots*, _____, or _____ to create their indexes.

4. Search _____ use people to review and decide which Web sites will be accepted into their search index.

5. A search that involves manually navigating through a series of topics or directories is called a _____ index search.

6. A search making a request using descriptive word(s) is considered a _____ search.

7. _____ logic uses operators to exclude or specify characteristics or terms to be included in a search.

8. _____ refers to programs that are dedicated to maintaining FTP site indexes.

9. _____ is a search engine for gopher sites.

The Internet was created to promote the exchange of information and ideas. It is often likened to a vast electronic library. However, finding the precise information that you require can feel like searching for a needle in a haystack. The goal of this chapter is to introduce you to common Internet search engines and explain effective search techniques by using these tools.

The Internet is constantly growing, and search engines grow with it, thus becoming more powerful and efficient. This chapter focuses on the way search engines work, including the ways they scan the Internet for appropriate sites and then present their findings to you. Ways to fine-tune your searches to make them more effective are also explored.

In addition, this chapter looks at directories and ferret programs and examines Archie, Veronica, and Gopher.

Search Engines

Explain the function of search engines and their use of keywords.

Search engines are a class of software that find a list of Internet addresses containing information that matches the search request that you provide. Think of the Internet as a huge library, and the search engine as the helpful librarian looking through the card catalog for you. Search engines are free and you can access them by visiting their respective Web sites. The Internet has no shortage of search engines and new ones appear every month. In fact, so many search engines exist that there are now Web sites dedicated to helping you locate and access the most popular of these.

Note   Web sites that list popular search engines include www.internet101.org/ browser.html, www.100topsearchsites.com/, and www.searchengines.net/.

Search engines use automated programs called *bots*, *spiders*, or *crawlers* to locate Web pages and collect information. Indexer programs compile the information into a list of keywords and cross-reference the keywords with the addresses of the sites that contain them, thus creating an indexed catalog. When you use the search engine, you enter one or more keywords and the search engine then scans the catalog and returns a list of Web addresses containing the keywords requested. These automated programs can update lists of new Web sites with current information more quickly and efficiently than search directories.

Keywords are simply words specified by a user to be used in a search. They describe the information that you seek. General words, such as "the," "and," or "was," are not keywords. Keywords are more clarified (for example, "Chicken Pox," "straw houses," or "apple cider vinegar").

Search directories resemble search engines because they provide users with a list of Web sites that match categories or topics. Some search directories, such as Yahoo!, are considered search engines because they present the user with a list of Web sites relating to a keyword request. *Search engines are not search directories.* Search directories and search engines differ in the way they gather a list of site addresses pertaining to a specific subject.

Web authors must submit their pages to a search directory, where a human being reads it and deems it acceptable or not. People, not programs, decide whether the page is good enough to be included in their database of sites. In fact, numerous submissions are turned down. Directories deal in quality—not quantity. Their directories may not yield as many Web pages as a search engine, but the pages returned in a search are more likely to match the request.

Search engines often answer your request by returning huge lists of Web pages that can overwhelm some users. Just because search directories return shorter lists doesn't mean that they are inferior. The relevancy of the Web content, rather than the volume of Web pages presented, produces the most favorable results.

The advanced search section of this chapter discusses techniques for narrowing a search to avoid receiving a huge list of Web sites in return.

Search Results

After you submit a request, search engines display results according to a ranking order. Typically, the search engine displays the number of matches that meet your request and lists the links to the top matches immediately below that number. Figure 4-1 shows the results of a search that was performed with the search engine Google.

Figure 4-1 displays the first 10 results of 45,100 possible matches. Of course, it is unrealistic to look through all 45,100 potentially matching Web pages. You usually find what you need within the first few suggested pages. However, there is no magic answer when searching for information over the Internet, and no particular search engine exists that can do everything for everyone. One useful search strategy is to try different search engines. If one search engine doesn't bring you the information that you desire, go to another one. Typing the same request into two different search engines can yield dramatically different results.

An interesting fact about Google is that it actually caches (saves a copy of) web pages it has indexed. This feature allows one to find desired information that may have been removed from its originating web site.

Links to Web pages   Shows ranking of search results

Figure 4-1: Results of a search engine displayed

Search engines differ in the way that they display results. For example, Google gives you the option of sorting the search results so that they are displayed by date. With Excite, you have three options: You can view full descriptions, titles only, or URLs. Lycos allows you to display results according to featured lists, popularity, and Web pages.

When a search engine's results are displayed according to a specific *ranking order*, pages ranked with lower numbers are considered by the search engine to be most likely to give you the information that you seek. Search engines rank results according to the following criteria:

✦ **Keyword frequency.** If I was searching for information on apple cider vinegar, and the search engine found these words at the beginning of a Web document in a heading, that page would have a higher rating than one mentioning the key words in the last paragraph of the page.

✦ **Keyword placement.** If the keyword appears many times on a page, the page will be given a higher rating than if the keyword only appears once.

✦ **Number of pages containing keywords.** If the keyword appears in many pages within a Web site, the site may be given a higher rating.

✦ **Links.** Pages with more links directed at them can get a higher ranking order.

✦ **Paying customers.** Web site owners can pay for placement to get their pages a higher rank.

✦ **Alliances.** Businesses in partnership with or connected to a search engine are often given a higher rating by that search engine.

✦ **Update frequency.** Some search engines can tell how frequently a page is updated. These engines rank frequently updated pages higher than older pages.

✦ **Hit frequency.** Some search engines can monitor how many hits a link gets after a search request. Pages that initially have a higher rating, but don't attract people to click the link to visit them, may be dropped to a lower ranking, and other pages may be boosted to a higher ranking if they attract more visitors.

Many variables affect the rank order of results from a search request. Each search engine gives different weight to each of the many variables.

Note   The placement and frequency of keywords in a Web page is very important. A Web page developer may repeat certain words often throughout the Web page in an attempt to have it appear high in Web page rankings. This approach is referred to as *stacking* or *stuffing*. This strategy works to a certain degree, but if you list a keyword too many times, it may be excluded altogether. Some search engines can detect when Web authors attempt to "spam" their search engine in this way, and won't include that site in their index as a result.

Promoting Your Web Site

Objective   Promote a Web site with enhanced search engines positioning.

If you want search engines to find your Web site, you need to register with them. The Web sites of search engines give information about how to register your site with them. Typically, you can find a link at the bottom of the home page that takes you to a screen where you can register your site.

The registration process typically requires you to submit a URL for your site and your e-mail address. After you give this information to the search engine, a robot or spider program belonging to the search engine will visit your site and index keywords.

Submitting your Web page

Search engines often provide several ways for Web authors to submit their Web pages. Usually, you can take advantage of a way to register without paying anything. Although you are not required to pay search engine sites to be listed, an option for Pay Submission is often included. With this option, you pay a fee when you submit your Web site to a search engine. This payment does not guarantee that your Web site will be listed in a search; it simply speeds up the process of having your site reviewed by the search engine. A third, and more expensive, option is called "pay for placement," and *does* guarantee a listing with a search engine.

Just because you register your site with a search engine doesn't mean that it will be indexed and make the "top ten" list in the searches. The following section discusses a method that you can employ in order to increase the ranking of your site and the likelihood that it will be chosen by a search engine.

Employing Meta tags

Web authors use Meta tags to increase the likelihood that their site will be noticed. A *Meta tag* is code that contains information read by search engines, and not by people visiting the Web site. Meta tags provide keywords and phrases that describe the Web document to the search engine. These tags may also give information about the author and a date specifying when the page was last updated. Meta tags don't necessarily guarantee that a search engine will choose your Web site, but they do increase its chances.

Cross-Reference For a more complete description of Meta tags and their attributes, refer to Chapter 9.

Querying Indexes

Objective Explain the functions of static, keyword, and full-text search indexes.

You query a search engine's database of Web page addresses in the hope that you get some acceptable matches. These databases can be cataloged or indexed by using the following indexes:

✦ Static index/site map

✦ Keyword index

✦ Full-text index

Some search utilities have only one type of index, but many include all three.

Static index site map

Directories, such as Yahoo!, index according to categories and subcategories, and typically provide site maps. The home page of the site contains general topics, and each of the main topics is a link to another page with subtopics that are linked to other subtopics and lists of Web pages. A site map's structure resembles a table of contents. The entire site map is structured like a directory tree. Yahoo!, LookSmart, MSN, GO, and Netscape have static index site maps. See Figure 4-2 for an example of Yahoo!'s site map.

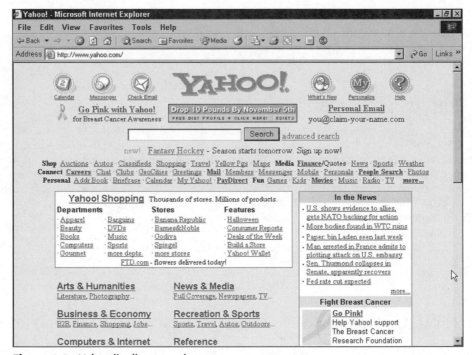

Figure 4-2: Yahoo!'s directory site map

By clicking on a series of heading links, you can navigate your way through the directory. Sites like this are very particular about the Web pages that they accept. The worthiness of each Web page is carefully considered.

Keyword index

Most search engines index according to keywords. These keywords are taken directly from the Web pages. Search engines such as Google have a place for you to enter a keyword(s). The search engine looks through its index to find matches to your entry and returns a list of likely Web addresses.

Full-text index

Full-text indexes store every word of a Web document, thus allowing people to search for a string of words within its index of Web pages. This type of indexing is often done within companies as a service to their employees to help retrieve information. This type of indexing is not used for Internet search engines because of the extensive storage requirements.

Search Basics

 Use Search engines to seek information.

The following search engines and directories are highlighted in the CIW curriculum:

✦ Yahoo!

✦ AltaVista

✦ Lycos

✦ Excite

 Examples and exercises within this book use the engines highlighted in the CIW curriculum and Google.

Yahoo!

Yahoo! (www.yahoo.com) was started in 1994 by Stanford University students David Filo and Jerry Yang. They wanted a way to keep track of their favorite places on the Internet. Eventually, their lists became lengthy and difficult to manage, so as a solution, they created categories and sub-categories, and the rest — as they say — was history.

Yahoo! now has 250,000 categories. You can find a desired site by clicking through these groupings. This site makes it easy for you to find varying items, such as maps, horoscopes, weather information, and addresses and phone numbers of businesses and people. You can find information on just about every general topic that you can think of, including the following:

✦ Arts and humanities

✦ News and media

✦ Travel

✦ Recreation

✦ Sports

✦ Entertainment

✦ Health

Yahoo! does not search the entire Internet; it searches only those sites that it judges worthy. Yahoo! gives you quality, not quantity, and may not always find what you need.

You can conduct a search through Yahoo by typing keywords. Although Yahoo! still functions as a directory, it has recently joined forces with Google, which is a search engine boasting the biggest index on the Internet. Although Yahoo! retains its browsing interface, Google provides search services for the site.

AltaVista

AltaVista (`www.altavista.com`), which was founded in 1995 by Digital Equipment Corporation, boasts one of the largest databases of information on the Internet. This search engine offers specialty searches, dedicated to finding the following:

✦ Images

✦ MP3 audio files

✦ Videos

✦ People

You can search AltaVista by using a directory, simple, or advanced search. The default simple search gives all-inclusive, wide-ranging findings. It is geared toward general search inquiries. AltaVista's advanced search works better for very specific searches.

AltaVista does not wait for Web submissions; rather, it sends out bots to gather information about Web pages. The pages in its index that are known to change are regularly checked for changes, and as a result, the index remains fairly up-to-date.

AltaVista rates Web sites according to how closely the findings match the keywords. Keywords in titles or at the beginning of the document are given a higher rating. AltaVista also assigns a higher priority to certain words and phrases.

Lycos

Lycos (`www.lycos.com`) was one of the first search engines to be used on the World Wide Web. This popular search engine allows two kinds of searching: simple, by using phrases and keywords, and advanced, by using Boolean operators to narrow the searches. Lycos also allows users to limit searches by selecting language limits. Lycos offers more language limits than any other search engine.

Excite

Excite (`www.excite.com`) supports keyword searches and cross references related words and topics. Excite's approach to searching the Web differs from other search engines, so you may want to give it a try if the engine that you normally use isn't giving you the pages that you want. Although its index is smaller than most other search engines, it is known for finding relevant sites for popular subjects.

Static index searches

Search directories typically provide static index searching. This process involves manually selecting categories and subcategories with your mouse until you reach a list of Web addresses that give you the information that you need. Some search engines also allow static index searches. Lab 2-1 in this chapter provides a standard index search exercise.

Keyword searches

Begin the most basic search by going to the search engine's Web site. Type a keyword or words into the search field and click the *search button* with your mouse or press the Enter key on your keyboard. For practice on simple searches, refer to Lab 2-2 at the end of this chapter.

Advanced Search Techniques

Search for Internet data using AND, OR, AND NOT, NOT, NEAR, wildcards, and minus signs.

Using advanced search strategies, you can narrow a search that has yielded too many irrelevant results, or you can broaden a search that returned no result.

Advanced search strategies use *search operators*. Search operators can be text commands, symbols, or punctuation. You can manually type search operators into the search field of a search engine. The following are some examples:

✦ **Quotation marks.** If you do a search for *apple cider vinegar*, the search engine will return results containing "apple," or "cider," or "vinegar." This search will probably bring you many irrelevant pages. If you place quotation marks around the words, as in "apple cider vinegar," when doing the search, however, the search engine returns only those pages that have "apple cider vinegar" written together.

✦ **Wildcard.** *Wildcards* are symbols that can be used to represent one or more characters in a search. For example, if you search for "promo*", the asterisk acts as a multi-character wildcard, thus causing the search engine to return any Web page that contains any keywords beginning with the letters "promo". The results may include keywords, such as "promo," "promote," "promoting," and "promoter."

   • Another common wildcard is the question mark "?". Similar in function to the asterisk, it represents a single character. Searching for "b?t" results in the search engine looking for keywords, such as "bat," "bet," "bit," "bot," and "but."

   • The ellipsis "..." is used as a positional operator when placed between two words and is an indication to the search engine that the two words must appear in the results, and that the first word must appear before the second word. Searching for "blue...sky" will return any pages containing both words with the word *blue* appearing before the word *sky*.

- The minus sign (-) is the exclusion operator. For example, "winter sports-hockey" requests all winter sports with the exception of hockey.

- The plus sign (+) indicates what must be included. The query "+flowers+perennials" finds sites that refer to both flowers and perennials.

In the Real World   Many search engines (such as Google) eliminate the need to manually use such operators due to the design of their advance query pages.

You can access advanced searches by clicking on the advanced link that takes you to a more complicated search form that offers more options.

Boolean search operators

Objective   Use Boolean operators in an advanced Web search.

Boolean operators use Boolean logic to search the Internet. Boolean operators are used in advanced search techniques to direct your search. These operators allow you to specify or exclude certain characteristics. Effective use of Boolean operators can either cut down or increase the number of possible sites that a search engine returns to you, depending on your needs. If you are looking for a needle in a haystack, like a very specific statistic, you want to cut down the total number of results. However, if you were looking for a vast amount of information on a given topic (say, for a research paper), then you would use Boolean operators to increase the number of results you see.

For example, perhaps you want a recipe for tomato soup that does not use basil as an ingredient. Boolean operators such as And, Or, and Not let your browser know which key words should be included or excluded, and how these words should appear in relation to each other.

AND

The AND operator is used when more than one word must appear on a page (but not necessarily in positions beside each other). Some search engines search this way by default—but many don't, and you may need to create a query using an AND operator from time to time. For example, "tomatoes AND recipes" is the same as using "+tomato+recipes". This example instructs the search engine to find Web pages where both "tomato" and "recipe" appear.

OR

Using the OR operator in a search statement demands that at least one of a set of words appear within a Web page. For example, "hamburger OR beef" requests pages with the word *hamburger* or *beef* or both. Some search engines, such as AltaVista, search with an OR condition by default when more than one word is requested. For example, "ground beef, hamburger" is the same as using "beef OR hamburger.'

NOT

In some search engines, this operator is written as NOT. In others, it is written as AND NOT. This Boolean operator excludes keywords; for example, "Chocolate NOT bar" is the same as using "+Chocolate-bars". In this example, the search engine returns the addresses of Web pages containing the word *chocolate* but not the word *bar*.

NEAR

The NEAR operator is used to request pages that contain two words that should appear in close proximity, but not necessarily next to each other on the pages found.

Combining Boolean operators

You can use more than one Boolean operator together if you include parentheses. For example, "elm trees AND (disease OR beetles)" requests pages containing the words *elm* and *disease*, or *elm* and *beetles*, or *elm* and *disease* and *beetles*.

Advanced options

For a list of Boolean operators and their uses, see Table 4-1.

Table 4-1 Boolean Operators		
Search Engine	*Use of Boolean*	*Comments*
Google	Automatic AND between words	Does not support NOT or searching with nested Boolean operators. Supports OR but must be in uppercase.
Lycos	Automatic AND between words	Accepts a plus (+) for AND, and a minus (–) for NOT. No Boolean operators. Under advanced search.
AltaVista	Default OR search (before May 2001 search requests with one to four words were automatically OR, while five or more words were automatically AND).	Supports all Boolean search operators, but operators should be written in uppercase. You may also use (+) for AND, (-) for NOT, and (~) for NEAR. Allows double quotes to search for phrases.
Excite	Multiple terms OR	Boolean operators must be in uppercase. Supports (+), (-), AND, NOT. Supports Boolean operators nested in parentheses.
Yahoo!	Sometimes does an OR, sometimes defaults to AND	Does not support Boolean operators in searches. Does allow (+) for an AND condition and (-) for excluding keywords.

Other Specialized Searching

 Objective   Search for graphics, people, and mailing lists on the Internet.

Besides Web pages, many search utilities are dedicated to searching for a variety of items on the Internet, including images, people, or mailing lists. The CIW course-ware and exam focus on searches in these three areas.

Image searching

Most of the popular search engines have links to a specialized search utility to find graphic images. These specialized search engines, which are contained within the major search engines, focus on finding graphics within the pages rather than text subject matter. When you search for an image, thumbnail pictures appear with text links to the original Web site. Figures 4-3 and 4-4 show the results of searching for a picture of a bowl of fruit.

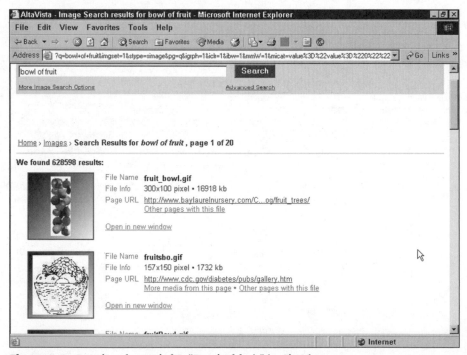

Figure 4-3: Results of search for "Bowl of fruit" in AltaVista

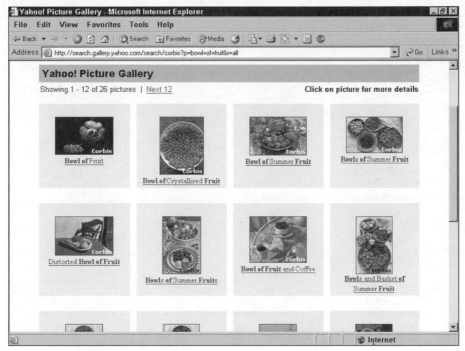

Figure 4-4: Results of search for "Bowl of fruit" in Yahoo!

At both AltaVista and Yahoo!, you can find a link to the original Web page from which the image originated. When you get to the Web page, you can download the image by right-clicking the image and choosing Save picture as from the short menu of Explorer, or Save image from the short menu of Netscape, as shown in Figures 4-5 and 4-6.

Figure 4-5: Saving a picture with the short menu in Internet Explorer

Open Link in New Window
Edit Link in Composer
Back
Forward
Reload
Stop
View Page Info
View Image
Bookmark this Link
Save As...
Save Link As...
Save Image (89426501)...
Select All
Copy
Prefill Form
Save Form Data
View Stored Data
Copy Link Location
Copy Image Location
Properties

Figure 4-6: Saving a picture in Netscape

After you select the Save image or Save picture command, choose the drive and folder location for storing the file. You may want to create a special folder to hold your downloaded image files.

In addition to AltaVista's built-in image search utility, you may want to try the following:

✦ Google Advanced Image search:
http://images.google.com/advanced_image_search

✦ Image request: site for finding free images: www.imagerequest.com/

✦ Public File Libraries: www.surfmadison.com/libsearch.htm

✦ Yahoo! picture gallery: http://gallery.yahoo.com/

✦ At the Excite directory homepage, you can select a photos search option and the search engine will return thumbnail image examples, as shown in Figure 4-7.

Copyright rules apply to all image files downloaded from the Internet. People and companies who use image files for advertising or profit without the permission of the artist or photographer can be prosecuted and fined.

People searching

Many major search engines have links to specialized utilities that are dedicated to searching for information about people and businesses. Through these search features, you can find phone numbers, mailing addresses, e-mail addresses, and URLs for business Web sites. Search engines for companies are often referred to as *yellow pages*, while search engines for individuals are known as *white pages*, *people search,* or *people finders.*

Figure 4-7: Options for accessing an image search at Excite

When you search for a business or person, you are usually presented with fields to enter information specifying location (city, country, and postal code) and names (first and last). You are not required to enter information into all the fields, but the more information that you can provide, the better your search results will be. See Figure 4-8 for an example of a people search.

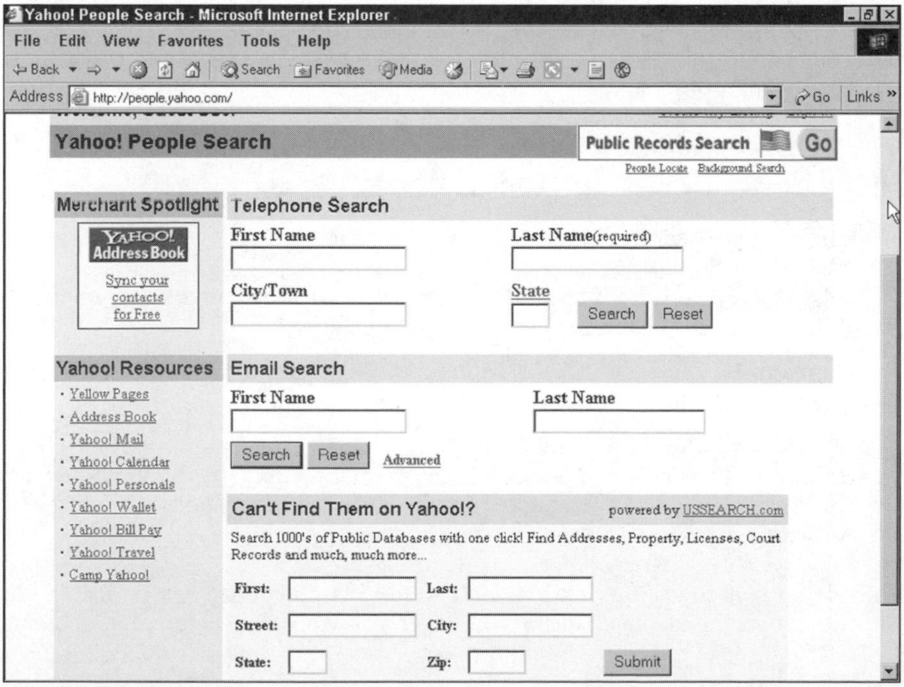

Figure 4-8: Yahoo!'s people search form

Most major search engines and directories display a link option on their homepage that takes you to a page with a form for submitting a people search. The information for these indexes comes from public phone listings. Many sites have online forms giving users the option of listing themselves with an index.

The following are some of the more popular people search engines:

✦ **People search engine** (`www.people-search-engines.com`): This site gives the option of searching by name, e-mail address, phone number, or mailing address.

✦ **SuperPages.com** (`http://yp.gte.net/`): This site offers both people pages and yellow pages, and provides Web page directory searches.

✦ **Yellow pages.com** (`www.yellowpages.com/`): This site searches for both yellow and white page listings.

Different indexes contain different lists of people. If you can't find the person that you are looking for at one source, simply try another engine. Remember, if someone truly does not want to be found, you may not find information on him or her anywhere.

Searching for mailing lists

Mailing list sites are discussion forums that can be subscribed to by e-mail. Your name is added to the list so you receive e-mail messages relating to the topic to which you subscribe.

Cross-Reference   For more information regarding mailing lists, see Chapter 3.

The following are search utilities dedicated to mailing lists:

✦ **List Universe.com** (`http://list-universe.com`): This search engine contains hundreds of indexed and searchable lists.

✦ **E groups** (`http://groups.yahoo.com/`): On this site, you can both search for mailing lists or start your own.

✦ **NeoSoft's Publicly Accessible Mailing Lists** (`http://paml.net/`): This website reports to be the Internet's premier Mailing list Directory. Thousands of publicly available Mailing lists can be located through both Keyword and indexed searches.

Many other search utilities are available to help you in your search for mailing lists. You can subscribe or unsubscribe whenever you want. See Figure 4-9 for a sample mail list search.

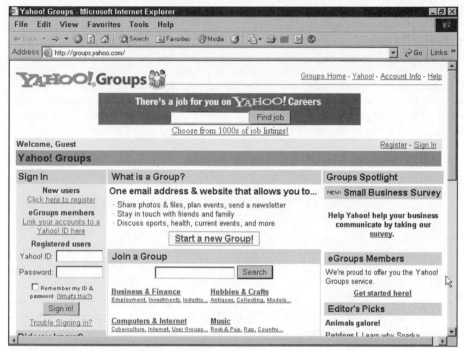

Figure 4-9: E-groups is a specialty mail list search utility at Yahoo!

Early Web Searching

Objective

Describe the purposes of Archie, Gopher, and Veronica.

When the Internet was young, Archie, Veronica, and Gopher were the tools used to search the Internet. Although their use today is quite limited, you should still be aware of their existence for the CIW Foundations exam.

Gopher

Gopher refers to an Internet protocol and software that was developed at the University of Minnesota. Gopher was created to provide a way for people to find files on the Internet. This text-based, menu-driven search utility indexed articles from universities, government offices, public libraries, and businesses. Users navigated through the hierarchical headings until they found the information that they needed.

Although Gopher sites still exist, they have become obsolete—replaced by Web documents, directories, and search engines.

Cross-Reference

Gopher is discussed further in Chapter 14.

Archie

Archie Software is used to search FTP sites. Archie is a spider program that searches and indexes files from FTP servers that contain anonymous FTP sites. Archie checks queries against its index and presents the user with the results. You can access Archie through Telnet by logging onto a computer as a user with specified permissions or through an ArchiePlex, which is a Web page that allows you to do an Archie query. Search engines of the World Wide Web have largely replaced Archie and most Archie sites no longer function.

 Anonymous FTP gives people the right to use File Transfer Protocol sites without telling the server who they are. The user ID is entered as "anonymous," and the user does not need to know a password to enter a site.

 FTP is discussed in more detail in Chapter 14.

Veronica

Veronica works very much like Archie, but searches for Gopher sites. It finds Gopher servers that contain files that match general information topics. Gopher sites are becoming fewer and fewer in number on the Internet and finding information with Veronica is arduous and time-consuming. As Gopher's significance decreases, so does Veronica's.

Power Searching

Meta search engines conduct a search by using many powerful search engines at one time. Some Meta search engines include the following:

✦ **Google** (www.google.com)

✦ **Profusion** (www.profusion.com)

✦ **Dogpile** (www.dogpile.com/index.gsp)

✦ **Highway 61** (www.highway61.com)

This list is by no means comprehensive because you can access numerous other Meta search sites. Some sites, such as the multi-search engine site at www.bjorgul.com/#met, let you simultaneously choose the engines that you want to search with.

You can install specialized search utility software called *ferrets* on your local machine and use them to search multiple search engines simultaneously. The advantage of these programs is that you can save a search request along with the results and then return to it anytime you want. You can delete individual search results and organize your results in a way that suits you. Copernic is one such program, and you can download it from `www.copernic.com`. See Figure 4-10 for an example of this utility.

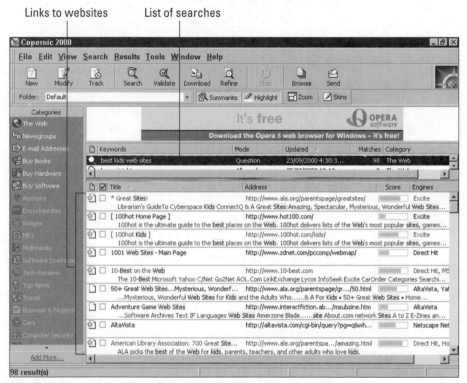

Figure 4-10: Copernic search utility

Copernic allows you to store many search requests. The Search requests are shown near the top of the window. When you select a search request, results display at the bottom of the window. To submit a new search request, click the New toolbar button, which is located at the top left side of the screen, to access a search form. See Figure 4-11.

Toolbar button to activate
new search request   Search request form

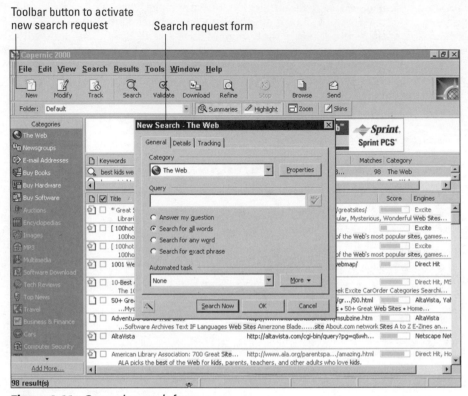

Figure 4-11: Copernic search form

Key Point Summary

✦ Search directories help users find sites just like search engines, but they are not search engines. They differ in the ways they seek and present information.

   • Web pages can be submitted to search sites by their authors. At these sites, people read the pages and deem them acceptable or not. Sites that compile Web pages this way are search directories.

   • Search engines use automated programs called bots, spiders, or crawlers to search the Internet for appropriate sites. Indexer programs compile a catalog from the Web addresses obtained by the spider.

✦ Keywords are words specified by a user to be used in a search. The words are usually present in Web sites, and describe the information that you seek.

✦ Search engines display results according to a ranking order. Pages ranked with lower numbers are considered by the search engine to be most likely to give you the information that you seek. Results are ranked according to the following:

- Keyword frequency

- Keyword placement

- Number of pages containing keywords

- Links

- Paying customers

- Alliances

- Update frequency

- Hit frequency

✦ You may submit your site to a Web engine to have it included in relevant search results.

✦ Many search engine sites use automated programs (or even people) to visit sites on the Internet and add them to their catalog of possible results.

✦ A static index site map indexes Web sites according to categories and subcategories and resembles a table of contents.

✦ These keyword index search engines match your keywords to their index entries and return a list of likely Web addresses.

✦ A full-text index search engine stores every word of a Web document. This type of indexing is not used for Internet search engines because of the extensive storage requirements.

✦ Advanced search strategies allow you to narrow a search that has yielded too many irrelevant results or to broaden a search that returned no result.

✦ Advanced search strategies use search operators such as the following:

- Quotation marks (" ")

- Wildcards (*) or (?)

- Boolean Operators (AND, OR, NOT, and NEAR)

✦ Specialized search engines allow you to search for the following:

- Graphics

- People

- Mailing lists

✦ Early search tools include the following:

- Gopher – Internet protocol and software that finds files on the Internet by navigating through a series of hierarchical headings.

- Archie – Search utility for anonymous FTP sites.

- Veronica – Search utility for gopher sites.

✦   ✦   ✦

STUDY GUIDE

Assessment Questions

1. Choose all statements that correctly describe the term *search engine*:

   A. Search engines are a class of software that finds a list of Internet addresses.

   B. Similar in concept to a library's card catalog, search engines contain indexes of Web addresses that match keywords.

   C. All search engines are search directories.

   D. Users must pay a fee to use them.

2. The ranking order of search engines display results based on: (Choose all that apply)

   A. The number of users visiting the found Web sites at the time of the search

   B. Keyword frequency and placement

   C. Alliances between the search engine and businesses

   D. How frequently information is updated

   E. All of the above

3. True or false: Static index site maps, keyword indexes, and full-text indexes are all querying index types used to search the Internet.

4. Which of the following search utilities was the first search directory?

   A. Lycos

   B. WebCrawler

   C. Excite

   D. AltaVista

   E. Yahoo!

5. Which of the following search engines searches the Web by cross-referencing keywords?

    A. Lycos

    B. Excite

    C. Google

    D. AltaVista

6. When doing a keyword search using more than one word with AltaVista, the search defaults to a:

    A. Boolean AND search

    B. Boolean OR search

    C. Boolean NEAR search

    D. Boolean NOT search

7. True or false: Excite supports Boolean operators nested in parentheses.

8. The correct syntax for an AND search at Lycos is:

    A. crib, cards

    B. +crib+cards

    C. AND crib AND cards

    D. crib+cards

    E. crib AND cards

9. What is Veronica used to search for?

    A. Anonymous FTP sites

    B. Gopher sites

    C. Web sites

    D. Newsgroups

10. What does Archie search for?

    A. Anonymous FTP sites

    B. Gopher sites

    C. Web sites

    D. Newsgroups

Lab Exercise 4-1

You may use Internet Explorer or Netscape Navigator to complete this exercise. Perform a search using Yahoo! by clicking on the various links of its directory.

1. Start your Browser Program.

2. Type `www.yahoo.com` into your browser's address field and press Enter. Your screen will look similar to Figure 4-12.

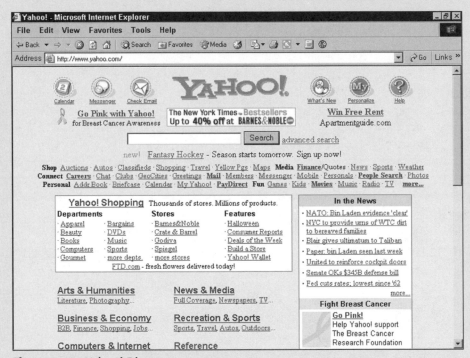

Figure 4-12: Yahoo! Directory

3. Find the directory heading Reference, the link to the Reference subdirectory. Click the link; it will take you to the directory shown in Figure 4-13.

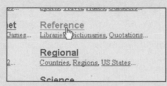

Figure 4-13: Reference link within Yahoo! directory

In the reference directory, you will see a list of other directories. There are links to directories of dictionaries, encyclopedia, and quotations, among other things. See Figure 4-14.

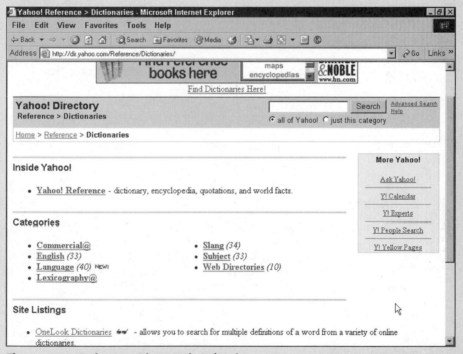

Figure 4-14: Reference Directory in Yahoo!

4. Access the English Category directory. Locate the Category directory heading and link to the Dictionary subdirectory. Then click the English link. Figure 4-15 shows this directory.

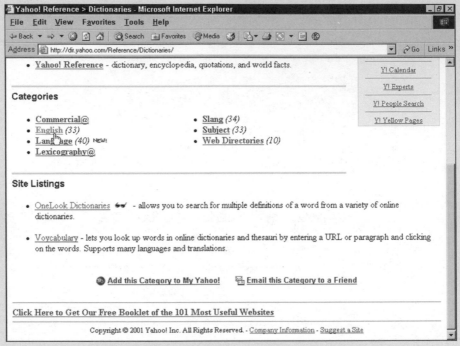

Figure 4-15: Reference Directory in Yahoo!

5. Scroll down the page and click the link to access the Merriam-Webster Dictionary. See Figure 4-16.

You should now be at the Merriam-Webster Dictionary Web site.

You have just completed a static index search by clicking a series of links to move through a series of directories. Other search engine sites allow you to find information by manually clicking through directories, but Yahoo! is a true search directory because the pages you access have been approved by a human being—and not a computer program.

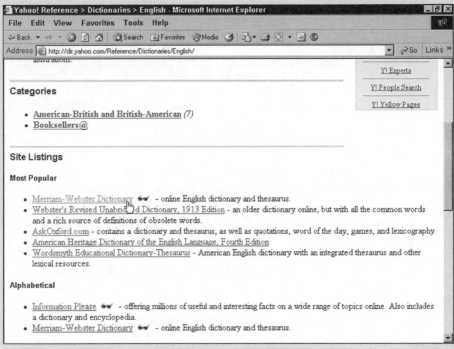

Figure 4-16: List of dictionaries

Lab Exercise 4-2

In this exercise, you will perform a simple keyword search in several different search engines, and then compare the results of those searches.

1. **Start** your **Browser** Program. To do this:

2. Use the Yahoo! search directory to perform a keyword search.

   a. Type **www.yahoo.com** into the address fields of your browser.

   b. Press **ENTER**.

   c. You should now be at the Yahoo Web site.

3. You will now do a keyword search for a tomato soup recipe.

   a. In the search box, enter **tomato soup recipe**.

   b. Click the Search button.

   c. You will be taken to a Web page displaying a list of Web matches.

4. Explore the list.

    a. Write down how many matches Yahoo! found for you.

    b. Click the link to one of these matches and observe the page.

    c. Click the **Back** button to return to the search list of Web addresses.

5. Use the AltaVista search engine to perform a keyword search.

    a. Type **www.altavista.com** into the address fields of your browser.

    b. Press **ENTER**.

    c. You should now be at the AltaVista Web site.

6. You will now do a keyword search for a tomato soup recipe.

    a. In the search box, enter **tomato soup recipe**.

    b. Click the Search button.

    c. You will be taken to a Web page displaying a list of matches.

7. Explore the list.

    a. Write down how many matches AltaVista found for you.

    b. Click the link to one of these matches and observe the page.

    c. Click the **Back** button to return to the search list of Web addresses.

You have probably found that AltaVista has displayed more links than you will ever have time to explore. You can make this list more manageable by putting quotation marks around the words *tomato soup recipe* when you do your search.

8. Combine keywords with quotation marks to narrow your search.

    a. In the search box, enter **"tomato soup recipe."**

    b. Click the Search button.

    c. You will be taken to a Web page displaying a list of Web matches. Note the difference in the number of matches displayed.

9. Use the **Lycos** search engine to perform a keyword search.

    a. Type **www.lycos.com** into the address fields of your browser.

    b. Press **ENTER**.

    c. You should now be at the Lycos Web site.

10. You will now do a keyword search for a tomato soup recipe.

    a. In the search box, enter **tomato soup recipe**.

    b. Click the Search button.

    c. You will be taken to a Web page displaying a list of Web matches.

11. Explore the list.

    a. Write down how many matches **Lycos** found for you.

    b. Click the link to one of these matches and observe the page.

    c. Click the **Back** button to return to the search list of Web addresses.

Note how Lycos displays its list in three groups under the following subheading: featured lists, popular, and Web pages.

12. Use the Excite search engine to perform a keyword search.

    a. Type **www.excite.com** into the address fields of your browser.

    b. Press **ENTER**.

    c. You should now be at the Excite Web site.

13. You will now do a keyword search for a tomato soup recipe.

    a. In the search box, enter **tomato soup recipe**.

    b. Click the Search button.

    c. You will be taken to a Web page displaying a list of Web matches.

14. Explore the list.

    a. Write down how many matches Excite found for you.

    b. Click the link to one of these matches and observe the page.

    c. Click the **Back** button to return to the search list of Web addresses.

Note

You can choose how you want to view the list of matches in Excite — Full description, titles only, or URL. Click the different viewing choices and observe your list. See Figure 4-17.

Figure 4-17: List of URLs displayed in Excite

Lab Exercise 4-3

In this lab exercise, you will perform an advanced search by using (+) and (-) parameters.

1. Perform a multi-word search at Excite.

   a. Start your browser.

   b. In the address bar, type **www.excite.com**.

   c. You should now be at the Excite Search engine Web site.

2. Do a search for tomato soup recipes.

   a. In the search field, type **tomato soup**.

   b. By default, Excite will do an OR search. Note the number of entries in the search response.

3. Do an AND search by using the (+) parameter. Excite will accept the (+) parameter as well as the Boolean AND operator.

   a. In the search field, type **+tomato+soup**.

   b. Compare these results to the first search. Note the volume and quality of these results.

4. At the Excite site, perform a search by using the (-) exclusion parameter. (Excite also recognizes Boolean NOT operator.)

    a. In the search field type, **-basil+tomato+soup**.

    b. Compare these results to the previous search. Note the volume and quality of these results.

Lab Exercise 4-4

In this exercise, you will use Boolean operators to improve your search results.

1. Search for a tomato soup recipe in AltaVista.

    a. In the address bar of your browser, type **www.altavista.com**.

    b. In the search field, type **tomato soup**.

    c. Note the search results. By default, AltaVista searches with an OR condition, pulling from all Web pages containing the word *tomato* or the word *soup*.

2. Search for tomato soup using the AND Boolean condition operator.

    a. In the search field, type **tomato AND soup**.

    b. The search engine will return results with Web pages containing both the words *tomato* and *soup*.

    c. Compare your results to the first search of this lab exercise.

    d. A second window containing source code will open — it will be a text-editing program with the source code for the current Web page displayed within it.

    e. Examine the source code.

3. Search by using the NOT Boolean operator.

    a. In the search field, type **tomato NOT soup**.

    b. The search engine will return a result of Web pages containing the word *tomato* without the word *soup*.

4. Use AltaVista to do a search using the Boolean NEAR operator.

    a. In the search field, type **lakes NEAR Canada**.

    b. Search results will include Web pages containing the words *lakes* and *Canada* that are placed within a few words of each other on a Web page.

5. Do a nested Boolean search using the AltaVista search engine.

　a. In the search field type **(birthday AND parties) AND (kids OR children)**.

　　Note: You must use parentheses in nested Boolean searches.

　b. The results of your search will contain the words *birthday, parties* and *kids*, or *birthday, parties,* and *children*.

6. Use the Google advanced search feature.

　a. In the address bar of your browser, type **www.google.com**.

　b. **Click** the link that says **advanced**. Your screen should now look like Figure 4-18.

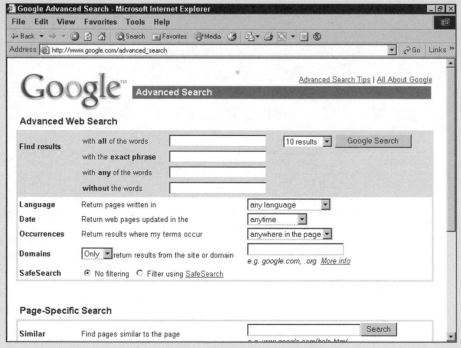

Figure 4-18: Google's advanced search form

　c. In the All the words field, type the words *virus* and *software*.

　d. Specify past three months from the drop-down menu of the Date – return pages updated in... option. Your form should look like Figure 4-19.

　e. Click the Google search button and observe search results.

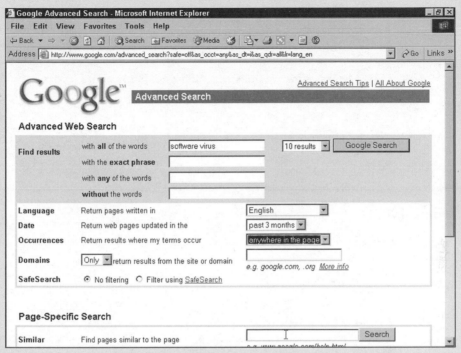

Figure 4-19: Google search form filled according to previous instructions

Lab Exercise 4-5

In this exercise, you will search for a graphic and a person.

1. Search for a graphic at Image Request.

   a. In the address bar of your browser, type
   http://www.imagerequest.com/.

   b. In the search field, type **mountains**.

   c. Right-click an image that you like and save it to your hard drive. Note the drive and folder you are saving the image to.

2. Conduct a people search.

   a. In the address bar of your browser, type `http://www.people-search-engines.com/`.

   b. On the left side of the screen, you can see links to search by: **name**, **e-mail**, **phone**, or **address**.

   c. Click the link **name**.

   d. Type your name.

   e. You may or may not find yourself listed. Perhaps you will find others with the same name.

3. Search for a mail list that gives information about growing orchids:

   a. In the address bar of your browser, type **www.Liszt.com**.

   b. In the search bar, type **orchids** and then click the search button.

   c. A list of potential links to mail groups appears.

   d. Pick one that interests you by clicking its link so that you can read more about it.

   e. You will be taken to a page that gives information for subscribing to this mail group.

Scenario 4-1

You are using search engines to research questions but have come across the following challenges:

1. A keyword search with your favorite search engine isn't yielding any relevant results. What should you do now?

2. When you tried to do a search using (+) and (-) operator at Lycos, the engine seemed to recognize the inclusion operator (+) but did not take the (-) into account when generating the result of your search. Why?

Answers to Chapter Questions

Chapter Pre-Test Answers

1. **Keywords** are used to submit search requests for Web addresses stored in search engine indexes.

2. **Search engines** are a class of software that find a list of Internet addresses containing information that match the search request you give it.

3. Search engines use programs called **bots**, **web crawlers**, or **spiders** to create their indexes.

4. Search **directories** use people to review and decide which Web sites will be accepted into their search index.

5. A search that involves manually navigating through a series of topics or directories is called a **static index search**.

6. A search making a request using a descriptive word(s) is considered a **keyword search**.

7. **Boolean** logic uses operators to exclude or specify characteristics or terms to be included in a search.

8. **Archie** refers to programs dedicated to maintaining FTP site indexes.

9. **Veronica** is a search engine for gopher sites.

Answers to Assessment Questions

1. Choose all statements that correctly describe the term *search engine*:

    A. A class of software that finds of list of Internet addresses.

    B. Similar in concept as a library's card catalog, search engines contain indexes of Web addresses that match keywords.

2. The ranking order of search engine display results is based on:

    B. Keyword frequency and placement

    C. Alliances between the search engine and businesses

    D. How frequently information is updated

3. **False**: Static index site maps and keyword indexes are used when searching for information on the Internet; however, full text indexes are not used for this purpose because of the vast amount of information that must be stored.

4. Which of the following search utilities was the first search directory?

    E. Yahoo!

5. Which of the following search engines searches the Web by cross-referencing keywords?

    b. Excite

6. When doing a keyword search using more than one word with AltaVista, the search defaults to a:

    B. Boolean OR search

7. **True**: Excite does support Boolean operators nested in parentheses.

8. The correct syntax for an AND search at Lycos is:

    B. +crib+cards

9. Veronica is used to search for:

    B. Gopher sites

10. Archie is used to search for:

    A. Anonymous FTP sites

Answers to Scenario Questions

1. A keyword search with your favorite search engine isn't yielding any relevant results. What should you do now?

   Try the same search on a different search engine. Different engines can yield very different results from each other.

   You may also change the order of the words that you type into the search field.

   Typing a synonym in place of the word that you used in the first search may also fix the problem.

2. When you tried to do a search using (+) and (-) operator at Lycos, the engine seemed to recognize the inclusion operator (+), but did not take the (-) into account when generating the result of your search. Why?

   The (-) should be placed before the (+). For example, if you search for the word *birthday* but want to exclude the word *party*, the search request should be -party+birthday.

Resources

✦ WebReference.com has existed since 1995. It is an established and respected Web site. For more information about search engines and searching, go to www.webreference.com/content/search/.

✦ For information on the history of the Yahoo! Search Engine, refer to http://docs.yahoo.com/info/misc/history.html.

✦ "Google, claiming largest index tapped by Yahoo!" Sam Costello; IDG News Service\Boston Bureau. June 26, 2000 www.idg.net/idgns/2000/06/26/GoogleClaimingLargestIndexTappedBy.shtml.

✦ For a list of specialty search engines, refer to www.searchability.com.

✦ You can find a chart comparing Boolean operators and various search engines at www.notess.com/search/features/.

✦ For information on Boolean operators, visit the Searchability Web site at www.searchability.com/boolean.htm.

✦ For a copy of the Copernic search utility, go to www.copernic.com.

Embedded Objects and Browser Plug-ins

EXAM OBJECTIVES

1. Define objects and their relationship to multimedia.

2. Explain the basics of C, C++, Java, JavaScript, ActiveX, JScript, VBScript, and describe how they relate to each other.

3. Describe the purpose of plug-ins.

4. Identify plug-ins and viewers, including RealNetworks RealPlayer, Macromedia Shockwave and Flash players, Apple Quicktime and Adobe Acrobat Reader.

5. Listen to and view multimedia objects within your browser.

6. Identify various file formats such as MPEG, MP3, MOV, AIFF, AU, WAV, AVI, EPS, TIFF, and RTF.

CHAPTER PRE-TEST

1. Why do Web developers embed objects on their Web pages?

2. What makes Java an ideal tool for Web development?

3. The MPEG-1 standard was developed to support what specific medium?

4. Are MP3 files an example of "streaming" or "non-streaming" multimedia?

5. What plug-ins enable you to take "virtual" tours of 3-D worlds on your Web browser?

6. Why is Macromedia Shockwave Flash an excellent tool for creating complex, Web-based animations?

7. What is the most likely reason that you are unable to view multimedia content, on a Web page that you know contains such content?

✦ Answers to these questions can be found at the end of the chapter. ✦

Multimedia enhances the way people interact with computers. Multimedia is used in many different ways, including instructional videos, voice and video memos, training materials, and sales presentations — just to name a few. Bringing multimedia to the Web poses many challenges because access speeds between browsers and servers can be quite slow. Many technologies, however, have been developed to address the special requirements of getting multimedia on the Web. This chapter discusses those technologies.

Embedded Objects and Active Content

Define objects and their relationship to multimedia.

Objects, in programming parlance, are self-contained structures that define properties and functionality. For example, an "audio" object may be included in a Web page to allow the Web page developer to play an audio clip when a user views a page. The object contains all the functionality required to interact with the user's computer — via the Web browser — to play the audio file for the user.

The ability to use these objects gives the Web developer the opportunity to deliver active multimedia content (most often referred to as "active content") by including the objects, which deliver the desired content, in the Web page design.

This process of including active content is known as "embedding." When an object is embedded, it becomes a part of the Web page and is delivered by the Web server to the user's browser, along with the static HTML content, such as text and fixed graphics. Typically, the Web developer embeds the active content by using the HTML <OBJECT> tag. The following HTML code shows an example of this method. Note that the Web site in the sample is fictitious. This listing is presented as an example of syntax only.

```
<HTML>
<HEAD><TITLE>Active Content Example</TITLE></HEAD>
<BODY>
<H1>An example of object embedding!</H1>
<OBJECT CLASSID="http://www.objectworks.com/testobject.py">
</OBJECT>
</BODY>
</HTML>
```

In the preceding example, the CLASSID attribute of the HTML <OBJECT> tag instructs the Web browser to download the object called testobject.py from the server at www.objectworks.com. The object will run after it has been downloaded, generally for as long as the Web page is being viewed.

Web pages that contain active content can be much more functional and enjoyable to use. As a result, active content embedding is becoming a common task for Web developers.

Programming and Scripting Languages

 Explain the basics of C, C++, Java, JavaScript, ActiveX, JScript, VBScript, and describe how they relate to each other.

The previous section discussed embedding objects into Web pages in order to provide active content. This section explores the programming languages that are used to create active content, and their relationship to older languages that don't provide object-oriented programming capabilities.

This section also discusses scripting languages that — although not used to create embeddable objects — can help to create active content.

C

C has traditionally been used as a development language for creating high performance applications and operating systems.

C programs are created from plain text source code files. A simple C program may have only a single file for the entire application. More complex programs may be comprised of many different source files, each of which represents a piece of the application. These source files, however, cannot be executed directly. They must first be converted to a format that is interpretable by the operating system on which they will run. Programmers do this conversion by "compiling" the source code files with a program called a "compiler". The compiler uses the source code that the programmer has created as an instruction set from which executable code is created. The resulting code makes up the application.

 The executable code is operating system and platform dependent. For example, a C program compiled on an Intel-based PC running Windows cannot simply be copied to a Macintosh computer.

However, the application's source files may be copied to the Macintosh and, if a C compiler is available on that machine, be compiled to executables that will run on the Mac. In theory this is a simple process, however, differences in the way that each platform operates make it necessary for all but the simplest of programs to be re-coded in order to conform to the platform's requirement, prior to compiling.

The source files (and, to some extent, the methods used to compile the code) also enable the programmer to employ various methods of debugging, such as tracing or stepping through the source code line by line, as the program executes to locate problems.

C is a "procedural language" — meaning the code controls program execution by calling procedures or functions that perform the bulk of the processing tasks. Object-oriented programming (OOP) is rapidly becoming the standard programming model and, as a result, C is being replaced by C++ and Java — both of which are OOP languages.

Object-Oriented Programming

Object oriented programming (OOP) is the process of developing applications from modular pieces of code called objects. These objects encapsulate both the data and functions that correspond to entities used in the development of an application. For example, suppose that an automated teller application is being created. The program must allow users to make deposits, withdraw cash, pay bills, and so on. To facilitate this, an "account" object could be created. The account object would contain account details, such as the account number, pin number, and balance. It may also contain the functions necessary to allow debiting and crediting of the account. By creating an account object, the programmer creates a reusable component that can be employed in the automated teller application. As the component is reusable, it may also be used in other applications, such as the application that a human teller works with behind the counter.

An object is developed in much the same way as any other program. Source code is created, either from a text editor or from a development environment such as Microsoft's Visual C++. The source code defines the object's details and functions. In OOP terminology, the object details are known as *properties* and the functions are called *methods*. After the coding is complete, the objects must be compiled. However, they are generally not compiled directly to executables. Instead, they are compiled into code that must be called upon by an executing program to be used. When the teller application needs to access an account, for example, it may create (through a process called *instantiation*) an instance of the account object. Several objects may be compiled together into a library file. Dynamic Link Libraries (DLLs) are an example.

Another way to think of objects, source files, and instantiations, is in an analogy of a custom built house. An architect is hired to design a house and produces a blueprint of the house (the source file and resulting compiled file). The blue print specifies the way that the house is to be built and several properties, such as the type of counters in the kitchen and the color of the shingles to name a couple. Now the house must be created (instantiated). The builder (the program which creates an instance of the object) follows the blueprint to produce an instance of the house that can actually be lived in (an object). If another house needs to be built, the builder can follow the blueprint to create a new house. As the design process is already complete and the blue print created, there is no need to get the architect involved. In addition, certain properties may be changed to make the new house unique. The color of the shingles, for example, may be different for each instance of the house.

C++

C++ is an extension of the traditional C programming language. It retains the same basic syntax as C but includes support for object-oriented programming. C++ is generally the language of choice for large, complex development projects. Because C++ compiles to native code, however, it is necessary to re-compile — and in some cases re-code — the application in order to move it to another hardware platform.

This lack of cross-platform portability has prompted developers who are developing software for the Internet — and heterogeneous networks in general — to consider Java as an alternative to C++.

Java

Java, which was developed by Sun Microsystems, is also an object-oriented programming language. In fact, Java has its roots in C++ and, has many of the same characteristics as C++. The syntax, data type, and program flow control of Java are nearly identical to C++ and, as a result, C++ programmers normally have little difficulty transitioning to the Java environment. The Java developers also examined the elements that made C++ difficult to use, such as manual memory allocation and deallocation, and wrote Java to manage these tasks automatically. These improvements have, in some ways, made Java an easier language to use.

Java was designed to be platform-independent. Java programs are not compiled to native, platform-specific executables, as is the case with C or C++. Rather, the Java compiler creates Java "object code," which is interpreted by an application called the Java Virtual Machine (JVM). As long as a JVM is available for a particular operating system, the Java program can be executed on that system with no need to re-code or re-compile.

Currently, JVMs are available for all major operating systems and environments, including Windows, Macintosh, and Unix/Linux. A Java interpreter, that performs the same function as the Java Virtual Machine, is also built into recent releases (version 3.0 or later) of Netscape Navigator and Internet Explorer Web browsers. Java's acceptance has promoted increased use of multimedia content.

When the Web was first becoming popular, HyperText Markup Language (HTML) was the primary tool used in development of Web pages. At that time, HTML was able to define the layout of static text and graphics and allowed linking between Web pages, but lacked an ability to provide any real dynamic content. Java, with its cross-platform acceptance and powerful programming capabilities, became the programming language of choice for developing multimedia content for Web pages. With Java, developers can create sophisticated graphical interfaces and deliver them across the Web to the user's browser, where they are interpreted by the browser's built-in Java interpreter. These applications are known as *Java applets*, which are discussed in greater detail later in this chapter.

In addition to creating applets, Java has the ability to create standalone applications that don't require a Web browser in order to execute.

Scripting languages

Scripting languages, unlike full programming languages, are typically not compiled. Rather, they are used to control functions that are built into applications, such as Web browsers.

Scripting enables a developer to create code that will perform certain tasks, usually in response to an event that has occurred in the browser environment, such as accessing a Web page, or passing the mouse pointer over an image. This is known as "event-driven" programming because the script functions don't execute until the appropriate "event" has occurred. Events are actions caused by the user, such as mouse clicks, key presses, or other such interaction, or actions caused by the browser, such as the opening or closing of a Web page.

Script programs are typically written inside the HTML documents that comprise Web page content. Alternately, you can create separate documents that just contain scripts; these documents are usually created as "libraries" of functions that can be used over and over in different projects.

The following HTML code shows a simple Web page, which displays a message in a pop-up dialog box when opened.

```
<HTML>
<HEAD>
<TITLE>Simple Web Page With Script</TITLE>
</HEAD>
<BODY onLoad="alert('Hello CIW Certification Candidate!')">
<H1> This has been a sample of scripting!</H1>
</BODY>
</HTML>
```

This simple example illustrates how events can be monitored and used to call built-in functions in the Web browser. In this case, the onLoad event, which occurs when the Web page loads, is captured in the <BODY> tag. The onLoad=... instruction is used to execute the built-in alert function. The alert function displays a message, defined by the developer, in a pop-up dialog box.

Although the preceding example uses JavaScript, the same functionality is available with other scripting languages, which are discussed in the following sections.

JavaScript

JavaScript was the first language developed specifically for the task of Web page scripting. Although JavaScript shares some syntactical similarities with Java, they are two completely separate and distinct languages. Java was developed by Sun Microsystems, whereas JavaScript began life as a language, called LiveScript, and was developed by Netscape.

Unlike Java, JavaScript is not a stand-alone programming language; it must be executed from within a Web browser or other application. JavaScript is also not limited to providing scripting capabilities in Web browsers; for example, many Web servers and various other programs use JavaScript for automating functions.

JScript

JScript is a subset of the JavaScript language and was produced by Microsoft as an alternative to supporting JavaScript in their earlier browser releases. Although JScript and JavaScript share some similarities, JavaScript may not function properly on older Internet Explorer versions, as the JScript interpreter does not recognize the full java command set, and JScript, which is not fully JavaScript compatible, may not function properly on Netscape Browsers (which only support JavaScript).

Visual Basic Script

Visual Basic Script (VBScript) is Microsoft's full scripting language, which competes directly with JavaScript. As its name implies, VBScript is based on the syntax and structure of Microsoft's popular Visual Basic programming language.

VBScript is capable of interacting with regular HTML content, such as HTML forms or other intrinsic Web elements, as well as with ActiveX objects and controls (which are discussed in the next section). For this reason, VBScript is the preferred language when using ActiveX content in Microsoft browsers.

VBScript, however, suffers from being a proprietary language, and is therefore not widely supported outside of Microsoft browsers.

Java Applets and ActiveX Content

To enable active, dynamic content, such as multimedia in a Web page, a developer can choose to make use of a number of different technologies, including Java applets and ActiveX controls.

Java applets

As previously mentioned, Java applets are Java programs that are designed to run within the Web browser environment. Applets are implemented in Web pages as embedded objects, and were actually the first such objects available for use in Web development. Java applets have become widely used to enable dynamic and interactive content in Web pages. This content may include:

✦ User interaction, such as with games or simulations.

✦ Audio and video playback.

✦ Graphical animations and reaction to user activity, such as opening menus or changing content based on where the user points the mouse.

✦ Real-time interfacing with external data, such as on-line chat programs, stock updaters, and other live-feed data.

These enhancements can make Web pages much more usable than plain static text and images.

Java Swing

To provide additional graphical capabilities and to enhance performance of Java applications and applets, Java Swing was developed. Swing enhances the original Abstract Windowing Tool kit (AWT), which adds support for a truly platform-independent graphical interface. With Swing, developers can create a graphical interface without having to worry about the underlying platform's capabilities. The JVM takes care of translation.

Unfortunately, Swing requires the Java 2 runtime environment to support Swing-based applets. At the time of this writing, Internet Explorer 5.x and prior versions, and Netscape Communicator 4.7x and prior versions don't support Java 2.

The solution to this problem lies in a component provided by Sun that is freely downloadable; this component is called the Java Plug-in (see `http://java.sun.com/products/plugin/index.html`). The Java Plug-in runs on a user's system and intercepts calls from Swing applets, thus providing support for Swing-based functions and interface components. The Plug-in Web site also has instructions on how to code your Web pages with HTML and JavaScript so that the latest Java Plug-in will be downloaded and installed automatically.

ActiveX

Another tool for enabling dynamic Web content is ActiveX. ActiveX was originally developed by Microsoft, but was later handed over to an organization called The Open Group. ActiveX is not a programming language, but rather a family of technologies and methodologies for creating reusable components or objects. ActiveX objects, sometimes called ActiveX *controls*, can perform the same functions as Java applets: Enabling sound, video, and interactivity in Web browsers. Like Java applets, ActiveX objects don't replace the static text or images found in Web pages. Instead, ActiveX enhances the Web page by providing additional functionality.

Unlike Java applets, however, ActiveX objects don't provide the same level of cross-platform support. Netscape Navigator, for example, doesn't support the use of ActiveX components. Java applets, on the other hand, are supported in all major browsers.

Objects and Security Issues

Both Java applets and ActiveX components are programs that — when downloaded into your Web browser — have the potential for causing problems, which can range from simple inconvenience to actual loss of data. Although the majority of applets and ActiveX controls that you encounter will be perfectly fine for download, you may stumble across a malicious one. For this reason, browsers provide the ability to disable active content, such as ActiveX controls and Java applets.

If you choose to disable these components, you will still be able to browse the static content of Web pages — you just won't see the active content. Nor will the browser report any errors because it is set to ignore active content. In the coding of the Web page, however, the developer may choose to insert a warning message that will appear as static text, but only if your browser does not support active content or if you have disabled the display of active content. The message is intended to inform you that the site has been designed with ActiveX or Java applets, and that you need to enable active content in order to realize the full effect of the Web page.

As an alternative to completely disabling active content, products have been created to help protect against malicious active content before it ever reaches the browser. These products are implemented as part of certain firewall solutions and examine active Web page content in an attempt to filter malicious programs (often referred to as "vandals"), or active content that is performing unacceptable operations. If, however, implementing such solutions is beyond an individual or organization's capabilities or budget, disabling active content at the browser may be the only option.

Introduction to Plug-in Technology

 Describe the purpose of plug-ins.

Plug-ins are programs that have been specifically written to provide a certain type of enhancement to your Web browser. The difference between plug-ins and Java applets or ActiveX controls is the fact that the plug-in is written to support a specific browser, for a specific enhancement. For example, a very popular set of plug-ins is the Macromedia Shockwave and Flash players. Each allows the playback of animations and interactive content produced with the Shockwave and Flash development tools. A separate plug-in is required for delivering each type of content — one for Flash and one for Shockwave. In addition, the plug-ins are not universal. You need a different plug-in for each operating environment, such as Internet Explorer, Netscape Navigator, and — for standalone use — in an operating system such as Windows 98, ME, or Macintosh. A single Java application, in contrast, is capable of running in both browsers (as long as it was created as an applet), and in every operating system that supports a Java Virtual Machine.

Plug-ins have an environment-specific nature because they are designed to interface directly with the underlying browser or operating system code without the overhead associated with a translation utility, such as the Java Virtual Machine. Also, the plug-ins are typically written in a high performance language, such as C++, which enables the plug-in to deliver the sophisticated multimedia content that they are designed to provide.

How do plug-ins work?

Plug-ins typically work by "streaming" the content that they are to deliver. In other words, when they are called into service, plug-ins begin to download the content and save it into a buffer. This buffer is usually located in the disk cache of your system in order to avoid using too much system memory.

For example, suppose that you are using a video player plug-in, such as RealAudio player or Microsoft MediaPlayer. When you access the movie file from your browser, the plug-in buffers a few seconds worth of data before it begins playback. When playback begins, you watch one part of the video while the plug-in brings down the next part and stores it in cache. Ideally, this provides uninterrupted playback of the content by storing enough of the stream in cache at any one time, so that the inevitable transfer delays caused by network traffic don't affect playback.

Some plug-ins, on the other hand, deal with non-streaming data. That is, the entire content that the plug-in is to deliver must be downloaded before playback can begin. This is generally an unacceptable situation for content that takes longer than a few seconds to download. As a result, streaming media plug-ins are becoming more and more popular as the size of the media files becomes larger and larger.

Plug-in appearance

Listen to and view multimedia objects within your browser.

When a plug-in is activated in a browser, it generally takes one of three forms:

✦ **Hidden.** A hidden plug-in does not have any visual interface. Instead, it runs in the background for delivery of content that does not require a visual environment, such as a background audio player.

✦ **Full Screen.** A full screen plug-in uses the entire display area of the browser's content window. Only the window border, title bar, tool bar, and menu bar remain visible. In some cases, the plug-in even hides all the bars and leaves only the border, thus maximizing the display space. Quite often, full screen plug-ins automatically launch a new browser window for the exclusive use of the content being delivered. After the content has been delivered, the window may be closed automatically, or the user may have to close it manually, depending on whether the plug-in closes the new browser window it has opened, or leaves it open for the user to close.

✦ **Embedded.** Embedded plug-ins appear as a part of the Web page, typically as a square or rectangular area. The content provided by the plug-in appears in this area. This is similar to how static images appear — with the obvious exception that the content is dynamic. Even though the plug-ins run as embedded areas of the Web page, however, they don't lack functionality in contrast to full screen plug-ins. Most embedded plug-ins have useable controls, which take a portion of their display space, and with which the user can manipulate the functioning of the plug-in. The RealPlayer plug-in, for example, has embedded controls for starting, stopping, and rewinding the video, as well as for adjusting the volume. Refer to Figure 5-1.

Figure 5-1: Embedded RealPlayer plug-in

Installing plug-ins

The methods that are used to install plug-ins share absolutely no consistency. Plug-in installation is initiated when a computer encounters content on a Web page that is not directly supported by the browser. In most cases, the download of the required plug-in begins automatically, but the process for actually installing it into the user's browser differs from plug-in to plug-in. In general, however, plug-in installation is done either *on-line* or *off-line*.

On-line installation

On-line plug-in installation does not require that the browser be closed. The user is given a warning that the content is unsupported and the user is prompted to allow the appropriate plug-in to be installed. Some plug-ins install completely "silently," which is another way of saying that no indication is given to the user that a plug-in has downloaded and installed.

Because some users are reluctant to allow silent installation of plug-ins or other active content, most browsers allow the user to prevent silent installation via configuration settings.

Off-line installation

Off-line installation requires that the browser be closed prior to running the plug-in installation program. In some cases, the installation requires that the computer be restarted prior to making use of the plug-in. You must follow the installation instructions carefully and provide any information that the plug-in installer requires, such as the location of the browser directory. Failure to follow the installation instructions, as with other software, often results in a plug-in that can't function properly.

Types of Browser Plug-ins

Objective Identify plug-ins and viewers, including RealNetworks RealPlayer, Macromedia Shockwave and Flash players, Apple Quicktime and Adobe Acrobat Reader.

There are as many (if not more) types of browser plug-ins as there are data types that need interpretation. This section explores some of these browser plug-ins.

In the Real World
BrowserWatch is an interesting Web site that contains listings of available browser plug-ins and ActiveX controls, as well as general browser news. Go to `http://browserwatch.internet.com/plug-in.html` to see their "Plug-in Plaza," which lists many different plug-ins, viewers, and productivity tools available for download from various manufacturers. Be warned, however, that just because a plug-in appears on a Web page doesn't guarantee its stability. Install all plug-ins at your own discretion.

Adobe Atmosphere

The Adobe Atmosphere Browser, which you can download from `www.adobe.com/products/atmosphere/betareg_player.html`, is a 3-D virtual reality plug-in. It allows you to move through 3-D virtual worlds, interacting with objects and even other users, through your computer persona (called an *avatar*).

The plug-in is installed off-line, but does not require a reboot of your computer. Figure 5-2 shows the Adobe Atmosphere download page.

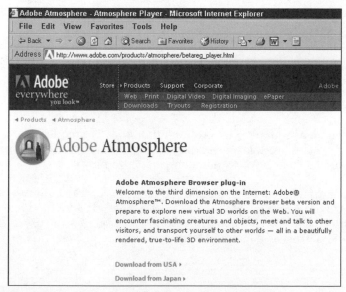

Figure 5-2: Adobe Atmosphere download page

Figure 5-3 shows Adobe Atmosphere running in Internet Explorer.

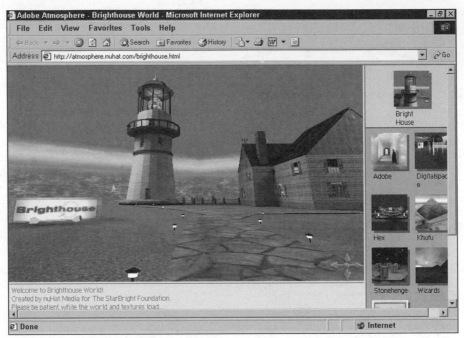

Figure 5-3: Adobe Atmosphere running in Internet Explorer. As of this writing, Adobe Atmosphere is still in beta format.

RealNetworks RealPlayer

RealNetworks first introduced the RealAudio streaming format and player in 1995. Shortly thereafter, they introduced the RealVideo player technology, which provides video using the same streaming format as RealAudio. Currently, the RealPlayer software handles playback of both video and audio.

RealPlayer is implemented as a standalone program that does not require a browser to operate. If you are browsing a Web page that contains a RealAudio or video clip, the browser can launch your standalone player to play it.

You may also implement the player as an embedded plug-in, as is done on the video site for NASA's Mars Odyssey mission at `www.jpl.nasa.gov/videos/mars/odyssey.html`, as shown in Figure 5-4. The embedded player allows the user a limited but capable set of controls as compared to the standalone player.

In this case, even though the video can play as an embedded object in the Web page, the page developer gave the option to launch the standalone player.

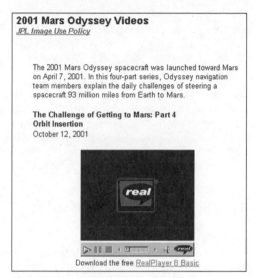

Figure 5-4: RealPlayer embedded in a Web page

Apple QuickTime

QuickTime, developed by Apple Computer, is a proprietary video/audio format with players available for both the Windows and the Macintosh platforms.

The QuickTime Movie (MOV) format makes use of the player's "fast start" feature, which begins playing the movie clip almost immediately upon receiving the first frame, while the remainder of the clip downloads in the background. This process is similar to other streaming formats previously discussed in this chapter.

The MOV format is supported in all versions of QuickTime and combines animation, audio, text, and video into one file. The extensions identifying files of this format are .mov, .moov, or .qt.

Also included with the installation of QuickTime is the ability to use QTVR, or QuickTime Virtual Reality, files. QTVR is similar to Adobe Atmosphere, which allows the exploration of virtual 3-D worlds.

Apple QuickTime 5 (the current version as of this writing) is available for download at www.apple.com/quicktime.

In the Real World

Both Adobe Atmosphere and QuickTime Virtual Reality are examples of plug-ins that allow the interpretation of a Virtual Reality Modeling Language, or VRML. VRML is actually a standards-based specification for 3-D content production, display, and manipulation.

Other examples of VRML-like technologies include ActiveWorlds from ActiveWorlds Corp. (www.activeworlds.com), Netscape Live3D (http://home.netscape.com/eng/live3d/index_v.html), and Computer Associates Worldview and Cosmo products (www.cai.com/cosmo).

Each 3-D package may use proprietary formats incompatible with VRML players that must written to support standards-based formats, such as VRML 1.0, VRML 2.0, or VRLM 97. More information about 3-D modeling on the Internet, visit the Web3D Consortium (www.vrml.org).

Windows Media Player

The Microsoft Windows Media Player provides support for both live and on-demand content.

Live content, as its name implies, is not pre-recorded. Instead, the data stream is captured as the audio or video is produced, and is then sent to the player. An example of live content is the broadcast of a live concert, via the Internet, or one of the live Internet radio stations that have become popular.

On-demand content is pre-recorded content, such as a recorded audio or video presentation, that is sent when the user demands it (usually by clicking a link to start the playback).

A major benefit of Windows Media Player is its ability to produce FM radio-quality sound. In addition, it has features that allow it to support pay-per-view services and piracy protection schemes, which protect copyrighted content from being saved to the user's hard drive.

MediaPlayer is available for both Windows and Macintosh, and is downloadable from www.microsoft.com/windows/windowsmedia.

Macromedia Shockwave and Flash players

Macromedia Shockwave allows users to embed a wide range of interactive multimedia content, including animation, movies, and audio. First released in 1995, Shockwave has become a popular method of providing interactive multimedia solutions.

To cope with the problems of limited bandwidth, Macromedia has also developed Flash, which has the same basic capabilities as Shockwave (in fact, when you get Shockwave, you also get Flash). However, Flash creates very small files that are ideal for transport across the Internet. These Flash files, which use a .swf extension, are optimized to provide very impressive multimedia and interactive capabilities in a very small amount of space. In addition, Flash makes use of content streaming, thus further enhancing usability and performance.

You can get additional information on the Macromedia Web site at `www.macromedia.com`.

Viewers

Viewers are necessary to display certain file types, which are produced by an application that is not installed on your computer. For example, suppose that you want to use a viewer to look at drawings produced in a Computer Assisted Design (CAD) package. Given that all you need to do is view the drawings — and not edit them — it makes sense to have a simple viewer rather than the full package.

Viewers, therefore, are scaled-down versions of applications (generally provided free of charge) that allow viewing of certain file types, but not permanent manipulation or editing of their content. If full editing capability is required, viewers will not suffice and the full application must be purchased. The following sections explore two commonly used viewer applications.

Adobe Acrobat Reader

Adobe Acrobat uses the Portable Document Format (PDF). The PDF format is platform-independent and features benefits such as true document format retention across platforms and high data compression. PDF is an ideal format for sharing documents on the Internet. PDF documents use the file extension .pdf.

The Acrobat Reader, which allows display of files in PDF format, is available free of charge from Adobe at `www.adobe.com/products/acrobat`.

Microsoft PowerPoint Viewer

The PowerPoint Viewer allows users to display presentations, or *slide shows*, created in Microsoft PowerPoint. The player enables users to present PowerPoint presentations without the need to have a licensed copy of Microsoft Office on their computers. This is ideal when space is limited (as is the case on a laptop computer), or when the full version of the software is not required.

Because PowerPoint has been around since the Microsoft Office 4.0 days, compatibility of the viewer with the data versions can pose a problem. Microsoft, however, has built backward-compatibility into their viewer product, so the latest version of the viewer should display both the latest, and prior, versions of PowerPoint files.

The PowerPoint Viewer (as well as other product updates) is freely available from the Microsoft Office Download Center located at `http://office.microsoft.com/Downloads/Default.aspx`.

Miscellaneous File Formats

 Objective Identify various file formats such as MPEG, MP3, MOV, AIFF, AU, WAV, AVI, EPS, TIFF, and RTF.

This section describes some additional file formats that you should be familiar with when working in multimedia environments.

Moving Picture Experts Group

The Moving Picture Experts Group (MPEG) format is an international standard for compression of digital video and audio, which provides extremely high quality and resolution. There are a number of different MPEG specifications, which are based on various screen sizes, or *resolutions*, and data throughput requirements. MPEG-1, for example, was developed for use with video CDs, whereas MPEG-2 was created for digital television applications.

 Caution The CIW material mentions MPEG-3 as the specification for High Definition Television (HDTV). Please remember this definition for exam purposes. As far as the exam is concerned, the definition is correct. However, a visit to the Moving Picture Experts Group Web site shows that MPEG-2 is the "...standard on which such products as Digital Television set top boxes and DVD are based..." In addition, the www.mpeg.org Web site further discusses standards, such as the U.S. Digital HDTV specification that is based on MPEG-2. There is, in fact, no MPEG-3 specification. MPEG-2 is followed instead by MPEG-4.

You can visit the MPEG site at www.cselt.it/mpeg/index.htm for additional information on the MPEG format.

MPEG Audio Layer-3

Based on the MPEG-1 audio standard, MPEG Audio Layer-3 (MP3) is a digital encoding scheme for stereo audio. It has become popular as a method for storing audio material in compressed files that retain a high degree of fidelity. The MP3 compression algorithm removes that data from the source audio file (representing sounds that are imperceptible to most listeners). This method results in files that are relatively small in size (about a tenth the size of the original) but provide good audio quality.

In order to use MP3 files, you must install an MP3 player, and many such players are available. Later versions of many players, such as the Windows Media Player, also include support for MP3 files.

MP3 is a non-streaming format, meaning that the files must be downloaded in their entirety before playback can start.

LiveVideo

LiveVideo supports the embedding and playback of Audio Video Interleave (AVI) files. AVI is the Microsoft standard for audio and video playback in Windows, known most commonly as Video for Windows.

LiveVideo was developed by Netscape to provide an ability to play AVI files in a Web page without the need to download the complete file for later playback.

RealTime Streaming Protocol

Co-developed by Netscape and RealAudio, the RealTime Streaming Protocol (RTSP) allows for the embedding and direct playback of RTSP format files in a Web browser. RTSP benefits from being cross-platform capable.

Audio file formats

Several audio file formats that you are likely to encounter are the Audio Interchange File Format (AIFF), Sun Microsystems audio format (AU), Musical Instrument Digital Interface (MIDI), and Microsoft Wave (WAV) formats.

Audio Interchange File Format

Audio Interchange File Format (AIFF) was developed by Apple Computer for storing high-quality sampled audio and musical instrument information. It is also used by Silicon Graphics and in several professional audio packages.

Microsoft Wave format

Microsoft Wave format (WAV) is the Windows standard for waveform sound files. WAV files predictably have the extension `.wav`.

AU

Developed by Sun Microsystems, the AU format has found wide acceptance in the Internet community, especially on UNIX systems. Most browsers, whether on a UNIX-based system, a PC, or a Macintosh, are capable of supporting this format. AU files have a file extension of `.au`.

Musical Instrument Digital Interface

Musical Instrument Digital Interface (MIDI — Pronounced "middy") is a standard that defines the interfacing of musical instruments into a digital network for the purposes of digitally controlling and recording musical tracks. The term is used to describe the standard itself, the hardware that supports the standard, and files that store information usable by the hardware. MIDI files are like digital sheet music. They contain instructions for musical notes, tempo, and instrumentation, and are widely used in game soundtracks and recording studios.

Apple Computer developed AIFF, WAV is the Microsoft standard audio format, and MIDI is used for interfacing of musical instruments. The AU format is used on Unix systems. Each format requires a plug-in or player; however, most audio plug-ins can support some — if not all — of the audio file formats mentioned. If the player is not available on the user's system, one must be downloaded and installed.

Encapsulated PostScript

Encapsulated PostScript (EPS) is a format that allows for the import and export of graphics files between operating systems and applications. EPS is similar to PostScript in that it includes embedded commands that help in the rendering of the file content. However, EPS also contains the actual bitmap data. Besides allowing cross-platform sharing of graphical information, EPS allows for the display of the included graphic in an alternate format for previewing. Three preview formats are available: PICT, for use on Macintosh systems, TIFF for IBM compatibles, and the EPSI format, which is platform-independent.

EPS is often used to transport graphics between applications as each application uses a proprietary file format. EPS acts as a translator between them, thus ensuring that all the graphical information is retained during the transfer.

You can identify EPS files by their .eps extension.

Tagged Image File Format

The Tagged Image File Format (TIFF) is a file format originally developed by Aldus Corporation as a universal file graphics file format that would work on various system platforms. However, over its lifetime, the TIFF format has been modified and adjusted and there are now many different varieties in existence, not all of which are compatible. The latest revision, dated June, 1992, is 6.0.

The TIFF format is commonly used where high resolution and high color is required, such as in medical imaging or desktop publishing. The TIFF format supports 1-bit monochrome (black and white), 16 and 256-level grayscale, 8-bit color, and 24-bit color. TIFF is supported in many applications, making it a good format choice for exchanging graphical images. TIFF files use either a `.tiff` or `.tif` extension.

Rich Text Format

Rich Text Format (RTF) is widely supported as a method of encoding format information and graphics in text-based documents. The format is one level above the DOS text format, which contains textual information only — not formatting details.

Originally developed by Microsoft, RTF is supported across most platforms and in most applications, such as Microsoft Word, Corel WordPerfect, Lotus WordPro, and others. Its wide acceptance makes it ideal for transferring files between applications whose native file formats differ. When using RTF, a separate converter (for example from Word to WordPerfect) is not required.

Key Point Summary

The HTML protocol, used in development of Web pages, is very capable in delivering static content. However, Web developers have not been satisfied with delivering simple, static Web pages. Multimedia content and interactivity are more and more the norm on Web sites. As this chapter has demonstrated, embedded objects, plug-ins, and viewers are enabling developers to deliver dynamic, interactive, multimedia rich pages to the users via their Web browser software.

✦ Objects enable the embedding of functions, such as the ability to play movies or audio clips.

✦ Movies, animations, audio, and other such multimedia effects are known as active content.

✦ Embedding is the process of including content other than the standard static text and graphics of simple HTML pages.

✦ C is a programming language, and because of its non-object oriented nature, is being gradually replaced by other languages, such as C++ and Java.

✦ C++ is an extension of the C programming language that supports Object-Oriented Programming (OOP) concepts and structures.

✦ Java is a programming language based on C++. It was developed as a platform-independent programming language, which would allow the same programs to run, without change, in various hardware and software environments.

✦ Java can produce standalone applications, as well as programs called applets, which must execute in a browser environment.

✦ Java applets were the first embedded objects that could provide true multimedia effects capabilities and user interaction in the Web environment.

✦ Netscape first introduced JavaScript as LiveScript.

✦ JavaScript was designed as a scripting language that would give automation capabilities to HTML-based Web pages.

✦ JavaScript is usually coded to call functions based on Web events, such as when the Web page opens or when a user clicks a link or points the mouse at a graphic.

✦ JScript is Microsoft's version of JavaScript. It is a subset of JavaScript.

✦ JScript and JavaScript, while sharing basic similarities, are different enough from each other to cause problems in portability.

✦ Microsoft originally developed ActiveX. Microsoft later turned it over to The Open Group.

✦ VBScript is Microsoft's answer to JavaScript. However, VBScript is not widely supported outside the Microsoft family or products.

✦ Both ActiveX and Java applets download and run on your system. This makes them a potential source of security concerns.

✦ Internet Explorer, Netscape Navigator, and most other browsers support the disabling, via user settable options, of Java applets and other active content, such as ActiveX.

✦ Plug-ins are applications associated with certain file formats or data types.

✦ Plug-ins extend the capabilities of your Web browser to add support for multimedia and other content.

✦ Plug-ins work by integrating with the browser and launching when a supported data type is encountered in a Web page.

✦ Various media types are supported by plug-ins and include both streaming and non-streaming data sources.

✦ Streaming is a process of starting playback of the media content prior to completing the download. As a part of the media is playing, the remainder is being downloaded in the background.

✦ Non-streaming content must be fully downloaded before playback can begin.

✦ Plug-ins can appear as hidden, embedded, or full-screen objects.

✦ Plug-ins are installed by connecting to the plug-in provider's Web site, downloading the plug-in software, and installing it.

✦ Online plug-in installation can be done with the browser open, and does not generally require a reboot.

✦ Off-line installation generally requires that the browser be closed (after the plug-in setup files have been downloaded) during installation. A reboot of your computer is then often required.

✦ Many types of plug-ins are available, including the following:

  • RealNetworks RealPlayer. Provides support for RealAudio and RealVideo data formats.

  • Macromedia ShockWave and Flash Players. Provide support for multimedia content and interactive Web pages.

  • Apple QuickTime Player. Provides support for Apple's QuickTime audio/video format as well as support for QuickTime Virtual Reality (QVTR).

- Windows Media Player. Provides support for many multimedia formats in the Windows and Macintosh environments.

- Adobe Atmosphere Player. Provides support for Adobe Atmosphere, which is a 3-D virtual reality development environment.

✦ Virtual Reality Modeling Language (VRML) plug-ins are available from many vendors and support high speed VRML file viewing, animation, and 3-D navigation of sites created with a VRML language.

✦ Viewers are scaled-down versions of applications that allow opening and viewing of an application's files when the full application is not required.

✦ Microsoft PowerPoint Viewer and Adobe Acrobat Reader are examples of viewer applications.

✦ PowerPoint allows for the viewing of Microsoft PowerPoint presentations.

✦ Adobe Acrobat Reader allows for the viewing of documents coded as Adobe Portable Document Format (PDF) files.

✦   ✦   ✦

STUDY GUIDE

The following materials will aid you in preparing for the portion of the CIW Foundations exam covered in this chapter. Several assessment questions will, as much as possible, mimic the feel of the actual exam. Some scenario questions test your knowledge of how to apply, in real world situations, the information that you have received in this chapter. These are typically essay-type questions that you won't find on the actual exam, but are useful in solidifying your understanding of the chapter topics. In addition, there are a number of labs that may or may not have questions associated with them, but which allow you to install and make use of some of the plug-ins and active content discussed.

After you have been through the assessment questions and scenarios, check your answers in the section Answers to Chapter Questions, which immediately follows the scenarios.

Assessment Questions

1. What are the two methods of plug-in installation? (Choose two)

    A. Online installation

    B. Demo installation

    C. Registered installation

    D. Off-line installation

2. You need to install a plug-in that will allow for the viewing of files with an .swf extension. Where would you look for such a plug-in? (Choose the best answer)

    A. The distribution CD for Windows 98 Second Edition.

    B. The Macromedia Web site.

    C. The media directory on a Windows computer.

    D. There are no such files.

3. What kind of Web pages are you viewing if you were required to install the Adobe Atmosphere plug-in?

    A. A meteorological information site.

    B. A site concerning air pollution.

    C. A site with "mood" music.

    D. A site with 3-D, interactive, virtual reality content.

4. What should users do to limit the possibility of damage caused by malicious components downloaded from a Web site? (Choose the best answer)

  A. Keep current backups of the system available.

  B. Disable active content and Java applet support in the browser options.

  C. Enable RSACi content tracking.

  D. Stop surfing the Internet.

5. Which of the following are examples of Object Oriented Programming (OOP) languages? (Choose all that apply)

  A. C

  B. C++

  C. JScript

  D. VBScript

  E. Java

6. Why is Java popular for programming Web content? (Choose two)

  A. Java is platform-independent.

  B. Java is much simpler to use than other programming languages.

  C. Java is faster than other languages.

  D. Java supports the creation of programs that can be embedded in Web pages.

7. When a streaming video file is viewed in a browser, what best describes the process involved? (Choose the best answer)

  A. The Web browser launches the appropriate plug-in. The plug-in starts to download the video file into a buffer maintained in cache. After a sufficient portion of the file has been buffered, the plug-in begins playback, and continues to download the remainder of the file in the background.

  B. The Web browser downloads the video file, placing it in a buffer maintained in cache. After the file has finished downloading, the browser starts the plug-in for the video file type. The plug-in then plays the video.

  C. The browser analyzes the file format and re-directs the user to the Web site of the manufacturer of the video file. From there, the appropriate playback application is launched and the user watches the video on the manufacturer's site. When finished, the user is re-directed back to the page that they launched the video from.

  D. The browser launches the appropriate plug-in, which begins download of the video file. As soon as the first frame arrives, the plug-in begins playback of a sample video until the entire download is complete. The downloaded file is then loaded and played.

8. You need to view a file in PDF format. Which plug-in or viewer should you get? (Choose the best answer)

   A. Microsoft PowerPoint Viewer.

   B. Adobe Acrobat Reader.

   C. Adobe PageMill.

   D. Adobe Atmosphere.

9. What type of program could you use RTF files to share information with a similar program from another manufacturer?

   A. Word processor.

   B. Database.

   C. Spreadsheet.

   D. Real time forecasting applications.

10. What type of file would have an .au extension?

   A An audio file.

   B. A video file.

   C. A spreadsheet file.

   D. None of the above.

11. What does MPEG stand for?

   A. Movie Player Extended Graphics.

   B. Motion Picture Enhancement Group.

   C. Moving Picture Experts Group.

   D. Multimedia Playback Experimental Group.

12. What platforms is the Microsoft Windows Media Player supported on? (Choose two)

   A. Linux.

   B. OS/2.

   C. Windows.

   D. Macintosh.

13. What type of content does the RealPlayer support? (Choose the best answer)

   A. Video.

   B. Audio.

   C. Video and Audio.

   D. None of the above.

14. Which audio format specification is more commonly referred to as MP3?

    A. MPEG Audio Layer-3.

    B. RealAudio.

    C. Microsoft MediaPlayer audio.

    D. Media Partners Advanced Audio Association.

15. Apple Computer developed which audio format?

    A. AU.

    B. MIDI.

    C. WAV.

    D. AIFF.

Scenario

1. As a Web designer, you have been approached to consult on the creation of a Web site for a local art gallery. The client wants to be able to offer a virtual tour of the gallery in order to expand the market for the artists featured. Specific requirements for the site are:

   - The visual interface should invoke the feeling of actually being in the gallery.

   - The user should be able to move to various "rooms" where individual artists will be showcased.

   - Audio descriptions of each work of art will be available. The user will click an icon to start the audio playback.

   - If the artist produces 3-D works (i.e. sculpture), the user should be able to view the piece from all sides. If the work is "flat," as in a picture or photograph, the user should be able to select a full screen view of the item.

2. The customer wants you to recommend a strategy for development of the site content. Included in your design is a required a list of all plug-ins or viewers. The customer wants to provide, on the first page of the site, a complete list of URLs for each of the required plug-ins.

3. In your solution, provide the type of technology that you will recommend, and which design goal it will fulfill. Also, provide the names of any plug-ins or viewers that will be required, and the URL of the site from where they can be downloaded.

Lab Exercises

The following lab instructs you to download and install the Macromedia Flash Player.

Lab 5-1 Downloading and installing Macromedia Flash Player

1. Open your Web browser and navigate to the Macromedia Web site at `www.macromedia.com`.

2. Find the Downloads link and select it to navigate to the software download page.

3. From the download page, click the Macromedia Flash Player link.

   You should be taken to the installation page. Find the Install Now button and click it to continue the installation of Flash Player. Figure 5-5 shows the format of this page, as of the writing of this book. The installation may take a few moments, depending on the speed of your Internet connection.

Figure 5-5: Macromedia Flash Player installation page

4. After the Flash Player installation is complete, you should see a small flash movie playing in the browser window. This is to indicate that the installation was successful. Figure 5-6 shows how this confirmation page was formatted as of the writing of this book.

   This is an example of an online installation.

Figure 5-6: Flash Player confirmation movie

Lab 5-2 Viewing Macromedia Flash sites

In this lab, you will view several Web sites that incorporate Macromedia Flash in their design.

1. Open your Web browser (if it is not already open from the previous exercise). If you have just finished Lab 5-1, then the Flash plug-in will already be on your system. If you do not have Flash, follow the instruction in Lab 5-1 to download and install the plug-in. Then return here to continue with this lab.

2. Using your browser, navigate to the Jaguar of Australia site at `www.jaguar.com.au`. There are a large number of elements on this site, both static and dynamic, so give it a moment or two to load completely. Refer to Figure 5-7.

Figure 5-7: Jaguar of Australia home page

3. After the page fully loads, locate the Flash content on the page.

Tip

It is not always easy to spot what content is produced by what plug-in. Some developers strive for this kind of seamless integration whereas some are not so concerned.

If it is not obvious whether an area of a page is Flash content, you can find out by pointing at it and right-clicking to produce the shortcut menu. If you see a menu like the following, then the content is Flash. Refer to Figure 5-8.

Figure 5-8: Macromedia Flash shortcut menu

4. Select the link for the Flash intro. Notice that as the full Flash presentation is downloading, the developer has used an introductory or "splash" screen providing an indication that the presentation is loading, and gives you the opportunity to skip the intro and proceed directly to the main site.

Notice also, that the Flash introduction loads in a separate browser window.

After you are finished viewing the site, continue with the next step.

5. You will now view the Macromedia Flash Web site. From there you can access many pages that have been created with Flash, and are being showcased by Macromedia. Browse to www.macromedia.com/showcase. Refer to Figure 5-9.

Figure 5-9: Macromedia showcase Web site

6. From the showcase product list, at the right of the page, click the Flash link.

7. The Flash showcase page has many additional sites incorporating Flash that you can visit. A navigator, located at the bottom of each page, will take you between the showcase pages, thus allowing you to access all of the sites in the showcase. Refer to Figure 5-10.

Figure 5-10: Macromedia Flash showcase, case study navigator

At the time of this writing, 90 sites (Macromedia calls them case studies) were available.

8. Choose some sites and try them out. Some will have lots of interactive content, whereas others will be mostly presentation.

Lab 5-3 VRML Plug-in installation

In this lab, you will download and install the Active Worlds Browser and explore a 3-D virtual reality environment.

1. Navigate to www.activeworlds.com. Refer to Figure 5-11.

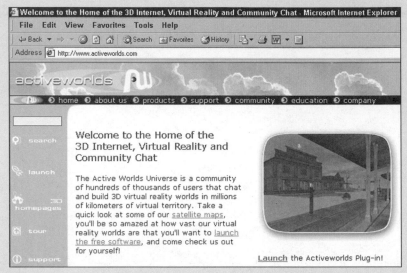

Figure 5-11: Active Worlds home page

2. Click the link to launch the Activeworlds Plug-in. If you don't already have the plug-in installed in your browser, the software will be downloaded and installation will start. After it starts, you will be prompted to accept the license agreement for use of the plug-in. You may choose to accept or reject this agreement by clicking OK or Cancel. Refer to Figure 5-12.

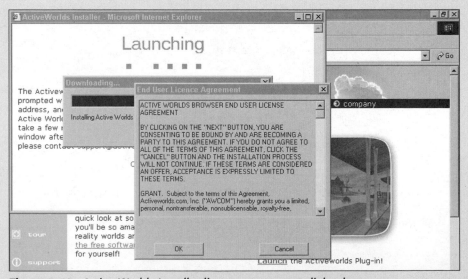

Figure 5-12: Active Worlds Installer license agreement dialog box

3. If you decide to accept the agreement, click OK and continue with the next step. Otherwise click Cancel. You won't be able to complete the exercise if you choose to cancel.

4. After you have accepted the agreement, the Active Worlds Browser will finish installing and you will be presented with the Internet Connection properties window. Refer to Figure 5-13.

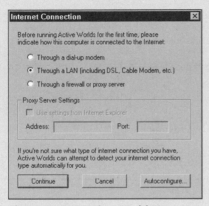

Figure 5-13: Active Worlds Internet connection dialog box

5. Configure the settings for your system. If you aren't sure of the settings appropriate for your system, select the defaults and continue. Alternately, you can try to let the browser detect the appropriate settings for you by clicking the Autoconfigure button. If you choose to do an auto configure, the installer will take a few minutes to determine the best method for connecting.

6. After your Internet connection is configured, you will be required to log in to the Active Worlds server. Simply choose a name that others will see you as in the environment and enter it into the first text box. Enter your e-mail address in the second text box and click OK. Refer to Figure 5-14.

Figure 5-14: Active Worlds welcome dialog box

If you have visited an Active World before, you are probably already a "citizen." If so, click the Citizen button to log in to your previously created account. You may also, from the Citizen dialog box, choose to connect as a tourist, if you prefer not to create an account. Refer to Figure 5-15.

Figure 5-15: Active Worlds Citizen sign-in dialog box

To enter as a tourist, click the Tourist button. If you do this, you will still need to enter a name and e-mail address, but a permanent account won't be created. You may also choose to cancel, which will prevent you from viewing any Active Worlds.

7. After you are logged in, you will be presented with the Active Worlds Browser. Refer to Figure 5-16.

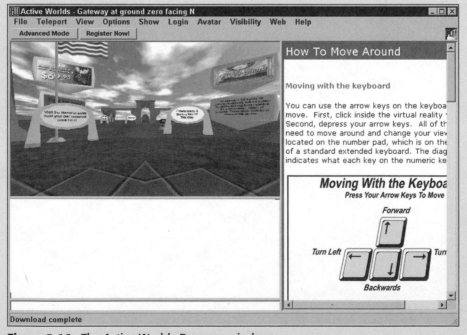

Figure 5-16: The Active Worlds Browser window

The browser has a number of "panes" that help in navigating the "world" that you are visiting. The top left pane is the 3-D environment where you will interact with the 3-D world and with other visitors. The bottom left pane is used for conversing with other visitors and for entering commands. The pane on the right is used for getting help.

8. Spend a moment reading through the help information, and then go exploring. After you are finished, simply close the Active Worlds Browser.

Answers to Chapter Questions

Chapter Pre-Test

1. Objects are designed as components that provide a specific function. A developer uses, or embeds, them on a Web page to provide functionality to the page that it otherwise would not have. For example, a sound object may be embedded in a Web page to provide background music.

2. Java is an ideal tool for Web development because it is platform-independent and allows for the creation of Java applets, which are components that can be embedded into Web pages to provide additional functionality.

3. MPEG-1 was developed to support digital audio.

4. MP3 (MPEG Layer 3) files are examples of non-streaming multimedia.

5. Virtual Reality Modeling Language (VRML), or similar plug-ins, such as Adobe Atmosphere, allow exploration of 3-D virtual space.

6. Macromedia Flash files are optimized for delivering complex graphics, audio, video, and interaction in a small file size. This makes them ideal for delivery across the World Wide Web because they aren't as affected by low bandwidth as larger file formats. In addition, Flash streams content, thus further enhancing performance.

7. Most likely, your browser doesn't have the necessary plug-ins or viewers installed.

Assessment Questions

1. **A, D**. Online component installations can happen while the browser is open. Off-line installation requires that the browser be shut down prior to installing the component.

2. **B**. The .swf extension is used with Shockwave Flash files. Shockwave and Flash are complementary products from Macromedia.

3. **D**. Adobe Atmosphere allows for the creation of 3-D, interactive, virtual reality environments. The Atmosphere plug-in allows the browser to interpret the Atmosphere files and lets the user navigate through, and interact with, the environment created by the Atmosphere developer.

4. B. Disabling active content and Java applets stops Java applets, ActiveX controls, and other active content from being downloaded to your computer. The ability to disable active content is provided through user settings in the browser software.

5. B, E. Of these languages, only C++ and Java are considered true OOPs. Although JScript and VBScript interact with objects, they are scripting rather than programming languages. C does not support OOP programming. It is a procedural language.

6. A, D. Java is truly platform-independent, due to its interpreted nature. As long as there is a Java Virtual Machine (JVM) available for the platform or Web browser that the developer is targeting, the Java application will run on it. Also, Java supports the creation of applets, which are Java programs that can be embedded in Web pages, providing additional functionality.

7. A. Streaming content is designed to reduce the time it takes to start playback, while at the same time, reducing the pauses associated with inconsistent transfer rates on the Internet. The solution is to buffer, in cache, enough information so that continuous playback can take place, without having to wait for the entire file to be downloaded.

8. B. The Adobe Acrobat Reader, implemented either standalone, or as a browser plug-in, is designed specifically to display PDF files and so is the best choice for viewing such content.

9. A. Word processors (i.e. Microsoft Word, Corel WordPerfect) use RTF as a format that is transportable between applications for formatting textual documents.

10. A. An .au extension is used on audio files commonly found on the Unix platform.

11. C. MPEG stands for the Moving Picture Experts Group, which is an organization concerned with audio and video standards determinations.

12. C, D. Windows Media Player is supported in the Windows and Macintosh environments.

13. C. The RealNetworks RealPlayer software supports a wide range of video and audio formats.

14. A. MPEG Audio Layer 3.

15. D. Apple Computer developed the AIFF audio format.

Scenario

This Web site can be developed with a number of different technologies; however, given the desire to have 3-D interaction as indicated by the criteria, a "Virtual Reality" implementation would likely be the best choice.

Adobe Atmosphere can be used to create the site, incorporate video, still graphics, and audio. It also allows the user to navigate to virtual rooms designed to hold the images of the different art pieces. Sculpture objects can be photographed from multiple angles and "rotated" with the software by the user.

Refer to the following table for additional Adobe information:

Technology Recommended	Adobe Atmosphere
Design Goal(s) Satisfied	3-D Navigation, virtual reality object manipulation, produces the "feel" of being at the gallery, has audio playback
Plug-in or viewer required	Adobe Atmosphere Browser
URL for download	www.adobe.com/products/ atmosphere/betareg_player.html

Internet Security Issues

CHAPTER PRE-TEST

1. A text file placed on your local machine's hard drive that remembers your preferences at a Web site is called a _____.

2. What is the name of the file that Netscape Navigator uses to save your cookie information?

3. A server that caches your Web requests in order to make future requests quicker is called a _____.

4. What type of device do you deploy to protect your company's assets from unauthorized access and to safeguard your private internal network?

5. The program that you use to secure your personal e-mail with encryption is called _____.

6. You can protect your data during transmission with _____.

7. The _____ _____ will allow you to password protect your browser in order to prevent access to inappropriate content on the Web.

8. What can you use to protect your operating systems from damage caused by a virus?

9. What system is used to ensure the security of financial transactions on the Internet?

10. What will help to establish your credentials before you make transactions on the Internet?

✦ Answers to these questions can be found at the end of the chapter. ✦

Chapter 5 discussed browser plug-ins and basic Internet browser viewers. This chapter ventures into the realm of Internet security by introducing you to the fundamentals and foundations of Internet security, including the following topics:

✦ Cookies

✦ Secure data transmissions

✦ User authentication

✦ Digital certificates

✦ Encryption

✦ Viruses

✦ Proxies

✦ Firewalls

This chapter should leave you feeling more comfortable about surfing the Internet and will prepare you for this section of the CIW Foundations exam.

Cookies

 Understand cookies.

A *cookie* is a simple text file on your hard drive that stores information about your visit to a particular Web site. Web developers can use this collected information to customize or personalize the page the next time you return to the site. You can locate these files by searching your local machine for a folder called `cookies`. The location of the `cookies` folder varies among operating systems. The browser you use also determines where the cookies are located. After you find this folder, you can open it to display many of these text files, as shown in Figure 6-1.

Figure 6-1: An example of what cookies look like on the local machine

A server places a small amount of information on your hard drive, in the form of a cookie, when you visit a Web site hosted on that server. The information that the cookie carries allows the Web site and server to remember your personal data. When you return to the site, your cookie is examined for data that may help provide better service and a relevant surfing experience. A cookie can make a record of your preferences for that site. When you log into a forum, it may ask you to enter a password and to establish your preferences. Based on this information, a cookie is created, placed on your hard drive, and stored there. The next time you visit the forum, the server retrieves the information stored in this cookie, and you are able to begin working immediately without the hassle of logging in. Not all Web servers deploy this technology, but be assured that your passwords are safe because you will be asked to "allow" for this functionality to happen (saving the username and password to be used later). Even if you select to use this technology, the information is safely encrypted in the cookie text file. Some Web servers may not allow you to use their sites unless you allow them to store cookies on your hard drive; you must have cookies *enabled*. So if you are disabling cookies (this is discussed later in this chapter), you may have problems.

Internet Explorer

Internet Explorer stores each cookie as a separate text file in a folder (or directory) on the local hard drive. This directory is found in different locations, depending on the version of Windows you are running. If you are running Windows 98, you can find the `cookies` folder under the Windows directory. If you're running Windows 2000 Professional, you can find your `cookies` folder under the logged-in user's profile. In other words, the `cookies` folder is on the hard drive where Windows is installed, under the `Documents and Settings` folder.

Netscape Navigator

Netscape Navigator stores all your cookies in a single `cookies.txt` file located on your local hard drive. The browser stores all entries in one file called `cookies.txt`, which can be viewed with Notepad. The browser saves the `cookies.txt` file to the `X:\Program Files\Netscape\Users\default` directory where "X" is the drive to which you installed Netscape Navigator.

To view the `cookies.txt` file within Windows Explorer, perform the following steps:

1. Go to the `Program Files` folder and open the `Netscape` folder.

2. Open the users folder and then click the subfolder labeled `Default`.

3. Find the `cookies.txt` file in the `Default` folder. Double click the file's icon to open it. You will see the cookie entries, as shown in Figure 6-2.

The full path that you will use to locate the `cookies.txt` file is `C:\program files\Netscape\users\default`.

```
# Netscape HTTP Cookie File
# http://www.netscape.com/newsref/std/cookie_spec.html
# This is a generated file! Do not edit.

.netscape.com      TRUE  /  FALSE  1293832086  UIDC      172.144.154.145:0963792049:176874
.lycos.com         TRUE  /  FALSE  2145916866  p_uniqid  5cplmMzWThlZplnrED
.mediaplex.com     TRUE  /  FALSE  1245628800  svid      966206463907423838268951160162
.mediaplex.com     TRUE  /  FALSE  1245628800  mojo1     10sb186635
.shockwave.com     TRUE  /  FALSE  1191233537  vid       80c206fe.25077.399647bb.11055
```

Figure 6-2: An example of what the `cookies.txt` file looks like

Opera

Opera stores your cookies in a single file called `cookies.dat`. This file can be found in the `program files\opera` folder. Although this is not as easy to view as a text file, you can still view it by double-clicking the `cookies.dat` file. From the Open with dialog box, select Notepad, but be sure you don't check the box that forces all future files to be opened in Notepad (because it will change the file association of the `cookies.txt` file). You can now view the contents of the cookies file in Notepad.

Enabling and disabling cookies

Enabling cookies on your browser is not difficult because browsers are generally set up to accept cookies by default. On the other hand, disabling them can take a little work. You need to carefully consider the consequences of enabling or disabling cookies. As mentioned earlier in this section, having cookies enabled is an outstanding way to enhance your Web surfing experience — no more bothersome dialog boxes asking you for passwords and a customized page when you visit a site. However, what if you want privacy? If you don't want a recording of your actions, then you may want to disable cookies.

Another disadvantage to disabling cookies, however, is that you may not be able to visit a particular site. If you configure the cookies to "prompt" you for acceptance, then surfing the Web can be a hassle — each site you visit will be accompanied by a dialog box asking you to accept cookies. In any case, you need to make a decision on what you want. This chapter will provide you with the tools to make that decision and how to make the actual changes to your browser.

In the following section, I use Internet Explorer (versions 5.x and later) to illustrate how to disable or configure the options that affect the use of cookies. Within the Internet Explorer properties, you can find the options to change cookie settings by carrying out the following steps:

1. Open the Internet Explorer browser.

2. From the Tools menu, select Internet Options.

3. Select the Security tab, as shown in Figure 6-3.

Note   If you're using Internet Explorer 6, then the cookie settings appear on the privacy page tab.

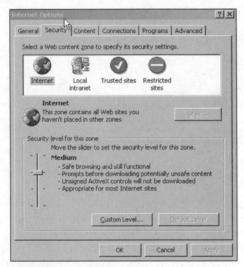

Figure 6-3: The Security tab within the Internet Explorer Properties dialog box

The Security tab contains options to change security settings. You can see the settings to alter cookies in Figure 6-4.

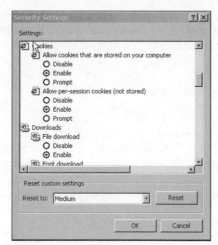

Figure 6-4: The cookie settings within Custom Internet Properties

The cookies settings allow you to do the following:

✦ **Store cookies on your local hard drive.**

✦ **Use cookies only temporarily.** Cookies are stored in memory for the session that you are holding with the Web server and then discarded when the session is terminated.

✦ **Set the browser to prompt you to manually accept a cookie from the server.** This is a great option, but it can become very annoying to be asked every time whether you want to accept a cookie. This issue is explored further in a lab at the end of this chapter.

✦ **Disable or enable the use of cookies.** Be aware that disabling cookies can cause problems when accessing a site that requires cookies to be enabled.

To configure cookies in Netscape Navigator, you need to first open the Netscape browser. After it is opened, follow these steps:

1. Choose Edit ➪ Preferences.

2. Select the Advanced option from the menu to the left of the dialog box.

3. Select one of the choices within the dialog box.

4. Your first choice is to "Accept all cookies," which is the best choice, as well as the easiest choice.

5. Your second choice is to "Accept only cookies that get sent back to the originating server," which is another good choice because your computer will not send a cookie to a server that did not originate it. This is a safety precaution.

6. Your last choice is to "Disable cookies."

7. A final setting, which appears as a check box instead of a radio button, is used to "Warn before accepting a cookie." This is the selection that may annoy you because from the moment you select this check box, every time you visit a site that uses cookies, you are going to be asked if you want to accept the cookie. Virtually all sites deploy this technology, so you may be bothered after the first few hundred times of being prompted with a dialog box and find yourself turning this feature off.

Secure Data Transmission

 Understand the components necessary for secure data transmission.

Securing data transmission hides your data from prying eyes during transmission. Securing information that is going to travel across the Internet is an important concept, especially for those that expect to perform online transactions involving the exchange of private information, such as a credit card number supplied to an e-commerce Web site. Numerous technologies are available that are designed to secure data transmission. SET, SSL, and PGP are a few examples of these technologies.

Secure Sockets Layer

Secure Sockets Layer (SSL) is a protocol that provides a secure channel between a client and a Web server during a session over the Internet. SSL can easily layer itself over TCP/IP layers and provide security to many different application-layer protocols. SSL is mainly used with Microsoft- and Netscape-based Web browsers (SSL can also be used with any application that supports it). SSL provides end-to-end encryption and authenticates a merchant's Web server. If the connection to a merchant is successful, it means the Web client trusts the merchant's server because a Certificate Authority (CA) has endorsed it.

SSL provides security for two items only: Applications that support SSL, and the Process and Application Layer of the DOD TCP/IP model, which incorporates Layers 5-7 of the OSI. IPSec provides lower layer protection.

Secure Electronic Transaction

Secure Electronic Transaction (SET) is often used to secure financial data transactions over the Internet. MasterCard, Visa, and many other credit card companies fully support its use because of the protection that it offers. A user is issued a *digital certificate* (also called a *wallet*). A transaction is completed upon verification of the digital certificate and the digital signatures of the merchant, the purchaser, and a bank. This process makes online shoppers more comfortable purchasing goods over the unsecured Internet. SET uses Secure Socket Layer (described in the next section) and Secure HTTP.

 Cross-Reference   Digital certificates are covered in more detail later in this chapter.

Pretty Good Privacy

Pretty Good Privacy (PGP), developed by Philip R. Zimmerman, encrypts and decrypts e-mail and files over the Internet. PGP also makes sure that the data is not intercepted and altered en route by verifying the sender's identity. You can download PGP for free from the Internet for personal use. As with most freeware, PGP is free until you use it for commercial purposes, at which point you are required to buy a license. PGP is a very reliable method of ensuring that e-mail is secure while in transit over the Internet and conveniently snaps into applications such as Microsoft Outlook and Outlook Express. Refer to Figure 6-5.

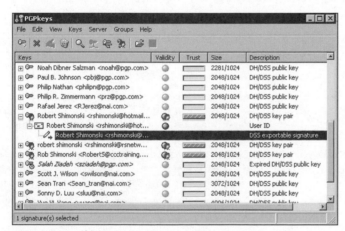

Figure 6-5: The PGP application dialog box setup screen

Understanding Encryption

 Objective   Understand encryption.

Although implementation and thorough comprehension of encryption algorithms can be confusing, the idea is actually quite basic. If you want to send a message to your friend over an unsecured channel, but you don't want anyone other than your friend to be able to read it, send your message in code. For example, design a code in which each letter in the alphabet corresponds to a number. You write a message that you want to send and use the code to encrypt it. Send the code to your friend so that the message can be decrypted when it arrives. After the message is encrypted, you can have a messenger deliver it to your friend. The messenger will look at the message and be unable to read it.

The Internet is a public infrastructure that anyone can use. The only way to protect your data in transit is to encrypt it so that, if the data is intercepted, it can't be read.

Authentication

Explore user authentication.

To successfully traverse and do business on the Internet, you must prove who you are. Digital Certification, Certification Authorities, Digital Signature, and a Public Key Infrastructure allow you to authenticate your identity.

Digital Certificates

Understand digital certificates.

A digital certificate electronically identifies an individual. Consider it similar to an "electronic" birth certificate. A digital certificate establishes your credentials so that you can perform business over the Internet. Many digital certificates conform to the X.509 standard. It is very important to understand why you need a digital certificate in the first place: It proves your identity to the requestor. Whenever you do business on the Web, you generally do not know exactly whom you are transacting business with, so it is imperative that you have some form of "proof." This certificate is your proof of identity. Digital certificates contain the sender's personal information, such as the following:

- ✦ Sender's name
- ✦ Public key
- ✦ The expiration date of the sender's public key
- ✦ The issuer of the certificate
- ✦ The certificate's serial number
- ✦ The digital signature of the certificate issuer

A Certificate Authority issues the digital certificate.

Certificate Authority

A Certificate Authority (CA) issues and manages public keys. The CA works with the Registration Authority (RA) to make sure that the information requested via the digital certificate requestor is valid. If the information is valid, the CA issues a certificate. A CA is part of a public key infrastructure.

Public key infrastructure

A public key infrastructure (PKI) allows users in an uncertain network environment, such as the Internet, to safely exchange data. This safe exchange is done via a public and a private cryptographic key pair that is first obtained and then shared through a Certificate Authority. The following are components of a Public Key Infrastructure:

✦ The Certificate Authority (issues and verifies the digital certificate)

✦ A Registration Authority (holds the digital certificates)

✦ A certificate management system

Securing a Browser

 Secure a browser.

You can use Content Advisor to control access to Web content on the Internet. Because the Internet is a free media, you need to be careful about securing content that is accessed via the browser. For example, you may want to prevent small children from accessing content of a sexual or violent nature. Content Advisor gives you the power to restrict access to certain content and allow only material that meets your criteria to be displayed in the browser. You can adjust Content Advisor's default settings to tighten security as desired. You can view the configurable settings in Figure 6-6.

You can protect your Content Advisor settings with a password so that no one else can alter them. (Secure your password carefully, because it requires a registry hack to reset it.) A password change is illustrated in Figure 6-7. Content Advisor allows you to view and change the ratings settings for the following four topics:

✦ Language

✦ Violence

✦ Sex

✦ Nudity

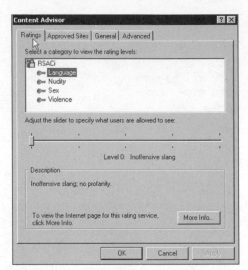

Figure 6-6: Content Advisor settings

Keep in mind that not all Internet content is rated and unrated sites can still be accessed via the Web browser and may contain explicit content. The Content Advisor's default settings are very conservative and need to be adjusted to make security tighter.

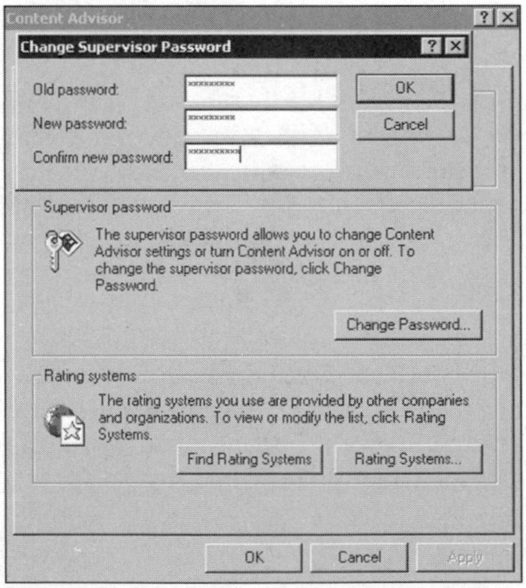

Figure 6-7: Configuring the Supervisor Password on the Content Advisor

Computer and Network Viruses

 List computer and network viruses.

Thinking about computer viruses can conjure up images of lost data, e-mail, or word processing documents. Viruses introduce the possibility of losing crucial company information due to a problematic piece of code traversing your computer systems.

A virus is usually a small program or application that, when activated or opened, performs a mischievous task. Viruses can be very destructive and, because they are common, must be protected against. Generally, a virus is designed to automatically replicate and spread to other computers via the program itself or files or e-mail passed between users. Viruses can be transmitted as attachments to an e-mail or can be in the e-mail itself so that just opening the e-mail can activate the virus. Viruses can be broken down into the following three main categories:

✦ File infectors

✦ Boot record infectors

✦ Macro viruses

File infector viruses

File infectors attach themselves and wreak havoc to any form of data on the machine, including word documents, program files, and spreadsheets. File infectors can be created to activate separately or as part of an affected program file when you (the user of the file) click on it and active it yourself. Not only do you have to beware of activating one of these programmed viruses when it's in plain sight, but — worse yet — these File infectors can be hidden or masquerading as something else, such as a script within a file attachment or e-mail.

Boot record viruses

Boot record viruses are usually received via an infected floppy disk. When you load the floppy disk and boot up your machine, the machine is infected and the hard drive becomes inaccessible. The boot record is the location of the logical pointer to the operating system; if it is compromised, then the machine won't boot to the operating system that the user has configured on the machine. If this happens, users of the machine are paralyzed because they can't boot up the operating system. This, of course, may not seem so bad to an avid user of Windows because it can be repaired quickly with an antivirus boot disk and a Windows startup disk (run SYS C: at the command prompt after booting to the A:\ Prompt), but the non-computer-savvy user won't know this repair task and therefore, won't be able to fix his or her machine. The creator of the boot record virus knows this and is able to affect a great many users. If you do get infected, the only way to clean the machine is to use a boot disk that is equipped with anti-virus software, which is discussed later in this chapter. Boot record viruses are generally a chore to fix, but they don't cause irreversible damage.

Macro viruses

Macro viruses are small, script-based programs that are added to Microsoft Office documents to create mischief rather than severe damage. W97.Marker is the most common example of a macro virus. Macro viruses are easily cleaned with anti-virus software and occasionally destroy their host Word documents; they are attached to templates such as `Normal.dot`. Beware of macro viruses when accepting Word documents from other users or via e-mail.

Other forms of malicious code

The following sections detail other forms of malicious code of which you should be aware.

Worms

A *worm* is a more problematic virus because it self-replicates. Worms reside in the memory of the systems that they infect and repeatedly replicate themselves. Worms are usually difficult to find with memory-scanning anti-virus software. They can be located by investigating network and computer system slowdowns, which occur because the worm takes over much of your system's resources, such as memory and CPU time.

Trojan horses

You may be familiar with the story from Homer's *Iliad*, in which a horse hiding the enemy Greeks was presented to the citizens of Troy. During the night, the soldiers piled out of the horse to take over and capture the city. This is much the case with the Trojan horse virus. You think you are looking at a program that is safe, but when you open, execute, or run it, the Trojan horse emerges and begins causing problems.

A Trojan horse is a program that neither replicates nor copies itself to anything; it causes damage and compromises the security of a computer when you open it and let it in. Trojan horses are generally sent to you (usually by e-mail), but you must remember that it does not arrive like a worm.

Protection with Anti-Virus Software

Anti-virus protection for your systems is easy to implement but difficult to maintain. Anti-virus software searches the system on which it is installed for viruses. The anti-virus program is loaded with definitions that guide its search. Owners of anti-virus software can download these definitions on a subscription basis — usually weekly — and production systems are usually scanned on a daily basis. A *virus definition* (or *signature*) is a description used to "update" the virus engine or application to combat a particular virus. In other words, the application must be updated with "what to look for." Think about it — new viruses come out almost daily, so how does your antivirus application know about them? You must tell it what to look for with a virus definition. Generally, you download the virus definition as a program file and it updates the antivirus software automatically when executed. You must continually update the definitions because new viruses are made, distributed, and found regularly. Failing to update your system may lead to an infection of your systems.

No system is immune to viruses, but Microsoft-based technologies are prone to getting viruses because many client-based machines use Microsoft products. Microsoft systems aren't actually targeted — the virus attacks occur more often on these systems simply because of the volume of systems using Microsoft products. In fact, every system can be — and is — the target of malicious intent and attack. To prevent viruses, take time when you receive an e-mail to check the sender and type of attachment (if any). If the sender is someone you've never heard from, use caution when opening the message — or simply don't open it at all. Also use caution if the attachment ends in .vbs. Files that end with a vbs extension contain a Visual Basic script, and by opening the documents (hence executing the script), you will run whatever program was created inside, which can range from changing a setting on your system to erasing precious data on your hard drive. Scanning your system for viruses is essential. Refer to Figure 6-8.

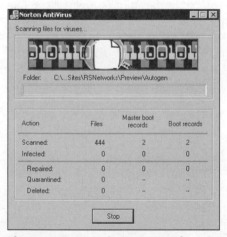

Figure 6-8: Scanning a System for Viruses

Tip   When scanning your systems for a suspected virus, adjust the default of "only" scanning system files to a "full" scan. If you don't set it to do a full scan, then it will only check your system files, which may only be a small percentage of all your data.

Proxy Servers and Firewalls

 Explain proxy servers and firewalls.

To make your World Wide Web experience faster and more secure, you may need to invest in a proxy server, a firewall, or both. However, be aware of your needs before you make this investment. Consider this: If you are connected to the Internet for Web-surfing, then you may want technology to either *accelerate* it (make it faster) or *secure* it (protect it from attacks with some sort of firewall device). The first thing to decide is what you need—acceleration, security, or both. Do you want to secure your Internet connections? Do you want to accelerate your Internet connections?

Like most organizations, you may need to provide for both acceleration and security. With today's product lines, the distinction between security with a firewall and acceleration with a proxy server has blurred. The following sections examine each technology and discuss how they either protect or enhance your Internet experience.

Proxy servers

A proxy server acts on behalf of the clients attached to it. Organizations who use proxy servers configure each Internet client computer to send the request to the proxy server, then the proxy server goes out on the Internet to find the requested object (typically a Web page) on behalf of the client. The proxy server then returns the requested object to the Internet client machine that had requested the page. When you access the Internet from behind a proxy server, you are technically letting the proxy server connect for you so that your IP address and identity are kept secret, thus making your network more secure because only the IP address of the proxy server is exposed to the Internet. A typical proxy server setup is shown in Figure 6-9.

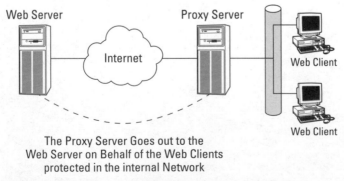

The Proxy Server Goes out to the
Web Server on Behalf of the Web Clients
protected in the internal Network

Figure 6-9: A proxy server that is set up on behalf of network clients

Proxy servers also speed up your Internet connection by caching requested pages for future viewing. *Caching* is the simple task of pulling your Web page for you, keeping it local to the proxy server's hard drive and giving it directly to you when you request it. How does it stay updated? The proxy server is smart enough (after you configure it) to pull a fresh page for you and place it in its cache on a timed basis. For example, when you (the client) request a Web page, the proxy server finds the site, pulls the page down to the server's cache, and simultaneously stores and delivers the page to you. The next time that the page is requested, the client only needs to go as far as the proxy server, which is normally on your company's private network. How do you make sure the cached content is current or updated? The servers cache can be configured with an automatic refresh time, or it can be cleared and updated manually.

When configuring a proxy server, pay attention to its minimum hardware and software requirements. When accessing the Internet, you need a high-powered machine that can handle requesting and downloading multiple Web pages simultaneously. Memory requirements on proxy servers have always been higher than on most other types of servers. Skimping on these requirements can seriously impact network- and Internet-based performance.

Proxy servers can be configured in an array. This configuration allows content to be handled and cached across multiple proxy servers that work together to provide Web resources for network clients. This is a good design to implement when you need to service many clients and don't want to overtax a single server. By adding more servers, you can balance the load of the requests over multiple machines, instead of depending on just one.

Firewalls

A *firewall* is a group of components and programs set up between two or more networks to control the data moving between your private network and any outside network, as shown in Figure 6-10.

A firewall is a combination of hardware and software that protects your internal systems or hosts from outside access. A firewall should be an entry point to your network.

A firewall protects and controls access to your company's internal resources, which can be a database of secret information or other protected assets from the outside world (namely the Internet). An administrator can allow specific access to the internal (and protected) network by adjusting the basic *rule sets* that firewalls provide. A rule set is what you can configure to either allow or disallow access through the firewall. Additionally, a firewall examines each packet that attempts to pass through it and checks the passing data against the configured rules. Any packet that contradicts or doesn't conform to the rules is automatically dropped. Firewalls also log activity for later analysis and so that patterns or problems can be identified. Firewalls can be any of the following:

✦ Appliances dedicated to the purpose of analyzing packets

✦ Routers configured with access lists

✦ Servers with firewall software installed

✦ A combination of all three

Tip   Use your firewall to log access from external and internal client-based attacks. Attacks often come from within a private network.

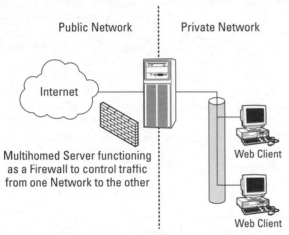

Figure 6-10: Typical firewall setup in a network

Network Address Translation

Network Address Translation (NAT) is a technology used in conjunction with any device that will allow you the functionality of Network Address Translation. NAT can be configured on a NAT-based device to translate IP addresses.

NAT translates IP addresses used within one network into different IP addresses known to another network. This translation enables both networks to avoid changing their address assignments. NAT is also very popular with Internet-based connections in which a private address range is used on an internal network, and users are connecting to the public Internet that uses a public IP address range via the NAT server.

One of the reasons that NAT is such a "hot" technology is because of the different versions of TCP/IP. To be more exact, version 4 of the Internet Protocol (IP) is in use today and version 5 is being tested and now on the horizon. With IPv4, the amount of available addresses quickly diminished with the onslaught of users trying to get on the Web. In other words, the Internet ran out of possible addresses. To keep the Internet expanding, two technologies were developed that allow for this growth beyond a dead end. With NAT, you can be issued a few public IP addresses from an ISP (Internet Service Provider) and configure this block of numbers as your NAT or Network Address Translation Pool. Then, you can address your entire internal and private network with an entire range of numbers that "translate" to the few that you received from your ISP. The other technology that provides more numbers is IP Version 6, but this has not been fully tested yet and is problematic because you have to reconfigure many of the devices on your network. Because of this fact, NAT is a simple solution, has been heavily used, and has kept the movement to IPv6 or IP Next Generation from being ruled out quickly.

NAT also improves security by hiding the private client-based range of IP addresses from the public Internet. The client accesses the device performing NAT on one interface with a private IP range, and the proxy accesses the Internet after translating to a public IP address. Security is enhanced because each outgoing and incoming request must go through a translation process. Refer to Figure 6-11.

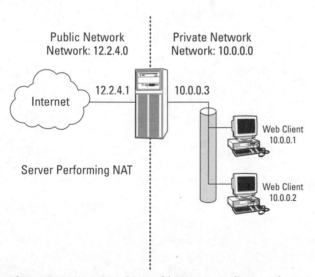

Figure 6-11: NAT performed between a client and a proxy server

Demilitarized zone

A demilitarized zone (DMZ) is the network segment between a company's private network and the outside public network. The DMZ (also called an Isolation LAN) is an isolated segment populated with Bastion Hosts. Bastion Hosts are servers set up and configured to have public access to the Internet like a DNS server, a Web server, and an FTP server. The DMZ allows controlled access to publicly accessible resources, that need to be reached via the Internet, without jeopardizing internal resources such as your mainframes, database, or other private assets.

The DMZ is usually set up from an Ethernet port (or NIC card) that hangs off of your firewall. Figure 6-12 illustrates the basic setup of a DMZ with Bastion Hosts.

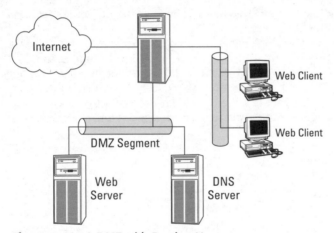

Figure 6-12: A DMZ with Bastion Hosts

Key Point Summary

- ✦ Cookies are small text files used to record preferences from a Web server.
- ✦ Cookies are stored in different places depending on the browser and operating system that you are using.
- ✦ Cookies can be enabled, disabled, or can be accepted manually via a prompt from the browser.
- ✦ Secure Electronic Transaction (SET) provides secure financial transactions online.
- ✦ Secure Sockets Layer (SSL) provides a layer of security at the "Socket" level of transmission between client and server.

✦ Pretty Good Privacy protects files and e-mail through the use of encryption and is freely available on the Internet.

✦ Digital certificates are electronic birth certificates that prove identity.

✦ A certificate authority (CA) verifies the identity of users by issuing digital certificates.

✦ Public Key Infrastructure (PKI) uses secure methods to build an infrastructure for safe data transmittal.

✦ Content Advisor is an Internet Explorer utility that allows you to control content accessed via the browser based on nudity, sex, violence, and other explicit content.

✦ Password protection can be implemented on the Content Advisor to secure settings that regulate content.

✦ Encryption is the use of codes and algorithms to make your data unreadable without decryption.

✦ Viruses are small programs designed infected machines and cause harm or mischief.

✦ Worms are self-replicating viruses that reside in memory.

✦ Trojans are viruses hidden within another program and executed inadvertently.

✦ Anti-virus software is installed on a machine and uses definitions to search for and eliminate known viruses. The definitions must be updated on a regular basis.

✦ A proxy is a server that acts on behalf of its clients to retrieve requested content from the Web.

✦ Requested Web pages are cached so that clients connected to the proxy server have quicker access in the future.

✦ Proxy servers can be set up in an array to provide better performance for clients.

✦ A firewall protects a company's assets by disallowing and logging unauthorized access.

✦ Network Address Translation (NAT) translates one IP address into another. This translation separates two similar networks or to allows a private network to access a public network via valid IP addresses.

✦ The demilitarized zone (DMZ) is where bastion hosts (or public servers) reside for public access from the Internet. This keeps it separate from your internal private network and still assessable from the public Internet.

✦　　✦　　✦

STUDY GUIDE

Assessment Questions

1. You want to set up a protected segment on your network where you can build a Web server with a Web site that is accessible via the public Internet. Where would you put this server?

    A. Public network

    B. Private network

    C. NAT

    D. DMZ

2. If you realized that you had a virus on your local machine, what would be your first course of action?

    A. Install a service pack.

    B. Install a hot fix.

    C. Run anti-virus software and perform a full scan.

    D. Delete the C Drive.

3. What type of virus self-replicates and resides in your machine's memory?

    A. Trojan

    B. Shell

    C. Worm

    D. Boot Sector

4. Which technology protects financial transactions online?

    A. NAT

    B. SET

    C. IKES

    D. DMZ

5. If you had a range of IP addresses set up on your private internal network that were not valid on the Internet, such as the 10.0.0.0 range, what would you implement on your NAT Device to allow clients to access the Web?

   A. Private

   B. Public

   C. NAT

   D. Outside

6. What freeware application snaps into Microsoft Outlook Express and helps you to personally encrypt your e-mails and files?

   A. PGP

   B. SET

   C. DMZ

   D. IPS

7. Which file houses cookies in Netscape Navigator?

   A. `cookie.dat`

   B. `cookies.txt`

   C. `cookie.sys`

   D. `cookies.msc`

8. Which one of the following is not a choice on the Content Advisor's list of configurable options?

   A. Sex

   B. Nudity

   C. Violence

   D. Brutality

Lab Exercises

The following lab exercises allow you to apply concepts covered in this chapter.

Lab 6-1 Disabling cookie acceptance within Microsoft Internet Explorer

1. Open Internet Explorer. (This lab is done with version 5x or above.)

2. Go to the Tools menu and select Internet Options. You will see the Internet Explorer properties dialog box.

3. Select the Security tab and select Internet in the top left side of the dialog box.

4. Click the Custom-level button at the bottom of the dialog box to open a new dialog box called Security settings.

5. Scroll down to cookies and select to the option to disable "allow cookies that are stored on your computer."

6. Select OK. If you are prompted with a question asking you to confirm that you want to make changes to the zone, select yes.

7. Your cookies are disabled. Surf the Web with the new settings. You may find that you get rejected from some sites because you do not have cookies enabled.

Lab 6-2 Prompting cookie acceptance within Microsoft Internet Explorer

1. Open Internet Explorer. (This lab is done with version 5x or above.)

2. Go to the Tools menu and select Internet Options. You will see the Internet Explorer Properties dialog box.

3. Select the Security tab and select Internet in the top left side of the dialog box.

4. Select the Custom-level button at the bottom of the dialog box to open a new dialog box called Security settings.

5. Scroll down to cookies and select to manually prompt to "allow cookies that are stored on your computer."

6. Select OK. If you are prompted with a question asking you to confirm that you want to make changes to the zone, select yes.

7. Your cookies are set for prompt. Surf the Web with the new settings to see if Web sites prompt you to accept cookies because you don't have cookies automatically enabled.

Lab 6-3 Enabling cookie acceptance within Microsoft Internet Explorer

1. Open Internet Explorer. (This lab is done with version 5x or above.)

2. Go to the Tools menu and select Internet Options. You will see the Internet Explorer Properties dialog box.

3. Select the Security tab and select Internet in the top left side of the dialog box.

4. Select the Custom-level button at the bottom of the dialog box to open a new dialog box called Security settings.

5. Scroll down to cookies and select Enable to "allow cookies that are stored on your computer."

6. Select OK. If you are prompted with a question asking you to confirm that you want to make changes to the zone, select yes.

7. Your cookies are enabled. Surf the Web with the new settings to see how Web sites operate when your cookies are accepted by default.

Lab 6-4 Tighten the Content Advisor content settings

1. Open Internet Explorer. (This lab is done with version 5x or above.)

2. Go to The tools menu and select Internet Options. You will see the Internet Explorer Properties dialog box.

3. Select the content tab.

4. Select the Enable button at the top of the dialog box to open a new dialog box called Content Advisor. (You are now in the Content Advisor.)

5. Select violence from the content category keys.

6. Adjust the rating level for violence by dragging the slider to Level 3, Killing with blood and gore.

7. Select OK. Your new settings tighten the control of content accessible on the Web.

Note   When you click OK, you will be prompted to set a supervisor password. This is similar to the exercise in Lab 6-5. Enter a password that you can remember and then hit OK.

Lab 6-5 Set and change the Content Advisor password

1. Open Internet Explorer. (This lab is done with version 5x or above.)

2. Go to The tools menu and select Internet Options. You will see the Internet Explorer Properties dialog box.

3. Select the Content tab.

4. Select the Enable button at the top of the dialog box to open a new dialog box called Content Advisor.

5. Select the General tab.

6. In the middle of the dialog box you will see the content advisor "supervisor password." Select change password and you will be prompted to change the current supervisor password.

7. Enter your new password.

Caution   As previously mentioned, if you forget this password, the only way to change it quickly is to journey into the Registry.

Chapter Pre-Test Answers

1. Cookie

2. cookies.txt

3. Proxy server

4. Firewall

5. PGP (Pretty Good Privacy)

6. Encryption

7. Content Advisor

8. Anti-virus software

9. SET

10. A digital certificate

Answers to Assessment Questions

1. **D.** The DMZ is where bastion hosts (or public servers) reside for public access by the Internet. This placement keeps publicly assessable servers separate from the internal private network where your company databases may reside.

2. **C.** Anti-virus software searches for and eliminates known viruses on the machine on which it is installed.

3. **C.** A worm is self-replicating and resides in your machine's memory.

4. **B.** SET (Secure Electronic Transaction) is used to secure financial transactions on the Web

5. **C.** NAT translates one IP address into another to separate two similar networks or to allow a private network range to access a public network via valid IP addresses.

6. **A.** PGP is an application used by Microsoft Outlook Express to encrypt and secure your e-mail and files.

7. **B.** The file cookies.txt is used in Netscape Navigator to store cookie entries.

8. **D.** Brutality is not a configurable option within Content Advisor.

Resources

✦ www.sans.org/newlook/home.htm

✦ www.novell.com/info/security/

✦ www.microsoft.com/security/

✦ www.sarc.com

Introduction to Electronic Commerce

EXAM OBJECTIVES

1. Define electronic commerce and compare it to traditional commerce.
2. Identify the principal features of Electronic Data Interchange (EDI) and Secure Electronic Transactions (SET).
3. Discuss the advantages and key issues of e-commerce.
4. Define Payment models for e-commerce.
5. Identify the international issues involved with e-commerce.
6. Describe the functions and advantages of smart cards.
7. Explain the issues involved with copyrights, licensing, and trademarks.

CHAPTER PRE-TEST

1. What is the main identifying feature of electronic commerce?

2. What benefits can a small business owner realize by setting up shop on the Internet?

3. What challenges might a small business owner — or any organization — face when entering the e-commerce arena?

4. What are the current standards governing electronic communications between systems involved in e-commerce?

5. Why are smart cards considered a valuable tool in e-commerce transactions?

6. Is the display of copyrighted information on a commercial Web site a violation of copyright law, even if the copyrighted material is not being sold?

✦ Answers to these questions can be found at the end of the chapter. ✦

Electronic commerce, or e-commerce, is no longer just on the wish list — it is a necessity for businesses with competitors that have embraced e-commerce as a way of expanding their market share and providing convenient service to their customers.

E-commerce on the Internet is also often referred to as *Web commerce* or *Internet commerce*. Whatever the term, it is rapidly expanding the way people perceive and use the Internet.

Business owners can find do-it-yourself e-commerce kits in most software stores — many are available for under $100. The only additional requirement for getting started in e-commerce is an Internet connection. With this simplicity of setup, many businesses are diving into the e-commerce waters — sometimes without checking to see what dangers lurk just beneath the surface.

This chapter describes the fundamentals of e-commerce — from what it is to what it does and how it works — and also explains the dangers and benefits of entering the e-commerce arena.

Electronic Commerce

 Define electronic commerce and compare it to traditional commerce.

Before you can fully grasp the concept of *electronic commerce*, you must first understand the concept of commerce. *Commerce* is the trading of goods or services in exchange for something of value — generally currency.

Electronic commerce has been defined as commerce that makes use of electronic services for a portion, or all of, the process of conducting a transaction.

For example, you participate in commerce when you buy a CD at a music store and pay by credit card. You participate in electronic commerce when the store clerk uses an online system to authorize your card and record the transaction. This is actually a mix of traditional commerce and e-commerce because the transaction that transfers the money to the vendor's bank and records it against your available credit is done electronically, while you are physically present in the music store.

E-commerce on the Internet is an extension of electronic commerce. Because the Internet is a fusion of various systems, organizations, services, and individuals, e-commerce is concerned with highly complex transactions affecting the buyer, the seller, and the financial services that interact between the two. Additionally, because the Internet is such an open environment, e-commerce must deal with security and data management in ways that have not been required in older e-commerce systems.

E-commerce, therefore, must integrate the buyer, seller, service providers, and financial institutions into a common framework that defines security, communications, and data management.

Three main elements of electronic commerce address the major issues of the new e-commerce environment:

✦ **Communications:** Services that support the electronic transfer of information between the buyer, the seller, and any intermediaries, such as financial institutions. Communications standards must provide a common digital language by which various systems — which are often from various vendors and run on different hardware and software platforms — can communicate.

✦ **Security:** Mandatory methods for identification and authentication of parties involved in transactions, as well as for ensuring the integrity and privacy of transferred data. The buyer no longer sees the goods, necessarily, nor the merchant sees the customer. Security must build a bridge of trust between these remote parties.

✦ **Data Management:** Robust methods that maintain the transaction details and respond to inevitable breakdowns in communication. In addition, data management must include common data formats and access languages.

Comparing Traditional and E-Commerce

Electronic commerce and traditional commerce employ different methods of sharing information and carrying out transaction processes.

In traditional commerce, information is shared directly. A visit to a store, a telephone call, or a mail order are all ways in which information that defines the transaction may be shared. Additionally, a person generally handles the information. For example, if a customer makes a phone order to a store, someone must receive the call and deal with the sale.

In electronic commerce, direct contact is virtually eliminated. Transaction information is shared via purely electronic means, and the information is processed through automated, rather than manual, means.

Because of this lack of personal contact, electronic commerce must provide automation that can provide the same service as a direct contact purchase. For example, merchants must gather identification from the client for check-cashing purposes. A traditional commerce merchant usually asks for a driver's license or other suitable form of identification to verify that the buyer actually owns the checking account.

Another example is proof of sale; in traditional commerce, proof of sale typically consists of a printed or written sales receipt. It is this receipt that proves when and from where the customer bought the item. This receipt is necessary in case the customer needs to exchange or return the purchased item for some reason.

In both scenarios, the commerce merchants are concerned with identification and *non-repudiation*. Non-repudiation is a non-refutable proof of identity and origin of a piece of data. In the traditional commerce scenario, the driver's license is considered non-refutable proof of identity (especially licenses that contain photographs of the license holder). The sales receipt is also considered non-refutable proof of the date of purchase and the location where the item was purchased.

In e-commerce, methods of providing for these issues must be addressed without the benefit of direct contact between the buyer and seller.

Two models, the business-to-business model and the business-to-customer model, define the ways that clients deal with business and the ways that businesses deal with each other in the e-commerce arena.

The business-to-business model

When businesses want to deal with other businesses via an e-commerce arrangement, higher volumes with lower prices typify the transactions. For example, an automobile parts manufacturer will make arrangements with a retailer who owns a chain of car parts stores. The manufacturer's transactions with the retailer will be high in volume (a large number of parts will be ordered in order to stock the stores) and low in price (a discount will be offered due to the volume purchased).

The business-to-customer model

The transactions between a business and a customer are typically lower volume with higher prices. Each customer won't purchase as many of a particular item (as the retail store purchased), so the price is naturally higher. The auto parts manufacturer *could* also sell to individuals, but would charge more for the same part, given the lower individual volumes.

Regardless of the model, e-commerce generally combines the ability to reach a greater number of customers and/or to generate a substantial increase in volume while reducing the costs associated with that increase. These factors have prompted many companies to implement a business-to-customer model (B2C) or a business-to-business model (B2B) strategy — or even both.

Electronic Data Interchange

 Identify the principal features of EDI and SET.

As previously discussed in this chapter, e-commerce requires automated transaction processing. For the transaction process to succeed, an e-commerce merchant must have a standard method for moving transaction data from business-to-business or from business-to-customer. Electronic Data Interchange (EDI) is one such method.

EDI is a standard that defines how documents may be exchanged between organizations in a standard format, directly from computer to computer. EDI is also sometimes described as *workflow automation* or *form-based automation*. Consider the following example of a retailer and a wholesaler: In traditional commerce, the retailer determines the required products, fills out a purchase order, and sends it to the supplier or suppliers. The supplier fills the order, sends out the product, and produces an invoice to send back to the retailer. EDI replicates this purchase order and invoice process through electronic transfers rather than paper transfers.

As this example implies, EDI was designed to fill a need for standardized information exchange between businesses, and as such, was created with certain goals in mind:

✦ **To enable simple and cost-effective communication of structured transaction information throughout the transaction life.** *Transaction life* is the time necessary to complete the required transactions, such as when a product is ordered, invoiced, paid for, and funds are transferred to cover its cost. Additionally, if the product is being shipped, the transaction is not considered complete until the buyer notifies the seller of receipt of the goods.

✦ **To reduce the occurrences of data being captured, so as to limit the possibilities of data error or corruption.** As a result, the amount of time spent rectifying such errors is reduced, thus making the transaction more efficient.

✦ **To decrease the time associated with the transaction process, thus making the entire process more profitable.**

Early acceptance of EDI was limited; in fact, less than one percent of U.S. businesses made use of EDI in 1993. EDI is typically found in specific industries where standard data formats are easier to agree upon. The chemical and electronics industries, for example, have been successful in implementing their own versions of EDI that are specific to their industry, but not necessarily compatible across all industries.

As the Internet draws more and more business into e-commerce relationships, EDI is being standardized not just within a particular industry, but also across industries. Current EDI standards dictate a data format defined by the ANSI X12 and UN/EDIFACT specifications.

EDI also initially suffered due to prohibitive implementation costs; however, as well-defined standards began to emerge, EDI became an important element for tying together the different transaction processes of e-commerce.

Many companies are implementing EDI as a result of numerous factors, including:

✦ To reduce the costs associated with repetitive transactions.

✦ To exist in an environment where profit margins are small and cost controls are extremely important.

✦ To implement more efficient business practices as a result of competition.

✦ To successfully fulfill business commitments in a timely manner.

✦ To follow suit of partner companies that have implemented EDI.

Secure Electronic Transactions

The Secure Electronic Transaction (SET) protocol is a new protocol that has been undergoing resolute testing, but has emerged with the promise of significantly enhancing both business-to-business and business-to-customer e-commerce.

MasterCard originally proposed SET as a standard for securing transaction information. At the same time, Visa proposed a protocol in direct competition with SET, but SET was shown to be the superior protocol in test circumstances. Now, both organizations support the SET standard.

Japan, Switzerland, and Denmark have deployed SET and are using it in live transactions in an ongoing commercial basis. MasterCard, IBM, and others have conducted live transaction tests for verification purposes. All indications thus far have shown that SET is ready for implementation. The following sections describe the features of SET.

Identification

SET requires that all participants in a transaction make use of digital certificates to identify themselves. This requirement enables all handlers of transaction data to be verified at each step of the transaction process, and ensures that the data is encrypted by the keys of the communicating parties, which significantly decreases the risk of data being pulled off the network by uninvited users. This strengthened communication security makes online bill paying more secure than calling in a payment over the phone.

Reduced rates

The enhanced security provided by encrypted transactions has also prompted financial institutions to lower the rates charged for credit card usage, from between 6 and 12 percent for "card not present" or standard Internet credit card transactions, to 1 to 3 percent for SET transactions. Both MasterCard and Visa have indicated that they will consider SET transactions to be equivalent to "card present" transactions, which is considered a traditional credit card purchase.

Reduced risk

SET also reduces the risk of credit card information being either fraudulently or inadvertently misused. With SET, merchants never get the card information. Instead, the merchant's system redirects the cardholder to the bank's system, where the cardholder enters his or her credit card information. After the card information is processed, the bank forwards a success or failure message concerning the transaction back to the merchant's system, which then completes or cancels the transaction appropriately.

Ease of use

Aside from assuring secure transactions, SET was designed with financial transactions in mind. As such, it specifies methods for credits, returns, and transaction reversals. Without SET, these functions would have to be written into the payment systems (often called *payment gateways*). Accounting for these necessities in the protocol eliminates the need for each vendor to develop a means to deal with them.

The features of SET are summarized in the following list:

✦ Enhanced identification of the parties involved in the transaction processes via digital certificates.

✦ Credit card information is communicated directly from the customer to the financial institution. The merchant is not responsible for the information and never has access to it.

✦ Non-repudiation, data integrity, authentication, and privacy are assured through the use of encryption. Each party is required to have a digital certificate, which is used to sign the transactions and encrypt the data.

✦ SET was designed with all aspects of financial transaction processing in mind, including details, such as returns, credits, and transaction reversals.

Advantages of E-Commerce

 Discuss the advantages and key issues of e-comerce.

Both individuals and businesses stand to benefit from e-commerce. Consumers can avail themselves to a much wider range of products from around the world. Businesses can be set up online for far less cost than a standard brick-and-mortar store.

The following list summarizes some of the benefits of e-commerce:

✦ Purchasing processes are streamlined and less expensive than similar manual or paper-based processes. Orders placed online require no paper chase or intervention.

✦ Reduction in time required for completion of business transactions.

✦ Reduction in paperwork and other administrative tasks means more time to concentrate on the business and customer service.

✦ New business opportunities.

✦ Larger target audiences, and a built-in method of reaching them. Businesses can easily create mailing lists for distribution of a newsletter or a customer satisfaction survey by using data gathered from the customer database. This list of customers can then be contacted via e-mail, rather than expensive and labor-intensive snail-mail campaigns.

✦ The business is open all the time, and is available from any Internet-enabled computer, which significantly increases the chances of generating business.

✦ Reduction of errors, time, and costs involved in processing orders.

Conducting Business on the Internet

E-commerce is not without its issues, which demand consideration prior to implementing an e-business.

With increased visibility comes increased vulnerability. Imagine the disruption in business if a hacker deletes, or steals, the customer and order databases from an online store.

In addition, e-commerce businesses should consider several other issues:

✦ How to protect intellectual property (which is a difficult task when the info is placed online)?

✦ How to collect and submit taxes when dealing with customers from around the world?

✦ How to resolve issues of legality? Customs and trade agreements must be honored. With the world as your marketplace, it's important to define how to do business with various countries. What is considered legal in one country may not be legal in another country.

✦ How to deal with regulations (which hinder security or invade privacy)?

✦ How to deal with fraud in an e-commerce situation? What is the cardholder liable for and what are the merchant's responsibilities?

✦ How to gain customer trust? With no personal contact, and no storefront, an e-commerce business could be gone in an instant. How can a business assure customers that their patronage is warranted?

Setting up an e-commerce site deals with more concrete issues that are discussed in the following sections.

Setting up for Web-based business

Starting a Web-based business can be deceptively easy. You get some Web space, you spend a few hundred dollars on software, and suddenly, you're in business. However, a startup such as this usually ends in failure because creating a successful online business involves much more.

After a business has identified and dealt with all the factors regarding management and implementation of the system, the prospective business must also decide whether to create an in-house solution, in which all the hardware and software is owned and operated by the business, or to go with a pre-packaged or "instant storefront" solution. Instant e-commerce software is readily available, and often includes software and arrangements for connection to such services as online payment processing, which can greatly reduce the costs involved in setting up the online business. The instant storefront is particularly attractive for small companies, who seldom have the budget, time, or expertise required for a fully customized solution. The storeowner needs little or no programming experience to customize the storefront software. The only other necessity is some Web space from which to host the storefront.

Instant storefronts

If a business owner decides to incorporate an instant storefront, then he or she must make another decision: whether to use an "on-line" or "off-line" instant storefront.

On-line storefronts house all the software on the e-commerce service provider's systems. The business owner then simply pays for the service and maintains the store by updating catalogs, prices, pictures of goods, and so on. The service provider is responsible for ensuring that the data is secure and that transactions are performed appropriately. Also, the service provider is responsible for all hardware and software, including maintenance and upgrades.

Off-line storefronts are generally built on the business's computers, are tested, and are then uploaded to a service provider for hosting. The advantage of this approach is that the retailer has more control over the design of the site while passing off hardware and software responsibilities to the service provider.

In-house systems

If an organization decides to host their Web-based business in-house, they take on the responsibility for all aspects of e-commerce. This responsibility extends to not only the physical maintenance of the site, but also to the data management issues of integrity, privacy, availability, and security of the data. This can be a substantial investment both monetarily and logistically.

An advantage to the in-house approach, however, is the complete control that the business has over their Web site. The question that the business must answer, therefore, is whether the benefits of an in-house solution justify the costs. Regardless of the way in which an e-commerce site is implemented, certain issues must be resolved in order for the site to be secure and successful.

Security

The need for security — in every aspect of the e-commerce process — can't be stressed enough. From the time the user accesses a Web page that asks for private information to the point where the user's transaction is finalized, each exchange of data must be made as securely as possible.

Issues of security, however, have become a stumbling block in getting people to shop online. It is important, therefore, to inform customers that every precaution has been taken to ensure their privacy, and to remind them that, due to enhanced security, online transactions are often safer than phoning in an order or giving a waiter your credit card.

A business can take several steps to assure their customers, including procuring a digital certificate for the site, and using secure HyperText Transfer Protocol (HTTPS) and Secure Sockets Layer (SSL) to encrypt the data. The business needs to make sure that the customers realize that the order page is secure and that security also extends to the underlying transactions.

International currencies

Identify the international issues involved with e-commerce.

If your business plans to support a global market, you must be prepared to deal with different currencies. Large sites can employ software with built-in support for multiple currencies. Smaller operations that don't have the budget for such software can make use of manual currency conversions.

International shipping

Shipping outside of your home country can be a challenging task. The costs involved with shipping vary and must be made apparent to the customer at the time of the order. This way, you can charge for shipping along with the purchase. This method eliminates the problem of goods being returned when customers refuse to pay collect shipping charges, or when shipping charges are billed to them at a later date. In order to facilitate the shipping charge process, you need some form of cost calculator to determine the cost of shipping to the product's intended destination. Most major shipping companies provide software that you can incorporate into your Web site for this purpose. Some software is available as applets or plug-ins that are directly incorporated into your site, while other forms of software are hosted by the shipper, which you link to from your Web pages.

Shipping costs from a single location can be prohibitively expensive. To alleviate this cost, some organizations set up distributed warehouses to reduce the distances involved in reaching customers. Before going this route, however, ask yourself these questions: Can these remote warehouses be maintained properly? If you decide to use couriers, does the courier deliver to all countries that you deal with?

Multi-language support

Your business must be able to support multiple languages if you plan to deal with customers from around the world. Providing that support, however, can be time-consuming and expensive. Consider that each page must be translated and presented based on the geographic region or personal choice of your customers. If you decide to translate your site, you can use translation software; however, be aware that most software is not 100 percent accurate.

In addition to translation, you also face the issue of displaying international characters. To alleviate this problem, you should employ Unicode because it is a standard that supports most of the languages in the world through a 16-bit encoding scheme. This scheme gives Unicode the ability to encode over 65,000 characters as opposed to the 8-bit ASCII standard, which is currently the most common character encoding, and supports either 127 or 256 characters, depending on the scheme in use.

Unicode is currently in its third revision and may eventually replace ASCII.

Payment processing

 Define payment models for e-commerce.

An e-commerce site must accept online payments to be successful. The merchant must be able to accept payment information in whatever format they choose to support. Approval must be quick, preferably while the customer is online, rather than via an e-mail confirmation at a later time.

The following are the three general models for accepting payment in an e-commerce setting:

✦ The cash model

✦ The check model

✦ The credit model

In addition, the *smart card* is starting to become available as a fourth payment option, but so far, is in limited use.

The cash model

The cash model mimics real world monetary transactions through the use of electronic cash, or e-cash. E-cash is equivalent to real money, except that it is in the form of digital markers or tokens. Consumers purchase e-cash from e-cash vendors, such as banks. The e-cash tokens are stored in a digital wallet, which is a piece of software and accompanying data structure that is located on the buyer's computer. When the consumer purchases something, they pay for it with e-cash. The wallet program then communicates with the vendor, effectually transferring e-cash from the buyer to the seller like in a traditional transaction. The merchant then deposits the e-cash that they have collected with their bank in exchange for actual currency.

One advantage offered by e-cash is that the customer suffers no delay and no background processing. If you have sufficient funds in your digital wallet, you can make the purchase. No further verification is required.

A number of vendors offer e-cash; however, DigiCash is considered to be at the forefront. More information on e-cash is available at `www.digicash.com`.

 In the Real World

DigiCash is now known as eCash Technologies, Inc. The CIW materials still list them as DigiCash; therefore, remember this name for exam purposes. Be aware, however, that if you follow the preceding link, you will arrive at the eCash Technologies Web site.

The check model

The electronic check is similar to electronic cash; the only real difference is in the names. The electronic check still makes use of a program and data (called a *digital checkbook*) that stores a user's available fund balance.

The transaction of an electronic check is somewhat different from e-cash. When the buyer issues a digital check to an online merchant, the merchant's system deducts the appropriate amount from the user's checkbook. The merchant's system then verifies the check by contacting the merchant's financial institution, which, in turn, contacts the buyer's financial institution, which then reports availability of funds.

A disadvantage of this system is that the transfer of funds to the merchant's account is not instantaneous, as in the cash model.

More information on electronic check services can be found at `www.checkfree.com`, which is one of the leading e-check service vendors.

The credit model

The credit model is probably the most familiar model to Web users. This model simply employs the use of a credit card to make purchases on the Web. Much of the infrastructure for providing this service already exists, and most merchants — if they are coming from a traditional storefront environment — already have their merchant accounts in place.

Typically, in brick-and-mortar retail operations, merchants are already verifying credit card purchases electronically by swiping the buyer's card through a reader, which contacts the merchant's bank, which then verifies the buyer's card and initiates the funds transfer.

Moving this process to the Web simply involves a service that replaces the manual scanning of the card. The rest of the process is already in place.

In order to be able to accept online credit card payments, the merchant must usually ask their banks to have their accounts enabled to accept online payment. As mentioned previously, most credit card companies charge a higher transaction fee for online orders. Therefore, the merchant's accounts are normally not enabled for online processing by default.

Optionally, a merchant may choose to employ a third-party payment acceptance service if they don't have their own merchant accounts, or if they feel that the merchant transaction charges are prohibitively high.

Smart cards

Describe the functions and advantages of smart cards.

Smart cards may eventually replace traditional credit cards and ATM, or debit, cards. They are gaining popularity and acceptance, and provide more capability than traditional cards.

Unlike traditional credit or bankcards, which have a magnetic strip, the smart card uses a small integrated circuit. This makes current smart cards a little thicker than a traditional credit card.

The smart card circuit integrates CPU and memory. In fact, some cards can store almost 100 times the amount of information stored in the magnetic strip on a traditional card. Some cards, such as optical memory cards, can hold up to 4 MB of information.

In addition to storing information, the card's circuitry can send, receive, and process information, thus giving it the ability to perform substantial services.

Some of the services that a smart card can perform include enhanced authentication, encryption of data, currency conversions, and data storage, such as transaction records, which you can later download to a PC in order to track spending.

The main disadvantage of smart cards, however, is cost. Standard bank or credit cards can cost less than ten cents to produce and distribute, whereas a standard processor carrying smart cards costs about ten dollars, at the least.

Like most technology, however, the cost of using smart cards will decrease as it matures and gains more support. Organizations such as Microsoft, MasterCard, and IBM, along with some government programs, are already starting initiatives to make smart cards more common. Visa has also announced its own initiative — GlobalPlatform — which is a forum established to promote global standardization of smart card technology.

Site statistics

Tracking your visitors' activities on your site can help you make decisions regarding the content of your site. In addition, you can give the information that you gain by tracking site usage to different individuals in your organization. The number of visits to the sales page, for example, can go to the sales team, and the general site information may be of great interest to a manager.

You can employ simple site tracking in the form of counters that increment with each connection to the Web page. Web server software usually allows for some form of site tracking. Most software allows for the customization of the tracking reports that give you the data that you are most interested in. An owner of a Web site may be most interested in how many repeat visits the site is getting. This is an indication that the content is valuable to viewers. If the owner is trying to promote advertisement on the site, the number of unique visitors may be of the greatest value as proof to potential advertisers of the audience the site attracts. In general, however, site statistics indicate who was looking at what and when they were looking. Additionally, the duration of the visit, either on a per page basis or over the entire site, is generally part of the available information.

This information can prompt you to change the format of your site. If the overall site statistics show a decrease in the number of visits to the site, it may indicate that visitors are bored with the site and that it needs to be updated more frequently. If you find that a certain part of your site is getting more traffic than others, you may consider providing more of the same kinds of information or services.

Paying close attention to site statistics can make the difference between a well-maintained and visitor-oriented site, and one that, while it may have enjoyed substantial traffic when it was new, has lost its appeal due to its static nature.

Copyrights, Trademarks, and Licensing

 Explain the issues involved with copyrights, licensing, and trademarks.

Due to its global nature, the Internet presents special challenges in the enforcement of copyright, trademark, and licensing laws. Because each country has its own laws governing the issues of copyright infringement, trademark usage, and licensing agreements, it can be difficult to apply hard-and-fast rules and to determine who has jurisdiction when a case of infringement is brought forth.

Copyrights

The CIW materials define *copyright laws* as those laws, which "...protect original works of authorship that are fixed in a tangible medium of expression." The basic defining elements are expression, which is the medium in which your work is conveyed, and originality, which deals with the content delivered by your work.

Works of authorship can include music, graphics, sound recordings, and literary productions, as well as motion pictures, animations, and almost anything else that has been developed or created. You can find many instances, for example, of graphics artists who distribute their works on Web pages. Most artists, who submit their works to such sites, allow the graphics to be used by individuals, free of charge, for non-commercial purposes. They prescribe a fee, however, for use in a commercial environment. This practice implies that the material is copyrighted; however, there is no such thing as an international copyright. For works to be truly copyright protected, the country in which the artist resides must grant copyrights. In order to apply for a copyright, you must contact the appropriate government agency. In the U.S., you can visit `www.loc.gov/copyright` and download the appropriate forms for making a copyright application.

If any pages in your site contain copyrighted materials, they should be clearly marked with the copyright symbol and the date of the copyright. This information is usually included at the bottom right of each page. Even though copyright symbols are not required, they are recommended as a clear indication that the material contained in the page is protected under the copyright laws of the owner's country.

The nature of the Internet makes copyright enforcement difficult. Laws governing the use of copyrighted material on the Internet are not yet clear, although some court cases have made precedent for the solidification of such laws.

In order to structure copyright law in relation to digital material, an organization known as the Information Infrastructure Task Force, or IITF, was formed in 1993. A working group formed under the IITF was given the task of defining intellectual property rights as they applied to the digital era. This group determined a need for review of existing copyright laws, given the ease and rapidity with which intellectual material can now be disseminated. In 1994, this group distributed a report, called the "Green Paper," outlining their findings and recommendations in this regard.

One organization that assists in the worldwide enforcement of intellectual property laws is the United Nations agency called the World Intellectual Property Organization (WIPO). With more than 170 countries (174 as of March 14, 2001) holding active membership, the WIPO encourages cooperation between members in enforcing copyright law. This cooperation allows for prosecution of copyright violators in not only the country where the copyright is registered, but also in the country where the offense was committed (given that the two countries are WIFO members). The WIPO Web site, located at `www.wipo.org`, has more information, including a list of copyright offices in each member country.

As mentioned previously, a number of court cases have brought copyright issues to the forefront in relation to intellectual property rights violations on the Internet. Probably the most publicized case was that of the Recording Industry Association of America versus Napster.

The sharing of artist's material in the form of MP3 files is a case of copyright violation, according to the RIAA. Napster claims that because they didn't charge a fee (members copy MP3s among themselves — Napster simply provides the servers and the software) for the files, they aren't in violation of copyright. The RIAA wants to see artists paid a royalty for the copying of their materials via the Napster service, just as they would if their music was played on radio or other traditional mediums.

As of this writing, Napster has been forced to limit their operations. The U.S. Ninth Circuit Court of Appeals ruled that Napster can no longer carry on as a host for shared music and other files, as long as the material being shared is not in the public domain. This has effectively shut down their service, until such time as reasonable filters can be put in place that will restrict the distribution of copyrighted materials via the Napster service.

The CIW materials also mention the cases of Sega Enterprises versus MAPHIA, and Playboy versus George Fena, in which copyright violations were claimed due to the copying and downloading of game software in the case of Sega, and photographs in the case of Playboy. Both MAPHIA and Fena ran electronic Bulletin Board Systems, or BBSs, and were allowing the download of the aforementioned copyrighted materials. Both Sega and Playboy were successful in their legal actions.

Trademarks

Another area of contention is the use of trademarks, which are words, slogans, graphics, or other methods of "branding" or creating brand recognition for a product or service. Pentium(is an example of a trademark; in this case, it is the brand name of a CPU created by Intel.

The purpose of having a trademark is to create uniqueness for a product, which makes it distinguishable among other products of the same type. Companies may expend considerable resources in creating a trademark, which they feel gains them an advantage in what may be a crowded marketplace.

Trademark law protects this investment by making it illegal for one organization to use another's trademarks without permission. An example of trademark violation is if a CPU manufacturer, other than Intel, used the word *Pentium* to market their CPUs.

Registering a trademark is much like applying for a copyright. The intent is to limit the use of the trademark to the registered party, thus ensuring that the party is effectively distinguished in the marketplace. Forms for applying for a trademark registration are available from the U.S. Patent and Trademark Office (www.uspto.gov), in the United States, and from the Canadian Intellectual Property Office (http://cipo.gc.ca) in Canada.

Trademarks are also protected by cooperation of the member countries of the WIPO.

Licensing

The preceding discussions make it clear that you can't simply use someone else's copyrighted materials without seeking, and receiving, their permission. This process is known as *licensing*.

In order to license the use of copyrighted material, you must contact the copyright owner, who may or may not choose to grant the right to use their materials. Usually, the copyright owner will make some stipulation as to how the material may be used. Seeking legal assistance in drawing up the licensing agreement is a best practice. This is true whether you are the licensee or the licensor, and helps to ensure that no ambiguities exist in the license agreement. The agreement generally defines how the licensed material may be used and what, if any, royalties or lump sum payments are to be made in exchange for the license.

A common example of licensing occurs when PC manufacturers place labels on the outside of their systems with slogans like "Pentium Inside," showing the Intel Pentium processor logo. All of these materials are registered trademarks or copyrighted materials of Intel, the CPU manufacturer. In order for these labels and slogans to appear on the machine, the right to use this material is granted to the PC manufacturer, under license.

It is important to note, when speaking of licenses, that the responsibility for obtaining permission to use copyrighted materials — to obtain a license agreement — is entirely the end user's. Until such agreements are in place, the end user must not assume that it is allowable to use the materials, unless an interim agreement is granted by the copyright holder.

Key Point Summary

The Internet has redefined the way that business is done and information is transferred between the parties involved in a business transaction. Businesses are able to "set up shop" on the Internet with little time and investment. Understanding the risks and how to reap the benefits of e-commerce, however, is vital if the business is to succeed.

This chapter presents e-commerce fundamentals and discusses some of the technologies and issues involved in the e-commerce arena. Keep the following points in mind.

✦ Electronic commerce on the Web is also known as Web commerce, Internet commerce, or e-commerce.

✦ Commerce is the trading of goods and services in exchange for currency or something of equal value.

✦ E-commerce must deal with security and data management in non-traditional ways.

✦ The following are three major elements of e-commerce:

- **Communications** — Services supporting the electronic transfer of information between all parties in an electronic transaction.

- **Security** — Methods for identification and authentication of parties involved in an electronic transaction. In addition, the integrity and privacy of the communicated data must be assured.

- **Data management** — Methods of maintaining transaction details and responding to breakdowns in communication. Must also employ a common data format and access language.

✦ In traditional commerce, information is shared directly. In e-commerce, information is shared indirectly because the entire transaction is handled electronically.

✦ Electronic means of ensuring identification, authentication, and non-repudiation must be used. These include the use of digital certificates and encryption.

✦ The two main e-commerce models are the Business-to-Business (B2B) model and the Business-to-Customer (B2C) model.

✦ The Business-to-Business model is typified by high volume, low price transactions.

✦ The Business-to-Customer model is typified by low volume, high price transactions.

✦ Electronic Data Interchange (EDI) is a standard defining how documents, in a standard format, may be exchanged directly between computer systems.

✦ EDI deals with the electronic transfer of information, such as purchase orders or sales invoice data, which is traditionally paper based.

✦ EDI seeks the following goals:

- Enable simple and cost-effective communication of structured transaction information throughout all stages of a transaction's life.

- Reduce the occurrences of data capture so as to limit the possibility of data error or corruption, thus reducing the time required to correct such errors.

- Decrease the time associated with the transaction process in order to increase profitability.

✦ EDI was initially limited in acceptance due to factors of perceived cost and lack of a universal EDI standard.

✦ EDI has found niche acceptance in various industries, such as chemical, electronics, and others, which have developed their own specific forms of EDI.

✦ The growing desire for doing business on the Internet has prompted the formalization of EDI standards. Currently the ANSI X12 and UN/EDIFACT specifications are being accepted across industries.

✦ Reasons for implementing solutions that incorporate EDI follow:

- To reduce the cost involved in repetitive, manual transactions.

- To implement tighter cost controls in low-profit margin environments.

- To match competitor implementations to maintain competitive levels.

- To ensure completion of business commitments in a timely manner.

- To maintain compatibility with partner organizations that are implementing EDI solutions.

✦ Secure Electronic Transaction (SET) is a protocol with significant benefits for B2B and B2C e-commerce.

✦ MasterCard originally proposed SET. Visa originally proposed a competing standard. Now, both organizations endorse the SET standard.

✦ Japan, Switzerland, and Denmark have deployed SET for on-going, live transactions. MasterCard, IBM, and others have completed live transaction tests of the protocol.

✦ The primary features of SET follow:

- All parties must use digital certificates to identify themselves and to provide for digital signing of their involvement in the transaction. This ensures non-repudiation and reduces the chances of transaction tampering.

- Data is encrypted via the keys of each party's digital certificate. This ensures the secure transfer of transaction information between parties.

- Reduction of the risk of credit card fraud because the merchant never receives a customer's credit card information. Rather, the buyer submits their credit card information directly to the financial institution, which will process the transaction and inform the merchant that the payment has been received.

- SET was designed to accommodate transactions, such as returns, credits, and transaction reversals.

✦ Some benefits of e-commerce include the following:

- Purchasing processes are streamlined and inexpensive.

- Business transactions can be completed in a more timely manner.

- Reduction in paper-based management means more time spent on customer service.

- Larger target audiences, and more efficient ways of reaching them.

- Unlimited business hours.

- Reduction of errors, time, and cost involved in order processing.

✦ E-commerce sites can be set up as either instant storefronts, or as complete in-house systems.

✦ Instant storefronts make use of pre-packaged software, which can be customized, with little or no programming experience, in a very short time.

✦ Online instant storefronts house all the storefront software on the e-commerce service provider's site.

✦ Off-line instant storefronts are created on the merchant's systems and then hosted by a service provider after the design is complete.

✦ The online storefront offers less customization in exchange for a simpler setup.

✦ The off-line storefront offers more customization, but requires the business owner to have more in-house expertise.

✦ In-house systems are created and hosted by the business owner.

✦ In-house systems, while allowing complete customization, require substantial investment in funds, logistics, and expertise.

✦ The main question to ask when considering an in-house solution is: Do the benefits outweigh the costs?

✦ Security is absolutely necessary, but can discourage users from patronizing an online business.

✦ Secure Socket Layer (SSL) and secure HyperText Transfer Protocol (HTTPs) can be used to secure communications between customer and business.

✦ Customers need to be educated in security measures, to reduce their fears in using online business services.

✦ When customers shop from around the world, international currency conversion is an important feature of your site. Smaller sites may make use of manual conversion, while larger sites may employ software to convert currency at the time of the transaction.

✦ International shipping must be addressed in terms of who will deliver to what countries, and what are the costs.

✦ Some organizations develop distributed warehouse solutions to overcome international shipping problems.

✦ Storefronts should provide a shipping calculator to provide buyers with a concrete shipping cost, which can be included in their purchase price.

✦ Online business should employ Unicode character coding because it supports international character sets.

✦ Site translation to other languages should be considered if the site is intended to target international locations.

✦ Translation can be done either manually or by software.

✦ Manual translation is usually quite expensive. Software-based translation, even though it can cost less, is not always 100 percent accurate.

✦ The three payment models used in e-commerce are cash, check, and credit models.

- ✦ The cash model uses digital cash, or tokens, stored in a digital wallet on the customer's computer.

- ✦ The cash model allows instant transfer of funds to the merchant's account.

- ✦ The check model is similar but uses a digital checkbook instead of a digital wallet.

- ✦ The check model benefits the buyer, but does not immediately transfer funds to the merchant account.

- ✦ The credit model mimics traditional credit card usage.

- ✦ Because credit card transactions are generally verified electronically, the only addition required to automate the credit model is the secure electronic collection of credit card information.

- ✦ Smart cards are also becoming available as an alternate means of payment.

- ✦ Smart cards may potentially replace credit and ATM cards.

- ✦ Smart cards use CPUs and memory to store and process information.

- ✦ Smart cards have the potential of storing far greater amounts of information than traditional magnetic strip cards. Some cards have storage capacities of up to 4 MB.

- ✦ Recording site statistics helps to tune an online business for maximum profitability.

- ✦ Site statistics generally report on the number of visits (hits) to an overall site or to specific pages.

- ✦ Copyright, trademarks, and licensing are legal issues that need to be dealt with in e-commerce.

- ✦ Copyright laws are defined as laws that protect original works of authorship in a particular medium.

- ✦ The basic defining elements of copyright are expression and originality.

- ✦ There is no such thing as international copyright law.

- ✦ Copyright must be registered in the country in which the author or artist resides.

- ✦ The World Intellectual Property Organization (WIPO) assists in international copyright protection through the cooperation of its member states.

- ✦ More than 170 countries belong to WIPO.

- ✦ Trademarks are words, slogans, graphics, or other devices that uniquely differentiate a product or service from those of its competitors.

- ✦ Trademarks are also protected through cooperation of the members of the WIPO.

✦   ✦   ✦

STUDY GUIDE

The following materials will aid you in preparing for the portion of the CIW Foundations exam that is covered in this chapter. Several assessment questions will, as much as possible, mimic the feel of the actual exam. Some scenario questions will test your knowledge of how to apply, in real world situations, the information that you have received in this chapter. These are typically essay-type questions that you won't find on the actual exam, but are useful in solidifying your understanding of the chapter topics

After you have been through the assessment questions and scenarios, check your answers in the section Answers to Chapter Questions, which immediately follow the scenarios.

Assessment Questions

1. What terms are often used to describe electronic commerce on the Internet? (Choose all that apply)

    A. Web commerce

    B. On-line shopping

    C. E-commerce

    D. Internet commerce

2. What are the three main elements of electronic commerce?

    A. Digital wallets

    B. Communications

    C. Encryption

    D. Data Management

    E. Security

3. For systems participating in an electronic transaction to communicate successfully, what must they have in common? (Choose only one)

    A. They must all use the same operating system.

    B. They must all be based in the same hardware platform.

    C. They must all have a common communication language, or protocol.

    D. They must all be Web servers.

4. In comparing electronic and traditional commerce, what feature of traditional commerce is virtually eliminated in e-commerce scenarios? (Choose only one)

    A. There are never any sales promotions is the e-commerce.

    B. There is no direct contact between buyer and seller in e-commerce.

    C. Payment methods, other than by credit card, are not used in e-commerce.

    D. E-commerce sites never advertise.

5. Which definition best defines the term *non-repudiation* as it relates to transaction processing in e-commerce?

    A. A non-refutable proof of the identity and origin of transaction data by some electronic means, such as digital signing.

    B. An online sale is final and non-refundable.

    C. An online vendor can't be held responsible for the type of products sold online.

    D. A vendor can't be held responsible if a hacker steals the vendor's customer information database and fraudulently uses information contained in it.

6. What two models of e-commerce define how businesses and customers deal with each other?

    A. Business-to-business

    B. Supplier-to-retailer

    C. Customer-to-bank

    D. Business-to-customer

7. What typifies business-to-business transactions?

    A. Only purchase order and invoice forms are sent in business-to-business transactions.

    B. Low volume, high price transactions.

    C. High volume, low price transactions.

    D. Business-to-business transactions are always verified via e-mail.

8. What does EDI stand for?

    A. E-commerce Data Interface

    B. Electronic Data Interface

    C. Electronic Data Identification

    D. Electronic Data Interchange

9. What best describes the type of data exchanged in an EDI transaction? (Choose only one)

   A. Credit card verification and transaction status.

   B. Electronic documents such as electronic equivalents of purchase orders and invoices.

   C. Identification only. EDI is not responsible for the actual transport of data.

   D. Electronic check information.

10. What are three design goals of EDI?

    A. Enable simple and cost effective communication of structured transaction information.

    B. Reduce the occurrences of data capture so as to minimize opportunity for data error.

    C. Enforce data integrity through the use of digital certificates.

    D. Decrease the time associated with the transaction process, making the entire process more profitable.

11. Approximately how many U.S. businesses were using EDI in 1993?

    A. More than 75 percent

    B. Less than 50 percent

    C. Less than 10 percent

    D. Less than 1 percent

12. What two standards represent current EDI specifications? (Choose two)

    A. EDI Phase I

    B. UN/EDIFACT

    C. ANSI X12

    D. EDI Phase II

13. What characteristics best describe organizations that can benefit from implementing EDI? (Choose all that apply)

    A. Partner companies are implementing EDI, thus forcing compliance.

    B. A desire to reduce the time spent on repetitive transactions.

    C. Low margins are demanding as much efficiency in the business process as can be achieved.

    D. All of the above.

14. Who was the original proponent of the Secure Electronic Transaction protocol?

   A. MasterCard

   B. American Express

   C. Diner's Club

   D. Visa

15. What two features best distinguish SET from other protocols? (Choose two)

   A. It is being used live in Japan, Denmark, and Switzerland for on-going live transactions.

   B. SET requires the use of digital certificates by all transaction participants.

   C. SET is only used between financial institutions.

   D. SET was designed with financial processes such as returns, credits, and transaction reversals in mind.

16. What are some advantages of e-commerce over traditional commerce? (Choose all that apply)

   A. Reduction of errors, time, and cost involved in transaction processing.

   B. Business owners can ignore their businesses for months at a time, due to the level of automation.

   C. The purchase process is streamlined and inexpensive.

   D. None of the above.

17. Instant storefronts allow businesses to get into the e-commerce game quickly and easily. What are the two major types of instant storefronts?

   A. On-line storefronts

   B. On-line DVD sales

   C. Off-line storefronts

   D. Off-line gaming download sites

18. What is the biggest disadvantage of in-house solutions for setting up an e-commerce site? (Choose only one)

   A. The business owner must have considerable monetary, logistical, and technical resources available.

   B. Due to the complexity of the software, very little uniqueness can be built into in-house systems.

   C. In-house systems take years to develop.

   D. In-house systems can't be integrated into networks to provide online payment processing.

19. What steps can the developer take to ensure that the form that the customer enters their credit card information on is secure? (Choose two)

   A. Enable Secure Socket Layer functionality at the Web server.

   B. Refer the customer to a payment service specializing in secure payment processing.

   C. Make sure that the page is securely transported via HTTPS.

   D. Don't accept payments online.

20. What factors can have a significant effect on the way a Web site with an international audience is designed? (Choose three)

   A. Use of translation services for translating pages into other languages may be required.

   B. Currency conversion programs may need to be linked to, or integrated into the Web site.

   C. Unicode encoding should be used to support international character sets.

   D. A graphic of the flag of each supported country should be placed on the page to indicate that shipping can be done to that country.

21. What three payment processing models are currently used in e-commerce transactions?

   A. The e-barter model

   B. The cash model

   C. The check model

   D. The credit model

   E. The ATM model

22. What device, containing a CPU and memory, may eventually replace standard ATM and credit cards?

   A. Smart cards

   B. Ram cards

   C. PC cards

   D. Hand-held computers

23. What international organization helps to enforce copyright and trademark law in various countries?

   A. The United Nations

   B. The International Standards Organization

   C. The World Intellectual Property Organization

   D. The World Wide Office of Patents and Trademarks

24. What can site statistics do to aid in managing a Web site? (Choose all that apply)

   A. Can indicate the most popular pages, so more of that particular content can be offered.

   B. Can determine when the Web site is getting old due to a decrease in overall visits.

   C. Can help determine the type of audience the site hosts by showing the times of day that the most hits are recorded and to what pages the viewers navigate.

   D. All of the above.

Scenarios

You are a consultant hired to recommend an e-commerce implementation strategy to an existing retailer. The retailer wants to ease into the e-commerce marketplace by offering a specific line of antique books for sale on the Internet. These books will appeal to a select, but international audience.

The retailer wants to show pictures of the front covers of each book, as well as a small description of the book, and its price, next to each picture. There will be approximately 50 individual books for sale at any given time, and book pictures and descriptions will be updated only when new books are acquired or sold. The business owner wants the ability to update the pictures and descriptions, but has minimal computer experience.

The owner doesn't want to be responsible for computer equipment or communications facilities. He does, however, insist that he be provided with reports on how many users are viewing the site and that his company retain the ability to update the product information.

Online payment is required, but the retailer does not want to obtain merchant accounts for many different credit cards.

Given these criteria, what would you recommend that the business do in setting up their online operation? Should they have an application developed for them? Should they bite the bullet and host everything in-house or hire a service provider? How are updates to the site, site reports, and payments to be handled?

Answers to Chapter Questions

Chapter Pre-Test

1. The main identifying feature of electronic commerce is the lack of direct contact between the parties involved in the transactions. This is the primary requirement for additional attention to be paid to issues such as security, communications, and data management. Automation must take the place of direct customer interaction.

2. There are many benefits that a small business may derive from going online including the following:

   • Longer hours of operation with no increase in expense.

   • The ability to reach a substantially larger audience.

   • The ability to quickly and efficiently take orders, thus reducing the cost associated in the order process.

   Note   The section titled "Advantages of E-commerce" provides additional information in this regard.

3. The challenges in getting online can be many. Some of the most immediate include the following:

   • Should the company attempt to build their own solution, or contract it to a qualified developer?

   • Should the company invest in the infrastructure to host their own business, or should they make use of an online service?

   • What payment methods will the business accept and what services are required to facilitate those methods?

   Note   See this chapter's section "Conducting Business on the Internet" for further information.

4. The primary standards governing the electronic communication of data between systems in the e-commerce environment are the Electronic Data Interchange (EDI) specification and the Secure Electronic Transactions (SET) protocol standard.

5. Smart cards provide the opportunity to bring true processing capabilities to the credit or ATM card. They allow a wide range of possibilities in terms of simple and secure funds transfer, both in traditional transactions and in e-commerce transactions. Through the use of a specialized reader, a Smart Card has the ability to actually interface with the e-commerce software, thus interacting with it in a way that is not currently possible. See the section "Smart Cards" for additional information.

6. Online merchants who display copyrighted information must obtain the copyright owner's permission to use their materials, whether they are for sale or not. Using another's copyrighted material without obtaining permission is a copyright infringement. Some copyright owners will allow the use of their materials for nothing more than an acknowledgment; others will want payment. Regardless, the burden is on the party that desires to use the material to seek the right to use it. See the section "Copyrights, Trademarks, and Licenses" for more information.

Assessment Questions

1. **A, C, D**. Web commerce, Internet commerce, and e-commerce have become synonymous for business conducted on the Internet. Online shopping is simply one of the services provided.

2. **B, D, E**. Communications, Data Management, and Security are the main elements in electronic commerce. Encryption is a method of providing secure communications. Digital wallets are simply the term used to describe the software that holds e-cash on a user's computer.

3. **C**. A common communication language, or protocol, must be established defining the structures and methods used to communicate transactional information. This is above and beyond the transport and network level protocols, such as TCP/IP. Examples of e-commerce protocols are EDI and SET.

4. **B**. In traditional commerce, direct contact between the buyer and seller was common. In e-commerce this is virtually eliminated.

5. **A**. Non-repudiation, in e-commerce terms, is the proof that a transaction was handled by a particular party, and was not forged by someone who has substituted a counterfeit message for a legitimate one. This is primarily accomplished through the use of digital signatures and encryption.

6. **A, D**. Business-to-business and business-to-customer are the two models defining how businesses and customers interact in an e-commerce setting.

7. **C**. Business-to-business transactions typically have high volumes and low prices per transaction. This is simply "volume buying," which typically occurs between businesses.

8. **D**. EDI stands for Electronic Data Interchange.

9. **B**. EDI describes the means by which structured data, such as forms, are communicated between organizations. These forms are electronic documents describing transaction information or requests, such as purchase orders and invoices.

10. **A, B, D**. EDI was designed to decrease costs, increase profitability, and reduce errors in the transaction process, which helps to fulfill the first two goals.

11. **D**. According to the CIW materials, less than one percent of U.S. businesses were using EDI as of 1993.

12. **B, C**. EDI is defined by the UN/EDIFACT and ANSI X12 specifications.

13. **D**. All of these are typical reasons that organizations will implement EDI. See the "Electronic Data Interchange (EDI)" section of this chapter for further information.

14. **A**. The original proponent of SET was MasterCard. Visa originally had a competing specification proposal, but SET proved to be more powerful.

15. **B, D**. SET enforces strict security by demanding the use of digital certificates for data signing and encryption. Also, it was designed with financial transactions of all types in mind, so it provides built-in support for refunds, exchanges, credits, and other such transactions.

16. **A, C**. E-commerce can substantially reduce the amount of time spent in transaction processing by automating most of the mundane aspects of the process. As such, the purchase process is streamlined and reduced in expense because manual handling of the information is not required. However, simply opening an online store doesn't mean that the owner can, from that point forward, leave the business in electronic hands. Such management practices will result in an electronic store closure as surely as they would for a traditional operation.

17. **A, C**. Online and off-line storefronts are the two types of instant storefronts that a prospective Web business can choose from. Online storefronts are the simplest because all the software is hosted by the service provider. Off-line storefronts require the installation of some software at the merchant's side, which they will use to configure the store. The completed store site is then uploaded to the service provider for hosting.

18. **A**. In house solutions involve substantial investment, both monetarily and otherwise. Equipment and software must be purchased, sufficient communications connections, such as high-speed (T1 or better) lines, must be installed, and sufficient expertise to implement and maintain the systems must be available.

19. **A, C**. The developer should enable (or have enabled) SSL and HTTPS. This combination allows encrypted communication between the browser and Web page, protecting the data being submitted on the form.

20. **A, B, C**. Translation into languages of the intended audience countries, acceptance of their currencies, and Unicode encoding to ensure proper display of non-English character sets may be desirable to ensure the greatest acceptance of a site that services different countries.

21. **B, C, D**. The cash, check, and credit models are payment methods used in e-commerce.

22. **A**. Smart Cards, due to their extended capabilities, may eventually replace ATM and credit cards, as their cost comes down, and the maturity of their software and hardware increases.

23. **C**. The World Intellectual Properties Organization helps to enforce copyright and trademark laws through cooperation of member countries. If a copyright infringement takes place, prosecution can take place in all WIPO member countries, where the offense took place, rather than just in the country where the owner filed the copyright.

24. **D**. The overall intent of site statistics is to show how many hits a site is receiving in a given period, and which content on the site is generating the most interest. This information can, if monitored regularly, aid in site management by pointing out what viewers appear to like and dislike about the site.

Scenarios

Because the owner doesn't want to get involved in setting up or maintaining equipment, the most obvious solution is an online, instant storefront.

Most such services provide the ability for at least basic modification of a "product catalog" that would likely be sufficient for the picture, descriptive text, and price of each book. In addition, a "shopping cart" program that can collect the items that a buyer wants to purchase, and forward them to a payment or "check out" page is often included. Payment services are most often included, although typically a charge is levied on every transaction because it is the service provider that is taking the responsibility for providing the credit card merchant accounts.

The service provider generally provides an online management utility that the owner can use to update the catalog, whenever he desires.

An in-house solution is more than this owner wants to deal with, at least at this time. The amount of product that is to be offered does not warrant much more than a simple catalog and support services, as mentioned previously.

The major task in this case is to find a few service providers capable of hosting the site, comparing their costs and offerings, and determining which one suits the owner's desire for catalog update, reporting, and payment collection processes.

In addition, some time is required to get the owner comfortable with the processes involved, and teaching him what the site statistics mean and how to interpret the data so that he can derive some meaningful benefit from the reporting.

Fundamentals of Web Authoring

This part presents essential information regarding the process of Web page authoring.

Web Page Authoring Basics

1. Distinguish between creating Web Pages using an HTML text editor and a GUI HTML editor.

2. Identify different types of GUI HTML editors that create HTML automatically.

3. Define HTML.

4. Describe the origins of HTML.

5. Identify strategies for developing accessible Web pages.

6. Describe the standards organization that controls the various versions of HTML.

7. Identify the HTML 4.01 varieties.

8. List the benefits of Extensible HTML (XHTML).

9. List the benefits of Extensible HTML (XHTML) and how it relates to HTML and the Extensible Markup Language (XML).

10. Explain how HTML is related to XHTML.

11. Determine which browsers support which versions of HTML.

12. Identify strategies for developing accessible Web pages.

13. Identify front-end Web page design issues, such as the interface.

14. Define the concepts of creative design and branding standards, and illustrate their importance to business.

15. Identify back-end Web design issues, such as bandwidth and page names.

16. Explain Web document naming conventions.

17. Identify the issues that affect Internet site functionality.

CHAPTER PRE-TEST

1. Using a _____ editor, you can create Web pages with a simple point-and-click of your mouse.

2. If you use a _____ editor, you must manually type HTML tags into your Web page document.

3. Often referred to as "the language of the Web," _____ is used to create Web pages.

4. What variety of HTML uses cascading style sheets and no depreciated tags?

5. The HTML version that allows frames in a Web page is called _____.

6. HTML is a subset of what language?

7. True or False: Content, tables, and forms are examples of back end issues.

8. Approximately how long will a 110Kb file take to download over a 56Kbps modem connection?

9. XHTML is based on which two markup languages?

10. What error do you see when the file that you requested is not on the Web server?

✦ Answers to these questions can be found at the end of the chapter. ✦

Creating a Web document is not like creating a printed document; you must have more than just interesting ideas, snazzy graphics, and easy-to-use software programs. You also need the tools and ability to create an engaging, usable Web page.

This chapter discusses the many tools that make the task of creating a Web page easier. This chapter also examines HTML, how it has evolved, and how these changes can affect the viewing of your Web files. With so many choices, you have many decisions to make. The tools that you choose won't be effective unless you have defined a plan for your site. This chapter covers the planning basics of a Web site by looking at "front end" and "back end" issues, software, and markup languages.

Constructing Web Pages

When your friend tells you that she is creating a Web page, what exactly does she mean? Many people confuse the terms *Web page* and *Web site*. A Web page is a document or file on the World Wide Web that you access by typing its URL into a browser address bar. The Web page may contain any or all of the following:

✦ Text

✦ Video

✦ Graphics

✦ Sound

✦ Forms

✦ Links to other pages

A Web site is a collection of Web pages. Think of the World Wide Web as a great big library. Then, think of each Web site as a book, and Web pages as chapters within the book. Your *home page* is the first page of your Web site. It works like an index or table of contents by providing links to all the other pages.

 Cross-Reference For more information about URLs and Web browser basics, see Chapters 1 and 2.

Web-authoring software

 Distinguish between creating Web Pages using an HTML text editor and a GUI HTML editor.

Web developers create Web pages from Hypertext Markup Language (HTML) by using some type of Web-authoring software. This software falls into one of two categories: *text editors* and *GUI Editors*. The following sections compare these two.

GUI editors

 Identify different types of GUI HTML editors that create HTML automatically.

Graphical User Interface (GUI) editors allow you to create Web pages without typing HTML code. Many books and Web sites use the phrase What You See Is What You Get (WYSIWYG) to describe a GUI editor interface. Working with a GUI editor is like editing your Web page through your browser. With a simple point-and-click of your mouse on various menu and toolbar commands, you can design your page the way you desire while the program automatically enters the appropriate HTML code for your file. Unlike the text editor, a GUI editor allows you to see how the page will be displayed and formatted as you create it.

 Caution Don't be misled — the browser interpretation of your Web page may differ dramatically from what you see in your GUI editor.

Some GUI editors work better with specific browsers. To make your page easily accessible to all browsers, you may need to manually edit HTML code. Most GUI editors provide this ability. Unfortunately, your GUI editor sometimes overlooks the code that you manually enter or uses it incorrectly. Another downside to GUI editors is that they don't seem to change as quickly as HTML, so your editor may not be able to use the hottest new tags.

The Web page that you create may look great on your computer — with your browser software and monitor display settings. However, to someone else using different browser software — or even a different version of the same browser — it may look dreadful. Each of the numerous browsers has different versions and all of them differ somewhat in the way they interpret HTML commands. HTML started out as a very simple language with few commands, but it has evolved to meet the new needs of developers and now has around 100 tags. Not all editors and browsers have kept pace with the changes, however (more detail on this later in the chapter). Remember this best practice rule: Always test your Web files with different browsers — you may be surprised by what you see. Refer to Figure 8-1.

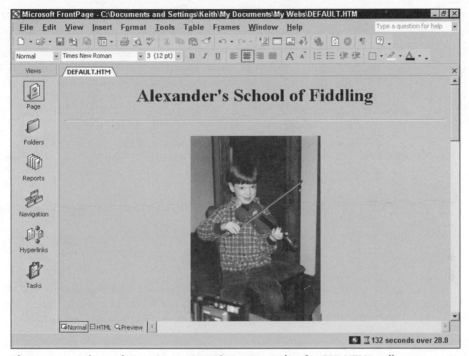

Figure 8-1: Microsoft FrontPage 2000 is an example of a GUI HTML editor.

A list of some popular HTML editors follows:

✦ Dreamweaver (Macromedia)

✦ FrontPage and FrontPage Express (Microsoft)

✦ FusionMX (NetObjects)

✦ GoLive (Adobe)

✦ HomeSite (Allaire)

✦ IMS Web Dwarf (Virtual Mechanics Inc.)

✦ Netscape Composer (Netscape)

✦ WebSphere HomepageBuilder for Linux (IBM)

You can read about these and other HTML editors at the following Web sites:

✦ www.stars.com/Vlib/Authoring/HTML_Editors.html

✦ www.webreference.com/authoring/languages/html/editors/

Text editors

Text editors are applications that save unformatted text files. When you use a text editor to create Web pages, you must manually type all text and HTML tags. (HTML and HTML tags are discussed in greater detail later in this chapter.) Despite their crudeness, text editors give you complete control over the content and "look and feel" of the page. With a text editor, you can easily update your Web pages to a newer standard by typing new tags into your file. Using a text editor, however, requires more time to complete a Web page.

If you are interested in using a text editor, you need only look as far as your operating system. Examples of text editors in the various operating systems include the following:

✦ Notepad (Microsoft Windows)

✦ vi (Linux/UNIX)

✦ SimpleText (Macintosh)

Several text editors contain features that insert HTML tags so you don't have to manually type them. However, you still need to know when to use each tag. Figure 8-2 demonstrates how the screen looks to edit a Web page in a text editor.

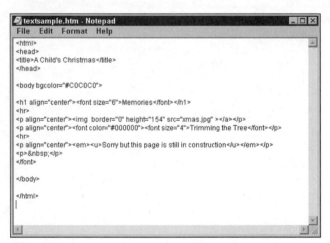

Figure 8-2: HTML editing in Notepad, the text editor in Microsoft Windows

As you can see from the preceding example, text editors don't really give you a feel for how your file will actually look on the Web; to accomplish this, you must open the file in a browser.

Some other popular editors follow:

✦ TextPad (www.textpad.com)

✦ BBEdit (www.barebones.com)

✦ UltraEdit (www.ultraedit.com)

Tip UltraEdit has great resources on their site as well. Go to http://www.ultraedit.com/downloads/additional.html.

For a comprehensive list of text editors, visit the following Web sites:

✦ http://texteditors.anydownloads.com/

✦ www.webdevelopersjournal.com/software/html_editors.html

✦ www.w3.org/Tools/

Hypertext Markup Language

Objective Define HTML.

HTML (Hypertext Markup Language) is the set of markup symbols or codes inserted in a file intended for display on a World Wide Web browser page. The markup tells the Web browser how to display a Web page's words and images for the user. Each individual markup code is referred to as an element (but many people also refer to it as a tag). Some elements come in pairs that indicate when some display effect is to begin and when it is to end.

An example follows:

```
<H1>The History of Balloons</H1>
```

In the preceding example, the content, "The History of Balloons," is contained within two tags, <H1> and </H1>. These tags tell the interpreter to format the text in the style of a heading. The angle brackets on either side of the tag are used to differentiate between tags and text. Although all browsers display the file content according to the tags' instructions, the appearance of the subject matter varies from browser to browser. The font style and font size for this tag may be different among the language interpreter software packages.

Do not confuse the terms *markup language* and *programming languages*. HTML is a markup language — not a programming language. Program languages, such as COBOL, give tasks for the computer to complete. HTML simply "marks up" or describes how a browser should display a particular file.

Cross-Reference Chapters 9 and 10 explain some of the many tags you can use.

History

Describe the origins of HTML.

HTML was born in 1989 when Tim Berners-Lee and Robert Caillau collaborated to make an information system that could be accessed by computers running on different platforms. HTML 2.0 is the basis for the core HTML features that are used on the World Wide Web. Like natural languages, this markup language's roots are in other languages.

HTML was built from Standard Generalized Markup Language ((SGML), which is a more complicated and very robust markup language. SGML provides codes to describe text structure, thus categorizing the various parts of a document. This language provides a method for describing electronic text that works across multiple platforms. Like SGML, HTML describes the logical structure or context of a document. The tags carry formatting for a particular context. For example, headings will be a larger font than body text, and they may be bolded. The actual font size, type, and other attributes of the tags vary from browser to browser. Although formatting is attached to these tags, the interpretation of these formats also varies among the many different browsers. Although SGML wields more power than HTML, the simplicity of HTML and its ease of use have made it popular.

Standards and controls

Describe the standards organization that controls the various versions of HTML.

Over the years, different standards or *versions* of HTML have been released. The World Wide Web Consortium (W3C) publishes models for the Web community to follow. This international, vendor-neutral organization is comprised of 500 members and 60 full-time staff members who uphold communication standards between hardware and software over the Internet. The W3C provides a forum for discussion and publishes recommendations, turning new advancements into accepted standards.

Note

You can read these recommendations by going to the W3C Web site at www.w3.org/. This Web site gives information on HTML, XML, XHTML, and various other Internet specifications. It is a reliable guide for Web developers who want to conform to the latest W3C standards.

When referring to recommendations at the W3C Web site, don't use suggestions from the working drafts documentation; instead, refer to final recommendations.

In 1996, the W3C approved HTML version 3.2. This version of HTML was backwards-compatible with HTML 2.0 interpreters. Version 3.2 included changes for small programs (applets), tables, and text flow around images. You will still find pages written in this version of HTML today.

HTML 4.0 followed in 1998, and allowed for additional scripting languages, multimedia options, style sheets, and improved printing. Version 4.01, which was released in 1999, repaired some of the bugs present in version 4.0 that caused browsers to crash.

Exam Tip The CIW Foundations exam and course treats versions 4.0 and 4.1 as one version by using their elements interchangeably.

The varieties of HTML 4.01

Objective Identify the HTML 4.01 varieties.

HTML 4.01 is available in three different types: Transitional, Strict, and Frameset. None of these varieties are superior to the others; you can design interesting and effective Web pages with any of them. You must use the variety that best meets the needs of your clients and organization.

HTML 4.01 Strict

This variety of HTML gives the author extensive control over the design and appearance of the document. You can use Cascading Style Sheets (CSS) and Document Object Models in HTML Strict to increase your choices. You should not, however, use Depreciated tags. Some older Web browsers can't read HTML Strict and will display errors when attempting to do so.

Note The W3C uses the term *Document Object Model,* Microsoft uses *dynamic HTML,* and Netscape uses *Object Model* to describe the same element: A series of new tags that enhance the Web page, such as changing heading text color when a mouse is passed over the text. Some of these tags can actually make your Web page resemble a desktop application; for example, users can "drag and drop" images. Although both the Netscape and Microsoft browsers support this variety of HTML, there are some things that both browsers won't support. Netscape has developed some Object Model tags that don't work with Internet Explorer, and Microsoft has developed some dynamic HTML tags that don't work with Netscape.

HTML 4.01 Frameset

Web pages that use frames must be created in HTML 4.01 Frameset. *Frames* divide a Web page into more than one section. They give added options to Web developers, allowing them to incorporate features such as banners, sidebars, and tables of content. This variety supports more tags than HTML Transitional by using all the tags from HTML 3.0. Although HTML Frameset is supported by more browsers than can support HTML 4.01 Strict, some browsers still can't interpret Frameset correctly.

HTML Transitional

Of the three specifications, the HTML Transitional variety reaches the widest audience because almost all browsers interpret it correctly. Transitional HTML uses style sheets but, unlike HTML Strict, it does not use them to define everything. In this variety, you may use depreciated tags, which are HTML components that will be eventually phased out. You should use HTML Transitional if you suspect that the people trying to access your Web pages are using older browsers.

Markup languages and browsers

Determine which browsers support which versions of HTML.

Which HTML variety should you use? The CIW Foundations exam is based on HTML 4.0 and 4.01 standards and, as a result, the next couple of chapters focus on these standards. W3C suggests that you use the latest recommendation. Editors create pages and browsers interpret them. But not everyone keeps up with the latest standards; older browsers (still used by many people) don't understand newer HTML tags, and many GUI editors don't use the latest tags, either. The challenge is addressing these discrepancies.

The most popular browsers belong to Netscape and Microsoft, and have evolved over time as these companies released different generations or versions of their browsers. Newer versions take advantage of the more current HTML tags, while older versions can't read the newest tags. Newer Web pages also use other languages to deliver text, graphics, and video. Some of these languages are built into certain browsers, and some require that you downloaded plug-ins, such as Flash or Shockwave. Those in the general public don't always upgrade their browser software. If you use the latest tags and specifications to make your Web site, you will potentially alienate certain people from your site.

To further complicate matters, the latest versions of the Microsoft and Netscape browsers are diverging in the way that they interpret Web pages. Both companies have developed specific tags that only work with their specific browser.

In the Real World
You can run programs called *validators* to check the compatibility of your Web page with other browsers.

To maximize your efforts, decide which browsers are worth targeting, and use the HTML that best meets your needs. Table 8-1 compares the HTML types to browsers that can interpret them correctly.

Table 8-1 HTML Browser Issues	
HTML Variety	**Browsers**
2.0 & HTML Transitional	All browsers understand this HTML.
HTML 3.2 & HTML Frameset	Early browsers can't handle frames. Internet Explorer 4.01 and Netscape Navigator 4.03 can handle these specifications, but they may have some problems handling tables. The newer browsers should have no difficulty interpreting this HTML.
HTML 4.0 Strict	This is meant for the newest browsers. You will be excluding people using older browsers if you use the newer tags of this HTML. Also Netscape and Microsoft have each developed proprietary tags that don't work in the other's browser.

XHTML or HTML 5.0

 List the benefits of Extensible HTML (XHTML) and how it relates to HTML and the Extensible Markup Language (XML).

Explain how HTML is related to XHTML.

HTML will gradually be replaced by Extensible Hypertext Markup Language (XHTML) because HTML in its present form won't be able to meet all future Internet demands. XHTML is a combination of the best parts of two languages: HTML and XML (Extensible Markup Language). Both HTML and XML languages are subsets of the more complicated and robust Standard Generalized Markup Language (SGML).

Alternative browsing platforms, such as Personal Digital Assistants (PDAs), Personal Information Managers (PIMs), and Handheld PCs (HPCs), are rapidly growing in popularity. A recent study states that by the year 2002, only 25 percent of users accessing the Internet will use PCs, whereas 75 percent will use technologies such as PDAs and other personal devices. These alternative Internet access methods don't have the processing power needed to interpret HTML, and Web developers must rise to the challenge of making their content available to people using these devices. XHTML is the solution: Like XML, it is easily read across many platforms, and both PCs and wireless devices easily interpret this language.

XHTML files are text files comprised of tags and content. HTML and XML also use tags, but that's where the similarity ends. The differences between XHTML tags and HTML and XML language tags appear in the way the tags are used and what they represent. HTML began as a very simple language with only a few tag codes, and when coding in HTML, you must use existing tags — you can't make up your own tags. Although new tags have been added to the language, developers still need more to address security issues, audio and video streaming, specialized math formulas, and more. Due to this lack of extendibility, HTML is said to be *non-extensible*. Conversely, SGML, XML, and XHTML are examples of *metalanguages*, which are languages that allow you to develop language extensions as you need them. You can develop new custom tags as required. In other words, you can extend the language.

Consider the following sample text and corresponding tags:

```
<h1>Pinto</h>
```

When the preceding example is interpreted in HTML, the text "Pinto" will format as a heading. In XML, the same tags can be used to define "Pinto" as a heading, or you can also use the tag <h1> to represent types of horses or something else entirely, like addresses of houses. You can "extend" the language to meet your own needs. Tags separate chunks of data in XML, and the parsing of this data can be based on meaning. XML is as powerful as SGML, yet easier to use. The XML qualities adopted by XHTML compensate for the tags that are lacking in HTML. XHTML plays by XML rules, allowing the author to create tags that address new ways of presenting information. XHTML also adopts many HTML codes, so if you already know HTML, you don't need to relearn everything. XHTML may be viewed and interpreted by the same tools that you use for XML, which are also backwards-compatible with HTML.

The XML language requires precision; there is no room for sloppiness. Forgetting to close a tag properly or omitting a character can cause your file to be unreadable. HTML is more forgiving in this respect because browsers that read the HTML files compensate for errors and shoddy programming.

XML documents must be "well-formed." They must contain the following:

- ✦ A document declaration tag (DTD)
- ✦ A root element
- ✦ Correctly declared tags

XHTML is more like XML in this respect.

In the Real World The CIW Foundations exam focuses on HTML 4.01, but for real world situations, you may want to start coding by XHTML rules so that new browser platforms can read your Web pages.

For more information about XHTML, go to www.w3.org/TR/xhtml1/ .

Designing a Functional Site

 Identify strategies for developing accessible Web pages.

Identify the issues that affect Internet site functionality.

An effective Web page is a well-designed Web page. In the world of Web surfing, first impressions definitely count. The next section discusses important planning considerations from front-end planning issues to back-end planning issues.

The *front end* refers to the layout of the Web page and the ease with which a visitor can navigate through information. Front-end planning issues include the updating and presentation of content and links, and the choice of graphics and the design of forms. Included in front-end detail is the art of putting together an interface that reflects the company or organization you represent and appeals to your target audience.

Back end refers to the Web server and network. The speed with which your Web page is downloaded onto computers is a result of back-end issues usually related to your ISP. Ideally, your Web site should download quickly into most computers. Download speed, however, isn't entirely in your control, but you can compensate for slow modem connections and old browsers in some ways, such as limited graphics usage.

Front-end issues

 Identify front-end Web page design issues, such as the interface.

Your content and the way you choose to display it are front-end design issues. In fact, the way you place elements on your page can make or break your Web site. Consider the following:

Graphics and images
You see them on almost every Web page. Choosing the image that best conveys your message can be a tricky task. Visual appeal of graphic elements can help capture and keep a visitor. Too many graphics or large complex graphics, however, may frustrate people who must wait as they download.

Content

You must make many decisions about your content. For example, how frequently will you need to update your content? Nobody wants to read "old news." Exactly how much content will be placed on each page? If you have too much content on each page, your visitors may have to scroll down the document too many times.

Tables

A *table* is an alternative method of displaying data. Tables give more options for the overall design of the Web page. Tables can hold graphics, and not just text. However, not all browsers interpret tables the same way, and it is important to test your tables on different browsers. Figure 8-3 demonstrates a simple example of an HTML table.

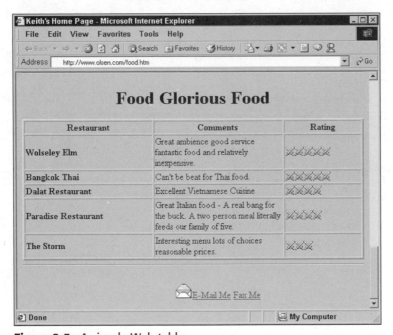

Figure 8-3: A simple Web table

Forms

Do you need to collect information from your Web pages' visitors? If so, you can use forms to collect the data. Determine what you want to ask and make it easy for your visitors to "fill in" and send the forms. You will probably have to incorporate script languages to process the information on the Web server, so your form must also be designed well. Figure 8-4 displays an example of a Web form.

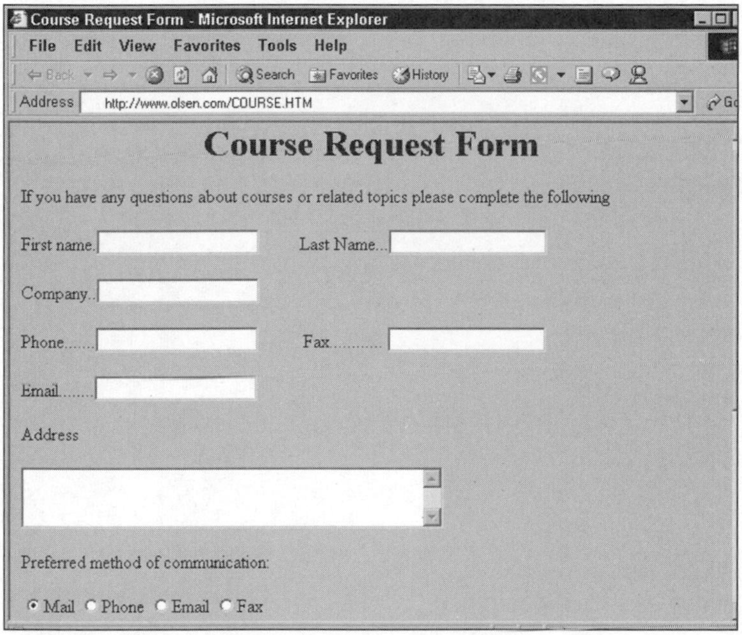

Figure 8-4: An example of a Web form

Links

Where will you place the links on your page? Where will your users be taken? The number and placement of links is important because the links should be obvious, easy to find, and should always work. Keep in mind that navigating between pages and ideas should be easy for your visitors. All Web users know the frustration of clicking a link that goes nowhere. If you are considering using external links, you must be prepared to test and update them frequently to ensure that they work and remain appropriate. Links to pages that no longer exist will often result in the "HTTP 404 — File not found" error. This is a Web server's way of telling you that the server is functioning but the Web page that you are looking for does not exist. Figure 8-5 displays the HTTP 404 error.

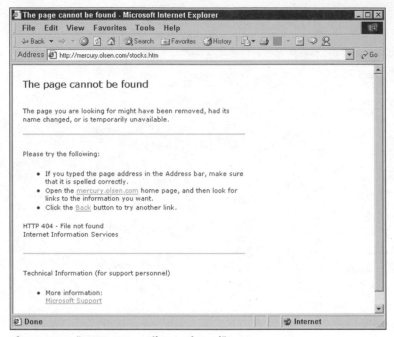

Figure 8-5: "HTTP 404 — File not found" error

Image maps

An *image map* is a graphic on a Web page. Image maps are not ordinary graphics, however, because they are divided into different sections called *hot spots*. Each hot spot is linked to a URL. Clicking the hot spot of the image map is like clicking a hyperlink. Image maps can be stored and interpreted on either the client side or the server side. Providing hyperlinks as well as image maps accommodates people who change their browser settings, so that images are not downloaded.

Creative design and branding standards

 Define the concepts of creative design and branding standards, and illustrate their importance to business.

The number of Web sites that represent companies, organizations, and special interest groups has been increasing exponentially. The Web is big business. As a Web author, you will find that marketing strategies influence design strategies.

For the CIW Foundations exam, you need to be familiar with the term "name and brand recognition," which is the identification of a logo or symbol with a company name. The pouncing cat ornament on the hood of a Jaguar makes you think "Jaguar." The picture of the colonel on the bucket of chicken is synonymous with KFC. These images that have become so closely associated with products are examples of name and brand recognition.

The term *mind share* is connected to name and brand recognition; it is part of branding standards and appeals to more than the sense of sight. Using jingles, music, and slogans creates associations with products. Wendy's "Where's the beef?", Volkswagen's "Driver's wanted" slogans, and Chevy Truck's "Like a Rock" song are all examples. You may not be the one who designs the logo or jingle, but you may be expected to incorporate them into your Web site.

Exam Tip   Be able to explain the terms *mind share* and brand recognition.

Many large companies have rules pertaining to use of font style, colors, and logo. The appearance of your Web page must mirror the appearance of the advertisements, stationary, and signage already existing within a company. These rules assure consistency in the presentation of company image. Numerous books, Web sites, and classes explain marketing goals and strategies and how to achieve them through various media, including Web pages. The fine art of branding standards, however, goes beyond the scope of the CIW Foundations course and this book.

Back-end issues

Objective   Identify back-end Web design issues, such as bandwidth and page names.

Ideally, you want your Web site to be accessible to everyone. A user-friendly Web site downloads quickly and facilitates accessibility. Download time is vital to the success of your Web site because people have limited patience waiting for a Web page to load. The Internet is somewhat unpredictable, and many factors that affect your Web page's download time are out of your control.

Exam Tip   Be able to define bandwidth and download time. Know that they are back-end issues, and know which factors that affect download time are within your control and which factors are out of your control.

Download time is the length of time necessary for a Web page to load onto a computer. When you type a URL, the request for that Web page is sent to the server, and the server sends the file to your computer. Download time is dependent on bandwidth and the size of the file being downloaded.

Bandwidth

Bandwidth is the rate at which data travels over a network connection in a fixed amount of time. Typically, this rate is given as the numbers of bits of data transferred per second. The greater the bandwidth, the faster the data can be transferred. Less bandwidth means more time must be taken to download a file. Bandwidth is dependent on many factors; for example, download time is affected by the activities of people who share connections. More traffic means less bandwidth and results in a longer wait time for Web page requests.

To understand this scenario better, think of bandwidth as a highway or road, and think of the packets traveling across the wire as vehicles on that road. When traffic is light, you are able to get to your destination much faster because there is more room to travel (larger bandwidth). Increased traffic lowers the amount of space available for traveling, or the bandwidth, thus slowing down the process. Bandwidth is a direct result of how a computer is connected to the Internet. A computer connecting to the Internet with a 56K modem will have a smaller bandwidth than one connecting with a T3 line.

You have few options when trying to optimize your bandwidth because the amount of traffic accessing the Web server and the user connection speed is out of your control. You also may have no input regarding the speed of your network connections. As the Web designer, however, you can control the file size. The smaller the file size, the more quickly it is transferred. A larger bandwidth can transfer larger files in a reasonable amount of time, but large files are not transferred as quickly over a smaller bandwidth. HTML files are small, but the graphics files that you insert into them are generally big, increasing the overall size of your Web page.

When you design your Web page, you must take into account the users who will be connecting at lower bandwidth levels. You may need to limit the number of graphics to assure a positive Web browsing experience for everyone who visits your site. Software tools, such as Adobe ImageReady and Macromedia Fireworks, can help decrease graphics file size.

Calculating approximate download time

You can estimate approximate download time by dividing the total size of your Web page by the speed of your network.

You must remember that the Web page file size includes the HTML file and all other associated files — graphics, programs, etc. The number that you use to represent your network speed is an estimate based on connection speeds. For some examples of network connection speeds, refer to Table 8-2 below. Please note that, in reality, the connection speeds will probably be slower than the optimum speed shown in Table 8-2.

Table 8-2
Common Connection Speeds

Speed	Method of Connecting to the Internet
28.8 Kbps	Very Slow Modem Speed
33.6 Kbps	Slow Modem Speed
56 Kbps	Popular Modem Speed
960 Kbps	High Speed DSL connection
1.544 Mbps	Full T1 internet connection

File size is measured in kilobytes, while bandwidth is measured in kilobits or megabits. Bits and bytes are not the same. Before you can do a calculation using file size and connection speed, you must know how to convert them into the same unit, either bytes or bits, as shown in Table 8-3.

Table 8-3
Conversion Chart

Unit	Equivalent
1 bit	Smallest unit of data, either a 1 or a 0
1 kilobit	1,000 bits
1 megabit	1,000,000 bits
1 byte	8 bits
1 kilobyte	1024 bytes
1 megabyte	1024 kilobytes

After you have converted the speed of the network or file size, you are ready to calculate the download time of your file.

To calculate Web page download time, use the following steps:

1. Find the total Web page size. Add your HTML file size to the sizes of all other associated files. For example, suppose that you have an HTML file that contains text and uses pictures that are stored in an individual image file. If the HTML file is 4 kilobytes, and the associated images files is 90 kilobytes, then the total Web page size is 94 kilobytes.

2. Find the network or modem speed. For this example, assume that the file will be downloaded using a 56Kbps modem.

3. Convert the file size and network speed to a common unit.

   In Step 1, you calculated the size of your file in kilobytes. Your modem speed, however, is listed as 56 kilobits per second (not kilobytes). In order to figure out the transfer time, you must convert both of these values to a common unit. For this example, convert everything to bits. The modem speed is 56Kbps, which is equal to 56,000 bits. The file size is 94 kilobytes; to convert this to bits, simply multiply the file size by 1024 to determine total number of bytes (94*1024 = 96,256). Multiply the total number of bytes by 8 to determine the total number of bits (96,256 bytes = 770,048 bits).

Exam Tip   A kilobyte is approximately 1000 bytes. If you use this number instead of 1024, the calculation will be easier and the final result should be very close to the correct answer.

4. Calculate the connection speed (file size/modem speed). Divide the file size of 770,048 bits by the connection speed of 56,000 bps to get a result of 13.75 seconds.

The calculation that you just performed is meant to be used as an estimate. Even though a modem may be rated at a certain speed, such as 56Kbps, seldom does the connection actually approach that speed. Network traffic and other variables cause computers and network connections to operate at speeds slower than the optimum. It is very likely that a person using this modem will have to wait even longer than the calculated time for this page to download. A good rule of thumb is to keep any Web page and its associated files no larger than 100KB. The best way to determine the download time to a 56Kbps modem is to actually download an item by using a 56Kbps modem and a stopwatch.

Exam Tip   You should know how to calculate download times by dividing file size by modem speed.

Naming your Web file

Always check with your Internet Service Provider (ISP) before naming your HTML file for the first time. Web development is performed on your local computer, and when you are ready to publish, the page is uploaded onto a Web server. Filenames that work on your desktop computer when you create your page won't necessarily work on a Web server, and filename restrictions differ slightly among the various Web servers. Here are some key things to remember when naming the Web file.

✦ **Be descriptive yet concise.** Most network operating systems support long filenames; in other words, you can give your file almost any descriptive name. However, strive to be as concise as possible. Avoid cryptic names, but don't make your filename 255 characters.

✦ **Include extensions.** Your file must have an extension, usually the extension.htm or .html. Macintosh operating systems typically require four-letter extensions, whereas Windows and UNIX require three-letter extensions. Java Script files have .jsp extensions. You can also place .pdf files onto Web sites. Check with your Web server administrator to determine the right extension for you.

✦ **Use lowercase filenames.** Most Internet users expect lowercase filenames, and UNIX servers distinguish between cases. Users who access a file from this type of server must remember which letters are capitalized if a combination of uppercase and lowercase letters are used. For example, if you ask someone to visit your URL called `www.ashley.org/MYWEBPAGES`, the users must request the file with the capital letters. If a user requests `www.ashley.org/mypages`, he or she will receive an error message stating that "the Web page could not be found."

The home page is typically the first page that people see when they visit a site. Typing a Web server's name redirects you to that server's home page. For example, if you go to the W3C Web site by typing `www.w3c.com` in the address bar of your browser, you will be presented with W3C's home page. The actual document that produces this page is usually saved with a name that the server recognizes as a home page name. For example, Microsoft's IIS Web server looks for a file called `default.htm`, while Apache Web servers look for a file called `index.html`. These are the default filenames. The administrator, however, can change these. Ask your Web server administrator which default document name you should use.

The following are common default page names:

✦ Home

✦ Index

✦ Welcome

✦ Default

They may have any of the following extensions:

✦ htm

✦ html

✦ asp

✦ jsp

Key Point Summary

The following is a summary of the key points in this chapter:

✦ Web authoring software falls into one of two categories: text and GUI editors.

✦ Text editors

  • Must enter HTML manually into your file

  • Require a knowledge of HTML

  • Must open the file in a browser to see how it will look

✦ GUI editors

  • Allow you to design a Web page using a GUI WYSIWYG interface

  • Allow you to create an HTML file with little or no knowledge of HTML

✦ HTML is an authoring language used to create Web pages.

✦ HTML is made up of content and tags.

✦ Tags are instructions for document structure and formatting.

✦ W3C publishes recommendation models for the Web community to follow.

✦ W3C provides a guide to the various versions and flavors of HTML.

✦ HTML 2.0 was the first HTML version to be widely used and became the basis for core HTML features used today.

✦ HTML 3.2

  • Backwards-compatible with HTML 2.0

  • Added futures included incorporation of small programs (applets), tables, and text flow around images.

✦ HTML 4.0/4.01

  • Allows for additional scripting languages

  • Includes multimedia options

  • Includes style sheets

  • Improved printing

  • HTML 4.01 mainly repaired HTML 4.0 bugs that caused browsers to crash

✦ The three HTML varieties are Strict, Frameset, and Transitional.

✦ HTML 4.01 Strict

  • Uses cascading style sheets

  • No depreciated tags allowed

  • Only the browsers are able to interpret this variety correctly

✦ HTML 4.01 Frameset

- Supports more tags than transitional—uses all tags from HTML 3.2

- Used for Web pages that use frames

- Divides Web documents into two or more sections

- Includes features like banners and sidebars

✦ HTML 4.01 Transitional

- Interpreted by almost every browser

- May use depreciated tags

✦ XHTML

- Will gradually replace HTML

- A language built from XML and HTML

- Can be used by alternative browsing platforms, such as PDAs

- Comprised of tags and content

- Allows you to create your own tags, thereby "extending" the language

✦ Front-end issues or design elements that affect your interface include:

- Graphics and images

- Content

- Tables

- Forms

- Links

- Image maps

✦ Creative design and branding standards define consistency in the presentation of a company or organization's image.

✦ Creative design and branding standards elements include font style, colors, and logo.

✦ Words, phrases, or jingles that help the public identify a product or company are referred to as *mind share*.

✦ Download time is the length of time it takes for a Web page to load onto a computer.

✦ Download time is dependent on bandwidth and file size.

✦ Download time can be calculated by dividing the total size of your Web page by the speed of your network.

✦ Bandwidth is the speed at which data travels over a network connection in a set amount of time, usually measured in bits per second (bps).

✦ The greater the bandwidth, the faster the data can be transferred.

✦ Bandwidth is dependent on network traffic and the type of network connection.

✦ Limit graphics to cut Web file size.

✦ Keep the size of the Web page and its associated files to no more than 100 kilobytes.

✦ Always check with your ISP before naming your HTML file for the first time.

✦ The home page is the first page that people see when they visit a site.

✦ Examples of default home page file names include home, index, welcome, and default.

✦ Common Web page file name extensions include .htm, .html, jsp (Java server page), and .asp (active server page).

✦   ✦   ✦

STUDY GUIDE

This chapter covers basic concepts of Web page authoring. The following questions will test your understanding of these concepts. The answers to these questions are found at the end of the chapter.

Assessment Questions

1. Web authoring standards are controlled by

  A. The American Government

  B. W3C

  C. Microsoft and IBM

  D. Web languages council

2. Which HTML variety requires the use of style sheets?

  A. Strict

  B. Transitional

  C. Frameset

  D. Loose

3. In HTML 4.01, _____ lets you incorporate elements such as banners, sideboards, and tables of content.

4. In HTML 4.01 Transitional you are allowed to use which of the following?

  A. Depreciated tags

  B. Style sheets

  C. Frames

  D. Dynamic HTML

5. True or False: Text editors can't be used to create frames.

6. True or False: HTML 4.0 is the latest published Internet standard.

7. Which of the following are true about HTML Strict? (Choose all that apply)

    A. Uses depreciated tags

    B. Is successfully interpreted by most browsers

    C. Uses cascading style sheets

    D. Of all the varieties, HTML strict gives the most control over the design and appearance of the document

8. Which of the following are meta-languages? (Choose all that apply)

    A. HTML

    B. XHTML

    C. XML

    D. SGML

9. Which one of the following is a reason for avoiding HTML GUI editors?

    A. Difficult to use

    B. They don't keep up with new HTML tags

    C. Manual tag editing is not allowed

    D. They don't allow depreciated tags

10. Hand-held devices and other alternative browsers are able to read pages created with which of the following languages?

    A. XML

    B. HTML

    C. XHTML

    D. WML

11. If Ashley wants to use CSS exclusively to define her HTML page, she should use HTML _____.

12. Which of the following are both back-end and front-end issues?

    A. Content

    B. Tables

    C. Graphics and Images

    D. Links

13. Ideally, your Web page should be no larger than

    A. 50 Kilobytes

    B. 100 Kilobytes

    C. 150 Kilobytes

    D. One megabyte

    E. None of the above

14. Your HTML page and its associated files have a combined size of 110 kilobytes. Approximately how long will it take to download these files with a 56Kbps modem?

    A. One second

    B. 16 seconds

    C. 27 seconds

    D. 2.7 minutes

    E. 27 minutes

15. Which of the following could be default filenames for your homepage?

    A. home.html

    B. welcome.htm

    C. Ashley.html

    D. index.asp

    E. default.jsp

    F. None of the above

    G. All of the above

Scenario

Simple Simon School of Humor and Hilarity (SSSHH) is a clown school that graduates 100 certified clowns each year. The school has 35 staff members and approximately 200 students. Sandy Spinach, SSSHH's executive director wants to "raise its profile" and recruit more students. To this end, Sandy decides SSSHH should develop its own Web site.

The goals for this Web site follow:

✦ Advertise courses and prices.

✦ Provide information about the atmosphere and uniqueness of the school.

✦ Highlight backgrounds of star instructors.

✦ Provide links to clown support sites and humor databases.

✦ Allow all internal employees and students to access class schedule information via their Web browsers.

Due to budget limitations, staff member Harry Peaches, one of the computer-savvy clown instructors, is recruited to design the Web site.

With the aid of a GUI editor, Harry creates the Web site incorporating sounds, pictures, and even animation. After he finishes, he asks staff members to test his Web site and provide feedback on their experiences. To his delight, most staff members give his Web site excellent reviews. Harry is so excited, he calls Sandy at home to tell her the site is ready. Sandy immediately sits down at her computer and connects to the Web site. Unfortunately, Sandy's experience is not as rewarding as it was for other staff members.

First, Sandy waits a long time for the Web page to appear on her screen. After it fully appears, she finds that she has to scroll up and down and right to left to see everything on the page. Some graphics elements don't look right and others don't appear at all.

The following is a complete list of Sandy's Web site concerns:

✦ The download time from home is slow.

✦ Colors and graphics don't reflect the atmosphere of the school.

✦ Many links don't function properly, and often go nowhere.

✦ The Web site looks good with one of the major browsers, but does not display properly in another.

✦ Clowns are not able to access the site with their cell phones, PDAs, and other wireless devices capable of accessing the Web.

✦ Some of the board of directors thought that the school colors and logo should have been incorporated.

Using the information you learned in this chapter, answer the following questions:

1. What are some of the front-end planning issues that should have been considered so that the personality of the school was truly captured on the Web site?

2. What is the likely reason for the slow download times for people accessing the Web site from home?

3. What languages other than HTML should have been considered in the creation of the Web site to make it possible for people to obtain information through their PDAs and other hand-held devices?

4. Basil's home page and associated files are 150 kb in size. How long will it take for a computer with a 56K modem to download this page?

5. What is a simple testing technique that Harry could have employed to ensure that his Web site was compatible with all common browsers?

6. Marie, another SSSHH employee, has been using the same Internet browser for the past five years. When she views the Web page, her browser can't read the Web site properly. What variety of HTML did Harry probably use to create the site?

Answers to Chapter Questions

Chapter Pre-Test

1. Using a **GUI** editor you can create Web pages without typing HTML code.

2. If you use a **text** editor, you must manually type HTML tags into your Web document.

3. Often referred to as "the language of the Web," **HTML** is used to create Web pages.

4. HTML Strict uses cascading style sheets and no depreciated tags.

5. The HTML flavor that allows frames in a Web page is called HTML Frameset.

6. HTML is a subset of SGML.

7. False. Content, tables and forms are examples of front-end issues.

8. It would take approximately 16 seconds to download a 110 kb file over a 56Kbps modem connection.

9. XHTML is based on HTML and XML.

10. "HTTP 404 File not found" is the error that you see when the file you request is not on the Web server.

Answers to Assessment Questions

1. Web authoring standards are controlled by

   D. W3C

2. Which HTML variety requires the use of style sheets?

   A. Strict

3. HTML 4.01 Frameset lets you incorporate elements such as banners, sideboards, and tables of content.

4. In HTML 4.01 Transitional, you are allowed to use which of the following?

   A. Depreciated tags

   B. Style sheets

5. **False.** Text editors can be used to create frames. It is just more difficult than using a GUI editor.

6. **False.** HTML 4.01 is the latest published Internet standard.

7. Which of the following are true about HTML strict?

   C. HTML strict uses cascading style sheets.

8. Which of the following are meta-languages?

   B. XHTML

   C. XML

   D. SGML

9. Which one of the following is a reason for avoiding HTML GUI editors?

   B. They don't keep up with new HTML tags.

10. Hand-held devices and other alternative browsers are able to read pages created with which of the following languages?

    A. XML

    C. XHTML

11. If Ashley wants to use CSS exclusively to define her HTML page, she should use HTML **Strict**.

12. Which of the following are both back-end and front-end issues?

    C. Graphics and Images

13. Ideally, your Web page should be no larger than

    B. 100 Kilobytes

14. Your HTML page and its associated files have a combined size of 110 kilobytes. Approximately how long will it take to download these files with a 56Kbps modem?

    B. 16 seconds

15. Which of the following could be default filenames for your homepage?

    A. home.html

    B. welcome.htm

    D. index.asp

    E. default.jsp

Answers to Scenario Questions

1. Basil should have considered the school's branding standards, such as the use of the school logo, school colors, and perhaps a motto.

2. The slow download times are likely due to the size of the files being downloaded across the dialup lines.

3. XML or XHTML can be supported over PDAs and other hand-held devices.

4. It will take approximately 22 seconds to download 150 kb worth of files over a 56Kbps connection.

5. Basil should have tested the Web page in a variety of different browsers.

6. Basil likely used HTML 4.01 Frameset, which is not supported by older browsers.

Resources

The following are suggested additional resources for Web authoring fundamentals:

✦ W3C — World Wide Web Consortium Web site: www.w3c.org

✦ Internet Development Resource Center:
www.wayoutthere.com/idrc/resources

✦ Marchel Benoit, *XML By Example*, Que Books. 2001

✦ The World Wide Web: A short personal history by Tim Berners-Lee:
www.w3.org/people/Berners-Lee/ShortHistory.html

HTML Basics

◆ ◆ ◆ ◆

EXAM OBJECTIVES

1. Identify HTML document structure tags.

2. Explain the <META> tag and the Document Type Declaration (DTD).

3. Apply proper HTML tag usage.

4. Create simple HTML pages.

5. Format paragraphs and text with HTML tags.

6. Add horizontal rules to your Web pages and work with horizontal rule attributes.

7. Incorporate image files as standalone graphics.

8. Use the Web-safe color palette.

9. Change the page background color.

10. Use a tiled image across the page background.

CHAPTER PRE-TEST

1. Tags that work in pairs are called _____ tags. Instruction tags that don't need a closing tag are called _____ tags.

2. What are the three main document structure tags?

3. The _____ tag gives information about a particular Web page. It tells what the page is about, who wrote it, and when the page was last updated. It is what search engines look for and read.

4. The _____ tag is optional in HTML; it describes the version and the flavor of HTML being used in a particular document.

5. A _____ level element affects one or more paragraphs, whereas a _____ level element affects sentences, words, or characters.

6. How many heading styles or levels can you choose from?

7. What code adds horizontal rules to your Web pages?

8. The tag that makes text appear in the title bar of the browser is the _____ tag.

9. The _____ text elements are meant to describe structure and not just formatting of a character, whereas the _____ text elements describe the way text is formatted with no connection to structural meaning.

10. What attribute should always be included with the IMG (image tag) to compensate for text-only browsers?

11. Name the three image file formats that are suitable for Web pages?

12. The tag and attribute to change background color is _____?

13. The 216 colors that are rendered correctly across multiple browsing platforms are taken from the _____.

✦ Answers to these questions can be found at the end of the chapter. ✦

E ven if you don't intend to author Web pages, you will benefit from knowing how HTML works. After all, it is the language behind most Web documents. HTML has evolved and changed; with new tags, style sheets, and depreciated tags, even seasoned Web authors can be confused. Despite the dynamics, however, certain rules continue to prevail. All Web pages and tags have a precise consistent structure, and specific tags must be present in every HTML document because without them, a browser can't render a document successfully. This chapter examines structure tags, and tag elements, attributes, and values. This chapter also explores the differences between container tags and empty tags. By the end of this chapter, you will understand how to build a basic HTML Web page with body text, headings, graphics, and color enhancements.

HTML Tag Construction

 Objective   Apply proper HTML tag usage.

HTML is comprised of text and tags. Tags are often referred to as code, and give instructions to browsers or other interpreters. Tags are comprised of a *text command* that is located between *angled brackets* (< >), also known as *wickets*. The role of angled brackets is to specify the way content within a document should be displayed. The angled brackets separate commands from the actual content of the Web page. The following code is an example of content and code:

```
<tag name> Content - The words the browser displays </tag name>
```

The previous code is an example of an HTML element. Elements typically consist of three parts: a *start tag*, also referred to as an *opening tag*, content, and an *end tag*, also referred to as a *closing tag*. Your entire HTML file consists of a series of page elements. The tags themselves are not elements, but rather serve to describe or define the elements, as shown in Figure 9-1.

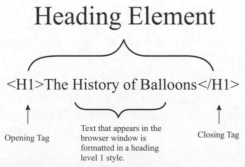

Figure 9-1: Elements and tags

The element shown in Figure 9-1 is put together like a sandwich; the tags, or bread, contain the text, or meat, of the element. The first unit is a heading tag <H1>. The element's initial tag, or opening tag, represents the beginning of the element. The content to be displayed by a browser comes next, followed by a closing tag, which denotes the end of the element. A closing tag always has a forward slash character, </ tag name>, before the tag name.

Caution   Some books and individuals confuse the terms *elements* and *tags*, but they are not the same thing. Tags are part of an element. Although an element typically consists of an opening tag, content, and a closing tag, some elements, such as the HEAD element, is always present — even when the opening and closing HEAD tags are omitted in the source code.

Tags come in two basic categories: container tags and empty tags. *Container tags* work in pairs; they have an opening tag at the beginning of the element and a closing tag at the end of the element, as shown in Figure 9-1. The opening tag starts an instruction and the closing tag stops the instruction. For example, an opening tag may instruct a browser to begin bolding the text that follows. The corresponding closing tag instructs the browser to stop bolding text.

Empty tags are opening tags that don't have a corresponding closing tag. The line break tag <BR>, the list tag <LI>, and the horizontal line tag <HR>, are examples of empty tags. You will see examples of empty tags as you work through this chapter. Figure 9-2 shows examples of container tags and empty tags.

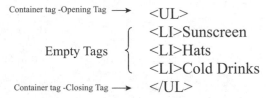

Figure 9-2: Container tags and empty tags

The unordered list tag <UL>, shown in Figure 9-2, is an example of a container tag that contains other tag elements. The list tags <LI>, also in Figure 9-2, is an example of an empty tag. As you can see from this example, elements can reside within other elements. Although container tags comprise most of the elements in HTML documents, empty tags can also represent elements.

Some tags are meant to be container tags and some are meant to be empty tags. If you examine the source code of some HTML documents, you will see some authors omit closing tags of certain HTML element tags that are, in fact, container tags. For example, browsers can correctly read the </P> paragraph without its closing tag.

Leaving out closing tags is not recommended — even though most browsers compensate for their absence. Many browsers, however, predict XHTML, which will replace HTML as the recognized W3C standard. XHTML demands closing tags, and newer browsers built to work with XHTML may not compensate for sloppy coding. Get into the habit of closing your elements properly so you won't have to go back and update them.

Attributes and Values

Tags may consist of more than wickets (< >) with an element label — they may also consist of attributes and values. An *attribute* indicates or identifies a specific characteristic about the element, while the *value* precisely defines a characteristic. Whenever elements and attributes are included in tags, they are structured in the following format: tag name, then attribute name, followed by an equal sign with the value enclosed by quotation marks.

```
<TAGNAME ATTRIBUTE NAME="value">
```

For example:

```
<HTML LANG="en">
```

This code example shows the LANG element attribute of the HTML tag. The attribute LANG states *language* as the element's characteristic to be defined, and the "en" value specifies *English* as the language of this document. The value doesn't have to be English; it could be French or German or whatever language you choose to write in. Throughout this chapter, you will see many examples of tags using elements and attributes.

Exam Tip   You must know how the element name, the attribute, and the value differ, and the correct coding syntax for all three.

CIW courseware and exam questions are based on the W3C HTML 4.01 specifications. The W3C Web site recommends that element names be typed in uppercase letters, and that attribute names be typed in lowercase letters to enhance readability. The CIW courseware presents both the element and the attribute in uppercase letters because CIW feels this way of presenting the code draws more attention to attribute names, making it easier to discuss them. The goal of this book is to help you pass the CIW exam, so all the code is in accordance with CIW courseware.

In the Real World   If you decide to code in XHTML, you must type both the attribute and the element name in lowercase letters.

Document Structure Tags

 Identify HTML document structure tags.

Apply proper HTML tag usage.

All HTML documents require three document structure tags: HTML, HEAD, and BODY. These structure tags provide the basic foundation for the Web document; they are containers for the rest of the tags. HTML tags are a subset of SGML, and as a result, most tags have contextual significance attached to them. Emphasis is placed on defining structure, not text formatting. The following is a simple example of HTML code using document structure tags:

```
<HTML>
  <HEAD>
          <TITLE>Sample document</TITLE>
  </HEAD>
<BODY>
<P>This is an example of a web document. The three document
structure tags: HTML, HEAD, and BODY used in the construction
of this file are all container tags.</P>
</BODY>
</HTML>
```

The three HTML structure tags, <HTML>, <HEAD>, and <BODY>, all hold other tag elements. The <HTML> opening tag is placed at the beginning of the document, and the </HTML> closing tag is placed at the very end of the document. Therefore, the HTML tag contains all the tags of the Web page and is hierarchically placed at the topmost tag level. Your HTML file is made up of two main parts: the HEAD and the BODY. The HEAD and BODY tags serve as containers for the rest of the tags that comprise an HTML file.

Certain rules must be followed when placing tags within tags. The following is an example of correct tag placement order:

```
<BODY><P>This is my paragraph</P></BODY>
```

Note that in the preceding code, both opening and closing body tags appear outside the paragraph tags. Proper coding should not mix the order of tags. The following is an example of what not to do:

```
<BODY><P>This is my paragraph</BODY></P>
```

The preceding example has not kept the paragraph tag contained within the body container tag. Sloppy coding can cause errors in browsers and will create more work for you later.

<HTML>

The opening and closing tags (<HTML> and </HTML>) hold all the tags of your document. Technically, the <HTML> tag is optional if you use the DTD, which specifies the HTML version. The language attribute of this tag helps browsers to find appropriate pages. Using the language attribute (lang), you can identify the language that the HTML document is written in, as shown in the following example:

```
<HTML lang="en">
```

This example specifies English as the language of the document.

<HEAD>

The <HEAD> tag describes facts about the document. Search engines (not people) read most of the information found in this tag. The title tags and META tags reside within the Header tags. You should always include a title tag in your HTML file. The text that appears between the title tags is displayed on the title bar of your browser. To see how the following code will look in a browser, see Figure 9-3.

```
<HTML>
  <HEAD>
        <TITLE>Sample document</TITLE>
  </HEAD>
<BODY>
<P>This is an example of a Web document. The three document
structure tags: HTML, HEAD, and BODY used in the construction
of this file are all container tags.</P>
</BODY>
</HTML>
```

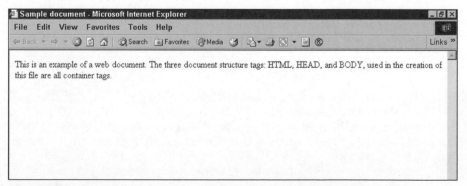

Figure 9-3: The result of using the <Title> and </Title> tags is shown here. Notice the words "Sample document" shown in the Title bar of this window.

Note that in the preceding figure, the text in the title bar of the browser matches the text within the title tags of the HTML code.

<BODY>

The BODY element encases all the information that will be read by people visiting your Web site. It holds the content that is displayed in the browser and most of the tag elements. Some of the many elements found within the BODY tag will be discussed throughout this chapter.

Document Type Declaration Tag – DTD

Explain the <META> tag and the Document Type Declaration (DTD).

The Document Type Declaration (DTD) tag is an SGML statement that describes the markup language used to create the document so that it may be interpreted correctly. DTD is typically the first tag you see in an HTML file, and does not necessarily appear in every document published on the Web. Although it is possible for an HTML document to be rendered without the <!DOCTYPE> tag, thus making it optional, it's best to include this tag because omitting it may cause problems. The absence of this tag may restrict the use of advanced browser features, and this tag is essential if you are using a validator to test for coding inaccuracies.

For more information about validators, see Chapter 8.

The purpose of the DTD is strictly to inform. This tag specifies the version and flavor of the markup language that is used in a particular document. The following is an example of a DTD tag:

```
<DOCTYPE HTML PUBLIC "-//W3C//DTD HTML 4.01 Transitional//EN"
    "http://www.w3.org/TR/html4/loose.dtd>
```

The first part of the DTD is the tag name information. All DTDs begin with `<!DOCTYPE HTML PUBLIC "-W3C//DTD`. The next section of the DTD gives information about the markup language that is used to create the document. The preceding code example shows that the markup language used was HTML 4.01, Transitional flavor. The next section of the DTD is optional; the EN states that the Web page is created in English. This language information helps search engines find pages in the appropriate language. Different letter symbols represent each language; for example, FR represents the French language.

A list of document declaration tags appears in Table 9-1.

Table 9-1
Document Declaration Tags

Markup Language	Corresponding DTD
HTML 4.01 Transitional	<!DOCTYPE HTML PUBLIC" -//W3C//DTD HTML 4.01 Transitional//EN" "http://www.W3C.org/TR/html4/loose.dtd">
HTML 4.01 Strict	<!DOCTYPE HTML PUBLIC" -//W3C//DTD HTML 4.01 Strict//EN" "http://wwwlw3.org/TR/html4/strict.dtd">
HTML 4.01 Frameset	<!DOCTYPE HTML PUBLIC" -//W3C//DTD HTML 4.01 Frameset//EN" "http://wwwlw3.org/TR/html4/frameset.dtd">
HTML 3.2	<!DOCTYPE HTML PUBLIC "-//W3C//DTD HTML 3.2 Final//EN">
HTML 2.0	<!DOCTYPE HTML PUBLIC "-//W3C//DTD HTML 2.0//EN">
XHTML transitional	<!DOCTYPE HTML PUBLIC "-//W3C//DTD XHTML 1.0 Transitional//EN" "http://www.w3.org/TR/xhtml1/DTD/xhtml-transitional.dtd">
XHTML Strict	<!DOCTYPE HTML PUBLIC "-//W3C//DTD XHTML 1.0 Strict//EN" "http://www.w3.org/TR/xhtml1/DTD/xhtml-strict.dtd">
XHTML Frameset	<!DOCTYPE HTML PUBLIC "-//W3C//DTD XHTML 1.0 Frameset//EN" "http://www.w3.org/TR/xhtml1/DTD/xhtml-frameset.dtd">

Using a DTD enhances the page's capability to perform with a browser. Although this tag is not present in all documents, it is typically the first tag you see in the Web document coding.

META tag

The purpose of the META tag is to provide information about your Web site. This tag is optional, but when used correctly, it can be extremely useful. META tags are different from most HTML tags. For example, they don't give instructions to browsers; instead, they describe the HTML document for search engines. Search engine Spider Programs scan META tags of Web sites as they look for appropriate URLs for search requests. The information that you place in your META tag can increase the chances of your site being found by search engines and accessed by users.

META tags can include the following:

✦ Keywords that describe your Web page

✦ A brief synopsis of the page's subject matter

✦ Information about you as the author

✦ Instructions for refreshing the page

The META tag is always contained between the <HEAD></HEAD> container tags. The following is an example of a META tag showing the subject of the file by listing *descriptive words* within the tag.

```
<META NAME="Keywords" CONTENT="Internet, History, Tim Berners
Lee, HTML">
```

The next example shows a META tag describing the subject of a Web page using *sentences*. When you use a META tag this way, you must be descriptive yet brief.

```
<META NAME="Description" CONTENT="This page recounts the
History of the World Wide Web with emphasis on the evolution of
HTML and contributions made by Tim Berners Lee.">
```

The following example shows how to identify the Web author within your META tag:

```
<META NAME="Author" CONTENT="Keith Olsen">
```

When using the META tag to refresh your page automatically, you must include the number of seconds after which your page should be refreshed, and the URL of your Web site, as shown in the following sample code:

```
<META HTTP-EQUIV="Refresh" Content="8;
URL=http://www.typeyourhostnamehere.com>
```

META tags provide a means for you, the author, to have some control over how your Web page is accessed. Tapping into the true power of META tags goes beyond the scope of the CIW Foundations course and exam and this book. Numerous Web sites and books are available that can provide excellent information of how to use this valuable mechanism effectively. Table 9-2 provides a summary list of tags that provide structure to HTML documents.

Table 9-2
Document Structure Tags

Tag Name	Description
BODY	Container tags for the document. Includes all the text.
DTD Document Type Declaration	Located at the beginning of the document. Describes version and flavor or HTML or XHTML used in creation of the document.
HEAD	Designates one of the main parts of the document, referred to as the HEAD. This section contains the Title tag and the META tags.
HTML	Describes document type.
TITLE	Container tag that displays the text in the title bar of the browser. This text describes what the document is about. Usually concise and descriptive.
META	Optional tag that contains information about the Web page that search engines will read.

The three main structure tags are HTML, HEAD, and BODY. The TITLE tags, META tags, and DTD tags have also been included in this table; their main purpose is communication with browsers and search engines to describe the entire document, and not specific text elements.

Style Elements

 Apply proper HTML tag usage.

Create simple HTML pages.

Format paragraphs and text with HTML tags.

Armed with the tags examined prior to this point in the chapter, you could create a Web file, but your file wouldn't be aesthetically pleasing. For example, text is more meaningful and easier to follow when it is broken into paragraphs, headings, and lists. This section focuses on two types of element style: block-level elements, which affect one or more paragraphs, and text-level elements, which affect units smaller than a paragraph, such as sentences, words, or characters.

Web authoring is unlike the grammatically correct paragraphs you learned about in grade school. Paragraphs in Web authoring can be as short as one word; for example, a heading is considered a paragraph. A new paragraph is represented by a paragraph break that occurs automatically with a tag. The paragraph tags, <P> and </P>, and Headings tags are examples of block-level elements. Both are container tags and both come with automatic breaks after the closing tag.

Block-level structure elements

When you use tags that designate text as headings or paragraphs, you are designing for structure—not formatting. Text enclosed by paragraph tags will be rendered as a paragraph within the browser, but the way that the paragraph is formatted is beyond your control. The browser will designate the font size, type, and line spacing. The same situation is true for heading tags. When text is tagged at a certain heading level, it will appear that way, but the browser decides the formatting applied—not you. If you have been accustomed to working with word processors, this concept may seem bizarre. To truly understand block elements, you must be aware of the contextual information attached to these tags.

Heading tags

Most Web pages contain at least one heading. In HTML, you may have up to six different heading levels. Heading designation Level 1 has the most important rank, and Heading designation Level 6 has the least important rank. The following is the syntax for the various heading levels:

```
<H1>The text for your Heading goes here</H1>
```

As you can see, the heading tag is a container tag, and as such, has both an opening and closing tag. The preceding code example shows text that will be formatted at the highest heading level. This means that the formatting of the text will have more emphasis than the formatting of text at Levels 2 through 6. Table 9-3 shows all heading tags, and Figure 9-4 shows how these heading levels appear in a browser.

Table 9-3 Heading Tags		
Heading Level	*Tags*	
Heading Level 1	<H1>	</H1>
Heading Level 2	<H2>	</H2>
Heading Level 3	<H3>	</H3>
Heading Level 4	<H4>	</H4>
Heading Level 5	<H5>	</H5>
Heading Level 6	<H6>	</H6>

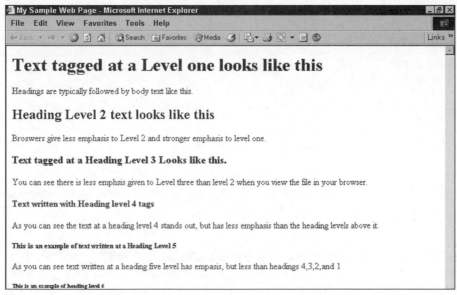

Figure 9-4: Text within heading tags as displayed by a browser

As Figure 9-4 demonstrates, the headings are formatted hierarchically. The most important heading, labelled H1, appears bigger and bolder than the other heading levels and the body text. Note the paragraph breaks that occur automatically at the end of each heading element. Although the interpreter controls how the text appears when it is displayed, the formatting will always be consistent with the structural meaning of the text.

The paragraph tag <P>

Written text is typically divided into paragraphs and does not appear as one big long block. To divide your text into basic paragraphs, use the paragraph container tags <P> and </P>. Originally, this element was a one-sided tag, and as such, you could omit the paragraph closing tag from your code (although not recommended) and it would still work. However, the exercises in the CIW courseware treat this tag as a container tag and XHTML requires both opening and closing tags for this element. The newer browsers created to work with XHTML may also treat this tag as a container tag. Therefore, in order to prevent having to redo code for new browsers, it is best to get into the habit of using both the opening and closing tags for this command.

The following code does not have paragraph tags. Look at the text between the <BODY> tags and then examine Figure 9-5 to see how the text is displayed in the browser.

```
<!DOCTYPE HTML PUBLIC "-//W3C//DTD HTML 4.01 Transitional//EN"
"http:/www.w3.org/TR/html4/loose.dtd">
<HTML>
<HEAD>
<TITLE>My Sample Web Page</TITLE>
</HEAD>
<BODY>
This is an example of a paragraph typed into a Web page.
Ideally you need to have paragraph codes to divide your text
into different paragraphs. Simply pressing the enter key
doesn't work to separate paragraphs into different sentences

Look at the following screen shot to see how this file looks
without using the correct code.
</BODY>
</HTML>
```

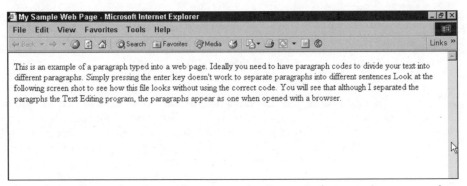

Figure 9-5: The results of not using <P> and </P> tags when creating paragraphs. Notice how both paragraphs appear as one.

Note that in the text file showing HTML code, a hard return separates paragraphs; within the browser, however, no distinction is made between the two paragraphs that are present. You can't separate the blocks of text into two paragraphs by pressing the Enter key, either. To display your text properly, you need to use the <P> and </P> tags. The following code is similar to the previous code, except that it has used the paragraph tags to separate paragraph blocks.

```
<!DOCTYPE HTML PUBLIC "-//W3C//DTD HTML 4.01 Transitional//EN"
"http:/www.w3.org/TR/html4/loose.dtd">
<HTML>
<HEAD>
<TITLE>My Sample Web Page</TITLE>
</HEAD>
<BODY>
<P>
```

```
This is an example of a paragraph typed into a Web page.
Ideally you need to have paragraph codes to divide your text
into different paragraphs. Simply pressing the enter key
doesn't work to separate paragraphs into different sentences
</P>
<P>
Look at the following screen shot to see how this file looks
without using the correct code. You will see that although I
created separate paragraphs in the text editing program, the
paragraphs appear as one when opened with a browser.
</P>
</BODY>
</HTML>
```

Compare the code to the browser display shown in Figure 9-6, and pay particular attention to the <P> tags; note that these tags divide the text into paragraphs.

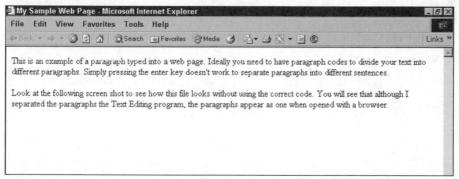

Figure 9-6: The result of using the <P> and </P> tags to separate paragraphs. Notice the two paragraphs do in fact show as two distinct paragraphs.

The line break tag

The <BR> tag creates breaks within the structure of the text, by inserting a line break. A line break appears wherever this tag is placed. Look at the following code and note the <BR> tag.

```
<!DOCTYPE HTML PUBLIC "-//W3C//DTD HTML 4.01 Transitional//EN"
"http:/www.w3.org/TR/html4/loose.dtd">
<HTML>
<HEAD>
<TITLE>My Sample Web Page</TITLE>
</HEAD>
<BODY>
<P>
This is the first line,<BR>
```

```
and this is the second line.
</P>
<P>This is another paragraph within the document. There is no
line break in this paragraph. Notice the difference? There is
more space between paragraph breaks than between line breaks. A
line break simply brings text to the next line while a
paragraph break separates block of text. It makes a structural
distinction between paragraphs.
</BODY>
</HTML>
```

Figure 9-7 shows a line break that has been inserted wherever the <BR> code was placed in the text file. This tag changes the structure of the text block by inserting a line break. It is a depreciated (older) tag, but is still used with HTML 4.01 transitional coding.

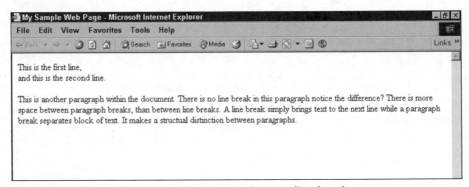

Figure 9-7: The result of using the <BR> to insert a line break

Exam Tip   Be sure you understand the differences between paragraph breaks and line breaks.

The <PRE> tag

Up to this point in the chapter, the paragraph, heading, and line break tags have been used to change the placement of text. In previous examples, you saw that spaces created by pressing the Enter key or the spacebar more than one time don't get displayed when your file is opened in a browser. However, you can gain some flexibility over where text is placed in your browser display by using the PRE tag. With this tag, you can add spaces and place text more or less where you want.

The PRE tag is a container tag that formats text in a fixed width font, and makes the text appear in the browser window in more or less the same way that it appears in your text editor.

Tip   *Fixed width* fonts display each letter taking up the same width. Courier is an example of a fixed width font.

The following code shows an example of text placed at different positions by using the PRE tag. Compare this code to Figure 9-8.

```
<!DOCTYPE HTML PUBLIC "-//W3C//DTD HTML 4.01 Transitional//EN"
"http:/www.w3.org/TR/html4/loose.dtd">
<HTML>
<HEAD>
<TITLE>Container tag example</TITLE>
</HEAD>
<BODY>
<H1>Poetry</H1>
<PRE>

                This is an example
             of text formatted
                      using a pre tag.

</PRE>
</BODY>
</HTML>
```

See Figure 9-8 to view the code in a browser.

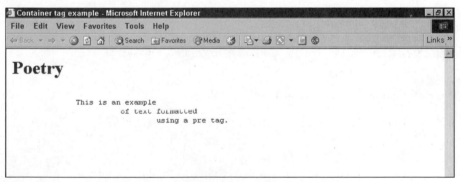

Figure 9-8: The result of using a PRE tag as displayed by a browser

The PRE tag works well for displaying poetry, for example. This tag is also excellent for displaying tabular data. Tables can also render this effect, but in some cases, the PRE tag may be a faster way to get the result you need. Refer to the following code for an example of using the PRE tag to create a tabular effect.

```
<!DOCTYPE HTML PUBLIC "-//W3C//DTD HTML 4.01 Transitional//EN"
"http:/www.w3.org/TR/html4/loose.dtd">
<HTML>
<HEAD>
<TITLE>Container tag example</TITLE>
</HEAD>
<BODY>
```

```
<H1>My Expenses</H1>
<PRE>
   Expenses             Amount
   Travel expenses      $2034.00
   Food                   800.00
   Entertainment          790.00

</PRE>
</BODY>
</HTML>
```

Figure 9-9 shows what this code looks like when displayed in a browser.

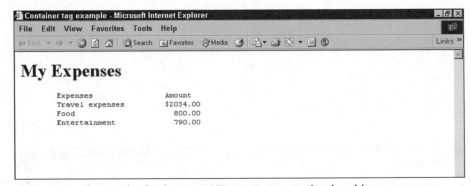

Figure 9-9: The result of using a <PRE> tag to create simple table

The PRE tag can also be used to create ASCII art. See the sample code that follows:

```
<!DOCTYPE HTML PUBLIC "-//W3C//DTD HTML 4.01 Transitional//EN"
"http:/www.w3.org/TR/html4/loose.dtd">
<HTML>
<HEAD>
<TITLE>Container tag example</TITLE>
</HEAD>
<BODY>
<H1>Peek a Boo Cat!</H1>
<PRE>
              /\-/\
             (     )
             ( 0 0  )   Meow
             (((\J/))
         _____/ _____
       ____|(_)|(_)_|__|
      _|___|____|____|_
       __|___|____|____|_
</PRE>
</BODY>
</HTML>
```

Figure 9-10 shows what this code looks like when displayed in a browser.

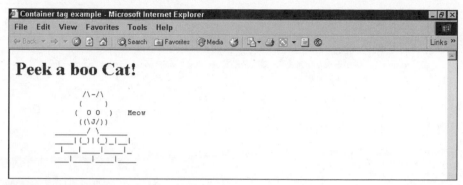

Figure 9-10: PRE tag used for ASCII art

As you can see, the PRE tag is not only useful but also fun. Although this tag has been depreciated in favor of using style sheets to achieve the same effect, it continues to be used in many Web sites.

<BLOCKQUOTE> tag

This block-level tag represents block quotations. It carries with it contextual information that specifically designates text as a block quotation. Block quote text displayed within a browser is often centered and indented. Some people use this tag to center and indent text — a task considered by many to be misusing the tag, which was created to depict the structure of the document, and not text formatting. The BLOCKQUOTE tag can contain paragraph tags, but conversely, it can't be contained within a paragraph tag. The following code and Figure 9-11 show the syntax of the tag within the text editor and how it is displayed within a browser.

```
<!DOCTYPE HTML PUBLIC "-//W3C//DTD HTML 4.01 Transitional//EN"
"http:/www.w3.org/TR/html4/loose.dtd">
<HTML>
<HEAD>
<TITLE>Container tag example</TITLE>
</HEAD>
<BODY>
<BLOCKQUOTE>This text is defined as a blockquote element.
Although this browser has centered and indented the text, not
all browsers will format block quotations this way. This tag
should be reserved for displaying long quotations.
</BLOCKQUOTE>
<P> Compare the blockquote text to the text in this paragraph.
All the text in this paragraph is defined by the paragraph
tags.
</P>
</BODY>
</HTML>
```

Figure 9-11 shows what this code looks like when displayed in a browser.

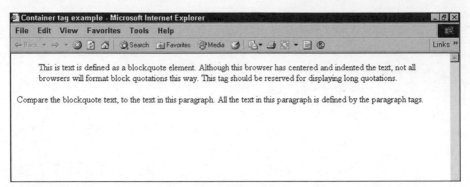

Figure 9-11: The result of using a BLOCKQUOTE tag as displayed in a browser

<DIV> tag

Although the PRE tag offers added flexibility for text placement, it is not the only alternative; the <DIV> tag has an ALIGN attribute that changes alignment to one of three values: *left*, *center,* or *right*. By default, all text is left-aligned. The following code shows how the DIV tag changes the alignment of text within a paragraph. Note also that you can use this tag for more than just text Alignment in tables and alignment of graphics are just a couple of other attributes that can be attached to this tag, too.

```
<!DOCTYPE HTML PUBLIC "-//W3C//DTD HTML 4.01 Transitional//EN"
"http:/www.w3.org/TR/html4/loose.dtd">
<HTML>
<HEAD>
<TITLE>Text alignment & indents example</TITLE>
</HEAD>
<BODY>
<H1><DIV ALIGN="center">My Title is Centered</DIV></H1>
<P><DIV ALIGN="right"> This text is Right aligned</DIV></P>
</BODY>
</HTML>
```

Figure 9-12 shows the effects of the DIV tag with the ALIGN attribute as they appear in a browser.

Tip   If you want to practice using the PRE, BLOCKQUOTE, and DIV tags, refer to Lab Exercise 9-2 and 9-3 in the Lab Exercises section at the end of this chapter.

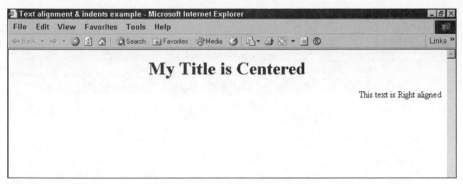

Figure 9-12: Effects of the DIV tag with the ALIGN attribute displayed in a browser

List tags

List tags are block-level elements that are typically contained within a paragraph tag. List tags come in two types: numbered lists, which are referred to as *ordered lists*, and bulleted lists, which are referred to as *unordered lists*. The list type tag specifies the list that you will be using: ordered <OL> or unordered <UL>. When you define a list, you must use two sets of tags. The list type tag is a container tag that holds the list item container tags. The following bullet list displays the different types of list tags:

✦ <OL> </OL> — Ordered list tags

✦ <UL> </UL> — Unordered list tags

✦ <LI> </LI> — List item tags

The following code shows the construction of an ordered list. Both the <OL> container tag and <LI> tags are necessary to create a numbered list. The two sets of tags used to define a list make this a *compound* element or tag.

```
<!DOCTYPE HTML PUBLIC "-//W3C//DTD HTML 4.01 Transitional//EN"
"http:/www.w3.org/TR/html4/loose.dtd">
<HTML>
<HEAD>
<TITLE>Ordered list example</TITLE>
</HEAD>
<BODY>
<H1>Directions:</H1>
<P>
<OL>
<LI>Put the key into the ignition.
<LI>Turn the Key.
<LI>Put the vehicle into DRIVE.
</OL>
</P>
</BODY>
</HTML>
```

Figure 9-13 shows how this code appears when it is opened in a browser.

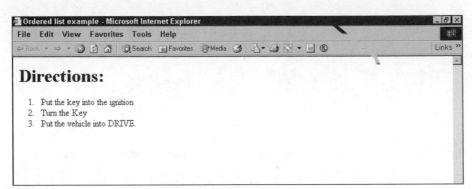

Figure 9-13: An ordered list rendered in a browser

For the list to be rendered properly, the list item tag <LI> must be contained within the ordered list tags <OL> </OL>. Unordered lists are structured like ordered lists. The following code is an example of an HTML document with a bulleted list:

```
<!DOCTYPE HTML PUBLIC "-//W3C//DTD HTML 4.01 Transitional//EN"
"http:/www.w3.org/TR/html4/loose.dtd">
<HTML>
<HEAD>
<TITLE>Ordered list example</TITLE>
</HEAD>
<BODY>
<H3>Bring the following to the Party :</H3>
<P>
<UL>
<LI>Sunglasses
<LI>Sun Screen
<LI>Cold Beverage
<LI>Insect Repellent
</UL>
</P>
</BODY>
</HTML>
```

Figure 9-14 shows how this code appears when opened in a browser.

The list tags mark text as a list item, but the formatting is left up to the browser. Some browsers may format your unordered list with round bullets, other browsers may format it with square bullets, and still another browser may use an asterisk to represent the bullets.

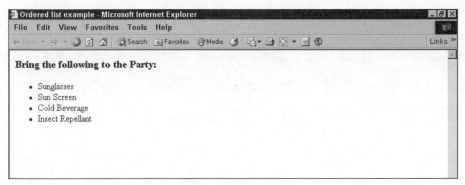

Figure 9-14: An unordered list rendered in a browser

Text-level elements

Although paragraph elements affect an entire block of text, text-level elements make changes within paragraph-level elements. A text-level element changes a word, a character, or phrase so that it looks different from the text that surrounds it. These text-level elements can be further subdivided into font style elements and phrase elements.

Font style elements and *phrase* elements differ from each other in their intentions for the changes that they make. The phrase elements describe structure, and not just formatting. The *font* elements describe the way text is formatted, with no connection to structural meaning.

Font style elements

The purpose of font style elements is to describe the physical appearance of text. No structural meaning is connected with these elements. The following is a list of font style tags:

✦ **<B>** — Applies bold formatting

✦ **<BIG>** — Formats text in large font size

✦ **<I>** — Applies italics to text

✦ **<SMALL>** — Applies small font to text

✦ **<SUB>** — Makes text subscript, smaller font and slightly lowered below the surrounding text

✦ **<SUP>** — Makes text superscript, smaller font and slightly raised above the surrounding text

✦ **<STRIKE>** — Strikethrough text; depreciated in 4.0

✦ **<TT>** — Fixed-width font

✦ **<U>** — Underline; depreciated in 4.0

Figure 9-15 illustrates how these tags are displayed in Internet Explorer.

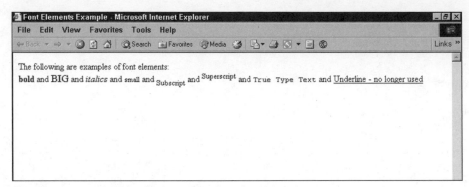

Figure 9-15: Font style attributes displayed within a browser

Some browsers, wireless devices, and speech recognition interpreters won't be able to interpret font style element tags.

Phrase elements

Phrase elements affect text appearance, but also change formatting according to what the text structurally represents. The following is a list of some common HTML phrase elements.

✦ **<CITE>** — Reference to a book, article, report, or Web site

✦ **<CODE>** — Describes typed samples of program code

```
<P><CODE>type some program code here</CODE></P>
```

✦ **<DFN>** — Describes a definition; the word being defined is emphasized

```
<P><DFN>font elements</DFN>>     
describe the text formatting of the characters it
defines</P>.
```

Note The multiple "nbsp"'s has been added to the above code to add some space between the word and it's definition.

✦ **<EM>** — Applies emphasis to the word or characters. The formatting for this particular code will cause text to stand out or be emphasized. Browsers will often italicize the text.

```
<P>The fire burned <EM>furiously</EM>while the crowd watched
with horror.</P>
```

✦ **<KBD>** — Describes text that is to be typed by the person reading the text. This is frequently used with a set of directions.

```
<P>Type the following:<KBD>The quick brown fox jumped over
the lazy dog.</KBD></P>
```

✦ **<SAMP>** — Similar to <CODE> and used less frequently; meant to show a sequence of characters from programs or scripts.

✦ **<STRONG>** — This tag gives more emphasis than the <EM> tag. Strong text is displayed with bold formatting.

```
<P><EM>Boil</EM>on high for <EM>10 minutes</EM>, then remove
for the heat and allow to <EM>cool</EM> for <EM>30
minutes</EM>
```

✦ **<VAR>** — Represents changeable reference names within programs.

Tip   Style sheets give added options to the effects presented by text element tags.

As stated previously, HTML documents are designed for structure, not formatting. In contrast, font style elements focus on formatting, which can cause problems in certain situations. Most HTML tags are meant to show more than physical formatting. HTML documents may also be interpreted by devices that have speech output, not just visual output. Phrase element tags show more than text formatting; emphasis, variable, and strong tags are interpreted by their meaning, not simply by the way text is displayed. In contrast, font style elements, such as bold, italics, and small, simply describe text. Table 9-4 compares font style elements to phrase style elements that appear with similar text formatting on a browser.

Table 9-4
Font and Phrase Style Comparison Chart

Font Style	Phrase Style	Appearance
<B>	<STRONG>	Bold text
<I>	<EM>	Italics
<TT>	<CITE>	
<SAMP>		
<VAR>		
<KBD>	True type font	

Whenever possible, use a phrase style element rather than a font style element so that the structural meaning can be better conveyed to alternative interpreters.

Hidden comments

You can leave comments within your code for yourself or others who update the HTML file. These comments are part of the source code but are not displayed by HTML interpreters. The following is an example of how to enter a comment into your code:

```
<!-- Write your comment here -->
```

You can use comments to document the last time you changed part of a page, or to generally describe what you've done.

Special characters

HTML files are simple text files with no formatting or decorative characters. In other words, you are not permitted to directly insert special characters into your HTML file using a keystroke combination with any key except for the Shift key. You can hold down the Shift key to create a character, but you can't use the Alt key or the Ctrl key to create your characters. Inserting a special character, such as an *e* with an accent (é) or the copyright symbol ((c)) directly into your HTML document may produce some unwanted results. Although these or similar characters may look right some of the time; they undoubtedly won't look right most of the time. For example, your character may be substituted for another or it may appear as gibberish. Remember this rule: Only characters that you see on your keyboard may be included in your HTML file. Additionally, certain characters, such as the greater than sign <, the less than sign >, and quotation marks, are reserved for HTML tags, and therefore, can't be entered by simply typing them.

You can include the copyright symbol or letters with accents or cool bullets if you use *character entities*, which are particular character code sets interpreted correctly by browsers. The character code set can be represented with names or numbers. ANSI code sets are numeric, and HTML code sets are represented by words. All character entities begin with an ampersand (&) and end with a semicolon. Some special characters have both numeric and name codes. Table 9-5 illustrates some of the more popular numeric and name codes.

Table 9-5 Special Character Entities			
Description	*Numeric Code*	*Name Code*	*Character*
Degree sign	&#176;	&deg;	_
Copyright symbol	&#169;	&copy;	(c)
Registered trademark	&#174;	&reg;	(r)
Lowercase *e*, acute accent	&#233;	&eacute;	é

In addition to the special symbols, some characters are reserved for HTML tag functions that can't be typed into the tag itself. These reserved characters include the greater than sign, the less than sign, quotation marks, and the ampersand. If you want any of these characters to appear in your browser, you must use special character codes to represent them. Table 9-6 illustrates codes for character tags.

Table 9-6
Codes for Characters Used by Tags

Character	Description	Code
<	Less than sign	&lt;
>	Greater than sign	&gt;
&	Ampersand	&amp;
"	Quotation marks	&quote;

Graphics

Almost every Web page that you visit these days has them. Graphic elements add visual appeal, contribute to design structure, and can serve as another way for you to present your message. By the end of this section, you will be able to add decorative horizontal lines to a Web page and insert standalone graphics.

Caution   Using graphics without permission is both illegal and unethical. Graphics and text that are present at a particular Web site are the property of that Web site.

Horizontal rules

Objective   Add horizontal rules to your Web pages and work with horizontal rule attributes.

A *horizontal rule* is a straight line extending across a page; they are much like lines that you draw with a pencil and ruler on paper. Horizontal rules within HTML documents contribute to the aesthetic design of the page, and provide for a physical division between document content. A horizontal line is displayed at the point where the <HR> code is placed. This tag is not associated with any text and needs no closing tag. The following sample source code uses the <HR> tag.

```
<!DOCTYPE HTML PUBLIC "-//W3C//DTD HTML 4.01 Transitional//EN"
"http:/www.w3.org/TR/html4/loose.dtd">
<HTML>
<HEAD>
<TITLE>Horizontal Rule Example</TITLE>
```

```
</HEAD>
<BODY>
<H1>Bring the following to the Party:</H1>
<HR>
<P>
<UL>
<LI>Sunglasses
<LI>Sun Screen
<LI>Cold Beverage
<LI>Insect Repellent
</UL>
<IIR>
</P>
</BODY>
</HTML>
```

Figure 9-16 shows how this code is rendered in a browser.

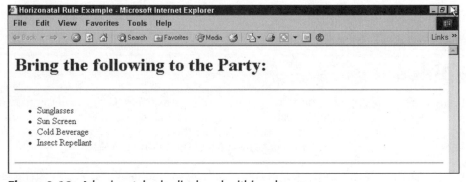

Figure 9-16: A horizontal rule displayed within a browser

By default, the horizontal rule extends from left to right across the entire screen, and has a 3-D shadow effect, as shown in Figure 9-16. You can use attributes to change the default settings of the horizontal rule. For example, you can use the <HR> tag to specify line length, thickness, alignment, and 3-D effects. These attributes were deprecated in HTML 4.1, with preference given to attaining the same results with style sheets. However, the <HR> attributes are still used in many Web sites and are part of the CIW curriculum and exam.

Changing thickness of <HR>

The thickness of the line is specified by the *size attribute*. The syntax for this attribute is as follows:

```
<HR size ="3">
```

The value number "3" in the preceding example represents the number of pixels that make up the thickness of the line. The higher the value number, the thicker the line. A lower value number results in thinner lines.

```
<HTML>
<HEAD>
<TITLE>Horizontal line widths example</TITLE>
</HEAD>
<BODY>
<H1>This line is three pixels</H1>
<HR size="3">
<H1>This line is five pixels</H1>
<HR size="5">
<H1>This line is ten pixels</H1>
<HR size="10">
</BODY>
</HTML>
```

Figure 9-17 shows value variation of the size attribute for the <HR> tag.

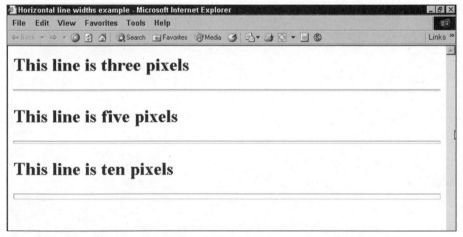

Figure 9-17: A horizontal rule with different values associated with the size attribute

Varying length of <HR>

The length of the horizontal line is controlled by the *width* attribute. The value after the width attribute is written as a percent of the width of the screen. The syntax for this attribute is as follows:

```
<HR width="50%">
```

The following code shows variations of the width attribute.

```
<HTML>
<HEAD>
<TITLE>Horizontal line widths example</TITLE>
</HEAD>
<BODY>
<H3>Width 5%</H3>
<HR width="5%">
<H3>Width 15%</H3>
<HR width="15%">
<H3>Width 25%</H3>
<HR width="25%">
<H3>Width 50%</H3>
<HR width="50%">
<H3>Width 100%</H3>
<HR width="100%">
</BODY>
</HTML>
```

Figure 9-18 shows how the width variation specified in the code above appears in a browser.

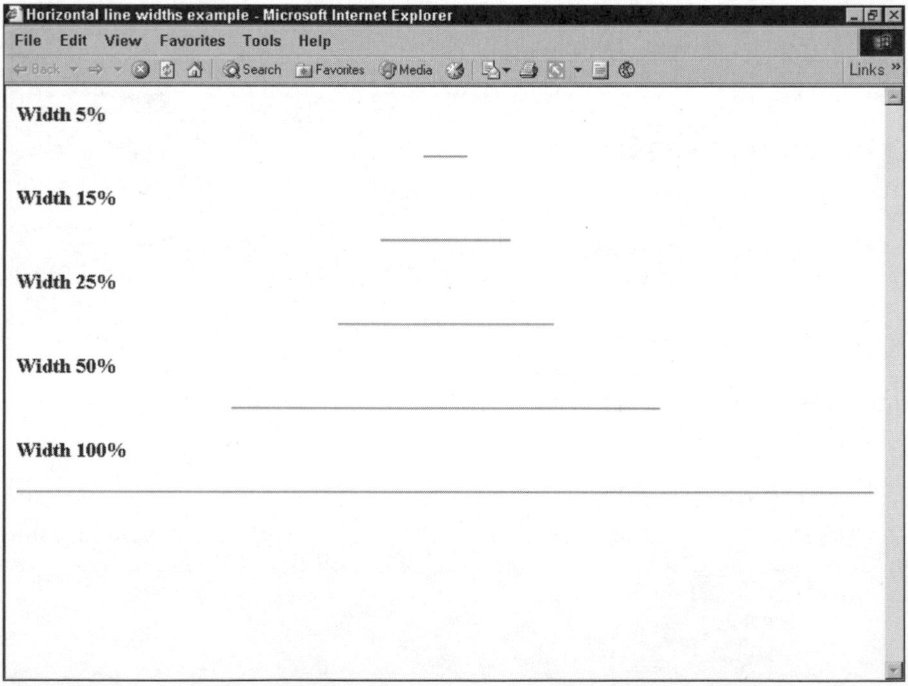

Figure 9-18: Variations in the width attribute of the <HR> tag as displayed on Internet Explorer

Changing alignment of horizontal line

You can control the alignment of your horizontal line with the ALIGN attribute. This attribute works only if your line is not the full width of the screen. Choose from three values: left, which is the default, right, and center.

```
<HR align="right">
```

Figure 9-19 shows variations of the alignment attribute for the HR tag as displayed in a browser.

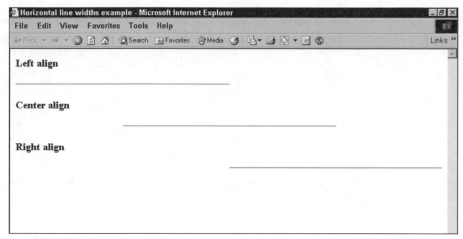

Figure 9-19: Variations of the ALIGN attribute with the <HR> tag

NOSHADE

You can remove the 3-D shadow effect that you see by default with the NOSHADE attribute. This attribute is different from most other attributes in that it doesn't have any values associated with it; simply having it present takes away the shadow.

```
<HR NOSHADE>
```

Figure 9-20 compares horizontal rules with the NOSHADE attribute to those without this attribute.

You can achieve similar effects to the horizontal rule by using other methods; for example, a graphics image in the form of a bar can render the same effect on an Internet browser that the horizontal rule does. However, the horizontal line may be more appropriate than a graphic; it will be more likely to work within the various browsers and alternative interpreters because this tag also carries with it information regarding document structure.

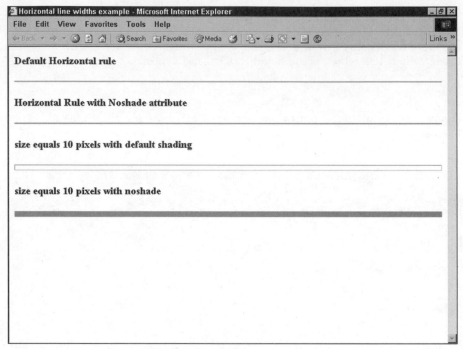

Figure 9-20: Displays NOSHADE attribute in a browser

Images

Incorporate image files as standalone graphics.

You can use three image formats with Web pages: Graphics Interchange Format (GIF), Joint Photographic Experts Group (JPEG), and Portable Network Graphics (PNG). Actually, you can use a fourth type, which is Bitmap image files, but Microsoft Internet Explorer is the only browser that can interpret Bitmap (BMP) files. You may be excluding a percentage of your audience if you choose to use Bitmap images.

GIF

Graphics Interchange Format, or (GIF), is one of the most widely used image file formats on the Web. It supports excellent quality, high-resolution graphics, and provides for the storing and sharing of 2D raster-based graphics. Due to their small file size, GIFs can be downloaded quickly. Two versions of GIFs are available: GIF 87a and GIF 89a. The most popular, GIF 89a, supports three different GIF types: transparent, interlaced, and animated.

Tip   Raster graphics are comprised of pixels, which are small dots of color. Graphics constructed this way can be complex and still have a small file size.

Transparent GIFs

This file format blends into the background color of the Web page by designating one color as "transparent." Most images consist of a major image with a background color. The background color is assigned to be transparent, causing the image to blend into the background. Transparent GIFs are also called *Spacer GIFs* because this effect decreases the space taken up by the graphic, thus effectively adding space to the Web page. This technique works even when the user changes the default background color of the browser.

Interlaced GIFs

GIFs that are interlaced appear to fade onto the screen, giving the impression that the image is not taking as long to download. Interlacing enhances the Web browsing experience of people with slow Internet connections, while individuals with high-speed connections probably won't notice any difference between interlaced and non-interlaced images.

Animated GIFs

Animated GIFs appear in motion. Images of waving hands and letters that grow or spin are probably animated GIFs, although these same effects can also be made by other tools, such as Flash or Java. Animated GIFs are popular because they are fairly easy to create and their file size is smaller than other types of animations. Animated GIFs are able to loop continuously, providing non-stop animation, or can be made to stop animation after a specified sequence.

JPEG

JPEG is one of the two most popular image formats found on Web pages. The acronym JPEG stands for *Joint Photographic Experts Group*, named after the committee that created it. This format works best with photographs and realistic artwork; line drawings, lettering, and cartoon-like drawings work best as GIFs.

JPEG reduces file size through lossless compression methods. As a result, JPEG images are sometimes referred to as "lossy" because an image is changed when it's converted. A bit of the picture quality is exchanged for a smaller file size.

This reduced image quality is not necessarily noticeable to the eye because of the way the parts of the image are changed. The compression methods take advantage of restrictions of the human eye, essentially fooling the eye so that you may be completely unaware of the changes to the brightness and color. When converting a file to JPEG, you have control over the amount of compression. The smaller the file, the more noticeable the decreased quality.

Progressive JPEGs are similar to Interlaced GIFs; they fade into view, first appearing fuzzy and out of focus and then sharp. Progressive JPEGs are not used as frequently anymore because of the higher connection speeds now being accessed by the general public.

PNG

Portable Network Graphics (PNG) is the newest image format to be used across the Web. PNG is superior in image quality to GIFs. With this format, you can control *opacity*, which is the degree of transparency. The file size tends to be smaller than GIFs, and PNGs are therefore downloaded more quickly. Interlaced PNG files load more quickly than GIFs. PNG also allows for many features that the GIF format doesn't, including 254 levels of transparency (GIF supports only one), more control over image brightness, and support for more than 256 colors. This format possesses many positive features and is quickly gaining popularity among Web developers.

Tip   Unisys, the company that owns the GIF format, has a patent restricting software developers from creating software to build these images without a license. PNG file format carries with it no such restrictions.

The Image tag

Choosing an image in the correct format is the first step to inserting graphics into your Web page. After you have selected an image, you need the image tag <IMG> to attach your picture to your Web file. Similar to the <HR> tag in that it has no closing tag, the image tag <IMG> simply commands the browser to display the graphics file. This tag requires one attribute, the SRC, for a graphic to load correctly. The following is an example of image tag with the SRC attribute:

```
<IMG SRC="imagefilename.gif">
```

or

```
<IMG SRC="imagefilename.jpeg">
```

The graphics file to be displayed is the value for the SRC and must always be enclosed in quotation marks.

Exam Tip   The preceding code example works only if the image file and Web page are stored in the same location. You can enter the value in other ways so that an image stored in a different file or on a different computer can be accessed. However, these specifics go beyond the requirements of the CIW Fundamentals exam and course.

The following code uses the IMG and SRC to insert a picture of a sailing ship into the Web page. Both the image file and the HTML file reside in the same folder.

```
<HTML>
<HEAD>
<TITLE>Sailing in the 1800's</TITLE>
</HEAD>
<BODY>
<DIV ALIGN="center"><H1>Life on a Sailing Ship</H1></DIV>
<IMG SRC="smallShip.jpg">
</BODY>
</HTML>
```

Figure 9-21 shows how this code appears in a browser.

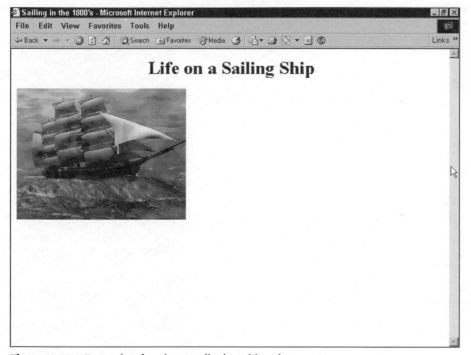

Figure 9-21: Example of an image displayed in a browser

By default your image appears left-aligned. The DIV tag, used earlier in this chapter to alter text alignment, can also be used with the IMG tag to change the alignment of your graphic. The following code is an example of the two tags used together:

```
<DIV ALIGN="center"><IMG SRC="name of file.gif"></DIV>
```

Note how the image tag is nested within the DIV tag. Figure 9-22 shows what the file in Figure 9-21 looks like when the DIV tag is used to center the image.

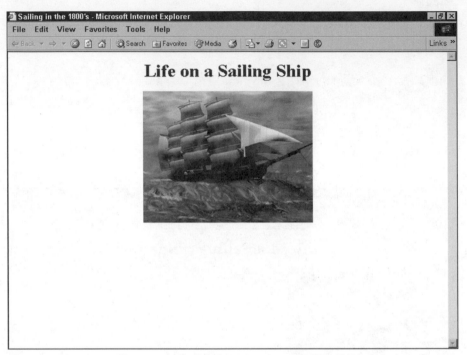

Figure 9-22: Image file centered with the DIV tag as displayed in a browser

Although the DIV tag is useful, it may not meet all your alignment needs. The alignment attribute works well to align your image in relation to the text on the Web page. The following is an example of code for the ALIGN attribute within the IMG tag:

```
<IMG SRC="Imagefilename.gif" ALIGN="alignmentvaluehere">
```

You can use five different alignment values: Right, Left, Top, Bottom, and Middle:

- ✦ **Right alignment image attribute** — The image appears on the right side of the text, with the top of the image placed at the same level as the first line of adjacent text. Paragraph text wraps along the left side of the image.

- ✦ **Left alignment image attribute** — The image appears on the left side of the text, with the top of the image placed at the same level as the first line of adjacent text. Paragraph text is wrapped along the right side of the image.

- ✦ **Top alignment image attribute** — Places the top of the image at the top edge of the adjacent graphic or line of text.

- ✦ **Bottom alignment image attribute** — This is the default; places the bottom of the image in line with the baseline of the text beside the image.

- ✦ **Middle alignment image attribute** — Places the center of the image at the baseline of the text situated next to the image.

ALT attribute

Many Web users can't view images. Text-based browsers like Lynx don't show images, and people with slow Internet connections disable graphics viewing in order to speed up their Web page viewing. For these reasons, you should include the *ALT attribute* with all IMG tags. In the event that the image can't be displayed, this ALT attribute places a text description in its place. The following is an example of code syntax for this attribute:

```
<IMG SRC picture.jpg ALT="type text to describe picture here">
```

Figure 9-23 demonstrates how an image appears when image loading is disabled on Internet Explorer. Text-only browsers display the word image in parentheses — and if the picture is a link, the link will be kept.

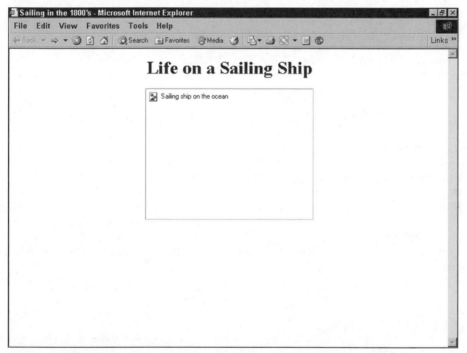

Figure 9-23: Internet Explorer showing a Web page with the alternative text displayed in place of an image

The ALT attribute is required with HTML 4.0 Strict and XHTML 1.0 specifications, and the inclusion of the ALT attribute is considered good coding practice.

Height and width attributes

You can increase or decrease the size of your picture by using two attributes: height and width. Image size is measures in pixels, and that's the value changed with these two attributes. More pixels result in a larger picture; less pixels result in a smaller picture. The syntax for these attributes is as follows:

```
<IMG SRC="picture.gif" height="NoOfPixels" Width="noOfPixels">
```

Suppose that you have a graphic that is 200 pixels wide and 100 pixels tall. If you want to decrease this image by a quarter of its original size, you would change the width to 150 pixels and the height to 75 pixels. Height and width should be adjusted in proportion to each other.

What if you don't know the dimensions of your picture and you want to adjust its size? In this case, you should use either the height or the width attribute—not both. Changing the value of one of these attributes results in the other being adjusted, with the original picture size proportions intact. See the following code:

```
<IMG SRC="picture.gif" height="NoOfPixels">
```

or

```
<IMG SRC="picture.gif" Width="NoOfPixels">
```

If you know the height and width of your picture, it's best to include it—even when you don't intend to alter the size of your graphic. With this extra information, browsers can download the image into the client computer more quickly.

Don't forget that when you work with graphics, the appearance of your Web page changes when it is viewed at different resolutions. Many software programs are available that can help you design your own graphics or edit graphics. Always take into account download speeds and various screen resolutions when you work with graphics.

Color Attributes

Use the Web-safe color palette.

Change the page background color.

Use a tiled image across the page background.

The Web isn't strictly black and white. Color adds interest, style, and fun to your page. This section examines how to change colors of the background, text, and text links. Table 9-7 shows BODY tag attributes and code syntax for making color changes.

Exam Tip Style sheet specifications in HTML 4.0 have replaced color attributes illustrated in this section of the chapter. Although these tags and attributes are depreciated, they are still used, and you will see questions about them on the CIW exam.

Table 9-7 BODY Tag Attributes		
Body Color Attribute Name	**Code Example**	**Element Changed**
GBCOLOR	<BODY BGCOLOR="color">	Background color
TEXT	<BODY TEXT="color">	Text color (Does not affect text with links)
ALINK	<BODY ALINK="color">	Color of a link when it's selected
LINK	<BODY LINK="color">	Color of links before they have been selected or visited
VLINK	<BODY VLINK="color">	Links that have been visited
BACKGROUND	<BODY BACKGROUND="filename">	An image file specified by the value is tiled in the background

Note Although the BACKGROUND attribute is an image file, and not a color, it is included in this discussion because of the relation to the BODY tag.

Before you change the color of text and background, you need to know the rules for picking colors to use on the Web. Not every shade and color hue in existence will work with all Internet browsers. The value for a color can be represented by a word, such as *green*, or it can be represented by a set of three hexadecimal numbers. However, it is best to draw from the Web-safe color palette that represents colors as hexadecimal values whenever possible.

Netscape and Internet Explorer both display colors when the attribute is written as a word, such as *white*, *black*, *gray*, *blue*, *yellow*, and so on. You have a limited number of word colors to choose from, which makes this color palette limited. Even Netscape and Internet Explorer differ from each other in the way they display some of these colors.

Exam Tip Know about the Web-safe color palette and the colors represented by hexadecimal numbers.

When a color is not supported by a particular system, the computer makes up for the discrepancy by dithering. *Dithering* is the process of estimating the color by mixing a combination of RGB. In the process of dithering, the computer is essentially guessing the color. As you can imagine, this process can sometimes result in some unsightly color combinations.

Web-safe color palette

Also referred to as the *Netscape-safe palette* or the *browser-safe palette*, the *Web-safe color palette* is a list of 216 colors that can theoretically be displayed consistently across multiple platforms. Each color is a mixture of red, green, and blue light. A hexadecimal number represents the amount of each color that is mixed together to produce the color on the screen, as shown in Figure 9-24.

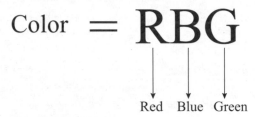

Figure 9-24: A breakdown of red, blue, and green light mixed together to create Web-safe color

Red, blue, and green light mixed together results in the color you see on your monitor. The intensity of each light color is represented by a number; the higher the number, the lighter the color. The numbers range from 0 to 255 and are written in hexadecimal. See Figure 9-25 for an example of how the color white is represented with hexadecimal numbers.

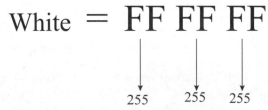

Figure 9-25: This diagram shows the color white represented in hexadecimal.

You can access these Web-safe colors through an image-editing program. There are Web sites that also help match the hexadecimal color number with a color. For example, the FastBoot Web site displays a color-safe grid that allows you to hover your mouse over the color that you want to use and see the corresponding hexadecimal number displayed at the bottom of the screen. Go to `http://www.fastboot.com/safecolor_pallette.html` to give it a try.

What are hexadecimal numbers?

Our normal number system is based on the factors of ten (which is why it is often called the "base ten" system). Each digit of a number represents a different factor of ten. The first position (starting from the right) represents the number of ones (which is a factor of ten because 10 to the zero power is 1); the second digit represents the number of tens (10^1), the third digit represents the number of hundreds (10^2), and so on. For example, the number 2,453 means 2 thousands, 4 hundreds, 5 tens, and 3 ones.

The hexadecimal system is a similar number system; however, it is based on factors of 16 instead of 10. So the first digit of a number (starting again from the right) represents the number of ones (which is a factor of 16 because 16^0 is 1). The second digit represents the number of 16s (16^1), the third digit represents the number of 256s (which is 16^2), the fourth digit represents the number of 4,096s (16^3), and so on. Therefore, the number 8,754 in hexadecimal really means eight 4,096s, seven 256s, five 16s, and four 1s. Adding this all together (8*4,096) + (7*256) + (5*16) + (4*1) gives you the decimal equivalent of 34,644.

An additional feature of hexadecimal is the number of digits used. The base ten system uses ten different digits: 0 through 9. Hexadecimal uses 16 digits; the first ten are 0 through 9, but the remaining six are the letters A, B, C, D, E, and F. A is equivalent to a 10, B is an 11, and so on, up to F as a 15. Therefore, a hexadecimal number, such as 3AE, means three 256s, ten 16s and fourteen 1s, or (3*256) + (10*16) + (14*1) = 942.

Table 9-8 compares our number system to the hexadecimal system.

Table 9-8
Hexadecimal Comparison Chart

Top number in each cell represents hexadecimal number & bottom number is our base 10 number system equivalent.

1	2	3	4	5	6	7	8	9	A	B	C	D	E	F	10
1	2	3	4	5	6	7	8	9	10	11	12	13	14	15	16
11	12	13	14	15	16	17	18	19	1A	1B	1C	1D	1E	1F	20
17	18	19	20	21	22	23	24	25	26	27	28	29	30	31	32
21	22	23	24	25	26	27	28	29	2A	2B	2C	2D	2E	2F	30
33	34	35	36	37	38	39	40	41	42	43	44	45	46	47	48
31	32	33	34	35	36	37	38	39	3A	3B	3C	3D	3E	3F	40
49	50	51	52	53	54	55	56	57	58	59	60	61	62	63	64
41	42	43	44	45	46	47	48	49	4A	4B	4C	4D	4E	4F	50
65	66	67	68	69	70	71	72	73	74	75	76	77	78	79	80
51	52	53	54	55	56	57	58	59	5A	5B	5C	5D	5E	5F	60
81	82	83	84	85	86	87	88	89	90	91	92	93	94	95	96
61	62	63	64	65	66	67	68	69	6A	6B	6C	6D	6E	6F	70
97	98	99	100	101	102	103	104	105	106	107	108	109	110	111	112
71	72	73	74	75	76	77	78	79	7A	7B	7C	7D	7E	7F	80
113	114	115	116	117	118	119	120	121	122	123	124	125	126	127	128
81	82	83	84	85	86	87	88	89	8A	8B	8C	8D	8E	8F	90
129	130	131	132	133	134	135	136	137	138	139	140	141	142	143	144
91	92	93	94	95	96	97	98	99	9A	9B	9C	9D	9E	9F	A0
145	146	147	148	149	150	151	152	153	154	155	156	157	158	159	160
A1	A2	A3	A4	A5	A6	A7	A8	A9	AA	AB	AC	AD	AE	AF	B0
161	162	163	164	165	166	167	168	169	170	171	172	173	174	175	176

Key Point Summary

The key point summary highlights major topics covered in this chapter.

✦ HTML is made up of text and tags.

✦ Tags are comprised of a text command between angled brackets (< >) and are used to specify the way a document should be displayed.

✦ Container tags work in pairs with both an opening and a closing tag.

✦ Closing tags always begin with a forward slash (/).

✦ Empty tags are singular opening tags that don't require a corresponding closing tag.

✦ An element is both a tag and the contents described by the tag. The following are features of an element:

   • The tag name is the name for an element.

   • Elements can be contained within elements.

   • Elements typically have three parts to them: opening tag, content, and end tag (unless the opening tag is an empty tag).

✦ An attribute indicates or identifies a specific characteristic of the element. The following are features of an attribute:

   • Appears after the element name

   • Is followed by an equal sign and the attribute

✦ The value precisely defines the attribute and always appears in quotation marks.

✦ The three main document structure tags are:

   • HTML

   • HEAD

   • BODY

✦ <HTML> is an optional tag if DTD is part of the document.

✦ The <HEAD> and <BODY> elements are within the <HTML> container tag.

✦ <HEAD> describes facts about the document:

   • The TITLE tag is placed within the HEAD element.

   • The META tag is placed within the HEAD element.

✦ <BODY> tags encase all the information displayed on the browser.

✦ Tags appearing within the BODY element include:

- Paragraph tags: <P> </P>

- Heading tags: <H1> </H1>

- List tags: <UL> </UL> or <OL> </OL>

✦ The Document Type Declaration (DTD) tag is technically an SGML statement, not an HTML tag; it describes the markup language used to create the document and is optional in HTML 4.01. The advantages to using this tag include the following:

- It can give you better access to advanced features of browsers.

- Use of it may eventually be required by newer browsers.

- It is essential if you are using validators to test for coding inaccuracies.

✦ <META> is contained between <HEAD> </HEAD> tags. It is used to describe your HTML document and can be used to help search engines select your Web site. <META> gives information in the following ways:

- **Keywords** — a listing of words describing the subject

- **Subject** — descriptive sentence(s) depicting the subject matter

- **Author** — identity of the Web author

- **Refresh** — command to refresh your page automatically within the time frame you specify.

✦ Block-level elements affect one or more paragraphs. They are used to change the structure of blocks of text. Examples of block-level tags include:

- **<P> </P>** — separates paragraphs with paragraph breaks.

- **<Hn> </Hn>** — used to identify a Heading; n is any number from 1 to 6.

- **
** — a depreciated empty tag used to creates a line break.

- **<PRE>** — gives flexibility for text placement by allowing text to be displayed on the browser the way it was typed into a text editor.

✦ There are two categories of lists: numbered lists and bulleted lists.

✦ Numbered lists (also referred to as ordered lists) require:

- **<OL> </OL>** — ordered list container tags

- **<LI>** — list item tag

✦ Bulleted lists (also referred to as unordered lists) require:

- **<UL> </UL>** — unordered list container tags

- **<LI>** — list item tag

✦ Text-level elements change a word or character or phrase so that it looks different from the text that surrounds it. These can be further subdivided into two groups: font style elements and phrase elements.

✦ Font style elements describe how the text should look with an emphasis on formatting. The following are all considered font style tags:

- **<B>**
- **<BIG>**
- **<I>**
- **<SMALL>**
- **<SUB>**
- **<SUP>**
- **<STRIKE>**
- **<TT>**
- **<U>**

✦ Phrase elements change formatting according to what the text structurally represents. The following are all considered phrase element tags:

- **<CITE>**
- **<CODE>**
- **<DFN>**
- **<EM>**
- **<KBD>**
- **<SAMP>**
- **<STRONG>**
- **<VAR>**

✦ A horizontal rule is a straight line extending across a page. It is specified by using the empty tag <HR>. The following are attributes that may be used with the <HR> tag:

- **SIZE**—Changes line thickness
- **WIDTH**—Changes line length
- **ALIGN**—Changes alignment of horizontal rule
- **NOSHADE**—Removes 3-D shading

✦ To insert images into your Web site, you need two things:

- A file in the appropriate image format
- An image <IMG> tag

✦ There are three image formats you can use for Web pages:

- **GIF** — best suited for line drawings, lettering, and cartoon-like drawings. There are two versions available: GIF 87a and GIF 89a. GIF 89a is used the most because it supports transparent, interlaced, and animated GIFs.

- **JPEG** — suited for photographs and realistic artwork. It uses lossless compression methods to exchange picture quality for smaller file size.

- **PNG** — Similar to GIFs, but offers superior quality, smaller file size, and increased flexibility when controlling degree of transparency within graphic.

✦ The <IMG> image tag attributes include:

- **SRC** — References the name and location of image files.

- **ALIGN** — Aligns graphic in relation to text or other graphics using one of five alignment values: bottom, middle, top, left, and right.

- **ALT** — Displays text in place of a graphic either for a text-based browser or when image viewing is disabled.

- **Height and width** — Used to alter the size of a graphic. Values are used to represent the number of pixels.

✦ Colors can be adjusted for text, background, and links.

✦ The Web-safe Color Palette includes 216 colors that are rendered correctly across multiple browsing platforms. Each color is represented by a hexadecimal number. The higher the number, the lighter the color.

✦ When a color is not supported by a particular system, the computer makes up for the discrepancy by dithering.

✦   ✦   ✦

STUDY GUIDE

Using the information covered in this chapter, you can now create a Web document. The scenario questions and lab exercises will give you an opportunity to apply your knowledge of basic HTML concepts. The assessment questions and scenario questions review the major topics covered in this chapter.

Assessment Questions

1. Which of the following does not require a closing tag?

   A. <H1>

   B. <HEAD>

   C. <HR>

   D. <UL>

2. Select container tags from the choices below. Select all that apply.

   A. <BODY>

   B. <LI>

   C. <HR>

   D.

3. _____ tags are found in pairs, whereas _____ tags appear by themselves without a closing tag.

4. Which of the following code examples could generate errors in a browser because it is not coded correctly?

   A. <HTML LANG="en">

   B. <HTML LANG=en>

   C. All of the above

   D. None of the above

5. True or False: The word *element* in HTML means *tag*.

6. True or False: HTML 4.01 specification recommends that elements and attributes be written entirely in uppercase.

7. Which of the following statements is true regarding META tags?

    A. Located within the HEAD container tag

    B. Not a true HTML tag, but rather an SGML statement

    C. These tags are optional in HTML 4.01

    D. All of the above

    E. A and C only

    F. A and B only

    G. B and C only

8. Which tag can specify the refresh rate for an HTML tag?

    A. <TITLE>

    B. <META>

    C. <DTD>

    D. <DIV>

9. Which statement or statements are true with regards to the BR tag?

    A. This tag inserts manual paragraph breaks

    B. It is depreciated

    C. Can be used with HTML 4.0 transitional flavor

    D. All of the above

    E. None of the above

    F. A and B

    G. A and C

    H. B and C

10. You want to type a stanza of poetry. The beginning of each line does not begin at the same place horizontally on the page. What tag could you use to achieve a desirable result?

11. Which of the following are text-level element tags? (Choose all that apply)

    A. <H>

    B. <I>

    C. <EM>

    D. <DTD>

    E. <TT>

12. Identify all phrase-level tags. (Choose all that apply)

    A. <B>

    B. <SUB>

    C. <KBD>

    D. <CITE>

    E. <SMALL>

13. Identify all text-level tags. (Choose all that apply)

    A. <STRONG>

    B. <CODE>

    C. <BIG>

    D. <I>

    E. <DFN>

    F. <SUP>

14. Which of the following are attributes for the HR tag?

    A. ALIGN

    B. NOSHADE

    C. LENGTH

    D. WIDTH

    E. SIZE

    F. All of the above

15. Which HR attribute is used to specify the thickness of the HR line?

    A. WIDTH

    B. SIZE

    C. THICKNESS

    D. DEPTH

16. Which of the following can be a type of GIF file?

    A. Transparent

    B. Interlaced

    C. Animated

    D. Glossy

    E. PNG

17. Which of the following will correctly change background colors on a Web page?

    A. <BODY BGCOLOR="#FF0000">

    B. <BODY BACKGROUND="#FF0000"

    C. <BODY COLOR="#FF0000">

    D. <COLOR=BLUE>

18. Select all statements that are correct.

    A. The Web-safe color palette is made up of 255 colors.

    B. It is possible to change the color of text links on your Web page.

    C. Colors on Web pages are made by mixing red, yellow, and blue light.

    D. The numbers that represent each light color mixed on your monitor can range from 0 to 255.

Lab Exercises

Now you have the opportunity to use the tags that you have been reading about throughout this chapter. This "hands-on" practice will help you remember what all these tags do. There are a total of six exercises, and it is recommended that you do them in the order in which they are written because they build upon each other to create one file at the end.

Lab 9-1

Create a simple Web page by using document structure tags.

1. Begin by starting a text-editing program. Type the following code:

```
<!DOCTYPE HTML PUBLIC "-//W3C//DTD HTML 4.01
Transitional//EN" "http:/www.w3.org/TR/html4/loose.dtd">
<HTML>
<HEAD>
<TITLE>My Sample Web Page</TITLE>
</HEAD>
<BODY>
This is an example of a paragraph typed into a web page.
Simply pressing the enter key doesn't work to separate
paragraphs into different paragraphs.

When you open your file in a browser it these 2 paragraphs
will appear as one paragraph.
</BODY>
</HTML>
```

2. Save this file. Call it "Sample.htm".

3. Start your browser and open this file in your browser. It should look like the file in Figure 9-26.

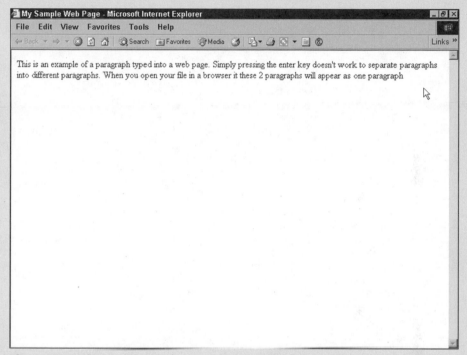

Figure 9-26: If your HTML code is entered correctly the result in your browser should resemble this screen shot.

Note the title bar. You should see the text that appeared between the TITLE tags displayed on the title bar of your browser. All the text that you typed within the BODY tag appears as one block of text.

Lab 9-2

You will build on the files that you started in Lab 9-1. To your file you will add these block level tags: <P>, <H1>,<H2>, <H3>, <H4>, <H5>, <H6>, and <BLOCKQUOTE>.

In the following code example, the text represented in bold text highlights the text that you will be adding to your file. The bold formatting directs your attention to the new tags. Don't apply bold formatting to these tags in your document.

1. Your text-editing program should be running and the Sample.htm file should be open.

2. Look at the following code and add the new tags to your code. (All new tags are bolded in this code example.)

```
<!DOCTYPE HTML PUBLIC "-//W3C//DTD HTML 4.01
Transitional//EN">

"http:/www.w3.org/TR/html4/loose.dtd"
<HTML>
<HEAD>
<TITLE>My Sample Web Page</TITLE>
</HEAD>
<BODY>
<H1>Using HTML</H1>
<H2>The Paragraph Tag</H2>
<P>This is an example of a paragraph typed into a web page.
Simply pressing the enter key doesn't work to separate
paragraphs into different paragraphs. The paragraph tag
creates paragraph breaks.</P>
<P>If you use the paragraph container tags, when you open
your file in a browser it these 2 paragraphs will now appear
as two paragraphs.</P>
<H2>The Blockquote Tag</H2>
<BLOCKQUOTE> This is an example of text typed with the block
quote tag. Blockquote is a container, block level tag that
represents block quotations. Note the differences between
this text and text that appears between the paragraph tag.
Although this block of text probably appears centered and
indented, text within this tag will not necessarily appear
this way within every browser. </BLOCKQUOTE>
</BODY>
</HTML>
```

3. Save your file.

4. Open this file in your browser. (If this file is already open in your browser, you can update the display by clicking the Refresh command if you're using Internet Explorer, or the Reload command if you're using Netscape. (Both commands are found on the View menu.) Your file should look like the file shown in Figure 9-27.

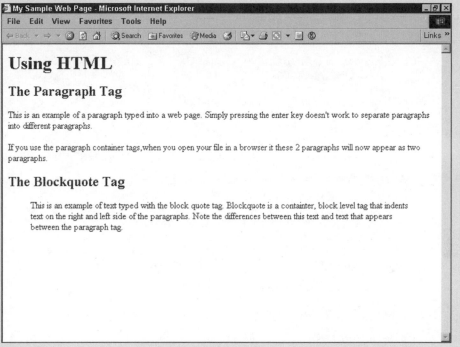

Figure 9-27: Your file opened in a browser should resemble the above screen image.

If you are using Netscape or Internet Explorer, text within the BLOCKQUOTE tags will be indented and centered. The paragraph tags divide blocks of text into paragraphs, and text between the heading tags will be emphasized.

Lab 9-3

You will now use the <BR> and <PRE> and <DIV> block-level tags. Just as in the previous exercise, all new code and text that you will be adding to your file is highlighted in bold.

1. Your text-editing program should be running and the Sample.htm file should be open.

2. Examine the code below.

```
<!DOCTYPE HTML PUBLIC "-//W3C//DTD HTML 4.01
Transitional//EN"

"http:/www.w3.org/TR/html4/loose.dtd">
<HTML>
```

```
<HEAD>
<TITLE>My Sample Web Page</TITLE>
</HEAD>
<BODY>
<DIV ALIGN="center"><H1>Using HTML</H1> </DIV>
<H2>The Paragraph Tag</H2>
<P>This is an example of a paragraph typed into a web page.
Simply pressing the enter key doesn't work to separate
paragraphs into different paragraphs. The paragraph tag
creates paragraph breaks.</P>
<P>
If you use the paragraph container tags, when you open your
file in a browser it these 2 paragraphs will now appear as
two paragraphs.</P>
<H2>The Blockquote Tag</H2>
<BLOCKQUOTE> This is an example of text typed with the block
quote tag. Blockquote is a container, block level tag that
represents block quotations. Note the differences between
this text and text that appears between the paragraph tag.
Although this block of text probably appears centered and
indented, text within this tag will not necessarily appear
this way within every browser. </BLOCKQUOTE>
<H2>The Pre tag </H2>
<PRE>With this tag
                you can place text
                        where you want it to be
</PRE>
<H2>The Break tag</H2>
<P>This tag also creates breaks <BR>
within the structure of the text,<BR>
by inserting a line break. Wherever this tag is placed,<BR>
a line break appears.</P>
</BODY>
</HTML>
```

3. Save changes to your file.

4. Now open this file within your browser. If the file is already open, use the Refresh or Reload command (depending on your browser) to update the screen and view changes. Your file should resemble Figure 9-28.

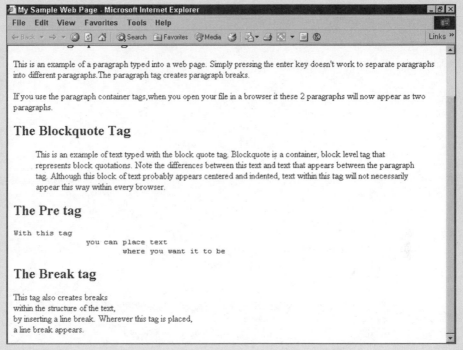

Figure 9-28: Your file opened in a browser

The first heading should now be centered. If the entire document is centered, check the closing DIV tag—it might be missing a forward slash, or it might be missing altogether. Text between the PRE tags will appear in a fixed-width font, and there should be a line break after each of the BR tags.

Lab 9-4

The focus of this exercise is lists. You will create both a numbered and a bulleted list.

1. Begin by starting a text-editing program. Type the following code:

```
<!DOCTYPE HTML PUBLIC "-//W3C//DTD HTML 4.01
Transitional//EN" "http:/www.w3.org/TR/html4/loose.dtd">
<HTML>
<HEAD>
<TITLE>Using Lists</TITLE>
</HEAD>
<BODY>
<DIV ALIGN="center"><H1>Using HTML list tags</H1></DIV>
<H2>Numbered Lists</H2>
<P>
<OL>
<LI>This is a numbered list item
```

```
<LI>requires compound tags
<LI>list item tag and ordered list tag
</OL>
</P>
<H2>Bulleted Lists</H2>
<P>
<UL>
<LI>simply lists items
<LI>Also requires 2 sets of tags
<LI>Uses the unordered list tag
<LI>Also uses the list item tag
</UL>
</P>
</BODY>
</HTML>
```

2. Call this file "lists example.htm".

3. Open this file in your browser. This file should look like the file shown in Figure 9-29.

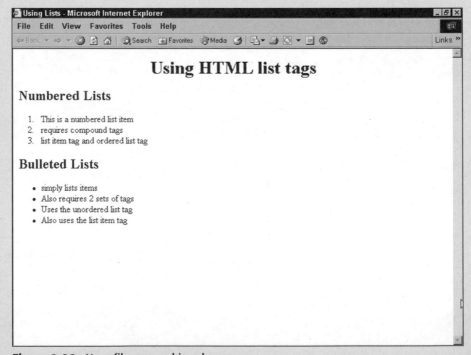

Figure 9-29: Your file opened in a browser

You have now successfully created a numbered list and a bulleted list.

Lab 9-5

Up to this point, the focus of these exercises has been on block-level elements. Now you can use text-level elements.

1. Enter the following code into your text editor:

```
<!DOCTYPE HTML PUBLIC "-//W3C//DTD HTML 4.01
Transitional//EN" "http:/www.w3.org/TR/html4/loose.dtd">
<HTML>
<HEAD>
<TITLE>Using HTML Text level elements</TITLE>
</HEAD>
<BODY>
<DIV ALIGN="center"><H1>Text Level Elements</H1></DIV>
<P>While paragraph elements affect an entire block of text,
text level elements make changes within paragraph level
elements. These text level elements can be further subdivided
into: Font style elements & Phrase elements.
<H2>Font Style Examples</H2>
<P>The purpose of font style elements is to describe the
physical appearance of text. You can make text <B>bold</B>,
<BIG>BIG</BIG>, <I>Italicised</I>, <SMALL>small</SMALL>,
<SUP>in Superscript</SUP>, <SUB>in subscript</SUB>, or in
<TT>True Type</TT> font.</P>
<H2>Phrase style examples</H2>
<P>Phrase elements affect text appearance, but also change
formatting according to what the text structurally
represents. The following are some examples of some HTML
phrase elements.
<CITE>Reference to a book, article, report, or
website</CITE>, <EM>emphasis</EM>, <STRONG>strong</STRONG>.
Feel free to experiment with other phrase elements.</P>
</BODY>
</HTML>
```

2. Name and save this file.

3. Now open this file in your browser. Your file should look like the file shown in Figure 9-30.

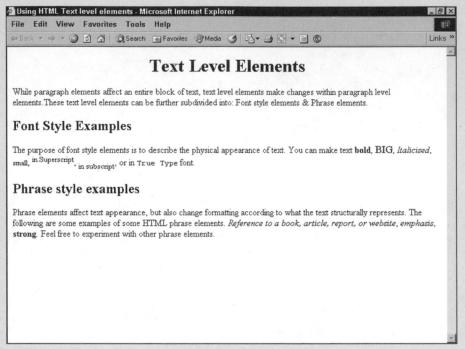

Figure 9-30: The previous code displayed in the browser

Note that all the new tags used in this lab exercise are container tags. If your file is not displayed properly, check that all closing tags are present, spelled correctly, and contain a forward slash.

Lab 9-6

This exercise gives you the opportunity to insert a horizontal graphics line to your file and make changes to it. You will also insert a picture and change its alignment and the text wrapping around the picture.

Before you begin this exercise, search for a picture of a train and copy it to the same folder as this file. Call this picture file "trains." This will be the picture that appears on your Web page.

1. Type the following code:

```
<!DOCTYPE HTML PUBLIC "-//W3C//DTD HTML 4.01
Transitional//EN"
"http:/www.w3.org/TR/html4/loose.dtd">
<HTML>
```

```
<HEAD>
<TITLE>I love Trains</TITLE>
</HEAD>
<BODY>
<DIV ALIGN="center"><H1>Train Talk</H1></DIV>
<HR>
<IMG SRC="trains.jpg"> <ALT="Picture of a Train Engine">
<P> The popularity of train travel has been lost in this day
and age of planes and automobiles. Sadly few people
experience the magic of travelling a great distance by train.
The historical significance of the train itself and the
effect it had to our culture is lost to most people. </P>
<P>
When you travel via a train there is time to you can think or
sleep and leave all the concentrating to the engineer,
tremendously more relaxing that driving your car. You also
get to see the countryside you are travelling past. There is
a comforting transition that you simply don't get when you
travel quickly by air.</P>
</BODY>
</HTML>
```

2. Open this file in your browser and compare it to Figure 9-31.

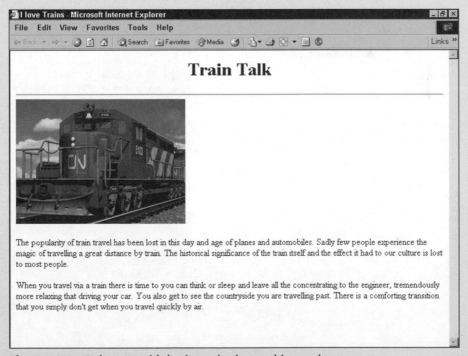

Figure 9-31: Web page with horizontal rule, graphics, and text

3. You now have a Web page with a horizontal rule and a graphic. To make the horizontal rule shorter and thicker without the 3-D shading, edit your code as shown in the following:

```
<HR WIDTH="75%" NOSHADE ALIGN="center" SIZE="20">
```

4. Look at this file in your browser. (You can update the display by clicking the Refresh command if you're using Internet Explorer or by clicking the Reload command if you're using Netscape. Both commands are found on the View menu.) Your file should look like the file shown in Figure 9-32.

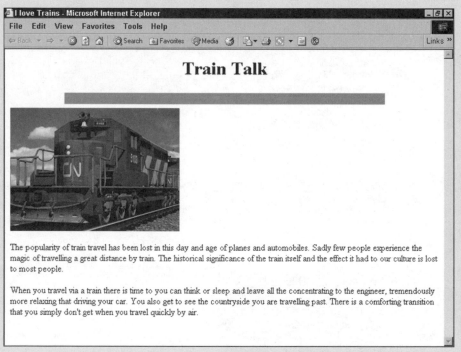

Figure 9-32: Web page with a horizontal rule increased in thickness, decreased in length, centered, and with 3-D shading removed

5. Now make the following changes to your graphic: right align it, decrease picture size by adjusting the width (you may have to use a different number for your picture), and adjust the space between text and the image (HSPACE). Use the following code as a guide:

```
<IMG SRC="trains.jpg" ALIGN="right" Width="200" HSPACE="10"
ALT="Picture of a Train Engine" >
```

Open this file in your browser and compare it to Figure 9-33.

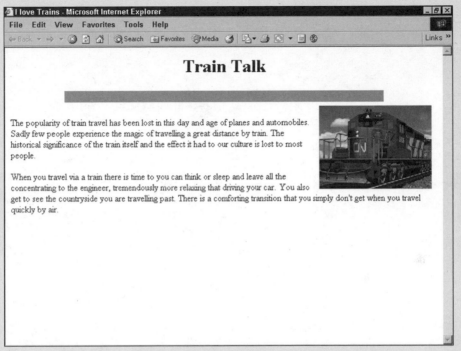

Figure 9-33: Web page with image right-aligned and in a smaller size

Congratulations! You now have the basics for creating Web pages in HTML. You used document structure tags, block-level tags, and text-level tags. In the next two chapters, you create Web pages with tables, forms, and links. You also use style sheets to get some of the same effects that you just created.

Scenario

1. You have been contracted to help with a History of Travel Web site. One of the staff started a Web page, but couldn't get it to display properly. Read the following code and then compare the code to the image in Figure 9-34 showing how the code is displayed in a browser. Then answer the questions that follow.

```
<!DOCTYPE HTML PUBLIC "-//W3C//DTD HTML 4.01
Transitional//EN"
"http:/www.w3.org/TR/html4/loose.dtd">
<HTML>
<HEAD>
<TITLE>How to Organize a Block Party</TITLE>
</HEAD>
<BODY>
```

```
<DIV ALIGN="center"><H1>Neighbourhood Block Parties</H1><DIV>
<HR WIDTH"75%" ALIGN="right>
<IMG SRC="Party.jpg"><ALT="Picture of a neighbourhood block
party">
<H2>What is a Block Party?</H2>
<P>It's a chance for neighbours to meet. It can be a quiet
affair with lemonade, balloons and cookies or it can be a big
Barbeque with games, prizes and entertainment.</P>
<H2>Why have a Block Party?</H2>
<P><UL>
<LI>Safety
<LI>Build Community Spirit
<LI>A Way to Address Neighbourhood Issues

Our neighbourhoods become safer when we know each other.
Knowing who belongs on a street and watching those who don't
is an excellent way to reduce crime in a neighbourhood. Block
parties get people together so they can address neighbourhood
issues. Finally, it is a way to enjoy your neighbourhood for
a day. It is an opportunity to enjoying the company of the
people around you, and build community spirit. </P>
</BODY>
</HTML>
```

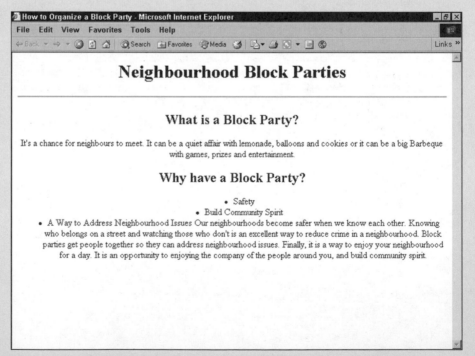

Figure 9-34: The scenario code opened up and displayed in a browser

Based on the information provided and what you have learned in this chapter, answer the following questions:

a. Why is everything in the Web page centered? Only the title should be centered. The HR should be right-aligned, paragraph text should be left-aligned, and the horizontal rule should be right-aligned.

b. What are some likely reasons for the image not being displayed properly?

c. The horizontal rule should be only 75 percent of the width of the Web page. The horizontal line is displayed to take up the full width of the screen.

d. There should be a break for a new paragraph after the last bullet list item. What can you do to fix this?

e. How can you make text display in place of the image if someone has disabled image viewing on his or her browser?

Answers to Chapter Questions

Chapter Pre-Test

1. Tags that work in pairs are called **container tags**. Instruction tags that don't need a closing tag are called **empty tags**.

2. What are the three main document structure tags? **<HTML> <HEAD> <BODY>**.

3. The **META** tag gives information about a particular Web page. It tells what the page is about, who wrote it, and when the page was last updated. It is what search engines look for and read.

4. The **DTD or Document Type Declaration** tag is optional in HTML; it describes the version and flavor of HTML being used in a particular document.

5. A **block-level** element affects one or more paragraphs, whereas a **text-level** element affects sentences, words, or characters.

6. There are **six** heading styles or levels.

7. The **<HR>** tag adds horizontal rules to your Web pages.

8. The tag that makes text appear in the title bar of the browser is the **<TITLE>** tag.

9. The **font style** text elements are meant to describe structure and not just formatting of a character, whereas the **phrase style** text elements describe the way text is formatted.

10. The **<ALT>** attribute should always be included with the IMG (image tag) to compensate for text-only browsers.

11. The three image file formats suitable for Web pages are: **GIF, JPEG,** and **PNG**.

12. The tag and attribute to change background color is **BODY, BGCOLOR**.

13. The 216 colors that are rendered correctly across multiple browsing platforms are taken from the **Web-safe color palette**.

Assessment Questions

1. Which of the following does not require a closing tag?

    C. <HR>

2. Select container tags from the choices below. Select all that apply.

    A. <BODY>

3. Container tags are found in pairs whereas Empty tags appear by themselves without a closing tag.

4. Which of the following code examples could generate errors in a browser because it is not coded correctly?

    B. <HTML LANG=en>

5. False: The word *element* in HTML does not simply mean *tag*. The element is also the content associated with the tag.

6. False: HTML 4.01 specification recommends that elements appear in upper-case and that attributes appear in lowercase.

7. Which of the following statements is true regarding META tags?

    D. All of the above

8. Which tag can specify the refresh rate for an HTML tag?

    B. <META>

9. Which statement or statements are true with regard to the BR tag?

    H. B and C. The BR tag is depreciated, and it can be used with HTML 4.0 transitional flavor. Answer A is wrong because the BR tag inserts line breaks, not paragraph breaks.

10. You want to type a stanza of poetry. The beginning of each line does not begin at the same place horizontally on the page. What tag can you use to achieve a desirable result?

    <PRE> tag

11. Which of the following are text-level element tags? (Choose all that apply)

   B. <I>

   C. <EM>

   E. <TT>

12. Identify all phrase-level tags. (Choose all that apply)

   C. <KBD>

   D. <CITE>

13. Identify all text-level tags. (Choose all that apply)

   C. <BIG>

   D. <I>

   F. <SUP>

14. Which of the following are attributes for the HR tag?

   A. ALIGN

   B. NOSHADE

   D. WIDTH

   E. SIZE

15. Which HR attribute is used to specify the thickness of the HR line?

   B. SIZE

16. Which of the following can be a type of GIF file?

   A. Transparent

   B. Interlaced

   C. Animated

17. Which of the following will correctly change background colors on a Web page?

   A. <BODY BGCOLOR="#FF0000">

18. Select all statements that are correct.

   B. It is possible to change the color of text links on your Web page.

   D. The numbers that represent each light color mixed on your monitor can range from 0 to 255.

Scenarios

1. The answers to this chapter's scenario questions are as follows:

   a. The closing DIV tag used to center the first heading doesn't have a forward slash to close it properly.

   b. The filename is written incorrectly: misspelled or wrong file extension. Or perhaps the file is stored in a different location than the Web file and needs the correct path to be entered into the SRC value.

   c. There is no equal sign between the attribute name and value.

   d. Using a paragraph tag <P> would fix this.

   e. By entering the ALT attribute with a text value in quotation marks that describes the picture, text can replace the image when image viewing is disabled.

Resources

The following URLs sites provide some further useful information in the area of HTML:

✦ www.w3.org/MarkUp/html3/text.html

✦ www.w3.org/MarkUp/html3/logical.html

✦ www.w3.org/TR/REC-html40/present/graphics.html

✦ www.w3.org/TR/REC-html40/struct/text.html

✦ http://Webreference.com/dev/graphics/palette.html

Intermediate HTML

EXAM OBJECTIVES

1. Reference full and partial URLs.

2. Create hyperlinks for text.

3. Create hyperlinks for images.

4. Link to local files.

5. Link to remote sites.

6. Create an internal anchor and link to that anchor within the same file.

7. Create simple and complex HTML tables.

8. Add or remove table borderlines.

9. Format table rows and cells using attributes.

10. Identify HTML form elements.

11. Construct a Web form using all the HTML form elements.

12. Test your Web form using a public test engine.

CHAPTER PRE-TEST

1. Links that take you to another spot within the same Web page are called _____ links.

2. Links that take you to a separate Web file are called _____ links.

3. A link to a remote Web site must contain a _____ to that site.

4. Internal links require two parts: a _____ and an _____.

5. You can create links from text or _____.

6. The default vertical alignment for text within a table is _____?

7. A basic table must contain the following three tags: _____, _____, and _____.

8. The attribute used to adjust the horizontal alignment of text within a table is _____.

9. What container tag is needed to create a form?

10. The form-submitting attribute that defines the way that the form is sent is: _____.

✦ Answers to these questions can be found at the end of the chapter. ✦

In the last two chapters, you learned about the basics of Web authoring. This chapter takes you to a higher level of Web authoring. It builds on the topics covered in the previous chapters, and focuses on three important subjects:

✦ Links

✦ Tables

✦ Forms

Tables enhance the presentation of your information, forms assist with the collection of data, and links make the Web a fun experience.

Links

Links connect one page to another page within the same site, or to some page across the world. They catch your attention, draw you in, and allow you to dive deeper and deeper into the topic that interests you. Links are one of the most basic components of your Web page. Without them, the World Wide Web would not exist.

You activate a link by clicking it with your mouse. A link is easy to identify because your mouse pointer changes to a hand when it hovers over a link. This "jumping off point" can be either *text* or an *image*. An *internal link* takes you to another spot within a Web page. Links that send you to a separate Web file are called *external links*. This chapter explains the following link types:

✦ Links to text

✦ Links to images

✦ Links to local files

✦ Links to remote sites

A lab section at the end of this chapter offers exercises that give you practice creating the various links discussed.

Creating a Link

 Objective

Reference full and partial URLs

Create hyperlinks for text

Link to local files

Link to remote sites

To create a link, you need anchor container tags — <A>...</A> — which surround the text or image to be used as the link source. Within the start anchor tag, include the *hypertext reference,* or *HREF, attribute.* The value for the *HREF* attribute identifies the link target or site that you will be hooked up to. The following sample code displays an example of how to compose a link in HTML:

```
<A HREF="type name of file or URL here"> Text or Image tag </A>
```

The two URL types that you can specify by the HREF attribute are *fully qualified URLs* and *partial URLs.* When linking to a page stored within the same folder as your Web page, type the name of the file into your code as follows:

```
<A HREF="Filename with extension">text for link</A>
```

For example:

```
<A HREF="planning.htm">Planning a Block Party</A>
```

The preceding code sample references an external file by using a partial URL. This way of referencing links works well when two HTML files that are being linked together are stored within the same folder.

 Cross-Reference

URLs are discussed in more detail in Chapter 1.

Partial URLs can reference more than just files within the same folders. They can reference a file stored on the same computer, but within a different folder. When you link a file this way, you must include the pathname with the filename.

```
<A HREF="/blockparties/organizing.htm">
```

In this case, blockparties is the path, and organizing.htm is the filename. The preceding code syntax references an external link with a partial URL. Partial URLs can direct you to a file stored on a different computer. The partial URL must include the protocol, hostname, and domain name in order for the link to work.

```
<A HREF="http://www.colsen.com/">
```

In this example, the protocol is `http`, the hostname is `www`, and the domain name is `colsen.com`. The preceding example will take you to the default home page of the Web site referenced.

You can use a *fully qualified URL* to reference a link to a home page document or to a specific file within an external Web site. The syntax for a fully qualified URL is as follows:

```
<A HREF="Protocol://servername.domainname/filename.htm">
```

Refer to Chapter 8 for more information on default home page filenames.

When you use a fully qualified URL, find out the name of the default file. Names for default files are usually something like `home.htm` or `index.htm`. The following code is an example of a fully qualified URL referenced in a link to a homepage:

```
<A HREF=" http://www.yury.f2s.com/start.html">Sample link to an
external site</A>
```

Using a fully qualified URL to link to a specific file within a site works exactly like linking to the default home page. (Lab Exercise 10-1 will give you practice in creating both of these basic links.)

Image links

Create hyperlinks for images

The previous example created text links. Creating links from images works the same way as creating text links. The anchor <A> tags are placed on either side of the image tag, and the HREF attribute must be included to reference the link, as in the following example:

```
<A HREF="planning.htm"><IMG SRC="picture.jpg"></A>
```

When an image is also a link, a colored border surrounds the image. If your mouse is held over the image link, the mouse pointer becomes a hand. You can create image links by using partial URLs or fully qualified URLs. (Lab Exercise 10-2 will provide practice in creating image links.)

Internal links

Create an internal anchor and link to that anchor within the same file

Occasionally, you may need to create links to other parts of the same document. These *internal links* allow a user to jump to a specific point in a page quickly rather than having to scroll.

Creating internal links involves two steps: the first is creating an *anchor*, and the second is creating the *link*.

An anchor is the location in the page to which you want a link to jump. To create an anchor, use the <A> tag with the NAME attribute using the following syntax:

```
<A NAME="Anchor reference name"> Text or image to jump to</A>
```

The following is an anchor code example:

```
<A NAME="Interests">My Hobbies</A>
```

In this example, I have created an anchor to the text "My Hobbies." The name that will be used as a reference to this anchor is "Interests."

An example of a link that would jump to the above anchor follows:

```
<A HREF="#Interests">To see a list of my hobbies click
here!</A>
```

As you can see, the HREF attribute value references an anchor within a document. When you click the link, you are taken to that anchor. The value for the HREF attribute must always include the hash symbol (#) before the reference name of the anchor. This symbol instructs the browser to search for the anchor inside the current page. Omitting the symbol will cause the link to fail. (Lab Exercise 10-4 provides practice in creating internal links.)

Tables

 Create simple and complex HTML tables.

Tables serve many purposes. For example, they display tabular text and place text in specific locations. By placing text and images within table cells, you achieve more flexibility for aligning these elements both vertically and horizontally. Tables have been part of HTML since version 2.0. Over the years, the code has extended to offer extra options.

Tables can be simple or complex. Regardless of the complexity, certain elements are common to all tables. To compose a basic HTML table, the following three elements are mandatory:

✦ Table
✦ Table row
✦ Table data

Also common, but not mandatory, are *header* and *table caption* elements. To see how these basic elements are used together to form a simple table, study the following HTML code:

```
<HTML>
<HEAD>
<TITLE>table example</TITLE>
</HEAD>
<BODY>
<TABLE>
<CAPTION>Children's Activities</CAPTION>
<TR>
<TH>Time</TH><TH>Activity</TH>
</TR>
<TR>
<TD>2:00 - 3:00</TD><TD>Scavenger Hunt</TD>
</TR>
<TR>
<TD>3:00-3:30</TD><TD>Cameron the Clown</TD>
</TR>
</TABLE>
</BODY>
<HTML>
```

Figure 10-1 shows how this code will be rendered in a browser.

Figure 10-1: An example of a table created from the five basic tags displayed in a browser.

Table

The <TABLE> container tags hold all the elements that describe the table. They define where the table starts and ends. All other table elements must appear between the table container tags.

Table caption

The table caption is typically the first element to appear within the table tags. This element is optional and gives a brief description of the table. Captions are appropriate sometimes, but you won't need them at other times. In Figure 10-1, for example, the caption "Children's Activities" appears centered across the top of the table.

Table row

Table row <TR> container tags identify the beginning and end of each row. This element is required to define the structure of the table, and must be present in all tables. Table row elements contain the table heading and table data.

Table heading

Nested within table row tags, the table heading <TH> tags define the *beginning* and *end* of heading text. Table headings are typically placed in the *top row*, or in the *first column*. Figure 10-1 shows an example of a table heading as rendered in a browser. As you can see in this figure, the text "Time" and "Activity" is emphasized, making it appear as a heading. Because not all tables require a heading, this element is optional.

Table data

Table data tags <TD> mark the beginning and end of text within each table cell. This element is absolutely necessary, except when the table heading element is used. These tags are nested between the table row tags.

Changing table defaults

Add or remove table borderlines.

Format table rows and cells using attributes.

The chapter text and examples to this point have discussed how to create very simple tables. The browser did not display the table borders, however; instead, the browser decided how to display the following: text alignment, table width, table background colors, and so on. This chapter will now examine attributes that let you, rather than the browser, dictate how your table will look.

Border

By default, the table borders are not displayed by browsers. If you want lines showing the borders of cells within your table, you need the border attribute. This attribute also allows you to specify the border width. See the following code sample:

```
<TABLE BORDER="2">
```

The value "2" that follows the BORDER attribute in the preceding code tells the browser to render a table with a border of two pixels. To increase border thickness, increase the number of pixels for the border attribute.

Width

By default, browsers determine the width of your table. The width attribute allows you to specify how wide the table will appear on the computer screen. With this attribute, you can specify the width by a percentage or by pixels, as in the following example:

```
<TABLE WIDTH="60%">

The preceding code results in the table width taking up 60
percent of the total screen. You can also specify the exact
width of your table in pixels, as in the following
example:<TABLE WIDTH="400">
```

The value of the preceding width attribute is 400 pixels. Increasing the table width increases the white space around the text within the cells. The width attribute determines how wide your table will be displayed by the browser.

In the Real World Specifying table width in pixels can result in a table that is larger than the width of the screen. Because you have no control over the browser and monitors used by people viewing your pages, it is best to specify width in percentages.

Cell padding

The CELL PADDING attribute is another way to control the white space within your table. This attribute enables you to adjust the space between the table border and text within cells of the table. The value for the CELLPADDING attribute is a number that represents the number of pixels. The syntax for this attribute is as follows:

```
<TABLE CELLPADDING="12">
```

The space between the contents and table border is measured in pixels. The higher the number of pixels, the more space added. A value of zero means that the cell contents and borders come into contact with each other.

Height

You can adjust the height of a row or cell with the HEIGHT attribute. This attribute was depreciated in HTML 4.0, but is included in the CIW courseware. It is used with the TR, TD, and TH tags.

Background color

You can change the background colors in your table with the BGCOLOR attribute. This attribute works like the BGCOLOR attribute that is used with the <BODY> tag;

a word or a hexadecimal number can represent its value. The following is an example of the code syntax:

```
<TABLE BGCOLOR="RED">
```

Or

```
<TABLE BGCOLOR="FF0033">
```

The first code example represents the color value with a word; the second code example specifies the color value with a hexadecimal number. When you place the BGCOLOR attribute within the <TABLE> tag, you change the background color of your entire table. You also have more options; for example, you can change the background of selected parts of your table. What this attribute changes depends on where it is placed.

 For more information about hexadecimal numbers, the BGCOLOR attribute, and colors, see Chapter 9.

Using the BGCOLOR attribute within the <TABLE> tag changes the background color of the entire table. Similarly, when placed within the <TR> tag, this attribute changes the background color of a specific row. You can even specify the background of individual cells by placing this attribute within the <TD> tag or <TH> tags. See Table 10-1 for examples.

Table 10-1
BGCOLOR Attribute

TAG used with BGCOLOR	Code Example	Element changed
<TABLE>	<TABLE BGCOLOR="color">	Background color of table
<TR>	<TR BGCOLOR ="color">	Background color of a row
<TD>	<TD BGCOLOR ="color">	Background color of a table data cell
<TH>	<TH BGCOLOR ="color">	Background color of a table heading cell

 Some color changes are rendered differently in Explorer and Navigator. This is also true of many table attributes. You will need to observe your table in both browsers frequently to ensure that the table is displayed correctly.

Alignment

You have many alignment options when working with tables. You can control the horizontal alignment of the entire table on your Web page, or you can control the alignment of specific parts of your table. You can use all of the following to change alignment:

✦ <DIV> tag

✦ VALIGN attribute

✦ ALIGN attribute

<DIV> TAG

When the table container tags are nested within the DIV tags, you can control the alignment of your entire table. By default, your table is left-aligned. The DIV tag can either center or right-align your table.

```
<DIV ALIGN="center">
<TABLE>
<TR>
<TH>Designation</TH>
<TH>Wages</TH>
</TR>
<TR>
<TD>Level 1</TD>
<TD>$25,000</TD>
</TR>
<TR>
<TD>Level 2</TD>
<TD>$30,000</TD>
</TR>
<TR>
<TD>Level 3</TD>
<TD>$35,000</TD>
</TABLE>
</DIV>
```

Note how the DIV tags are placed outside the TABLE tags in the preceding code. For an example of how this code displays within your browser, refer to Figure 10-2.

Cross-Reference For more information about using the DIV tag to center text and images, see Chapter 9.

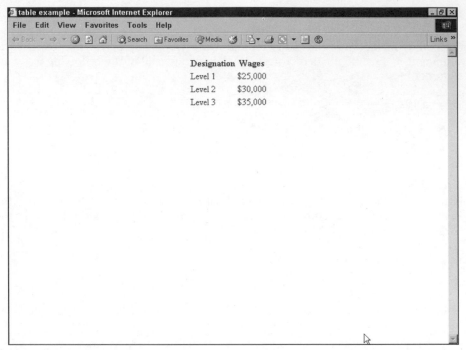

Figure 10-2: The DIV tag used to center a table as displayed within a browser.

The ALIGN Attribute

The DIV tag is not the only means of changing the alignment of an entire table: You can use the ALIGN attribute with the <TABLE> tag to center or right-align a table. The ALIGN attribute has three values: left, right, and center. The following is an example of code using the ALIGN attribute:

```
<TABLE ALIGN="center">
<TR>
<TH>Designation</TH>
<TH>Wages</TH>
</TR>
<TR>
<TD>Level 1</TD>
<TD>$25,000</TD>
</TR>
<TR>
<TD>Level 2</TD>
<TD>$30,000</TD>
</TR>
<TR>
<TD>Level 3</TD>
<TD>$35,000</TD>
</TABLE>
```

To see how the preceding code displays within a browser, refer to Figure 10-3.

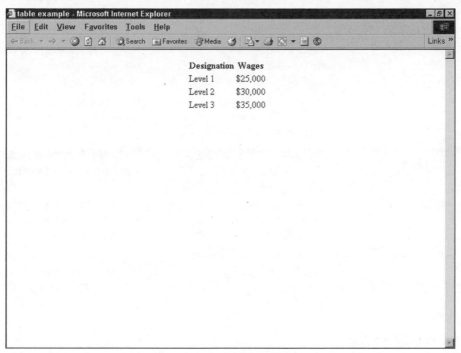

Figure 10-3: The ALIGN attribute used with the center value causes the table to appear centered in the browser.

You can also use the ALIGN attribute to change the alignment of specific parts of your table. For example, when the ALIGN attribute is used within the <TR> tag, it indicates changes to the alignment for the contents of that row. By using the ALIGN attribute within the <TD> or <TH> tags, you also have the flexibility of changing the alignment of contents within a single cell.

The ALIGN attribute has one more use within tables: If you use this attribute with the <CAPTION> tag, you have the option of placing your caption under your table. By default, the caption will always appear at the top of tables. The following is a code example for changing the placement of your table caption:

```
<CAPTION ALIGN="bottom">My example</CAPTION>
```

For a summary of how the ALIGN attribute can be used with various elements, refer to Table 10-2.

Table 10-2
ALIGN Attribute

TAG used with ALIGN	Code Examples	Element changed
<TABLE>	<TABLE ALIGN="right">, <TABLE ALIGN="left">, <TABLE ALIGN="center">	Horizontal alignment of entire table; By default, the table will be left-aligned
<TR>	<TR ALIGN ="right">, <TR ALIGN ="left">, <TR ALIGN ="center">	Horizontal alignment of a table row
<TD>	<TD ALIGN ="right">, <TD ALIGN ="left">, <TD ALIGN ="center">	Horizontal alignment of table data; by default, table data is left-aligned.
<TH>	<TH ALIGN ="right">, <TH ALIGN ="left">, <TH ALIGN ="center">	Horizontal alignment of table heading; by default, the table headings are centered.
<CAPTION>	<CAPTION ALIGN="top">, <CAPTION ALIGN="bottom">	Alignment of table caption; by default, the caption will appear at the top of a table.

The VALIGN Attribute

The VALIGN attribute controls vertical alignment of the information within a table. The values for VALIGN are top, middle, and bottom. The VALIGN attribute enables you to control the vertical alignment within rows or cells. See Table 10-3 for a summary of tags that you can use with this attribute.

10-3
VALIGN Attribute

TAG used with ALIGN	Code Examples	Element changed
<TR>	<TR VALIGN ="top">, <TR VALIGN ="middle">, <TR VALIGN ="bottom">	Vertical alignment of a table row
<TD>	<TD VALIGN =" top ">, <TD VALIGN =" middle ">, <TD VALIGN =" bottom ">	Vertical alignment of table data
<TH>	<TH VALIGN =" top ">, <TH VALIGN =" middle ">, <TH VALIGN =" bottom ">	Vertical alignment of table heading

To truly see the effects of changing vertical alignment, you must first increase the height of the cells. Read the following HTML code that incorporates the VALIGN attribute. As also demonstrated in the preceding figure (10-3), the VALIGN attribute can place text at the top of a cell.

```
<TABLE>
<TR VALIGN="bottom">
<TH HEIGHT="55">Designation</TH>
<TH>Wages</TH>
</TR>
<TR>
<TD HEIGHT="50">Level 1</TD>
<TD VALIGN="top">$25,000</TD>
</TR>
<TR>
<TD>Level 2</TD>
<TD>$30,000</TD>
</TR>
<TR>
<TD>Level 3</TD>
<TD>$35,000</TD>
</TR>
</TABLE>
```

Spanning

Occasionally, you may want to have a heading span the width of multiple columns or across multiple rows. The attributes ROWSPAN and COLSPAN allow you to do this. These attributes are placed within <TH> or <TD> tags. The value for these attributes is a number representing the number of columns or rows over which they should span, as in the following examples:

```
<TH COLSPAN="2">My title</TH>
```

Or

```
<TD ROWSPAN="5">
```

Figure 10-4 shows an example of a heading spanned across multiple rows.

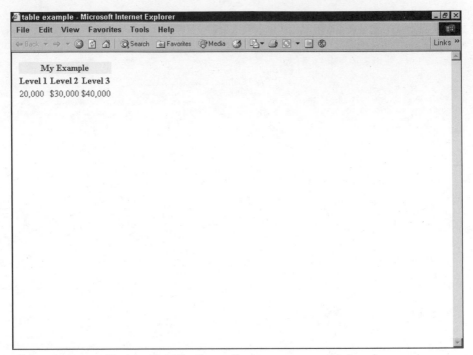

Figure 10-4: A table in which the first cell spans across multiple columns as a result of using the COLSPAN attribute.

Forms

 Identify HTML form elements.

Construct a Web form using all the HTML form elements.

Test your Web form using a public test engine.

If you have ever visited a Web site and filled out information about yourself or a product or service that you were interested in, then you have used what is known as a *Web form*. Web forms gather information from users. Web forms are used for many purposes, including the following:

   ✦ Online surveys

   ✦ Information requests

   ✦ Online shopping

   ✦ Banking

To create a Web form, you combine HTML elements and *controls*. The controls are simply the elements of a form that can be used to enter data. Common controls include text boxes, checkboxes, or radio buttons. (These controls are discussed in more detail in this chapter.)

All forms contain a *submit button*, and most forms include a *reset button*. Clicking the submit button sends the information to a server designated to manage it. Clicking the reset button clears a form of all data and allows the user to begin again.

Information sent to the server through the use of a form is typically processed by the server using *Common Gateway Interface* (CGI) scripts. What these scripts do with the data varies depending on the intended purpose of the form.

Some of the more common scripting languages used to create these scripts include the following:

✦ Practical Extraction and Reporting Language (PERL)

✦ C Programming Language

✦ VBScript

✦ JavaScript

These CGI scripts are typically *server-side scripts*, meaning that they are processed on the server rather than on the client. Because all processing is done on the server, this type of scripting can slow down a busy Web server that is hosting or running a Web Site.

The CIW courseware states that CGI can be used as either server-side script or client-side script; however, most other sources define CGI as a strictly server-side scripting solution.

Client-side scripts process forms on the client computer. Typically, client-side scripts are intended to give the user information. These scripts can be ActiveX, JavaScript, VBScript, or Java applets.

For more information about HTML form processing, refer to Chapter 17, which details server-side scripting, database connectivity, and the server handling of HTML forms.

Form elements

The *form* <FORM> </FORM> *container tag* defines where your form begins and ends. It is a block-level element always begins a new line. This element contains the following:

✦ All the form controls

✦ Directions for the management of submitted forms

✦ Text and text-level elements

✦ Other block-level elements, such as paragraphs and lists

The following example shows code for a typical form:

```
<DOCTYPE HTML PUBLIC "-//W3C//DTD HTML 4.01 Transitional//EN"
"http://www.w3.org/TR html4/loose.dtd">
<HTML>
<HEAD>
<TITLE> Form Example</TITLE>
</HEAD>
<BODY>
<FORM
  ACTION="http//myserver.com/cgi-bin/script"
  METHOD="post">

Enter Your ID Number: <INPUT TYPE="text" NAME="ID"
SIZE="35"><P>

Enter your e-mail address<INPUT TYPE="text" NAME="Email"
SIZE="40"><P>

Would you like to receive our newsletter?<BR>
<INPUT TYPE="radio" NAME="AddToList" VALUE="Yes" CHECKED> Yes
<INPUT TYPE="radio" NAME="AddToList" VALUE="no">No
<P>

<INPUT TYPE="SUBMIT"> <INPUT TYPE="RESET">
</FORM>
</BODY>
</HTML>
```

Don't worry about the code elements in the preceding list that are new to you — they will be explained in more detail later in this chapter. At this point, compare the code to Figure 10-5, which shows how this simple form will appear in a browser.

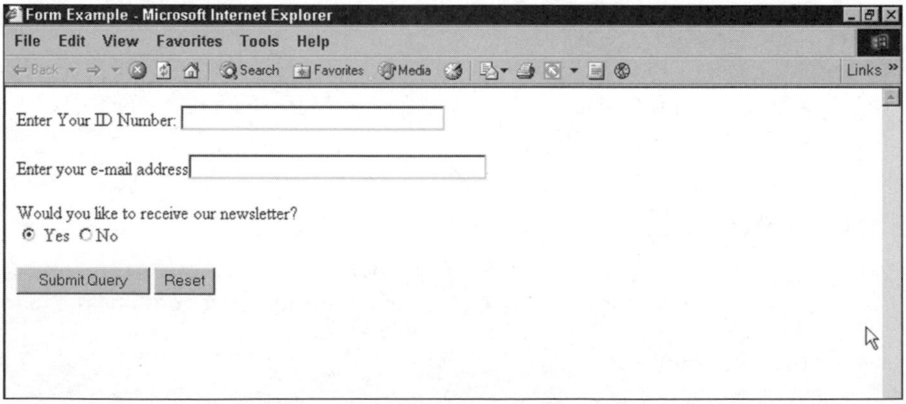

Figure 10-5: Sample form displayed within a browser.

As you can see from the figure, the<FORM></FORM> container tag holds all form elements. You must always enter the closing tag for the form element. Omitting the closing tag can result in certain browsers being unable to display your form, and although it's possible for some browsers to display the form correctly, they probably won't be able to send it correctly. A form that can't be processed is useless.

Form submitting attributes

You will often see two elements associated with the opening form tag: METHOD and ACTION. The METHOD attribute defines the way that form information will be transferred from the client's browser to the Web server. This attribute uses two values: "get" and "post". See the following syntax examples:

```
<FORM
  METHOD="get">
```

Or

```
<FORM
  METHOD="post">
```

The "get" value places the user-input data into a URL that is used as a query string. This method is typically used when the user wants to "get" information.

Note You often see this when you fill out a search request at a Web search engine site. The words that you are searching are appended to a URL and are used to display your list of found links.

The "post" value is typically used to send a large amount of data obtained from a form — usually with the intent of posting it to a database. With "post", the data is directed to a specific location identified by the ACTION attribute. The ACTION attribute typically contains a URL that points to a specific CGI script in order to process the data from the form. What the script actually does with the data depends on the script.

Form fields

After you have the specified the submission method for the form's information, you are ready to create fields for your form. You can use several tags for this purpose, including **<INPUT>**, **<SELECT>**, and **<TEXTAREA>**.

In the Real World The CIW course focuses on very few of the many possible form fields available.

The <INPUT> tag is used to create the following:

✦ Check boxes

✦ Text boxes

✦ Radio buttons

✦ Submit buttons

✦ Reset buttons

The <SELECT> tag is used to create the following:

✦ Select lists

✦ Multiple select lists

The <TEXTAREA> creates a scrolling text field.

Within each of these tags, you must enter the appropriate attributes. The following attributes are used with these tags in this chapter: TYPE, NAME, and VALUE.

The TYPE attribute is used with the tags <INPUT>, <SELECT>, and <TEXTAREA>. The TYPE attribute is used to identify the type of field that you are creating. Specific field types are connected to specific tags. For example, the INPUT tag combined with the TYPE attribute can be used to make text boxes, radio buttons, and lists.

```
<INPUT TYPE="text" NAME="ID" SIZE="35">
```

The NAME attribute is used with all tags that create form fields. Each field has a unique name. When a user enters information into a field, the information is sent for processing with the field name. For example, if a user entered "555-1234" into a field named "PhoneNo", the server will receive the data as: "PhoneNo=555-1234". These value-to-field associations help manage and organize data. The following code shows the name attribute with the value "PhoneNo".

```
<INPUT TYPE="text" NAME="PhoneNo" SIZE="35">
```

The client sends the form data to the server. The form data information comes to the server as plain text. If you examined this data, you would see something similar to the following example:

```
ID=colsen&e-mail=colsen@olsen.com&age=29
```

This example represents three fields of data (ID, e-mail, and age). An ampersand (&) separates the data into fields, and equal signs (=) separate fieldnames from data entered into the field. A CGI script running on the server can be used to examine the data string, extract the relevant information, and organize it in a way that is easy to read. For example, after the preceding data has passed through the CGI script process, it can be placed into a format similar to the following:

```
ID Badge: colsen
E-mail Address: colsen@somedomain.net:
Age: 29
```

Text boxes

Text boxes provide places for users to type information, such as ID badge number, e-mail address, age, name, and so on. Text boxes are useful for any instance where the required information can be almost anything. Name, phone number, address, and e-mail address fields are all good candidates for using a text box.

Text boxes are created with the <INPUT> tag. The basic syntax for a text box is structured like the following:

```
Field label: <INPUT TYPE="text" Name="FieldName">
```

The following is an example of this code syntax:

```
Enter Your Phone Number here: <INPUT TYPE="text"
NAME="PhoneNo">
```

Figure 10-6 shows how this code will look as interpreted by a browser.

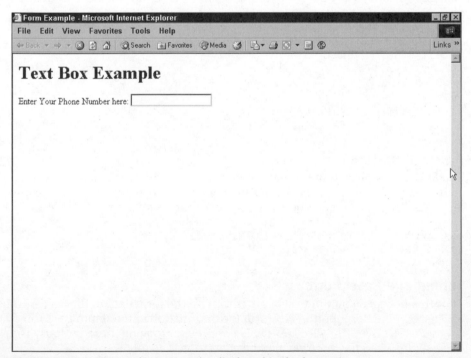

Figure 10-6: Basic text box example, displayed in the browser

Along with the mandatory attributes, TYPE and NAME, three other attributes are commonly used when creating text boxes. These attributes follow:

✦ VALUE

✦ SIZE

✦ MAXLENGTH

The VALUE attribute

You can use the VALUE attribute when you want default text to appear within your field. Code using this attribute is structured as follows:

```
<INPUT TYPE="text" NAME="FieldNameHere" VALUE="DefaultTextHere">
```

A specific example follows:

```
Country of Birth: <INPUT TYPE="text" NAME="country" VALUE="Canada">
```

The SIZE attribute

The SIZE attribute changes the width of the text box that is rendered in your browser by specifying the value in number of pixels. This SIZE attribute does not change the number of characters that may be entered into the field. Code using this attribute is structured as follows:

```
<INPUT TYPE="text" NAME="FieldNameHere"
SIZE="EnterNoOfPixelsHere">
```

A specific example follows:

```
Last Name: <INPUT TYPE="text" NAME="FieldNameHere"
SIZE="EnterNoOfPixelsHere>
```

The MAXLENGTH attribute

The MAXLENGTH attribute contrasts the SIZE attribute by restricting the number of characters that can be displayed in a field while having no effect on the field width displayed by the browser. Code using this attribute is structured as follows:

```
<INPUT TYPE="text" NAME="FieldNameHere"
MAXLENGTH="NoOfCharacters">
```

Submit and Reset buttons

All forms need a Submit button in order to send the form data to the server to be processed. The Reset button clears all the information entered into the form so the user can start over. The <INPUT> tag is required for making these buttons. The code syntax used to create each of these buttons is as follows:

```
<INPUT TYPE="SUBMIT">
<INPUT TYPE="RESET">
```

Figure 10-7 shows the display of both the Submit and the Reset button.

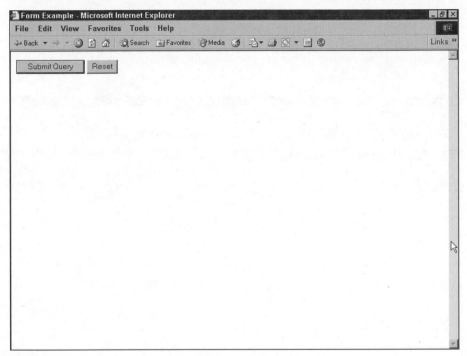

Figure 10-7: Submit and Reset buttons as displayed by a browser.

Radio buttons

Radio buttons are used when only one item from a list can be selected. These buttons are frequently used for answering "yes" or "no" questions. You can create these buttons by using the <INPUT> tag with the NAME and VALUE attributes.

The code syntax for these buttons is as follows:

```
<INPUT TYPE="radio" NAME="FieldNameHere" VALUE="TypeValueHere">
```

Many forms have one radio button selected by default. To do this, add the CHECKED attribute to the appropriate radio button's tag.

```
<INPUT TYPE="radio" NAME="FieldNameHere" VALUE="TypeValueHere"
CHECKED>
```

A specific example follows:

```
Do you like broccoli?<BR>
Yes <INPUT TYPE="radio" NAME="preference" VALUE="yes" CHECKED>
No <INPUT TYPE="radio" NAME="preference" VALUE="no">
```

To see how these radio buttons are rendered in a browser, refer to Figure 10-8.

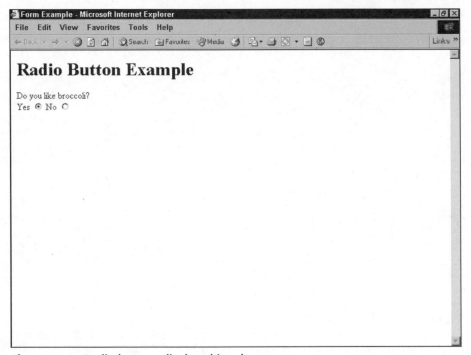

Figure 10-8: Radio buttons displayed in a browser

In the preceding example, the radio buttons share the same control name, which restricts the user to selecting only one of the two buttons. Radio buttons are usually entered as mutually exclusive data sets.

Check boxes

Check boxes provide users with the option of selecting more than one choice from a list. These fields appear as boxes that appear "checked" when the user clicks on them. As with radio buttons, you use the <INPUT> tag, with the TYPE and NAME attributes. The following is the syntax code for creating check boxes:

```
<INPUT TYPE="checkbox" NAME=" FieldNameHere" VALUE>
```

The following code creates word processor, spread sheet, graphics, and e-mail check boxes:

```
Select types of software you have installed on your
computer:<BR>
<INPUT TYPE="checkbox" NAME="words">Word Processor <BR>
<INPUT TYPE="checkbox" NAME="numbers"> Spread sheets<BR>
<INPUT TYPE="checkbox" NAME="pictures"> Graphics <BR>
<INPUT TYPE="checkbox" NAME="mail"> E-mail
```

Refer to Figure 10-9 to see how this code is rendered in a browser.

Figure 10-9: Check boxes displayed in a browser

With check box fields, you have the option of storing a group of check boxes under the same database field, or storing each check box under separate fields. The previous code example showed text boxes that will be stored under separate field names.

To group boxes under the same name, they must share the same name attribute, as in the following example:

```
Select types of software you have installed on your
computer:<BR>
<INPUT TYPE="checkbox" NAME="Software">Word Processor <BR>
<INPUT TYPE="checkbox" NAME=" Software "> Spread sheets<BR>
<INPUT TYPE="checkbox" NAME=" Software "> Graphics <BR>
<INPUT TYPE="checkbox" NAME=" Software "> E-mail
```

In this second code example, the information from all four check boxes will be stored under the "Software" field.

Select lists

Select lists are drop-down lists that contain many options from which the user can choose. You can choose from two types of select lists:

✦ **Single Option Select Lists** restrict the user to one selection.

✦ **Multiple Option Select Lists** allow the user to select multiple options.

The basic syntax of these two options is the same. To create a select list field, use the <SELECT> container tag with the NAME attribute. The <OPTION> tag follows the <SELECT> tag. The <OPTION> tags provide the menu choices for the field. The following is an example of the code syntax:

```
<SELECT NAME="fieldnamehere">
<OPTION>1ST Option
<OPTION>2nd Option
<OPTION>3rd Option
            .
            .
            .
<OPTION>Last Option
</Select>

The following is an example of  HTML code which will produce a
Single Option Select list:Select your favorite color:
<SELECT NAME="color">
<OPTION>Red
<OPTION>Blue
<OPTION>Yellow
<OPTION>Green
<OPTION>Orange
<OPTION>Purple
</SELECT>
```

Refer to Figure 10-10 to see how this will appear in your browser.

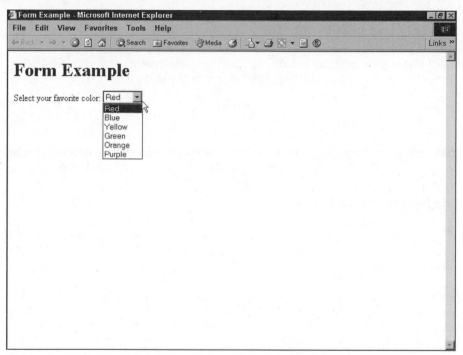

Figure 10-10: Select List Field as displayed in a browser

You will usually have to scroll the list of items that are available to you. By default, you can only select one item from the list. The inclusion of the MULTIPLE attribute within the <SELECT> tag makes it possible for users to select multiple items from the list. By following the MULTIPLE attribute with a value number, you can restrict the number of items a person picks. The following is an example of this syntax:

```
Select your favorite colors. Choose no more than three.
<SELECT NAME="color" MUILTIPLE=3>
<OPTION>Red
<OPTION>Blue
<OPTION>Yellow
<OPTION>Green
<OPTION>Orange
<OPTION>Purple
</SELECT>
```

You can select the multiple options by holding down the Shift key or Control key while clicking in a Windows environment or with a simultaneous command and click for Macintosh environments.

What you display in your list options sometimes differs slightly from the value that you want to send to the server. For example, suppose that you will display a list of numbers written as words, but you want the numeric values sent to the server. In this case, add the VALUE attribute to the <OPTION> tag, as in the following example:

```
<OPTION VALUE="2">Two
```

Using the VALUE option also works well if you have text strings showing in the drop-down list, but you prefer one-word responses sent back to the server.

Scrolling text area box

Earlier in the chapter, a text box field was used to gather text information from a user. Sometimes, however, you need to obtain more than a few words of text. In this situation, use a Scrolling Text Area Box field to collect your information. This field allows a user to enter multiple sentences or paragraphs.

To create this field, use the Text area container tag <TEXTAREA> </TEXTAREA>. Any text placed between the opening and closing TEXTAREA tags will be used as default text within the field. The user can edit or change this text as desired. Several attributes commonly used with this tag are COLS, ROWS, and WRAP.

The COLS and ROWS attributes together specify how much text can be placed in the field. The COLS attribute defines how many text characters are allowed across the width of the text box. The ROWS attribute identifies how many rows of text may be entered into the box. The following is an example of the code syntax for this field:

```
<TEXTAREA NAME="Suggestions" COLS="30" ROWS="6" WRAP="none">
</TEXTAREA>
```

See Figure 10-11 for an example of a scrolling text box.

The WRAP attribute has two values: none and virtual. If the value of *none* is specified, text that the user enters will stay in one continuous line, making it necessary for the user to scroll to the right to read the entry. The *virtual* value automatically wraps text to the next line when text reaches the border of the box. This text is sent to the server as one long text string. The wrap attribute is allowed in HTML 4.01 Transitional but has depreciated in favor of style sheets.

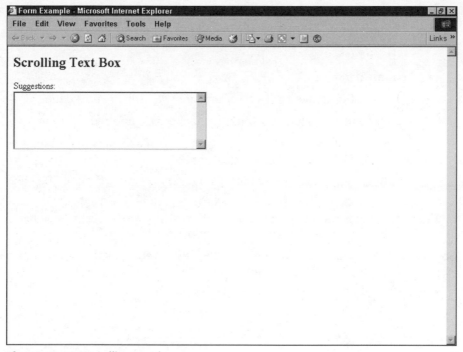

Figure 10-11: Scrolling text box

Key Point Summary

The key point summary highlights the major topics covered in this chapter.

✦ Links are one of the most basic components of your Web page.

✦ A link is easy to identify because your mouse pointer changes to a hand when it hovers over a link.

✦ An *internal link* takes you to another spot within a Web page.

✦ An External Link takes you to a separate Web page.

✦ To create a link, you need anchor container tags — <A HREF>...</A>.

✦ The *HREF* attribute identifies the link target.

✦ Internal Links require both the link and an anchor .

✦ An anchor is created by using the <A> tag with the NAME attribute.

✦ The following three elements are mandatory for HTML tables:

- Table

- Table row

- Table data

✦ Controls are the elements of a form that allow a user to enter data.

✦ Common controls include text boxes, checkboxes, and radio buttons.

✦ Information sent to the server through the use of a form is processed by the server using *Common Gateway Interface* (CGI) scripts.

✦ CGI scripts are typically processed on the server rather than on the client.

✦ *Client-side scripts* process forms on the client computer. Typically, client-side scripts are intended to give the user information. These scripts can be ActiveX, JavaScript, VBScript, or Java applets.

✦ The METHOD attribute for the Form tag defines the way that form information will be transferred to the server (get or put).

✦ The <INPUT> tag is used to create the following:

- Check boxes

- Text boxes

- Radio buttons

- Submit buttons

- Reset buttons

✦ The <SELECT> tag is used to create the following:

- Select lists

- Multiple select lists

✦ The <TEXTAREA> tag is used to create a scrolling text field.

✦   ✦   ✦

STUDY GUIDE

Assessment Questions

1. Which of the following are examples of fully qualified URL links? (Choose all that apply)

   A. <A HREF="www.example.com">

   B. <A HREF="http//example.com">

   C. <A HREF="http://example.com/index.htm">

   D. <A HREF="http://www.example.com/internet/links.htm">

2. What needs to be included when creating a link to an external site? (Choose all that apply)

   A. <LINK> tag

   B. HREF attribute

   C. <A> tag

   D. Partial URL

   E. Fully qualified URL

3. True or False: A fully qualified URL must be referenced when creating a link to an external site.

4. Which of the following are examples of internal links? (Choose all that apply)

   A. <A HREF="#airlines">Airlines that fly to the Carribian</A>

   B. <A HREF="http:/www.keitho.com">Keith's Homepage</A>

   C. <A HREF="airlines/Europe.htm">European Airlines</A>

   D. <A HREF="wildflowers">Wildflowers of North America

5. Which of the following tags are used to create form fields? (Choose all that apply)

   A. <INPUT>

   B. <METHOD>

   C. <SELECT>

   D. <TEXTAREA>

   E. <POST>

6. True or False: Explorer and Netscape interpret tables and table attributes in exactly the same way.

7. You may use the ALIGN attribute with which of the following tags?

    A. <TABLE>

    B. <TR>

    C. <TD>

    D. <TH>

    E. <CAPTION>

8. The BGCOLOR attribute can be used with which of the following tags? (Choose all that apply)

    A. <TABLE>

    B. <TR>

    C. <TD>

    D. <TH>

    E. <CAPTION>

9. The <INPUT> tag can be used to create the following: (Choose all that apply)

    A. Check boxes

    B. Text boxes

    C. Radio buttons

    D. Submit buttons

    E. Select lists

    F. Scrolling text field

10. Which of the following attributes can be used with text boxes?

    A. TYPE

    B. NAME

    C. VALUE

    D. SIZE

    E. WRAP

Lab Exercises

Lab 10-1

In this lab you will create an HTML file using several of the Tags and concepts learned thus far. You will save this file and then create a second file which will link back to the first.

1. Start your text editor.

2. Type the following code:

```
<!DOCTYPE HTML PUBLIC "-//W3C//DTD HTML 4.01
Transitional//EN"
"http:/www.w3.org/TR/html4/loose.dtd">
<HTML>
<HEAD>
<TITLE>Planning a Block Party</TITLE>
</HEAD>
<BODY>
<DIV ALIGN="center"><H1>Planning Checklist</H1></DIV>
<P>The following is a list of things you must make sure are
done if you are to have a successful block party:
<UL>
<LI>Approach your neighbours
<LI>Set a date, time, and place.
<LI>Approach your city for permission to block the street
<LI>Secure funding - donations from local business, political
representatives, and neighbours.
<LI>Decide on the menu
<LI>Activities and Entertainment
<LI>Invitations for the neighbours
</UL>
</P>
</BODY>
<HTML>
```

3. Save this file in a folder called "block", and call this file blockplan.htm.

    The file that you just created will be the one you link to. Open the file in your browser.

4. Close this file. You will now create the file with the link codes.

5. In your text editor, type the following:

```
<!DOCTYPE HTML PUBLIC "-//W3C//DTD HTML 4.01
Transitional//EN"
"http:/www.w3.org/TR/html4/loose.dtd">
<HTML>
<HEAD>
<TITLE>How to Organize a Block Party</TITLE>
</HEAD>
<BODY>
<DIV ALIGN="center"><H1>Neighbourhood  Block
Parties</H1></DIV>
<H2>What is a Block Party?</H2>
<P>It's a chance for neighbours to meet. It can be a quiet
affair with lemonade, balloons and cookies or it can be a big
Barbeque with games, prizes and entertainment. Our
neighbourhoods become safer when we are on familiar terms
with each other. Block parties are an opportunity to enjoying
the company of the people around you, and build community
spirit.
</P>
<H2>Organizing the Party</H2>
<P><UL>
<LI>Introducing the Idea to your neighbours
<LI><A HREF="blockplan.htm">Basic Planning steps</A>
<LI>Creative tips for Getting Donations
<LI>Game & Entertainment Suggestions
<LI>Food Ideas
</UL>
</BODY>
</HTML>
```

6. Name and save this file. Call it `blockinfo.htm`.

7. Open this file in your browser.

8. The text *Basic Planning Steps* should be underlined and blue in color indicating that it is a link. Click on this link, and you will be taken to the file `blockplan.htm`, which gives you information on planning steps for a block party.

Lab 10-2

In this exercise, you will link to an external Web site using a fully qualified URL and a container tag.

1. Open the file `sample.htm` from Lab Exercise 9-3 (from the previous chapter) in your text editor.

2. Add the code displayed in bold below:

```
</HEAD>
<BODY>
<DIV ALIGN="center"><H1>Using HTML</H1> </DIV>
<P>This document highlights some of the most commonly used
tags. For more information go to:<BR>
```

```
<A HREF="http://www.w3.org/TR/REC-html40/intro/intro.html">
W3C Introduction to HTML 4</A>
<H2>The Paragraph Tag</H2>
```

3. You have just created a link to the W3C Web site. Save your changes to the file and open it in your browser.

4. The text that is your link will stand out from the rest of the text; it is colored and underlined. Now click the link to test it. You should end up at the W3C Web site. If your link doesn't work, check the spelling of your URL.

Lab 10-3

In this exercise, you will use an image to link to another file.

1. Start your text editor and type the following:

```
<!DOCTYPE HTML PUBLIC "-//W3C//DTD HTML 4.01
Transitional//EN"
"http:/www.w3.org/TR/html4/loose.dtd">
<HTML>
<HEAD>
<TITLE>Train Story</TITLE>
</HEAD>
<BODY>
<DIV ALIGN="center"><H1>Train Stories</H1></DIV>
<HR WIDTH="75%" NOSHADE ALIGN="center" SIZE="20">
<P>I first rode the train when I was 12 years old. It was not
only the first time I travelled by train, but it was my first
experience travelling alone. A real adventure! Although I
must confess, in the beginning I did not see it as an
adventure. My mother had recently died of cancer and my
father had no time to deal with me that summer. I was on my
way to stay with my grandparents. Little did I know how that
train ride would affect the rest of my life.
</P>
</BODY>
</HTML>
```

2. Name and save this file. Call it stories.htm.

3. Open this file in your browser to see how it looks.

4. Go back to working in your text editor. Open the file train.htm from Lab Exercise 9-6 (from the previous chapter).

Note

For this exercise to work, the file train.htm, its image file, and stories.htm must all be stored in the same file.

5. Add the following code that is formatted in bold text. (The text is bolded so that you can differentiate between code that was already there, and the code that you need to add.)

```
<DIV ALIGN="center"><H1>Train Talk</H1></DIV>
<HR WIDTH="75%" NOSHADE ALIGN="center" SIZE="20">
<A HREF="stories.htm"><IMG SRC="trains.jpg" AlIGN="right"
Width="200" HSPACE="10"
ALT="Picture of a Train Engine" > </A>
```

6. Now open the file trains.htm in your browser. The image on your Web page now has a colored border and when your mouse pointer changes to a hand when it is placed over the picture.

7. Click your link to test it. You should be taken to stories.htm.

If this exercise did not work for you, check the location of all your files. The image file, and both stories.htm and trains.htm should be saved in the same directory or folder.

Lab 10-4

In this exercise, you will create internal links within a long document so that you can easily navigate to that part of the document.

1. Start your text editor and open the file called exercise 10-4.htm.

2. Add the code shown in bold font in the following section. You will be creating anchors using the Anchor tag <A> and NAME attribute. Then you will enter links using the anchor tag <A> and the HREF attribute.

```
<!DOCTYPE HTML PUBLIC "-//W3C//DTD HTML 4.01
Transitional//EN"
"http:/www.w3.org/TR/html4/loose.dtd">
<HTML>
<HEAD>
<TITLE>My Sample Web Page</TITLE>
</HEAD>
<BODY>
<DIV ALIGN="center"><H1>Using HTML</H1> </DIV>
<P>This document highlights some of the most commonly used
tags. For more information go to:<BR>
<A HREF="http://www.w3.org/TR/REC-html40/intro/intro.html">
W3C Intoduction to HTML 4</A>
<UL>
<LI>
Anchor Tag<LI>
<A HREF="#Blockquote">Blockquote tag</A><LI>
Body tag<LI>
Bold<LI>
```

```
<A HREF="#break">Break Tag</A><LI>
Div tag <LI>
Emphasis<LI>
Heading Tags<LI>
Horizontal Rule<LI>
HTML Tag<LI
Image Tag<LI>
Italics<LI>
Ordered Lists<LI>
<A HREF="#Pre">PRE Tag</A><LI>
<A HREF="#Paragraph">Paragraph tag </A><LI>
Strong<LI>
Unordered lists</LI>
</UL>
<A NAME="Paragraph"><H2>The Paragraph Tag</H2></A>
<P>This is an example of a paragraph typed into a web page.
Simply pressing the enter key doesn't work to separate
paragraphs into different paragraphs.The paragraph tag
creates paragraph breaks.</P>
<P>
If you use the paragraph container tags, when you open your
file in a browser it these 2 paragraphs will now appear as
two paragraphs.</P>
<A NAME="Blockquote"><H2>The Block quote Tag</H2></A>
<BLOCKQUOTE> This is an example of text typed with the block
quote tag. Block quote is a container, block level tag that
represents block quotations. Note the differences between
this text and text that appears between the paragraph tag.
Although this block of text probably appears centered and
indented, text within this tag will not necessarily appear
this way within every browser.
</BLOCKQUOTE>
<A NAME="Pre"><H2>The Pre tag </H2></A>
<PRE>With this tag
                you can place text
                        where you want it to be
</PRE>
<A NAME="break"><H2>The Break tag</H2></A>
<P>This tag also creates breaks <BR>
within the structure of the text,<BR>
by inserting a line break. Wherever this tag is placed,<BR>
a line break appears.</P>
</BODY>
</HTML>
```

3. Now that you have added the anchors and links, you need to test them.

    a. Open this file in your browser.

    b. Scroll through your file. All links will appear in blue and will be under-
        lined, but the browser makes no formatting changes to the anchors.

Lab 10-5

In this exercise, you will create a basic HTML table.

1. Open your HTML editor. Type the following code:

```
<!DOCTYPE HTML PUBILC"-//W3C//DTD HTML 4.01
Trainsitional//EN"
"http://www.w3.org/TRhtml4/loose.dtd">
<HTML>
<HEAD>
<TITLE>
Clown Class Schedule
</title>
<BODY>
<TABLE>
<CAPTION>Autumn Course Schedule</CAPTION>
<TR>
<TH>Course</TH>
<TH>Start Date</TH>
</TR>
<TR>
<TD>Balloon Building</TD>
<TD>September 12,2001</TD>
</TR>
<TR>
<TD>Makeup 101</TD>
<TD>September 13</TD>
</TR>
<TR>
<TD>Improv</TD>
<TD>September 14</TD>
</TR>
</table>
</BODY>
</HTML>
```

2. Name and save this file. Call it `table.htm`.

3. Open the file in your browser to see how it looks.

Lab 10-6

In this exercise, you will make changes to the default settings of a basic table. You will add and increase borders, white space within cells, add color, and make alignment changes.

1. Open file `table.htm`.

2. By default, the table borders are not displayed by browser.

3. Add the BORDER attribute to the table tag, so that a table border will be displayed.

```
<TABLE BORDER="2">
```

4. Save changes to your file

5. Open your file in a browser and observe the changes. If possible, open this file in both Explorer and Netscape to view the differences.

6. Increase white space with the WIDTH attribute

```
<TABLE BORDER="2" WIDTH="90%">
```

Save your changes.

7. Open your file in a browser and observe the changes. If your file is already open, refresh your screen. If possible, open this file in both Explorer and Netscape to view the differences.

8. Change the table's background color to yellow.

```
<TABLE BORDER="2" WIDTH="90%" BGCOLOR="yellow">
```

Save your changes.

9. Switch to your browser program, refresh your screen and observe the difference.

10. Change cell height and width options. Add the following code that is in bold:

```
<BODY>
<TABLE Border="2"WIDTH="90%"BGCOLOR="yellow">
<CAPTION>Autumn Course Schedule</CAPTION>
<TR>
<TH Height="55">Course</TH>
<TH>Start Date</TH>
</TR>
<TR>
</BODY>
```

11. Save changes to your file.

12. Look at this file in your browser. Refresh your browser screen. The top row should be wider as a result of using the height attribute.

13. Change the alignment of text in specific cells by using the align attribute. Changes should be made in your text editor. Refer to the following code:

```
<TH>Start Date</TH>
</TR>
<TR>
<TD>Balloon Building</TD>
<TD ALIGN="center">September 12,2001</TD>
</TR>
<TR>
<TD>Makeup 101</TD>
<TD ALIGN="center">September 13</TD>
</TR>
<TR>
<TD>Improv</TD>
<TD ALIGN="center">September 14</TD>
</TR>
```

14. Save your changes.

15. Switch to your browser program, refresh the screen, and observe changes.

16. Center your table by using the align attribute. Adjust your code in accordance to the following code:

```
<TABLE Border="2"WIDTH="90%"BGCOLOR="yellow"ALIGN="center">
```

17. Save your changes.

18. Switch to your browser program, refresh the screen, and observe changes.

19. Switch to your text editor. Delete your table caption and add a row to the top of your table that spans across three columns. Adjust your code in accordance to the following code:

```
<TABLE Border="2"WIDTH="90%"BGCOLOR="yellow"ALIGN="center">
<CAPTION>Autumn Course Schedule</CAPTION>
<TR>
<TH COLSPAN="3" HEIGHT="60">Autumn Course Schedule</TH>
<TR>
<TH Height="55">Course</TH>
```

20. Save your changes.

21. Switch to your browser program, refresh the screen, and observe changes.

22. Create a cell that spans across multiple rows. Make changes to your file in your text-editing program.

```
<TH COLSPAN="3" HEIGHT="60">Autumn Course Schedule</TH>
<TR>
<TD ROWSPAN="4"WIDTH="20%">Free balloons and Hats for the
first 100 clowns to register!</TD>
<TH Height="55">Course</TH>
<TH>Start Date</TH>
```

23. Save your changes.

24. Switch to your browser program, refresh the screen, and observe changes.

25. Change the vertical alignment of text. Do this in your text-editing program. Adjust your code in accordance to the following:

```
<TD ROWSPAN="4"WIDTH="20%">Free balloons and Hats for the
first 100 clowns to register!</TD>
<TH Height="55" VALIGN="bottom">Course</TH>
<TH VALIGN="bottom">Start Date</TH>
</TR>
<TR>
<TD>Balloon Building</TD>
```

26. Save your changes.

27. Switch to your browser program, refresh the screen, and observe changes.

Lab 10-7

In this exercise, you will create a form. You will start by entering the <FORM> tag and the METHOD and ACTION attributes.

For this exercise, you will create an action link to your e-mail address so that you can test the form. Normally, the action link references the server containing the script that processes the form data, but not everyone reading this book will necessarily have access to a server and scripts.

Many sources recommend using the mailto link as an option to using server scripts. This is, however, not a good idea. The value within the ACTION attribute should technically be a correctly formed URL. This means that the mailto: link will not work in all situations. To achieve the best results from this exercise scenario, we recommend that you use Internet Explorer as your browser and use Outlook Express as your e-mail program.

Your form will also include the following: Text box fields, Send button, and the Reset button.

1. Enter the form tag and processing instructions by starting your HTML editor and typing the following code:

```
<DOCTYPE HTML PUBLIC "-//W3C//DTD HTML 4.01 Transitional//EN"
"http://www.w3.org/TR/html4/loose.dtd">
<HTML>
<HEAD>
<TITLE>A Form Example</TITLE>
</HEAD>
<BODY>
<H1>Request Form</H1>
<FORM
   ACTION="mailto:Type your e-mail address here"
   METHOD="POST">

</FORM>

</BODY>
</HTML>
```

2. Name and save your file. Call it formexample.htm.

3. Add code displayed in bold to create text box form fields.

   a. Move your mouse curser so that it is between the opening and closing form tags.

   b. Add the following code:

```
<FORM
   ACTION="mailto:Type your e-mail address here"
   METHOD="POST">
Enter Your NickName: <INPUT TYPE="text" NAME="Nname"
SIZE="45"> <P>

Enter Your E-Mail Address: <INPUT TYPE="text" NAME="Email>
<P>

Enter Your Phone Number: <INPUT TYPE="text" NAME="Phone">
<P>
</FORM>
```

4. Start your browser and open your `formexample.htm` file.

5. Enter source code to create Submit and Reset buttons.

   a. You should be in your text editing program and working in the file called `formexample.htm`.

   b. Add the following code that is displayed in bold text:

```
Enter Your Phone Number: <INPUT TYPE="text" NAME="Phone">
<P>
<INPUT TYPE="Submit"> <INPUT TYPE="reset">
</FORM>
```

6. Save changes to your file.

7. Observe the changes that you have made to your form in your browser, and test your form.

   a. Switch back to your browser.

   b. You should have the file `formexample.htm` open.

   c. Press F5 function key or click the refresh button.

   d. Enter some text into one of the fields.

   e. Now click the Reset button to clear contents of all form fields.

   f. Fill in the form and click the send button, and the form will be sent to your e-mail address.

8. Open the e-mail message that contains the form information. The form information will arrive as a file attachment.

9. Save this file with a .txt extension, and then open it. You will see other control information in with the form data.

Lab 10-8

In this Lab exercise you will add check box fields, and radio button fields onto the file formexample.htm that you created in Lab 10-7.

1. To add check box fields, start your text editor, open the formexample.htm, and type the following bold font code:

```
Enter Your Phone Number: <INPUT TYPE="text" NAME="Phone">
<P>
Clown Certifications (Select all that apply)
<INPUT TYPE="checkbox" NAME="Certifications">Balloon Building
<BR>
<INPUT TYPE="checkbox" NAME="Certifications">Improvisation
<BR>
<INPUT TYPE="checkbox" NAME="Certifications">Props Design
<BR>
<INPUT TYPE="checkbox" NAME="Certifications">Jokes & Humour
<BR>
<INPUT TYPE="checkbox" NAME="Certifications">Costume Design
<BR>
<INPUT TYPE="checkbox" NAME="Certifications">Creative Makeup
<P>
<INPUT TYPE="Submit"> <INPUT TYPE="reset">
</FORM>
```

2. Save changes to your file.

3. Observe the new fields in your browser.

4. Add radio buttons to your file.

   a. Switch back to your HTML editing program

   b. Check that the file form example.htm is open and displayed on your screen.

   c. Type the following code that appears in bold text:

```
<INPUT TYPE="checkbox" NAME="Certifications">Creative Makeup
<P>
Would you like us to send you an application form and class
schedule for our school of Clowning and Humor?<BR>
<INPUT TYPE="radio" NAME="application" VALUE="yes"
CHECKED>Yes
<INPUT TYPE="radio" NAME="application" VALUE="no">No<BR>
<P>
<INPUT TYPE="Submit"> <INPUT TYPE="reset">
</FORM>
```

5. Observe the changes that you have made to your form in your browser, and test your form. (Press the F5 function key or click the refresh button.) Fill in the form and click the send button, and the form will be sent to your e-mail address.

8. Open the e-mail message that contains the form information. Compare this information with the e-mail you received in Lab 10-7.

Lab 10-9

In this exercise, you will add Select lists and a scrolling text area box to your `formexample.htm` file.

1. Start your text editor, open the `formexample.htm`, and add a single option select lists field by typing the following bold font code:

```
<INPUT TYPE="checkbox" NAME="Certifications">Creative Makeup
<P>
Would you like us to send you an application form and class
schedule for our school of Clowning and Humour?<BR>
<INPUT TYPE="radio" NAME="application" VALUE="yes"
CHECKED>Yes
<INPUT TYPE="radio" NAME="application" VALUE="no">No<BR>
<P>
Select your Clown Act Specialty
<SELECT NAME="Specialty">
<OPTION>Music
<OPTION>Jokes
<OPTION>Mime
<OPTION>Slap Stick
</SELECT>
<P>
<INPUT TYPE="Submit"> <INPUT TYPE="reset">
</FORM>
```

2. Save changes to your file.

3. Observe the new field in your browser.

4. Add a scrolling text box to your file.

   a. Switch back to your HTML editing program.

   b. Check that the file `form example.htm` is open and displayed on your screen.

   c. Type the following code that appears in bold text:

```
<OPTION>Slap Stick
</SELECT>
<P>
Recommendation to Clown ethics commission:<BR>
<TEXTAREA NAME="recommendations" COLS="30", ROWS="5"
WRAP="virtual">
</TEXTAREA>
<INPUT TYPE="Submit"> <INPUT TYPE="reset">
</FORM>
```

5. Observe the changes you have made to your form in your browser, and test your form.

    a. Switch back to your browser.

    b. You should have the file `form example.htm` open.

    c. Press F5 function key or click the refresh button.

    d. Fill in the form and click the send button, and the form will be sent to your e-mail address.

8. Open the e-mail message that contains the form information. Compare this information with the e-mail you received in Lab Exercise 10-8.

Scenario

You have created a Web page with both external and internal links. Some of the links require fully qualified URL' and others can work with partial URLs. Your links have many problems. Only about half of them work and they must be fixed.

The following list outlines the problems:

1. None of the internal links work. You were careful to create anchors for the parts of the page that you want to link to. You know your anchors were written with the correct syntax using the NAME attribute, and your text links are formatted as links within your browser, yet when you click the link, the browser can't find the link. What could be the cause of this problem?

2. One of the links to an external file was written like this:

```
<A HREF="wildflowers.htm">Wildflowers</A>
```

The browser can't find this page. Why?

Answers to Chapter Questions

Chapter Pre-Test Answers

1. Links that take you to another spot within a Web page are called **internal** links.

2. Links that take you to a separate Web file are called **external** links.

3. A link to a remote Web site must contain a URL to that site.

4. Internal links require two parts: a **link** and an **anchor**.

5. You can create links from text or an **image**.

6. The default vertical alignment for text within a table is **middle**

7. A basic table must contain the following three tags: **<TABLE>**, **<TR>** table row, and **<TD>** table data.

8. The attribute used to adjust the horizontal alignment of text within a table is **ALIGN**.

9. What container tag is needed to create a form? **<FORM> </FORM>**

10. The form submitting attributes that defines the way that the form is sent is: **METHOD**.

Answers to Assessment Questions

1. Which of the following are examples of fully qualified URL links? Select any that apply.

   c. <A HREF="http://example.com/index.htm">

   e. <A HREF="http://www.example.com/internet/links.htm">

2. What needs to be included when creating a link to an external site? Select all that apply.

   b. HREF attribute, c. <A> tag

3. True or **False**: A fully qualified URL must be referenced when creating a link to an external site.

4. Which of the following are examples of internal link? Choose all that apply:

   a. <A HREF="#airlines">Airlines that fly to the Carribian</A>

   Answer d isn't correct because it is missing a hash symbol; the link won't work without it.

5. Which of the following are tags used to create form fields: (Select all that apply).

   a. <INPUT>, c. <SELECT>,d. <TEXTAREA>

6. **FALSE:** Explorer and Netscape interpret tables and table attributes in exactly the same way.

7. You may use the ALIGN attribute with which of the following tags:

   a. <TABLE>, b. <TR>, c. <TD>, d. <TH>, e. <CAPTION>

   All of them

8. The BGCOLOR attribute can be used with the following tags: (Choose all that apply)

   a. <TABLE>, b. <TR>, c.<TD>, d. <TH>

9. The <INPUT> tag can be used to create the following: (Select all that apply)

    a. check boxes, b. text boxes, c. radio buttons, d.submit buttons

10. Which of the following attributes can be used with text boxes?

    a. TYPE, b. NAME, c. Value, d. Size

Answers to Scenario Questions

1. None of the internal links work. You were careful to create anchors for the parts of the page you want to link to. You know your anchors were written with the correct syntax using the NAME attribute, and your text links are formatted as links within your browser, yet when you click the link, the browser can't find the link. What could be the cause of this problem?

   You probably forgot to type the hash sign # before the anchor name when you referenced it in the opening link tag.

2. One of the links to an external file was written like this:

   ```
   <A HREF="wildflowers.htm">Wildflowers</A>
   ```

   The browser can't find this page. Why?

   Perhaps the file you are referencing is not in the same directory or folder as your web page. You could fix this by either: Moving the file, so that it is in the same default location as your web page, or by including the path name with the filename when you reference the link.

   ```
       I.E.   <A HREF=lists/wildflowers.htm">
   ```

Resources

✦ For an excellent reference for HTML form creation information go to: http://www.w3.org/TR/REC-html40/interact/forms.HTML

✦ Great beginners resource for information regarding form processing: http://www.isolani.co.uk/newbie/mailto.html

✦ Loads of information regarding CGI scripting including sample code: http://cgi.tj/

Advanced HTML

EXAM OBJECTIVES

1. Create client-side image maps.

2. Define rectangle, circle, and polygon areas in an image.

3. Define image transparency.

4. Describe image interlacing.

5. Identify animated GIFs.

6. Define frames and the purpose of the frameset document.

7. Use the <FRAMESET> and <FRAME> tags, and list several attributes of each.

8. Identify the purpose of the <NOFRAMES> tag.

9. Target links from one frame to another.

10. Specify default targets using the <BASE> tag.

11. Create borderless frames.

12. Describe the effects of Cascading Style Sheets (CSS) on design.

13. Identify the purpose and uses of JavaScript.

14. Describe the benefits of Dynamic HTML (DHTML).

15. Explain the function of the Document Object Model (DOM) and how it relates to browsers.

16. List the benefits of Extensible HTML (XHTML) and explain how it relates to HTML and the Extensible Markup Language (XML).

CHAPTER PRE-TEST

1. The areas, as defined by an image map, that control linking to a target location, are often referred to as what?

2. Which graphic formats support transparency?

3. What is the name of the document that defines frame layouts and characteristics?

4. What are the four methods of incorporating Cascading Style Sheets into Web pages?

5. Why is JavaScript considered an object-oriented scripting language?

6. What purpose does the Document Object Model serve?

7. What two specifications are combined in the XHTML specification?

8. XML is a derivative of what language?

9. What is the purpose of an XSL document?

10. What element is required in an XML document but is optional in an HTML document?

✦ Answers to these questions can be found at the end of the chapter. ✦

This chapter deals with advanced features of HTML, including image maps, frames, and HTML extensions. Learning these HTML features will not only prepare you for the CIW exam, will give you a better understanding of the more advanced aspects of HTML coding. You can put this knowledge to immediate use if you like to code by hand or if your favorite GUI editor isn't giving you exactly what you want.

Images

Well-placed graphics can make a Web page attractive and interesting. In fact, the viewer's eye is drawn first to your graphics, whether they are simple clip-art or bitmap masterpieces. So why not incorporate your graphics as active components of your pages? Turning graphics into links, or incorporating them as user interface components, can greatly enhance the way a viewer interacts with your site.

To see an example of interesting ways to use graphics, take a look at `http://maps.map.net/start`. For this Web site, the designers have turned a fairly dry activity—doing an Internet search—into a graphical experience, where categories of information are laid out and linked together, through the use of maps, which represent the information that users are searching.

This site goes to the extreme—incorporating images as navigable components. Although you don't need to use graphics as extensively, you can implement them in much the same way on your site by using HTML and various graphic techniques.

Image maps

 Create client-side image maps.

Image maps allow you to define areas on your graphics that the user can interact with. You can create these areas, which are also known as "hot spots," with image map tags, which are covered later in this chapter. Think of the image map as a transparent screen—like a touch pad—over your graphic. With your help, this screen divides the graphic into the regions, or hot spots, that determine what the user has selected. When a user touches (or clicks, or moves the mouse over) a hot spot, an event will be triggered that you can capture and process.

The map on the Web site that you visited at the beginning of this chapter was divided up into regions, just like the divisions representing individual countries on a continental map. The hot spots were created, using image maps, to exactly follow the outline of each of these regions. When you create image maps for your own site, you will define the regions on your graphic that will be used as hot spots through a coordinate system.

Coordinate system

Suppose that you want to link to three different Web pages from the graphic shown in Figure 11-1. You want users to be taken to a page about squares, circles, or polygons when they click inside the respective shape on the graphic.

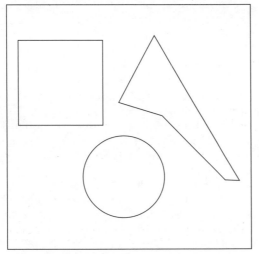

Figure 11-1: Graphic to be used as a map

In order to accomplish this, you need to create an image map that defines the coordinates of the square, circle, and polygon on the graphic. Without it, the browser has no way of knowing where the user clicked. Defining an image map is the process of determining the set of coordinates that outline the hot spots and coding them in HTML.

The coordinate system that you use to define your map is pixel-based. The graphic in Figure 11-1 is 300 pixels wide by 300 pixels high. Therefore, the graphic contains 9000 individual pixels. By stating a pixel's position in terms of its horizontal and vertical location, you can describe any point on the graphic. Your image map defines the individual points on the graphic that will determine the boundaries of the hot spot regions. The standard method of defining a point is to measure from the upper-left corner of the graphic. This point is called the *origin* and its coordinate is 0-X by 0-Y, or just 0,0.

Graphics incorporated into Web pages are always rectangular (even though the graphic may not look like a rectangle). The lower-right corner represents the *extent* of the graphic, which is exactly opposite the origin. The extent of the graphic in Figure 11-1 is located at the coordinate 299,299. (Remember that the origin is at 0,0, so if the graphic is 300 pixels square, the last pixel on each axis is at 299.) Figure 11-2 illustrates the axes, origin, and extent of a graphic.

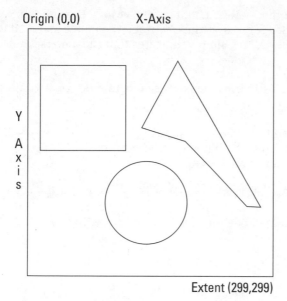

Figure 11-2: Graphic axes, origin, and extent

Defining the image map

Now that you know the origin of your graphic and how to determine individual points on the graphic, you are ready to gather those points and define your image map. You can create either server-side or client-side image maps based on the coordinates you have gathered. Server-side image maps require the use of a CGI script. Client-side image maps are much easier to implement and are, therefore, used far more often.

To define a client-side image map, enter the coordinate information directly into HTML by using the <MAP> and </MAP> container tags and the <AREA> tags. The overall image map is defined by the <MAP> tag, which uses the NAME attribute to uniquely identify the map (you can have multiple maps in your page, with each defined for a different graphic).

The <AREA> tag, which is coded inside the <MAP> section, defines the shape and coordinates that comprise the boundaries of a hot spot. You use one <AREA> tag for each hot spot on the graphic that you want to define.

After you have defined your map, you can use the USEMAP attribute of the <IMG> tag to attach the map to a graphic image. The following code demonstrates the syntax for defining an image map with three hot spot areas, and then attaching it to an image.

```
<MAP NAME="myMap">
<AREA SHAPE="shape" COORDS="coordinates" HREF="URL">
<AREA SHAPE="shape" COORDS="coordinates" HREF="URL">
<AREA SHAPE="shape" COORDS="coordinates" HREF="URL">
</MAP>
<IMG SRC="myGraphic.gif" USEMAP="#myMap">
```

Notice the relationship between the NAME attribute in the <MAP> tag and the USEMAP attribute in the <IMG> tag. This is the link between the image map and the graphic. The # symbol in the USEMAP tag simply indicates that the map is defined in the same HTML document.

The <AREA> tag, as shown in the listing, also makes use of a number of attributes, including the following:

✦ The SHAPE attribute is used to indicate the type of shape that the area will take. Legal values for the SHAPE attribute are "rect," "circle," and "polygon" for rectangular, circular, and irregular areas, respectively.

✦ The COORDS attribute is a list of the coordinate pairs that are used to describe the shape.

✦ The HREF attribute is used to define the link location, either in the same HTML document or in an external file.

Defining the shape of an area

Define rectangle, circle, and polygon areas in an image.

As mentioned previously, you can define our hot spots as rectangles, circles, or irregular shapes (polygons). Each particular shape requires different sets of coordinates.

Defining a rectangular area

Rectangles are defined by two points: the upper-left corner and the lower-right corner. Both corners are defined as points (remember that a point is comprised of an x,y coordinate pair) and are entered into the COORDS attribute as a string of comma-separated integers. Figure 11-3 illustrates how the area for the square in the graphic should be coded.

The following code dictates how the area for the square in the preceding figure should be coded.

```
<MAP NAME="myMap">
<AREA SHAPE="rect" COORDS="30, 30, 130, 130"
HREF="squares.html">
<MAP>
<IMG SRC="figure11-3.png" USEMAP="#myMap">
```

In Figure 11-3, the top-left corner of the square is 31 pixels to the right and 31 pixels down from the origin. That is a coordinate of 30,30 (remember that the origin is at 0,0). The square is 100 x 100 pixels, so the bottom-right corner is at 130,130. These four numbers, or two pair of coordinates, are entered as the COORDS attribute values. Notice also the SHAPE attribute value of "rect."

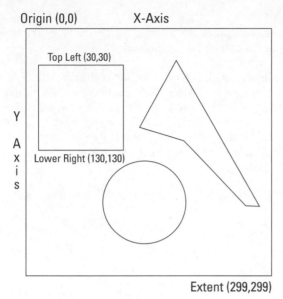

Figure 11-3: Rectangular coordinates in the graphic.

Defining a circular area

Circular area coordinates are defined by stating the x,y coordinate of the circle center, followed by the radius of the circle in pixels. The radius is one half the circle's width, or the distance from the center to any point on its edge. Figure 11-4 illustrates the coordinate and radius definition for a circle.

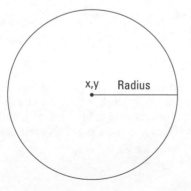

Figure 11-4: Circle attributes are used to define the COORDS values.

The syntax for defining the <AREA> tag for a circle is:

```
<AREA SHAPE="circle" COORDS="x, y, radius" HREF="URL">
```

Defining a polygon

The polygon area can define any shape that is not a circle or a rectangle. Triangles, parallelograms, or oddly shaped areas can all be defined with the polygon.

Polygon coordinates are simply a listing of all the points that comprise the corners of the shape. In fact, these coordinates look just like the connect-the-dots games that you may have played as a child. You start at one point and go around the shape, stating the coordinate of each corner. When you have reached the last corner, you simply stop. The system takes care of "closing" the polygon for you. Figure 11-5 illustrates the coordinates that are used to describe a polygon.

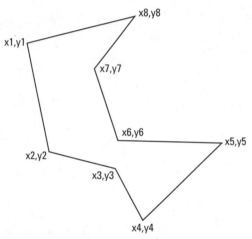

Figure 11-5: Polygon coordinates

The syntax for defining a polygon in the <AREA> tag is as follows:

```
<AREA SHAPE="polygon" COORDS="x1,y1, x2,y2, ... xn,yn"
HREF="URL">
```

The key item to remember when defining the coordinates of a polygon is to go in sequence. You can't define coordinates that will cause the line, which makes up the boundary of the polygon, to cross. For example, if you try to define the coordinates of the polygon in Figure 11-5 as "x1,y1; x6,y6; x3,y3; x7,y7;" you'd get an area definition that won't work.

Putting it all together

Most image maps will require more than a single area definition. If you are making a map for a complex or irregular image, then you may have to combine the rectangle, circle, and polygon shapes to make your map effective. The following code will insert the graphic shown in Figure 11-1 into the page and define an image map for it.

```
<IMG SRC="figure11-1.png" USEMAP="#fullmap">
<MAP NAME="fullmap">
<AREA SHAPE="rect" COORDS="30, 30, 130, 130"
HREF="aboutsquares.html">
<AREA SHAPE="circle" COORDS="150, 200, 50"
HREF="aboutcircles.html">
<AREA SHAPE="polygon" COORDS="150, 100, 200, 250, 200, 270,
200,30" HREF="polygons.html">
</MAP>
```

Image transparency

Define image transparency.

As stated previously in this chapter, all images inserted into a Web page are rectangular, even though the content of the image may not be. Because of this shape, you may have difficulty achieving a blended look unless you have graphics that contain nothing but square corners. Figure 11-6 is an example of a graphic that loses a lot of impact because of the shape.

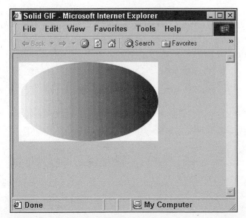

Figure 11-6: Images are always rectangles.

If you make the background of your image transparent, however, it blends much more cleanly into the Web page, as shown in Figure 11-7.

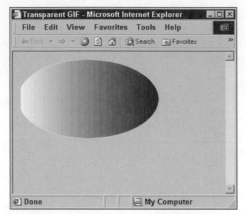

Figure 11-7: Using a transparent image background

To give an image a transparent background, follow these two steps:

1. **Specify a color in the image as the transparency color.** After you have selected a transparency color, it won't be displayed when the graphic is rendered. Instead, whatever is behind the graphic (usually the background of the Web page) will show through. Note that you can specify any color in your image as the transparency color. You should be careful not to specify a color for your background that will appear elsewhere in your image because, if you do, the background and portions of the image will both become transparent.

2. **Save the image in a file format that supports transparency.** Currently, the GIF89a and PNG formats are the only graphic formats optimized for the Web that support transparency. Of the two, the GIF89a format is the most widely used. In fact, most Web developers refer to any image that has a transparent component as a "transparent GIF" — even though the PNG format also supports transparency.

The specific method of setting transparency depends on your graphics package. Most graphics editors that allow you to save an image in GIF89a or PNG format will also allow you to specify a transparency color.

Interlacing

 Describe image interlacing.

Most graphics embedded in Web pages are downloaded as complete images. If you've ever watched a large graphic load, you've seen the rendering start at the top of the graphic and move to the bottom. If it is a very large graphic, or if the user's

Internet connection is slow, waiting for the graphic to download can pose an unacceptable delay. Image interlacing can be used to make the downloading of large images less tedious for the user.

Interlacing is the process by which an image is saved progressively, or in stages. The following list details these stages, for interlaced GIF images. Other image formats that support interlacing perform this task in much the same manner:

✦ The first stage saves only about 13 percent of the detail of the entire graphic. Suppose that you have a graphic that is 240 lines (pixels) high. The first stage will save approximately every eighth line of this graphic. If you looked at just this information, you would probably recognize the image, but the image would lack sharp detail.

✦ The next stage saves every fourth line of the remaining lines. Then, every second line of the remaining original lines is saved in the next stage, and the final stage saves the remainder.

This format allows an image to "fade in" as it is being downloaded, thus decreasing the apparent download time. The actual download time may increase, however, because interlacing often increases the size of the graphic. This increase in size is generally negligible and is considered a fair trade-off for the apparent increase in download speed.

The only Web-friendly graphic formats that support interlacing are GIF87a, GIF89a, and PNG.

Animated GIFs

 Identify animated GIFs.

The GIF9a format allows you to store multiple images in the same physical file, which enables the format to perform animations. To better understand the way that animated GIFs work, think of each individual image as a frame in a movie. When a movie is filmed, the camera snaps pictures at a fairly rapid rate — 24, 25, and 30 frames per second being the standard for film and video. When the film is played back through the projector at the same rate at which it was captured, your eye "sees" smoothly flowing motion pictures, even though it is a rapid succession of individual still images that are being displayed. The rapid speed that the images were captured and subsequently replayed at fool your eye into seeing motion.

In order to create an animated GIF, you must use a GIF animation program. The program will allow you to specify the images that make up each frame, the delay between frames, and looping information. Many shareware and commercial packages are available for creating animated GIFs. A good source for these and other utilities is TUCOWS, located at www.tucows.com.

Frames

Define frames and the purpose of the frameset document.

HTML frames allow you to create Web pages that are divided into separate panels. Each panel contains a complete and separate HTML document.

Each frame is independent of the other frames. In other words, you can scroll through the content of one frame, and the other frames will maintain their state. Web designers often employ frames when they want to keep static information, such as the page banner or navigation bar, visible while the user scrolls through the site content.

Frames were first supported in Netscape Navigator 2.0 and were considered to be an extension of the HTML standard 3.2. The World Wide Web Consortium (W3C) officially adopted frames as a part of the HTML standard into the HTML 4.01 specification.

Frames are comprised of two distinct entities: *frames* and *framesets*. The frame is the pane that contains an HTML document, and the frameset is a description of all the frames that comprise a document.

When developing a frame-based page, a developer first considers the intended layout, divides it into rectangular areas (each rectangle will represent a frame), and then defines the frameset and frame HTML tags that will accommodate the design.

Figure 11-8 illustrates a simple frame-based Web page. The frame on the left contains the links for site navigation, and the frame on the right contains the content of the HTML document that is currently selected.

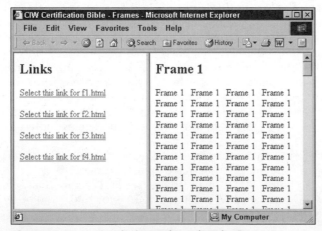

Figure 11-8: A simple frame-based Web site

The two frames are treated almost as if they were each in a separate browser. They can contain different HTML documents and they can be scrolled independently. However, they are still in the same browser window and, as such, can work together to create a unified page.

The HTML <FRAME> and <FRAMESET> tags

Use the <FRAME.SET> and <FRAME> tags, and list several attributes of each.

As mentioned previously, frame-based sites are defined through the use of frames and a frameset. The frames contain the documents that comprise the Web site and the frameset defines the frames. In this section, you will learn the details of the <FRAME> and <FRAMESET> tags.

<FRAMESET>

The <FRAMESET> tag is used as the layout control for the frame-based site. The following code shows the syntax for the frameset document that was used to produce the Web page shown in Figure 11-8.

```
<HTML>
<HEAD><TITLE>CIW Certification Bible - Frames</TITLE></HEAD>
<FRAMESET COLS="45%,55%">
<FRAME SRC="links.html">
<FRAME NAME="mainFrame" SRC="f1.html">
</FRAMESET>
</HTML>
```

As you can see from the preceding listing, a frameset document does not contain a <BODY> tag. The use of the <BODY> tag in a frameset document is not supported by some browsers, and will result in a blank page being displayed instead of your framed page. To help you remember this, simply think of the <FRAMESET> tag as providing the same function as the <BODY> tag. Because its function is being provided for, the <BODY> tag is not needed.

The lack of a <BODY> tag is one characteristic of a frameset document that makes it unique. The other unique aspect of the frameset document is that it is never visible; it simply defines how the frames of the site will be arranged.

A frameset document can have a header (defined with the <HEAD> and </HEAD> container tags), so you can define a title — or any other items normally contained in the header, such as META tags.

The <FRAMESET> tag, as shown in Listing 11-4, defines the layout of two frames that are arranged in columns. The number represents the space allocated to each frame in relation to the width of the browser window. In this case, the first frame gets 45 percent of the available space and the second frame gets 55 percent of the space.

You can also specify that the frames be arranged horizontally by using a <FRAME-SET> tag, such as the following:

```
<FRAMESET ROWS="50%, 50%">
```

In this case, two frames will be defined — one above the other — and each will occupy half of the available vertical space in the browser window. Figure 11-9 shows how a frameset of this type would be arranged.

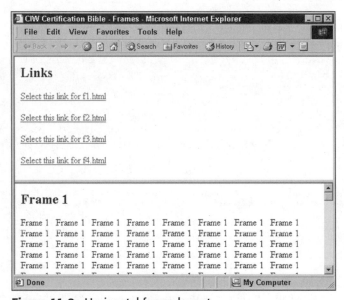

Figure 11-9: Horizontal frame layout

In addition to allocating space to the frames as a percentage, HTML also supports the use of pixel allocation and wildcards. *Pixel allocations* are simply the number of pixels that you want to allocate to a frame. *Wildcards*, which are indicated by the asterisk (*), tell the frame to use up whatever amount of browser space that hasn't already been allocated to other frames.

```
<FRAMESET COLS="160, *">
```

This frameset tag defines two frames arranged in columns; the first frame is allocated 160 pixels and the second frame is allocated the amount of pixels remaining, horizontally, in the browser window. You can do the same with the ROWS attribute.

```
<FRAME>
```

The <FRAME> tags, which are defined inside the <FRAMESET> and </FRAMESET> container tags, define the contents of each frame.

The <FRAME> tags define the content of the two columns defined by the <FRAME-SET> tag. The first frame is defined as follows:

```
<FRAME SRC="links.html>
```

The SRC attribute of the <FRAME> tag names the document, which will occupy this frame's space in the layout. The source attribute can specify either a local document or the full URL of an external document.

The second <FRAME> tag is defined as follows:

```
<FRAME NAME="mainFrame" SRC="f1.html">
```

In this case, the SRC attribute again names the document that will occupy this frame. Notice also the use of the NAME attribute, which allows you to define a name for your frame. This attribute is important in order to allow your links to "target" a particular frame. Frame targets are examined in a later section of this chapter.

Keep in mind the following details concerning frameset documents and frames:

✦ The frameset document does not have a <BODY> section. Instead, the <FRAMESET> section takes the place of the body.

✦ The <FRAMESET> tag can contain either the COLS attribute or the ROWS attribute, but not both at the same time.

✦ The <FRAME> tag's SRC attribute contains the name of the document that will occupy the frame.

✦ The <FRAME> tag's NAME attribute can be used to provide a reference name for the frame.

<NOFRAMES>

Identify the purpose of the <NOFRAMES> tag.

Some older browsers are unable to support the use of frames. In order to ensure that your Web pages are available to the widest possible audience, you can use the <NOFRAMES> tag to assist those users with browsers that can't deal with frames. The following code demonstrates how to use a <NOFRAMES> section in a frameset document.

```
<HTML>
<HEAD><TITLE>CIW Certification Bible - Frames</TITLE></HEAD>
<FRAMESET COLS="45%,55%">
<FRAME SRC="links.html">
<FRAME NAME="mainFrame" SRC="f1.html">
<NOFRAMES>
This site uses frames. Please select the following link
to our <A HREF="noframes.html">frame free site.</A>
</NOFRAMES>
</FRAMESET>
</HTML>
```

As this listing demonstrates, you can use the <NOFRAMES> section to provide a link to a non-frames portion of your site. Even if you don't provide such a link, you can at least provide a message indicating that the site uses frames, so users won't think your site is blank.

Frame targeting

 Target links from one frame to another.

A well laid-out set of frames is of no value unless you can automatically target those frames to display your content.

The sample site shown in Figure 11-8 makes use of links in the left frame to display documents in the right frame. The tricky part is making the document appear in the intended frame instead of in the current frame. You can do this by using the <FRAME> and <A HREF> (anchor) tags and their respective NAME and TARGET attributes.

The <FRAME> tag is defined as follows:

```
<FRAME NAME="framename" SRC="URL">
```

The corresponding anchor tag is defined as follows:

```
<A HREF="URL" TARGET="framename">
```

The two tags work together; the <FRAME> tag provides the frame name and the anchor tag uses this name in its TARGET attribute.

The following code shows the links.html that targets the right frame in the sample site.

```
<HTML>
<HEAD>
<TITLE>Links</TITLE>
</HEAD>
<BODY>
<H2>Links</H2>
<P><A HREF="f1.html" TARGET="mainFrame">Select this link for
f1.html</A></P>
<P><A HREF="f2.html" TARGET="mainFrame">Select this link for
f2.html</A></P>
<P><A HREF="f3.html" TARGET="mainFrame">Select this link for
f3.html</A></P>
<P><A HREF="f4.html" TARGET="mainFrame">Select this link for
f4.html</A></P>
</BODY>
</HTML>
```

Notice in this listing that the anchor tags use the TARGET attribute to cause the linked document to appear in the mainFrame. The name attribute of <FRAME NAME="mainFrame"...> is the intended target.

Keep the following in mind when targeting named frames:

✦ If your anchor (<A HREF>) tags don't specify a TARGET, the document will open in the same frame that the link is in.

✦ If your anchor tags specify a TARGET frame that matches the name of any of the frames in your frameset, the browser will launch a new window and open the linked document in it. This is an interesting effect, but is quite possibly not what you had in mind.

Base target

 Specify default targets using the <BASE> tag.

Targeting frames is a fundamental task in frame-based designs. However, you normally target the same frame from multiple anchor tags. This task normally requires that you enter the TARGET attribute in every anchor. However, you can take advantage of an easier way to perform this task.

If most of your links target the same frame, you can set a *base target*, or default frame, that your links will automatically use. The base target is set in the header section of your document that contains the anchor tags, and is coded as such:

```
<BASE HREF="URL" TARGET="framename">
```

The <BASE> tag uses the TARGET attribute to specify the name of the default frame. The optional URL attribute allows you to specify the base URL of your Web site. This is useful in the event that the document containing the links gets moved out of the Web site; for example, if a user saves your link page to his or her local hard drive. In this case, the URL attribute will allow the system to find your Web site again.

If you do incorporate a <BASE> tag, you can still indicate a different frame for a link by using the anchor tag's TARGET attribute, as previously shown.

Frame borders

 Create borderless frames.

The example frames in the links.html document use a visible separator, or border, between them. If you don't want the border to be visible, use the FRAME-BORDER attribute of the <FRAME> tag. The <FRAME FRAMEBORDER="0" attribute will turn the border off. The FRAMEBORDER="1" attribute will turn it on.

You can also specify the distance between a frame's borders (whether visible or not) by using the MARGINWIDTH and MARGINHEIGHT attributes of the <FRAME> tag. These attributes specify the number of pixels of blank space between the content of the frame, and the frame's left and right, and top and bottom, borders, respectively. These attributes help to enhance the visual appearance of your site. If you use them, however, you must specify a value greater than 0. If you don't, the default value, which differs from browser to browser, will be used.

HTML Extensions

HTML extensions are an addition to the HTML standard, which provides additional functionality while leaving the basic HTML standard unchanged. This helps to ensure that newer capabilities don't invalidate older development practices; that is, until sufficient time has passed to validate the new methods and get site updates underway.

As users become more sophisticated in their use of computers and the Internet, they are beginning to demand that the same types of capabilities be delivered — regardless of the environment they are working in. Most users don't care if an application is running locally or is being delivered across the Web. They want to be able to interact with Internet applications the same way that they interact with local applications.

As a result, Web developers are faced with the task of presenting sophisticated user interfaces via the Web browsers, where they are accustomed to working with static text, graphics, and links.

HTML extensions provide developers with the tools that they need to create the types of user interfaces that clients are demanding. Without them, developers would be faced with the task of developing their Web applications in development languages like Java. However, by using technologies such as Cascading Style Sheets (CSS), JavaScript, Dynamic HTML (DHTML), Extensible HTML (XML), and others, developers can create Web-based applications with far greater capabilities than HTML can deliver on its own.

The following section explores some of the technologies that enhance and extend HTML capabilities.

Cascading Style Sheets

 Describe the effects of CSS on design.

One of the biggest challenges when designing visual interfaces — whether they are computer-based or otherwise — is to create a consistent format or "look." Cascading Style Sheets (CSS) aid in this task by allowing developers to define unique formatting styles and to apply them to individual elements in their Web pages. In this way, if the style requirements change, only the style sheet needs to be updated. The elements of the Web page or pages will automatically take on the new appearance as dictated by the style sheet.

CSS can be implemented in four different ways:

✦ Linked Style Sheets

✦ Imported Style Sheets

✦ Embedded Style Sheets

✦ Inline Styles

Linked and imported style sheets offer the most flexibility. Style definitions are stored in a file separate from the HTML documents. The style sheet is then linked into the Web pages, thus allowing them to use the style elements in the linked sheet. This is extremely useful because by modifying the style sheet, and not every Web page, you can change the formatting of the entire site.

Embedded style sheets are coded directly into an HTML document. These style sheets offer you the ability to change the formatting of the entire Web page through the style attributes, and only the individual Web page is affected.

Inline styles are coded directly into the tag that they are to affect. For example, a paragraph tag can have an embedded style to change the appearance of the text in that paragraph only.

Each type of implementation has its own area of expertise. Linked style sheets are best for global design, embedded style sheets are best for page-centric formatting, and inline styles are best for unique, one-time changes to specific regions of the page.

Currently, two CSS specifications are available—CSS1 and CSS2. CSS1 is concerned with basic formatting and layout, and CSS2 extends the capabilities of CSS1 by including support for additional media types, such as printers, and improved support for HTML tables.

The HTML 4.01 specification has adopted both CSS1 and CSS2 as the preferred method for controlling formatting in Web pages. Older formatting options, such as the bold (<B>), italic (<I>), and centering (<CENTER>) tags are now deprecated in favor of the format options provided by CSS.

In the Real World

The term *deprecated* means to diminish the value of or discourage the use of something. When an HTML tag is deprecated, the standards developers have discouraged its use in favor of a method that more fully conforms to the current standards. It does not mean that your Web page will suddenly stop working; it is simply a suggestion that you use the newer "standard" way of accomplishing the task, and that developers should consider implementing the new standard in their current development and possible existing works. HTML tags will continue to be introduced, used and deprecated as Web standards evolve.

How CSS works

Cascading Style Sheets are implemented through rules. A *rule* is a complete style definition that includes a *selector* and one or more *properties*, each with corresponding *values*. Consider the following CSS rule:

```
H1 {color: green}
```

In this example, H1 is the selector, color is the property, and green is the value.

The result of using this rule is that all text affected by the <H1> heading tag is rendered in green.

The following code shows a simple HTML document with no special formatting. Figure 11-10 shows how the page looks in Internet Explorer.

```
<HTML>
<HEAD>
<TITLE>No CSS Styles</TITLE>
</HEAD>
<BODY>
<H1>This line's style comes from the H1 tag.</H1>
This text is displayed in the style of the BODY tag.
</BODY>
</HTML>
```

Figure 11-10: The document from the preceding code rendered in Internet Explorer

The following code makes use of an embedded style sheet to modify the format of the <H1> and <BODY> tags, resulting in the output shown in Figure 11-11.

```
<!DOCTYPE HTML PUBLIC "-//W3C//DTD HTML 4.01//EN"
"http://www.w3c.org/TR/html4/strict.dtd">
<HTML>
<HEAD>
<TITLE>CSS Embedded Styles</TITLE>
```

```
<STYLE>
<!--
H1 {color:green; font-family:Comic Sans MS, sans-serif; font-
size:18pt; text-align:center}
BODY {color:brown; font-family:Celtic, serif; font-size:12pt}
//-->
</STYLE>
</HEAD>
<BODY>
<H1>This line's style comes from the H1 tag.</H1>
This text is displayed in the style of the BODY tag.
</BODY>
</HTML>
```

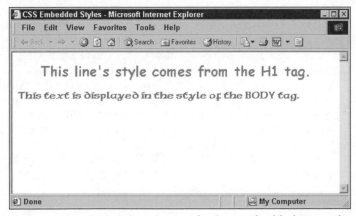

Figure 11-11: Formatting as a result of an embedded CSS style

These examples show that the style sheet embedded between the <STYLE> and </STYLE> container tags causes the document format to change — even though the tags within the body of the document stay the same. The selectors, H1 and BODY, correspond to the <H1> and <BODY> HTML tags. Any text within the influence of these tags is rendered according to the corresponding rule.

A rule can consist of one or more properties. In the code example immediately preceding Figure 11-11, the H1 selector uses the color, font family, font size and text align properties in defining the rule. Each property is followed by a colon (:) and a value. A semicolon (;) always separates the list of properties. Curly braces {} enclose the list of properties and values for each individual rule. These properties are always true when using embedded or external style sheets. However, inline styles (which are discussed later in this chapter) don't make use of the braces.

Multiple values are allowed on certain properties. If a property contains more than one value, commas separate them. The multiple font family values allow the system to select an alternate font — if one is not available. In this case, if the Comic Sans MS font is not available, the standard sans-serif font will be used.

> **In the Real World**
> Remember that your Web page may be viewed on many different systems, and you have no guarantee that all systems will have the same fonts installed. It is a good idea to incorporate as much flexibility in your design as you can by listing the fonts you want to use in the font family property, in the order of preference, and include a "generic" font as the last option. The generic fonts — sans-serif, serif, cursive, fantasy and monospace — will render appropriately on all systems.

CSS inheritance

All changes made through CSS styles are inherited throughout the HTML document. You can create rules that define different property values in separate style sheets, embedded style sections, or even inline styles, to affect only those properties. However, due to inheritance of styles, a combination of the styles, which are imparted by all rules that affect a particular selector, will be applied to the document. For example, suppose that you give one designer the responsibility of defining all the color styles, and you give another designer the task of defining the appropriate fonts. Each designer can define separate style sheets using the same selectors, but with color properties defined in one set of rules, and font properties defined in the other. When combined in the same HTML document, however, the document will inherit the properties of both sheets, in much the same way that people inherit different characteristics from each parent.

Appling CSS style to HTML documents

Now that you've seen an example of how CSS controls formatting, you need to explore the options for implementing style sheets. At the beginning of this chapter, you learned that you can use four ways to incorporate style sheets: linked, imported, embedded, or inline. The following section explains the use of each of these methods.

Linked style sheets

A *linked style sheet* is one that is created outside of the Web page and stored as a simple text file. This file becomes known as a CSS file or a style sheet. A style sheet file generally has a .css extension.

A CSS file looks almost identical to an embedded style sheet, as shown in the previous code example. It does not, however, use the <STYLE> and </STYLE> tags.

The following code shows a sample CSS file.

```css
BODY {
  background: White;
  color: Black;
  font: Verdana, Geneva, Arial, Helvetica, sans-serif;
  font-size: 10pt;
}

H1 {
  background: White;
  color:Blue;
  font: italic Verdana, Geneva, Arial, Helvetica, sans-serif;
  text-align: center;
  font-size: 36pt;
}

P {
  background: Black;
  font: normal Verdana, Geneva, Arial, Helvetica, sans-serif;
  color: White;
  font-size: 10pt;
  text-align: left;
}
```

Note the formatting of the rules in this style sheet. It is not required that each property be listed on a separate line, but it does improve readability.

After you have created a style sheet file, you must link it into your Web documents by using the <LINK> tag. The following code demonstrates how to incorporate the style sheet by using the <LINK> tag in an HTML document.

```html
<!DOCTYPE HTML PUBLIC "-//W3C//DTD HTML 4.01//EN"
"http://www.w3c.org/TR/html4/strict.dtd">
<HTML>
<HEAD>
<META http-equiv="Content-Type" content="text/html;
charset=iso-8859-1">
<TITLE> Linked Style Sheet</TITLE>
<LINK rel="stylesheet" type="text/css" href="sample.css">
</HEAD>
<BODY>
<H1>This style comes from the H1 tag.</H1>
This text is displayed in the style of the BODY tag.
<P>This text is affected by the Paragraph tag</P>
</BODY>
</HTML>
```

Note that in this listing, the <LINK> tag is placed in the header section of the HTML document. This is required because the style sheet must be fully linked into the document before the body of the document is rendered.

The `rel` attribute specifies the relationship between the linked file and this HTML document and, in the case of CSS linking, always reads "stylesheet."

The `type` attribute is specifying the MIME type for style sheets and will generally read "text/css."

Finally, the `href` attribute indicates the file to which you are linking. In this case, it is a relative reference because the `sample.css` file is in the same directory as the Web page.

The result of displaying this Web page in a browser is shown in Figure 11-12.

Figure 11-12: An HTML document with linked style sheet

Imported style sheets

Imported style sheets are similar to linked style sheets in that they are defined in an external document. However, an imported style sheet must have an `@import` directive as its first line, as shown in the following code:

```
@import url(imported.css)
```

In this case, the name of the style sheet is `imported.css`.

The following code shows how an imported style sheet is to be included in an HTML document.

```
<!DOCTYPE HTML PUBLIC "-//W3C//DTD HTML 4.01//EN"
"http://www.w3c.org/TR/html4/strict.dtd">
<HTML>
<HEAD>
<TITLE>Imported Style Sheet Sample</TITLE>
<STYLE type="text/css">
@import url(imported.css);
</STYLE>
</HEAD>
```

Note in these examples that the name of the style sheet is `imported.css`. You can name your style sheet anything that you want, however.

 The use of imported style sheets is not recommended because of the inconsistent ways in which the various browsers support it; problems range from styles not being imported properly to system crashes.

Inline styles

Another method of incorporating CSS rules into your Web documents is through *inline styles*. Inline styles are incorporated directly into the HTML tag that you want to affect by using the tag's STYLE attribute. For example:

```
<H1 STYLE="color:green; background:black; font-family: sans-
serif; font-size:36pt">
```

In this example, the style has been applied to the <H1> tag. Any text between the <H1> and </H1> tags is rendered in the style shown.

If you have a range of text to which you want to apply a style, but you don't want to define a separate STYLE attribute for each tag, you can use the <SPAN> and </SPAN> container tags to enclose the area of the document that you want to affect, and set the STYLE attribute on the <SPAN> tag.

The following code illustrates the use of the <SPAN> tag with an inline STYLE.

```
<!DOCTYPE HTML PUBLIC "-//W3C//DTD HTML 4.01//EN"
"http://www.w3c.org/TR/html4/strict.dtd">
<HTML>
<HEAD>
<META http-equiv="Content-Type" content="text/html;
charset=iso-8859-1">
<TITLE> Linked Style Sheet</TITLE>
</HEAD>
<BODY>
<H1>This style comes from the H1 tag.</H1>
This text is displayed in the style of the BODY tag.
```

```
<P>Paragraph 1</P>
<SPAN STYLE="font-family:Arial; color:white; background:black">
<P>Paragraph 2</P>
<P>Paragraph 3</P>
<P>Paragraph 4</P>
</SPAN>
<P>Paragraph 5</P>
</BODY>
</HTML>
```

In this example, the <SPAN> tag will cause Paragraphs 2, 3, and 4 to be formatted according to the tag's STYLE attribute.

Embedded styles

As Listing 11-8 demonstrates, embedded styles place the CSS rules in the header of the HTML document between the <STYLE> and </STYLE> tags. Also note the use of the comment tags (<!– and //–>) before and after the rules. These tags are used so that older browsers that don't understand CSS styles will simply ignore the rules, and not print them as text to the browser window.

Browser compatibility

Cascading Style Sheets promise the benefits of easy, consistent formatting of Web pages. However, you must be aware that the various browsers interpret the style information differently; for example, your page may be difficult or impossible to use in one browser, and it may be perfectly fine in another browser. You can do little to control this situation other than testing your pages in as many browsers as possible. This is not an excuse for not using style sheets, however. As browser technologies mature, adherence to standards, such as the CSS1 and CSS2 specifications, will become more consistent. Until then, however, test your pages carefully and avoid CSS formats that are known to cause browser problems or that are inconsistently implemented. A very helpful site is the House of Style CSS Browser support page, located at:

```
http://www.westciv.com.au/style_master/academy/browser_support/
index.html
```

JavaScript

 Identify the purpose and uses of JavaScript.

Scripting allows developers to build interactive functionality into their Web pages. JavaScript is the most universally supported of the scripting languages. With it, developers can create client-side and server-side scripts. In this section, however, you will deal exclusively with JavaScript at the Web browser, or client-side.

JavaScript can provide many capabilities, including:

✦ Displaying pop-up dialog boxes

✦ Enabling rollovers where the image or text can change in response to mouse movements

✦ Manipulating cookies

✦ Creating banner, marques and other dynamic content

✦ Enhancing copyright protection

Because JavaScript is a scripting language, it must be contained within an application. Most people think of the Web browser, but many other applications support the use of JavaScript.

Programmers who have dealt with traditional programming languages, such as C, C++, and others, can easily transition to the JavaScript world. Those familiar with Object Oriented Programming languages, such as C++ or Java, have an even easier time. These folks enjoy easy transitions because JavaScript is an *object-oriented* scripting language. In other words, your JavaScript programs deal directly with the objects that comprise the environment that your script runs in. For example, when you write the following pop-up message, you are using JavaScript to call the alert method (function) of the browser's window object:

```
window.alert("I just wrote an alert");
```

Object-Oriented Programming concepts

Because JavaScript is object-oriented, you should be somewhat familiar with standard Object-Oriented Programming (OOP) concepts and terminology before continuing.

An *object* is any programming construct that encapsulates both form and function. In other words, an object contains data that define the object and one or more functions that allow the object to perform some kind of task.

In OOP terminology, the *data* of the object are considered its *properties*. The *functions* embedded in the object are its *methods*. All objects are comprised of methods and properties, and with an object-oriented language, such as JavaScript, you can make use of them.

For example, consider the window object in this simple line of code:

```
window.alert("I just wrote an alert");
```

A window object has properties, such as *status* (the status message at the bottom of the browser), *outerheight,* and *outerwidth* (the height and width of the browser windows) — as well as others. It also has methods, such as *alert*, *close* (used to close a window), and *confirm* (another pop-up dialog box method that allows the user to select either an OK or Cancel button response).

As you can see, objects allow you to access the underlying functionality of the environment that you are programming in.

In addition to using built-in objects, JavaScript allows you to define your own objects if you find it beneficial to your development tasks.

Why use JavaScript?

JavaScript offers many features that make it an ideal language for creating dynamic Web content. These features include:

✦ **Platform independence.** JavaScript is supported on the largest number of platforms and in the largest number of Web browsers.

✦ **Reduced learning time.** Because JavaScript is much more relaxed in terms of syntax and programming rules, it is easier to learn than traditional programming languages.

✦ **Rapid development.** JavaScript does not need to be compiled. The Web browser interprets it, so testing your code is as easy as opening the browser and trying it out.

✦ **Ease of development.** The only tool that you need to create JavaScript is a text editor. No additional compilers, linkers, or other development tools are required.

User interface design in JavaScript

As mentioned previously, JavaScript promotes rapid development. For example, JavaScript is able to interact with and control objects in the browser. In terms of user interface, this can include HTML forms and all the accompanying controls, such as buttons, text boxes, lists, and so on. The JavaScript developer doesn't necessarily need to be the one to create these forms. The HTML developer can create the forms and the JavaScript developer can create functions that manipulate the data from the forms. This is an important advantage because HTML developers are generally concerned with the overall look of the site, so they will design the form to match the visual design. This decreases the JavaScript programmer's time and allows that person to concentrate on automation rather than design.

Using JavaScript in HTML documents

You can embed JavaScript into your HTML documents just like with Cascading Style Sheets.

You can create script sections in your document by enclosing your JavaScript inside the <SCRIPT> and </SCRIPT> container tags. This is somewhat similar to using the <STYLE> and </STYLE> container tags, except that you don't have to limit your use of them to the header section of your document. Script containers can also go in the body of your document. Even though you can place script containers in either the body or the header sections of your page, they are usually contained in the header. This allows the script *functions* (reusable code components that perform a specific task) to be easily located, and ensures that the functions will be loaded prior to being called, as the header section is always the first to load.

You can also implement JavaScript inline — again much like CSS — by placing the script command directly into appropriate HTML tags. This is often done in anchor tags to trigger a change in the appearance of a link when the user rolls the mouse over the link.

Together, your JavaScript functions in the <SCRIPT> containers and your inline JavaScript provide you with the means to automate the Web page.

The following code shows a Web page with JavaScript to illustrate how a typical set of JavaScript functions and inline code will be embedded into a Web document.

```
<!DOCTYPE HTML PUBLIC "-//W3C//DTD HTML 4.01 Transitional//EN"
"http://www.w3.org/TR/html4/loose.dtd"
<HTML>
<HEAD>
<META http-equiv="Content-Type" content="text/html;
charset=iso-8859-1">
<TITLE>Examples of JavaScript</TITLE>
<SCRIPT>
  function popUpMessages(cname)
  {
    window.alert("This is an alert dialog, " + cname);
    if(window.confirm("Close the Web page now, " + cname +
"?"))
    {
      self.close();
    }
  }
</SCRIPT>
</HEAD>
<BODY>
  <SCRIPT>
    var candidateName;
    candidateName = window.prompt("Please Enter you Name","");
```

```
        document.write("<H3>Hello CIW Candidate, " + candidateName
  + "</H3><BR>");
      popUpMessages(candidateName);
    </SCRIPT>
  </BODY>
</HTML>
```

In this listing, you can see the use of the <SCRIPT> containers in both the header and the body of the document.

The following list details the sequence of events, which take place under script control:

1. When the document loads, the script within the body executes.

2. A prompt dialog box appears, asking for the user's name.

3. After the user has entered his or her name and clicked the OK button, thus closing the prompt, the *document.write* method is called to write a message out to the user, including his or her name, which has been captured into the variable *candidateName*.

4. Finally, the function *popUpMessages*, which is coded in the document header, is called with the *candidateName* passed as an argument.

The popUpMessages function performs two tasks: First, it calls the window.alert method to display a message to the user. Next, after the user closes the alert dialog box, a confirm dialog box is presented, asking whether the browser should now be closed. If the user clicks OK, the browser will close—otherwise, it will stay open.

This completes the script for this page. Note that no script is written here to respond to user interactions other than the prompts. This is very much a procedural script that simply starts, performs its functions, and then stops. Most Web-based programming is not so procedural. Instead, the developer writes code to respond to *events*, and as such, works in an *event-driven* environment. Events take place in response to user interaction with the Web page, such as when a user clicks a link, or when an action like opening or closing a window has taken place. Event-driven programming is the process of writing code to respond to these events.

Controlling where your Web page can appear

Many Web site designers opt for the easy way of creating content for their pages by including links to other designer's pages from within their own. This practice is not uncommon, and it's not wrong—just as long as developers linking to this other content are not trying to pass it off as their own work. This is, in effect, a violation of copyright, and it usually happens on Web sites that are designed with frames. Because any frame in a site can contain an HTML document from any URL, it can appear that the pages in all the frames belong to the site doing the linking, and not to the original developer.

Even if you are not concerned about copyright, you probably didn't originally intend that your document appear in someone else's frame. You may choose this scenario because your page won't format properly in a smaller frame.

To keep your pages from being displayed in a frame, you can incorporate a very simple JavaScript placed in the header of your page. The script ensures that your page appears at the top of the browser's window, and not inside a frame in the browser, thus effectively "breaking out" of the frame site.

The following code uses JavaScript to aid copyright protection.

```
<HTML>
<HEAD>
<TITLE>Break Out of Frames</TITLE>
<SCRIPT LANGUAGE="JavaScript">
<!--
if (self != top) top.location.href = location.href;
//-->
</SCRIPT>
</HEAD>
<BODY>
</BODY>
</HTML>
```

As you can see from this listing, when the header is loaded (this happens before anything else in the page loads), the Web page (self) is compared against the *top* property, which is a reference to the top document in the window. If the self is not the top, then the document is placed in the top position by the code `top.location.href = location.href`.

JavaScript provides a very powerful way of creating active content. Many excellent resources on the Web and in bookstores are available that you can turn to for reference.

Dynamic HTML

 Describe the benefits of DHTML.

Dynamic HTML (DHTML) is a combination of scripting, HTML, Cascading Style Sheets, and an object collection called the Document Object Model, which allows for the creation of dynamic and interactive Web page content.

Using DHTML Web developers can incorporate:

✦ Text animations.

✦ New document content based on user actions.

✦ Position control. You can specify the exact placement of components (such as images or text areas).

DHTML is currently inconsistently supported between browsers, but will likely become standardized with time.

To employ DHTML effectively, you must understand HTML, scripting, and CSS1 and CSS2 specifications. Additionally, you must be familiar with the Document Object Model (DOM).

Document Object Model

 Explain the function of the DOM and how it relates to browsers.

The Document Object Model (DOM) is a description of all the objects that control the way a document appears within a Web browser. The DOM is intended as a vendor-neutral specification with which to standardize the methods of creating interactive and dynamic Web content. Using the objects defined in the DOM, you can accomplish tasks such as controlling the physical size of the browser window, turning on and off toolbars and menu bars, and controlling the content of areas of your document, such as SPANs and DIVs. Additionally, you can dynamically change formatting issues, such as the issues previously mentioned in the DHTML section.

Unfortunately, the DOM is not supported or implemented exactly the same way in all browsers. Each of the major browsers implements its own version of the DOM, so you are forced to deal with a new DOM for each browser that you want to support. Fortunately, the DOMs are similar enough so that basic scripting will work in each browser. Certain capabilities, however, still need to be coded on an individual basis. As support for a standard DOM grows, however, this concern should be alleviated. In order to work with a DOM, you must program with a scripting language, such as JavaScript. JavaScript is the most universal of the scripting languages, yet it is not the only one available. Microsoft browsers support the use of both JavaScript and VBScript, which is Microsoft's answer to JavaScript. VBScript is only supported, however, in Microsoft browsers, so it suffers from lack of cross-platform support.

Because each browser has a specific DOM, you may encounter a situation in which your code is not understood in one browser, while it works perfectly well in another browser. This is simply a fact of life when dealing with the various DOMs, but you can take advantage of workarounds. These are beyond the scope of this book, however, but many good references are available on how to deal with browser incompatibilities. The Web Standards Project (www.webstandards.org/index0901.html) is an example of one such Web site that includes reference material for dealing with various browser incompatibilities, as well as providing information on the organizations and issues surrounding Web standardization.

Extensible HTML

 List the benefits of XHTML and explain how it relates to HTML and XML.

Created in January of 2000, Extensible HTML (XHTML) is a combination of the HTML 4.01 and XML 1.0 specifications. The full specification for XHTML is available at www.w3.org/TR/xhtml1, and is called the XHTML 1.0 specification. The World Wide Web Consortium describes XHTML 1.0 as "... a reformulation of HTML 4 as an XML 1.0 application, and three DTDs corresponding to the ones defined by HTML 4."

In other words, XHTML is considered an application under XML specifications. XML, the Extensible Markup Language, is a specification for developing "well-formed" documents that deliver a "... universal format for structured documents and data on the Web" (quoted material is from the W3C XML site, located at www.w3.org/XML). XML describes document content and functionality in standard terms, which are universally understandable.

XHTML, then, takes the features of HTML and combines them with the universal nature of XML, thus providing a more standard way of dealing with Web pages as applications, rather than static display spaces.

Extensible Markup Language

Extensible Markup Language (XML) is a language that supports the universal description of a document's content and the way in which that content is to be dealt with. With XML, you can create any type of document and define the way the information in that document is to be interpreted. In effect, XML provides you with the ability to create your own tags, which will then be used to define your document. You can define a tag to describe a portion of your own documents in the same way that the <BODY> tag defines the main body content of a Web page. In this way, XML becomes a language, which is used to describe the language, which describes your document.

Banks and other financial institutions use XML to define transactions in terms of universal function — and not according to the strict details of how that function is to be performed. For example, suppose that Bank A wants to transfer some funds for a client to Bank B. If Bank A and Bank B are using completely different computer systems and software to maintain their account information, how can they communicate this transaction? XML is a solution that allows the transaction to be defined in broad terms. The XML document doesn't deal with issues such as which kind of database needs to be updated, because this is the job of the underlying accounting software. XML simply provides a method for both parties to communicate a need for a function to be performed, which, in this case, is a transfer of funds.

XML is like a subset of the Standardized General Markup Language (SGML) that has been in use for years, and which is considered a meta-language for the creation of other languages. XML inherits this ability while eliminating a lot of the complexity of SGML.

The structure of a well-formed XML document

A "well-formed" document organizes the tags that define the data in a structured hierarchy. In addition, an XML document must contain a Document Type Definition (DTD) and a *root* element, or tag, from which all others are derived.

The following code demonstrates an example of implementing an actual XML document:

```
<?xml version="1.0"?>
<INVENTORY>
  <SOFTWARE>
    <TITLE>How to play winning golf</TITLE>
    <FORMAT>Windows 95/98</FORMAT>
    <PUBLISHER>Joes Sport Software</PUBLISHER>
  </SOFTWARE>
  </HARDWARE>
    <TYPE>Mouse</TYPE>
    <MANUFACTURER>Mouse Makers, Inc.</MANUFACTURER>
  </HARDWARE>
</INVENTORY>
```

This example shows only one instance of the SOFTWARE and HARDWARE elements. In an actual implementation, you would likely see many instances of each.

Although this document is well formed (meaning that all the elements are arranged properly) it is lacking a DTD to make it complete.

Document Type Definitions

XML documents should include a Document Type Definition (DTD). HTML documents don't demand their use, but it is a good practice to use one. The DTD defines the validity of the tags in the XML document. Without a DTD, the XML document won't function.

The DTD describes the meaning and function of every tag in your XML document. In this way, the language that you have used (your tags and their relationship to one another) will be made known to whatever system will be interpreting your document. Without the DTD, your document is unusable because it doesn't contain a description of the syntax, structure, rules, and vocabulary of your document. Even well-formed XML documents are meaningless without their DTDs. For this reason, you may consider the DTD to be the most important part of the XML document; in reality, however, the two work together to provide a usable solution.

DTDs are normally placed in files separate from the XML document. You can, however, place the DTD in the XML document if you prefer. The advantage of keeping the DTD in a separate file is that it can be referred to in all XML documents of the type defined in the DTD. This is similar to linking CSS files into an HTML document.

Extensible Stylesheet Language

Because XML documents don't directly provide formatting tags like HTML, a style sheet appropriate for use in the XML environment is required in order to format the output from your XML documents.

One method of formatting an XML document is to use CSS. The other formatting method is to implement the Extensible Stylesheet Language (XSL). The advantage of XSL is that it can, in addition to formatting your XML document, provide transformation or translation to other document formats. For example, an XSL can transform your XML document into an HTML page, so it can be viewed in a Web browser. XSL and CSS can also be used together.

You can find more information regarding XSL on the W3C site, located at `www.w3.org/Style/XSL/`.

Key Point Summary

This chapter has examined various technologies that can work together to provide dynamic, interactive Web content. You learned about image methods and formats, creating frame-based sites, and HTML extensions that extend the ability of HTML to provide active content. These extensions include Cascading Style Sheets, JavaScript, DHTML, the Document Object Model, XHTML, and XML.

The following points summarize the major concepts of this chapter:

✦ Image maps allow you to define areas of an image for use as links to other documents, or areas inside the current document.

✦ Image maps are defined with the <MAP> tag and include the SHAPE attribute to define the general shape (rect, circle, or polygon) of the hot spot, and the COORDS attribute to specify its actual location on the image. The HREF attribute indicates the target location to link to when the user clicks on the corresponding hot spot.

✦ Transparency is the elimination of certain colors of an image in order to let the Web page background show through. Currently the only Web-friendly graphic formats that support transparency are the GIF89a and PNG formats.

✦ Interlacing is used to progressively store a graphic so that it appears to download more rapidly. GIF87a, GIF89a, and PNG are the only Web-friendly formats to support interlacing.

✦ Animated GIFS provide a means of creating animated images. This is done by storing individual frames, like the frames of a movie, in a single file, which will play the frames back in sequence when incorporated into a Web page.

✦ Frames are used to divide a Web page into unique and individually controllable sections or panes. Each frame contains a separate HTML document.

✦ Frameset documents are HTML documents that control the placement of the individual frames. A frameset document replaces the HTML <BODY> tag with the <FRAMESET> tag. Each frame is then defined within the <FRAMESET> with individual <FRAME> tags.

✦ The <FRAMESET> tag uses the ROWS or COLS attributes to define the number of frames on a page, and determines whether they will be arranged in rows or columns. An individual <FRAMESET> can use only ROWS or COLS — not both at the same time.

✦ The <NOFRAMES> tag allows you to provide material on your Web page for browsers that don't support frames. The content provided in the <NOFRAMES> section of the <FRAMESET> is generally a link to a non-frame site, or an explanation of why the Web site won't appear in the browser.

✦ Frame targeting refers to directing the document accessed via a link to appear in a specific frame of the Web page. The <FRAME> tag's NAME attribute names the frame. The anchor (<A>) tag's TARGET attribute then specifies the destination frame by its name. The <BASE> tag and its TARGET attribute can be used to specify a default frame, rather than setting the TARGET attribute of each anchor tag.

✦ Cascading Style Sheets are used to provide overall formatting for your documents. They can be implemented in four different ways: linked, imported, embedded, or inline.

✦ CSS1 and CSS2 specifications have been adopted into the HTML 4.01 specification.

✦ Imported style sheets are not recommended because they often cause problems due to inconsistent implementation in different browsers.

✦ JavaScript is an object-oriented scripting language that you can use to build interactive functionality into your Web pages.

✦ JavaScript is not a compiled language. The browser interprets it.

✦ When developing interactive Web pages, developers use JavaScript to control objects in the HTML environment, such as the *window* and *document* objects. This allows developers to make use of pre-defined functions and properties inherent in the browser environment.

✦ JavaScript is embedded in HTML documents through the use of the <SCRIPT> and </SCRIPT> container tags. Script sections can appear in the header section, body section, or both.

✦ Dynamic HTML is a combination of scripting, HTML, and the Document Object Model, and provides for the creation of dynamic Web content.

✦ The Document Object Model (DOM) is a description of all objects in the browser and Web page environment, and specifications regarding their methods and properties.

✦ Each browser makes use of a different DOM. Although similar, the differences in each can cause a script to function incorrectly in one browser, but work fine in another.

✦ Extensible HTML is a combination of the HTML 4.01 specification and the XML 1.0 specification.

✦ Extensible Markup Language (XML) is a derivative of the Structured General Markup Language (SGML).

✦ XML defines the way a document is structured, rather than the actual data that the document contains. That definition is left to the document creator through the use of a Document Type Definition, or DTD.

✦ The DTD defines the syntax, structure, rules, and vocabulary of an XML document. Every XML document must have a DTD, which can be stored separately from the XML document, or embedded in it.

✦ The Extensible Stylesheet Language (XSL) provides formatting and transformation capabilities in XML documents. Transformation means changing an XML document into another type of document, such as an HTML document. XSL provides this capability by acting as a translator between the two document definitions.

✦   ✦   ✦

STUDY GUIDE

The following materials will aid you in preparing for the portion of the CIW Foundations exam, 1D0-410, covered in this chapter. Several assessment questions will, as much as possible, mimic the feel of the actual exam. In addition, this section offers a number of labs—which may or may not have questions associated with them—that allow you to get hands-on experience with some of the chapter subject matter.

After you have been through the assessment questions and labs, check your answers in the Answers to Chapter Questions section, which immediately follows the scenarios.

Assessment Questions

1. Client side image maps are implemented in HTML by what tag?

   A. <MAP>

   B. <IMAP>

   C. <IMG>

   D. <IMAGEMAP>

2. What shapes are allowed in defining the image map hot spots? (Choose all that apply)

   A. Triangle

   B. Rectangle

   C. Polygon

   D. Circle

3. To define the coordinates of your image map, all measurements are made from the graphics origin. What does this refer to?

   A. The URL that the graphic is loaded from.

   B. The upper-left corner of the graphic image.

   C. The center of the graphic image.

   D. The bottom-right corner of the graphic image.

4. What tag defines the hot spot in an image map?

    A. <HS>

    B. <SPOT>

    C. <TARGET>

    D. <AREA>

5. How is an image map associated with a graphic on your Web page?

    A. By setting the TARGET property of the anchor tag to the name of your image map.

    B. By setting the TARGET property of the <IMG> tag to the name of your image map.

    C. By setting the IMAGE property of the image map to the name of your image.

    D. By setting the USEMAP property of the image to the name of your image map.

6. Image transparency is supported by which of the following Web-friendly graphic formats? (Choose two)

    A. BMP

    B. EPS

    C. PNG

    D. GIF89a

7. Interlacing is used to accomplish what? (Choose all that apply)

    A. Speed up the actual download of graphic images.

    B. Decrease the apparent download time of images.

    C. Decrease the size of graphic images.

    D. Ease user frustration over large image download times.

8. Animated GIFs are supported by which Web-friendly graphic format or formats? (Choose all that apply)

    A. BMP

    B. GIF89a

    C. GIF87a

    D. PNG

9. An HTML frameset document can't contain which HTML section?

   A. <SCRIPT> section

   B. <BODY> section

   C. <HEAD> section

   D. <STYLE> section

10. Which two attributes of the <FRAMESET> tag can't be used together in the same frameset?

   A. <BORDER>

   B. <MARGINLEFT>

   C. <ROWS>

   D. <COLS>

11. What tag is used to define a frame inside of a frameset?

   A. <FRAME>

   B. <ROW>

   C. <COL>

   D. <TABLE>

12. What attribute of the <FRAME> tag enables a link to send its document to the frame for display?

   A. TARGET

   B. NAME

   C. BASE

   D. LINK

13. Where does the <NOFRAMES> section of a frameset document appear?

   A. Inside the <FRAMESET> tags, usually after the final <FRAME> tag.

   B. Just after the </FRAMESET> tag, but before the </HTML> tag.

   C. In a separate HTML file.

   D. In the header section of the frameset document.

14. What two "flavors" of Cascading Style Sheets are incorporated into the HTML 4.01 specification?

    A. CSS1

    B. CSS2

    C. XSL

    D. CSS3

15. Which of the following is not a method of implementing CSS in a Web page? (Choose all that apply)

    A. Creating embedded style sheets with the <STYLE> and </STYLE> container tags.

    B. Creating inline styles by using the STYLE attribute of most HTML tags.

    C. Linking external style sheet files with the <LINK> tag.

    D. Using a "style format" program to format your HTML text prior to publishing.

16. The combination of a CSS selector, property and value is referred to as what?

    A. A rule

    B. A format

    C. A style

    D. Cool

17. Which method of implementing CSS in Web pages is seldom used due to inconsistencies in browser implementation?

    A. Importing style sheets

    B. Embedding style sheets

    C. Linking style sheets

    D. Using inline style properties

18. How is JavaScript commonly implemented in HTML documents? (Choose all that apply)

    A. By embedding JavaScript code in the document header with the use of the <SCRIPT> and </SCRIPT> tags.

    B. By embedding JavaScript code in the document body with the use of the <SCRIPT> and </SCRIPT> tags.

    C. By writing script into the supporting HTML tags such as the anchor tag.

    D. All of the above.

19. DHTML stands for:

   A. Deprecated HTML

   B. Deliverable HTML

   C. Dynamic HTML

   D. Dead HTML

20. The Document Object Model defines objects available for manipulation through scripting in the browser environment. Why, then, will the same script often work differently in different browsers? (Choose all that apply)

   A. Each browser incorporates its own, unique version of the DOM, which may not be compatible with another browser's implementation.

   B. Scripting languages need to be recompiled for the various browsers that they will execute on.

   C. Developers need to rewrite code before moving to different browsers, and may have made mistakes.

   D. None of the above.

21. XML provides a framework for defining elements of a document, which describe the type of content in the document. These elements are called what?

   A. Verbs

   B. Nouns

   C. Trees

   D. Tags

22. XML documents must have one, but it is optional in HTML documents. What is it?

   A. A header section

   B. A body section

   C. A Document Type Definition

   D. A style section

23. XSL provides what two services for XML documents?

   A. Security

   B. Formatting

   C. Re-usability

   D. Transformation

Lab Exercises

In the following labs, you will create a frame-based Web site that uses a graphical interface for navigation (via an image map), implements transparent and opaque graphics, and makes use of Cascading Style Sheets for formatting. You will start by creating the basic frame structure for your Web pages.

Lab 11-1 Creating a frame-based document

1. Using a text editor, create a frameset document with the following characteristics:

   Split the page vertically, allocating 150 pixels for the left column and the remainder of the space available for the right column. The left column will be used for site navigation, and the right column will display the content of each of the pages.

   Set the SRC attribute for the first <FRAME> tag to "navpage.html."

   Set the SRC attribute for the second <FRAME> tag to "mainpage.html."

2. Save the frameset document to the directory of your choice. Call the file index.html. For a sample of how to create the frameset document, see the Labs portion of the Answers to Chapter Questions section at the end of the chapter.

3. Create two more HTML documents. Call one navpage.html and the other mainpage.html. Save these to the same directory as your frameset document. From now on, store all files in this directory unless instructed otherwise.

4. Modify your two new pages as follows:

   navpage.html

5. Create four anchor tags on the page. The link text should be "Home Page," "GIF Formats," "Cascading Style Sheets," and "JavaScript." Set the HREF attributes for each to "mainpage.html," "gifspage.html," "csspage1.html," and "jspage.html," respectively. Here is an example of how the first should look:

   ```
   <A HREF="mainpage.html">Home Page</A><BR>
   ```

   The <BR> tag following the anchor will ensure that the next link starts on the line following. Create the remaining three anchors on your own, using this one as a reference.

6. Save your changes to navpage.html.

   mainpage.html

7. In the body section of `mainpage.html`, enter a line of text to serve as the heading. The actual text is up to you, but should have something to do with the fact that this is the home page of your site. Use the `<H2>` tag to format your text.

8. Create a short paragraph describing your site. Something about CIW Certification is appropriate, but again, the actual text is up to you. Use the paragraph tag (`<P>`) to start this paragraph of text

9. Save your changes to `mainpage.html`

10. You will now add the HTML pages for each of the links. You've already done the home page, so start with `gifspage.html`. For now, just put a heading formatted with the <H3> tag, on the pages and save them. Use the following table as a guide:

Filename	*Title Text*
`gifspage.html`	GIF Formats
`csspage1.html`	CSS Formatting
`jspage.html`	JavaScript

11. Test your Web site by launching the frameset document, `index.html`, in your browser.

12. What do you notice when you click on the links in the left frame? Why does this happen?

13. You will now change your navigation links to target your right frame. Open your `navpage.html` file in your text editor and edit the anchor tags to use the TARGET attribute. The TARGET attribute will send the Web page in this anchor's HREF attribute to the frame named in the TARGET. Edit the anchor tags as follows:

    ```
    <A HREF="mainpage.html" TARGET="mainframe">Home Page</A>
    ```

    Edit the other tags using the previous tag as an example.

14. Save your changes to `navpage.html`.

15. Open your frameset document, `index.html`, and edit the second frame tag to include the NAME attribute. The tag should look like this:

    ```
    <FRAME SRC="mainpage.html" NAME="mainpage">
    ```

16. Save your changes to `mainpage.html`.

17. Open or refresh your `index.html` frameset document in your browser. Try the links. What is different from the last time you navigated the Web site?

18. Can you think of another way of targeting the linked documents to the *main-page* frame, without having to create a separate TARGET attribute for each anchor tag?

19. (Optional) Implement the alternate targeting method you created in Step 18 above.

In this lab, you created a frameset document that split your Web page into two columns. Each column represents a separate frame in the Web page. You saved your frameset document as `index.html`. This is typical of real-world Web development because `index.html` is a default first page name for most Web servers, and the frameset document should be the first page to be displayed.

You also created a number of documents in addition to the frameset to function as the content of your Web site. One, `navpage.html`, is used to hold links to the content pages that should appear in the right frame.

Finally, you added targeting control to your links to allow the content pages to appear in the right frame.

In the next lab, you will modify your `gifspage.html` document to display opaque and transparent GIF images.

Lab 11-2 Working with images and image maps

1. You are going to add a background image to your `gifspage.html` document. Open `gifspage.html` in your text editor.

2. Edit the <BODY> tag of the page to include the BACKGROUND attribute. Change the tag as follows:

```
<BODY BACKGROUND="bgimage.gif">
```

3. Save the page and open it in your browser, or view your index page in your browser and navigate to the GIF Formats page.

4. Now add two GIF files to the page. One will be opaque and the other transparent. Open `gifspage.html` in your editor and add the following lines of code, in the body section, but after the heading line.

```
<TABLE BORDER="0">
<TR>
<TD><IMG SRC="opaque.gif" HEIGHT="100" WIDTH="100"></TD>
<TD>Opaque GIF Image</TD>
</TR>
<TR>
<TD><IMG SRC="transparent.gif" HEIGHT="100" WIDTH="100"></TD>
<TD>Transparent GIF Image</TD>
</TR>
</TABLE>
```

5. Save your changes and try to view the page in your browser. Notice how the background of the Web page shows through the background of the second GIF image. The second GIF was saved with white selected as the transparency color. As a result, all occurrences of white in the image are transparent.

In this lab, you have updated the `gifspage.html` document to include a background image and created a table to display an opaque and a transparent GIF image. In the next lab, you will create an image map to facilitate a graphical navigation image, which will replace your text links in the `navpage.html` document.

Lab 11-3 Creating a graphical navigation image and an image map.

1. Start by opening your `navpage.html` document in your text editor.

2. Delete each of the anchor tags. Remember the settings for the HREF and TARGET attributes.

3. Enter the following line of code in the body section of the document. This will load the image that you will use for navigation:

```
<IMG SRC="navimg.gif" HEIGHT="200" WIDTH="125">
```

4. Save your work, and open your `index.html` document in your Web browser. The navigation image that you created should now appear in the left frame and the links should be gone.

5. You will now create the image map for the *navimg* GIF that you just added to your navigation page. Start by loading your `navpage.html` document into your editor.

6. Edit the <IMG> tag, adding the attributes in bold:

```
<IMG SRC="navimg.gif" HEIGHT="200" WIDTH="125" BORDER="0"
USEMAP="#navmap">
```

7. Now, add the code to create an image map. The code can come before or after the <IMG> tag, but should be inside the body section. Remember that the image map uses the <MAP> and </MAP> container tags, within which you define the hot spots with the <AREA> tag. The AREA tag uses three attributes: SHAPE, COORDS, and HREF, which define the shape and coordinates of the hot spot and the URL of the document to link. As you are working on a frame site, you should also include the TARGET attribute. The first <AREA> definition is already done for you. Use the information in the following table to complete the rest.

```
<AREA SHAPE="rect" COORDS="39, 28, 88, 58"
HREF="mainpage.html" TARGET="mainpage">
```

LINK	SHAPE	COORDS
GIF Formats	rect	15, 71, 110, 96
CSS	circle	63, 123, 18
JavaScript	polygon	14, 147, 23, 173, 98, 173, 110, 147

8. After you have finished coding your image map, save your work and open the `index.html` document in your browser. You should now be able to navigate with the image in the navigation frame. If it does not work, check your code and try again. If you need a hint in completing this portion of the lab, refer to the Lab Answers section at the back of the chapter.

You have now completed incorporating an image to use for navigation of the site, and an image map to enable links from the image. The next lab instructs you to create and implement Cascading Style Sheets.

Lab 11-4 Creating and applying Cascading Style Sheets.

1. You'll start by creating a Cascading Style Sheet file. Create a new file in your text editor and save it with the name `chapter11.css`. Enter the following code in your style sheet. Be sure to observe the punctuation and get it in the proper places.

```
H2  {
   color:red;
   font-family: Comic Sans MS, sans-serif;
   font-size: 24pt;
   text-align: center;
   }
H3  {
   color:blue;
   font-family: fantasy;
   font-size: 16pt;
   text-align: center;
   }
BODY  {
   background: url(bgimage.gif);
   color: black;
   font-family: Comic Sans MS, sans-serif;
   font-size: 12pt;
   text-align: left;
   }
```

2. Save the changes to your document.

3. Now, incorporate the `css` document that you just created into the `main-page.html` document by linking it into the document. Do you remember the method for doing this? If you need a hint, look at the Lab Answers section.

4. Open your `index.html` document in your browser and view the effect of your linked `css` document. If you see no difference, check your linking.

5. Try navigating to different pages. Notice that the formatting defined in your CSS document only applies to the home page (the background in the GIFs page was done manually in the last lab).

6. Include the following code after the <H3> heading line, in your `csspage1.html` document to summarize the changes made by your stylesheet:

```
The chapter11.css style sheet defines the format for these
tags:<BR>
<H1>The H1 Tag</H1><BR>
<H3>The H3 Tag</H3><BR>
And the body tag.
```

Link the `chapter11.css` file into your other Web pages and observe the changes.

In this lab, you created a Cascading Style Sheet and linked it into your Web pages.

The final lab illustrates the use of JavaScript in your Web site. You will create a pop-up message (an alert) that will appear each time the JavaScript page is viewed. Also, you will be prompted to enter your name, which will be included in a greeting printed on the page.

Lab 11-5 Implementing JavaScript code in a Web page.

1. Open your `jspage.html` file in your editor.

2. In the body section of the document, enter the following code:

```
<SCRIPT>
<!--
var userName;
window.alert("Welcome to the JavaScript Page");
userName = window.prompt("Please enter your name","");
document .write("<H1>Welcome " + userName + "!");
//-->
</SCRIPT>
```

3. Save your changes and open your index page in your browser. Navigate to the JavaScript page. You should be given an alert. When you close the alert dialog box, you should be prompted for your name. Enter your name and click OK. The prompt dialog box disappears and you are left at the JavaScript page. This sequence of events should happen every time you visit the page.

   Notice the use of the comment tags (<!– and //–>). It is good coding practice to include these around your script to prevent the lines of code from being rendered as text in browsers that don't understand the <SCRIPT> tags.

In this lab, you implemented a JavaScript that prompted you for information and dynamically wrote a message to the Web page.

Answers to Chapter Questions

Chapter Pre-Test

1. The areas used in defining links through image maps are often referred to as "hot spots." This is the location of the image defined through the AREA attribute of the <MAP> tag that provides a link to other documents or other areas of the same document. See the section "Defining the image map" for more information.

2. Currently, the only Web-friendly graphic formats that support transparency are the GIF89a format and PNG. Although others may support the use of transparency, these two are considered the best for use in a Web environment.

3. The HTML document that defines the way frames are arranged is called the *frameset document*. It includes the <FRAMESET> and <FRAME> tags that define the shapes and locations of the frames, as well as their content. See the section "The HTML <FRAME> and <FRAMESET> tags" for more information.

4. The four methods of incorporating CSS into HTML documents are linking, importing, embedding, and inline. See the section "Cascading Style Sheets (CSS)" for further information.

5. JavaScript is considered an object-oriented scripting language because it can be used to access methods and properties of objects in the environment that the script runs in. This can be in a Web browser, Web server, or almost any other application. See the section "Object-Oriented Programming concepts" for additional reading.

6. The Document Object Model describes the objects and their methods and properties found in the browser environment. The DOM acts as an instruction guide for how the objects that comprise the environment relate to each other, and what functionality can be derived from them. See the "Document Object Model" section of this chapter for further information.

7. XHTML is a combination of the HTML 4.01 and XML 1.0 specifications. For further reading on XHTML, refer to the "Extensible HTML (XHTML)" section of this chapter.

8. XML is considered a derivative of the Structured General Markup Language (SGML), although it eliminates a lot of the complexity associated with SGML. The section of this chapter "Extensible Markup Language (XML)" contains additional information on the XML language.

9. XSL, or Extensible Style Language, allows formatting information to be applied to XML documents. It also allows transformation of one XML document type to another for use in differing environment. See the "Extensible Style Language" section for further details.

10. An XML document requires the use of a DTD. As mentioned previously, a DTD defines the tags that make up an XML document. These tags can be defined by the developer in the creation of the XML document, and are, therefore, not universally understood. The DTD provides the description of how the tags are structured and the type of data that they contain to software making use of the XML document. See the "Document Type Definitions (DTDs)" section for additional detail.

Assessment Questions

1. A. The <MAP> tag is used to implement client-side image maps.

2. B, C, D. The rectangle, polygon, and circle are all shapes allowed in image maps.

3. B. A. graphics origin is its upper-left corner, which represents the coordinate 0,0.

4. D. The <AREA> tag, through the use of the SHAPE and COORDS attributes, defines the hot spot.

5. D. The USEMAP property of the <IMG> tag is used to associate an image map with an image.

6. C, D. PNG and GIF89a.

7. B, D. Interlacing makes images appear to download faster, easing user frustration.

8. B. GIF89a is the only format to support animation.

9. B. The <FRAMESET> tag replaces the <BODY> tag of a regular HTML document. If a frameset document has a <BODY> tag, it will render as a blank page on some browsers.

10. C, D. A single <FRAMESET> tag can specify either ROWS or COLS, not both at the same time.

11. A. The <FRAME> tag defines the frame. There is one <FRAME> tag for each row or column specified in the <FRAMESET>.

12. B. The <FRAME> tag's NAME attribute allows a name to be associated with the frame that a link may use to target the frame.

13. A. The <NOFRAMES> section appears inside the <FRAMESET>. Convention places it after the last <FRAME> tag.

14. A., B. CSS1 and CSS2 are incorporated into the HTML 4.01 spec.

15. D. HTML documents aren't pre-formatted because the browser looks for style instructions during rendering. These instructions are given through style commands in the document.

16. **A.** A CSS rule is the name by which the selector, properties, and values of the style are collectively referred to.

17. **A.** Using the @import directive is inconsistently implemented in the browsers so it is not recommended.

18. **D.** Each of these methods is valid for implementing JavaScript code.

19. **C.** DHTML stands for Dynamic HTML.

20. **A.** Even though the DOM is a W3C specification, browser manufacturers have implemented their own versions. The version differences cause problems when trying to make a script function across browsers.

21. **D.** Tags define the content of your XML document. XML defines the framework by which these tags can be defined.

22. **C, A.** Document Type Definition (DTD) is required to give meaning to, and validation for, tags in your XML document.

23. **B, D.** XSL provides formatting and transformation services in XML.

Labs

This section provides sample code and answers to question for each lab and step in the lab where you are expected to provide code or answer a question. For example, step 2 of Lab 11-1 asks you to save the frameset document as index.html. The code listed below provides one possible solution to that step. The other code samples also provide possible solutions for the tasks assigned in each lab, or answers to questions posed.

Lab 11-1

Step 2. A sample frameset document (index.html)

```
<HTML>
<HEAD>
<META http-equiv="Content-Type" content="text/html;
charset=iso-8859-1">
<TITLE>Lab 11 Frameset Document</TITLE>
</HEAD>
<FRAMESET COLS="150, *">
  <FRAME SRC="navpage.html">
  <FRAME SRC="mainpage.html">
</FRAMESET>
</BODY>
</HTML>
```

Step 11. Creating the navpage.html and mainpage.html documents.

navpage.html

```
<HTML>
<HEAD>
<META http-equiv="Content-Type" content="text/html;
charset=iso-8859-1">
<TITLE>Lab 11 Navigation Page</TITLE>
</HEAD>
<BODY>
<A HREF="mainpage.html">Home Page</A><BR>
<A HREF="gifspage.html">GIF Formats</A><BR>
<A HREF="csspage1.html">Cascading Style Sheets</A><BR>
<A HREF="jspage.html">JavaScript</A>
</BODY>
</HTML>
```

mainpage.html

```
<HTML>
<HEAD>
<META http-equiv="Content-Type" content="text/html;
charset=iso-8859-1">
<TITLE>Lab 11 Home Page</TITLE>
</HEAD>
<BODY>
<H2>CIW Certification Bible - Chapter 11 Home Page</H2>
<P>This Web site is used for the exercises at the end of
    Chapter 11 in the CIW Foundations Certification Bible.</P>
</BODY>
</HTML>
```

Step 12. What do you notice when you click on the links in the left frame? Why does this happen?

As you click on the links, the document appears in the left frame, not in the right. This happens because the anchor tags don't have the TARGET attribute set.

Step 17. What is different from the last time you navigated the Web site?

The documents now appear in the right frame.

Step 18. Can you think of another way of targeting the linked documents to the *mainpage* frame, without having to create a separate TARGET attribute for each anchor tag?

Implement a <BASE TARGET="mainpage"> tag in the header of the `navpage.html` document, such as follows:

```
<HTML>
<HEAD>
<META http-equiv="Content-Type" content="text/html;
charset=iso-8859-1">
<TITLE>Lab 11 Navigation Page</TITLE>
<BASE TARGET="mainpage">
</HEAD>
```

Lab 11-3

Step 8. Coding the image map.

The following code segment illustrates a proper image map definition for the `navimg.html` document.

```
<MAP NAME="navmap">
 <AREA SHAPE="rect" COORDS="39,28,88,58" HREF="mainpage.html"
TARGET="mainpage">
 <AREA SHAPE="rect" COORDS="15,71,110,96" HREF="gifspage.html"
TARGET="mainpage">
 <AREA SHAPE="circle" COORDS="63,123,18" HREF="csspage1.html"
TARGET="mainpage">
 <AREA SHAPE="poly" COORDS="14,147,23,173,98,173,110,147"
HREF="jspage.html" TARGET="mainpage">
</MAP>
<IMG SRC="navimg.gif" HEIGHT="200" WIDTH="125" USEMAP="#navmap"
BORDER="0">
```

This code should be placed in the body section of the document.

Lab 11-4

Step 3. Linking a Cascading Style Sheet into a Web page.

The correct way to do this is to incorporate the <LINK> tag into the header of each Web page that the style sheet is to apply to. The following code segment shows the link tag that should be incorporated in the Web pages of your sample site:

```
<HEAD>
existing header code
<LINK rel="stylesheet" type="text/css" href="chapter11.css">
</HEAD>
```

Network Fundamentals

T his part focuses on basic networking concepts. Although there is some overlap with concepts presented in Part I, the thrust of these chapters is on general networking concepts and how they apply to all networks (not just the Internet).

The Basics of Networking

EXAM OBJECTIVES

1. Define "networking" and explain this concept's importance in today's data communications marketplace.

2. Identify and describe the functions of servers, workstations, and hosts.

3. Define the term Internetwork, and define its role and usage as related to the Internet.

4. Relate Internetworks to the concept of the corporate enterprise network.

5. Identify networking architectures and provide at least two defining characteristics of each.

6. Describe the basic network topology characteristics.

7. Identify the major network operating systems, including Microsoft Windows NT/2000, Unix, and Novell NetWare and their respective clients.

CHAPTER PRE-TEST

1. Two or more computers connected together for the purpose of sharing and managing resources are referred to as a _____.

2. List two disadvantages of the Mainframe approach to networking.

3. Where does processing occur in the client/server model of networking?

4. An _____ is formed when an organization opens up their intranet to selected external users.

5. What are the two main network architectures?

6. A network that connects all computers in an organization is referred to as an _____ Network.

7. A network topology describes the _____ layout of a network.

8. List at least three common network topologies.

9. What are the three most common Network Operating Systems?

✦ Answers to these questions can be found at the end of the chapter. ✦

In the scope of time and technology, computer networks are still very much in their infancy. Despite this fact, however, their popularity and use has grown faster than anyone could have imagined. Networks now appear in every corner of the earth and beyond. Networks are in our businesses, schools, homes, coffee shops, bookstores, banks — even our laundry mats. Thousands of different networks literally link millions of computers. Despite their vast numbers, all networks are based on some very basic network concepts. The goal of this chapter is to introduce you to some of the most fundamental of these concepts and to provide you with a foundation of information to build on in future chapters.

What Is a Network?

Define "networking" and explain this concept's importance in today's data communications marketplace.

A network, simply defined, is two or more computers connected together for the purpose of sharing and managing resources. Of course, this definition does not truly capture the essence of most networks being used in today's high-tech world. In addition to computers, many other devices are attached to modern networks including, but not limited to, the following:

✦ Printers

✦ Copiers

✦ Plotters

✦ Fax machines

✦ Cash registers

✦ Instant-teller banking machines

✦ Alarm systems

✦ Hotel room doors

✦ Furnaces

✦ Video cameras

Basic networking terminology

Identify and describe the functions of servers, workstations, and hosts.

Understanding the terminology used in networking is important for passing the CIW Foundations exam and also for your understanding of networks in general. The most fundamental terms include: networking, Internetworking, server, client, workstation, node, and host.

Networking and Internetworking

Networks have a huge impact on peoples' day-to-day lives. You will often interact with the networks you encounter. The term *networking* is often used to describe this interaction. Many people (including the people who put together the CIW foundations exam) expand the definition of this concept by using the term *Internetworking* to describe the act of networking on the Internet.

Server

One of the most important functions that a computer can perform in a network is that of a server. In networking, a *server* is any computer that provides services or resources for other computers. Common resources that are provided by servers include files, applications, and printers. A server may also provide a service, such as security, to protect those resources.

Workstation, client, host, and node

The terms *workstation*, *client*, *host*, and *node* are often used interchangeably when discussing networks. You should be aware, however, of subtle differences between these items.

✦ At one point, the term *workstation* was reserved for fairly high-powered desktop computers. These computers were typically used for high-end, processor- and graphics-intensive programs, such as desktop publishing or Computer Aided Drawing (CAD) applications. In recent years, the term *workstation* has expanded to include any computer on which people run applications. Workstations — unlike clients, hosts, and nodes — don't have to be part of a network.

✦ A *client* is any computer attached to a network that can access services or resources from a server. If a workstation is attached to a network and can be used to access network resources, then the workstation is considered to be a client. If a particular server requires a service or resource from another server, then it can also be a client.

✦ The general definition of a *host* is any computer that provides information to other computers via a network. The term *host* is also commonly used to refer to any computer attached to a TCP/IP-based network, including a client or a workstation.

✦ If a device has a Network Interface Card and its own network address, then it can be considered a network *node*. Many devices can act as nodes; common examples of nodes include workstations, servers, routers, and printers.

The three basic elements of networks

Networks are available in many different shapes, sizes, and configurations, and —
despite these differences — all networks have the following three basic elements in
common:

✦ **Protocols:** These are the communication rules to which all components of the
network must adhere. Think of protocols as a language that is shared between
nodes of a network. In order for two network devices to communicate with
each directly they must share a common protocol.

✦ **Transmission Media:** The manner in which the various components of the
network connect. The many different types of transmission media include network cable, microwave, and radio transmission.

✦ **Network Services:** Resources that are to be shared with network users, such
as files, applications, printers, fax machines, copiers, and cameras — the list is
almost endless.

Protocols are discussed in detail in Chapter 13; transmission media in Chapter 14;
and network services in Chapter 15.

History of Computer Networks

Computer networks have been around for several decades. Like all computer-
related technologies, these networks have greatly evolved since they first
appeared. The most significant change has occurred in the design model of the network. Networks have moved from a mainframe model of networking to a
client/server model.

Mainframe network model

The first networks were based on what is known as a *mainframe* or *centralized network* model. In this model, a central computer, or the mainframe, controls all network devices. The mainframe is responsible for all information processing on the
network. As such, these mainframes were huge machines that filled entire floors of
buildings and required a small army of engineers and operators to keep them running. To access the resources on the network, users had to use devices called *terminals*. These terminals consisted of a screen, a keyboard, and a connection to the
mainframe. Terminals transmitted the information that was typed by the users
directly to the mainframe and displayed that information on the screen per the
instructions of the mainframe. Terminals had no processing power, and without a
constant network connection to the mainframe, they were basically useless, earning
them the nickname "dumb terminals." Figure 12-1 displays a network setup following the mainframe model.

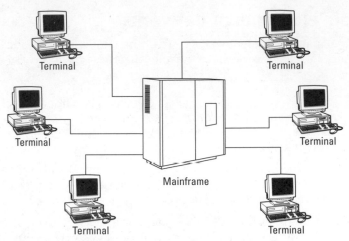

Figure 12-1: Centralized network model showing the mainframe as the central component

Disadvantages of the mainframe model

Although many networks in the world still use mainframes, the general trend is moving away from them. This trend is mainly due to the following disadvantages:

Single point of failure

Many of the problems associated with this network model resulted from the fact that users of the network had to rely on the mainframe for all of their data processing needs. In many cases, *when* these central computers failed, the production of an entire organization came to a complete standstill. Many people (including this author) have sat, staring blankly at a frozen screen, wishing, hoping, and praying that the network would suddenly spring back to life in order to continue working.

Network congestion

In a true mainframe network, the mainframe performs most tasks, including interpreting every keystroke at each terminal and instructing each terminal what to display on its screen. In many circumstances, the constant flow of information back and forth between the terminals and the mainframe can result in an extreme amount of network traffic, which in turn, slows the network response. Additionally, mainframe processors (like any computer processor) can become overburdened with too many processing requests, resulting in a bottleneck inside the mainframe. The ultimate outcome of this scenario is slow or nonexistent network response and frustrated operators.

Note   In computing terminology, a *bottleneck* is any process that may cause a decrease in performance.

Cost

Initially, running a mainframe network was so expensive that only very large, well-funded organizations, such as the U.S. government, universities, and large companies, were able to own one.

As time progressed, computing devices shrunk in size and cost, and grew in power and reliability. By the mid-70s, these developments allowed even small to midsize organizations to set up their own networks. Instead of using huge mainframes, many organizations were able to run their networks using a *minicomputer*. As its name suggests, a minicomputer is basically a scaled-down version of the mainframe. These minicomputer-based networks, however, are still a form centralized computing and thus suffer the same disadvantages as mainframe-based networks.

Be sure to know the major disadvantages of the mainframe model.

Client/Server Network Model

By the late 1970s, it became feasible to create a computer small enough to sit on a desk, yet powerful enough to process information without the aid of a larger mainframe or minicomputer. These *microcomputers* or *personal computers* (PCs), as they became known, allowed for a major shift in the structure of many modern networks. Networks began to move away from the mainframe's centralized computing model to the client/server or, as is it often referred to, the distributed model of networking.

In a client/server network, the processing of information is split between a client computer and a server computer. If you have a client/server network, as shown in Figure 12-2, the workstation computer is the client or *front end*, and the server is the *back end*.

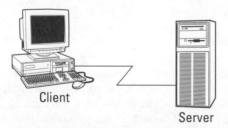

Client

Server

Figure 12-2: A simple client/server network

In a typical client/server network, communication between computers usually begins when a client computer requests information from a server. The server processes the request, retrieves the required information, and returns it to the client. At this point in the communication process, the client machine works with the data and places it into a desirable format for the user. If you have ever browsed Web pages on the Internet, you have seen this client/server relationship in action. Consider the following example:

Kaleigh sits down at her computer to play a game. She opens her Web browser, clicks her mouse into the address line, and types the following URL: `www.reallyfungamesite.com`. In a few minutes, Kaleigh's browser displays the game site's home page. She chooses a game and begins to play.

In this example, Kaleigh's computer is the client and the Web server at the game site is the server. Both computers need to process information in order for Kaleigh to see her desired Web page. Kaleigh's computer is responsible for running the browser software. This software must interpret Kaleigh's actions and respond accordingly. When Kaleigh types the URL in the address line, her computer must then locate the appropriate Web server and request the home page. The server is responsible for locating the requested page and passing it back to Kaleigh's computer. Kaleigh's computer is responsible for displaying the page on the screen.

Most of the advantages of this network model are a result of its distributed processing power. In other words, one machine is no longer doing all the work. Servers can now satisfy more requests than were possible in the traditional central processing model because they have much less work to do with each request. Network traffic also decreases because the server is no longer responsible for individually controlling each user's screen nor for processing each user's keystrokes.

Two-tier computing

Another term for the client/server interaction is *two-tier computing*. In two-tier computing, the workstation is the first tier and the server is the second tier.

Three-tier computing

In an effort to further offload some of the processing requirements on a server, many organizations have added a third computer, or "third tier," to the previous two-tier model. In this configuration, the first tier is still the workstation, the second tier is an intermediary application server, and the third tier is usually a database server. To illustrate how two-tier computing works, consider the following example:

Rubber Chickens-R-Us, Inc. (RCRU), a large retail novelty company, has created a Web site to promote their products. They have incorporated an online catalog into this Web site, and because RCRU produces thousands of items, they have designed the catalog so that customers have the ability to view subsets of products based on their individual preferences. To facilitate this, RCRU has implemented a three-tier solution, as shown in Figure 12-3.

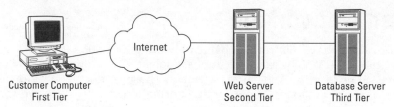

Figure 12-3: The three-tier networking solution of RCRU, Inc.

As the Figure 12-3 indicates, the first tier is the customer's computer, or, more specifically, the browser software on the computer. The second tier is a Web server to which the customers will connect. The third tier is a database server that is used to hold and manage the product information.

In the Real World Notice in this diagram that the Internet is depicted as a cloud. A cloud in a network diagram typically refers to any semi-public or public network.

Consider the following example:

Grant, a potential customer, uses his computer and browser software to connect to the RCRU Web site. Interested in what RCRU produces, Grant decides to explore the online catalog. He clicks the appropriate link, and shortly thereafter, his Web browser displays a form. The form asks him to choose the types of products he is interested in. He makes his choices and pushes the on-screen Submit button. Grant sits back and waits for his catalog to download to his computer. After a brief wait, he is presented with his requested price list. Grant has quickly and easily found the information that he was looking for.

In this example, Grant's computer is the first tier computer. This computer accepts his input (his mouse clicks and keystrokes), formats it, and passes it on to the Web server. The second tier Web server processes the information received and passes the Web page and blank form back to the client machine for it to display. After Grant fills out his request form and presses the Submit button, the information that he entered is sent back to the second tier for processing. The Web server, which has no product information, must now ask the database server for this information. The Web server formulates a request, called a *query,* for Grant's data. The database server assumes the role of the third tier, which retrieves the product information requested and sends the data back to the Web server. The Web server places the data received into an HTML format and passes it back to Grant's computer. Grant's computer processes the HTML code and displays the product information in the browser. This is a typical example of a three-tier networking solution.

Note Although the CIW Foundations exam only focuses on Two-tier and Three-tier you can find examples of Four-tier, Five-tier, and so on. These types of networking solutions are often referred to as N-tier, where N can represent virtually any number.

Web-Based Networking

Web-based, or *collaborative*, networks provide network information to clients in a format compatible with Web-based applications, such as Web browsers. Many organizations have set up internal Web-based networks. These *intranets* allow individuals within the organization to locate corporate information via their Web browser. This corporate information may include information on the following:

✦ Customers

✦ Meetings

✦ Sales

✦ Job postings

✦ Corporate news

✦ E-mail

Think of intranets as private versions of the Internet.

An *extranet* is formed when an organization opens its intranet to external users. These users may be clients, customers, suppliers, or perhaps even business partners. Extranets are ideal for situations in which multiple organizations are working on joint projects, or if one organization wants to share information in a customer/supplier environment.

The true benefits of Web-based networking are its ease of use and the user's ability to obtain a large variety of information without the need for custom client software. All the user typically needs is a Web browser. Web-based networking combines the power of the mainframe computers with the scalability of the client/server network model.

In the Real World   The term *scalability* refers to a network's ability or computer's ability to handle increased demand. An example of a highly scalable network is a network that suddenly grows from 100 workstations to 200 workstations, yet the users of the network notice little, if any, decrease in the network's response time.

Networking Categories

Objective   Identify networking architectures and provide at least two defining characteristics of each.

A network's architecture refers to its design or structure. These architectures fall into two basic categories: peer-to-peer and server-based.

Peer-to-peer networks

A *peer-to-peer* network is a network where the security and resources are not centralized or protected via a centralized source. In other words there is no one authority for the network. Network resources can be distributed across any and all hosts on the network and each host is responsible for providing security (if any) for the resources it is providing.

A typical peer-to-peer network arrangement is shown in Figure 12-4. In this particular network each workstation can act as both a client and a server. For example, Workstation 3 can be configured to share its plotter with the rest of the network. If a user sitting at Workstation 4 sends a drawing through the network to Workstation 3's plotter, then Workstation 4 is the client and Workstation 3 is the server for that transaction. Conversely, if a user at Workstation 3 accesses the modem connected to Workstation 5, then Workstation 3 is the client and Workstation 5 is the server.

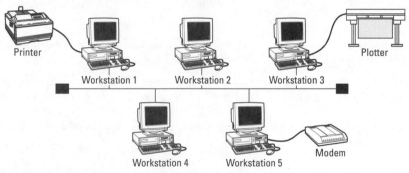

Figure 12-4: Peer-to-peer network architecture

The following operating systems have been designed to participate in a peer-to-peer network:

✦ Microsoft Windows for Workgroups 3.11

✦ Microsoft Windows 95/98/Me

✦ Artisoft LANtastic

✦ Novell NetWare Lite

Peer-to-peer benefits

Peer-to-peer networking is an ideal network solution for small organizations of ten or fewer users, or for homes with several computers. This network solution offers two major benefits:

✦ **Cost:** To run this network, you need only computers with basic operating systems. The equipment and software required is typically inexpensive. The user has no need for high-end server operating systems or their associated hardware.

✦ **Ease of use:** Due to the lack of complexity in the operating systems used, administrators and users usually require minimal training.

Peer-to-peer disadvantages

Peer-to-peer networks also have disadvantages. The most significant are the following:

✦ **Weak security:** Typically, the operating systems that are used on these networks are not designed with security in mind.

✦ **Designed to support very few users (ten or fewer):** With no central server, managing large networks of this type can be very cumbersome. Resources, such as data files, can be spread throughout the network—potentially on every computer. Network file management, such as backup and even locating files, can be difficult.

Server-based networks

In a true server-based (also referred to as client/server based) network, a host on the network is either a server or a client—but typically not both. The servers are computers dedicated to providing services and resources to clients. These services may include file storage and retrieval, security, printing, and application access. In a large network, several servers may provide each one of these services. Unlike peer-to-peer based networks, server-based networks security is centralized. A user in need of network resources must first prove their identity to a centralized authority before any resource access is allowed.

Note   Providing proof of one's identity to a network security authority is referred to as authentication.

Cross-Reference   For more information about methods of authentication see Chapter 18

The resources available can vary from user to user based on rights and privileges as granted to the user by the network administrators.

In a small server-based network, as shown in Figure 12-5, one server may provide all services.

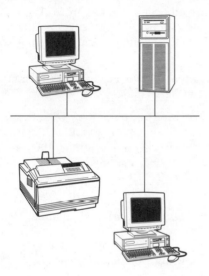

Figure 12-5: A server-based network

The following network operating systems have been designed for server-based networks:

✦ Novell NetWare

✦ Microsoft Windows NT

✦ Microsoft Windows 2000

✦ Microsoft LAN Manager

✦ Unix

✦ Digital Advantage Networks

✦ Banyan Vines

✦ AppleTalk network for Macintosh

Server-based network benefits

For many years, server-based networks have dominated the networking world because of the benefits gained by using such architecture. These benefits include the following:

✦ **Security:** Most server-based networks will implement some form of access control to monitor and prevent unauthorized access to resources. Typically, at least one server on the network manages security. This server authenticates users, verifies rights and permissions to resources, and audits network access

✦ **Large network support:** If implemented correctly, a large network with many servers can service hundreds, even thousands of clients.

✦ **Greater access to very powerful software:** Many applications are intended to run on dedicated server computers. Software, such as high-end SQL database applications, e-mail applications, and Web-hosting applications often require the speed, size, and security usually found on high-end dedicated servers.

Server-based network disadvantages

As with many things in life, nothing good comes without a price. Remember the following disadvantages of server-based networks:

✦ **Cost:** The server software, licensing, and the supporting hardware can be very expensive.

✦ **Usually requires full time administrators:** Network operating systems and the applications designed to run on them can be very complex, requiring a high degree of training and abilities to keep the network working correctly and efficiently.

Exam Tip   Memorize the advantages and disadvantages of both the peer-to-peer and the server-based networks. Knowing when each network design is appropriate to use is also important.

Enterprise networks

Objective   Define the term Internetwork, and define its role and usage as related to the Internet.

Relate Internetworks to the concept of the corporate enterprise network.

Large organizations may have many LANs situated in the various geographic locations in which they operate. In some larger locations, they may implement a server-based network topology. In smaller locations, the organizations may decide to go with simple peer-to-peer networks. Early in the growth of an organization, these networks may be fully independent; however, most companies will eventually link these networks together to form an *enterprise network*. Because many of these enterprise networks began as individual networks, incompatibilities exist that must be overcome for communication to work. Some systems often have to act as translators or gateways between networks.

Cross-Reference   For more information about LANs and WANs, see Chapter 15.

At the beginning of this chapter, *Internetworking* was defined as networking on the Internet. This term also refers to the act of combining multiple Local Area Networks (LANs) together to form a larger Wide Area Network (WAN). An enterprise network is "Internetworking" within an organization. However, an Internetwork is limited to the boundaries of one organization. A great example of this is the Internet, which is really an Internetwork of thousands of autonomous networks that are owned and operated by many organizations all over the world. In fact, this is how the Internet got its name.

Network Topologies

Objective   Describe the basic network topology characteristics.

A network's *topology* describes the shape or physical layout of the network. In other words, the topology describes how all the nodes on the network are connected. The five main topologies are bus, star, ring, hybrid, and mesh.

Cross-Reference   For more information about the hardware used in the various topologies, see Chapter 15.

Bus topology

In a bus topology, all network devices, or *nodes*, connect to a single cable, as shown in Figure 12-6.

The main cable is referred to as either the *bus* or *trunk*; it is typically a coaxial cable (and is similar to the wire running out of your television — if you have cable TV). In a bus network, a computer places data on the bus when it needs to send the data to another computer. This data travels the entire length of the cable in both directions and passes all the nodes. Each node examines the message as it travels by to see if it is the intended recipient. If it is, the node reads the message in its entirety and processes it accordingly. If a node determines that it is not the intended recipient, it does not process the message. Eventually, the data reaches the ends of the cable, where it is absorbed by small devices called *terminators*. Without the terminators, the signal — upon reaching the end — would actually echo back down the wire and disrupt network communication.

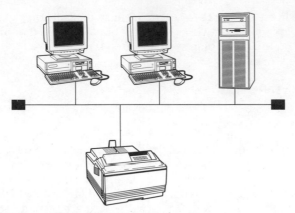

Figure 12-6: A bus network topology

 Note   Although not shown in the diagram one of the two ends of the bus must be grounded.

Bus topology advantages

Bus networks offer several advantages that have made them an attractive network topology option in many situations. Some of these advantages include the following:

✦ **Simple to install**

✦ **Inexpensive**

✦ **Reliable**

Bus topology disadvantages

The two main disadvantages associated with using a bus network follow:

✦ **Difficult troubleshooting:** A break in the cable will stop all network traffic and may be difficult to isolate.

✦ **Possible poor network response:** As network traffic increases on the network, the network response time will diminish. Due to the advantages, the bus topology has been very commonly used. However, due to its disadvantages and the fact that the cost of equipment for other topologies has decreased, use of this form of network is also decreasing.

Star topology

As shown in Figure 12-7, all nodes in a star topology connect to a central device. This device, usually a *hub* or *concentrator*, handles the job of passing information from one node to another.

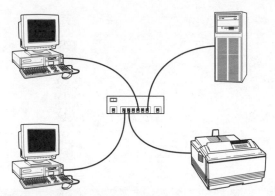

Figure 12-7: A star topology showing all nodes connected to a central device.

Star topology advantages

The main advantages offered by star topologies are the following:

✦ **Easy expansion and reconfiguration:** Simply connect and disconnect nodes as required. Disconnecting a node won't affect traffic.

✦ **Centralized management:** Because all data must pass through a central device, network management and monitoring can be centralized. These advantages have made the star topology one of the most preferred and often-used network topologies.

✦ **Fault Tolerance:** If a cable is bad or a workstation gets disconnected it does not bring down the entire network, as is the case with a bus topology

Star topology disadvantages

The star topology suffers from the following two major disadvantages:

✦ **More cable is required than with a bus topology:** A cable must run from the central device to all nodes on the network.

✦ **Single point of failure:** If the hub fails, then all network traffic stops.

Ring topology

In a ring topology, nodes are connected to form a ring, as shown in Figure 12-8.

All data travels in the same direction around the ring. When computers send data, they will pass it on to their neighboring computer. The neighbor then examines the data to see if it is the intended recipient; if not, the data is passed to the next node in the ring. This continues until either the intended recipient receives the data or the message returns to the sender.

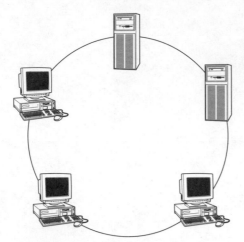

Figure 12-8: A ring topology

Ring topology advantages

Several advantages offered by ring topologies have resulted in this topology being widely implemented:

✦ **Equal network access for all nodes:** Networks of this type usually support the idea of a *token*, which is a small piece of data that travels around the ring, stopping at every node. A computer can send data only when it has possession of the token. Because this token must circle the ring, every node attached to it will get a chance to send data.

✦ **Designed to perform well — even with heavy network traffic:** Ring-based networks don't suffer from network data collisions like other topologies. Excessive collisions are a hindrance to good network performance.

For more information about ring-based networks, see Chapter 14.

Ring topology disadvantages

The disadvantages of using the ring topology include the following:

✦ **Single point of failure:** If a node fails, it won't be able to pass data to its neighbor.

✦ **Network reconfiguration or expansion may affect network communications:** In some implementations of the ring topology, disconnecting a computer may break the ring and cause communication to stop.

Hybrid networks

When you combine two or more of the topologies discussed in this chapter (star, ring, and bus), you form a *hybrid network*. You should be familiar with two common hybrids: star-bus and star-ring.

Star-bus hybrid

A star-bus network is formed when at least two star networks are connected in a bus fashion, as shown in Figure 12-9. In this arrangement, the cable joining the star networks is referred to as the network's *backbone*.

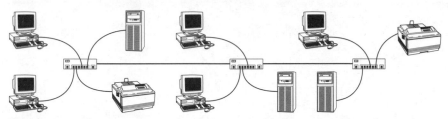

Figure 12-9: Three star networks are connected by a trunk cable to form a star-bus hybrid network.

Star-ring hybrid

Another fairly common hybrid is the *star-ring topology*. In this arrangement, multiple star networks are connected in a ring fashion, as shown in Figure 12-10.

Hybrid topology advantages

Hybrid networks offer many advantages — the most beneficial include the following:

✦ **Easy network expansion:** The use of hubs makes the task of adding new nodes very simple.

✦ **No single point of failure:** A failure in one node can't bring down the entire network.

Hybrid topology disadvantage

If the trunk cable or ring fails, then interconnectivity between networks is lost. Connections between nodes connected to each star will still be able to continue.

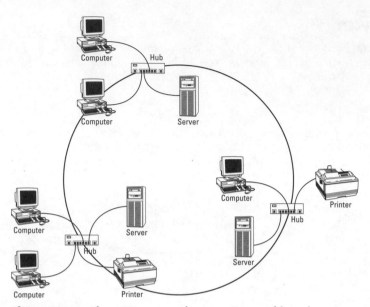

Figure 12-10: Three star networks are connected in a ring to form a star-ring topology.

Mesh topology

A mesh topology is an arrangement in which multiple paths exist between devices or between networks, as shown in Figure 12-11. Devices such as routers determine the destination of data and route the data down the most efficient path. If that path is unavailable, then an alternate path can be chosen.

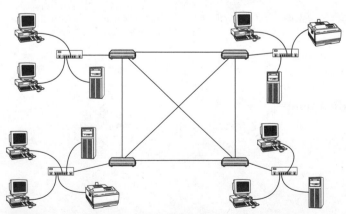

Figure 12-11: A mesh topology showing multiple paths between networks

Mesh topology advantages

You will gain the following two advantages by implementing a mesh topology:

✦ **High degree of reliability:** The redundant data paths allow networks to function despite connection failures.

✦ **Increase in network efficiency:** Routers can be configured to ensure that data will travel down the best route in given network conditions.

Mesh topology disadvantages

The main disadvantages of using a mesh topology include the following:

✦ **Cost:** Additional hardware may make costs prohibitive.

✦ **Complexity:** Administrators must possess knowledge of routers and routing.

Exam Tip　Know the five main topologies, along with their various advantages and disadvantages.

Network Operating Systems

Objective　Identify the major network operating systems—Microsoft Windows NT/2000, Unix, and Novell NetWare—and their respective clients

A *network operating system* (NOS) manages and provides access to resources and services on the network. Typically, these operating systems provide for user management, file access, printer access, and network security. The software that provides these functions is divided into two pieces: the client and the server.

Popular network operating systems

The most popular network operating systems include Microsoft Windows NT/2000, Unix, and Novell NetWare. Each of these systems has strengths and weaknesses. Organizations commonly use only one particular brand of NOS. However, it is becoming more common for organizations to use two or even all three of these operating systems, which is made possible by a certain level of built-in interoperability.

Tip　If a network uses more than one NOS, it is said to be a *heterogeneous network*. Conversely, if a network uses only one NOS, then it is referred to as a *homogenous network*.

Novell NetWare

Novell Corporation released NetWare in 1983. Since its inception, NetWare has grown to become one of the most popular families of networking operating systems to date. As of this writing, NetWare 5.1 is the latest version of NetWare, but Novell is testing version 6, and by the time this book goes to print, it will likely be released to the public. This network operating system features standalone servers to provide network services. Originally, the main protocol used to communicate with a NetWare server was Novell's IPX/SPX protocol; however, limited support for TCP/IP became available in NetWare 4.11, and full support for TCP/IP was incorporated into NetWare 5 and above. This has broadened NetWare's interoperability with other operating systems.

Cross-Reference Protocols are discussed in depth in Chapter 14.

Microsoft Windows NT and Windows 2000

Windows New Technology (NT) has been around since 1993. This family of operating systems began life as Windows NT 3.1 and went through several version number upgrades until it was radically redesigned and renamed Windows 2000 in the summer of 2000. Each version of NT (including 2000) has been released in a few different variations to address a variety of different business needs. Microsoft has produced both Windows NT Workstation and Windows NT Server. Windows NT Workstation was designed for use as either a workstation in a server-based network or as a peer in a peer-to-peer network. NT Server was designed as a full-blown server operating system for use in true server-based networks. As stated previously, Windows 2000 has replaced Windows NT as Microsoft's predominant NOS. Windows 2000 Professional was designed to replace NT Workstation 4.0, and Windows 2000 Server was designed to replace NT Server 4.0.

Note In the fall of 2001 Microsoft released Windows XP Professional as an upgrade to its Windows 2000 Professional product. This upgrade is intended to provide a greater level of stability, enhanced security, and improved performance along with several other enhancements. For more information you may want to visit Microsoft's Web site at http://www.microsoft.com/windowsxp.

Microsoft has also announced that it will be updating the Windows 2000 Server family by introducing a new server group, known as Microsoft .NET Servers. In addition to all of the features found in Windows 2000, the .NET operating systems will offer many new and powerful features. For more information see http://www.microsoft.com/windows.netserver.

Unix

Unix and its many variants have been a mainstay in the world of computer networks since 1969. From the beginning, Unix was designed to be a multiuser operating system. Two key components of a Unix server are its *kernel* and its *shell*.

The kernel

The kernel is a portion of the operating system responsible for memory management, process and task management, and disk management. The kernel was developed to run on a variety of hardware platforms. Due to this portability, as well as its flexibility and power, Unix has become the leading operating system for all non-PC based computers. Many hardware vendors have developed their own variants of Unix, based on this kernel. In fact, over the past several years, the PC-based variant, Linux, has started to make a move in the Microsoft dominated world of personal computers. Some of the more popular versions of Unix include the following:

✦ Red Hat Linux

✦ Sun Solaris

✦ Digital Unix

✦ SCO Unix

✦ IBM AIX

✦ FreeBSD

✦ Hewlett Packard's HP-UX

The shell

A Unix shell is the interface that the user works with to interact with the operating system. In other words, the shell is what users see on the screen. For most of its existence, Unix has had text-based shells and users have had to contend with learning hundreds of commands to fully operate Unix. To make the world of Unix more user-friendly, several graphical user interfaces have been developed — the most popular of which is X-Windows or Motif GUI.

Key Point Summary

The following is a summary of the key points in this chapter:

✦ A network consists of two or more computers connected together for the purpose of sharing resources.

✦ All networks consist of three basic elements:

• Protocols

• Media

• Network services

✦ Networks are typically based on two network models:

• Mainframe

• Client/Server

✦ Web-based networking is a method of providing network information in a format compatible with Web-based applications, such as a Web browser.

✦ Networks generally fall into one of two network categories:

- Peer-to-peer: All computers can act as both clients and servers; resources are typically distributed throughout the network. There is no one security authority for the network.

- Client/server: Each node on the network is either typically a server or client, but seldom both. Server based networks security is centralized and a user in need of network resources must first prove their identity to a centralized authority before any resource access is allowed.

✦ A network's topology describes the physical layout of the network.

✦ The five standard topologies are:

- Bus Topology: All network devices, or nodes, connect to a single cable

- Star Topology: All network nodes connect to a central device

- Ring Topology: Network nodes are connected in such a manner that they form a ring

- Hybrid Topology: A combination of two of the ring, bus, and star topologies with the most common topologies being the Star-Bus and the Star-Ring

- Mesh Topology: An arrangement in which multiple paths exist between devices or between networks

✦ A network operating system (or NOS) is responsible for managing and providing access to resources and services on the network.

✦ The most popular network operating systems include Microsoft Windows NT/2000, Unix, and Novell NetWare.

✦ ✦ ✦

STUDY GUIDE

The following assessment questions will test your memory on some of the key topics covered in this chapter. The scenario questions will test your understanding of the basic networking concepts by presenting you with a real life scenario in which you will have to answer chapter-related questions.

Assessment Questions

1. Mainframe computing is an example of

   A. Distributed processing

   B. Singular processing

   C. Haphazard processing

   D. Centralized processing

2. Which network model has a dumb terminal at the client side?

   A. Client/Server

   B. LAN

   C. Mainframe

   D. None of the above

3. In client/server networking the _____ is referred to as the *back end*, whereas the _____ is referred to as the *front end*.

4. Which type of computer is usually the third tier in three-tier computing?

   A. Client

   B. Web server

   C. Database server

   D. Node

5. True or False: A peer-to-peer network is ideal for networks in which security is important.

6. True or False: Peer-to-peer networking is recommended for large networks mainly because it does not support sharing of data files.

7. All networks consist of the following basic elements: (Choose all that apply)

   A. Routers

   B. Network services

   C. Protocols

   D. Trunk cables

   E. Transmission media

   F. Printers

   G. Meshes

8. Bus and Star are two examples of:

   A. Network classifications

   B. Back-end clients

   C. NOSs

   D. Network topologies

   E. Network architectures

9. Terminators are placed at the end of trunk cables to:

   A. Stop information leak

   B. Power the network cable

   C. Stop data bounce

   D. Ensure data echo

10. An organization has six employees in a small building. They want to connect the computers of all their employees and make a network without much expenditure. The organization wants data to be shared among all the computers without any restrictions. What is the most likely network architecture they will choose?

    A. Server-based

    B. Peer-to-peer

    C. Mainframe

    D. Web-based

11. Which of the following statements about the star topology is false?

 A. If one computer fails, the entire network fails.

 B. Network nodes are connected through a central device.

 C. Network expansion is relatively simple.

 D. Network management can be centralized.

12. Which of the following statements about the ring topology is false?

 A. All computers have equal access to the data.

 B. It performs well, even with heavy traffic.

 C. Network expansion won't affect the operation.

 D. A failure of one node on the network can effect network operation.

13. Many corporations have now set up internal Web-based networks that are referred to as:

 A. Intranets

 B. Extranets

 C. Internets

 D. Ubernets

 E. Webnets

14. The level of interoperability in a network operating system (NOS) defines how well it can do what?

 A. Operate on the Internet

 B. Communicate with its clients

 C. Operate on an extranet

 D. Operate in conjunction with other NOSs

 E. None of the above

15. Which of the following operating systems are appropriate for server-based networks?

 A. Novell NetWare

 B. Unix

 C. Windows Me

 D. Apple AppleTalk

 E. Windows NT Workstation

 F. Windows NT Server

Scenario

Big Bad Wolf, Inc. (BBW), is a pork product manufacturer that employs over 500 people at its head office in Brickhouse, North Dakota. BBF also has processing plants set up in Strawhouse, Maryland, and Stickhouse, Iowa. Approximately 80 people are employed at these two sites. BBW is a very successful operation and has had several expansions at its head office and at both processing plants within the past two years. They expect more expansion in the next few years as well. BBW currently has a mainframe network at the head office and two small networks at the processing plants — both of which use the Windows 98 operating system for clients and servers. The head office network has been plagued with problems that are manifested by slow network response and lengthy downtimes resulting in lost production. Competition in the pork industry is cutthroat and in an effort to stay competitive, BBW has decided to upgrade its network infrastructure at all locations. The following are the key goals of the new network:

✦ Replace the mainframe and terminals with up-to-date PCs and servers.

✦ Reduce downtime due to network problems as much as possible.

✦ Provide security and centralized monitoring of all networks.

✦ Provide redundant links between all locations.

✦ Allow all internal employees and key customers and suppliers to use their Web browsers to view information about products and production-related information.

Based on the information provided and what you have learned in this chapter, answer the following questions:

1. What network architecture does BBW currently use at its processing plants? What information led you to this decision?

2. What are some likely reasons for the slow response times at the head office?

3. What network model would you suggest for the three networks?

4. What are some key factors that led you to that decision?

5. What network topology should BBW use in its head office network and why?

6. What network topology should BBW use when linking its three sites? State some reasons for your decision.

7. What operating systems should BBW consider for its servers?

8. Allowing employees, key customers, and suppliers the opportunity to view corporate information by using a browser is called _____ based networking. After implementation, this is an example of a _____.

9. Customers will be able to browse to the BBW's Web server and view a list of products based on search criteria. This is an example of _____ tier networking.

Answers to Chapter Questions

Chapter Pre-Test

1. Two or more computers connected together for the purpose of sharing and managing resources are referred to as a **network**.

2. The two disadvantages of the mainframe approach to networking are **single point of failure and cost.**

3. In the client/server model of networking, processing occurs at both the client and the server.

4. An **extranet** is formed when an organization opens up their intranet to selected external users.

5. The two main network architectures are **Peer-to-Peer** and **Client/Server**.

6. A network that connects all computers in an organization is referred to as an **enterprise** network

7. A network topology describes the **physical** layout of a network.

8. Common network topologies include bus, star, ring, hybrid, and mesh.

9. The three most common NOSs are Novell NetWare, Windows NT/2000, and Unix.

Assessment Questions

1. Mainframe computing is an example of:

   D. Centralized Processing

2. Which network model has a dumb terminal at the client side?

   C. Mainframe

3. In client/server networking, the **server** is referred to as the *back end*, whereas the **client** is referred to as the *front end*.

4. Which type of computer is usually the third tier in three-tier computing?

   C. Database server

5. **False**: A peer-to-peer network is ideal for networks in which security is important

6. **False**: Peer-to-peer networking is recommended for large networks mainly because it does not support sharing of data files.

7. All networks consist of the following basic elements: (Choose all that apply)

    B. Network services

    C. Protocols

    D. Transmission media

8. Bus and Star are two examples of:

    D. Network topologies

9. Terminators are placed at the end of trunk cables to:

    C. Stop data bounce

10. An organization has six employees in a small building. They want to connect the computers of all their employees and make a network without much expenditure. The organization wants data to be shared among all the computers without any restrictions. What is the most likely network architecture they will choose?

    B. Peer-to-peer

11. Which of the following statements is false about the star topology?

    A. If one computer fails, the entire network fails.

12. Which of the following statements is false about the ring topology?

    C. Network expansion won't affect the operation.

13. Many corporations have now set up internal Web-based networks that are referred to as:

    A. Intranets

14. The level of interoperability in a network operating system defines how well it can do what?

    D Operate in conjunction with other NOSs

15. Which of the following operating systems are appropriate for server-based networks?

    A. Novell NetWare

    B. Unix

    C. Windows NT Server

Scenario

1. BBW uses the peer-to-peer networking model because they are using only Microsoft Windows 98.

2. The slow response time is probably due to the processing demands on the mainframe or the overabundance of terminal control traffic on the network.

3. The model of network that BBW should choose is Client/Server.

4. Some of the key factors should include network size, need for security, and centralized administration.

5. BBW should use either a star network or a hybrid (star-bus) because both of these designs will allow the network to continue should one computer fail. They also allow for easy expansion without disrupting the current network.

6. BBW should use the mesh topology when linking sites together. This will provide for backup data paths if one link fails.

7. Unix, Novell NetWare, or Windows NT/2000 should be considered for NOSs because they are all true client/server-based network operating systems.

8. Allowing employees, key customers, and suppliers to view corporate information using a browser is **Web**-based networking. After implementation, this is an example of an **extranet.**

9. Customers will be able to browse to the BBW's Web server and view a list of products based on search criteria. This is an example of **three**-tier networking.

Resources

The following are suggested resources in the area of networking fundamentals:

✦ Derfler, Frank and Les Freed, *How Networks Work*. Ziff Davis, 1996.

✦ Microsoft Press: *Networking Essentials, 1997*

✦ Lowe, Doug, *Networking For Dummies*, Hungry Minds, 2000

✦ Webopedia: Online Computer Dictionary for Internet Terms and Technical Support: www.webopedia.com

Internetworking Concepts

1. Discuss the Open Systems Interconnection Reference Model (OSI/RM), Including the layers and functions at each layer.

2. Explain packets and describe packet creation.

3. Differentiate between protocols that reside at the Network, Transport and Application Layers of the OSI/RM.

4. Identify key internetworking protocols and explain the need for multi-protocol networks.

5. Define the nature, purpose, and operational essentials of TCP/IP.

6. Compare, contrast, and discuss the functions of networking protocols.

7. Bind protocols to a Network Interface Card.

CHAPTER PRE-TEST

1. The OSI/RM can best be described as a set of _____.

2. Name the seven layers of the OSI/RM in hierarchical order.

3. What is the proper name for a unit of data that is transmitted across a network?

5. What are the three main elements of a packet?

6. Which layer of the OSI/RM provides network services to applications?

7. Which layer of the OSI/RM is responsible for routing?

8. When sending data, what is the only layer the Transport layer can directly communicate with?

9. Name three application protocols.

10. Connecting to the Internet requires the use of which protocol suite?

11. The _____ order determines the order in which an operating system will try protocols when attempting to communicate across a network.

✦ Answers to these questions can be found at the end of the chapter. ✦

If you were to examine a typical network, you would most likely find a mixture of hardware and software from a variety of different manufacturers and vendors. For the most part, network components are developed independently, yet they are able to function together to form a heterogeneous network. This chapter examines some of the key network features that enable this level of interoperability.

Standards for Internetworking

A key factor in the growth of networks, such as the Internet, is that it's relatively easy to purchase and install a network component that is interoperable with your existing components. Modern computer components and operating systems have been developed with interoperability in mind; designers have followed well-developed communication standards that allow you to create heterogeneous networks, such as the Internet. Most notably, designers have followed the standards set forth in the OSI/RM.

OSI/RM explained

 Discuss the Open Systems Interconnection Reference Model (OSI/RM), including the layers and functions at each layer.

In 1977, the International Standards Organization (ISO) began work on a set of specifications that — if followed — would allow dissimilar devices to communicate with each other in a networked environment. The original model was released in 1978 and gained some acceptance. These specifications didn't really catch on until 1984, when ISO revised the specifications and released them as the Open System Interconnection Reference Model (OSI/RM). This model is now internationally known as *the* standard for network communications.

 Understand the OSI/RM and the role that it plays in modern networks.

The OSI/RM outlines the process of preparing data for transmission across a network. When users follow the standards in the OSI/RM, an application running on one computer can send information to an application running on another computer — regardless of the type of computers, operating systems, or applications running on both machines. The OSI/RM describes how the data should be treated when it leaves the application, gets passed through the operating system, and is eventually transmitted on to the network cable (or whatever transmission media is being used). The OSI/RM also describes the process that should occur after the data is received by the destination computer (or other network device).

The OSI/RM divides this process into seven layers. Figure 13-1 shows these layers in order and their position in processing relative to the network cable. Take note of both the names of the layers and their corresponding numbers because the layers are often referred to by either name or number.

Figure 13-1: The seven layers of the OSI/RM

| 7. Application |
| 6. Presentation |
| 5. Session |
| 4. Transport |
| 3. Network |
| 2. Data Link |
| 1. Physical |

A device that follows this model will use a combination of hardware and software to perform the tasks that are defined in each of the layers. As data is being prepared for network transmission, it passes through each layer, as displayed in Figure 13-2. The data begins its journey at the actual application running on the computer; from there, the data moves down to the Application Layer, then through the Presentation Layer, on to the Session Layer, and so on until it finally passes into the Physical Layer where it encounters the transmission media. The data then flows to the destination computer where it is processed again through these layers — only this time, in the opposite direction, starting at the Physical Layer and moving up to the Application Layer, where it then gets passed to an application or service.

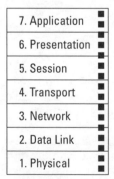
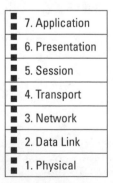

Data Flow ■ ■ ■ ➤

Figure 13-2: Data traveling through the OSI/RM layers

Functions of the OSI/RM layers

Each of the seven layers is responsible for very specific functions when sending or receiving data. The following paragraphs detail some of the more important functions of each layer.

 Exam Tip Know these layers in order. You can use a mnemonic device to make remembering a little easier. Here are two popular ones:

Please **D**o **N**ot **T**ease **S**limy **P**urple **A**liens (bottom to top)

All **P**eople **S**eem **T**o **N**eed **D**ata **P**rocessing (top to bottom)

Application Layer

Despite what the name may suggest, you won't find applications in the Application Layer. Applications communicate with the Application Layer when they need to request or send data on the network. In other words, the Application Layer provides network services to applications. These applications are any program or operating system service that requires access to the network. Most applications must contact the Application Layer with an Application Programming Interface (API) to send data across a network.

An API is a set of routines, protocols, and tools for building software applications. A good API makes it easier to develop a program by providing all the building blocks; a programmer puts the blocks together. Most operating environments, such as Microsoft Windows, provide an API so that programmers can write applications consistent with the operating environment. Although APIs are designed for programmers, they are ultimately good for users, as well, because they guarantee that all programs using a common API will have similar interfaces. Similar interfaces make it easier for users to learn new programs and for developers to write them.

For example, suppose that you're using a word-processing program, such as Word Perfect or MS Word. You type a letter and you want to save it to a folder that is shared on a network server. You push the Save button on your screen and, when prompted, you type both the filename and the path to the shared folder. The word-processing program can't save the data on the network, so it contacts the Application Layer, informing it that the data needs to be saved on the network. Then, the word-processing program passes the data along to the Application Layer. At this point, the application sends the data to the network.

Presentation Layer

The Presentation Layer performs many functions — the most significant of these functions are translation, compression, and encryption.

Translation

For the computer sending data, the Presentation Layer is responsible for translating the data that comes down from the Application Layer into a standard, machine-independent, network data format. For the receiving computer, the Presentation Layer translates the data received back into its original format.

Presentation

To make the sending of data as efficient as possible, the Presentation Layer may also perform some compression techniques on the data. This compression reduces the amount of data that actually has to travel across the network. The Presentation Layer of the receiving computer uncompresses the data before handing it up to the Application Layer.

Encryption

Networks commonly carry sensitive data. For example, many people use the Internet to do their banking. Most of these people expect that all data traveling between the bank and their computer will be transferred in a secure manner. Banks often set up their Web sites to scramble (or encrypt) all data before it is sent across the network. The Presentation Layer on the sending computer performs this encryption. The Presentation Layer on the receiving computer performs the decryption of this data.

 Chapter 19 delves into more detail regarding network security and encryption.

Session Layer

In many instances, the sending device should notify the receiving device that data is being sent between a server and a client application. The Session Layers on both devices negotiate the terms of the transfer, so both can be assured that the data will arrive correctly and in its entirety. This process is referred to as setting up a *session* or *connection*.

 Chapter 16 discusses this process in more detail.

The Session Layer (along with the Transport Layer) is responsible for data flow control. Unfortunately, just like luggage in an airport, it is not uncommon for data that is being transmitted between network devices to be damaged or lost in transit. In most cases, when a file is being transferred, the entire file must get to the destination. If even the smallest part of that file is damaged or lost, the entire file is useless. Without proper flow control, the only way to remedy data loss or damage is for the client machine to request the entire file again.

Many of the files that computers transfer across networks are substantial in size. If you have ever downloaded files, programs, music, or video from the Internet, you know that you may have to wait several minutes — or even hours — to complete the transfer. Therefore, asking for an entire file again because one little part has a problem seems unreasonable. The Session Layer offers a solution to this problem: It decides how much data is to be sent before a *checkpoint* is added to the data. A checkpoint is a marker that the sending computer adds to transmitted data. When the receiving computer gets the checkpoint, it examines the data that arrived prior to the checkpoint. If this data is valid and complete, the computer sends back an acknowledgement of receipt. If the sending computer does not get an acknowledgment to one of its checkpoints in a reasonable amount of time, it resends all the data that it sent since the last acknowledged checkpoint. This reduces the need to resend all data from the beginning of the session.

To help visualize the idea of a checkpoint, consider Figure 13-3. In this example, you can see a server sending data to a client. Assume for this example that the server has agreed to send a checkpoint to the client after every 12K of data. The client is also expected to acknowledge this checkpoint. After the client receives Checkpoint 1, it analyzes the first 12K of data to ensure that the data is sound. If so, the client sends an acknowledgment packet back to the server. It repeats the process for Checkpoint 2 as well as for Checkpoint 3. However, suppose that Checkpoint 4 never arrives, or perhaps it does arrive but the preceding data is unreadable. Whatever the case, the client never sends back an acknowledgment of the last checkpoint. The server, realizing that the acknowledgment has not been sent, resends all the data since the last good checkpoint. In this case, the server resends only the data after Checkpoint 3.

Figure 13-3: Checkpoints placed in the data stream

Transport Layer

The main goal of the Transport Layer is to provide reliable data transportation between the source and destination devices. A major function of the Transport Layer is to break up large amounts of data into smaller, more manageable chunks (referred to as *fragments*). For example, if you send a 500-page document to a server for storage, the Transport Layer on your computer breaks up your document into many small fragments. Each fragment includes reassembly information (1 of 40, 2 of 40, and so on.) as well as some error control information. As fragments arrive at the destination computer, its Transport Layer examines each fragment, analyzing error control information to determine whether the packet has been damaged in transit. If all is in order, the Transport Layer uses the reassembly information to put all the fragments back together. Depending on the type of data being transferred, the receiving computer may send back confirmations for the good packets and replacement requests for damaged packets. The sending computer usually resends any fragments for which it has not received confirmations.

Network Layer

The Network Layer is responsible for organizing data into *datagrams*. A datagram is a combination of the data received from the Transport Layer and *addressing information*. The addressing information includes both the destination and source network addresses. The Network Layer is responsible for obtaining this information and for choosing a route for the data to follow to its destination. The choice of routes may depend on many factors, including network conditions, data sensitivity, and so forth. On the receiving computer, the Network Layer is responsible for verifying the identity of the destination computer. If it is not the correct destination, the packet is either routed to the real destination or discarded.

Chapter 16 delves into more detail about routing and routing protocols.

Data Link Layer

On the sending side, the Data Link Layer takes data from the Network Layer and passes it down to the Physical Layer. In order for the Physical Layer to understand the data, it must be placed into a raw bit format (1s and 0s). On the receiving end, the Data Link Layer translates the raw bits that come from the Physical Layer into data frames that can be understood by the Network Layer. In other words, the Data Link Layer prepares data for actual transmission across the physical transmission media and for reading and translating data coming from the physical transmission media.

The term *data frame* refers to a structured package of data. The format of the data frame depends on the network topology or encapsulation method.

The Data Link Layer is divided into two sublayers: the Logical Link Control (LLC) Layer and the Media Access Control (MAC) Layer. The LLC Layer is responsible for error checking and regulating the flow of data from the Physical Layer to the Network Layer. The MAC Layer is responsible for gaining access to and placing data on the transmission media.

Physical Layer

The Physical Layer converts the raw bits from the Data Link Layer into signals to be passed over the transmission media. On the receiving side, the Physical Layer translates the signals back to raw bits. It is at this level that voltage levels and electrical properties of the media are dealt with.

Take the time to learn the function of each layer in the OSI/RM because you'll probably be questioned about them.

Layer-to-layer communication

Two features characterize the communication between layers: Peer Layer-to-Peer Layer communications and Vertical communications.

Peer Layer communications

You may have noticed when reading through the functions of each of the layers that what a layer does to the data on the sending computer is also intended for the corresponding layer (Peer Layer) on the receiving computer, as shown in Figure 13-4. For example, the sending computer's Presentation Layer may compress data before sending it; whereas the Presentation Layer on the receiving computer decompresses the data as it arrives. Another example of this situation occurs when the sending Transport Layer chops a large piece of data into several smaller fragments. The Transport Layer on the receiving computer puts all of these fragments back together again.

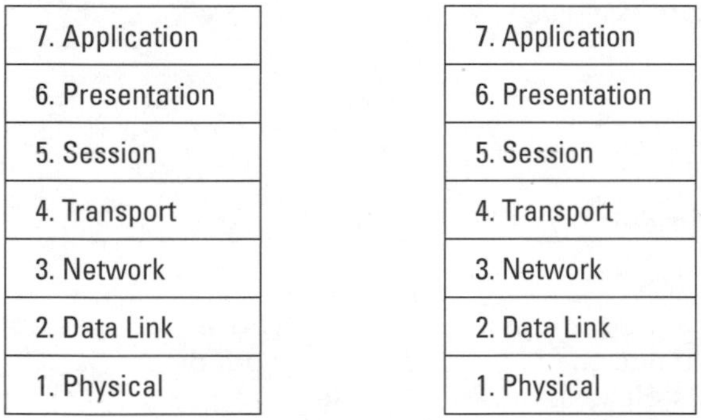

7. Application
6. Presentation
5. Session
4. Transport
3. Network
2. Data Link
1. Physical

7. Application
6. Presentation
5. Session
4. Transport
3. Network
2. Data Link
1. Physical

Figure 13-4: Peer Layers on both computers will communicate with each other.

Vertical communications

The various layers may only pass data on to a layer that is directly below it when sending data and directly above it when receiving data, as shown in Figure 13-5. For example, the Application Layer on the sending computer only passes data directly to the Presentation Layer, which, in turn, only passes it to the Session Layer and so on. On the receiving side, the Physical Layer passes data to the Data Link Layer, which, in turn, passes the data up to the Network Layer and so forth until the data gets to the Application Layer. At that point, the Application Layer passes it to an actual application or service running on the destination computer.

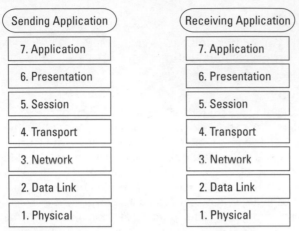

Figure 13-5: A layer will only pass data to the layer directly above it or directly below it, depending on whether the computer is sending or receiving data.

Packet Creation

 Explain packets and describe packet creation.

A *packet* is a unit of data transmitted across a network. Packets are created anytime a network device needs to send information to another network device. A packet consists of three main elements: Header, Data, and Trailer.

Packet header

When data is passing through the OSI/RM layers of a sending computer, each layer (with the exception of the Physical Layer) adds its own information to the front of the packet. This information is used to pass information on to the next layer, as well as to its Peer Layer on the destination computer. Each layer on the receiving computer processes the header from its peer, removes the header, and passes the remainder of the packet up to the next layer. Figure 13-6 demonstrates this process:

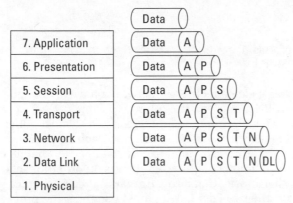

Figure 13-6: Each layer adds its own header when sending data and removes its peer's header when receiving data. Note that the Data Link Layer also adds trailer information.

Packet data

The data is the cargo of the packet. When data needs to be sent, it goes through transformations on its way through the OSI/RM layers. For example, when data travels through the Presentation Layer, it may be compressed, translated, or encrypted. When data passes through the Transport Layer, it may be split into smaller fragments, each of which is contained in its own packet. Therefore, the packet data may really be a translated, compressed, and encrypted fragment of the original data that was sent.

Trailer

The trailer of the packet contains error-checking information. Recall that the Logical Link Control sublayer of the Data Link Layer checks for errors. On the sending computer, the LLC Layer performs a mathematical calculation called a *Cyclical Redundancy Check* (CRC) on the data that is in the packet to be sent. The LLC Layer stores the result of this calculation in the trailer of the message and sends the packet on its way. When the receiving computer gets the message, its LLC Layer performs the same CRC calculation on the packet. It compares its result against the result in the trailer; if they match, the LLC Layer allows further processing of the packet to continue. If the results don't match, the destination LLC Layer assumes that the packet has been damaged in transit and discards the packet.

Layered Protocols

Differentiate between protocols that reside at the Network, Transport, and Application Layers of the OSI/RM.

Protocols are one of the three basic elements that all networks have in common (Transmission Media and Network Services are the other two elements). *Protocols* are the communication rules to which all components on a network must adhere. Think of protocols as the language of the network. Recall that each layer of the OSI/RM on a sending computer places information into the data packet that its corresponding Peer Layer on the destination computer interprets. In order for this to be true, each layer must place this information into a format that can be understood by its peer. In other words, the two Peer Layers must use the same protocol.

Cross-Reference

See Chapter 12 for more information about protocols.

In order for two computers to be able to communicate on the network, they must share a common set of protocols that address each layer of the OSI/RM. These sets of protocols are referred to as *protocol suites* or *protocol stacks*. Some of the more popular protocol suites include the following:

- ✦ TCP/IP
- ✦ IPX/SPX
- ✦ NetBEUI
- ✦ AppleTalk
- ✦ SNA
- ✦ DLC

Cross-Reference

For an overview of each suite, see the section "Major Networking Protocol Suites" located later in this chapter.

Protocols within each suite are generally divided into four categories:

- ✦ Application
- ✦ Transport
- ✦ Network
- ✦ Data Link

As depicted in Figure 13-7, these categories roughly map to the OSI/RM layers.

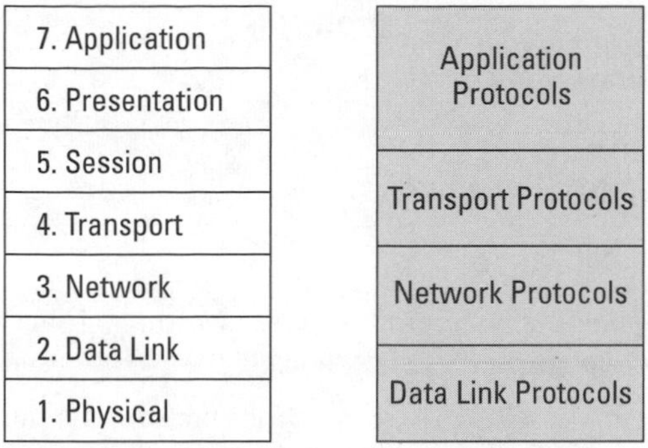

7. Application	Application
6. Presentation	Protocols
5. Session	
4. Transport	Transport Protocols
3. Network	Network Protocols
2. Data Link	
1. Physical	Data Link Protocols

Figure 13-7: The four protocol categories mapped to the OSI/RM

Application protocols

As the name suggests, application protocols allow applications to talk to each other over the network. Table 13-1 shows some common Application Layer protocols with their respective protocol suites and a brief explanation.

Table 13-1
Application Protocols

Protocol	Suite	Description
HTTP	TCP/IP	Hypertext transfer protocol — used to request and transmit Web pages. Web Browsers and Web Server applications will use this to communicate.
SMTP	TCP/IP	Simple Mail Transfer Protocol — used to send electronic mail.
FTP	TCP/IP	File Transfer Protocol — used to request and transfer files between an FTP client and an FTP server.
SMB	Various	Server Message Block Protocol — primarily found in Microsoft networks, it allows files and printers to be shared.
NCP	IPX/SPX	NetWare Core Protocol — enables file and printer sharing in a NetWare environment.
NFS	TCP/IP	Network File System — allows a computer to access files across the network as if they were local.

Transport protocols

Transport protocols allow reliable data delivery during network communications. Table 13-2 lists some of the more common transport protocols.

Table 13-2 **Transport Protocols**		
Protocol	**Suite**	**Description**
TCP	TCP/IP	Transmission Control Protocol — used to ensure reliable data delivery through the use of sessions.
SPX	IPX/SPX	Sequenced Packet Exchange Protocol — provides the same services as TCP but in an IPX/SPX environment.
NWLINK	IPX/SPX	NetWare Link Protocol — Microsoft's version of the IPX/SPX protocol suite; it is implemented both at the Transport and Network Layers of the OSI/RM.
NetBEUI	NetBEUI	NetBIOS Extended User Interface — transport protocol supported by all Microsoft network systems; it is considered both a Transport and Network Protocol.
APPC	SNA	Advanced Program-to-Program communication — part of IBM's SNA protocol suite.

Network protocols

Network protocols provide addressing and routing services. Table 13-3 includes the most common network protocols.

Table 13-3 **Network Protocols**		
Protocol	**Suite**	**Description**
IP	TCP/IP	Internet Protocol — responsible for packet addressing, routing, and forwarding services.
IPX	IPX/SPX	Internetwork Protocol Exchange — provides the same services as IP but in an IPX/SPX environment.
NWLINK	IPX/SPX	NetWare Link Protocol — Microsoft's version of the IPX/SPX protocol suite; it is implemented both at the Transport and Network Layers of the OSI/RM.
NetBEUI	NetBEUI	NetBIOS Extended User Interface — Transport protocol supported by all Microsoft network systems; it is considered both a Transport and Network Protocol.

Data Link protocols

Data Link protocols allow communication over a specific network architecture. These protocols are not associated with any particular suite. The suites are layered over the top of a Data Link protocol.

 Cross-Reference   Network architectures are covered in detail in Chapter 15.

Table 13-4 describes the two most common Data Link protocols.

Table 13-4 Data-Link Protocols	
Protocol	**Description**
Ethernet	This widely used protocol was co-developed by Digital Equipment Corporation, Intel, and Xerox.
Token Ring	Second only to Ethernet in popularity, this protocol and its associated network architecture were originally developed by IBM in the 1970s.

An example of the layering of protocols

When a packet is built, it typically contains protocol information from each of the four categories. An examination of a complete packet shows that each protocol used is actually layered on top of the next in an order that matches their position in the OSI/RM. To illustrate this, I used the Microsoft Network Monitor program to capture a packet that was part of a file transfer from an FTP server to an FTP Client, as shown in Figure 13-8. On the left side of this figure, I circled the protocols that Network Monitor has found in this packet. This captured packet uses the FTP Application protocol, TCP Transport protocol, IP Network protocol, and the Ethernet Data Link protocol. Notice that the order in which the protocols appear in Network Monitor matches the order in which they are processed after this packet reaches its destination.

The FTP protocol is present because this is a file transfer from an FTP server to an FTP client. If you examined this portion of the packet in more detail, you would see that this is where the transferred file resides, or at least a fragment of it. The TCP protocol is present to provide error checking, acknowledgment, and fragmenting information about where this packet belongs in relation to the entire file. The IP protocol is present because it contains addressing information, including where this packet is coming from and where it is going. The Ethernet protocol is present because this packet was found going across an Ethernet-based network.

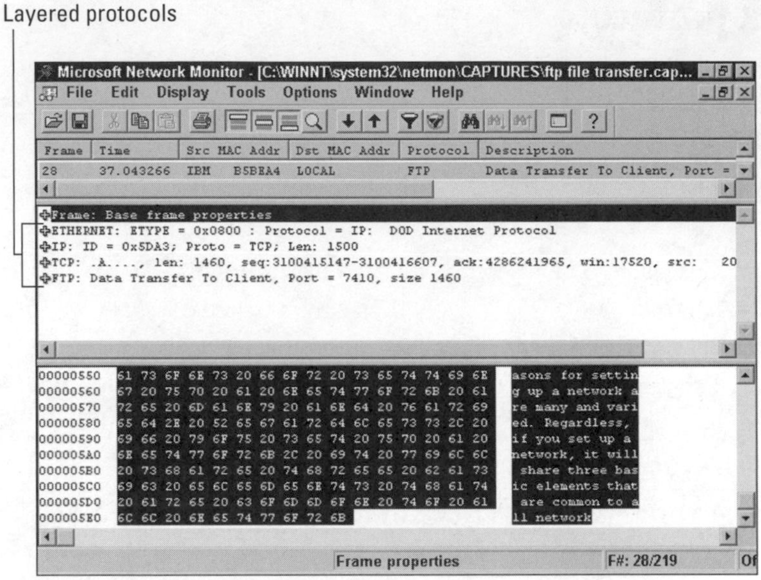

Layered protocols

Figure 13-8: Microsoft Network Monitor shows the protocols that make up a FTP file transfer packet.

Major Networking Protocol Suites

Objective

Identify key internetworking protocols and explain the need for multi-protocol networks.

Compare, contrast, and discuss the functions of networking protocols.

Protocol suites are, in a way, very much like human languages. In order for one human to fully understand another human, both must speak the same language. Similarly, in order for a computer to understand data from another computer, both must understand the same protocol suite.

Protocol routing abilities

Protocol suites typically fall into one of two categories: *routable* or *non-routable*. A protocol suite is routable if its packets can be deciphered and passed by a router; otherwise, it is non-routable. Routable protocol suites include TCP/IP and IPX/SPX. Non-routable protocol suites include NetBEUI, SNA, LAT, and DLC. This is an important consideration when deciding on a protocol suite.

Cross-Reference

Routing and routers are covered in detail in Chapter 14. TCP/IP is covered in-depth in Chapter 15.

The following sections give you an overview of some of the more common protocol suites in use. You should be able to recognize these protocols and understand where and why they are used.

TCP/IP

Originally developed in the early 1970s, TCP/IP gained worldwide acceptance in 1983 when it was adopted as the protocol suite of the Internet. Several reasons can account for this occurrence—not the least of which is the fact that TCP/IP is a routable protocol, making it ideal for a large distributed network, such as the Internet. TCP/IP is also an *open standard* protocol suite. In other words, TCP/IP is not associated with any one vendor, such as Microsoft or Novell. Any vendor can adopt TCP/IP, so it is an ideal protocol suite for a heterogeneous networking environment. In fact, TCP/IP is now the default protocol for UNIX, Netware 5, Windows NT, and Windows 2000.

The name *TCP/IP* is derived from two of its core protocols: Transport Control Protocol (TCP), and Internet Protocol (IP). TCP is a Transport Layer protocol, and IP is a Network Layer protocol that gives TCP/IP its routability. Although important, these two protocols are certainly not all of the protocols in the suite. TCP/IP is comprised of many protocols that are used at almost all layers of the OSI/RM. Some of these include the following

- ✦ FTP
- ✦ SNMP
- ✦ HTTP
- ✦ ARP
- ✦ DNS,
- ✦ SMTP
- ✦ ICMP
- ✦ UDP

Cross-Reference

TCP/IP and many of its member protocols are discussed in detail in Chapter 15.

IPX/SPX

Like TCP/IP, the name *IPX/SPX* is derived from two of its core protocols: Internetwork Packet Exchange (IPX), and Sequenced Packet Exchange (SPX). Unlike TCP/IP, however, the first protocol (IPX) is a Network Layer protocol and the second protocol (SPX) is a Transport Layer protocol. IPX/SPX is a routable suite of protocols and can be used in a large routed environment. A major drawback, however, is that IPX/SPX is a closed standard protocol. Novell, Inc. developed IPX/SPX solely for use with its NetWare network operating system. Other vendors do offer support for IPX/SPX in their operating system (such as Microsoft with its variant — NWLINK protocol). However, because TCP/IP is the protocol suite of the Internet, IPX/SPX use is beginning to diminish. This is confirmed by the fact that, although still supported, IPX/SPX has been replaced by TCP/IP as the default protocol in Novell's NetWare 5 and beyond.

NetBEUI

NetBEUI is an oddity in that its full name contains an acronym. NetBEUI is short for NetBIOS Extended User Interface. NetBIOS, in turn, is an acronym for Network Basic Input/Output System. NetBIOS is a Session Layer protocol that allows applications to establish sessions with other applications across a network. NetBEUI is a small, fast, and efficient Transport Layer and Network Layer protocol. Although first developed by IBM, NetBEUI has been supported in all Microsoft network operating systems since the mid-1980s. Its speed and ease of use has made NetBEUI a very attractive protocol suite for small peer-to-peer based networks. The following are the major drawbacks of NetBEUI: It is a non-routable protocol and it is limited to Microsoft networks.

When first developed, NetBEUI and NetBIOS were considered part of the same protocol suite. Many vendors, however, have now implemented NetBIOS as an addition to other protocol suites. For example, consider the Microsoft Windows 2000 operating system. Figure 13-9 shows the Windows 2000 default setting for NetBIOS support with TCP/IP.

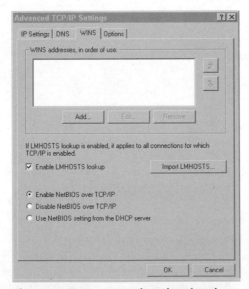

Figure 13-9: A screen shot showing the default NetBIOS support in the Microsoft Windows 2000 implementation of TCP/IP.

AppleTalk

As its name suggests, AppleTalk is a proprietary protocol suite that was designed by Apple Corporation for use by their Apple Macintosh computers to share files and printers in a networked environment.

DLC

Data Link Control (DLC) was originally developed by IBM as a protocol that allowed client machines to communicate with mainframes. Hewlett-Packard adopted DLC as the primary protocol used to communicate with printers using HP JetDirect network interface cards.

SNA

Still very prevalent in today's mainframe networks, Systems Network Architecture (SNA) was introduced by IBM in 1974 to provide a framework for connecting a variety of dissimilar networks together. This framework later became the basis for the OSI/RM. SNA includes a network topology and a protocol suite.

Multi-Protocol Networks

Multiple protocols are commonly supported within a single network environment. Cooperative support can add increased functionality to the network. For example, IPX/SPX is a required protocol in a Netware 4.11-based network. Using this single suite allows the individual components on the network to communicate with each other; however, if connectivity to the Internet is also required, TCP/IP must also be installed. Another reason to support multiple protocols may be to achieve greater performance; for example, NetBEUI is a very fast, efficient protocol in comparison to TCP/IP or IPX/SPX. To take advantage of this fact, you may have to configure a network to use this protocol for internal communications within a location. Due to NetBEUI's lack of support for routing, computers may also be configured to use a routable protocol, such as IPX/SPX or TCP/IP for communications beyond the local network.

Be aware of the downsides to using multiple protocols. When you increase the number of protocols on a network, you also typically increase the amount of traffic on the network. Many server-based services announce their presence by using every protocol configured. For example, consider the Computer Browser service that runs on Microsoft's networking products. The browser service is responsible for maintaining the list of computers that you find when you double-click the Network Neighborhood icon on your desktop. Servers periodically announce their presence in order to be included in this list. If these servers are configured to support multiple protocols, then the servers will make one announcement for every protocol configured. If three protocols are configured, you see triple the amount of announcements than would be seen if the server had only been configured with one protocol.

Network Protocol Binding Concepts

Bind protocols to a Network Interface Card.

Protocol binding is the process of assigning a protocol to a network interface card (NIC). If a NIC has multiple bindings, the network card is configured to use multiple protocols.

The method in which you bind or unbind protocols to network cards differs from operating system to operating system. In the Microsoft Windows 2000 and ME operating systems, protocols are bound to network cards by using the Network and Dial-up Connection icon in the control panel, as shown in Figure 13-10.

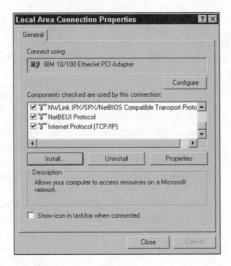

Figure 13-10: Windows 2000 connection property screen showing protocols currently bound to a network card.

Binding order refers to the order in which an operating system will try protocols when attempting to communicate across a network. Figure 13-11 displays the binding order for a Windows 2000 computer on which both TCP/IP and NetBEUI have been installed. The administrator of the machine has set the binding order in such a way that the operating system will first attempt communication by using TCP/IP; if this fails for any reason, the operating system will attempt to use NetBEUI.

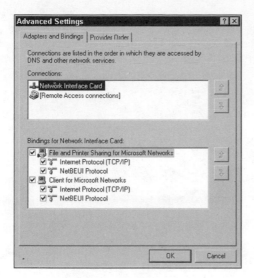

Figure 13-11: The network Advanced Settings dialog box showing the current protocol binding order on a Windows 2000-based computer.

When assigning multiple protocols to a single network card, the concept of binding order is important because it can have an impact on how quickly a computer can communicate with another computer on the network. Consider the following example:

You have a multi-protocol network, as shown in Figure 13-12. Computer A has been configured to use multiple protocols and the binding order of these protocols has been set to the following: NetBEUI first, IPX/SPX second, and TCP/IP third. Computer B uses only one protocol suite — TCP/IP. If a client application on Computer A requires services from a server application running on Computer B, Computer A will first attempt communication using NetBEUI. Computer B, not understanding NetBEUI, won't respond. After a brief wait, Computer A realizes that B is not responding to NetBEUI and tries to communicate using IPX/SPX. Once again, Computer B doesn't respond and, after a brief wait, Computer A attempts to communicate by using TCP/IP. Computer B, understanding TCP/IP, responds and the communication process proceeds. It should be fairly clear that this whole process could have been avoided if Computer A's binding order had been set to try TCP/IP first.

The network administrator should analyze the protocols in use on a network to help optimize its performance. Protocols should be chosen based on communication requirements. If possible, it is best to go with a single protocol on a network. If multiple protocols are necessary, consider configuring the protocol binding order to use the most commonly used protocol first.

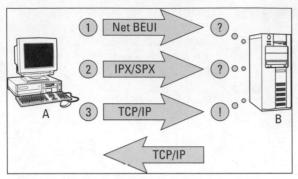

Figure 13-12: The effect of binding order in client/server communications

Tip   Because it is the client computer that normally initiates communication, setting the binding order on the client computers will yield the most benefits.

Key Point Summary

This chapter introduces the key concepts of Internetworking. The following is a review of the information covered in this chapter:

✦ Open System Interconnection Reference Model (OSI/RM) is a set of specifications developed by ISO that, if followed, allows dissimilar devices to communicate with each other in a networked environment.

✦ The following seven layers of the OSI/RM are listed top to bottom:

    7. Application

    6. Presentation

    5. Session

    4. Transport

    3. Network

    2. Data Link

    1. Physical

✦ Information placed in the header of a packet by an OSI/RM layer is intended for that layer's Peer Layer on the destination computer.

✦ Layers may only pass packets to the layer directly below it when sending, and only to the layer above it when receiving.

✦ A packet is a unit of data transmitted across a network consisting of the following three elements:

Header — Built by the layers of the OSI/RM

Data — Information being sent by the actual application

Trailer — Contains error-checking information, home of the CRC

✦ Protocols are communication rules that all components on a network must adhere to in order to communicate.

✦ Sets of protocols are referred to as protocol suites or stacks.

✦ Protocols within each suite are generally divided into the following four categories that map roughly to the OSI/RM:

- Application

- Transport

- Network

- Data Link

✦ Common protocol suites include the following:

- TCP/IP

- IPX/SPX

- NetBEUI

- AppleTalk

- DLC

- SNA

✦ Protocol bindings are the assigning of a protocol to a network interface card (NIC).

✦ Binding order refers to the order in which an operating system will try protocols when attempting to communicate across a network.

✦ Adjusting the binding order can affect the performance of the network.

✦ ✦ ✦

STUDY GUIDE

The assessment questions test your memory on some of the key topics covered in the chapter.

Assessment Questions

1. Who developed the OSI/RM?

   A. United States Department of National Defense

   B. ISO

   C. FTP

   D. IEEE

2. What is the OSI/RM?

   A. A set of standards

   B. A set of methods

   C. A set of laws

   D. None of the above

3. The OSI/RM is divided into _____ layers.

4. Most information added to a packet by a layer is placed in the _____.

   A. Trailer

   B. Data

   C. Header

   D. Node

5. True or False: The Network Layer of the OSI/RM places checkpoints into the data stream.

6. True or False: SMTP, FTP, SMB are all examples of Transport Protocols.

7. The CRC is placed into the trailer of a packet by which layer?

    A. Data Link

    B. Physical

    C. Transport

    D. Session

8. TCP and SPX are two examples of what?

    A. Application Layer protocols

    B. Network Layer protocols

    C. TCP/IP Suite protocols

    D. IPX/SPX Suite protocols

    E. None of the above

9. What is a name for a unit of data transmitted across a network?

    A. Session

    B. Packet

    C. CRC

    D. Signal

10. What layer is responsible for splitting up messages into fragments?

    A. Data Link

    B. Session

    C. Presentation

    D. Network

    E. Transport

11. What protocols are designed to allow reliable data delivery during network communications?

    A. Application protocols

    B. Transport protocols

    C. Network protocols

    D. Data Link protocols

Scenarios

1. High Flying Birdies, Inc. (HFB) is a badminton supply manufacturer in Overdanet, Saskatchewan, Canada. HFB's network consists of 300 Microsoft Windows 2000 Professional client computers and three Netware 4.11 servers. HFB's network connects to the Internet but Internet use by employees is fairly light. What protocol suites must be in use on the network? If you were responsible for optimizing the network response times, what binding order should you set for these protocols and why?

2. Ouch Brothers Corporation is trying to decide on the appropriate protocol suite for their enterprise network. Ouch Brothers have locations spread throughout North America and need connectivity between all of these branches and the Internet. They have a combination of Netware 5.1, UNIX, and Windows NT 4 servers. Which protocols must Ouch Brothers implement? Why? Is binding order on the client computers going to be important? Why or why not?

Answers to Chapter Questions

Chapter Pre-Test

1. The OSI/RM is a set of standards that, if followed, will allow dissimilar devices to communicate with each other in a networked environment.

2. The seven layers of the OSI/RM starting at the top are Application, Presentation, Session, Transport, Network, Data Link, and Physical.

3. A technique used to detect data transmission errors. The Cyclical Redundancy Check (CRC) is a mathematical calculation performed by the Data Link Layer on the packet to be sent. The result of the CRC calculation is stored in the trailer of the packet. After the destination computer receives the packet, the same calculation is performed and its result is compared to the result in the trailer. If the results match, the packet is considered good; if they don't match, the packet is considered damaged in transit and is discarded.

4. A unit of data transmitted across a network.

5. The three main elements of a packet are Header, Data, and Trailer.

6. The purpose of the Application Layer is to provide network services to applications.

7. The Network Layer is responsible for routing.

8. When sending data, the Transport Layer can directly communicate with the Presentation Layer.

9. Examples of Application protocols include HTTP, SMTP, FTP, SMB, NCP, and NFS.

10. TCP and SPX are considered transport protocols.

Answers to Assessment Questions

1. Who developed the OSI/RM?

   B. ISO

2. What is the OSI/RM?

   A. A set of standards

3. The OSI/RM is divided into __7__ Layers.

4. Most information added to a packet by a layer is placed in the

   C. Header

5. False: The Network Layer of the OSI/RM places checkpoints into the data stream.

6. False: SMTP, FTP, SMB are all examples of Transport Protocols.

7. The CRC is placed in to the trailer of a packet by which layer?

   A. Data Link

8. TCP and SPX are two examples of:

   B. Network Layer protocols

9. What is the name for a unit of data transmitted across a network?

   B. Packet

10. This layer may split up messages into fragments:

   E. Transport

11. What protocols are designed to allow reliable data delivery during network communications?

   B. Transport Protocols

Resources

The following are suggested resources for additional information on the topics discussed in this chapter:

✦ Microsoft Press: *Networking Essentials,* 1997

✦ Lowe, Doug; *Networking For Dummies*, Hungry Minds, Inc., 2000

✦ Berg, Glenn; *MCSE Training Guide: Networking Essentials*, New Riders, 1998

✦ *PROTOCOLS.COM Protocol Directory.* www.protocols.com/protoc.shtml

Introduction to Local and Wide Area Networks

◆　◆　◆　◆

1. Describe the basics of a local area network and a wide area network.

2. Identify and describe the function of network access points.

3. Explain how the various LAN/WAN devices work together, including NICs, repeaters, hubs, bridges, routers, brouters, switches, gateways, CSU/DSUs, modems, and patch panels.

4. Identify the differences between common transmission media used in networking, such as twisted-pair, coaxial, fiber optic cable, and wireless media.

5. Describe transmission types including asynchronous and synchronous, simplex, half duplex, full duplex, baseband, and broadband.

6. Explain the differences between logical and physical topologies.

7. Identify LAN standards, including the Institute of Electrical and Electronics Engineers LAN standards, Apple LocalTalk, and Fiber Distributed Data Interface.

8. Identify WAN standards, including X. 25 frame relay and asynchronous transfer mode.

9. Explain the function and types of T-carrier and E-carrier systems.

CHAPTER PRE-TEST

1. A network of computers in one geographical region is referred to as a _____ _____ network.

2. On the Internet, a junction between one high-speed network and another is referred to as a _____.

3. A _____ is used to strengthen a digital signal on a cable segment.

4. At what layer of the OSI/RM do bridges operate?

5. What device translates a digital signal into an analog signal?

6. UTP and STP are categories of what?

7. What is the maximum cable length of thicknet?

8. When a device can both send and receive information at the same time, that device is using a _____ duplex connection.

9. With _____ transmission both the sending and receiving devices share a common clock and transmission rate.

10. What layer of the OSI/RM does frame relay operate?

✦ Answers to these questions can be found at the end of the chapter. ✦

This chapter introduces you to the basics of Local Area and Wide Area Networks. This chapter explores the scope of both of these network forms and provides some insight into the technology that is used to implement such networks. You should note that a great deal of the information required to pass the CIW foundation exam will come from the topics presented in this chapter.

Local Area Networks

 Describe the basics of a local area network and a wide area network.

As the name implies, a Local Area Network (LAN) is a network in which all devices are situated within the same small geographical area (for example, a building or campus). Computers that participate in a Local Area Network will typically share the same resources.

Wide Area Networks

A Wide Area Network (WAN) is the interconnection of two or more LANs over a large geographic region (for example, between cities or countries). An organization may implement a variety of technologies to interconnect the various LANs, including — but not limited to — leased data lines, microwave transmission, satellite communications, radio, and possibly the Internet. WANs allow the nodes from the various LANs to share common resources. See Figure 14-1 for an example of a WAN.

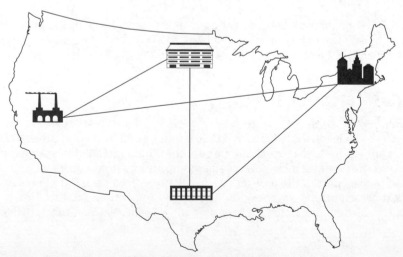

Figure 14-1: An example of a Wide Area Network

Network Access Points

Identify and describe the function of network access points.

The Internet is an interconnection of thousands of networks throughout the world. Each individual network is connected to an Internet service provider (ISP), which provides a connection to the rest of the Internet. Small ISPs in turn connect to larger ISPs, which connect to even larger ISPs. These major ISPs serve as the backbone networks of the Internet.

Tip   The term *backbone* is used to describe that portion of any Internetwork that carries the majority of network traffic.

Network Access Points (NAPs) are the points at which the major ISPs' high-speed networks interconnect. In the United States, for example, three main NAPs are run by the major telephone and telecommunication companies. These NAPs are located in New York, Chicago, and San Francisco.

Network Connectivity Devices

Explain how the various LAN/WAN devices work together, including NICs, repeaters, hubs, bridges, routers, brouters, switches, gateways, CSU/DSUs, modems, and patch panels.

To build a network, you must use a variety of different devices. The larger and more complex the network, the more devices you'll need to employ. The following section explains some of the more common devices used in modern networks.

Exam Tip   For the CIW Foundations exam, you will be responsible for knowing the purpose and appropriate use of the devices listed here. You will also be required to identify where each of these devices work in relation to the OSI Reference Model.

Network interface card

The *network interface card* (NIC), or the *network adapter card* (NAC) as it is sometimes called, is a device installed into a network node, such as a computer, to allow the node to connect to the network. Most often, the NIC is installed into an expansion slot inside the computer. However, some computer manufacturers include a network interface as part of the motherboard. NICs operate at the Data Link Layer of the OSI/RM, which means that besides serving as connection point to the network, the NIC is also responsible for preparing and sending data on the network transmission media. When receiving information, the NIC is responsible for translating the raw data signals coming off the wire and placing them into a bit format that the operating system can understand. When sending information, the opposite is true — the bit format is translated into raw signals that can be sent across the network transmission media. Figure 14-2 shows a diagram of an NIC.

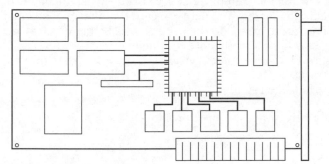

Figure 14-2: A typical NIC

Each manufacturer provides the NIC with a globally unique hardware number, known as a *MAC address*. Packets traveling on the network transmission media typically contain the MAC address of their intended destination computer. NICs examine packets as they go by to see if the destination MAC address in the packet matches their own. If a match is found, the network card keeps the packet for further processing; otherwise, the packet is ignored.

MAC addresses are 48 bits in length and are typically written in a 12-digit hexadecimal format, such as 00-04-AC-E8-47-2C. The first six digits represent a vendor code. This vendor code is a unique number that has been assigned to the network card manufacturer by the Institute of Electrical and Electronic Engineers (IEEE). Therefore, you can use the vendor code to identify the network card manufacturer. For example, the digits 00-04-AC identify an IBM network card. The manufacturer uses the remaining six digits of an NIC's MAC address to identify the actual card. The entire 12-digit address is globally unique.

Note   If you are interested in learning more about assigned vendor codes, visit
`http://standards.ieee.org/regauth/oui/index.shtml`.

NICs will accept packets addressed to their MAC address or to the following MAC address: FF-FF-FF-FF-FF-FF. The address FF-FF-FF-FF-FF-FF is known as a *broadcast address*. A computer will address a packet to a broadcast address when it wants to send a message to all nodes on the network.

The network's architecture is a key factor when choosing an NIC. The architecture of a network defines the structure, as well as the components that make a network function. Several standard architectures are currently in use — the most common architectures are Ethernet and Token Ring. If you want to attach a computer to a Token Ring network, you must install a Token Ring NIC into that computer. Likewise, if you want to connect a computer to an Ethernet network, you must install an Ethernet network card.

You must also consider the transmission media in use on the network when choosing an NIC. An Ethernet network, for example, can use coaxial, twisted-pair, or fiber optic cabling as its transmission media. The network card that you choose must have the appropriate connector to attach to the cable in use. Some NICs feature only one type of connector; other NICs are more flexible because they feature multiple connectors. Figure 14-3 shows an end view of a network card with the dual connectors.

Figure 14-3: End view of a dual-connector NIC

You should also consider speed when choosing a card. An NIC must be able to communicate at the same speed as the other components on the network. For example, if a particular Ethernet network communicates at a speed of 100 Mbps, then any NIC chosen for that network must be capable of communicating at 100 Mbps.

In the Real World   Many modern Ethernet cards are capable of two speeds (100 Mbps and 10 Mbps) and can sense the speed of the receiving transmission. It is possible, then, that a device using such a card can communicate with devices operating at either speed. Therefore, it is possible to have a LAN with multiple speeds operating upon it.

A key component of the network card is a *transceiver*. The transceiver's job is to transmit and receive data signals. The transceiver can be built directly on to the network card or, as depicted in Figure 14-4, it may be a small device attached directly to the network trunk cable and then connected to the network card via a transceiver cable.

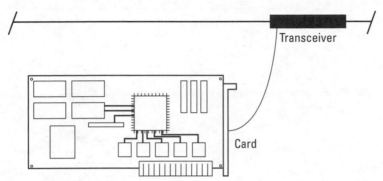

Figure 14-4: External transceiver

Repeaters

The longer the distance that data signals must travel down a cable, the greater the likelihood that the signals will degrade and perhaps be unreadable by destination nodes. Each type of cable is rated according to the length that a signal can travel before degradation becomes a problem. You can use a repeater when cable segments must run longer than the rated maximum length of the cable.

The purpose of a repeater is to regenerate and strengthen network signals. Installing a repeater onto the cable segment enables the network to go beyond its length limitations. Repeaters operate at the Physical Layer of the OSI. You can't use repeaters, however, to translate or filter data.

Tip   Degradation of signals over distance is often referred to as *attenuation*.

The top diagram in Figure 14-5 shows how a signal traveling across a long expanse of cable degrades. The bottom diagram shows a repeater being used to rectify the situation.

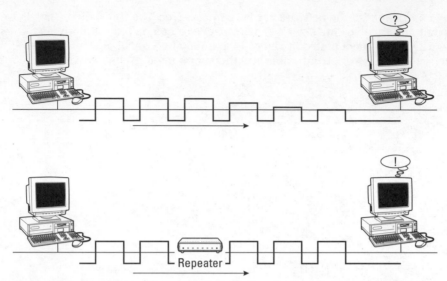

Figure 14-5: Data degradation before and after the installation of a repeater

Hubs

Hubs are devices that operate at the Physical Layer of the OSI/RM. They serve as the central connection point in a star topology network, as shown in Figure 14-6.

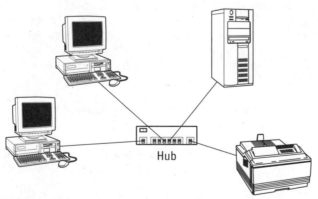

Figure 14-6: A hub is the central connection point in a star topology.

The *connectors* (or *ports*) of a hub allow connections to the various network devices. If you require more ports than are available on the hub, it is common practice to link multiple hubs together, as shown in Figure 14-7. This linking is referred to as *daisy-chaining or cascading.*

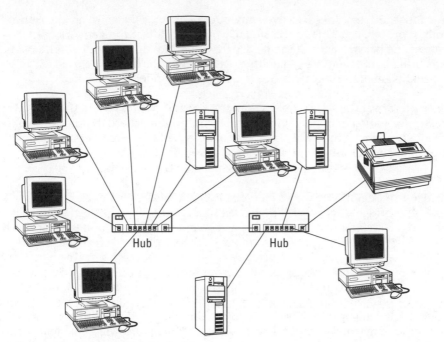

Figure 14-7: Daisy-chaining hubs

One of the main disadvantages of a bus network is that during network reconfiguration, such as adding or removing computers, the entire network may stop functioning until the reconfiguration is complete. This is not the case in a star topology, because the hub allows nodes to connect and disconnect at will — without adversely affecting network communications.

 For more information about bus networks, see Chapter 12.

Hubs are often referred to as *active hubs* because they accept signals from any node attached to them. They regenerate these signals and actively pass the signals on to all other attached nodes.

 Since hubs have the ability to regenerate signals before they pass them on they are often referred to as *multi-port repeaters*.

Bridges

Bridges are devices that divide a network into multiple segments or join separate networks together. One of the main reasons that you may want to break a network into multiple segments is to cut down on the amount of traffic that nodes on the network must process. Remember that an NIC examines every packet that passes by to see if it is the intended recipient. The more packets that pass by an NIC, the more it must process. An excessive amount of packets will lead to an excessive amount of processing. This processing may not only affect the network card, it may also affect the performance of the device in which the NIC is installed. When a network is broken into multiple segments with a bridge, the bridge acts as a filter to keep packets off of the segments not housing the intended recipient.

Bridges operate at the Data Link Layer of the OSI/RM, which means they use MAC address information contained in a packet to determine where that packet belongs. Bridges only examine the Data Link Layer of a packet; they aren't concerned with the protocol suites located in the higher layers of the OSI/RM. You can use a bridge — regardless of the protocol suites in use in the network.

If a bridge can't determine where a destination node is when a packet passes through, the bridge will forward the packet to all of the segments attached to it. When bridges are first turned on, they have no clue where any nodes are located on the network. Thus, bridges will allow many packets to pass to all segments. As these packets pass, however, the bridge examines the packets to determine the source (or sender's) MAC address. After examining the packets, the bridge knows where the correct node resides and, if a later packet is destined for that MAC address, the bridge will know which segment to forward that packet to. The longer a bridge is left running, the more it will know about locations of the various nodes and the more efficient the network will become. This in turn will make your oversaturated or broadcast-laden segments more reliable and improve overall speed of communications on your network.

See Figure 14-8 for an example of how a bridge operates. The network represented in this diagram has been divided into two segments by a bridge. Computers A and B are on one segment and Computers B and C are on the other.

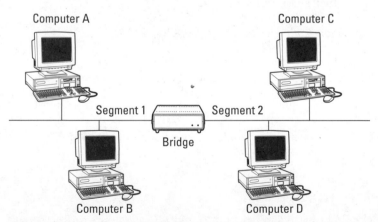

Figure 14-8: A network divided into two segments by a bridge

For the example shown in Figure 14-8, assume that the bridge has just been turned on and has no idea at this point where any of the computers on the network are located. Also assume that Computer A is sending a packet of data to Computer B. On a bus network, a packet of information that is sent from a computer travels in both directions across the entire length of the bus.

In this case, both Computer B and the bridge will receive the transmission. The bridge examines the destination MAC address of the packet to determine whether it should pass the packet on to the other segment. The bridge finds Computer B's MAC address, but because the bridge has no record of Computer B's location, it passes the packet onto Segment 2 where it is examined by Computers C and D and then ignored because these computers are not the intended destination. However, the bridge records that Computer A is on Segment 1; the bridge knows this because Computer A was the source of the packet and the packet came from Segment 1.

Next, assume that Computer B responds to Computer A's packet and sends a response packet back to Computer A. Once again, the packet is sent out over Segment 1. The bridge receives the packet and again examines the MAC address information. Because the packet is addressed to Computer A, which the bridge knows is on Segment 1, the bridge does not pass the packet on to Segment 2 and Computers C and D never see it. The bridge now records the location of Computer B; the bridge knows this information because the packet has Computer B listed as the source and the packet originated from Segment 1. From this point forward, all communication between Computers A and B will be contained in Segment 1, reducing the amount of traffic of Segment 2. Computers C and D will likely communicate on the network—when they do, the bridge will record their locations as well, further optimizing network communications.

Switches

Switches are devices that direct signals from a source to a destination. The type of source and the kind of destination depend on the type of switch. Three predominate types of switches are used in networks: Layer 2, Layer 3, and Layer 4.

Layer 2 switches

A Layer 2 switch is often used in place of a hub and can serve as the central connection point for a star topology-based network. The main difference between Layer 2 switches and hubs is how they deal with packets. When a hub receives a packet, it forwards the packet to all nodes attached to the hub, as shown in Figure 14-9. In this example, Computer A is sending a packet to Computer B. The packet arrives at the hub, which, in turn, forwards it to all computers attached to the hub. Each NIC must process the packet to some degree in order to determine the intended recipient of the packet.

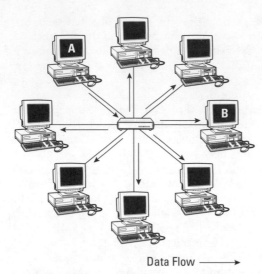

Data Flow ———→

Figure 14-9: A hub forwarding a received packet to all connected nodes

When a Layer 2 switch is used in place of a hub, only the destination node will actually receive the packet. Figure 14-10 demonstrates the same scenario as the preceding figure, but with a switch instead of the hub. When the switch receives a packet from Computer A that is destined for Computer B, the switch examines the destination MAC address and passes it on to Computer B only.

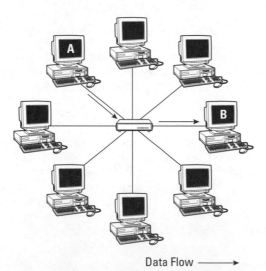

Data Flow ———→

Figure 14-10: A switch forwarding a packet to the destination node only. This technology offers several benefits:

✦ **Simple installation:** A switch is no more complicated to physically install than a hub. All cables and connectors are the same, so replacing a hub with a switch is a simple matter.

Note

Although this is true, to receive the full benefits of a switch there is some additional internal configuration that must be performed.

✦ **Faster network response:** Because an NIC will only see packets destined for it, there is less contention for wire space. Therefore, the NIC has the ability to send packets more often than in a traditional hub-based network. Add to this capability the fact that switches allow more than one sender/receiver pair to communicate at the same time.

✦ **More server bandwidth:** A server attached to a switch will have less traffic to contend with and can therefore respond to clients at greater speed.

Layer 3 switches

Layer 3 switches, or routing switches, function similarly to routers. They have the ability to examine the Network Layer information of routable protocols and can make routing decisions based on destination. The main difference between a Layer 3 switch and a true router is that routing switches use hardware-based algorithms to perform routing, and routers use software-based algorithms. The benefit of this difference is faster processing. The downside is less flexibility.

Layer 4 switches

Layer 4 switches, or Web switches, have the ability to examine the transport layer information and can route information based on very specific application information. For example, that specific information can be the header of a packet from a specific browser (like Netscape Navigator). The switch can look to see what browser a Web user is using and intelligently switch that user to a Web server hosting a site that is made specifically to exploit the benefits of that particular type of browser.

Note

This functionality is often referred to as "content smart switching."

Exam Tip

In-depth discussion of switches and how they operate go beyond the scope of the requirements for the CIW Foundations exam. Concentrate on the layers of the OSI/RM on which switches operate.

Routers

As with bridges, you can use routers to link networks together or to break a large network into smaller networks (often referred to as *subnets*, if addressed with TCP/IP and not IPX). However, unlike bridges, routers operate at the Network Layer of the OSI/RM, which means they can do a better job of filtering and forwarding data. Operating at this level, however, adds a degree of complexity, and routers typically perform their functions more slowly than a bridge.

Figure 14-11 shows a network environment with several networks interconnected with routers.

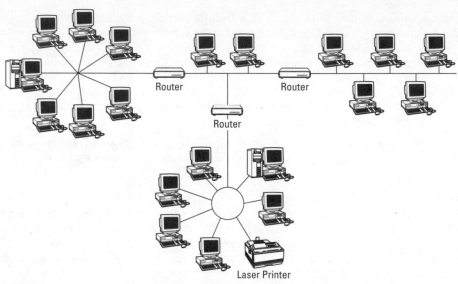

Figure 14-11: A series of networks interconnected with routers

Unlike bridges, routers don't find destination computers by examining the packets sent by those computers. In fact, routers (for the most part) aren't concerned with destination computers at all. Routers, for the most part, are concerned with the destination network. When a router receives a packet, it examines the packet for the destination network address. The router then consults its routing table to find a route to the destination network. If the router finds a route, the packet is forwarded on. If the router finds multiple routes to the destination network, you can configure the router to pass the packet by using the most efficient path. If a router can't find a route, it won't pass the packet at all. After the packet hits the destination network, the network's router must pass it on to the appropriate computer. This process is similar in concept to the way your modern postal services work; for example, when you mail a letter to a friend, the mail carrier doesn't care which individual in a household the letter is addressed to. The mail carrier's only concern is the house address. After the letter is dropped into the mailbox, it becomes the responsibility of the person who retrieves the mail to pass the letter on to the appropriate person.

Tip   A router's *routing table* is a list that contains known network addresses and the host address of routers that can pass information to those networks. A router administrator either manually enters these tables or routers learn the information by exchanging routing information with other routers.

In order to pass network packets, routers require the packets to be constructed in such a way that routers can determine which network they should be sent to. In other words, the packets must contain destination network addressing information. This information is only found in routable protocols, such as IP and IPX. These protocols support the idea of both network addresses and host addresses. When nodes are configured to operate in a TCP/IP environment, for example, they are assigned both a network address and a host address. All nodes on the same network (or, the same side of a router) have the same network address but each has a unique host address. A data packet that is sent by a computer includes both the destination network address and the destination host address.

Routers are protocol-specific. In other words, in order for a router to pass TCP/IP packets, the router must be designed to work in a TCP/IP environment. Similarly, to pass packets in an IPX/SPX environment, the router must be designed for IPX/SPX (which is a Novell Netware based routed protocol).

Cross-Reference TCP/IP routing is covered in more detail in Chapter 15.

Brouters

Because *brouters* operate at both the Data Link Layer and Network Layer of the OSI/RM, they combine the strength of both bridges and routers. Brouters are able to route routable protocol suites, such as TCP/IP and IPX/SPX. They are also able to bridge non-routable protocols, such as NetBEUI, DECnet, and LAT. A brouter is a good choice for a heterogeneous network environment in which both classifications of protocols exist.

Gateways

Gateways, or *protocol converters*, provide translation services from one protocol stack to another. For example, you can use a gateway to translate between TCP/IP and IPX/SPX. Microsoft offers a form of a gateway with its Windows NT server operating system: NT Server allows you to install Gateway Services for NetWare (GSNW). After you have installed GSNW, the NT server can advertise the resources available on the NetWare server as if they were on the NT server. This means that all NT server clients can access the NetWare resources — even if they don't use the same protocol suite as the NetWare server.

Modems

A traditional *modem* is a device that allows a computer to send data to other computers over a standard telephone line. When a computer sends data, the modem converts (or *modulates*) the digital signals used by the computer into analog signals, which can be carried over a common telephone line. When a computer receives the data, the modem converts (or *demodulates*) the analog signals back into digital signals, which are understood by the computer.

The term *modem* is currently used to describe any device that translates the computer's digital format into a format that can be carried over a communications network. For example, cable modems translate computer signals into a format that can travel over a cable TV network. Likewise, ISDN modems allow a computer to communicate over an Integrated Services Digital Network.

With modern computers and operating systems, installing and configuring a modem is usually as simple as plugging it in and turning it on. In some cases, however, you may be required to configure the modem so it won't interfere with the operation of existing devices on your computer. You may have to adjust the following three settings:

✦ **Interrupt request:** An *interrupt request* (IRQ) is a signal that a device sends to a computer's CPU to notify it that the device needs the processor's attention. *IRQ lines* are locations where devices, such as modems, can send their interrupt requests. Unfortunately, only a limited number of IRQ lines are available (usually 15 lines) and most devices don't support the sharing of those lines. Every device that requires the use of IRQs must be assigned a unique IRQ line. Figure 14-12 is a screen shot of a Windows 2000 server and shows its assigned IRQs. Typically, modems are serial devices and, as such, are usually assigned either IRQ Line 3 or IRQ Line 4.

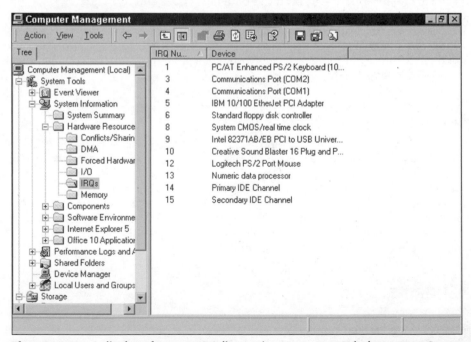

Figure 14-12: A display of current IRQ line assignments on a Windows 2000 Server

✦ **Input/Output address:** An Input/Output (I/O) address, or an *I/O Port address*, transfers data between the CPU and a device. Each device in a system must be assigned a unique I/O address. Because most modems are serial devices, they often have the same settings as standard serial ports. These settings are usually 3F0 to 3FF for COM1 and 2F0 to 2FF for COM2.

✦ **Modem (or port) speed:** The modem must operate at a speed equal to the speed of the modem with which it is communicating. Most modern modems automatically adjust their speed to match their communication partner. However, if a modem does not support this feature, you must manually adjust it.

CSU/DSUs

A CSU/DSU is a device about the size of an external modem that combines a Channel Service Unit (CSU) and a Data Service Unit (DSU). It operates at the physical layer of the OSI/RM and is used to format and send data from a LAN environment unto WAN transmission media and vice versa. The Channel Service Unit (CSU) receives and transmits signals from and to the WAN line and provides a barrier for electrical interference from either side of the unit. The CSU can also echo loopback signals from the phone company for testing purposes. The DSU component converts digital data signals used in LANs to and from bipolar signals, used over Wide Area Network transmission media such as T1 or T3 lines. CSU/DSUs operate at Layer 1 of the OSI/RM.

Figure 14-13 shows the placement of CSU/DSUs when connecting two LANs with a leased T1 line.

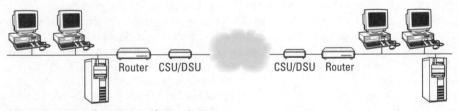

Router CSU/DSU   CSU/DSU Router

Figure 14-13: Placement of CSU/DSUs

Patch panels

A patch panel is a mounted hardware unit containing an assembly of port locations in a communications or other electronic or electrical system. In a network, a patch panel is generally static in nature (I've never seen them moved), using cables to interconnect computers within the area of a LAN, or to keep users moving to different switch ports more easily. A patch panel uses a patch cord to create each interconnection. A patch panel is also called a passive hub.

Data Transmission Terminology

 Describe transmission types including asynchronous and synchronous, simplex, half duplex, full duplex, baseband, and broadband.

You should become familiar with the data transmission and transmission media terms discussed in this section.

Bandwidth

The term *bandwidth* refers to the transmission capacity of any given medium (a cable, for example). Certain transmission media have a much higher bandwidth than others. For example, a fiber-optic cable has a much higher bandwidth than twisted-pair cable due to the fact that the fiber-optic cable can carry much more data than twisted-pair over an equal amount of time.

Baseband transmission

Baseband transmission is a means of transmitting digital signals over a transmission medium, such as a wire. When data is sent across a wire that uses baseband transmission, the message uses the entire bandwidth of the cable—leaving no room to carry any other signals. Baseband transmission is the most common transmission type used in local area networks.

Broadband transmission

Broadband transmission is another method for transmitting signals over a transmission medium. Using broadband, a single transmission media is divided into several channels using a process called *multiplexing*. Each channel is assigned a unique analog frequency and all transmissions over that channel are carried over that frequency. The use of the different channels allows several discrete communications sessions to occur simultaneously over the same transmission media. Cable TV transmission is a good example of broadband technology. The single cable connected to your TV allows you to receive several channels of information simultaneously.

Asynchronous transmission

Typically used by dial-up modems, *asynchronous transmission* refers to a data transfer method that breaks the data to be sent into one-byte frames. Before the frames are sent, each frame is prepared by adding start and stop information. To mark the beginning of a new character of data, a start bit is added to the front of the frame. Likewise, if configured to do so, the sending device performs a mathematical calculation on the data in the frame. The result of this calculation (either a 0 or a 1) is placed as a parity bit at the end of the data. When the receiving device analyzes the frame, it performs the same calculation as the sending device. The result that the receiving device obtains is compared to the result in the parity bit. If the results match, the receiving computer assumes that the received data was not damaged in transit. If the results don't match, the frame is considered to be damaged in transit and is discarded. Finally, depending on the configuration of the communicating devices, one or two stop bits are added to the end trailer of each frame to signal the end.

The benefit of this transmission method is that the sending and receiving computers don't have to rely on precise timing when sending or receiving data. In other words, the devices don't have to be in sync. The drawback of this transmission method, however, is that the start, stop, and parity bits can add as much as 50 percent overhead to all data being sent.

Synchronous transmission

Devices that transmit and receive data by using a synchronous transmission method eliminate the need for stop, start, and parity bits by coordinating clocks and transmission rates. Data is sent in a timed and controlled fashion, allowing data frames to be several bytes in length. The only additional data added to the transmission is start information, which is added at the beginning of the entire data transfer session, and stop information, which is added at the end of transmission. Throughout the transmission, additional synchronization information is also periodically added to keep the two devices in sync.

The benefit of synchronous data transfer is the reduction of the amount of data that needs to be sent. The downside of synchronous data transfer is that the two devices have to remain in sync throughout the entire message-sending process. A large number of Wide Area Network communications use synchronous transmission, including T1 lines.

Simplex data transmission

Simplex data transmission occurs when data can only flow in one direction. Examples of simplex data transmission are radio and TV broadcasts.

Half-duplex data transmission

Half-duplex transmissions are two-way communications in which only one device can transmit at a time. Ethernet networks employ half-duplex transmissions because all devices can send or receive, but only one can send at any given time. Citizen band (CB) radios are an example of half-duplex transmissions — you can talk or listen, but not at the same time.

Full-duplex data transmission

Full-duplex data transmission occurs when data can travel in two directions simultaneously. A common example of a full-duplex transmission is a phone conversation. Full-duplex switched Ethernet and several other networking technologies use full-duplex data transmission methods.

Types of Transmission Media

 Identify the differences between common transmission media used in networking, such as twisted-pair, coaxial, fiber optic cable, and wireless media.

One of the basic components found in all networks is a transmission media. In order for a node on a network to send information to another node, a transmission media must be present. This media may be cables or a form of wireless communication. The following section explains some of the more common transmission media types found in modern networks.

 Exam Tip Be sure that you can distinguish between the various transmission media types and know the appropriate use of each type.

Coaxial cable

For many years, coaxial cable was the most frequently used type of network transmission media. The popularity of coaxial cable was largely due to it being relatively inexpensive, flexible, and easy to work with.

A coaxial cable consists of several layers. The innermost layer is referred to as the *core*; it is typically either a solid or stranded copper wire. The core is the true transmission media for the electronic data signals. Surrounding the core is non-conducting insulating material, usually made of PVC or Teflon. This insulating material is, in turn, wrapped inside a metallic wire mesh or sleeve that acts as a ground and shields the core from outside interference. The outermost layer of the cable consists of another type of non-conductive material, such as plastic or rubber. Figure 14-14 shows the various layers of a coaxial cable.

Figure 14-14: The layers of a coaxial cable

Coaxial cable grades

Coaxial cable is available in two grades: Polyvinyl chloride (PVC) and Plenum. PVC is a fairly flexible plastic; as a result, it is often used in the construction of the insulation layers of the coaxial cable. You should know that in the case of a fire, PVC gives off a highly poisonous gas when it burns.

The term *plenum* refers to the space in many buildings between the false ceiling of one floor and the floor above. The plenum is often used to circulate air throughout the building, and, for this reason, fire codes are usually very strict regarding the type of cables that can be run through this area. Plenum grade coaxial cable uses special materials in its insulating layers that don't give off poisonous gases when burning. Plenum grade coaxial cable, however, is less flexible and more expensive than PVC cable.

Coaxial cable types

Many types of coaxial cables are used in a variety of situations. The CIW Foundations Certification exam concentrates on the two most common coaxial cables used in networking: Thinnet and Thicknet.

Thinnet

Thinnet — as its name suggests — is a fairly thin cable, about @@bf1/4 inch thick. This thickness allows it to be fairly flexible and easy to work with. Thinnet is the standard cable used in 10base2 Ethernet networks. 10base2 supports broadband data transmissions at 10 Mbps to a maximum of 185 meters (approximately 607 feet). Figure 14-15 is a representation of a British Navel Connector (BNC) typically used to connect devices to the cable.

Figure 14-15: A BNC connector

Thicknet

Until the advent of thinnet, thicknet was considered the Ethernet standard cable. With a thickness of @@bf1/2 inch, it is considerably less flexible and more difficult to work with than thinnet. Due to its thicker core and better shielding, however, thicknet can support data transfers over longer distances than thinnet. As the basic cable choice for the Ethernet 10base5 standard, it can carry a baseband signal at 10 Mbps over a distance of 500 meters (approximately 1,640 feet).

The terms *Ethernet*, *Broadband*, *10base2*, and *10base5* are described in more detail later in this chapter.

Twisted-pair cable

Twisted-pair cables are now the predominant network cable being used in LANs. Twisted-pair cables usually consist of multiple pairs of wires surrounded by a protective insulated layer (usually rubber or plastic). Each pair is made of insulated copper wires that have been twisted around each other throughout the entire length of the cable. This twisting reduces what is known as *crosstalk*. Crosstalk occurs when signals from one wire stray onto an adjacent wire, disrupting data communications.

Twisted-pair cabling are commonly used in telephone cables and in Ethernet 10baseT networks. 10baseT networks support a data transfer rate of 10 Mbps over twisted-pair cabling to a maximum length of 100 meters (328 feet).

Types of twisted-pair

Twisted-pair cables are available in two predominant types: UTP and STP. The following sections detail these types.

Unshielded twisted-pair

Unshielded twisted-pair (UTP) cabling is the most common type of twisted-pair cable because it is inexpensive and very easy to work with. The downside of UTP is that it literally provides no shielding for its incased wires, which means that the wires can suffer from the effects of electromagnetic interference (EMI). These effects may hinder or altogether disrupt data communications. EMI can originate from such sources as electric motors, power lines, and even high power radio signals.

Shielded twisted-pair

In shielded twisted-pair (STP) cables, the signal carrying wires are less prone to the effects of EMI because they are encased in a metal sheath. This shielding, however, reduces the flexibility of the cable making it harder to work with than UTP. The additional shielding also makes STP much more expensive than UTP.

Categories for twisted-pair cabling

Specifications for twisted-pair cables are outlined in the Electronic Industries Association and the Telecommunications Industries Association (EIA/TIA) 568 Commercial Wiring Standards. These standards outline five rating categories for twisted-pair cables. These five categories as well as Categories 6 and 7 (not yet standardized) are outlined in Table 14-1.

Table 14-1 EIA/TIA 568 Commercial Wiring Standards Twisted-Pair Categories	
Category	**Description**
1	Traditional UTP telephone cable that is certified to carry voice, but not data. Prior to 1983, this was the predominant type of telephone cable.
2	UTP cabling that is certified to carry data transmissions up to 4 Mbps. It consists of four twisted-pairs of wires.
3	Twisted-pair cabling that is certified to carry data transmission up to a speed of 10 Mbps. It consists of four twisted-pairs of wires.
4	Twisted-pair cabling that is certified to carry data transmission up to a speed of 16 Mbps. It consists of four twisted-pairs of wires. Common in Token Ring networks.
5	Twisted-pair cabling that is certified to carry data transmission up to a speed of 100 Mbps. It consists of four twisted-pairs of wires.
6	Twisted-pair cabling that is certified to carry data transmission up to a speed of 155 Mbps. It consists of four twisted-pairs of wires.
7	Twisted-pair cabling that is certified to carry data transmission up to a speed of 1000 Mbps. It consists of four twisted-pairs of wires.

In the Real World

Twisted-pair cabling is often referred to using the abbreviation "CAT." For example, category 5 UTP can be referred to as CAT 5. The category rating of a twisted-pair cable is often printed on the outside casing of the cable.

Twisted-pair wiring components

A variety of components are available for use with twisted-pair cables including the following:

✦ Register Jack-45 (RJ45) connectors

✦ Wall jacks

✦ Patch panels

RJ45 connectors are typically found on the end of a twisted-pair cable. To attach the connector to the cable, use a tool called a *crimper*. The RJ45 jack looks similar to the RJ11 connector, which is found at the end of your telephone cable. Despite their similarities, however, these two items are very different. The RJ45 houses eight twisted-pair wires, and the RJ11 houses only four. To accommodate the extra wires, RJ45 connectors are somewhat larger than the RJ11 connectors. NICs and hubs that support twisted-pair cabling also have an RJ45 jack (also known as a *socket*) that the RJ45 connectors can be plugged into. Figure 14-16 shows an RJ45 connector.

Figure 14-16: An RJ45 connector

Twisted-pair wiring is often used in a star topology network. To form the star, a connection must be made between each node in the network and a central hub. Hubs are typically placed in a centrally located wire closet in the building. Rather than running a single continuous strand of cable from each node all the way back to the hub, RJ45 wall jacks and patch panels are more commonly used. RJ45 wall jacks are simply RJ45 female connectors that are placed along the walls throughout the building. Each connector has a twisted-pair cable running inside the walls back to the wiring closet. At the wiring closet, each wall jack cable ends at a patch panel. A patch panel is a group of sockets (again female RJ45 cables) mounted on either a wall or a rack. Each socket is typically labeled with a number corresponding to the wall jack to which it is connected.

Fiber-optic cable

Fiber-optic cable is a type of cable through which data signals can travel as pulses of light. Most fiber optic cables consist of two or more glass or plastic strands. To keep the light inside the cable, a reflective layer of material called *cladding* surrounds each fiber.

Exam Tip   Be aware of both the advantages and disadvantages of fiber-optic cabling.

You gain several benefits by using light instead of electricity (which is used in coaxial and twisted-pair cables):

✦ **Speed:** Fiber-optic cables support very high transmission rates, in some instances well over a gigabit per second.

✦ **Distance:** Light signals don't degrade as quickly as electrical signals. The distances traveled can exceed several miles.

✦ **Security:** Unlike typical electrical cables, fiber-optic cables are difficult to tap to "listen in" on communications.

✦ **Reliability:** Fiber optic cables are not susceptible to EMI because they don't carry electrical signals.

You should be aware of a few downsides to choosing fiber-optic cables:

✦ **Cost:** Fiber optic cables and components can be much more expensive than standard copper cables.

✦ **Complexity:** Fiber optic installation professionals must often be hired to prepare and install the cable.

Wireless transmission media

Wireless transmission media offers all of the benefits of a network without the nuisance of cabling. Many types of wireless networking media are in use today, both for LAN and WAN connectivity. Some of the more popular wireless networking media include the following:

✦ Infrared

✦ Microwave

✦ Satellite

✦ Cellular

✦ Radio

Nodes that use wireless communication must have a wireless NIC and a transceiver (also known as an *access point*); the transceiver is used to send and receive network data.

Exam Tip   The CIW Foundations course and corresponding exam don't go into great wireless transmission detail. Understanding the basic concepts and the need for a transceiver should be sufficient for the exam.

Physical and Logical Topologies

Objective   Explain the differences between logical and physical topologies.

A network's physical topology describes the shape or physical layout of the network. In other words, the topology describes how the network's nodes are connected together. There are five main physical topologies:

✦ Bus

✦ Star

✦ Ring

✦ Hybrid

✦ Mesh

Along with the physical topology, networks are also described in terms of their logical topology. The logical topology of a network describes how data travels within the network.

See Chapter 12 for more information about network topologies.

In a typical Token Ring network, the nodes of the network are physically connected in a star pattern; all components are physically connected to a central device. The data packets, however, move from one computer to the next in a ring fashion. Therefore, the physical topology is a star and the logical topology is a ring.

IEEE LAN Standards

Identify LAN standards, including the Institute of Electrical and Electronics Engineers LAN standards, Apple LocalTalk, and Fiber Distributed Data Interface.

In an effort to standardize network technologies, the Institute of Electrical and Electronic Engineers (IEEE, pronounced "I triple E") published a series of standards referred to as the IEEE 802 standards. IEEE 802 defines network standards for the physical components of a network, including network adapter cards, LAN and WAN networking devices, and network cabling.

The IEEE 802 standards were originally broken up into 12 categories, as shown in Table 14-2.

Table 14-2 **IEEE 802 Network Standards**	
IEEE Number	*Category*
802.1	Internetworking
802.2	Logical Link Control
802.3	CSMA/CD (Ethernet)
802.4	Token Bus LAN
802.5	Token Ring LAN
802.6	Metropolitan Area Networks (MAN)
802.7	Broadband Communications
802.8	Fiber-Optics

IEEE Number	Category
802.9	Integrated Voice and Data Networks
802.10	Network Security
802.11	Wireless Networks
802.12	Demand Priority Access LAN

Table 14-2 is a complete list of the original IEEE standards. The CIW Foundations Certification exam, however, only requires that you fully understand IEEE 802.2, 802.3, 802.5, and 802.12. The following sections detail each of these standards.

IEEE 802.2: Logical Link Control

The 802.2 project committee was responsible for the task of dividing the Data Link Layer of the OSI/RM into two sub-layers: Logical Link Control (LLC) and Media Access Control (MAC). The LLC is responsible for error checking and regulating the flow of data from the Physical Layer to the Network Layer. The MAC Layer is responsible for gaining access to and placing data on the transmission media.

Cross-Reference   See Chapter 13 for more information about Logical Link Control.

IEEE 802.3: Ethernet

The 802.3 committee developed standards for networks based on the Carrier Sense Multiple Access with Collision Detection (CSMA/CD) access method. Ethernet is a networking technology that, although not 100 percent compatible, is very much based on 802.3 standards.

CSMA/CD defines a method for a device to gain access to a network. With CSMA/CD, a network node that wants to send data will "watch" the network to see if any other node is transmitting. If no communication is occurring, the node will transmit its data. If a transmission is already in progress, the node will wait until the line is free to transmit its data. Collisions often occur when two (or more) nodes on the network sense that the network is available and attempt to send at the same time. The collisions result in both data transmissions being corrupted. The nodes, sensing that their data has been destroyed, will wait a random amount of time and attempt to resend the failed transmission.

802.3 standards define a broadcast-based network in which all network transmissions are broadcast to all nodes. Each node analyzes a transmission to determine its destination. If a node detects that it is the intended recipient, it will process the transmission in its entirety; otherwise, the node will ignore the transmission.

The use of 10base2, 10base5, 10baseT, and fiber optic wiring standards are supported under 802.3.

Several extensions have been made to the 802.3 standards, most notably 802.3u, 802.3z, and 802.3ab.

The 802.3u standards define *Fast Ethernet*. Fast Ethernet is very similar to standard Ethernet but features a transfer rate of 100 Mbps as opposed to 10 Mbps. In order to use Fast Ethernet, all network components must support 802.3u.

802.3z and 802.3ab both define what is known as *Gigabit Ethernet*. Gigabit Ethernet is similar to standard Ethernet but features data transfer speeds of 1,000 Mps. 802.z defines standards for Gigabit Ethernet over specialty copper and fiber-optic cable. 802.3ab defines standards for Gigabit Ethernet over UTP cable.

Table 14-3 is a comparison of Ethernet, Fast Ethernet, and Gigabit Ethernet.

Table 14-3 Comparison of Ethernet, Fast Ethernet, and Gigabit Ethernet			
Feature	*Ethernet*	*Fast Ethernet*	*Gigabit Ethernet*
IEEE standard	802.3	802.3u	802.3z & 802.3ab
Access Method	CSMA/CD	CSMA/CD	CSMA/CD
Speed	10 Mbps	100 Mbps	1000 Mbps
Topology	Bus or Star	Star	Star
Wiring standards	10base2, 10base5, 10baseT, and 10baseFL	100baseTX, 100baseT4, and 100baseFX	1000baseT, 1000baseCX, 1000baseSX, and 1000baseLX

IEEE 802.5: Token Ring

The 802.5 standards were derived from IBM Corporation's Token Ring networking architecture. Token Ring networks are ring topology networks that base network access on a token traveling around the ring. The *token* is a small piece of data that travels around the ring, stopping at every node. The only time a computer can send data is when it has possession of the token. When a node needs to send data, it waits for the token. Upon receiving the token, the node places data on the wire in place of the token. The data is then sent to every node around the ring until it either reaches the intended recipient or returns to the sending node. The benefit of this type of network is that data collisions never occur.

Token Ring networks typically use twisted-pair cabling and operate at a speed of either 4 Mbps or 16 Mbps. Token Ring networks physically resemble star networks, but instead of using a hub (as in Ethernet), Token Ring networks use a Multi-station Access Unit (MAU) to serve as a connection point. The ring is contained within the MAU.

IEEE 802.12: 100VG-AnyLAN

Developed as a cooperative project between AT&T and HP and subsequently managed by the IEEE 802.12 committee, the 100VG-AnyLAN-network architecture is somewhat similar to a star-based Ethernet network in that all nodes are connected to hubs.

Networks based on the 802.12 networking standards use *demand priority* for controlling network access. The hubs control access to the network by allowing all nodes to transmit at any time. If two nodes transmit at the same time, the hub will service the transmission with the highest priority. If they have equal priority, the hub will randomly choose one, service it, and then service the other. The hubs act like switches in that they will only forward a transmission to its destination — not to every node on the network.

Non-IEEE Network Standards

You should be aware of two additional network standards for the CIW Foundations exam that are not defined in IEEE 802. They are Apple LocalTalk and FDDI.

Apple LocalTalk

Apple Corporation developed the LocalTalk network standard for networking their products. This networking standard uses Carrier Sense Multiple Access with Collision Avoidance (CSMA/CA) to control network access. With CSMA/CA, nodes broadcast their intent to transmit before they actually transmit data. This reduces collisions because the computers know when data is going to be transmitted. A major downside of this method, however, is the additional traffic that is created by the intent to send broadcasts.

Fiber Distributed Data Interface

Developed by the X3T9.5 American Standards Institute, the Fiber Distributed Data Interface (FDDI) specification details a high-speed, token-passing network. Unlike the 802.5 Token Ring standard, FDDI defines a network in which nodes are interconnected by two 100 Mbps, fiber optic, and counter-rotating rings (a primary and a Secondary). The dual rings provide redundancy in case either ring fails. Using fiber optics instead of copper allows each of these rings to extend up to 100 kilometers in length and can support 500 nodes. If the secondary ring is not required for backup, it can be used to carry data thus extending the length to 200 kilometers and doubling the support to 1000 nodes. FDDI rings are often used to interconnect multiple LANs within a small geographic area, such as a city or municipality, to form a *metropolitan area network* (MAN), as shown in Figure 14-17.

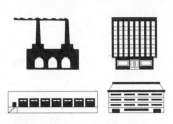

Figure 14-17: An FDDI based Metropolitan Area Network

WAN Technologies

Identify WAN standards, including X.25 frame relay, and asynchronous transfer mode.

Several transmission technologies are available for interconnecting LANs to form WANs. The following section deals with some of the more common technologies that you should know for the CIW Foundations Certification exam.

X.25

Implemented at the Network Layer of the OSI/RM, X.25 is a packet-switching technology that has been in use since the mid-1970s. Telecommunications companies that offer X.25 services provide multiple data paths on which data packets can travel. Despite being considered fairly slow (56Kbps or less) compared to today's more modern standards, X.25 is still used throughout the world due to its past popularity and its ability to ensure error-free delivery of packet data.

Frame relay

Frame relay is a high speed, variable-length, packet-switching telecommunication service provided by many telecommunications companies. This service is provided over fiber-optic and digital cables. Due to the high reliability of these connections, much of the error checking in older technologies, such as X.25, is removed. The frame relay network transparently offers multiple paths between source and destination networks. Connections between networks can be provided as an on-demand service. Bandwidth can be allocated as required with data transfer speeds ranging from 56Kbps to 1.544 Mbps. An organization can purchase a committed information rate (CIR) from a frame relay provider, this CIR, measured in bits per second, is used as a guarantee of service. The service provider will guarantee delivery of all data not exceeding the CIR; data exceeding the CIR may still be delivered but is not guaranteed.

If an organization uses frame relay to link two distant LANs to form a WAN, permanent virtual connections (PVCs) or switched virtual connections (SVCs) are formed between the LANS. These virtual circuits make it appear as if the two networks were connected at all times through a dedicated connection. For an SVC the connection is only set up when actual data is to be sent. Network bandwidth is allocated during the transmission of data, and unallocated upon completion. With a PVC, the connection remains permanently available.

Connection to a frame relay network is accomplished by connecting to a Point of Presence (POP) port. This POP port is a service provider's connection to the frame relay network.

Unlike X.25, frame relay (like most high-speed packet-switching networks) is implemented at the MAC sublayer of the Data Link Layer of the OSI/RM.

Asynchronous Transfer Mode

Asynchronous Transfer Mode (ATM) is a very advanced cell relay network technology capable of transmitting data at speeds between 155 Mps and 622 Mbps. Data to be transferred is broken down into 53-byte fixed length cells. Because all data is transferred in a fixed size, ATM network equipment can move data much more quickly than the corresponding equipment on variable-length packet-switching networks. Like frame relay, ATM is also implemented at the MAC sublayer of the OSI/RM.

T-Carrier and E-Carrier Systems

 Explain the function and types of T-carrier and E-carrier systems.

The T-carrier system, introduced in the 1960s by the Bell system, was the first transport system capable of supporting digital voice transmission. Currently, the T-carrier system supports high-speed transmission of voice and data across North America. Organizations that require high-speed connections to the Internet for their LANs or WANs will often lease T-carrier lines.

Several levels of T-carrier lines are available, starting with a T1 Line. A T1 line is composed of 24 individual channels—each of which can support up to 64Kbps. Thus, the full bandwidth of a T1 line is 24x64Kbps or 1.544 Mbps. Organizations that want to lease a T1 line usually have a choice of either leasing the entire T1 or a fractional T1. A *fractional T1* is a subset of the total 24 channels; a 768 Kbps Fractional T1 is 12 channels of a full T1 line.

Note The data rate standard of 64Kbps is known as DS-0, whereas 1.544 Mbps is known as DS-1. For this reason, T1 lines are often referred to as DS-1 lines, T2's are often referred to as DS-2 lines, T3s as DS-3 lines, and so on.

In order to connect over a T-carrier line, a network must use a CSU/DSU, a multi-plexer, and a router.

 Note A *multiplexer* is a device that combines (or multiplexes) multiple data streams together for transport across a carrier. On the receiving end, the data is de-multiplexed.

E-carrier services are the European equivalent to the North American T-Carrier system. Table 14-4 compares the North American T- carrier and European E-carrier systems.

Table 14-4
Comparison of North American T-Carrier
And European E-Carrier Systems

| Level | T – Carrier System | | E – Carrier System | |
	Channels	Speed	Channels	Speed
1	24	1.544 Mbps	30	2.048 Mbps
2	96	6.312 Mbps	120	8.448 Mbps
3	672	44.736 Mbps	480	34.368 Mbps
4	4032	274.176 Mbps	1920	139.268 Mbps
5	5760	400.352 Mbps	7680	565.148 Mbps

Key Point Summary

This chapter introduces you to the concepts of Local Area and Wide Area Networks. It explores the major components used in constructing modern networks. The following is a summary of the key points covered in this chapter:

✦ A Local Area Network is a network in which all devices are situated within the same small geographical area.

✦ A Wide Area Network is the interconnection of two or more LANS over a large geographic region, such as between cities or countries.

✦ The network interface is a device installed into a network node, such as a computer, to allow the node to connect to the network.

✦ A MAC address is a 48-bit address assigned by the manufacturer to an individual network card.

✦ MAC addresses are universally unique.

✦ A Repeater operates at the Physical Layer of the OSI/RM and is used to regenerate and strengthen network signals to increase the length of a network.

✦ Hubs operate at the Physical Layer of the OSI/RM and serve as the central connection point in a star topology network.

✦ Bridges operate at the Data Link Layer of the OSI/RM. Bridges are used to divide a network into multiple segments to increase bandwidth.

✦ Routers operate at the Network Layer of the OSI/RM. Routers are used to connect networks together or to divide a large network into smaller networks.

✦ Brouters operate at both the Data Link Layer and Network Layer of the OSI/RM. They combine the strengths of both Bridges and Routers.

✦ Three predominant types of switches are used in networks: Layer 2, Layer 3, and Layer 4.

✦ Gateways operate very high in the OSI/RM and can provide translation services from one protocol to another.

✦ A modem is a device that allows a computer to send data over standard telephone lines. The term *modem* may also refer to any device that translates a computer's digital format into a format that can be carried over a communications network.

✦ CSU/DSUs operate at Layer 1 of the OSI/RM and are used to prepare data from a LAN or transport across a WAN transport service (such as T-carriers) and vice versa.

✦ A patch panel is a collection of sockets mounted together for organizing network cables.

✦ The term *bandwidth* refers to the transmission capacity of a given medium (such as a cable).

✦ With baseband transmission, a send message takes all of the bandwidth of the cable—leaving no room to carry any other signals.

✦ With broadband, a single transmission media is divided into several channels using a process called *multiplexing*. This allows several discrete communication sessions to occur simultaneously over the same transmission media.

✦ With asymmetric transmissions, sending and receiving computers don't have to rely on precise timings when sending or receiving data.

✦ The synchronous transmission method eliminates the need for stop, start, and parity bits by coordinating clocks and transmission rates between communicating devices.

✦ Simplex data transmission occurs when data can only flow in one direction.

✦ Half-duplex transmissions are two-way communications in which only one device can transmit at one time.

✦ Full-duplex data transmission occurs when data can travel in both directions simultaneously across the same medium.

✦ Thinnet is the standard cable used in 10base2 Ethernet networks. 10base2 supports broadband data transmissions at 10 Mbps to a maximum of 185 meters.

✦ Thicknet is the basic cable choice for the Ethernet 10base5 standard; it can carry a baseband signal at 10 Mbps over a distance of 500 meters.

✦ 10baseT networks support a 10 Mbps data transfer rate over twisted-pair cabling to a maximum length of 100 meters (328 feet).

✦ Specifications for twisted-pair cables are outlined in the Electronic Industries Association and the Telecommunications Industries Association (EIA/TIA) 568 Commercial Wiring Standards.

✦ Fiber-optic cable is a type of cable through which data signals can travel as pulses of light.

✦ IEEE 802 defines network standards for physical components of a network, including network adapter cards, LAN and WAN networking devices, and network cabling.

✦ The 802.2 project committee divided the Data Link Layer of the OSI/RM into two sub-layers: Logical Link Control (LLC) and Media Access Control (MAC).

✦ The 802.3 committee develops standards for networks based on the Carrier Sense Multiple Access with Collision Detection (CSMA/CD) access method.

✦ In CSMA/CD, a node can only transmit if the wire is free of traffic.

✦ The 802.3u standards define Fast Ethernet. Fast Ethernet is similar to standard Ethernet but features a much higher transfer rate of 100 Mbps.

✦ 802.5 was derived from IBM Corporation's Token Ring networking architecture.

✦ Token Ring networks typically use twisted-pair cabling and operate at a speed of either 4 Mbps or 16 Mbps.

✦ FDDI defines a network in which nodes are interconnected by two 100 Mbps, fiber-optic cable, and counter-rotating rings. The dual rings provide redundancy in case either ring fails. Using fiber optics instead of copper allows each of these rings to extend up to 100 kilometers in length and can support 500 nodes.

✦ Implemented at the Network Layer of the OSI/RM, X.25 is a packet-switching technology that has been in use since the mid-1970s.

✦ Frame relay is a high speed, variable-length packet-switching telecommunication service with data transfer speeds ranging from 56Kbps to 1.544 Mbps.

✦ ATM is a very advanced cell relay network technology capable of transmitting data at speeds between 155 Mps and 622 Mbps. Data to be transferred is broken down into 53-byte fixed-length cells.

✦ T-carrier systems support high-speed transmission of voice and data across North America. Organizations that require high-speed connections to the Internet for their LANs or WANs will often lease T-carrier lines.

✦   ✦   ✦

STUDY GUIDE

The following assessment questions will test your memory on some of the key topics covered in the chapter.

Assessment Questions

1. An interconnection of two or more LANS over a large geographic region is known as a _____ _____ _____.

2. At what layer of the OSI/RM do NICs operate?

    A. Physical

    B. Data-Link

    C. Network

    D. Transport

3. Who assigns MAC addresses to NICs?

    A. ISO

    B. Network Administrator

    C. IEEE

    D. NIC Manufacturer

    E. Nobody, NICs don't have MAC addresses

4. Which device or devices can you use to regenerate and strengthen network signals?

    A. Repeaters

    B. HUBS

    C. Switches

    D. Patch panels

    E. Bandwidth Increasafier

5. Which of the following devices operates at the Network Layer of the OSI/RM?

   A. Bridge

   B. Gateway

   C. Router

   D. CSU/DSU

   E. Repeater

6. What are three settings that you may have to configure for a modem?

   A. IRQ

   B. RAM Block Port Number

   C. Port Speed

   D. I/O Address

   E. Assigned MAC addresses

   F. IP Address

7. In what type of transmission does a message take up the entire bandwidth of the cable?

   A. Baseband

   B. Broadband

   C. Full Duplex

   D. Simplex

   E. Half Duplex

   F All of the above

8. True or False: It is more efficient to send data using asynchronous data transfer methods than using synchronous data transfer methods.

9. A stadium's public address system is an example of what type of data transmission?

   A. Simplex

   B. Half-duplex

   C. Duplex

   D. Asynchronous

   E. Synchronous

10. PVC and Plenum are two grades of what?

    A. Coaxial Cable

    B. Routers

    C. Switches

    D. Twisted Pair Cable

    E. Fiber Optic Cable

11. Which cable supports baseband transmission at 10 Mbps over a distance of 500 meters?

    A. Thicknet

    B. Thinnet

    C. UTP

    D. STP

    E. Fiber

12. True or False: Category 5 cable is a coaxial cable that can support speeds up to 100 Mbps.

13. RJ45 connectors are the typical connector found at the end of what type of cable?

    A. Thicknet

    B. Thinnet

    C. UTP

    D. Fiber

    E. 10Basefx

14. True or False: The logical topology of a network describes how data travels within the network.

15. Which of the following defines standards for physical components of a network?

    A. OSI/RM

    B. IEEE 802

    C. EIA/TIA 568

    D. IEEE MAC

16. IEEE 802.5 defines standards for what?

    A. Token-Ring

    B. Hubs

    C. Ethernet

    D. Wireless networks

    E. Fiber-Optic networks

17. True or False: Token Ring networks are immune to data collisions due to CSMA/CD.

18. Which of the following WAN technologies is a very advanced cell relay network technology capable of transmitting data at speeds between 155 Mbps and 622 Mbps?

    A. FDDI

    B. ATM

    C. X.25

    D. T-Carrier

    E. Sparnet

Scenario

Red Riding Hood Industries (RRH) is a delivery company that primarily caters to seniors. You have been contracted by RRH to examine their existing network infrastructure and make recommendations to improve its performance and reliability. RRH's head office operates out of a single office building in Mythical Forest, New Hampshire. The existing network consists of 75 workstations and five servers interconnected by a physical bus topology. The bus consists of three segments of 10base2 cabling joined by two repeaters. The head office connects to a branch office by a X.25 leased line. Users are complaining of consistently slow network response when accessing both local and remote resources. The network also suffers from frequent downtime. When you examine the network, you determine that the slow response is due to a high volume of network traffic, and the frequent downtime occurs because the network administrator is adding or removing nodes from the network.

1. What is the maximum speed data transmission on the LAN?

2. What is the maximum length of each of the bus segments?

3. Why might you suggest replacing the repeaters with bridges?

4. What are some possible reasons to suggest replacing the 10Base2 cabling with Cat 5 UTP?

5. If RRH does implement Category 5 UTP, will this change the physical topology of the network? Will it change the logical topology?

6. When switching to CAT 5 UTP, besides the cabling, what other components of the network must be changed?

7. What is the most likely reason for suggesting that RRH switch from X.25 to a frame relay for WAN connection?

Answers to Chapter Questions

Chapter pre-test

1. A network of computers in one geographical region is referred to as a **Local Area** Network.

2. On the Internet, a junction between one high-speed network and another is referred to as a **Network Access Point** or a **NAP**.

3. A **repeater** is used to strengthen a digital signal on a cable segment.

4. Bridges operate at the **Data Link** Layer of the OSI/RM.

5. **Modems** are devices that translate a digital signal into an analog signal.

6. UTP and STP are categories of **twisted-pair cabling**.

7. The maximum cable length of thicknet is 500 meters.

8. When a device can both send and receive information at the same time, that device is using a **full** duplex connection.

9. With **synchronous** transmission, both the sending and receiving devices share a common clock and transmission rate.

10. Frame relay operates at the **Data Link** Layer of the OSI/RM.

Answers to Assessment Questions

1. An interconnection of two or more LANS over a large geographic region is known as a **Wide Area Network**.

2. At what layer of the OSI/RM does NICs operate?

    B. Data Link

3. Who assigns MAC addresses to NICs?

    D. NIC Manufacturer

4. Which device or devices can you use to regenerate and strengthen network signals?

   A. Repeaters

   B. HUBS

   C. Switches

5. Which of these devices operates at the Network Layer of the OSI/RM?

   C. Router

6. What are three settings that you may have to configure for a modem?

   A. IRQ

   C. Port Speed

   D. I/O Address

7. In what type of transmission does a message take up the entire bandwidth of the cable?

   A. Baseband

8. **False:** It is more efficient to send data using asynchronous data transfer methods than synchronous data transfer methods.

9. A stadium's public address system is an example of a device that uses what type of data transmission?

   A. Simplex

10. PVC and Plenum are two grades of what?

    A. Coaxial cable

11. Which cable supports baseband transmission at 10 Mbps over a distance of up to 500 meters?

    A. Thicknet

12. **False:** Category 5 cable is a coaxial cable that can support speeds up to 100 Mbps.

13. RJ45 connectors are the typical connector found at the end of what type of cable?

    C. UTP

14. **True:** The logical topology of a network describes how data travels within the network.

15. Which of the following defines standards for physical components of a network?

    B. IEEE 802

16. IEEE 802.5 defines standards for what?

    A. Token-Ring

17. False: Token Ring networks are immune to data collisions due to CSMA/CD.

18. Which of the following WAN technologies is a very advanced cell relay network technology capable of transmitting data at speeds between 155 Mps to 622 Mbps?

    B. ATM

Scenario Questions

1. The maximum speed of RRH's network is 10 Mbps because it is using 10Base2 cabling.

2. The maximum length of the three bus segments can't be greater than 185 meters because 10Base 2 is based on thinnet.

3. Bridges can help to reduce the amount of traffic on each of the three segments. This will improve network performance.

4. Switching to Cat 5 UTP will allow the use of hubs or switches, which will virtually eliminate the downtime associated with network reconfiguration. The use of switches will greatly reduce the problem of slow network response due to heavy network traffic. Cat 5 UTP supports speeds of up to 100 Mbps whereas the thinnet currently being used is limited to only 10 Mbps.

5. The physical topology will change from a bus topology to a star topology because UTP requires the use of a hub or a switch. The logical topology is still a bus.

6. NICs may have to be replaced if they don't support RJ45 connectors. Wall Plates, patch panels, hubs, or possibly switches will have to be added.

7. Frame relay is a faster WAN technology.

Resources

The following are suggested resources for additional information on the topics discussed in this chapter:

✦ Microsoft Press: *Networking Essentials, 1997*

✦ Lowe Doug; *Networking For Dummies*, Hungry Minds, 2000

✦ Glen Berg; *MCSE Networking Essentials*, New Riders, 1998

✦ techtarget.com's what is? computer term reference site. www.whatis.com

Understanding TCP/IP

EXAM OBJECTIVES

1. Describe the purpose of Request for Comments (RFC).

2. Define and describe the Internet architecture model and various Internet protocols.

3. Describe port numbers and their functions, including well-known and registered port numbers.

4. Explain IP addressing, address classes, and the concept of uniqueness.

5. Explain the use of private addresses.

6. Identify default subnet masks and explain their function.

7. Explain the routing process, including static versus dynamic routing, and interior versus exterior routing protocols.

8. Compare and contrast Routing Information Protocol (RIP) with Open Shortest Path First (OSPF).

9. Define the TCP/IP properties needed to configure a typical workstation.

10. Describe various diagnostic tools for troubleshooting TCP/IP networks.

CHAPTER PRE-TEST

1. What are the four layers of the Internet architecture model?

2. IP, ICMP, and ARP exist at what layer of the Internet architecture model?

3. Published documents that include detailed information about standardized Internet protocols are referred to as _____ _____ _____.

4. What TCP/IP protocol is used to transport HTML documents?

5. DNS is a protocol used to translate _____ to _____ addresses.

6. Which TCP/IP Transport Layer protocol provides session management?

7. _____ can be divided into two categories: Direct and indirect.

8. Routing Information Protocol (RIP) and Open Shortest Path First (OSPF) are examples of what?

9. Well-known port numbers lie between 0 and _____.

10. IP addresses are divided into _____ classes.

11. 220.120.12.1 is an example of a class _____ address.

12. What type of network address can't be routed on the Internet?

13. A subnet mask allows a node to distinguish between its _____ address and its _____ address.

14. What are the minimum three pieces of information that you must supply to a host in order for it to participate in a routed TCP/IP network?

15. Which TCP/IP diagnostic tool can you use to determine the communication path between two systems?

✦ Answers to these questions can be found at the end of the chapter. ✦

his chapter introduces you to the basics of the TCP/IP protocol suite. The discussion covers design aspects of TCP/IP, including the RFC standards process, TCP/IP suite structure, and common protocols. This chapter also introduces you to the basics of TCP/IP addressing, client setup, routing, and protocol diagnostic tools.

Introduction to TCP/IP

Originally developed in the early 1970s, TCP/IP gained worldwide acceptance in 1983 when it was officially adopted as the protocol suite of the Internet. This adoption occurred in large part because TCP/IP is an open standard routable protocol suite. The term *open standard* indicates that no single vendor controls its use or structure; therefore, any vendor can implement TCP/IP — making it an ideal protocol suite for heterogeneous networks like the Internet. The importance of this protocol suite is evidenced by the fact that most major network operating systems now include TCP/IP as their core protocol, including Novell. Because the Netware 5.0 product has moved away from its reliance on the IPX/SPX suite, Novell has introduced full TCP/IP use for both its Netware servers and their clients.

Request for Comments

Describe the purpose of Request for Comments (RFC).

Request for Comments (RFCs) are published standards documents that are maintained by the Internet Engineering Task Force (IETF). These documents establish specifications and standards for the various protocols and services that are currently being used on the Internet. Because TCP/IP is an open standard protocol suite, literally hundreds of vendors are developing and enhancing protocols and services for use with the suite. To ensure compatibility and acceptance, however, these new additions must be subjected to a thorough review and testing process before they can be considered an Internet standard. This review process begins by assigning both an *RFC number* and a *maturity state* to the protocol or service. The RFC number uniquely identifies the product or service, and the maturity state defines the level of acceptance that the protocol or service enjoys within the Internet community. The following is a list of the maturity states that currently exist in the RFC process:

✦ **Proposed:** The entry-level maturity specification. Internet specifications at this level are considered to be stable, well understood, and have been reviewed extensively by the Internet community. Further testing is recommended and this testing experience may result in a change or removal of the specification.

✦ **Draft:** These specifications are being seriously considered for full standard maturity. To obtain this specification, at least two independent and interoperable implementations of the protocol or service must have been developed and tested. Further testing is encouraged and results should be passed on to IETF. Specifications at this level may pass on to the final standard level or may drop back down to the proposed level.

✦ **Standard:** These specifications are considered to be an official standard; the specified protocol or service provides significant benefit to the Internet.

The following are additional non-standards track maturity levels that you should also be aware of:

✦ **Experimental:** New protocols and services are in a development and testing stage. These protocols may only be used in a controlled lab environment.

✦ **Historical:** Specifications for protocols or services that have been replaced by a more recent specification or have simply become obsolete.

✦ **Informational:** Specifications that are published for the general information of the Internet community. These specifications don't represent an Internet community consensus, recommendation, or standard.

Tip   For more information regarding RFCs and the standards maturity process, see `www.ietf.org/rfc/rfc2026.txt`.

TCP/IP Architecture

Objective   Define and describe the Internet architecture model and various Internet protocols.

TCP/IP is based on the four-layer Internet Architecture model. This model breaks up theTCP/IP communication process into the following four layers:

✦ Network Access Layer

✦ Internet Layer

✦ Transport Layer

✦ Application Layer

Note   It should be noted that there are several Internet architecture models in existence, such as the U.S. Department of Defenses (DOD) four-layer network model; however, the CIW Foundations exam focuses only on the Internet architecture model.

The relationship of Internet architecture layers to the OSI/RM layers is demonstrated in Figure 15-1.

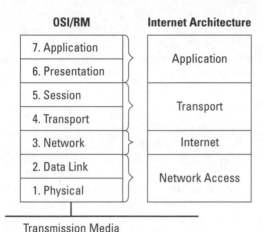

Figure 15-1: Mapping the four-layer Internet architecture model to the OSI/RM

Network Access Layer

The Network Access Layer of the Internet architecture model provides the same services as those found in the Physical and Data Link Layers of the OSI/RM. This layer is comprised of the physical connection to the network, the NIC, and its corresponding device drivers. For computers sending data, the Network Access Layer is responsible for accepting datagrams provided by the Internet Layer and transmitting them over the physical transmission medium. For computers receiving data, the Network Access Layer is responsible for accepting and formatting the incoming data transmissions. Accepted packets are passed up to the Internet Layer for further processing. The mechanics of the Network Access Layer are very much dependent on the underlying network architecture; for example, Ethernet, Token Ring, Frame Relay, and so on.

Internet Layer

The Internet Layer corresponds directly to the Network Layer of the OSI/RM. This layer is responsible for addressing and routing TCP/IP packets.

You need to be aware of several protocols that reside at this level. The following sections discuss these protocols:

Internet Protocol

According to RFC 791, the Internet Protocol (IP) provides two primary functions: addressing and fragmentation. The addressing function is responsible for two tasks: placing the appropriate address information on all packets to be sent, and choosing the appropriate route by which to send the packets. The fragmentation function is responsible for two tasks: determining the maximum packet size, also known as the *maximum transfer unit* (MTU), for the segment to which the computer is attached, and for fragmenting data packets when required.

Address Resolution Protocol

The Address Resolution Protocol (ARP) is used to find a MAC address associated with a given IP address. For example, if a computer sends a packet of data to an IP address in the same subnet, it will broadcast a request for the MAC address of the destination computer, as shown in Figure 15-2. All computers on the subnet hear the request, but only the computer whose IP address matches the request will respond with its MAC address. ARP is used by a device that has the IP address of another device that it wants to communicate with, but needs to find that device's MAC address. For additional information on ARP, consult RFC 826.

Figure 15-2: Use ARP to find a MAC address for a given IP address.

Reverse Address Resolution Protocol

Reverse Address Resolution Protocol (RARP) finds an IP address based on a particular MAC address. For example, diskless workstations will issue an RARP during their initial start up in order to obtain IP addresses. This RARP request contains the diskless workstation's MAC address. When a dynamic host configuration server sees the request, it typically sends the workstation the required information, as shown in Figure 15-3. You can find more information on RARP in RFC 903.

Figure 15-3: Use RARP to find an IP address for a given MAC address.

Internet Control Message Protocol

Internet Control Message Protocol (ICMP) is an error-reporting protocol typically used by routers and hosts. For example, if a router encounters problems when trying to determine the destination of a packet, it may issue an ICMP error packet informing the source of the problem, as shown in Figure 15-4.

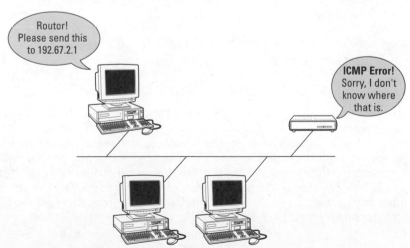

Figure 15-4: ICMP is an error-reporting protocol.

Several TCP/IP diagnostic utilities, such as Ping and Trace Route, rely on the ICMP protocol.

Cross-Reference   Ping and Trace Route are discussed in detail later on in this chapter.

Internet Group Management Protocol

IP supports three classifications of packets: Unicast, Broadcast, and Multicast. A Unicast packet is intended for only one recipient. A Broadcast packet is intended for any and all computers. A Multicast packet is intended for a group of computers (known as a *multicast group*). Internet Group Management Protocol (IGMP) is used to establish and maintain multicast groups.

Transport Layer

The Transport Layer of the Internet architecture model is responsible for providing communication sessions between computers. These sessions are supported by one of two transport layer protocols: TCP or UDP.

Transmission Control Protocol

Transmission Control Protocol (TCP), as defined by RFC 793, is a connection-oriented protocol; in other words, both the sending and receiving computers set up a communication session to govern the transfer of data. The two computers contact each other and negotiate the terms of the data transfer process. The intent of this negotiation is to ensure that all data being sent is complete and in sequence, and has no losses or duplications. TCP on the sending computer organizes the data to be sent into packets, each of which is assigned a unique sequence number. TCP on the receiving computer acknowledges all packets received and reassembles the data into its original form.

Note   The negotiation process that occurs in order to set up a TCP session is referred to as the "TCP three-way handshake."

User Datagram Protocol

User Datagram Protocol (UDP) is a connectionless transport protocol. A connectionless protocol does not require a session to be set up prior to the sending of data. UDP is considered to be an unreliable protocol because it makes no effort to ensure that all data arrives at the intended destination. The sending computer makes its best effort to send the data to the destination computer, but it does not expect nor desire any acknowledgement of the packets received by the client. The client machine must compensate for packets that don't arrive. Applications that use UDP typically transfer small amounts of data at a time. UDP is defined in RFC 768.

Application Layer

Corresponding with the Application, Presentation, and Session Layers of the OSI, the Application Layer of the Internet architecture model provides network access to applications. You need to be aware of several protocols that operate at this layer; the following sections detail these protocols.

Hypertext Transfer Protocol

As its name implies, Hypertext Transfer Protocol (HTTP) is used to transfer hypertext-based documents (HTML Web pages). Web browsers are typically the clients that make http requests for documents from http (Web) servers. HTTP is referred to as a *stateless protocol* because in HTTP 1.0, each page requested requires the setup of a separate protocol session. For large multi-page Web sites, the extra traffic required to set up these extra sessions is a potential bottleneck. To address this issue, HTTP 1.1 has been devised to use persistent connections with this protocol. HTTP 1.1 allows multiple page downloads to occur over a single connection, thus reducing the amount of traffic required. In order to benefit from HTTP 1.1, however, both the client and the server must support its use. HTTP is defined in RFCs 1945 and 2616.

File Transfer Protocol

File Transfer Protocol (FTP) is used to transfer files between client and server FTP applications. FTP requires TCP as a transport protocol to provide connection-oriented file transfers.

Many Web server applications contain an FTP server component that allows users running FTP client software to connect and transfer files. FTP servers require users to provide authentication information (user name and password) in order to access their services. In many cases, the FTP administrator will set up the server to accept the word *anonymous* as the user ID. This allows a user to connect without a unique user ID. Although many GUI FTP interfaces exist, most operating systems come with a simple command line FTP client utility, similar to the client in Windows 2000, as shown in Figure 15-5. In this example, a user on the client machine has logged on by using the "anonymous" user name and has requested and received a file called Game.exe from a server called ftp.olsen.com.

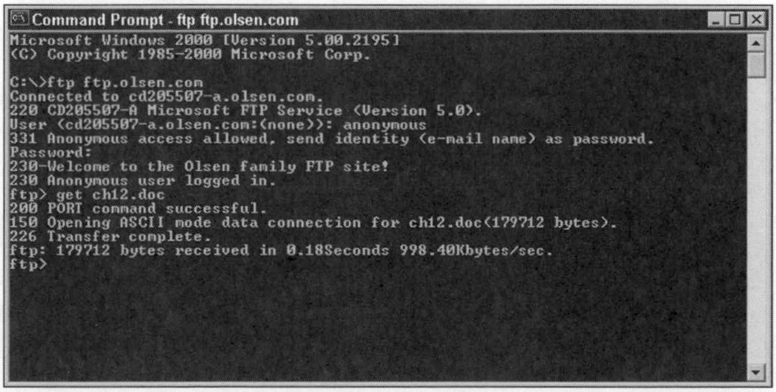

Figure 15-5: Windows 2000's FTP client

Trivial File Transfer Protocol

Trivial File Transfer Protocol (TFTP), similar to FTP, is used to transfer files between clients and servers. Unlike FTP, however, TFTP uses the UDP connectionless transport protocol and does not require nor support user authentication. These major differences make TFTP very small and simple. Diskless workstations and some routers often use this protocol to obtain configuration information during their startup processes. You can find the specifications for TFTP in RFC 1350.

Simple Mail Transfer Protocol

Simple Mail Transfer Protocol (SMTP) is one of the mail transfer protocols for the TCP/IP suite. SMTP sends e-mail from a client to a server or from one e-mail server to another. SMTP is typically used in conjunction with Post Office Protocol Version 3 (POP3) or Internet Message Access Protocol Version 4 (IMAP4). Mail client software typically uses SMTP to send mail and POP3 or IMAP4 to receive mail. When a mail server receives mail sent through SMTP, it typically stores it for later retrieval by the recipient. The recipient typically uses either a POP3 or an IMAP4 client to obtain this stored mail.

Cross-Reference   See Chapter 3 for more information on e-mail.

Network News Transfer Protocol

Network News Transfer Protocol (NNTP) is the protocol used to post, read, and distribute USENET news articles. USENET is a worldwide bulletin board system distributed over thousands of NNTP servers; most Internet service providers provide access to this system. USENET contains literally thousands of discussion-type bulletin boards that cover almost any topic you can imagine. Using an NNTP client application, users can read and contribute articles to bulletin boards of their choosing. Figure 15-6 shows Microsoft Outlook Express being used as an NNTP client.

Domain Name System

Domain Name System (DNS) is an Internet-related service that translates human-friendly computer host names into IP addresses. For example, when you type a name, such as `www.w3c.org`, into the address bar of your browser, your computer must resolve this name to an IP address. Your computer needs the IP address in order to route the information to the server hosting the Web service. One of the methods that your computer uses to resolve this IP address is to contact a DNS server and query it for the `www.w3c.org`'s address. The DNS server typically reacts to this request by finding the requested IP address and returning the result to your machine. After your machine has received this IP address, it can communicate with the Web server and request the desired home page. The DNS service and protocol are defined in RFCs 1034 and 1035.

Cross-Reference   DNS is discussed in more detail in Chapter 16.

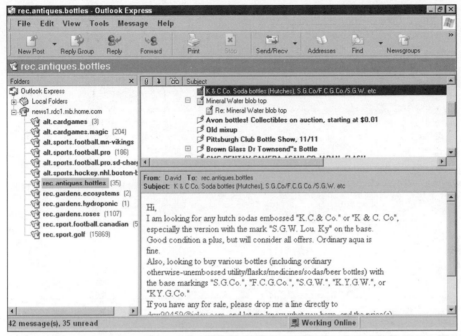

Figure 15-6: Outlook Express as an NNTP client

Simple Network Management Protocol

Simple Network Management Protocol (SNMP) is used to manage and monitor TCP/IP-oriented network devices. Many hardware vendors produce devices that allow administrators to manage them remotely from a management utility by using SNMP. For example, if a router supports SNMP, then an administrator can contact the router by using an SNMP management utility and query it for information regarding traffic, routing, errors, and other information. In some instances, it may even be possible for an administrator to use SNMP to reconfigure the router. RFC 1157 defines SNMP.

Telnet

Telnet is a protocol used to support terminal emulation sessions from a client to a server. Through a telnet session, clients can log on to a remote computer and carry out commands as if they were sitting at that computer in front of the server. Figure 15-7 shows an example of a user using Windows 98's telnet client to connect to a Linux server. Telnet is defined in RFC 854.

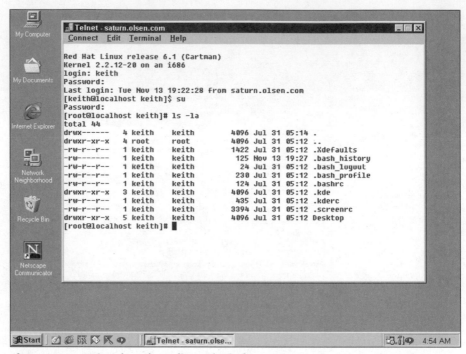

Figure 15-7: Using the telnet client of Windows 98 to connect to a Linux server

Bootstrap Protocol

Bootstrap Protocol (BOOTP) is an Internet protocol designed to allow a diskless workstation to discover its own configuration information. This information includes its IP address, the address of a server host, and the name of a file on that server host that can be executed to initialize an operating system for the client. BOOTP is defined in RFC 951.

Dynamic Host Configuration Protocol

Dynamic Host Configuration Protocol (DHCP), which is based on BOOTP, is used to assign IP addresses to hosts on a network. A DHCP client is a computer that hasn't been pre-assigned TCP/IP addressing information. During initialization, the client broadcasts a message across the network requesting IP information from a DHCP server. After a DHCP server sees the broadcast, it will respond with an available IP address, as well as other TCP/IP configuration information for the client. This other information may include a DNS server address, a router address, and a large list of other information for the client to use while participating on the network. For more information regarding DHCP, see RFC 2131.

Port numbers

Describe port numbers and their functions, including well-known and registered port numbers.

Many organizations have a single multi-use server that offers several services for a variety of clients. These offered services may include HTTP, FTP, SMTP, POP3, and SNMP—just to name a few. When a packet arrives at one of these multi-use servers from a client, it must contain information that directs the packet to the intended service. This information is kept in the Transport Layer of the packet and is referred to as a *port number*. Port numbers are 16-bit numbers that range from 0 up to 65535, and are used by both UDP and TCP to distinguish their various services.

The Transport Layer on a client computer places both a destination port number and a source port number into all packets intended for a particular service on a server. The destination port number directs the packet to the appropriate service on the server, and the source port number is used to indicate to which port on the client the server is to send replies. Figure 15-8 depicts a client computer sending an http request to port 80 of the server; it has indicated a port of 1672 as the source port. Therefore, the server response packets are sent from port 80 on the server to port 1672 of the client.

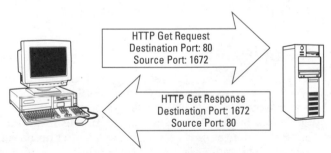

Figure 15-8: Data communication using port numbers

Reserved well-known port numbers

The port numbers from 0 to 1023 are referred to as *well-known ports*. These well-known ports are used to represent well-known TCP/IP services. These port numbers can only be used by a system, a kernel level process, or by any program that is run by a privileged user, such as an administrator in Windows NT or root in UNIX. The Internet Corporation for Assigned Names and Numbers (ICAAN) is responsible for assigning all well-known numbers.

Note   ICAAN has taken this responsibility over from the Internet Assigned Numbers Authority (IANA).

The following is a partial list of well-known port numbers used in TCP/IP:

- ✦ FTP = ports 20 and 21
- ✦ SMTP = port 25
- ✦ DNS = port 53
- ✦ HTTP = port 80
- ✦ POP3 = port 110
- ✦ Telnet = port 23

Registered port numbers

Port numbers from 1024 to 65535 are considered non-privileged. That is, these numbers are not controlled by ICAAN, and any process or service can use them.

When requesting services, client computers pick their source ports from the list of registered port numbers. These source ports are referred to as *ephemeral* or *temporary* ports.

In the Real World The CIW course material lists ports 1024 and above as reserved ports. However, the ICANN Web site lists ports 1024 to 49151 as registered ports and 49152 to 65535 as dynamic or private ports.

Multiplexing/demultiplexing

To fully understand the Internet architecture model and how it is used in the construction of a data packet, you should be familiar with the concept of *multiplexing*. Multiplexing describes how the protocols from various layers of the Internet architecture are combined to build a complete data packet. As data moves from the client application on the sending computer down through the Internet architecture, each layer adds header information intended for the corresponding layer on the receiving computer. As a result, the completed packet consists of several layers of protocol information. Each layer is then processed by the Internet architecture layers on the receiving computer.

Figure 15-9 demonstrates an example of the multiplexing process. This figure shows the various Internet architecture layers and their associated protocols multiplexed into a single data packet. This particular packet represents a simplified version of an HTTP get request used to request a Web page from a Web server. The top layer of the packet contains an HTTP header, which contains information regarding which page is requested from the Web server service on the destination computer. A TCP header is added to the packet to ensure that the request is received by the correct service on the Web server and that any response is directed to the correct application on the client computer. An IP header containing both the destination IP address and the source IP address is added to the packet to ensure that the packet can be directed to the correct computer and that the computer knows where to send a response, if any. Finally, the bottom header contains the Ethernet protocol used to specify both source and destination physical MAC addressing.

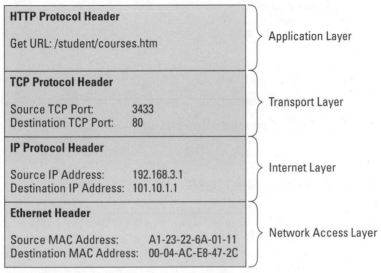

Figure 15-9: A fully multiplexed data packet

Demultiplexing refers to the method that the receiving computer uses to process the incoming packet.

1. The Network Access Layer examines the MAC addressing information to determine if the packet is truly destined for that computer.

2. After confirmation, the packet is passed up to the Internet Work Layer. The Internet Work Layer examines the destination IP address to ensure that the packet is truly intended for the computer and that no further routing is required.

3. The packet is passed up to the Transport Layer, where either TCP or UDP examines the destination port number to determine which service should receive the information.

4. The packet is passed up to the service that is using the appropriate application protocol.

5. The Application Layer retrieves the Web page query from the packet and passes it to the Web server.

Internet Addressing

Objective

Explain IP addressing, address classes, and the concept of uniqueness.

In order for a computer or any other network device to participate on a TCP/IP-based network, it must be assigned a unique Internet Protocol (IP) address. The IP address is required to uniquely identify the host. For a device participating on the Internet, the choice of address must be carefully considered because the address must be valid and unique to the entire world. To ensure this, the Internet Corporation for Assigned Names and Numbers (ICANN) controls the assignment of IP addresses.

Tip

For more information on ICANN and its services, visit www.icann.org.

The structure of an IP address

IP addresses are written in *dotted decimal notation* (also referred to as *dotted quad notation*). Using this notation, addresses are written as a series of four numbers separated by periods, such as 192.23.220.45. These four numbers, or *octets*, all fall in the range from 0 to 255. In fact, the name "octet" is derived from the fact that each represents one eight-bit (binary) number. Together, they form one complete 32-bit address. For example, the preceding IP Address can be expressed as the following 32-bit number: 10001001.00010111.11011100.0010110.

Exam Tip

You won't be responsible for converting an IP address to binary on the exam.

The IP address is used to define which network a host belongs to, and to uniquely identify the host on that network. To facilitate this process, the address consists of two components—a network ID and a host ID.

Network ID

The first part of any host's IP address is its network ID. The network ID identifies to which network, or more specifically, to which network *segment* a particular host belongs. All computers in the same network segment must have the same network ID, just as every person living on the same street has the same street name in their mailing address. No two networks within the same Internet work may share the same network ID.

Host ID

The last portion of an IP address is its host ID. The host ID is used to uniquely identify a particular host on a network segment, just as a house number uniquely identifies a house on a street.

Network address assignment example

To better understand the concepts of host IDs and network IDs, consider Figure 15-10. This example shows you a network divided into three network segments. Each segment has been assigned a unique network ID and each host has been assigned a unique host ID within their respective segments. Each computer's IP address is the combination of its network address and its host address. Computer A has an IP address of 75.0.0.10, Computer B has an IP address of 75.10.10.4, Computer C has an IP address of 205.12.1.5, and so on.

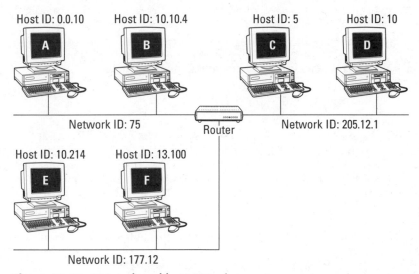

Figure 15-10: Network and host ID assignment

This example demonstrates that the networks have been assigned network addresses of different lengths; for example, Network Segment 1 was assigned network address 75, Segment 2 was assigned 205.12.1, and Segment 3 was assigned 177.12. This is perfectly acceptable as long as they are all unique and the hosts within each network have unique host IDs within their respective segments.

Internet address classes

Internet addresses are grouped into five classes: A, B, C, D, and E. These classes give some order to the assignment of Internet addresses. When applying for valid Internet addresses, an organization's size determines which class of network address it will obtain. An extremely large organization (over 16 million hosts) may be assigned a Class A network address, a medium organization (up to 65,534 hosts) may be assigned a Class B network address, and a relatively small organization (254 hosts or less) may be assigned a Class C network address. After a network address is assigned, no other organization is permitted to use the same network address.

Exam Tip   You must be able to identify a node's network class given its IP address.

Class A

Class A addresses are reserved for only the largest of organizations. When using a Class A address, only the first octet of any given IP address is used to determine the network ID, as shown in Figure 15-11. The three remaining octets determine the host ID. There are 127 Class A network addresses—each of which can have up to 16,777,214 hosts. With such a limited number of Class A network addresses allocated for the entire world, it should not surprise you that currently, none are available.

Figure 15-11: In a Class A network address, only the first octet is used to determine the network ID.

Class A addresses are easy to recognize because the first octet of the address always falls between 1 and 126. An address starting with 127 is also considered to be a Class A address; however, this Class A address has been reserved for testing purposes and is not assigned to any organization.

Class B

Class A addresses are reserved for medium to large organizations that can have up to 65,534 hosts each. A Class B address uses the first two octets of an IP address to determine the network ID and the remaining two octets determine the host ID, as shown in Figure 15-12.

Figure 15-12: In a Class B address, the first and second octets are used to determine the network ID.

The first octet in a Class B network address always falls between 128 and 191. This provides for 16,384 networks—each of which can have up to 65,534 hosts.

Class C

Class C addresses are reserved for relatively small companies. A Class C address uses the first three octets of an IP address to determine the network address, and only the fourth octet is used to identify the host ID, as shown in Figure 15-13.

201.38.12.100 **Figure 15-13:** In a Class C address, the first three octets
are used to determine the network ID.

Network ID   Host ID

The first octet in a Class C address always falls between 192 and 223. This allows for
2,097,152 networks — each of which can contain 254 hosts.

Class D

Class D addresses are a special class of addresses that have been set aside for a
form of network communication referred to as *multicasting*. Multicasts allow a computer to send a single packet of data to a group of computers. With multicasting, a
computer sends a packet of data to a multicast address, and client machines participating in the multicast run multicast client software. This software allows the
clients to recognize the destination multicast address as if the address were its
own. Nodes may share a common multicast address, forming *multicast groups*. Each
node can belong to several multicast groups. Each host, however, must still have a
unique IP address.

Class D addresses are never assigned to networks. You can easily recognize a Class
D address because the first octet always falls in the range of 224 to 239.

Class E

Class E addresses have been reserved for future use. You can easily recognize them
because their first octet always falls in the range of 240 to 247.

IP address class summary

Table 15-1 summarizes the five Internet address classes:

Table 15-1 IP Address Classes				
Address Class	**1st Octet Range**	**Octets used for Network ID**	**Number of Networks**	**Hosts per Network**
A	1-127*	1	126*	16,777,214
B	128-191	2	16,384	65,534
C	192-223	3	2,097,152	254
D	224-239	-	-	-
E	240-247	-	-	-

* The network ID of 127 is reserved for diagnostic testing.

Rules for assigning IP addresses

You must follow a few important rules when choosing an IP address for a host. The following sections outline these rules.

Rule 1 — Valid class addresses

Only addresses included in Classes A, B, or C may be assigned to a host. For example, the address of 238.2.3.200 can't be assigned to a network computer because it is a Class D address.

Rule 2 — Octet range

Each octet or byte of an IP address must fall between 0 and 255. For example, the IP address of 10.300.10.0 is invalid because its second octet is over 255.

Rule 3 — Broadcast addresses

Neither the network ID nor the host ID of any address may be all 255s because the address 255 has been reserved for network broadcast packets.

The following addresses are all invalid because they break Rule 3:

✦ **255.255.255.255**

   Reason: This address is reserved for limited broadcasts.

✦ **13.255.255.255**

   Reason: This is a Class A address; therefore, the host ID is all 255s.

✦ **152.10.255.255**

   Reason: This is a Class B address; therefore, the host ID is all 255s.

✦ **221.6.4.255**

   Reason: This is a Class C address; therefore, the host ID is all 255s.

Tip   When deciding whether an IP address breaks this rule, always look at the network class to which the address belongs, and then see whether the host ID is all 255s.

You should be familiar with the following four types of network broadcasts:

✦ **Limited Broadcast.** A *limited broadcast* is a packet sent to the address 255.255.255.255. All computers seeing a packet destined to this address will process the packet. This type of broadcast is usually contained within the segment of the network from which it originated because most routers don't pass this form of broadcast.

✦ **Net-Directed Broadcast.** A *net-directed broadcast* is a broadcast directed to all hosts on a network. For example, if a network has a Class C network ID of 212.13.4, then the net-directed broadcast is 212.13.4.255. If a network has a Class A network ID of 67, then the net-directed broadcast is 67.255.255.255.

✦ **Subnet-directed Broadcast.** A *subnet-directed broadcast* is a packet sent to a particular subnet within a larger network ID. Network IDs are commonly divided into different subnet IDs in large networks. For example, if the Class B address 172.10 was assigned to an organization, they may then assign portions of that address to different geographic locations within their Internetwork. The address 172.10.1 may be assigned to New York, 172.10.2 to Chicago, 172.10.3 to Vancouver, and so on. Therefore, a packet sent to 172.10.2.255 is a subnet-directed broadcast directed to all computers in Chicago.

✦ **All-Subnets-Directed Broadcast.** A broadcast across all subnets of a network is considered to be an *all-subnets directed broadcast*. Commonly replaced by multicasts, this type of broadcast is now obsolete.

Rule 4 – Special case addresses

The host ID or the network ID portion of an IP address can't consist entirely of zeros. The use of all zeros in the host portion of an address signifies a network address. For example, 155.15.0.0 is a Class B network address and therefore, can't be assigned to a node.

Exam Tip   Zeros are allowed in an address as long as the entire host or network address is not all zeros. For example, 155.15.0.13 and 167.0.21.0 are both considered valid.

All zeros in a network address can be used to denote a particular host. For example, in a Class B network, a host with an address of 165.4.14.200 can be referred to as host 0.0.14.200 on that network. However, you can't assign an address by using this form.

An IP address of all zeros (0.0.0.0) is a special-case address used by DHCP and BOOTP client computers prior to obtaining a valid address. This address allows the client to request broadcast requests for IP addressing information. In a device's routing table, this address is used to define a Default Route.

Note   Routing, Routing tables, and Default routes are discussed in detail later in this chapter.

Rule 5 – Loopback address

The network ID of 127 can't be assigned to a network because 127 is used to perform diagnostic testing of a node (as discussed previously in this chapter). The address of 127.0.0.1 is reserved as a *loopback address*. Packets of data sent to this address by a node are redirected back to the same machine. For example, if you open a Web browser and enter `http://127.0.0.1` in its address bar, the browser will attempt to contact the Web server that is running on your own computer. By using the 127.0.0.1 address, the packet is redirected back into the machine before it reaches the network, which means testing can occur without being physically attached to a network.

Be prepared to determine the validity of any IP address.

Private IP addressing

Objective Explain the use of private addresses

ICANN and its predecessor, Internet Assigned Numbers Authority (IANA), have reserved three ranges of IP addresses for use by those organizations that want to set up private networks.

The following ranges are reserved:

✦ 10.0.0.0 to 10.255.255.255

✦ 172.16.0.0 to 17.31.255.255

✦ 192.168.0.0 to 192.168.255.255

The significance of these ranges is that they are non-routable on the Internet. Internet backbone routers are configured to drop any data packet with a destination address that falls within these ranges.

ICANN recommends that organizations use these addresses if they want to set up a network for which Internet connectivity is not required, or if they want internal networked computers to connect to the Internet through a mediating gateway, such as a proxy server or an Application Layer gateway.

Cross-Reference For more information about proxy servers and Application Layer gateways, refer to Chapter 18.

You gain the following benefits by using reserved IP addresses:

✦ **Network flexibility.** Because an organization that uses a private network address can choose any size private network address, the network design has much more flexibility.

✦ **Security.** Host machines that use private addresses are not reachable directly through the Internet; therefore, they are much more difficult to compromise remotely.

✦ **Conservation of Internet addresses.** An organization using private addresses is not required to register its network addresses. This conserves the now limited number of Internet addresses available.

Be able to recognize the private network address ranges and be able to state the benefits gained by using them.

IP Version 6

Prior to this point, this chapter has addressed the features of IP version 4 (IPv4). A new version of this protocol, IPv6, is currently under review by the IETF standards committees. IPv6 will address some of the fundamental problems that are now being encountered with the current implementation of IP. The most pressing of these problems is addressing. IPv4 uses a 32-bit address scheme that yields approximately 4.2 billion unique addresses. Although this may seem like a lot of addresses, almost all of them have already been assigned and there is danger of running out. IPv6 uses a 128-bit address scheme that will support trillions of addresses. In fact, the number is very close to 340,282,366,920,938,000,000,000,000,000,000,000,000.

Other benefits of IPv6 include improved security, simplified administration, elimination of many routing related issues, and backwards-compatibility with IPv4.

It is estimated that IPv6 will be fully implemented between 2005 and 2015. However, several pilot implementations of IPv6 are already in existence today, and many vendors, such as Microsoft, have already built IPv6 support into their products.

IPv6 is also commonly known as *IPng* or *IP next generation*.

Subnet Masks

Identify default subnet masks and explain their function.

When configuring a computer for use with TCP/IP, not only must you assign an IP address, you should also assign a *subnet mask* (also referred to as a *net mask*). The subnet mask informs the computer which part of its IP address is the network ID and which part is the host ID.

As with an IP address, a subnet mask is a 32-bit number. Each bit of the subnet mask has a one-to-one correspondence with each bit of the IP address. A bit can only be 1 or 0, and if a bit in the subnet mask is 1, then the corresponding bit in the IP address is considered part of the network address; otherwise, it is considered to be part of the host address. For example, consider a computer with an IP address of 192.168.7.10 and a subnet mask of 255.255.255.0. With this subnet mask, the first 24 bits of the complete 32-bit subnet mask are 1s, so the first 24 bits or first three octets of the network address are considered to be the computer's network address. In other words, the network address is 192.168.7.

It is vital that a computer know its network address. When sending a packet of data, a computer will examine the destination network address to see if it matches its own. If the network addresses match, then the computer knows that it doesn't have to send the packet through a router.

Each of the three major network classes (A, B, and C) has a default subnet mask, as shown in Table 15-2.

Table 15-2
Class Default Subnet Masks

Class	Subnet Mask
A	255.0.0.0
B	255.255.0.0
C	255.255.255.0

Note   Classes D and E don't have associated subnet masks because the addresses in these classes are never assigned to hosts.

Routing and Routing Protocols

Objective   Explain the routing process, including static versus dynamic routing, and interior versus exterior routing protocols.

A host must be configured with three pieces of information in order to participate in a routed TCP/IP network environment. As this chapter has previously explained, the first two pieces of information are an IP address and a subnet mask. The third piece of required information is the *default gateway*. The default gateway is the IP address of a router to which a host can send packets if that host determines that the destination of those packets lies beyond the local subnet. To fully understand how and when a node uses the default gateway, you need to understand the basics of *routing*.

Routing is best described as the process that determines the path down which packets are sent in order to reach their final destinations. Critical to the routing process is the Internet Layer of the Internet architecture model and its associated protocol IP.

Routing has two general forms, direct and indirect, which are discussed in the following sections.

Direct routing

A computer uses direct routing when it needs to send a packet of information to another computer that is located on the same physical network, as shown in Figure 15-14. In this situation, a router is not required. A computer's NIC will pick up a packet of information if the packet has the NIC's MAC address listed as the destination. With direct routing, the sending computer must place the destination computer's MAC address onto the data packet. To accomplish this, the computer broadcasts a request (using the ARP protocol) for the MAC address of the destination computer. All computers on the subnet hear the request, but only the computer with the matching IP address in the request will respond with its MAC address. After it is obtained, the destination MAC address is placed into the Network Layer of the packet, which is then sent on its way.

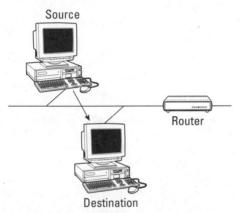

Figure 15-14: With direct routing, the source and destination nodes are on the same network segment.

Indirect routing

Indirect routing occurs between sending and receiving computers that are located on two different networks, as shown in Figure 15-15. In this example, the sending computer places the MAC address of the router onto the packet to be sent. The router, seeing its own MAC address on the packet, picks it up, analyzes the destination address, and routes the packet on to the appropriate destination network.

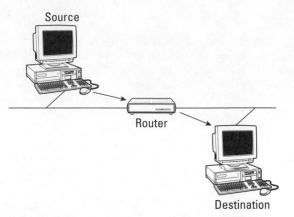

Figure 15-15: With indirect routing, the source and destination nodes are located on different network segments. Packets must be routed through the router.

Routing tables

When a router obtains a packet of data through indirect routing, it must determine the packet's intended destination. To accomplish this, the router consults its routing table. A routing table is a list of known networks, the path to those networks, and an indication of the location of those networks in relation to the router — often listed as a hop count. A *hop count* is a count of the number of routers that must be passed through in order to reach the final destination network. Many routers use this value to decide which route to use when multiple routes to the same network exist. A router that does so will typically choose the route with the lowest hop count. Figure 15-16 shows an example of information that is kept in a routing table; in this diagram, you can see a portion of the routing tables of three routers that are interconnecting four networks.

Categories of routers

Routers fall into one of two categories — static or dynamic. These categories indicate how a router's routing tables are built and maintained.

Statically configured routers

Static routers manually create and maintain routing tables. If a new network or route is added to the network, all static routers must have their routing tables manually updated in order to send packets to this network. In small, fairly stable networks, manually updating may not present a big problem, but the task of maintaining static routing tables for large networks may be overwhelming.

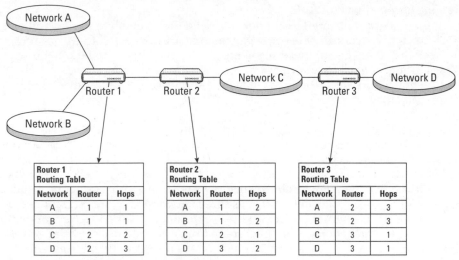

Figure 15-16: Routing information tables

Dynamically configured routers

 Compare and contrast Routing Information Protocol (RIP) with Open Shortest Path First (OSPF).

Dynamic routers build their routing tables by exchanging routing information with other routers. If a router detects a new route that has been added to the network, it will communicate with other routers and share this information. A router will also communicate with other routers when it learns that a route to a network is no longer available. Dynamic routers don't require manual intervention when network topologies change (one of the advantages that they offer).

Dynamic routers use routing protocols to communicate with each other. These protocols are divided into two classifications: exterior routing protocols and interior routing protocols.

Exterior routing protocols share routing information with routers that are external to an organization. The two most common exterior routing protocols are Exterior Gateway Protocol (EGP) and Border Gateway Protocol (BGP).

 The exam won't ask you for specifics of these two protocols. However, you should know the definition of "Exterior Routing Protocol" and be able to list EGP and BGP as examples.

Interior routing protocols share routing information with routers that are located within an organization's network. You should be aware of two common interior routing protocols: Routing Information Protocol (RIP) and Open Shortest Path First (OSPF).

Routing Information Protocol

Routers that are configured to support RIP send their complete routing tables every thirty seconds across all network segments that are connected to the router. Routers that share any of these segments receive the tables, update their own tables to reflect any new information, and then broadcast their tables across all network segments to which they are connected — thus propagating any changes across the network.

When a single destination has multiple routes, RIP routers always use the route with the lowest hop count to determine the best route. The disadvantage of this method of route selection is that it does not take into account available bandwidth or network conditions. As a result, a route over slow or congested network lines with a low hop count may be chosen over a faster route with a larger hop count. Figure 15-17, for example, demonstrates three networks that are interconnected in a mesh topology. If a packet of data is being sent from Network A to Network B, RIP router 1 will always choose the direct route from A to B across the relatively slow 56k line instead of the high speed T1 connections from A to C and from C to B.

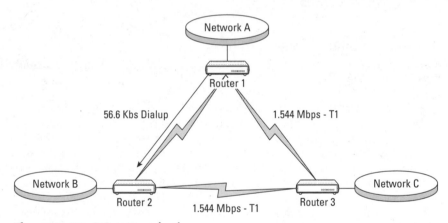

Figure 15-17: RIP route selection

RIP is an ideal protocol for small to medium networks because it requires very little administrative effort to maintain. In larger networks, however, RIP is less desirable because of the following factors:

✦ Frequent broadcasting of large routing tables

✦ Inability to perform variable route selection

✦ Absence of security

✦ Not allowing routes of over 15 hops

You can find more information on the two versions of RIP — RIPv1 and RIPv2 — in RFC 1058 and RFC 2453, respectively.

Open Shortest Path First

The interior routing protocol, OSPF, addresses many of the deficiencies of RIP. To reduce network traffic, OSPF only sends routing table update messages when changes actually occur — and even then, it only sends the changes (not the entire routing table).

A second OSPF advantage is variable route selection. When a destination network has two or more routes, you can configure OSPF routers to choose the best route, given the network conditions. You can also configure OSPF routers to perform load balancing by alternating traffic down the various routes to evenly distribute data across all segments.

Additional advantages offered by OSPF include the following:

✦ The ability to limit the transfer of routing table information to trusted routers only

✦ Acceptance of large route paths (greater than 15 hops)

✦ Support for network partitioning

OSPF is defined in RFC 2328.

Configuring a TCP/IP Client

Objective

Define the TCP/IP properties needed to configure a typical workstation.

A host must be properly configured in order to participate in a TCP/IP network environment. At a minimum, the host must have an IP address and a subnet mask. In a routed environment, a default gateway is also required. It's also common to configure additional information that allows the host to take full advantage of services that are offered on the network. Some additional settings follow:

✦ **Host name:** All hosts participating in a DNS-enabled network are required to have assigned host names. This enables both users and applications to locate the computer based on easy-to-remember names rather than hard-to-remember IP addresses. For example, a person can easily remember that an e-mail server is called "mail" rather than trying to recall an IP address of 192.134.201.211.

✦ **Domain name:** This is the name of the Internet domain to which the computer belongs. For example, if a mail server belongs to a company called "Keen Games, Inc.," then it is very likely that the host belongs to the Internet domain name `keengamesinc.com`. A host name can be combined with a domain name to form a fully qualified domain name (FQDN). For example, an FQDN for the Keen Games mail server may be `mail.keengamesinc.com`.

✦ **DNS server:** The IP address of a DNS server that provides host name resolution services for the client. Most clients allow the entry of IP addresses of at least two DNS servers — a preferred DNS server and a backup DNS server.

✦ **NetBIOS name:** On a Microsoft Windows-based network, all computers are required to have a NetBIOS name for identification purposes.

✦ **WINS server:** The IP address of a Windows Internet Name server (WINS) that provides NetBIOS name to IP address resolution.

The assignment of TCP/IP information for a host can be accomplished in two ways: statically and dynamically.

Static host configuration

When using static host configuration, you are responsible for manually configuring the TCP/IP addressing information at a host. In a Windows 95, 98, or ME computer, for example, this manual configuration involves accessing the Network icon in the control panel and completing the TCP/IP property pages, as shown in Figure 15-18.

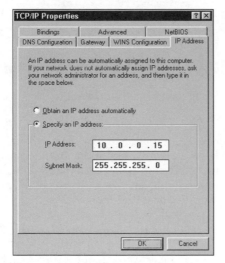

Figure 15-18: A TCP/IP Property configuration screen in Windows 2000

In a small network environment, static host configuration is a valid option; however, as a network grows in size, static host configuration may require extensive administration. For example, a change in the DNS server address requires a visit to each host to change the appropriate settings.

Dynamic host configuration

Dynamic host configuration simplifies the assignment of TCP/IP information in a large network environment. This form of configuration requires the use of a Dynamic Host Configuration Protocol Server (DHCP) and host machines that are set to obtain IP address information automatically, as shown in Figure 15-19.

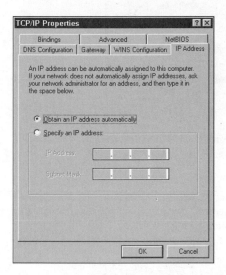

Figure 15-19: Configuring a client for dynamic host configuration

TCP/IP Diagnostic Tools

Describe various diagnostic tools for troubleshooting TCP/IP networks.

The following sections explore several diagnostic utilities that you can use to troubleshoot and optimize a TCP/IP-based network.

PING

Packet Internet Groper, or *ping*, is a simple utility that tests connectivity between systems in a TCP/IP environment by sending an ICMP echo request packet to a destination IP address. The node that receives the packet normally responds with an ICMP echo reply packet. If the sender receives the reply, then connectivity between the two systems must exist.

The following is the syntax of the ping command:

```
ping ip_address
```

Figure 15-20 shows an example of the ping utility successfully contacting a computer at IP address 192.168.2.1.

```
Command Prompt                                                _ □ X
Microsoft Windows 2000 [Version 5.00.2195]
(C) Copyright 1985-2000 Microsoft Corp.

C:\>ping 192.168.2.1

Pinging 192.168.2.1 with 32 bytes of data:

Reply from 192.168.2.1: bytes=32 time<10ms ITL=127
Reply from 192.168.2.1: bytes=32 time<10ms ITL=127
Reply from 192.168.2.1: bytes=32 time<10ms ITL=127
Reply from 192.168.2.1: bytes=32 time<10ms ITL=127

Ping statistics for 192.168.3.1:
    Packets: Sent = 4, Received = 4, Lost = 0 (0% loss),
Approximate round trip times in milli-seconds:
    Minimum = 0ms, Maximum =  0ms, Average =  0ms

C:\>
```

Figure 15-20: A successful connectivity test using the ping utility

An unsuccessful ping is an indication of source and destination communication problems. Pinging additional known operational computers or routers may give an indication as to where the problem lies. Refer to Figure 15-21.

```
Command Prompt                                                _ □ X
Microsoft Windows 2000 [Version 5.00.2195]
(C) Copyright 1985-2000 Microsoft Corp.

C:\>ping 192.168.2.23

Pinging 192.168.2.23 with 32 bytes of data:

Request timed out.
Request timed out.
Request timed out.
Request timed out.

Ping statistics for 192.168.2.23:
    Packets: Sent = 4, Received = 0, Lost = 4 (100% loss),
Approximate round trip times in milli-seconds:
    Minimum = 0ms, Maximum =  0ms, Average =  0ms

C:\>
```

Figure 15-21: An unsuccessful connectivity test using the ping utility

Caution

An unsuccessful ping doesn't always indicate a problem. For example, many organizations, for security reasons, have configured their network devices to not respond to external ping requests. Microsoft is one example. If you ping the address www.microsoft.com you won't get a response, but if you open a Web browser and attempt the same address, you will likely be successful.

Trace route utility

The trace route utility is used to show the network route taken by data between a source and a destination computer.

The syntax of this command varies from operating system to operating system. For example, in UNIX, the syntax is the following:

```
traceroute ip_address
```

In Microsoft Windows-based operating systems, the trace route syntax is the following:

```
tracert ip_address
```

The output of this command shows a list of all the routers and computers that packets pass through on the way to their destinations. For example, take a look at the output of the tracert command from my home computer to www. hungryminds.com, as shown in Figure 15-22. This example shows responses from 12 different machines (hops), all of which were involved in passing information from my computer to the Web server at Hungry Minds, Inc.

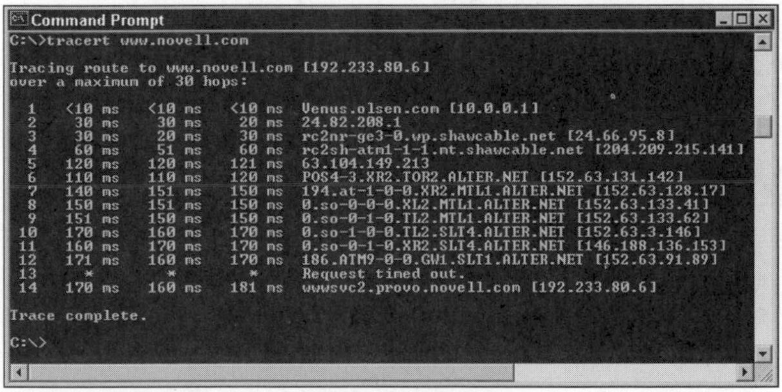

```
Command Prompt                                                    _ □ ×
C:\>tracert www.novell.com

Tracing route to www.novell.com [192.233.80.6]
over a maximum of 30 hops:

  1    <10 ms    <10 ms    <10 ms  Venus.olsen.com [10.0.0.1]
  2     30 ms     30 ms     20 ms  24.82.208.1
  3     30 ms     20 ms     30 ms  rc2nr-ge3-0.vp.shawcable.net [24.66.95.8]
  4     60 ms     51 ms     60 ms  rc2sh-atm1-1-1.nt.shawcable.net [204.209.215.141]
  5    120 ms    120 ms    121 ms  63.104.149.213
  6    110 ms    110 ms    120 ms  POS4-3.XR2.TOR2.ALTER.NET [152.63.131.142]
  7    140 ms    151 ms    150 ms  194.at-1-0-0.XR2.MTL1.ALTER.NET [152.63.128.17]
  8    150 ms    151 ms    150 ms  0.so-0-0-0.XL2.MTL1.ALTER.NET [152.63.133.41]
  9    151 ms    150 ms    150 ms  0.so-0-1-0.TL2.MTL1.ALTER.NET [152.63.133.62]
 10    170 ms    160 ms    170 ms  0.so-1-0-0.TL2.SLT4.ALTER.NET [152.63.3.146]
 11    160 ms    170 ms    170 ms  0.so-0-1-0.XR2.SLT4.ALTER.NET [146.188.136.153]
 12    171 ms    160 ms    170 ms  186.ATM9-0-0.GW1.SLT1.ALTER.NET [152.63.91.89]
 13     *         *         *      Request timed out.
 14    170 ms    160 ms    181 ms  wwwsvc2.provo.novell.com [192.233.80.6]

Trace complete.

C:\>
```

Figure 15-22: The tracert utility in Windows 2000

The trace route utility can be an effective troubleshooting tool when attempting to locate the source of network connectivity problems.

Windows IP configuration utility — `ipconfig`

The Windows IP configuration (`ipconfig`) utility displays current TCP/IP configuration information for a Windows NT/2000 host. The syntax of `ipconfig` is the following:

```
ipconfig {/option}
```

 The UNIX equivalent of the `ipconfig` is `ifconfig`.

In its simplest form, typing `ipconfig` at a command prompt yields information regarding the current IP address, subnet mask, and default gateway, as shown in Figure 15-23.

```
C:\WINDOWS\System32\cmd.exe                                          _ □ ×

C:\>ipconfig

Windows IP Configuration

Ethernet adapter Local Area Connection:

        Connection-specific DNS Suffix  . : Olsen.com
        IP Address. . . . . . . . . . . . : 10.0.0.201
        Subnet Mask . . . . . . . . . . . : 255.255.255.0
        Default Gateway . . . . . . . . . : 10.0.0.1

C:\>
```

Figure 15-23: Default results from using the ~~ipconfig~~ utility

You can learn extensive TCP/IP configuration information by using `ipconfig` with its `/all` switch. Besides the default information, the `/all` switch gives information such as host name, domain name, MAC address, and DNS server address, as shown in Figure 15-24.

For DHCP-enabled clients, `ipconfig` can be used to both release and renew IP configuration information. For example, if you want to release an IP address from a network card, you can use the following syntax:

```
Ipconfig /release adapter
```

You can use the `ipconfig` utility with the `/renew` option to renew or obtain IP configuration with the following syntax:

```
Ipconfig /renew adapter
```

```
C:\WINDOWS\System32\cmd.exe                                    _ □ ✕

C:\>ipconfig /all

Windows IP Configuration

        Host Name . . . . . . . . . . . . : neptune
        Primary Dns Suffix . . . . . . . : olsen.com
        Node Type . . . . . . . . . . . . : Unknown
        IP Routing Enabled. . . . . . . . : No
        WINS Proxy Enabled. . . . . . . . : No
        DNS Suffix Search List. . . . . . : olsen.com

Ethernet adapter Local Area Connection:

        Connection-specific DNS Suffix  . : Olsen.com
        Description . . . . . . . . . . . : AMD PCNET Family PCI Ethernet Adapter
        Physical Address. . . . . . . . . : 00-50-56-40-01-1F
        Dhcp Enabled. . . . . . . . . . . : Yes
        Autoconfiguration Enabled . . . . : Yes
        IP Address. . . . . . . . . . . . : 10.0.0.201
        Subnet Mask . . . . . . . . . . . : 255.255.255.0
        Default Gateway . . . . . . . . . : 10.0.0.1
        DHCP Server . . . . . . . . . . . : 10.0.0.4
        DNS Servers . . . . . . . . . . . : 10.0.0.4
        Lease Obtained. . . . . . . . . . : Tuesday, November 13, 2001 6:55:36 PM
        Lease Expires . . . . . . . . . . : Wednesday, November 21, 2001 6:55:36 PM

C:\>
```

Figure 15-24: Detailed information produced with `ipconfig/all`

Note   For a complete listing and description of all available options for `ipconfig`, type **ipconfig /?** at the command prompt.

Windows IP configuration utility — `winipcfg`

The Windows IP configuration utility (`winipcfg`) command is a graphical version of `ipconfig` utility for use with Windows 95, 98 or ME. The command `winipcfg` can be entered at either the command prompt or through the run command in the start menu. Figure 15-25 shows the IP configuration utility that appears when `winipcfg` is typed at either the command prompt or into the Run option from the start menu.

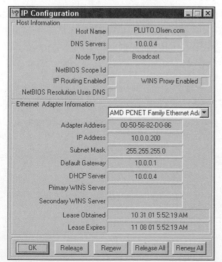

Figure 15-25: The `winipcfg` utility of Windows ME

The network statistics utility — `netstat`

The network statistics (`netstat`) utility displays protocol statistics and current TCP/IP network connection information. For example, type **netstat** at a Windows command prompt to display current active connection information similar to that shown in Figure 15-26.

Figure 15-26: The `netstat` command showing current active connections

You can find additional `netstat` options by typing **netstat -?** at the command prompt.

The `arp` command line utility

A host uses the ARP protocol to find MAC addresses for a known IP address. When ARP is successful, the result is placed into an IP-to-Physical address translation table (ARP Table). The `arp` command line utility can display and modify this table. To view the ARP table for a particular computer, enter the following at its command prompt:

```
arp -a
```

Figure 15-27 shows a typical result of this command.

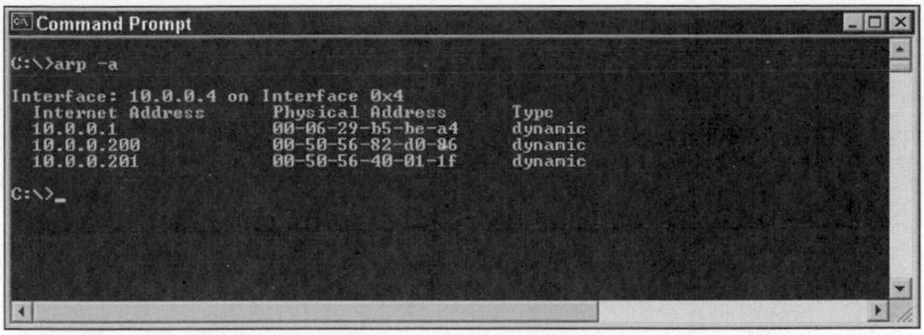

```
Command Prompt                                        _ □ X
C:\>arp -a

Interface: 10.0.0.4 on Interface 0x4
  Internet Address      Physical Address     Type
  10.0.0.1              00-06-29-b5-be-a4     dynamic
  10.0.0.200            00-50-56-82-d0-96     dynamic
  10.0.0.201            00-50-56-40-01-1f     dynamic

C:\>_
```

Figure 15-27: Using `arp -a` to display the current ARP table

To speed up communications, you can add permanent entries (also known as *static entries*) to the ARP table by using the following syntax:

```
arp -s ip_address mac_address
```

You can delete entries from the ARP table by using the following syntax:

```
arp -d ip_address
```

Network analyzers

Network analyzers, often referred to as *packet sniffers*, allow administrators to capture and analyze data crossing a network. This analysis can include network usage statistics, protocol analysis, and individual packet analysis.

Many types of network analyzers are available in a whole range of prices, from free to several thousand dollars. The abilities of these products are equally as wide ranging. The following are some common features found in network analyzers:

✦ **Packet gathering and analysis.** Most products have the ability to capture individual packets and save them for later analysis.

✦ **Alarms and alerts.** Many products have the ability to send notification alerts to operators if network problems arise.

✦ **Report generation.** Several products have the ability to produce detailed reports on network statistics, such as traffic patterns, high usage clients, and protocol distribution. Reports are often available in text format as well as chart or graph format.

✦ **Traffic Simulations.** Several products allow the creation of test packets to simulate the effect of traffic on specific devices or on the network in general.

A variety of network analyzer products are available on the market:

✦ Network General's Expert Sniffer

✦ Agilent Technologies' Advisor

✦ Network Associates' Sniffer Pro

✦ Microsoft's Network Monitor

Figure 15-28 demonstrates how captured packets can be analyzed in Microsoft's Network Monitor program. The top portion of the screen shows a listing of all packets that have been captured. The middle portion shows an in-depth analysis of a chosen packet, including its various layers and the information contained therein. The lower section of the screen shows both a complete hexadecimal and a text representation of the chosen packet.

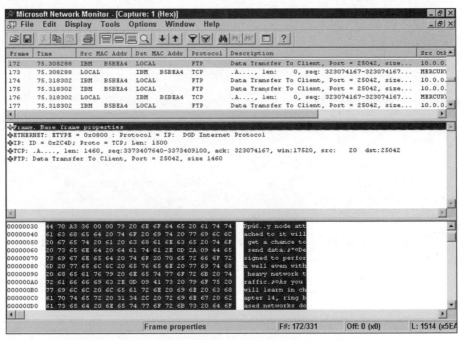

Figure 15-28: Using Network Monitor to analyze network traffic

Key Point Summary

The goal of this chapter is to introduce you to some of the fundamental concepts regarding the TCP/IP protocol suite. The following is a summary of the key points covered:

✦ TCP/IP was chosen as the protocol suite for the Internet largely because it is an open and routable suite.

✦ Request for Comments (RFCs) are published standards documents that are maintained by the Internet Engineering Task Force (IETF).

✦ RFCs lay out specifications and standards for the various protocols and services used on the Internet.

✦ Several maturities are associated with RFCs: Proposed, draft, standard, experimental, historical, and informational.

✦ TCP/IP is based on the following four-layer Internet architecture model:

- Network Access Layer: Provides the same services as those found in the Physical and Data Link Layers of the OSI/RM. Dependent on the underlying architecture of the network, such as Ethernet, Token Ring, etc.

- Internet Layer: Responsible for addressing and routing TCP/IP packets; protocols at this level include IP, ARP, RARP, IGMP, and ICMP.

- Transport Layer: Responsible for providing communication sessions between computers. Protocols at this level include TCP and UDP.

- Application Layer: Provides network access to applications. Protocols at this level include HTTP, FTP, TFTP, SMTP, NNTP, DNS, SNMP, BOOTP, and DHCP.

✦ Port numbers are used to identify a service to which network communication can be directed.

✦ Ports 0 through 1023 are reserved well-known ports. ICAAN controls their assignment and use.

✦ Ports 1024 to 65535 are registered port numbers that any process of service can use.

✦ Multiplexing describes how the various layers of the Internet architecture model are combined to build a complete data packet.

✦ Demultiplexing describes the method that the receiving computer uses to process the incoming packet.

✦ All devices participating in a TCP/IP network require a unique IP address.

✦ IP addresses are 32-bit numbers written in dotted decimal notation.

✦ An IP address contains both a network ID and a host ID. These IDs are used to identify which network a particular host resides on and uniquely identifies the host on that network.

✦ Internet addresses are grouped into five classes: A, B, C, D, and E.

✦ Class A networks use the first octet of an IP address to identify the network. These networks addresses have been reserved for extremely large organizations.

✦ Class B networks use the first two octets of an IP address to identify the network. Class B addresses are reserved for medium to large networks requiring up to 65534 host addresses.

✦ Class C networks use the first three octets of an IP address to identify the network. Class C addresses are intended for small networks with a maximum of 254 hosts.

✦ Class D addresses are reserved for multicasting.

✦ Class E addresses are reserved for future use.

✦ You must consider several rules when assigning addresses to hosts:

   • Addresses must come from Classes A, B, or C

   • Each octet must fall into the range between 0 and 255

   • The network ID or the host ID of an address may not be all 255s

   • The network ID or the host ID of an address may not be all zeros

   • The first octet of any address may not be 127 because this is reserved for the loopback address

✦ Private network addresses are not routable on the Internet and are reserved for those organizations that want to set up private networks.

✦ IPv6 is the next generation of the IP protocol, designed to address many of the deficiencies of the current IPv4 protocol.

✦ The role of the subnet mask is to tell the computer which part of its IP address is the network ID and which part is the host ID.

✦ There are two general forms of routing: Direct and indirect. Indirect routing requires the use of a router, indirect does not.

✦ Static routers require manual entry of routing table information.

✦ Dynamic routers build their routing tables by exchanging routing information with neighboring routers by using a routing protocol.

✦ Routing protocols fall into two classifications: Interior and exterior.

✦ Exterior routing protocols are used to share routing information with routers external to an organization. The two most common exterior routing protocols are Exterior Gateway Protocol (EGP) and Border Gateway Protocol (BGP).

✦ Interior routing protocols are used to share routing information among routes within an organization. RIP and OSPF are two commonly used interior routing protocols.

✦ The minimum TCP/IP configuration information required for a host in a routed environment is an IP address, subnet mask, and default gateway.

✦ Additional TCP/IP configuration may include host name, domain name, DNS server address, NetBIOS name, and WINS server address.

✦ Hosts can have TCP/IP configuration information statically assigned or automatically assigned by using Dynamic Host Configuration Protocol.

✦ The following are several TCP/IP diagnostic tools: PING, trace route, `ipconfig`, `winipcfg`, `netstat`, and `arp`.

✦ Network analyzers are commonly used to allow administrators to capture and analyze data crossing a network. The analysis can include network usage statistics, protocol analysis, and individual packet analysis.

✦   ✦   ✦

STUDY GUIDE

The following assessment questions test your memory on some of the key topics covered in this chapter. The scenario questions test your understanding of the basic networking concepts by presenting you with a real life scenario for which you must answer chapter-related questions.

Assessment Questions

1. Which of the following best describes TCP/IP?

   A. Non-Routable—Open Standard

   B. Routable—Closed Standard

   C. Routable—Open Standard

   D. Non-Routable—Closed Standard

2. Which of the following are maturity states in the RFC process? (Choose all that apply)

   A. Proposed

   B. Signed

   C. Draft

   D. Closed

   E. Discarded

3. In which layer of the Internet architecture model do UDP and TCP reside?

   A. Data Link

   B. Internet

   C. Network

   D. Applications

   E. Transport

4. Which of the following protocols is used to obtain a MAC address given an IP address?

   A. RARP

   B. BOOTP

   C. ARP

   D. DHCP

   E. ICMP

5. Which of the following is typically used as an error reporting protocol?

   A. RARP

   B. BOOTP

   C. ARP

   D. DHCP

   E. ICMP

   F. IGMP

6. Which protocol uses a three-way handshake to negotiate the terms of a data transfer session?

   A. TCP

   B. ARP

   C. UDP

   D. SNMP

   E. ICMP

7. True or False: UDP is considered a reliable protocol used to send large amounts of data.

8. True or False: POP3 is the send mail protocol.

9. Which of the following port ranges are reserved for well-known TCP/IP services?

   A. 1 to 127

   B. 0 to 1023

   C. 192 to 224

   D. 1024 to 65535

   E. 0 to 255

10. What is the port number associated with HTTP service?

    A. 25

    B. 53

    C. 80

    D. 110

    E. 143

11. True or False: Two hosts can't share the same network ID.

12. How many bits are there in an IPv4 address?

    A. 8

    B. 16

    C. 32

    D. 128

    E. 1043

13. What part of an IP address is used to uniquely identify a particular host on a network segment?

    A. Host ID

    B. Network ID

    C. Subnet mask

    D. Default gateway

    E. Ephemeral port number

14. Which of the following address classes can be used to support a network of over 5,000 hosts? (Choose all that apply)

    A. Class A

    B. Class B

    C. Class C

    D. Class D

    E. Class E

15. From which class of addresses does 193.22.33.1 come?

    A. Class A

    B. Class B

    C. Class C

D. Class D

E. Class E

16. Which of the following IP addresses can be assigned to hosts? (Choose all that apply)

   A. 0.12.11.13

   B. 2.0.0.1

   C. 127.2.1.12

   D. 197.255.255.1

   E. 224.0.0.1

17. Which of the following IP address ranges are reserved for companies that want to set up a private network? (Choose all that apply)

   A. 10.0.0.0 – 10.255.255.255

   B. 127.0.0.0 – 127.255.255.255

   C. 172.16.0.0 – 17.31.255.255

   D. 192.168.0.0 – 192.168.255.255

   E. 224.0.0.0 – 239.255.255.255

18. 255.255.0.0 is the default subnet mask for which IP address class?

   A. Class A

   B. Class B

   C. Class C

   D. Class D

   E. Class E

19. True or False: Direct routing does not require the use of a router.

20. True or False: Dynamic routers learn routing information through DHCP.

21. Which of the following are examples of exterior routing protocols?

   A. BGP

   B. RIP

   C. OSPF

   D. ESPF

   E. EGP

22. Routers using which of the following protocols always use the route with the lowest hop count to determine the best route?

   A. BGP

   B. RIP

   C. OSPF

   D. ESPF

   E. EGP

23. Which of the following TCP/IP settings is used to provide the host an address of a server that can provide host name to IP address resolution?

   A. Subnet mask

   B. Default gateway

   C. WINS server address

   D. DNS server address

   E. Domain name

24. Which of the following are TCP/IP typical configuration settings that can be assigned using DHCP?

   A. IP address

   B. DNS server Address

   C. MAC address

   D. Subnet Mask

   E. WINS server address

   F. DHCP server address

25. Which of the following is a simple utility used to test connectivity between systems in a TCP/IP environment?

   A. netstat

   B. ping

   C. tracert

   D. ipconfig

   E. winipcfg

26. Which of the following utilities can be used to display a node's current address resolution table?

    A. arp

    B. ping

    C. network monitor

    D. showtab

    E. winipcfg

27. Which utility is used to display protocol statistics and current TCP/IP network connection information?

    A. netstat

    B. ping

    C. tracert

    D. ipconfig

    E. winipcfg

28. Which of the following is a utility used to display current TCP/IP configuration information for a Windows NT/2000 host?

    A. netstat

    B. ping

    C. tracert

    D. ipconfig

    E. winipcfg

Scenario

Little Sister's Teasing, Inc. (LST) is a manufacturer of hair products in London, England. LST is currently in the process of setting up a network to support its internal operations.

The following are the key objectives that must be addressed in the new network:

    ◆ All 230 workstations and servers must be provided with Internet connectivity.

    ◆ Customers will have the ability to locate company information by visiting LST's Web site.

    ◆ All employees will be provided with the ability to both send and receive e-mails both in the office and remotely from home.

✦ Network administrators must have the ability to remotely monitor and maintain network connectivity devices, such as routers and switches.

✦ Network administrators should not be burdened with the task of manually configuring TCP/IP settings on every host computer.

✦ Employees must be able to use fully qualified domain names when accessing servers both internally and on the Internet.

To obtain these goals, LST has hired highly trained consultant, Alexander Pirate, to oversee the design and setup of the new network.

Based on the information provided and what you have learned in this chapter, answer the following questions regarding LST's network.

1. What class of IP addresses would Alexander request for LST's proposed network? Why?

2. Alexander is configuring a firewall for LST and needs to configure it with a list of all well-known port numbers that will be used on the network. What port numbers will he need to enter?

3. Which service will Alexander need to install to prevent LST administrators from having to visit each computer to configure TCP/IP settings?

4. What TCP/IP settings will need to be configured on each workstation within LST's network?

5. What protocol will likely be used by LST's administrators to remotely monitor and maintain network connectivity devices, such as routers and switches?

6. What service will allow employees to use fully qualified domain names when accessing servers both internally and on the Internet?

7. Alexander wants to analyze network traffic patterns in order to optimize its performance. What TCP/IP diagnostic tool will Alexander likely use?

8. Alexander wants to see the TCP/IP configuration information for his Windows ME-based computer. What command should he enter at the command prompt?

9. LST's final network design requires the use of several dynamic routers. To optimize network traffic, Alexander decides to use a routing protocol that will only send routing table updates when routing changes actually occur on the network. What routing protocol has Alexander most likely chosen?

Lab Exercises

The following labs give you some hands-on experience in working with some of the concepts presented in this chapter. These labs assume that you are using a Windows 95, Windows 98, or Windows ME-based computer and have a connection to the Internet.

Lab 15-1 Determining your TCP/IP settings

The objective of this lab is to show you how to view your current TCP/IP settings.

1. From the start menu, select Run.

2. Type **winipcfg** and press enter. You should receive a screen similar to the one shown in Figure 15-29:

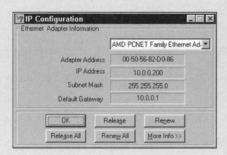

Figure 15-29: Windows IP Configuration Utility

3. Press the More Info button. You should now see a detailed listing of TCP/IP configuration information, similar to Figure 15-30.

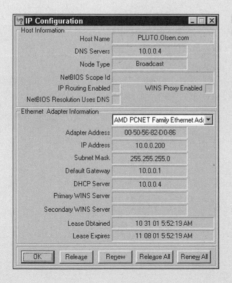

Figure 15-30: Windows IP Configuration Utility showing detailed information.

4. Click OK to close the IP Configuration dialog box.

Lab 15-2 Using ping to test connectivity

The following lab gives you hands-on practice working with the TCP/IP ping utility.

1. Open a command prompt window. Click Start ⇨ Programs ⇨ MS-DOS Prompt.

2. Use the ping utility to test connectivity to several well-known Web sites. For example, type **ping** www.yahoo.com.

3. Ping the address 127.0.0.1. Whose address is this?

4. Ping the address 10.0.25.122. Did it work? Why or why not?

Lab 15-3 Exploring additional TCP/IP utilities

This lab gives you hands-on practice with several TCP/IP utilities that are covered in this chapter.

1. Open a command prompt window. Click Start ⇨ Programs ⇨ MS-DOS Prompt.

2. Perform a trace route to several Web sites on the Internet. For example, type the following: **tracert** www.yahoo.com

Note   This command may produce limited results because some organizations filter out this type of traffic.

3. Use the arp utility to examine the entries in your computers address routing table. Type **arp –a**.

4. Use the `netstat` utility to display protocol statistics and current connection information. Try the following commands:

✦ `netstat`

✦ `netstat -e`

✦ `netstat -s`

✦ `netstat -?`

Answers to Chapter Questions

Chapter pre-test

1. The four layers of the Internet architecture model are: **Network Access, Internet, Transport, and Application**.

2. IP, ICMP, and ARP exist at the **Internet** Layer of the Internet architecture model?

3. Published documents that include detailed information about standardized Internet protocols are referred to as **Request for Comments (RFCs)**.

4. **HTTP** is a TCP/IP protocol used to transport HTML documents.

5. DNS is a protocol that is used to translate **host names** to **IP addresses**.

6. **TCP** is the TCP/IP Transport Layer protocol that provides session management.

7. **Routing** can be divided into two categories: Direct and indirect.

8. The two interior routing protocols are **OSPF** and **RIP**.

9. Well-known port numbers are between 0 and **1023**.

10. IP addresses are divided into five classes.

11. 220.120.12.1 is an example of a Class **C** address.

12. A **private** network address can't be routed on the Internet.

13. A subnet mask allows a node to distinguish between its **network** address and its **host** address.

14. The minimum three pieces of information that you must supply to a host for it to participate in a routed TCP/IP network are: **IP address, subnet mask, and default gateway**.

15. The trace route utility can be used to determine the communication path between two systems.

Assessment Questions

1. Which of the following best describes TCP/IP?

    C. Routable — Open Standard

2. Which of the following are maturity states in the RFC process? (Choose all that apply)

    A. Proposed

    C. Draft

3. In which layer of the Internet architecture model do UDP and TCP reside?

    E. Transport

4. Which of the following protocols is used to obtain a MAC address given an IP address?

    C. ARP

5. Which of the following is typically used as an error reporting protocol?

    E. ICMP

6. Which protocol uses a three-way handshake to negotiate the terms of a data transfer session?

    A. TCP

7. **False.** UDP is considered an unreliable protocol primarily used to send small amounts of data.

8. **False.** SMTP is the send mail protocol.

9. Which of the following port ranges are reserved for well-known TCP/IP services?

   B. 0 to 1023

10. What is the port number associated with HTTP service?

    C. 80

11. **False.** Two hosts must share the same network ID if they are on the same subnet; they can't share the same host ID or IP address.

12. How many bits are in an IPv4 address?

    C. 32

13. Which part of an IP address is used to uniquely identify a particular host on a network segment?

    A. Host ID

14. Which of the following address classes can be used to support a network of over 5,000 hosts? (Choose all that apply)

    A. Class A

    B. Class B

15. From which Class of addresses does 193.22.33.1 come?

    C. Class C

16. Which of the following IP address can be assigned to hosts? (Choose all that apply)

    B. 2.0.0.1

    D. 197.255.255.1

17. Which of the following IP address ranges are reserved for companies that want to set up a private network? (Choose all that apply)

    A. 10.0.0.0 – 10.255.255.255

    C. 172.16.0.0 – 17.31.255.255

    D. 192.168.0.0 – 192.168.255.255

18. 255.255.0.0 is the default subnet mask for which IP address class?

    B. Class B

19. **True.** Direct routing does not require the use of a router.

20. **False.** Dynamic routers learn routing information through communication with other routers by using a common routing protocol.

21. Which of the following are examples of exterior routing protocols?

    A. BGP

    E. EGP

22. Routers using which of the following protocols always use the route with the lowest hop count to determine the best route.

   B. RIP

23. Which of the following TCP/IP settings is used to provide the host an address of a server that can provide host name to IP address resolution?

   D. DNS server address

24. Which of the following are typical TCP/IP configuration settings that can be assigned using DHCP?

   A. IP address

   B. DNS server Address

   D. Subnet Mask

   E. WINS server address

25. Which of the following is a simple utility used to test connectivity between systems in a TCP/IP environment

   B. ping

26. Which of the following utilities can be used to display a node's current address resolution table?

   A. arp

27. Which utility is used to display protocol statistics and current TCP/IP network connection information?

   A. netstat

28. Which of the following is a utility used to display current TCP/IP configuration information for a Windows NT/2000 host?

   D. ipconfig

Scenarios Questions

1. Alexander will likely request a Class C network address because it will allow 254 hosts — more than LST requires.

2. Based on the information given in the scenario, Alexander will have to configure his firewall to pass packets destined to the following port numbers:

   • HTTP — Port 80 for customer Web server access

   • SMTP — Port 25 for employees to send mail.

   • POP3 — Port 110 for employees to check for received e-mail

   • DNS — Port 53 for DNS traffic

3. To eliminate the need for LST administrators to visit each computer to configure TCP/IP settings, Alexander should configure a server to provide the Dynamic Host Configuration Protocol (DHCP) service. Alexander should also have the clients configured to accept automatic IP addressing.

4. Each workstation at LST must be configured with at least the following information: A unique IP address, a subnet mask, a host name, a NetBIOS name, and the address of at least one DNS server.

5. The protocol most likely used by LST administrators to remotely monitor and maintain network connectivity is Simple Network Management Protocol (SNMP).

6. The domain name service (DNS) will allow employees to use fully qualified domain names when accessing servers both internally and on the Internet.

7. A network analyzer can be used to analyze network traffic patterns.

8. Alexander should use the `winipcfg` utility to see the TCP/IP configuration information for his Windows ME-based computer.

9. Alexander will likely choose the OSPF protocol because, unlike RIP, it only sends out routing table updates when routing changes actually occur on the network.

Resources

The following are suggested resources for more information regarding the topics covered in this chapter:

✦ Webopedia: Online Computer Dictionary for Internet Terms and Technical Support: `www.webopedia.com`

✦ WRQ tech support's IP addressing fundamentals tutorial: `http://support.wrq.com/tutotials/tutorial.htm`

✦ RFC Editor Site: `www.rfc-editor.org`

✦ Cisco's OSPF design guide for detailed information regarding OSPF and RIP comparison information: `www.cisco.com/warp/public/104`.

✦ For a complete listing of well known port numbers: `www.iana.org/assignments/port-numbers`.

Servers in a TCP/IP Internetwork

EXAM OBJECTIVES

1. Identify and describe the functions and features of file and print, HTTP, proxy, caching, mail, mailing list, media, DNS, FTP, news, certificate, directory, catalog, and transaction servers.

2. Describe how each type of networking server uses the TCP/IP suite protocols.

3. Describe access-security features of an HTTP server, including user names, passwords, and file-level access.

4. Define MIME, and explain how MIME types are used by HTTP and mail servers.

5. Describe the function of DNS, including the DNS hierarchy, root domain servers, top-level domains, and DNS record types.

6. Define daemon and identify the functions of the internet-related daemons.

CHAPTER PRE-TEST

1. Choose between LPR and LPD. Which is used to initiate print commands and which carries them out?

2. What are the three types of information usually collected in a Web server's logs?

3. What type of server enhances security and speeds up Internet access by caching frequently used documents?

4. What type of sever is most likely to use SMTP, POP3, and IMAP?

5. _____is used to identify and encode a file attachment when transmitting files via e-mail.

6. A _____ server is used to automatically forward SMTP e-mail messages to every member of a distribution list.

7. What type of server provides streaming audio or video over the Internet?

8. What file is stored locally on a computer and is used to resolve IP addresses from host names?

9. What is the highest domain level of the DNS name hierarchy?

10. What level of the DNS name hierarchy includes the following: .com, .edu, .ca, and .fr?

11. Name servers and name revolvers are two key components of _____?

12. What type of server does an MX DNS record identify?

13. The two protocols which serve as the basis for most directory services are _____ and _____.

14. Which UNIX daemon is used to launch Internet-related server applications such as smtpd and tftd?

✦ Answers to these questions can be found at the end of the chapter. ✦

The purpose of this chapter is to introduce you to the common server applications found in today's TCP/IP-based networks such as the Internet. This chapter should enable you to recognize and explain the concepts behind various network servers.

File and Print Server Fundamentals

 Identify and describe the functions and features of a file and print server.

Of all the types of servers in use in networks today, it is likely that the most common is the file and print server. Although a file server and a print server are often different servers, the two functions are commonly combined into one.

File servers

A file server is any computer that shares a file-system resource such as a file, a folder (also called a directory), or an entire disk (sometimes referred to as a volume). On a network, file servers typically act as central storage points for users to both save and access files.

 In a Microsoft network, shared file-system resources are referred to as "Shares."

Many organizations encourage (and sometimes require) users to save all files on the file server instead of saving files locally on their own computers. Reasons for this vary, but most often it is to simplify network file management. For example, keeping files in one location, as opposed to spread across the network, makes it easier to perform network backup and to regulate access to the files.

Drive letters are commonly used on users' computers to point to a shared area on a network. This way, saving files to a network server can be as easy as saving files to the local computer.

Figure 16-1 displays the My Computer window showing the drive letters available for the computer. Drive D, E, and F all point to different shared areas of a hard drive on a server called "Mercury." The user of this workstation can save data to these drives as simply as saving data to Drive C.

Figure 16-1: A My Computer window showing both local drives and drive letters pointing to shared areas on a file server

Almost all modern network operating systems, including client-oriented operating systems such as Windows 95, 98, and ME, have the capability of being file servers. In a large network environment, however, it is best to use a true server-oriented operating system that has appropriate security and data protection mechanisms built in. This operating system should also be installed on a fast computer capable of storing large amounts of data.

Print servers

Print servers allow multiple users access to the same physical print device. Using a print server eliminates the need to supply all users with their own printer. It also allows more flexibility for users because they can have access to more than one type of printer.

Jobs waiting to be printed are stored on the print server in a temporary holding area referred to as a *print queue*. The print queue is a storage area set aside on the hard drive of the print server. Print servers monitor print devices' availability and pass jobs from the queue to the print device.

Two additional network-printing terms that you should be aware of are Line Printer Daemon (LPD) and Line Printer (LPR).

Line Printer Daemon — LPD

The Line Printer Daemon is a print server service that typically runs in a UNIX/Linux environment but is also available in Windows NT/2000. Its main duty is to accept print requests and forward them on to managed print devices.

Line Printer — LPR

LPR is a client utility used to submit print requests to servers running the Line Printer Daemon.

Web Server Fundamentals

Identify and describe the functions and features of an HTTP server.

An HTTP server (a Web server) is a computer that runs the HTTP server service. The main purpose of this service is to supply HTTP clients with documents referred to as Web pages. HTTP clients, usually Web browsers, make requests for Web pages by issuing an HTTP Get Request to the server. The server receiving this request fetches or creates the requested document and passes it back to the client using an HTTP Response. This request and response exchange is a prime example of the client/server relationship between Web browsers and Web servers. The collection of Web servers on the Internet is referred to as the World Wide Web. Much of the traffic on the Internet is due to client/server interaction with the Web.

For the CIW Foundations exam there are several important Web server concepts of which you should be aware. The following sections will introduce you to these concepts.

Web pages

Most Web servers have a collection of Web page documents that they offer to clients. This collection is referred to as a Web site. These documents are typically stored in a Hypertext Markup Language (HTML) format, which is simply a series of instructions that tell a Web browser how and what information to display for the user.

Extensive information on HTML and how it is used is provided in Chapters 8–11.

Most Web pages are a combination of text and images but they can also incorporate multimedia such as video or sound. The text of a Web page is typically stored in an HTML document, whereas images and multimedia are stored as separate files on the Web server.

Root Web folders

Each Web server product has a default location in which its files are stored. This location is referred to as the Web root or Web Home directory. In Microsoft's IIS Web server, for example, the Web root is typically the folder "C:\inetpub\wwwroot." Administrators may wish to use the default root folder or change its location. Figure 16-2 shows the Microsoft IIS 5.0 default settings and options that an administrator must choose from when setting the location of the Web root.

Figure 16-2: Home Directory settings for Microsoft's IIS 5.0

Web browsers make a request for a Web page using a URL contained within an HTTP Get Request. Recall from Chapter 1 that a URL typically consists of the following elements:

- ✦ A Protocol followed by a colon and two forward slashes. For Web pages this would typically be http:// or https://.

- ✦ An address of a server that contains the resource. This would typically be the FQDN of the Web server.

- ✦ A path to the document or file on the server. This would be a file system path specified using the forward slash (/) in a UNIX style format — regardless of the actual operating system being used on the server.

- ✦ The name of the actual resource preceded by a forward slash. For web pages this is often an HTML document.

The path portion of the URL typically refers to the path relative to the server's Web root. For example, consider the URL `http://www.iisserver.com/ sales/prices.htm` directed to an IIS 5.0 Web server with an FQDN of `www. iisserver.com`.

This URL directs the Web server to the file called `prices.htm` which is located in a folder called `sales`. An IIS 5.0 server with default settings would interpret this path as `c:\inetpub\wwwroot\sales` and look for `prices.htm` there.

Virtual directories

Storing all files that are accessible from a Web server under the root folder is often not practical or recommended. Most Web server products build flexibility into Web site design by allowing the use of virtual directories. A virtual directory is simply a Web path name given to a physical folder. This physical directory can be a subfolder within the Web root, a separate folder on the server's file systems, or a file location on a different server. For example, the Web server www.iisserver.com can be configured to redirect all requests for Web pages in the directory products to the Web root folder on a server called www.apacheserver.com. If www.iisserver.com receives a request for the URL http://www.iisserver.com/products/copiers.htm, it redirects the client to www.apacheserver.com. The client would now request the page from this server. This interaction is shown in Figure 16-3.

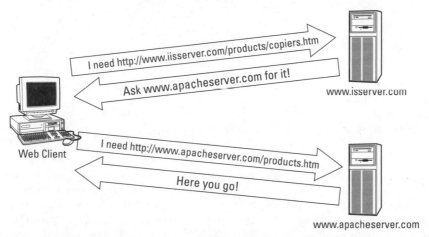

Figure 16-3: The result of using a Virtual Directory to redirect requests for Web pages

Virtual directories are also beneficial in simplifying Web page access. For example, suppose that a file called clients.htm is stored in the folder c:\inetdub\wwwroot\sales\canada\west\alberta\calgary\ on an IIS server named www.iisserver.com. To access this file, the following URL would have to be used: http://www.iisserver.com/sales/canada/west/alberta/calgary/clients.htm.

You can greatly simplify this process by creating a virtual directory, perhaps called calgary, that points to the above path. A client wishing to access the same file could then use the simplified URL of http://www.iisserver.com/calgary/clients.htm.

Note   This form of a virtual directory is often referred to as an alias.

Home pages

Generally when people visit Web sites they do not request a specific file. They merely wish to see that site's home page. The home page or initial page is the default Web page that the Web server hands out when no specific file has been requested. For most Web servers, the administrator can define any file name as the home page; however, many prefer to use their Web server's default. In the case of Microsoft's IIS product, this file is called `default.htm` and is stored in the Web server's root folder. Other common names include the following:

- ✦ `index.html`
- ✦ `main.html`
- ✦ `welcome.html`
- ✦ `default.asp`

Cross-Reference   For more information regarding home pages, refer to Chapter 8.

Dynamic Web pages

As previously stated, Web servers are responsible for sending requested Web pages to clients. These Web pages can be simple documents stored on the Web server itself or they can be complex documents consisting of data drawn from several sources and compiled together at the time of the request. Web pages offered by many Weather services, such as the one featured in Figure 16-4, are a good example of complex documents. The weather-related information such as temperature, humidity, cloud conditions, and so on are not hard coded into the Web page. Instead, they are obtained when the user requests the page. The appearance of the Web page can change throughout the day, which is why these types of pages are often referred to as dynamic Web pages.

Dynamic Web pages typically call on external applications to provide them with the content required to complete the page. These calls generally consist of Common Gateway Interface (CGI) scripts. The external applications are often database programs but can be any application that can handle input and output according to the CGI standard.

HTTP gateway

The terms Web gateway and HTTP gateway are used to describe a Web server process which acts as a gateway between a client and backend service process such as a database application. For example, Web pages commonly contain forms that accept user input for entry into a database. After the data is entered it is submitted to the Web server where a Web gateway process interprets the input and passes it on to a database application. The database application accepts the data and passes an acknowledgment back to the Web server, which in turn formats the acknowledgment as a confirmation page and passes it back to the Web client.

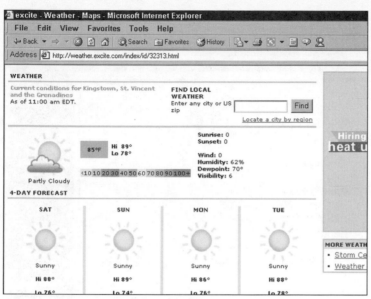

Figure 16-4: A dynamic Web page

For more information regarding Web gateways and CGI, see Chapter 17.

MIME types

 Define MIME, and explain how MIME types are used by HTTP and mail servers.

Links in Web pages often point to a variety of document types (not always HTML documents). For example, many software vendors offer links to product documentation that has been rendered in Adobe Acrobat. If the Adobe Reader plug-in has been installed in the browser, choosing this link displays the Adobe document in the Web browser. Another example of this technology is demonstrated in Figure 16-5, which shows a Microsoft Power Point presentation being displayed through Internet Explorer.

The ability to offer a variety of file types through a Web server and a Web browser can greatly add to the flexibility of Web pages and Web design. For this to work, there must be some coordination between server and client so the client knows how to properly render the file for the user. Web servers use either Multipurpose Internet Mail Extensions (MIME) or Secure Multipurpose Internet Mail Extensions (S/MIME) to inform the client of the file type that it is sending.

 S/MIME is a version of MIME in which all MIME related data is encrypted for secure transmission.

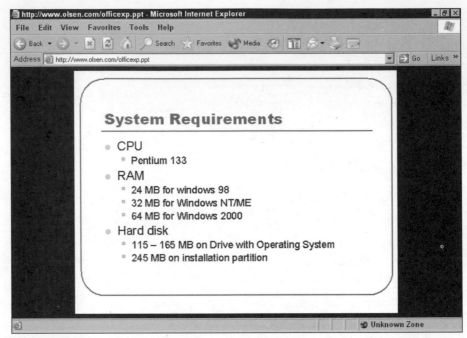

Figure 16-5: Power Point presentation displayed in Internet Explorer

At the beginning of a transmission, a server sends a label with the data that identifies the MIME type for the client. This label consists of two components: a content classification, including text, image, application, audio, or video, and a sub-classification by exact type. For example, the label sent when a server is sending a Graphics Interchange Format (GIF) image is `image/gif`. For a JPEG image the MIME label is `image/jpeg`.

The server selects the MIME type based on the extension of the file itself. When a client requests a file such as `history.html`, the server recognizes the `.html` extension as a simple text-based HTML document and assigns the label `text/html` to the file. When a client requests a file such as `officexp.ppt`, the server recognizes the `.ppt` extension as belonging to PowerPoint and selects the MIME type `application/vnd_powerpoint`. Similarly, if a client requests the file `outline.pdf` the server recognizes the extension `.pdf` as belonging to Adobe Acrobat and selects the MIME type `application/pdf`.

Note   The association between extensions and MIME types can typically be configured at the Web server.

Web server security

 Objective Describe access-security features of an HTTP server, including user names, passwords, and file-level access.

The two forms of security used with respect to Web servers are file permission security and access control security. An explanation of both follows:

File-level access permissions

Access to files on the Web server can be controlled using permissions. Permissions are restrictions typically placed on files or folders to limit the abilities of users to access or alter these files. For most Web servers, permissions can be defined through the underlying operating system or in the Web server software itself. The list of permissions available and the names given to these permissions differ between operating systems and between Web server applications. Typical permissions include the following:

✦ Read — Grants the ability to read the contents of a file.

✦ Write — Grants the ability to create, delete, or change the contents of a file.

✦ Execute — Gives the ability to run (execute) an executable file such as an application.

✦ Deny Access — Denies any access to the file or folder.

Figure 16-6 shows the standard file-level permissions that can be set when using Windows 2000.

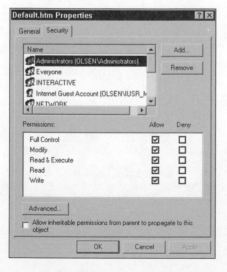

Figure 16-6: File-level permissions in Windows 2000

An administrator often uses both operating-system permissions in combination with Web-server permissions. Operating-system permissions usually take precedence over those set in the Web server application. If an administrator grants a user the right to read files on the Web server but denies that person access at the operating system file-level permissions, the user is denied access.

In the Real World

The official CIW curriculum mentions that the operating system (OS) permissions generally take precedence over Web server permissions. This is true because most administrators make OS permissions much more restrictive. However, when Web server permissions are more restrictive than the OS permissions, the Web server restrictions take precedence.

Access control

Access control defines who has access to a particular Web site or to a portion of a Web site. On the Internet most Web sites have been set up to allow anonymous access. This means they offer access to the general public without requiring any user identification.

Web sites also commonly restrict entry through the use of authentication. This means that a user must supply a valid user ID and password to access the site or page. The default authentication settings for an IIS 5.0 Web site are shown in Figure 16-7.

Figure 16-7: Authentication settings in Windows 2000's IIS 5.0

The list of users can be obtained by the Web server from the Host operating system, as is the case with Microsoft's IIS, or can be a database of users set up in the Web server application itself, as is the case with NCSA's HTTPd Web server. Many consider the second method more secure because there is a separation between the Web server and the operating system; if a Web server account becomes compromised (password stolen, for example), it cannot be used to compromise the operating system.

The Web server service is typically associated with a user account, often referred to as a service account. This account allows or restricts access to the operating system by the Web server itself. Assigning additional permissions to this account can further secure an operating system. For example, if an area of the hard drive of the local operating system should be off limits to the Web server, using the file-level permission "deny access" for the Web server's service account on that folder would disallow the Web server access.

The rule of thumb for all user accounts is to give a user account the minimum amount of permissions required to perform its tasks. Keeping this rule in mind, don't allow the Web server to use the administrator or the root account as its service account.

Web server logs

Most Web server applications allow the administrator to log events related to the server. The type and amount of information kept in a log varies between server products but most Web servers allow the logging of the following information:

✦ **Client access** — A server can log each request for service by HTTP clients. This can be an excellent indication of who is visiting a Web site and what information they are looking at.

✦ **Referrer data** — This gives an indication of how a client found your Web site. HTTP clients pass the Web page URL that contained the link to the server.

✦ **Error data** — Errors encountered by the Web server while processing client requests can be logged. These errors can result from invalid client requests or, potentially, from attempted security access violations.

A portion of a log taken from a Microsoft IIS 5.0 Web server is shown in Figure 16-8.

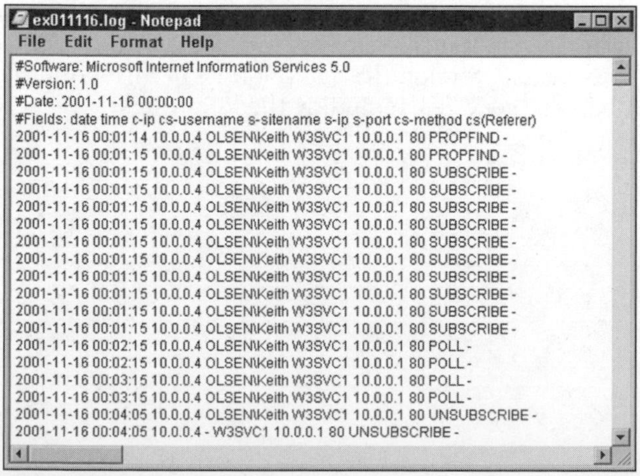

Figure 16-8: IIS 5.0 Web server log

Popular Web server products

Many Web server products are available on the market. The one chosen for a particular Web site depends on many factors, including the following:

- ✦ Host operating system
- ✦ Administrator expertise
- ✦ Product abilities
- ✦ Security
- ✦ Amount of client traffic

The following sections introduce you to a number of popular Web server products that you should be aware of for the CIW Foundations exam.

Apache Web server

The Apache Web server represents close to 50 percent of the Web servers used on the Internet today, largely because it's free, open-sourced, and powerful. Apache was developed and is maintained by a non-profit group called the Apache Software Foundation. Apache was originally developed for use with the UNIX operating system but is now supported under both Windows NT and 2000 as well. Apache is strictly an HTTP service and does not offer services such as FTP and Gopher, which are often offered in competing products.

Note   For a downloadable copy of Apache Web server or to obtain more information regarding Apache, visit the Apache Software Foundations Web site at `http://www.apache.org`.

Microsoft Internet Information Server

Microsoft's Internet Information Server (IIS) is close on Apache's heels in terms of Web server deployment. Versions of IIS are bundled with Windows NT server and Windows 2000 operating systems, and free updates are available for download from Microsoft. Unlike Apache, the current version (IIS 5 at the time of this writing) is bundled with many additional Web services, including the following:

- ✦ HTTP
- ✦ FTP
- ✦ NNTP
- ✦ SMTP
- ✦ Certificate services
- ✦ Active Server Pages
- ✦ Web site Indexing
- ✦ Transaction services

The one downside to IIS is that because of its tight integration with the underlying operating system it is only supported on the Windows NT, 2000, and XP operating systems.

Microsoft Personal Web Server – (PWS)

Personal Web Server is a simple Web server product for use on operating systems such as Windows 95, 98, ME, and NT Workstation. Although it lacks many of the features of full-blown Web servers, it can be a good solution for small organizations wishing to set up simple Intranets.

Lotus Domino

Developed and supported by IBM's Lotus Corporation, Domino is a full-blown Internet server application offering services such as HTTP, SMTP, FTP, and certificate services. It also features tight integration with Lotus Notes applications and databases and offers support for Java and Java servlets.

One of Domino's true strengths is its ability to run over a variety of different operating systems including, but not limited to, the following:

✦ AIX

✦ HP-UX

✦ Solaris

✦ Windows NT

✦ Windows 2000

✦ AS/400

iPlanet servers

iPlanet is an alliance of Sun Microsystems and Netscape Corporation. This alliance offers a large number of Internet-related application products including the iPlanet Web server, a highly stable server for enterprise Web sites. Similar to Lotus Domino, iPlanet's server applications typically run over a wide variety of operating systems.

Proxy Server Fundamentals

Identify and describe the functions and features of proxy servers.

A proxy server is a server that sits in between a client application and a server application. The typical arrangement of a proxy in a network is depicted in Figure 16-9, where the proxy has been set up between a corporate network and the Internet. A proxy's job is to intercept communication from the client and pass it on to the server as if the proxy server itself were making the request. Any response to the communication is returned to the proxy server, which in turn passes it on to the client. In essence, a proxy hides the client from the server. The most common use of a proxy is for Web access, but it can also be used for other client/server applications, such as FTP, Telnet, newsgroups, and mail.

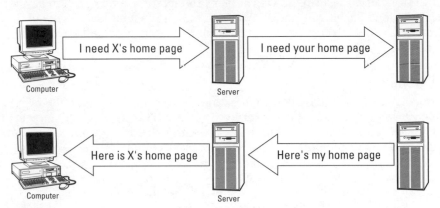

Figure 16-9: A proxy is used as an intermediary between clients and servers resources.

Client computers must be configured to handle the services of a proxy. This usually requires configuring each proxy-aware application with the IP address of the proxy server and the port number assigned to the proxy application on that server. Figure 16-10 shows the proxy configuration settings for Microsoft's Internet Explorer.

Figure 16-10: Proxy configuration in Internet Explorer

For those applications that do not directly support the configuration of a proxy, proxy client software can be installed on the computer. This software, typically included with the proxy server application directs all outgoing traffic to a proxy server, eliminating the need to configure each application.

Several advantages to using proxies are outlined below:

✦ **Increases network security** — When a proxy server makes a request for resources on behalf of a client, the proxy server uses its own IP address as the return address in the request, not that of the original client. The proxy server serves as a form of firewall and hides the internal network address from the outside world.

Cross-Reference

See Chapter 18 for information on firewalls.

✦ **IP Address conservation** — Because host computers in the internal network do not directly communicate with the Internet, they can use private IP addresses. This further increases security and allows an organization to use fewer live IP addresses.

Cross-Reference

See Chapter 15 for information on private IP addressing.

✦ **Speed up Internet access** — In a corporate network, multiple users often visit the same Web site. Without a proxy server, each request for pages from the same site requires each client computer to individually contact the Web server and download the page. To speed up access to commonly used pages, many proxy servers can be set up to cache Web pages. Caching proxy servers store Web pages for future requests. In other words, when a client machine requests a Web page from the Internet, the proxy checks its cache to see if it has already retrieved the page in the past. If so, the proxy passes the client the cached copy of the page, rather then re-requesting the page from the server. Caching reduces Internet traffic and increases performance of the corporate network.

✦ **Client transaction filtering** — Most proxy servers allow filters to be placed on outgoing traffic. In this way a proxy server can limit or restrict access to certain Web sites on the Internet. Filters can be based on the following:

- URLs
- IP addresses
- network addresses
- computer names
- user names
- Web page content

For example, a filter could deny users access to any Web page that contains offensive words or keep users from going to known gaming sites. Additional filters could be set up to allow Internet access only to select individuals or from select client computers on the network.

✦ **Transaction logging** — With most proxies, transactions performed by the proxy can be logged. Administrators can examine the log to determine such things as the following:

- Where users are going

- Number and details of requests filtered out

- Times and dates of transactions

✦ **Host server security** — Proxies can be set up in a reverse fashion so that requests from outside the corporate network are required to pass through a proxy to reach any internal resource. For example, an organization may register a proxy server as the corporate Web server. Requests from the Internet from HTTP clients are directed to the proxy first. As with any proxy, rules can be set up to deny or allow access based on specific criteria. If the proxy deems the traffic appropriate, it passes the information to the real Web server; otherwise it can be set to deny access and log the details of the attempted transaction. When this form of "reverse" proxy is used, a second proxy is commonly employed to handle outgoing traffic.

Caching Server Fundamentals

 Identify and describe the functions and features of caching servers.

Typically associated with a Web server and clients, a caching server is dedicated to storing data retrieved by users. Repeated requests for the same information can then be retrieved directly from the caching server as opposed to requiring clients to retrieve the data from the originating server. The benefit of a caching server is that it typically speeds up client data access.

Caching servers can be a component of a proxy server or can be a standalone application. The CIW curriculum mentions the term "cache-in-a-box" when referring to standalone caching server applications.

Mail Server Fundamentals

Mail servers store, retrieve, and forward electronic mail (e-mail) messages. E-mail and e-mail servers play a very important role in communication on the Internet and within corporate networks. The following sections deal with e-mail concepts with which you should be familiar.

E-Mail protocols

Recall from Chapter 15 that several protocols are associated with e-mail including the following:

✦ **SMTP** — Simple Mail Transfer Protocol (SMTP) sends e-mail messages. When a user of a client computer types an e-mail and submits the message for delivery, SMTP transfers the message from the client to the mail server. If the mail server determines that the destination of the message exists on a server other than itself, it uses SMTP to relay the message to its destination. In a UNIX environment, the sendmail program (or daemon) typically acts as the SMTP service.

✦ **POP** — Post Office Protocol is used to store and retrieve e-mails. The current standard, POP3, allows POP3-enabled client applications to download requests and messages that have been stored for a user on a POP3 server. With POP3, once the message has been downloaded to the client it is removed from the server.

✦ **IMAP** — The Internet Message Access Protocol (IMAP), similar to POP, allows a user to access e-mails currently stored on a mail server. Unlike POP, however, IMAP allows a user to browse and manage e-mails without downloading the e-mails first.

MIME, Uucoding, and BinHex

Define MIME, and explain how HTTP and mail servers use MIME types.

E-mail is commonly used to send text messages in addition to files attached to messages. The MIME, Uucoding, and BinHex mechanisms were developed to allow this to occur.

MIME

MIME is currently the most common method used to encode and decode file attachments. When the sender attaches a file to an e-mail message, MIME encodes the file into the message. A header is placed in the message to inform the recipient's e-mail application what type of file is attached and what method can be used to decode it. If a sender attaches a Word document to an e-mail, the recipient's e-mail application is able to decode the document and knows to display it in Word.

MIME types used with e-mail are identical to those used with HTTP covered earlier in this chapter.

Uucoding

UNIX to UNIX encoding (Uucode) is a method used to encode and decode e-mail attachments. Once extremely popular in the UNIX environment, this method has been largely replaced by MIME.

Although the official CIW curriculum uses the name Uucoding, it is more commonly known as Uuencoding.

BinHex

BinHex is an attachment encoding mechanism developed for use in the Apple Macintosh environment. BinHex encoded files can be identified by their .hqx extensions.

Mailing List Server Fundamentals

Identify and describe the functions and features of mailing list servers.

Mailing list servers allow the automatic distribution of e-mail messages to all members of a distribution list. A mailing list server typically allows the creation of mailing lists (also called distribution lists) for individuals interested in a particular subject. For example, an organization may set up a distribution list for people interested in a particular hobby or field of study. Users interested in joining a particular mailing list typically subscribe to it by contacting the mailing list's administrator. After a user has subscribed, any messages sent to the mailing list are forwarded to the user. Those users wishing to remove themselves from a mailing list can send an unsubscribe notice to the mailing list's administrator.

Several commercial e-mail programs, such as Microsoft Exchange, allow mailing list creation and management. There are also dedicated mailing list applications such as L-Soft's LISTSERV (www.lsoft.com), Lyris's ListManager (www.lyris.com), and the free UNIX-based Majordomo (www.greatcircle.com).

Many publicly accessible mailing lists are available on countless topics. Visit www.listserv.net for more information.

Media Server Fundamentals

Identify and describe the functions and features of media servers.

The job of a media server is to provide streaming media over a network. Streaming media is either video or audio provided by the server in a continuous fashion. Radio stations and TV stations commonly provide streaming media services across the Internet. Organizations also use streaming media servers to support real-time conferences, seminars, and presentations across their corporate Intranets. Common media server software available includes the following:

✦ RealNetwork's Realsystem G2 (www.real.com)

✦ Microsoft's NetShow (www.microsoft.com)

✦ Apple's QuickTime Streaming Server (www.apple.com)

Users wishing to listen to or view streaming media must have the appropriate client software, such as RealNetwork's RealPlayer, shown in Figure 16-11.

Figure 16-11: RealPlayer streaming media client

Domain Name Server Fundamentals

 Describe the function of DNS, including the DNS hierarchy, root domain servers, top level domains, and DNS record types.

One of the most important server services in today's TCP/IP networks is the Domain Name or DNS server. The main role of a DNS server is to provide Host name to IP address resolution services via the domain name system. In other words, when given a name such as www.novell.com, a DNS server with access to the Internet should come back with an IP address similar to 192.233.80.11.

 For more information regarding IP addresses, DNS, Host names, and FQDNs, refer to Chapters 1 and 15.

The truly amazing thing about the DNS system is that a user can enter the fully qualified domain name of any registered Web server in the world and within seconds his or her computer has the IP address of the Web server.

The host table

At one time, the Stanford Research Institute Network Information Center (SRI-NIC) managed a single text file referred to as the *host table*. This host table was a complete list of host names and IP addresses for every server resource on the Internet. Network administrators wishing to provide Internet name resolution services for their network would have to download this file to local name servers. As the Internet grew, so did the host table. To keep up to date, an administrator had to download this host file on a very regular basis. Eventually the file became too large and unmanageable, and another method for providing name resolution was needed. In 1984 Paul Mockapetris introduced the domain name system (DNS) to the world.

Similar in concept to DNS is a host file. This simple text file exists on TCP/IP-based computers and can be used by users or administrators wishing to speed up the name to IP resolution process. When trying to resolve an IP address from a name, most computers search this file for the answer before attempting any other methods of resolution. Placing the names and IP addresses for frequently-accessed servers in the host file can result in increased client performance. A sample host file is shown in Figure 16-12.

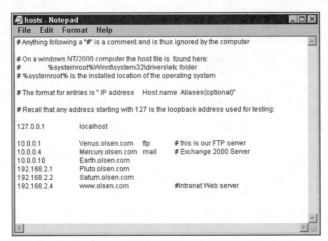

Figure 16-12: A sample Host file viewed in Window's Notepad.

The structure of the domain name system

DNS doesn't have one authoritative source of name to IP address mappings. DNS exists as a hierarchically structured, highly distributed database involving thousands of name servers spread throughout the world. The DNS hierarchy consists of three main layers of domains: root-level, top-level, and second-level.

Note   Top-level domains are often referred to as first-level domains.

The complete DNS database is referred to as the DNS name space. A portion of the DNS name space showing the hierarchical relationship between the domain layers is shown in Figure 16-13.

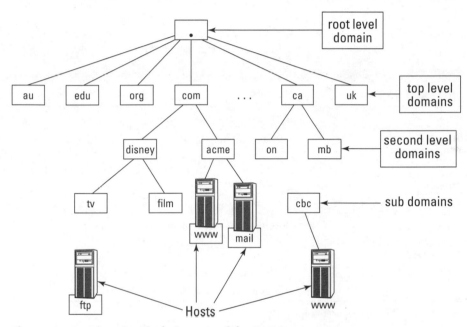

Figure 16-13: The Hieratical structure of the DNS name space

Root-level domain

The root-level domain, denoted simply by a period (.), serves as the highest level of the DNS name space. DNS servers at this layer, referred to as root servers, maintain the names and IP addresses of those servers responsible for the top-level domains. Host name queries received by a root-level domain server result in the root-level DNS server returning a list of servers responsible for whatever first-level domain the queried-for host belongs to. For example, if a root-level server is queried for the IP address of a host with an FQDN `www.acme.com`, the root-level servers will pass back the names and IP addresses of DNS servers responsible for the top-level domain ".com."

Note   Although FQDNs can include the period at the end, in most cases it is usually removed. For example, `www.olsen.ca.` is a valid name, but it is usually expressed as simply `www.olsen.ca` (no period at the end).

Top-level domains

Directly below the root-level in the domain name system are the top-level domains. These domains represent the right-most part of a fully qualified domain name. The purpose of a top-level domain is to organize the DNS name space into separate categories. These categories represent either geographical locations or types of organizations. A geographical location is represented by a two-character country code, and organizations use the current top-level domains shown in Table 16-1.

<table>
<tr><td colspan="2" align="center">Table 16-1
Top-Level Internet Domains</td></tr>
<tr><td>*Top-Level Domain*</td><td>*Purpose*</td></tr>
<tr><td>.com</td><td>Commercial organization</td></tr>
<tr><td>.edu</td><td>U.S. Educational Institutions such as universities</td></tr>
<tr><td>.gov</td><td>U.S. Government Institution</td></tr>
<tr><td>.int</td><td>International Organization (seldom used)</td></tr>
<tr><td>.mil</td><td>U.S. Military</td></tr>
<tr><td>.net</td><td>Internet Service Provider</td></tr>
<tr><td>.org</td><td>Nonprofit Organizations</td></tr>
<tr><td>.biz*</td><td>Business</td></tr>
<tr><td>.info*</td><td>Content and research</td></tr>
</table>

*.biz and .info became operational on June 26, 2001

Cross-Reference   For country codes and proposed future top-level domains, see Chapter 1.

DNS servers operating within the top-level domains are assigned to represent one of these categories. These DNS servers maintain the names and IP addresses of those DNS servers responsible for the various second-level domains registered within their respective categories. For example, a DNS server assigned to the `.com` domain contains a list of DNS servers and their corresponding IP addresses responsible for each second-level domain registered within .com, such as `acme.com`, `disney.com`, and `abc.com`. A top-level DNS server assigned to the `.ca` domain (the country code for Canada) will have a listing of DNS servers responsible for each second-level domain registered under `.ca` such as: `.mb.ca` and `.on.ca`. If a top-level DNS server is queried for the IP address of a host with an FQDN such as `www.acme.com`, the top-level servers pass back the names and IP addresses of DNS servers responsible for the second-level domain `acme.com`.

Second-level domains

Directly below the top-level domains are the second-level domains. These second-level domains represent organizations that have registered within a top-level domain category such as `microsoft.com` or `whitehouse.gov`. Second-level domains may also represent categories within a top-level domain. For example, the Canadian top-level domain, `.ca`, is further divided by province using second-level domains such as `.mb.ca` for Manitoba and `.on.ca` for Ontario.

DNS servers operating at the second level maintain a list of hosts and their corresponding IP addresses within their respective second-level domain. For example, in Figure 16-13, the DNS servers responsible for `acme.com` would have listings for `www.acme.com` and `mail.acme.com`. If a second-level DNS server for `acme.com` is queried for the IP address of a host with an FQDN such as `www.acme.com`, the second-level servers pass back the IP addresses of the actual host `www.acme.com` if it exists.

DNS servers operating within second-level domains that have been further divided by subdomains may also contain the names and addresses of DNS servers responsible for lower subdomains. For example, a DNS server responsible for `.mb.ca` has a listing of all DNS servers registered as representing organizations registered within `.mb.ca` (such as `cbc.mb.ca`).

Subdomains

Subdomains are further divisions of second-level domains. A large organization such as the Disney Corporation, for example, may decide to divide their second-level domain name into subdomains such as `tv.disney.com` and `film.disney.com`.

Domain Name Resolution

To fully understand DNS and how it resolves IP addresses from FQDNs, you must first recognize the following two critical components of DNS:

✦ **Name servers** — servers that can be called upon for name to IP address resolution.

✦ **Name resolvers** — client DNS software configured with at least one address of a name server that is used to resolve IP addresses from names unknown to the client. Both client computers and name servers themselves can be name resolvers.

The following example helps illustrate how the components of the domain name system work together to resolve IP addresses from FQDNs:

Sherri, an engineer with Buildem Construction Company, wishes to the see the home page for ACME Iron Works. She opens a browser and types the following URL into her Web browsers address bar: `www.acme.com`.

For the Web page to be located, Sherri's computer must resolve the IP address from the address www.acme.com. Her computer has been configured with the IP address of Buildem's corporate DNS server.

Figure 16-14 outlines the process that occurs.

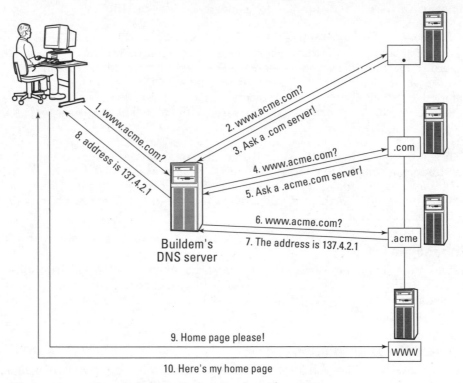

Figure 16-14: The resolution of www.acme.com

The steps involved in the resolution process are as follows:

1. Using its resolver software, Sherri's computer requests the required address from Buildem's DNS server.

2. Because Buildem's DNS server is not responsible for ACME's host addresses, it does not have the requested address. To find the address Buildem's DNS server contacts a DNS root server on the Internet and queries for the address. Buildem's DNS server acts as the resolver.

3. The root server has the addresses of DNS servers responsible for the top-level domain .com, of which www.acme.com is a member. The root server refers the Buildem DNS server to the .com DNS servers by supplying it with a list of their addresses.

4. Buildem's DNS server contacts a `.com` server and again queries for the address of `www.acme.com`.

5. If ACME has registered its second-level domain name, the `.com` server has the IP addresses of ACME's DNS servers, which it passes back to Buildem's DNS server.

6. Buildem's DNS server contacts one of ACME's DNS servers with a query for the IP address of `www.acme.com`.

7. Because the ACME DNS server is responsible for all ACME Internet host computer addresses, it has the appropriate address for `www.acme.com` and passes this back to the Buildem DNS server.

8. The Buildem DNS server passes the requested address on to Sherri's computer.

9. Sherri's computer uses the IP address to contact `www.acme.com` and request the home page.

10. The home page is passed back to Sherri's computer.

Note

DNS servers cache names for a period of time, so if another user requests access to `www.acme.com`, the server would not be required to repeat the entire process.

DNS Server types

Organizations that want to host services on the Internet or use DNS internally for name resolution must have at least one DNS server available to store their name to IP address records. In most cases, an organization uses several. Although a DNS server can be configured in a variety of ways, the CIW Foundations exam focuses on these three main DNS server types:

✦ **Root Server** – A DNS server used to identify the top-level domain servers on the Internet. Other DNS servers are configured to contact Root servers to help resolve FQDNs.

✦ **Primary Name Server** — The primary name server (the root server) holds the master copy of the entire DNS database for its domain. When new hosts are added to a domain, the primary server is updated with their names and IP addresses. The primary server is said to be authoritative for the domain. In addition to maintaining the records of the domain, the root server is responsible for resolving name queries for records within its domain and for contacting other root servers if it needs to resolve a name outside of its domain.

✦ **Secondary Name Server** — A secondary server also holds a copy of the entire domain, which it receives from the primary server. Updates to the domain cannot be made directly to a secondary server. A secondary server provides name resolution load balancing, fault tolerance in the event of a primary name server failure, and faster name resolution for clients in the same geographical location as the secondary server.

In the Real World   Secondary servers can be configured to receive updates from other secondary servers as well. This reduces the number of updates that a primary server must provide.

Introduction to DNS records

As you now know, DNS servers maintain information regarding the Domain over which they have authority. This information is stored by record type in a database. The record types you should know for the CIW Foundations exam are listed in Table 16-2.

Table 16-2
Important DNS Record Types

Record type Designator	Record Name	Description
A	Host address record	Used to associate a computer's host name with its IP address.
SOA	Start of Authority	The start of authority record is created on the primary server to be used as a reference containing information for that zone. For example, it contains the name of the primary server, how often secondary servers should be updating their records, and the name of the administrator responsible for the domain.
NS	Name Server	This record lists each name server responsible for the domain (both primary and secondary).
CNAME	Canonical Name or Alias	This record designates additional names for a particular host.
		For example, a server with a name of exchange.acme.com may perform the functions of a POP3 server, SMTP server, and a NEWS server. This one server can be given additional names such as pop3.acme.com, smtp.acme.com, and news.acme.com. When configuring clients for these services, the appropriate names can be used. If one of these services moves to another server, the CNAME record can be changed to reference the new server. Clients will not require changes to their configuration settings.
MX	Mail Exchanger	Identifies servers responsible for e-mail within the domain.

Exam Tip   Know these DNS record types for the exam.

Common DNS servers

The most common of all DNS servers currently found on the Internet is the Berkley Internet Name Domain (BIND) service, available on UNIX servers running the name daemon (named).

Although BIND is only supported on the UNIX platform, most other implementations of DNS are based on it, including Microsoft's DNS server found in Windows NT/2000 servers. Microsoft's version of DNS is installed as an optional networking service and allows the management of DNS domains and records in a GUI interface as shown in Figure 16-15.

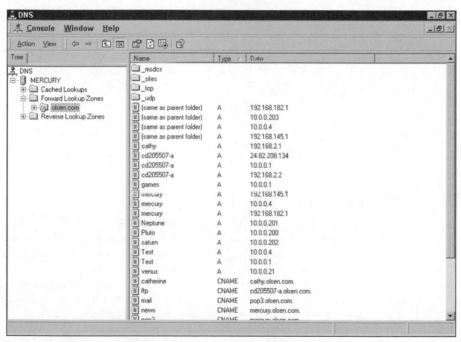

Figure 16-15: The DNS administration utility for Windows 2000

FTP Server Fundamentals

Objective   Identify and describe the functions and features of FTP servers.

An FTP server allows FTP clients to transfer files from the FTP server (read) or to the FTP server (write). Most operating systems and Web browsers now include FTP clients. The server component is typically an optional service with the operating system or is included as part of an Internet server suite such as Microsoft's Internet Information Server (IIS). After the service is installed and configured, an area of the server's hard drive is set aside for the files to be transferred to and from the server. As with HTTP servers, a user's access to the files can be controlled by setting permissions within the Web server or by using file permissions within the underlying operating system. Figure 16-16 shows the default file location and associated read and write permissions within a Windows 2000 FTP server.

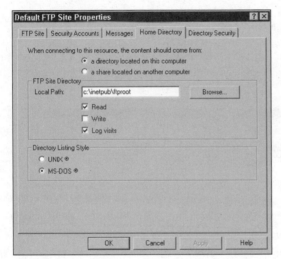

Figure 16-16: The default file settings in FTP Windows 2000

Considerations for using FTP

Although there are many methods of transferring files across a network, for larger files of two MB or greater, FTP should be considered. FTP is generally faster and more reliable than other methods. E-mail servers often have a size limitation placed on files, both for forwarding and for storing. The sending or receiving e-mail servers can reject a file that is too large. Large files sent to an individual's mailbox may be accepted but could put the recipient's mailbox over its maximum space allotment disabling the e-mail application to other incoming e-mails until the problem is rectified.

Exam Tip   Remembering that transferring files over two MB should be done using FTP could ensure one correct answer on the exam.

FTP security

Most FTP servers accept anonymous connections. This is actually considered a more secure method than password protecting FTP servers, because the FTP protocol itself requires user IDs and passwords to be sent in clear text, which makes them vulnerable to packet sniffing.

Cross-Reference   Packet sniffing and FTP security is discussed in Chapter 18.

FTP logging

FTP servers keep a connection log similar to the log kept by Web servers. This log, stored in text format, typically lists the details of client connections to the FTP server. As shown in Figure 16-17, information found in the log includes dates and times of user connections, names and passwords of connected users, and FTP file transfer commands carried out during the session. This log can be helpful to determine when clients connect to the server and what files are accessed most often.

```
ex011116.log - Notepad
File  Edit  Format  Help
#Software: Microsoft Internet Information Services 5.0
#Version: 1.0
#Date: 2001-11-16 18:02:43
#Fields: time c-ip cs-method cs-uri-stem sc-status
18:21:41 10.0.0.4 [5]USER anonymous 331
18:21:45 10.0.0.4 [5]PASS andy@bc.ca 230
18:22:24 10.0.0.4 [5]sent /ch12.doc 550
18:22:40 10.0.0.4 [5]sent /ch12.doc 226
18:38:38 10.0.0.4 [5]closed - 421
19:07:51 10.0.0.4 [6]USER anonymous 331
19:07:57 10.0.0.4 [6]PASS keith@a.z 230
19:08:28 10.0.0.4 [6]sent /ch12.doc 226
19:23:38 10.0.0.4 [6]closed - 421
22:24:13 10.0.0.4 [7]USER anonymous 331
22:24:34 10.0.0.4 [7]PASS Randy@machineshop.ca 230
22:24:51 10.0.0.4 [7]MKD test 257
22:25:13 10.0.0.4 [7]created betty.cer 226
22:25:29 10.0.0.4 [7]created Hammer.tif 226
22:25:31 10.0.0.4 [7]QUIT - 226
```

Figure 16-17: A Windows 2000 FTP server log

News Server Fundamentals

Objective   Identify and describe the functions and features of news servers.

A news server provides newsgroup access to NNTP clients. Newsgroups are discussion forums, similar to bulletin boards. Interested parties can access a newsgroup to read notices (referred to as postings), share ideas, ask questions, submit answers, and discuss topics of common interest in a text-based format.

Newsgroups categories

Thousands of publicly accessible newsgroups, referred to as USENET, are available on the Internet. USENET was originally developed as an open forum for discussion within the university community. Now it is available to anyone who wants to subscribe.

The content of newsgroups varies, so they have been organized by topic into various categories. The most popular, referred to as "the big-eight," are shown in Table 16-3.

Table 16-3 Popular Newsgroup Categories	
Category	**Description**
alt	Alternative or controversial topics
comp	Computer topics
misc	Miscellaneous
news	USENET information
rec	Recreational topics, such as hobbies and the arts
sci	Sciences and scientific research topics
soc	Topics regarding socializing and social issues
talk	General discussion groups for topics such as religion, politics, and so on

The newsgroup categories are divided into many subcategories, which, in turn, may also be divided into subcategories. The names of the newsgroups consist of these categories presented in a hierarchical format. For example, "comp.os. ms-windows.nt" is a general newsgroup for discussion on the computer operating system Windows NT, and "comp.os.linux.redhat" is a newsgroup dedicated to the Red Hat Linux operating system.

Figure 16-18 shows some additional newsgroup topics available under the "comp" category as viewed in Microsoft's Outlook express, a client newsgroup reader.

The distribution of newsgroups

Public newsgroups typically do not reside on one single newsgroup server. Instead, newsgroups are distributed among many servers throughout the world. Each server accepts messages posted by its users and passes these messages on to other news servers through a process referred to as *newsfeed*.

The owner of the news server can decide which public newsgroups it wants to host. An ISP, for example, may subscribe to thousands of newsgroups to make them available to their customers. A business, on the other hand, may decide to subscribe to a few specific newsgroups that deal with issues that are relevant to its employees.

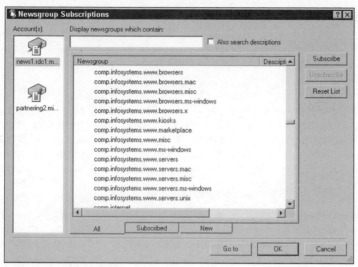

Figure 16-18: Viewing newsgroup categories in Outlook Express

Newsgroup content

Public newsgroups are often referred to as *Classic Internet newsgroups*. These newsgroups are typically available for free to anyone wants to subscribe. As a rule, classic newsgroups do not enforce any standards or regulations for posted messages. This openness can lead to inappropriate and offensive postings.

To combat the openness problems of classic newsgroups, many newsgroups are now offered in a moderated format. A moderated newsgroup administrator (a moderator) checks all postings for appropriateness. Messages that are deemed acceptable remain on the newsgroup, and all others are removed.

Many organizations choose to create their own private newsgroups. These newsgroups are often for the sole use of their employees within a corporate Intranet or for select individuals within a corporate extranet.

Private newsgroups can be used for many purposes, including discussion forums for project teams and departmental reference libraries. Private newsgroups often contain sensitive corporate information and employ security measures to limit the accessibility of this data. User access is secured through the use of user IDs and passwords, and data transmissions are often protected by encryption (using Secure Socket Layers or other technologies).

Cross-Reference   Data encryption using SSL is covered in more detail in Chapter 18.

Certificate Server Fundamentals

Objective

Identify and describe the functions and features of certificate servers.

One of the fundamental problems with using the Internet is the lack of security provided. Data moving between a client and a server on the Internet can pass through any number of intermediary networks and computers. The data could be intercepted and have its contents examined or even changed along the way. Companies or individuals wishing to send sensitive or personal information across the Internet need to be assured that the data sent is only available to the intended recipient. Certificate servers help in this process.

Certificate servers hand out and verify digital certificates or electronic keys. These digital certificates can be used to verify the identities of parties involved in electronic data exchange. Electronic keys contained within the certificate can also be used as part of a data encryption process to ensure that data passed between the parties is only readable by those parties. Figure 16-19 is an example of an electronic certificate generated by Microsoft's own certificate server.

Figure 16-19: An electronic certificate owned by Microsoft

Cross-Reference

Certificate servers, certificates, and electronic keys are covered in more detail in Chapter 18.

Directory Server Fundamentals

A directory server provides a centralized database of network resources. This database typically contains the listing of network users and resources, such as servers and printers, to which users may have access. Directory servers provide access to resources by verifying users' identities through network authentication (login). Once authenticated, if a user requests access to a network resource, the directory server determines whether or not the user has the necessary permissions and access is granted or denied.

A comprehensive set of information about each user can be stored in a directory services database. This data may include the following:

✦ User name

✦ User id

✦ Password

✦ Departmental information

✦ Phone numbers

✦ E-mail addresses

Figure 16-20 shows a subset of user information that can be kept on a Windows 2000 Active Directory directory server.

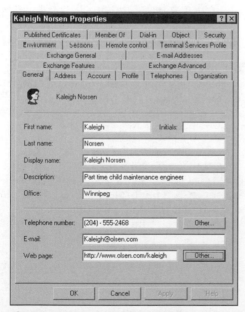

Figure 16-20: User information in Windows 2000 Active Directory

Additional Directory Service Functions

A true directory server service can act as a single centralized database for much of an organization's critical information. As such, it can replace the many individual databases often found in an organization that store redundant data. For example, the directory server can contain a complete list of employee information. This database can supply information for human resource applications, e-mail applications, and many other applications. Network resource information contained within the database can be used for hardware inventories or asset tracking.

To allow access to external applications and to facilitate communications with other directory servers, most directory services, including the popular Novell's NDS and Microsoft's Active Directory are based on two protocols: X.500 and LDAP.

X.500

The X.500 directory access protocol, also referred to as directory access protocol or DAP, creates a distributed directory service. A single directory service database may be distributed and shared between many directory servers, forming a global directory.

An X.500 compliant database is typically organized in a hierarchical fashion in which entries can be organized by criteria, such as their physical location or their function. For example, a large multinational company may design an X.500 database so that network resource entries can be added to the database according to the physical location of the resource. Figure 16-21 is a graphical representation of such a database.

X.500 databases offer the following features:

✦ **Scalability** — The complete database of resources can be divided between all directory servers in an organization, each having a small portion of the entire database. Because no one server needs to contain the complete database, the database can accommodate millions of entries. Even as the database grows in size, it can still be fairly easy to manage due to the hierarchical organization of the information.

✦ **Replication** — The directory service database or portions thereof can be replicated among multiple servers. Several servers can hold identical copies of the same data. These replicas can serve as a fault tolerant method of protecting data. If one server fails, the portion of the database that it held is still available on the replicas. The replicas can also reduce the workload of any one server because they can all respond to requests for resources held in the database.

✦ **Synchronization** — Synchronization enables replicas to keep data current by sending each other updates.

The design fundamentals of X.500 are extremely powerful. The X.500 protocol has had limited success due to its complexity.

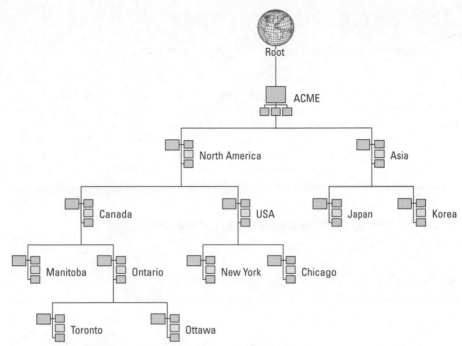

Figure 16-21: An X.500 database design based on geography

Lightweight Directory Access Protocol

The lack of success in using DAP has led to the development of the Lightweight Directory Access Protocol (LDAP). Although based on X.500, LDAP offers both a simplified directory structure and a simplified method of accessing this structure.

The LDAP structure is also hierarchical. It now forms the basis for many directory services, including Netscape's directory server.

An LDAP client, such as the one included with Microsoft's Outlook Express, allows you to use the LDAP protocol to search and retrieve data from LDAP-compliant databases. Many Internet-accessible organizations offer LDAP searching of their people databases so you can locate friends, family, acquaintances, or anyone for that matter. These include Yahoo's people search (`people.yahoo.com`) and Bigfoot's Internet Directory Service (`www.bigfoot.com`).

Catalog Server Fundamentals

 Objective

Identify and describe the functions and features of catalog servers.

A catalogue server indexes information distributed across a network. It allows users to look for information in one central location instead of going to each resource on a network. Catalog servers further simplify information gathering by allowing searches based on a variety of criteria, such as document creation dates, author name, key words contained in the document, and so on. As an example, Figure 16-22 shows a sample of some of the search criteria allowed in Microsoft's Portal Server, which features content cataloging.

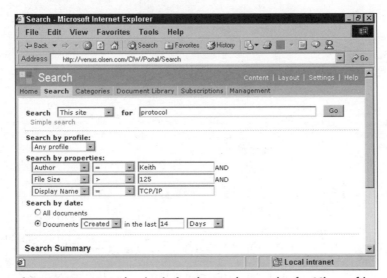

Figure 16-22: Search criteria for the catalog service for Microsoft's Portal Server

In addition to cataloging documents, many catalog servers also catalog the following:

✦ Web pages

✦ Databases

✦ E-mail

✦ Newsgroups

✦ Almost any other online format that data can be stored in

Cataloging and indexing functions are carried out by a process or program referred to as a spider or a robot. The robot "crawls" through the network looking for data files. When the files are found, the robot analyzes their contents and looks for key words that can be used to locate the file later. The file's name, key words, and any other relevant data (such as author, creation date, and time) are sent back to the catalog server and entered into the index. User searches are carried out against this index.

Transaction Server Fundamentals

 Identify and describe the functions and features of transaction servers.

Transaction servers have been in use for many years. Originally developed for the mainframe world of computing, they coordinate all of the tasks involved in completing an online transaction. These Online Transaction Processing (OLTP) servers are used in the following, often complex, types of systems:

✦ Payroll systems

✦ Retail distribution systems

✦ Airline reservation systems

✦ Banking systems

✦ Stock brokering systems

✦ Order entry systems

A transaction server does not constitute the entire system. It merely coordinates the interaction between all of a system's components when a transaction takes place. It ensures that all necessary updates occur to complete the transaction. For example, when an airline ticket is purchased, many updates must occur throughout the system. A seat must be reserved, the food services supplier must know that a meal is required, a ticket must be printed, invoicing and payment must be tracked, and so on. These updates often require interaction with a variety of individual databases. The person requesting the ticket does not want or need to know what databases must be updated, and doing so is up to the transaction server.

IBM's Customer Information Control System (CICS) is one of the most popular mainframe-based OLTP systems on the market. Several transaction server products exist in the client/server market as well; Microsoft's Transaction server is among the most popular. Transaction server has been designed to provide transaction services in a Web-based environment, through the use of Web servers and Active Server Pages. Transaction servers can serve as the central component in a three-tier (or multi-tier) network environment.

 For information regarding three-tier computing, See chapter 12.

Additional Internet Server Concepts

You need to understand two additional concepts concerning servers in a TCP/IP Internetwork for the CIW Foundations exam. The first is UNIX's Internet Daemon and the second is fault tolerance through the use of mirrored servers.

UNIX's Internet daemon fundamentals

Define daemon and identify the functions of the Internet-related daemons named inetd, and telnetd.

A daemon is a UNIX term used to describe any process running in the background that performs a specified operation in response to certain events. With respect to networking on a UNIX computer, the most important daemon is the Internet daemon, inetd. This super-server, typically evoked at system start up, listens to incoming network service requests corresponding to services configured on the server. Upon receiving these requests, inetd, starts up (or "spawns") the appropriate service and passes on the request to that service. For example, the Telnet server service on a UNIX computer is handled by a daemon called telnetd. When a request comes in from the network for Telnet services, inetd receives the request, determines that it is indeed for telnet, spawns the telnetd daemon, and passes it the request.

A file called inetd.conf is used to specify which service requests to listen for and which server service to pass them to. Of the many services available, the CIW Foundations courseware lists the following:

✦ telnetd — Telnet server daemon

✦ smtpd — Simple mail transfer protocol daemon

✦ tftd — Trivial File transport (TFTP) daemon

The inetd service runs with root privileges, which means any process spawned by it also runs with root privileges. Processes with root privileges can potentially have full control over the system. This represents a security risk, therefore limiting access to inetd.conf is recommended.

Mirrored servers

Because many of the servers discussed in this chapter provide "mission-critical" services, protecting these servers and, more importantly, the data on these servers is of prime importance. Organizations often go to great lengths to ensure that network systems services remain available and that data is protected in the event of a failure in a network component, including the loss of a server. Mirroring a server is a common way of providing such fault tolerance.

A mirrored server refers to a server that is a mirror copy of another. For example, if a file is saved to the hard drive on one of the two servers, that file is automatically saved on the other server as well. If one of the servers fails, the data it held is still available on the mirrored server.

The term "clustering" is often used in reference to this arrangement of mirrored servers.

Another technology for providing fault tolerance is mirrored drives. A single server with multiple physical hard drives can be configured to mirror data from one drive to another. If one of the two drives fail, the data is available on the second drive.

This type of data protection is often referred to as RAID level one, which is one form of the Redundant Array of Independent Disks (RAID) standard.

Key Point Summary

This chapter introduces you to some of the most common server technologies found in today's Internetworks. The following is a summary of the information presented:

✦ A file server is any computer that shares a file system resource such as a file or a folder.

✦ A file server should be a fast computer capable of storing large amounts of data.

✦ Print servers allow multiple users access to the same physical print device.

✦ LPD accepts print requests and forwards them to managed print devices.

✦ LPR is a client utility that submits print requests to servers running LPD.

✦ An HTTP (or Web) server's primary duty is to provide Web pages to HTTP clients, most often Web browsers.

✦ The collection of HTTP servers on the Internet is referred to as the World Wide Web.

✦ A virtual directory is a path name given in a URL, which maps to a physical folder. That physical folder might be contained within the Web root folder file structure, a separate folder location on the Web server, or a location on an entirely different server.

✦ The home page is the default Web page that the Web server hands out when no specific page has been requested.

✦ Dynamic Web pages are complex documents that may consist of data drawn from several sources compiled together at the time of the request.

✦ Dynamic Web pages call on external applications to provide them with the content required to complete the page. These calls from dynamic Web pages typically consist of Common Gateway Interface (CGI) scripts.

✦ A Web gateway or HTTP gateway is a Web server process that acts as a gateway between a client and backend service process such as a database application.

✦ The MIME mechanism allows network applications, such as HTTP and e-mail applications, to identify and exchange a variety of file types between clients and servers.

✦ Two forms of security are used with respect to Web servers; they are file permission security and access control security.

✦ File permissions are restrictions placed on files or folders that limit the abilities of users when accessing these files.

✦ File permissions can be defined in either the operating system or the Web server software.

✦ Operating systems permissions usually take precedence over those set in the Web server application.

✦ Access control defines who has access to a particular Web site or to a portion of a Web site.

✦ Most Web servers allow the logging of data regarding client access, referrer information, and errors encountered by the Web server while processing client requests.

✦ A proxy server sits in between a client application and a server application. The proxy server intercepts communication from the client and passes it on to the server as if the proxy server itself were making the request.

✦ Benefits and features of proxy servers include increased network security, conservation of Internet IP addresses, improved Internet access speed, transaction logging, and host-server security.

✦ A caching server stores frequently accessed data to speed client access to the same data in future requests.

✦ A Mail server stores, retrieves, and forwards electronic mail (e-mail) messages.

✦ SMTP is used to send e-mail messages.

✦ POP and IMAP store and retrieve e-mail messages.

✦ POP requires e-mails to be downloaded to a client. IMAP does not.

✦ MIME is currently the most common method for encoding and decoding file attachments within an e-mail message.

✦ UUCoding and BinHex are less popular alternate methods of encoding and decoding file attachments within an e-mail message.

✦ Mailing list servers allow the automatic distribution of e-mail messages to all members of a distribution list.

✦ Media servers provide streaming media over a network. Streaming media is either video or audio provided by the server in a continuous fashion.

✦ A DNS server provides host name to IP address resolution services via the domain name system.

✦ DNS is a hieratically structured and highly distributed database involving thousands of DNS servers spread throughout the world.

✦ The DNS hierarchy consists of three main layers of domains: root-level, top-level, and second-level. The complete DNS database is referred to as the DNS name space.

✦ Servers at the root-level (denoted by ".") in DNS are referred to as root servers.

✦ Top-level domains organize the DNS name space into separate categories.

✦ DNS servers at the top level are responsible for maintaining the names and IP addresses of those DNS servers responsible for second-level domains registered within their respective categories.

✦ Second-level domains represent organizations that have registered within a top-level domain or categories within a top-level domain.

✦ Subdomains are subdivisions of second-level domains.

✦ Name servers can be called upon for name to IP address resolution.

✦ A name resolver is client DNS software that has been configured with at least one name server address to be used when resolving IP addresses from names unknown to the client.

✦ The primary name server holds the master copy of the entire DNS database for a domain.

✦ A secondary name server holds a duplicate copy of the DNS database for a domain. Changes to the database can only be made on the primary name server.

✦ The most common DNS server on the Internet is the Berkley Internet Name Domain (BIND) service, available on UNIX servers running the name daemon (named).

✦ An FTP server allows FTP clients to transfer files from the FTP server (read) or to the FTP server (write).

✦ Files larger than two MB should always be transferred using FTP.

✦ News servers provide newsgroup access to NNTP clients.

✦ Updates between news servers are referred to as newsfeeds.

✦ Public newsgroups are referred to as Classic Internet newsgroups. Access to these public newsgroups is not restricted and content is not moderated.

✦ Private newsgroup content is typically moderated and protected using access control and encryption schemes such as SSL.

✦ A Certificate server hands out and verifies digital certificates, or electronic keys. These electronic keys are used to verify the identities of parties involved in electronic data exchange and to encrypt data sent between them.

✦ A directory server provides a centralized database of network resources.

✦ To allow access to external applications and to facilitate communications with other directory servers, most directory services are based on the X.500 and LDAP protocols.

✦ X.500 offers scalability, replication, and synchronization.

✦ A catalogue server indexes information distributed across a network to facilitate easy search and retrieval.

✦ Transaction servers coordinate all of the tasks involved in completing an online transaction.

✦ A daemon is a UNIX term that describes any process that runs in the background and performs a specified operation in response to certain events.

✦ The Internet daemon, inetd, listens to incoming network requests corresponding to services configured on the server. After receiving these requests, inetd "spawns" the appropriate service and passes on the request.

✦ Mirroring a server is a common way of providing fault tolerance, where data written to the hard drive of one server is mirrored (copied) to the other.

✦   ✦   ✦

STUDY GUIDE

This section is intended to test your understanding of the concepts covered in this chapter. The assessment questions are presented in a format similar to those on the real CIW Foundations exam. The assessment questions test you on key Internet server concepts that you are responsible for during the exam. The scenario questions further challenge your understanding of these concepts by presenting you with a real-life scenario about which you answer several chapter-related questions.

Assessment Questions

1. Which of the following servers uses robots to index information on a distributed network?

   A. Directory server

   B. Catalog server

   C. Transaction server

   D. LDAP server

2. Which of the following services is used to create a database of network resources?

   A. Directory server

   B. Catalog server

   C. Transaction server

   D. File and Print server

3. Which of the following is typically used to submit print jobs in a TCP/IP environment?

   A. LPD

   B. LPQ

   C. LPR

   D. LDAP

   E. LPUT

4. A Web client determines how to render a file based on the file's what?

    A. HTTP type

    B. URL

    C. Alias

    D. MIME type

    E. CNAME

5. Which of the following are examples of common initial Web document names? (Choose all that apply)

    A. initial.htm

    B. welcome.htm

    C. default.html

    D. default.asp

    E. hello.htm

6. Which of the following are not protocols related to e-mail? Choose all that apply.

    A. IMAP

    B. POP

    C. NNTP

    D. SMTP

    E. SNMP

7. Which of the following categories are found at the root-level domain of DNS?

    A. .com

    B. .org

    C. .ca

    D. .microsoft.com

    E. All of the above

    F. None of the above

8. True or False: Long URLs can be avoided with the use of virtual directories.

9. True or False: The name daemon is a UNIX client application used to resolve names from IP addresses.

10. Which of the following protocols is used to send e-mail?

    A. SMNP

    B. SNTP

    C. SMTP

    D. POP

    E. IMAP

11. Which of the following is used to limit access to system resources?

    A. Permissions

    B. SSL

    C. Virtual Directories

    D. SMIME

    E. System lock down parameters

12. Which of the following can be used to speed up access to frequently visited sites on the Internet?

    A. Web server

    B. Transaction server

    C. Proxy server

    D. Catalog server

    E. Media server

13. Which of the following can be used to filter out client requests to undesirable Web sites?

    A. Web server

    B. Transaction server

    C. Proxy server

    D. Catalog server

    E. Media server

14. Which of the following can be used to stream audio over the Internet?

    A. Web server

    B. Transaction server

    C. Proxy server

    D. Catalog server

    E. Media server

15. MIME is associated with which of the following servers?

    A. HTTP server

    B. Transaction server

    C. Mail server

    D. Caching server

    E. Media server

16. Which of the following are key components in the domain name system? (Choose all that apply)

    A. Name servers

    B. Resolvers

    C. Catalogs

    D. Requestors

    E. Uucode Decoders

17. Which of the following is said to be authoritative for a DNS domain?

    A. Root server

    B. Primary server

    C. Secondary server

    D. Master server

    E. Name server — inetd

18. Which of the following DNS record types is used to identify an e-mail server?

    A. NS

    B. A

    C. CNAME

    D. SOA

    E. MX

19. What is an NS record used to identify?

    A. Name servers for a domain

    B. News servers for a domain

    C. Alias for a specified host

    D. Mail servers

    E. Name status information for a registered domain

20. True or False: FTP is suitable for transferring files that are smaller than two MB.

21. True or False: USENET is a collection of private newsgroups strictly for user networks.

22. Two protocols associated with Directory servers are:

    A. SMTP

    B. X.500

    C. LDAP

    D. DSLP

    E. NNTP

23. Which of the following are used to address the issue of network data security?

    A. Certificate servers

    B. Name servers

    C. Transaction servers

    D. Mirrored servers

    E. All of the above

24. Which of the following server products is free, open sourced, and powerful?

    A. Apache

    B. IIS

    C. PWS

    D. iPlanet

    E. All of the above

25. Which of the following is an SMTP server whose primary job is to automatically forward e-mail messages to all members of a distribution list?

    A. Mailing List server

    B. News server

    C. Mail server

    D. Web server

    E. SMTP Go server

Scenario

Magic Carpet Travel Agency offers holiday planning and booking services over the Internet. Using Web browsers, clients can connect to the company's Web site at www.magictravel.uk and perform the following tasks:

✦ Find detailed information regarding holidays by performing key words searches through Magic Carpet's extensive online library of travel brochures and destination planning guides

✦ View streaming video footage of popular destinations

✦ Book airline tickets and hotel reservations on-line

✦ Make credit card payments on reservations

✦ Participate in electronic bulletin board discussion groups regarding travel topics of interest

✦ Join distribution lists for notifications of last minute travel specials and vacation travel bargains

Magic Carpet takes security very seriously and wants to make sure that all on-line booking and purchases are secure from electronic tampering.

Based on the information provided and what you have learned in this chapter regarding internetworking servers, answer the following questions about Magic Carpet's network.

1. What type of server does Magic Carpet likely use to index its library of travel brochures and planning guides?

2. What type of server supplies Magic Carpet's streaming video?

3. What type of server would Magic Carpet likely use to coordinate all the tasks that have to occur after a customer books a trip?

4. What type of server allows Magic Carpet's customers to participate on electronic bulletin boards? What protocol does it use?

5. What type of server can Magic Carpet employ so customers can join distribution lists?

6. What type of server can be used to help ensure that booking and purchase transactions are secure?

Answers to Chapter Questions

Chapter pre-test

1. **LPR** is used to initiate print commands and **LPD** carries them out.

2. Three types of information typically collected in a Web server's logs are **client access data, referrer data, and error data.**

3. A **proxy** server enhances security and speeds up Internet access by caching frequently used documents.

4. A **Mail** server is most likely to use SMTP, POP3, and IMAP.

5. **MIME** is used to identify and encode file attachments when transmitting files via e-mail.

6. A **Mail list** server is used to automatically forward SMTP e-mail messages to every member of a distribution list.

7. A **Media** server provides streaming audio or video over the Internet.

8. A **host** file is a file stored locally on a computer and is used to resolve IP addresses from host names.

9. **Root-level** is the highest domain level of the DNS name hierarchy.

10. The **top-level** domain in the DNS hierarchy includes com, edu, ca, and fr.

11. Name servers and name resolvers are two key components of **DNS**.

12. The **MX (mail exchanger)** DNS record identifies a mail server.

13. The two protocols that serve as the basis for most directory services are **X.500** and **LDAP**.

14. The UNIX daemon **inetd** is used to launch Internet-related server applications such as smtpd and tftd.

Assessment Questions

1. Which of the following servers uses robots to index information on a distributed network?

   B. Catalog server

2. Which of the following services is used to create a database of network resources?

   A. Directory server

3. Which of the following is typically used to submit print jobs in a TCP/IP environment?

   C. LPR

4. A Web client determines how to render a file based on the file's what?

   D. MIME type

5. Which of the following are examples of common initial Web document names? (Choose all that apply)

    B. welcome.htm

    C. default.html

    D. default.asp

6. Which of the following are not protocols related to e-mail?

    C. NNTP

    E. SNMP

7. Which of the following categories are found at the root-level domain of DNS?

    F. None of the above

    The root level is the highest level in DNS. .com, .org and .ca are found at the top-level, . micorosft.com is found at the second level, and none are found at the root level

8. **True**: Long URLs can be avoided with the use of virtual directories.

9. **False**: The name daemon is a UNIX server (not a client) application used to resolve names from IP addresses.

10. Which of the following protocols is used to send e-mail?

    C. SMTP

11. Which of the following is used to limit access to system resources?

    A. Permissions

12. Which of the following can be used to speed up access to frequently visited sites on the Internet?

    C. Proxy server

13. Which of the following can be used to filter out client requests to undesirable Web sites?

    C. Proxy server

14. Which of the following can be used to stream audio over the Internet?

    E. Media server

15. MIME is associated with which of the following servers? (Choose all that apply)

    A. HTTP server

    C. Mail server

16. Which of the following are key components in the domain name system? (Choose all that apply)

    A. Name servers

    B. Resolvers

17. Which of the following is said to be authoritative for a DNS domain?

   B. Primary server

18. Which of the following DNS record types is used to identify an e-mail server?

   E. MX

19. What is an NS record is used to identify?

   A. Name servers for a domain

20. True: FTP is suitable for transferring files that are smaller than two MB. FTP can be used for any size file and is recommended for all files greater than two MB in size.

21. False: USENET is a collection of public newsgroups available on the Internet.

22. Two protocols associated with Directory servers are:

   B. X.500

   C. LDAP

23. Which of the following are used to address the issue of network data security?

   A. Certificate servers

24. Which of the following server products is free, open sourced, and powerful?

   A. Apache

25. Which of the following is an SMTP server whose primary job is to automatically forward e-mail messages to all members of a distribution list?

   A. Mailing List Server

Scenarios Questions

1. **Magic Carpet likely uses a catalog server to create a searchable index of its library of travel brochures and planning guides.**

2. **A media server can provide Magic Carpet's streaming video presentations.**

3. **A transaction server would likely be used to coordinate all of the tasks that need to occur after a customer books a trip.**

4. **A News server, using the NNTP protocol, can be used to allow Magic Carpet's customers access to electronic bulletin boards.**

5. **Magic Carpet can employ a mailing list server so customers can join distribution lists.**

6. **A certificate server can be used to help ensure that booking and purchase transactions are secure.**

Extending Web Server Abilities

◆ ◆ ◆ ◆

EXAM OBJECTIVES

1. Explain the uses of server-side scripting and define gateways.

2. Define Common Gateway Interface (CGI).

3. Differentiate between client-side and server-side scripting.

4. Describe server programming interface alternatives to CGI, such as Java gateways, ActiveX Data Objects (ADO), and Server Application Programming Interfaces (SAPIs).

5. Explain server-side scripting applications, including Java Server Pages (JSP), Personal Home Page (PHP), Active Server Pages (ASP) and Server-Side JavaScript (SSJS).

6. Explain the functions of Java servlets and how they differ from scripting languages.

7. List the different types of databases and database management systems, including DBMS and RDMBS.

8. Differentiate between Open Database Connectivity (ODBC) and Java Database Connectivity (JDBC).

CHAPTER PRE-TEST

1. What tasks are typically associated with server-side scripting? What tasks are typically associated with client-side scripting?

2. CGI scripts are most commonly called from what location?

3. ISAPI and NSAPI are examples of which Web server extension technology?

4. DataBase Management Systems are responsible for what aspects of data management?

5. _____ is a Microsoft proprietary database connectivity standard, whereas _____ is developed by Sun Microsystems.

6. What is the primary difference between the operations of Java servlets compared to other server-side scripting technologies?

Web servers have an ability to present information in a hardware- and software-independent manner through the use of non-proprietary protocol standards. HyperText Transport Protocol (HTTP) defines the process of delivering linked pages of information across a TCP/IP network. HyperText Markup Language (HTML) defines universal formatting directives that are intended to make the Web page appear the same on all browsers, regardless of the platform on which they run.

As useful as these standards are, however, they don't directly present solutions for achieving inter-process and inter-server data access and manipulation. This type of interaction is becoming more and more common as the Internet is leveraged as a tool for information, entertainment, and commerce.

This chapter discusses methods and technologies that extend Web server capabilities and allow interaction between the Web browser, the Web server, and additional back-end servers, processes, and data.

Client-side and Server-side Scripting

 Differentiate between client-side and server-side scripting.

Client-side and server-side scripting are used as complimentary tools in the creation of complex and capable Web applications. Both scripting environments have their particular strengths and weaknesses, and you should understand where each fits into the overall application development strategy.

Client-side scripting

Client-side scripting is the process of writing code — most commonly JavaScript or VBScript — that is delivered to the Web browser on the user's computer (the client), along with the HTML document (the Web page) that the client is viewing. The script may be embedded in the Web page itself, or it may be contained in a separate file that is linked to one or more Web pages. The Web browser executes this code on the user's computer. Client-side script can improve the overall performance of the Web site by off-loading some of the processing requirements from the Web server, freeing it to serve more clients, or serve its existing clients in a more efficient manner. Client-side script usually handles interaction with the user, such as producing pop-up messages or initiating simple content changes based on what the user is pointing at. An example of client-side JavaScript follows:

```
<HTML>
   <HEAD>
   <TITLE>Client-Side Scripting Example</TITLE>
   <SCRIPT LANGUAGE="JavaScript">
   <!--
```

```
      function helloWorld()
      {
            alert("Hello World!");
      }
   -->
   </SCRIPT>
   </HEAD>
   <BODY onLoad="helloWorld()">
 <H1>Brought to you by JavaScript!"</H1>
   </BODY>
</HTML>
```

This simple example prompts a dialog box, called an *alert*, to pop up when the page is loaded. Note the use of the HTML `<SCRIPT>` and `</SCRIPT>` container tags, which enclose the script and set it apart from the rest of the document. The comment tags, `<!--` and `-->`, are used to hide the script from older browsers that can't interpret the script because they will ignore everything between the comment tags.

Server load reduction through client-side scripting

As mentioned previously, client-side script can effectively distribute the load of processing dynamic Web content by moving functions that can be efficiently performed by the client system out to the Web browser. For example, code that manages interactive content, such as pop-up menus or the changing images of rollover buttons, will run most efficiently on the client side. In fact, any function that accesses or manipulates properties of the client's system should be created with client-side script in order to reduce the communication between the client and the server, to free bandwidth, and to lessen the load on the Web server.

Client-side scripting restrictions

Given the ability to do fairly sophisticated client-side scripting, you may think that you can continue to increase Web server performance by off-loading even more functions to the client. In fact, through the use of programs such as Java applets or ActiveX components, you can create client-side functions that can make connections to database servers and other programs, independent of the Web server. Theoretically, this should increase performance by further reducing the workload on the server.

The opposite is true, however. Functions that create connections from the client to other data sources often have a negative impact on performance. Every network connection involves a certain amount of overhead in the form of message header information, which has nothing to do with the actual data that is requested. Therefore, it makes more sense to have the client communicate its data request to the Web server, which will then make a limited number of connections to the database server on behalf of the clients. This scenario is more efficient because it requires fewer connections, and — in terms of data transfer rates — because clients typically connect at slower rates (especially dial-up users) than network speeds used for connections between servers.

Common Client-side Script Usage

The following example illustrates a common method of implementing functions in client-side script.

The function `helloWorld` is defined in the header section of the HTML document. This is the recommended location for script functions because it assures that the functions are loaded with the document header prior to the body content from where the functions are normally called.

The `<BODY>` tag calls the `helloWorld` function by using the `onLoad` directive. This directive instructs the Web browser to look for and execute the function — in this case `helloWorld` — when the body of the HTML document loads.

Performance is not the only issue with overuse of client connections, however. Security is much more difficult to ensure if multiple connections are made from the clients to the database or application servers.

Consider an online store, for example. The store front application is accessed across the Internet from Web browsers. Data, such as user account information, user orders, and product catalogs are maintained on a dedicated SQL server. Assuming that many users (hundreds, thousands, and so on) will potentially connect to this system and need access to the data, how does the online store validate each user if it uses client-side directives to connect to the database?

In a local situation (such as a LAN or intranet) where the number of users is limited and the administrator knows each user, this validation is traditionally performed by creating a user account for each client. This account either resides at the data server or in the network security structure. If the account is maintained on the network, "pass-through" authentication is provided to the data server when a valid network user attempts to access the data server.

In the online store scenario, however, clients are not local users and therefore don't have local network accounts for authentication purposes. The application can be written to require the user to set up a "store account" when they first use the system, but unless the Web application employs some method of automatically creating a corresponding network user account with appropriate permissions, the network administrators have to create the accounts and set up the permissions for each new user of the Web application. Obviously, this is undesirable due to the workload involved for the administrators. In addition, most administrators don't appreciate any application creating and manipulating user accounts on their network — regardless of the validity of the concern.

To continue with the online store scenario, therefore, assume that the user is allowed to use the database because he or she already has a store account.

In this scenario, it makes sense to instruct the database to allow connections from the Web server, and not from individual users. To do this, simply create a service account in the security structure of the data server and code that identification into the connection request from the Web application. In this way, you can deny access to the data from anyone other than valid users of the Web application (those with store accounts). In addition, you can further protect the data server by instructing it not to service requests from systems other than the Web server. To facilitate communication between the Web server and the data server, it makes more sense to employ server-side scripting when making the data connection.

Server-side scripting

 Explain the uses of server-side scripting and define gateways.

Server-side scripting is the process by which the server carries out instructions embedded in the HTML documents that make up the Web site. This may entail including external files in the Web page, executing scripting code embedded into the page, or calling on scripts or programs completely outside of the HTML document.

For example, you can execute a *server-side include* from an HTML document by using the INCLUDE directive, as shown in the following simple example:

```
<HTML>
    <HEAD>
    <TITLE>Simple Include Example</TITLE>
    </HEAD>
    <BODY>
<H1>An Example Using a Server-Side Include</H1>
<P>
<!--#INCLUDE VIRTUAL="include_me.html"-->
    </BODY>
            </HTML>
```

A server-side include includes the content of an external file in the Web page. The Web page and the content of the included file are then sent to the browser. In the previous example, the content of the `include_me.html` file is included at the point where the sever encounters the INCLUDE tag. As far as the browser is concerned, the included file and the HTML document it is included in are interpreted as a single document.

If a process was dynamically updating the `include_me.html` file, then browsers would see that dynamic content whenever they viewed a Web page that included that file.

 For this example to work, the Web server must be set up to allow includes. In some cases, the server administrator will disable this ability due to its inherent security risk. For example, a hacker can quite possibly exploit the use of includes by gaining access to the Web server and replacing an exiting file, known to be used as an include, with a malicious file.

Another example of server-side scripting is the embedding of scripting commands in the HTML document, which will be acted upon by an interpreter. Such script is written in one of any number of scripting languages, such as Active Server Pages (ASP), Personal Home Page (PHP), or Server-Side JavaScript (SSJS). You can find more information about these scripting languages and definitions of their uses later in this chapter.

The following code is an example of ASP scripting embedded in an HTML document:

```
<HTML>
    <HEAD>
    <TITLE>Simple ASP Example</TITLE>
    </HEAD>
    <BODY>
<H1>An Example of Embedded ASP Script</H1>
<P>
Your Computer's IP address is:
<%=Request.ServerVariables("REMOTE_ADDR")%>
    </BODY>
</HTML>
```

This script uses the Request object, defined in ASP, to request that the server variable REMOTE_ADDR, which contains the IP address of the browser's computer, be displayed on the Web page. Note that the script itself is the code between the <%= and %> tags.

In the Real World In order for this script to run correctly, the Web server must support the use of ASP, which can't be guaranteed on servers other than Microsoft Internet Information Server (IIS) 4.0 (or later versions).

When choosing whether to use client-side or server-side scripting, the Web developer needs to recognize the advantages and disadvantages of each type. Generally, server-side scripting is best used for connection to back-end systems, such as database or application servers. Client-side scripting is more appropriate when manipulating client-contained information. The following table summarizes the appropriate uses of client-side and server-side scripting.

As you can see by looking at the table, both client-side and server-side scripting have their place in the development of a complete Web application. Don't think of one as better than the other; rather, use each one appropriately to create a Web application that will perform more efficiently and will be more appealing to the users.

Table 17-1		
Appropriate uses of Client-side and Server-side Scripting		
Function of Script	*Use Client-side Script*	*Use Server-side Script*
Access any data or properties of the client, such as type of browser or local time.	Yes	No
Access to data on any system other than the client.	No	Yes
Managing user interaction with Web page elements, such as menu selections or interactive images (i.e. roll-over buttons).	Yes	No
Creation of dynamic HTML content based on user's interaction with the Web site.	No	Yes

HTTP Gateways

An *HTTP gateway* is software that passes client HTTP requests on to other applications or servers, and then passes the application or server responses, in HTML format, back to the client.

Figure 17-1 illustrates the relationship between the Web browser or client, the Web server, and a database server or other service, such as an application server.

The HTTP gateway needs to provide capabilities outside the realm of client-side scripting or simple server-side includes. Many options for implementing HTTP gateways are available. The following sections discuss some of the most common implementations.

Common Gateway Interface (CGI)

Define common Gateway Interface.

Common Gateway Interface, or CGI, represents the most widely supported — and generally the simplest — method of deploying HTTP gateways. CGI programs, which are often called *scripts*, are written in languages such as Perl, Python, or C++. As Figure 17-1 illustrates, the CGI script accepts instructions from the HTTP server, accesses additional data or services, and returns that data, in the form of standard HTML code, to the HTTP server. This HTML response is then sent back to the client.

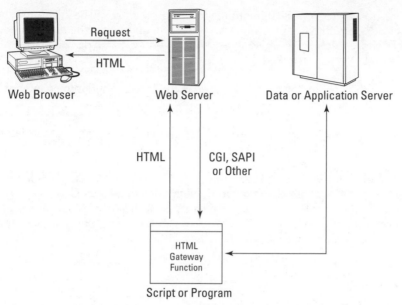

Figure 17-1: Information movement through an HTTP gateway

Benefits of using CGI

CGI benefits from the fact that it is tried and true; in fact, many developers know at least one of the common scripting languages, such as Perl, Python, or C++. This enables organizations that want to deploy a custom application to get their product developed and deployed in as short a time as possible, due to the abundance of qualified developers. It also ensures that — after the application is implemented — sufficient support resources will be available to maintain it.

Disadvantages of using CGI

Although CGI as a whole is a mature technology with a high degree of industry support, there are some disadvantages to implementing CGI.

CGI scripts can be difficult to debug because the development environments generally do not provide strong (if any) debug utilities. Without such tools, developers are forced to manually examine their code in an attempt to find problems.

Another disadvantage is that CGI applications are *stateless*, meaning that they don't have the ability to persist information between a user's sessions. For example, suppose that a user accesses a Web page and logs into a Web-based application. The user navigates to a form and begins filling it in. If the user's session is interrupted, the script has no way to *persist* (remember) the current state of the session. When the user reconnects to finish her task, she must log in and begin the entire process from scratch. Newer technologies, such as ISAPI, overcome this drawback by allowing state information to be tracked.

Note   ISAPI and similar technologies are discussed in the Server programming interfaces section later in this chapter.

CGI applications generally run *out-of-process*, meaning that they run as standalone processes outside of the Web server code and environment space.

When a user accesses a Web page that launches a CGI script, the script is loaded into the Web server's memory and executed. Each additional access to the script creates a new instance of the CGI application, on the Web server. This causes additional overhead and ultimately limits performance and the number of simultaneous users of the Web application, as shown in Figure 17-2.

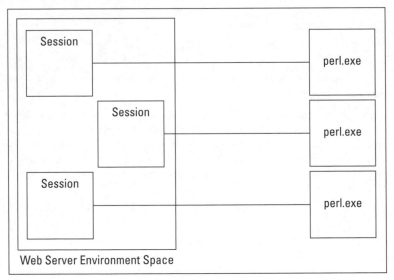

Figure 17-2: Out-of-process applications

In some implementations, the CGI interpreter is incorporated into the actual Web server code. In the Windows environment, this is done via dynamic link libraries (DLLs), which extend the functionality of the Web server. Implementing the interpreter via DLLs has the effect of bringing the CGI program *in process*. In-process applications run in the same code and environment space as the applications (in this case, the Web server) that called them. In addition, in-process applications are usually shared among all calling processes. If this is the case, the first call to the script will create an instance of the interpreter and subsequent calls to the script can share the same instance. This process reduces the overhead associated with running the script, boosts performance, and increases the number of simultaneous connections to the application.

Security may also be an issue in using CGI, particularly when run as out-of-process applications. Because out-of-process CGI applications call and execute external programs, a hacker can conceivably upload a malicious CGI script to a Web site and execute it. And because the script needs permissions to run on the server, the hacker can possibly gain access to the system through the permissions granted to the application.

CGI installation locations on the server

CGI scripts originated on UNIX-based systems, where they were placed in a directory called *CGI-BIN*. Because CGI scripts are generally platform-independent, the script file may be copied from one system to another, and is expected to perform the same function. To facilitate this process, CGI scripts are almost always placed in the CGI-BIN directory — regardless of the operating system.

Despite their drawbacks, CGI applications are still employed due to their mature nature, ease of implementation, and familiarity to a large number of developers.

HTML Form Processing

HTML forms are commonly used as the front-end data gathering mechanism for Web applications.

The HTML <FORM> tag is used to associate the form data with a CGI script or other server process. The form also includes a Submit button which, when clicked, will cause the data entered on the form to be submitted to the server. All controls between the <FORM> opening tag and the </FORM> closing tag are considered to belong to the same form and will be submitted when the form is submitted. The data is sent to the CGI application, or other gateway process, that is defined in the <FORM> tag, as shown in the following HTML form example:

```
<HTML>
<HEAD>
<TITLE>Simple HTML Form Example</TITLE>
</HEAD>
<BODY>
<H1>An Example of an HTML Form Submission</H1>
<P>
```

```
<FORM ACTION="http://www.w3prodesigns.com/cgi-bin/echo.pl"
  METHOD="POST">
    <TABLE>
    <TR>
    <TD>Enter your user name:</TD>
    <TD><INPUT TYPE="text" NAME="txtUserName"></TD>
    <TD><INPUT TYPE="submit" VALUE="OK"></TD>
    </TR>
    </TABLE>
</FORM>
</BODY>
</HTML>
```

The HTML document in the previous code presents a form to the user, asking for his or her user name, as shown in Figure 17-3.

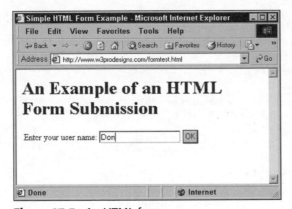

Figure 17-3: An HTML form

The user enters his or her user name and clicks OK, which causes the following Perl script to be called, resulting in the output shown in Figure 17-4.

```
#!/usr/local/bin/perl
use CGI qw/:all/;
($Second, $Minute, $Hour, $Day, $Month, $Year, $WeekDay,
$DayOfYear, $IsDST) = localtime(time);
$theTime = localtime;
print header();
print start_html();
print "<H1>Welcome " . param("txtUserName") . "</H1><BR>";
print "The time at the server is " . $theTime;
print end_html();
```

Figure 17-4: An HTML response from a Perl script

<FORM> tag attributes

The <FORM> tag provides the framework for defining what is included in the form, but the attributes of the <FORM> tag define how the data on the form is submitted and which application processes the data. Two attributes of the <FORM> tag are responsible for these actions: the METHOD and ACTION attributes.

ACTION attribute

The ACTION attribute specifies the URL of the CGI application, or other HTTP gateway, to which the form data will be sent for processing. In the HTML form, shown in Listing 17-4, the URL of the Perl script being called is www.somedomain.com/cgi-bin/echo.pl. When the user clicks the Submit button, the data on the form is packaged and sent to this URL, where the gateway application will process it.

METHOD attribute

The METHOD attribute specifies the transfer method that is used in sending the form data to the gateway application. Two methods are used in transferring data to the gateway: GET and POST.

The GET method appends the form field names and the data that the fields contain to the URL, and then passes it as part of the address call to the gateway application. This is usually considered undesirable, except for the most trivial of transfers, because the data is readily available to network monitors or *sniffers* (programs that allow capture and examination of the data flowing across a network).

The preferred method of transfer is POST because the data is packaged separately from the URL, which accesses the gateway location. This allows for tighter security because the POSTed data can take advantage of encryption in order to protect the content of the submitted information.

In the Real World   Not all Internet Service Providers (ISPs) will handle form submissions in the same way. You should contact the ISP to find out which methods are supported.

Server Programming Interfaces

Objective   Describe server programming interface alternatives to CGI, such as Java gateways, ADO, and SAPIs.

Although CGI is still a popular technology for implementing server-side functionality, the issues of performance and security raised by CGI have prompted the development of additional gateway software. These new options generally employ dynamically loaded object libraries, which run in process at the Web server, thus substantially reducing the overhead associated with out-of-process scripts. They also address the security risk associated with server-side scripts that run outside of the Web server, where a hacker can potentially upload and execute a malicious script.

Server Application Programming Interfaces (SAPIs) are an alternative to traditional CGI applications or scripts. SAPIs can be used in conjunction with — or as a replacement for — CGI scripts, as shown in Figure 17-1. SAPIs also offer a wider range of benefits, which will be discussed shortly.

Various vendors, such as Netscape, Microsoft, and others have developed SAPIs. Most have developed proprietary solutions rather than adhering to an open standard. Even so, numerous advantages can be gained by using SAPI technologies. The following SAPI implementations are some of the more popular technologies being used.

Internet Server Application Programming Interface

Internet Server Application Programming Interface (ISAPI) is a proprietary Web server extension that is supported only on Microsoft Web servers, such as IIS 4.0 or later versions, and on some proprietary third-party gateways.

ISAPI applications run as sub-processes of the HTTP server processes. As a result, they support more simultaneous requests than out-of-process applications can support with their additional overhead.

ISAPI processes are generally not executables. Instead, they are implemented as Dynamic Link Libraries (DLLs). These DLLs are simply libraries of functions that are loaded into the server process when they are needed. After they are loaded, the DLLs remain resident, reducing the access time to their functions for subsequent users. Also, the DLLs are generally shareable by multiple users, so memory is conserved — which equates to better overall performance.

Another advantage that ISAPI offers is its ability to persist client information in sessions. This makes it a state full process that provides the developer a method by which to track the client's actions across the Web application. CGI, on the other hand, can't persist this data from one instance to the next.

ISAPI supports both server-side and client-side scripting. It supports the Microsoft scripting languages VBScript and JScript (Microsoft's version of JavaScript).

Netscape Server Application Programming Interface

Netscape Server Application Programming Interface (NSAPI) is also an HTTP server extension that allows for the execution of in-process programs on the Web server. The main difference between NSAPI and ISAPI is their varying support of programming languages. NSAPI prefers JavaScript, whereas ISAPI prefers VBScript.

ISAPI and NSAPI file locations

Because both interfaces are implemented as DLLs, the files that make up the interfaces are stored in folders specific to the operating system or Web server. In a Windows environment, this is generally either the SYSTEM or SYSTEM32 folder, or a folder relative to the Web server's application folder.

Additional scripting technologies

 Explain server-side scripting applications, including JSP, PHP, ASP, and SSJS.

Other scripting technologies that enable connections from the Web application to databases and other processes include Netscape Server-Side JavaScript (SSJS), Allaire ColdFusion, and Microsoft Active Server Pages (ASP). These are each proprietary scripting languages that don't conform to any prescribed standard. They communicate with the Web application through the use of SAPI or CGI calls.

Two non-proprietary solutions are JavaServer Pages (JSP) and Personal Home Pages (PHP). JSP and PHP provide functionality similar to ASP and SSJS. The following sections discuss ASP, SSJS, PHP, and JSP.

Active Server Pages

Active Server Pages (ASP) is a Microsoft server-side scripting technology. ASP defines six objects that the scripting language interacts with and controls Web server processes and external connections (to a database server) via calls to ISAPI. Although ASP's object model is similar to the JavaScript model, and although it is possible to code with JavaScript or JScript, ASP favors the use of VBScript. This fact makes ASP attractive to developers who are already familiar with some form of Visual Basic (VB) programming.

You can implement ASP script by embedding ASP code into HTML documents (See Listing 17-3). You must also save the HTML document with an `.asp` as opposed to an `.html` extension. Besides the fact that the file now has an .asp extension, the Web server treats it as an HTML document. When the server receives a request for an ASP document, it scans the page for ASP code, executes it (if found), and forwards the page on to the client. The browser interprets the static HTML content of the page as normal. If the ASP code on the page resulted in a response that needed to be sent back to the client (for example, the result of a database query), the response will also be formulated as HTML code and sent to the browser. This makes the issue of browser compatibility with ASP documents a non-issue because the code is interpreted at the server, not the client.

Microsoft has designed ASP, Internet Information Server (IIS), and ISAPI to work together as complete solutions. ASP is provided as part of the full Microsoft IIS servers (on NT Server 4.0 or Windows 2000 Server), Personal Web Server 4.0 (for Windows 95/98 and ME), and Peer Web Server (NT 4.0 Workstation).

ASP has also been implemented as add-on software for numerous other Web servers that run on various operating platforms. Halcyon Software offers their Instant ASP product for Apache Web Servers and Netscape Enterprise Servers that run on NT, UNIX, and Macintosh systems.

Server-side JavaScript

Server-side JavaScript (SSJS) is Netscape's server-side scripting technology; it also relies on objects and is interpreted by the Web server. However, SSJS makes use of JavaScript, and the object model implemented by Netscape is different than the model implemented in ASP. Because JavaScript is more universally supported than VBScript, you may find that more developers able to code in JavaScript are available. You may want to keep this in consideration in terms of available development and support resources for a Web project. Despite these differences, however, the two systems are not radically different and porting from one to the other is relatively straightforward for those who understand scripting languages and are willing to take the time to learn both.

For example, the following HTML page with embedded SSJS performs the same function as the ASP example shown earlier in this chapter.

```
<HTML>
    <HEAD>
    <TITLE>Simple SSJS Example</TITLE>
    </HEAD>
    <BODY>
<H1>An Example of Embedded ASP Script</H1>
<P>
Your Computer's IP address is:
<SERVER>
write(ssjs_getCGIVariable("REMOTE_ADDR"));
</SERVER>
    </BODY>
</HTML>
```

As you can see, the structure of SSJS and ASP are very similar. The major difference is the syntax of the languages.

SSJS is supported on the Netscape Enterprise Server, which is also included in the full installation of Netscape SuiteSpot server — due to the fact that the JavaScript interpreter is implemented as part of the Enterprise Server.

Although ASP has been implemented on Windows, UNIX, and Macintosh systems, SSJS still leads in the number of different operating systems that it is supported on, including Windows, Novell, UNIX, OS/2, and Macintosh. Developers who need to deal with a wide variety of systems should keep this in mind. The fundamental difference between the two systems, however, is that JavaScript is used when coding SSJS and VBScript is the language of preference for writing ASP code.

Server-Side JavaScript is implemented either as standalone script files with a .js extension, or as code embedded in HTML documents. As with ASP, if SSJS is embedded in an HTML document, then the SSJS code is interpreted when the client requests the document. If the SSJS needs to send results to the user, the response is formatted as HTML elements and sent out to the browser.

Personal Home Page

Personal Home Page (PHP) is also a server-side scripting language that can be embedded in HTML documents and is interpreted by the Web server. It provides the same functionality as other server-side scripting languages for producing dynamic Web page content, as well as for connecting the Web server to other systems, such as database servers.

PHP is currently in its fourth version, known as PHP4. Because it is an interpreted language, the PHP interpreter must be installed, to allow the HTTP server to interpret PHP code. PHP interpreters are available for Apache Web server and Microsoft Internet Information Server (IIS). PHP can be downloaded for free from www.php.net. You can also find information on the use of PHP at this Web site. HTML documents with embedded PHP code use a .php extension. The following code shows a simple PHP page.

```
<HTML>
    <HEAD>
<TITLE>
PHP Hello World Test
</TITLE>
    </HEAD>
    <BODY>
<?php echo "Hello World<p>";?>
    </BODY>
</HTML>
```

In this example, the actual PHP script is between the <?php and ?> tags.

PHP competes directly with ASP and SSJS in terms of capabilities and performance. It is also portable between IIS and Apache servers due to its interpreted nature. The fact that it is free is an added bonus.

PHP is an example of software developed under open-source philosophies, the goal of which is to encourage the enhancement and customization of software by the users of that software for the benefit of all users. This is a communal arrangement where — in consideration of the fact that the software is free — users are encouraged to report bugs and suggest improvements as much as possible.

Java Server Pages

Java Server Pages (JSP) provide the same sort of functionality as other scripting languages. Instead of providing a script interpreter (as is the case with ASP, SSJS, or PHP), however, JSP employs a specialized Java *servlet* called the *JSP engine*. Servlets are small Java services that run on a Web server to extending their capabilities. JSP engines are available for NT, Novell, and most UNIX platforms. JSP is non-proprietary.

JSP is implemented in much the same way as ASP or PHP. The JSP Engine interprets the JSP code in a standalone file or embedded into an HTML document. JSP uses a .jsp file extension.

While functionally similar to other scripting languages, JSP can provide even more sophisticated data handling. In particular, JSP is ideal for processing information — contained in an HTML document — separately from the way it is displayed on the page. This enables JSP to deal with not only standard HTML and JSP script, but also with application-specific tags based on XML standard definitions.

JSP is also freely implemented on supported platforms, is vendor neutral, and is even more extensible than PHP. The Sun Microsystems JSP page, located at `http://java.sun.com/products/jsp/index.html`, allows you to download the JSP engine as well as specifications of JSP operation and instructions for its use.

Java servlets

 Explain the functions of Java servlets and how they differ from scripting languages.

As mentioned previously, Java servlets are small Java services that extend the Web server's capabilities. Java servlets are written in Java and compiled; they are not simply interpreted like the scripting languages discussed previously in this chapter.

Java is a full programming language. In addition to creating servlets, you can also use Java to create powerful standalone desktop applications and browser-based applets (applications that run in the browser). These applications are truly platform-independent because Java makes use of a run-time environment called the Java Virtual Machine (JVM). The JVM translates the platform-specific function calls for the Java program. As long as a JVM is available for a particular platform, a servlet, applet, or application will run on that platform without any re-writing or re-compiling. JVMs are currently available for Microsoft, Novell, Macintosh, and most UNIX systems, such as Linux and Solaris.

Due to the extensive support that Java enjoys, a developer can choose to use Java exclusively in creating applications that run both at the client and at the server. This reduces the number of programming languages that the developer needs to learn and support.

Java is also less difficult to program than most scripting languages, or other compiled languages, such as C or C++. The developers of Java purposely removed the elements that make other languages difficult to deal with in order to make it an efficient language to develop in. However, this doesn't mean that the language suffers from any reduction in capabilities; Java is simply easier and safer to code in.

Because servlets are self-contained, compiled pieces of code, they have the ability to be chained. In other words, one servlet can call upon the services of another servlet, which can call on another servlet, and so on. These servlets need not be all on the same system; a servlet can call another servlet anywhere in the network. This allows for distribution of services around the network, reducing the load on individual systems.

Because Java servlets run outside the server environment, they are independent of the life cycle of the Web-based application. That is, they have an innate ability to maintain state information from one session to another because they run independently of the Web services. Because of this ability, Web developers can track visitor information and save it in, for example, a database. The developer can then refer to that database in order to personalize a client's visit the next time he or she connects.

You can also accomplish this functionality by storing cookies on the user's system in stateless scripting languages. However, users have the ability to turn cookie storage off, which defeats the script's ability to retrieve state information from the browsers. Servlets that don't rely on cookies easily overcome this problem.

Java also provides support for the Common Object Request Broker Architecture (CORBA). CORBA is an industry standard architecture for communications between programs that are written in different languages. CORBA provides the common interface through which these programs communicate. By using CORBA to communicate with other applications or by making calls to other Java applications, Java servlets can call on services anywhere on the network.

Because Java servlets are less platform-specific than SAPIs, they have become popular in the implementation of Web services, such as HTTP gateways. In this way, they share similar functionality with CGI scripts. As mentioned previously, however, every user of a CGI script causes a new instance of the script to be created or instantiated. Java servlets, on the other hand, run in the JVM that allows, for example, sharing of the servlet. This means that the servlet will be instantiated upon the first call and then shared with all other processes that need to use it. The servlet instance's ability to be shared makes it more efficient than CGI scripts, allowing servlets to enhance Web server capabilities and performance.

Exam Tip   The CIW Foundations exam does not attempt to test your knowledge of server-side coding syntax. The code listings in this chapter show the similarities and differences between the scripting languages, and are for illustrative purposes only.

An Overview of Database Connectivity

Objective   List the different types of databases and database management systems, including DBMs and RDMBS.

A *database* is a storage location for information. Databases are arranged in either individual, standalone files, or in files that contain related data structures. Databases are at the heart of most online services and are essential in the e-commerce arena. For example, taking a customer's order online would be pointless if the transaction information could not be saved somewhere. *Transaction processing* is the process of updating database information as the transaction takes place. Online Transaction Processing (OLTP) is the name for the processing that happens as the transaction is being performed, capturing the information of the transaction into the database files in real time.

Databases are available in three types:

✦ Non-relational

✦ Relational

✦ Object-oriented

The object-oriented database is the newest of the three and works closely with data structures that are created in object-oriented programming languages, such as Java and C++. As organizations continue to rely more and more on Internet or online applications, relational and object-oriented databases are becoming more widely used. Developers should be familiar with them because these types of databases will almost certainly appear in development projects.

Databases — regardless of the category that they belong to — are controlled by software. In non-relational databases, this software is called the DataBase Management System (DBMS). In relational databases, it is called the Relational DataBase Management System (RDBMS), and the Object DataBase Management System (ODBMS) in object-oriented databases. Each type of database is responsible for managing the data stored in the database files, and for assisting in implementing the business logic that governs how the data is manipulated. Database management systems seldom exist in one location as a single identifiable entity. Rather, they are distributed throughout the network, with — in some cases — some portions located at the client. No single rule governs where services must exist. However, some standard practices dictate the kinds of database management services that should be placed at specific locations in the network. The following sections describe the different database management systems and illustrate where the services that comprise them are generally implemented.

Common database management system features

All database management systems share some common goals. They ensure that the data is accessible in an orderly manner. Connection to the data is controlled, rather than accepting multiple random accesses to ensure that the system can keep track of the information requests.

Another goal is data integrity. Updates to the data must be controlled so that only one user or service at a time can change the data. Also, data duplication is controlled by a database management system that won't allow data, which is required to be unique, to be stored more than once.

Finally, all database management systems are concerned with securing the data so that it is only available to valid users. In addition, the DBMS, RDBMS, or ODBMS may make it possible for users or services to have varying levels of access to the data, which makes control of the data easier to implement.

All DBMSs allow access with two general types of databases: Hierarchical and Network.

Hierarchical databases physically link one record to another and limit access to the records to one user at a time. Hierarchical databases are generally found on older mainframe systems.

Network databases, while providing record links, allow many users to access the record simultaneously.

Relational Database Management System

A Relational Database Management System (RDBMS) is software that manages relational databases. Microsoft Access is an example. Relational databases organize information into related structures called *tables*. The tables are linked together via fields of information called keys or key fields, which are stored in the table. The keys are responsible for providing the link between related tables. Also, the keys give the database designer the ability to tag the data that is to be kept unique in the table. The key field that is intended to hold unique, non-duplicating data is known as a *primary key*.

Consider an online retail business as a relational database example. The business will need data tables to store customer and order information. The customer table is designed with a field to uniquely identify each customer; this field is the *customer ID* or *customer number*. The customer ID should be unique, so it will be created as a primary key.

The order table, which will contain a list of all the orders that the customer has placed, needs to be related back to the customer table so that each customer's orders can be tracked. To facilitate this process, a customer ID field is also created in the orders table. However, because each customer may have placed more than one order, the customer ID field should not be unique in the orders table; it should simply be a key field that allows the customers to be associated with their orders.

Figure 17-5 illustrates the relationship between a customer table and an orders table.

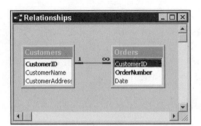

Figure 17-5: Table relationships in an RDBMS

This screen shot, taken from Microsoft's Access application, demonstrates the relationship between the customer and order tables. Other RDBMSs, such as Oracle 8 and 9, IBM DB2, Microsoft SQL Server, and Sun Microsystems NetDynamics Server, also define similar relationships between tables. The services that allow for the definition of the tables and their relationships are part of the RDBMS software.

RDBMS systems are generally distributed; in other words, some components will reside on the server that the data is stored on, and some will reside on servers separate from the database server. Services that reside at locations other than the data server are referred to as "middleware" services because they are located between the Web server, which services the client, and the database server, which services requests from the Web server. This middleware acts as an intermediary between the systems that are requesting data and the systems that provide the data. Most middleware applications use some form of Structured Query Language (SQL) to make requests to the database server for information retrieval or updates.

Object Database Management Systems

Rather than using tables to organize related data, Object Database Management Systems (ODBMS) organize information in structures that mimic real-world data relationships.

The benefits offered by ODBMS include increased performance and an ability to use object-oriented programming languages, such as Java, for defining the objects that will hold the data. Also, ODBMS systems are generally more robust than DBMS or RDBMS systems, meaning that they can recover from errors more readily.

Additionally, ODBMS systems are generally easier to maintain and simplify the querying process, so they are easier to interface with from a developer's standpoint. Rather than using SQL to formulate queries, developers use an Object Query Language (OQL) instead. OQL is a query language that is designed to work with the unique data structure presented by the ODBMS. ODBMS systems can also be used as bridges between older DBMS systems and RDBMS systems because they view data as flexible objects, and not strictly structured entities, such as tables.

Multi-tiered or n-tier computing

You will incorporate three major elements when designing the process by which data access will take place in your database system.

1. **User interface.** Determines how the user initiates a request for data, and how that data will be presented to the user.

2. **Process or business logic.** Places rules on how the data will be accessed in response to a user interface request. Generally makes use of SQL or OQL to communicate that request to the database server.

3. **Data storage.** The data storage element represents the database and the services that manage and control access to the physical data.

In a traditional data access model, the database is simply housed on a system that has no responsibility for the access methods that are used. The client (which may be the same computer that the database resides on) is responsible for providing the means by which to access, modify, and manage the data. This is known as a *one-tier model*.

A *two-tier model* moves the responsibility for managing the data to a separate system. In this case, the client is responsible for formulating the request for data and for displaying the results, but it does not control the physical access to the data, the process, or the business logic.

A *three-tier model* distributes the user interface, business logic, and data storage elements to separate systems.

The last model in multi-tier computing is the n-tier model, in which the middleware services are distributed among several systems, as shown in Figure 17-6. This model enhances the robustness of the overall system by providing for fault tolerance and load sharing among the middleware servers.

A "thin client" solution is an example of three-tier or n-tier architecture, and is becoming more common. In this scenario, a Web browser is used as the user interface or first tier. Process or business logic components are located either on the Web server or another server to which the Web server communicates; this server becomes the second tier. The third tier is the database server that controls physical access to the data.

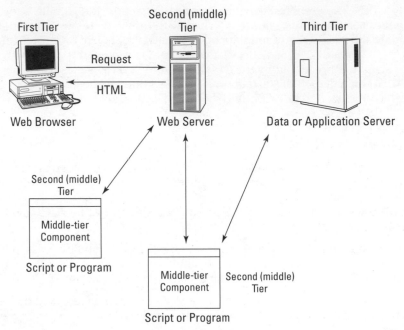

Figure 17-6: The n-tier computing model

In n-tier computing, tier-one represents the user interface software, often referred to as the *front end*. Data servers that manage data storage are often called the *back end,* and everything in between is called *middleware*.

The benefits of n-tier computing include performance enhancement — because each service runs on a system that is optimized to perform that function — and fault tolerance — because multiple systems can be associated with each process element.

Database connectivity

    Differentiate between ODBC and JDBC.

Database connectivity describes the process and technologies that are involved in actually connecting to, and working with, the data stored on a data server. This chapter has already discussed how gateways forward client queries in the form of HTTP messages to other systems or processes. If they are to pass a request on to a data server, the gateway programs, or scripts, need some way to access the functions that the data server understands. Instead of attempting to access the data files directly, the CGI scripts often attempt to access the system's registry in order to use the data access methods of the DBMS. Unfortunately, no standard method for CGI exists to accomplish this, so each system implementation generally employs a proprietary method of connecting to the data services.

Two standards have emerged, however, that define the rules and processes for generically accessing the various supported DBMS systems. These are the Open DataBase Connectivity (ODBC) and Java DataBase Connectivity (JDBC) specifications.

Open DataBase Connectivity

Microsoft developed Open DataBase Connectivity (ODBC), basing it on an industry standard called X-Open. X-Open defines a standard API for using SQL to access relational databases. ODBC is used in many Web-based solutions for implementing data access.

ODBC defines a database driver manager, through which it translates a client's standard ODBC data requests to requests that are understood by the underlying RDBMS. In this way, the developer can use the same function calls — regardless of the underlying database, whether it is a Microsoft SQL database, an Oracle Database, or even a data source of a non-traditional type, such as a spreadsheet or an e-mail address book. As long as the data source provides an ODBC driver, the data can be dealt with generically. After the ODBC driver connection has been established, the gateway application can access the data by making standard calls to the ODBC manager. Most commercial database products, such as Microsoft Access, Oracle, and IBM DB2, support ODBC. Microsoft has even built support for ODBC access into its Excel spreadsheet product, as have other manufacturers, such as Lotus. The near universal status of this standard has encouraged such acceptance.

You can implement ODBC by registering the DBMS ODBC driver with the operating system, and then making calls to it from the Web, gateway, or middleware applications. You accomplish this in the Windows environment by creating an ODBC connection with the ODBC manager application, which is found in the Control Panel. Other environments that support ODBC have similar mechanisms for defining these connections. When registering a database with ODBC, you are creating a Data Source Name (DSN) that describes the location of your data source, as well as any additional information necessary to connect to it, such as the driver version and authentication methods to use. This DSN then provides the information necessary to connect to the database.

Currently, two varieties of ODBC drivers are available: 16-bit and 32-bit. The newer 32-bit drivers provide better performance than their older 16-bit equivalents; however, the two are incompatible. Therefore, a database that only supports the older 16-bit drivers won't work with calls from a 32-bit ODBC DSN.

Java DataBase Connectivity

Javasoft, a subsidiary of Sun Microsystems, developed Java DataBase Connectivity (JDBC) as a non-proprietary database connectivity scheme. As in ODBC, JDBC also makes use of a driver to make the connection between the JDBC API and the underlying database. However, unlike ODBC (where the database driver is specific to the operating system it will run on), the JDBC drivers are platform-independent. Javasoft has taken the challenge of creating an effective open connectivity standard, rather than a proprietary one.

JDBC can use four different types of drivers. Type 1 drivers use bridging technologies to access the database. The JDBC-ODBC bridge, for example, translates JDBC API calls to ODBC calls and vice-versa, providing an ability to use JDBC in environments that will only support ODBC. Type 2 drivers use native drivers, which are called by JDBC but are written and provided by the database vendor. Type 3 drivers provide a generic network API that generates network-based access calls, which are translated at the data source. Type 4 drivers communicate directly with the compliant database engine.

Other database connectivity implementations

A number of additional technologies for supporting database connectivity are available. The following sections examine LiveWire, ColdFusion, ActiveX Data Objects (ADO), and Save As HTML.

LiveWire and server-side JavaScript

In the early releases of Netscape Enterprise Server, SSJS and LiveWire were considered to be one product, and the terms SSJS and LiveWire were often used to refer to the same item. However, between versions 2.0 and 3.0 of Enterprise Server, LiveWire was implemented as a service in its own right, which provides connectivity and manipulation of database objects. SSJS retained the role of creating active content for the Web application. As a result, it is now more accurate to view SSJS as the scripting language for Netscape Enterprise Server and LiveWire as the database connectivity component.

ColdFusion

ColdFusion was developed with the goal of simple database connectivity in mind. One of the design objectives was to create a robust and effective database connectivity product that even non-programmers could use. As a result, ColdFusion employs a programming structure called the ColdFusion Markup Language (CML), which is similar to HTML in that it uses tags as directives. Each CML tag (all start with the letters *CF*) is parsed by the server and executed by the ColdFusion API before the page is returned to the client. ColdFusion files are known as *templates* and are saved with the extension .cmf.

ColdFusion is implemented as a scripting engine, which can run in process with most supported Web servers, such as Microsoft IIS, Netscape Enterprise Server, and Apache Web sever. The ColdFusion engine uses the Web server's API to integrate database connectivity into the Web environment. ColdFusion is intelligent enough to automatically make calls to NSAPI, but if it is running on Netscape Enterprise Server, or to ISAPI if it is running on IIS, its ability to make these calls is still proprietary. This may be an issue if you must move to a different Web environment that doesn't support one of these SAPI implementations. In this case, you will have to use ColdFusion with CGI to interface with the Web applications. This is an unstable solution and is not recommended.

ActiveX Data Objects

ActiveX Data Objects (ADO) is Microsoft's standard for accessing data. ADO defines database objects that facilitate connection to the database via Microsoft's proprietary Object Linking and Embedding DataBase (OLE DB). OLE DB is similar to ODBC, except that it doesn't limit connection to traditional databases. Rather, it defines a means by which a connection can be established with almost any kind of data source, just as long as a compliant driver can be obtained. ADO can even work with ODBC to provide an interface from OLE DB to the data source. ADO is part of the Component Object Model (COM), as defined by Microsoft, which defines how applications may communicate with each other across a network, even if they are written in a different programming language.

ADO is most often implemented in Web applications by embedding ADO or ADO-enabled objects in ASP pages. However, you can implement ADO in client-side scripts through the use of ActiveX client controls.

ADO represents a robust, easy-to-use method for accessing data in a wide variety of locations from Web applications. Unfortunately, its proprietary nature means that you will be tying yourself tightly to the vendor. ADO, which is implemented on the client side with ActiveX, is particularly sensitive to this because ActiveX is simply not supported in browsers other than Internet Explorer.

A vendor-neutral alternative

The Common Object Request Broker Architecture (CORBA) is a vendor-neutral alternative to proprietary models such as ADO. The CORBA architecture is supported by a wide number of organizations because it addresses the need for a platform-independent service for connecting services from various vendors. You can obtain further information on CORBA by visiting www.corba.org.

Save as HTML

The premise behind Save as HTML technologies is to formulate the responses from data queries into either static or dynamic HTML. In the static solution, the data is formatted within HTML table cell tags and sent on to the client system. Dynamic HTML solutions generally require a product, such as IBM Net.Data.

Most Save as HTML engines are implemented as in-process DLLs that make use of either ISAPI or NSAPI calls to interface with the Web applications. As such, they can boast reasonable performance compared to out-of-process CGI scripts.

Key Point Summary

This chapter discussed methods of extending Web server capabilities by highlighting technologies that are available for providing active Web content, and connecting Web applications to data servers and additional services. This chapter also provided an overview of database management systems and presented a discussion of database connectivity options and issues. The following summarizes the key points discussed.

✦ Client-side scripting refers to code embedded in the HTML document, which is interpreted by the Web browser. It can reduce server load by performing tasks that the client can manage.

✦ Client-side scripting is appropriate for simple content changes on the Web page or for accessing client-side information, such as the browser name, but should not be used to create connections to services outside the client environment.

✦ Server-side scripting refers to code embedded in the HTML document, which is interpreted by the Web server, or by some form of scripting engine that runs in conjunction with the Web server.

✦ Server-side scripting is appropriate for accessing information on the server side, or for initiating a connection to and requesting services from, another server or process on the network.

✦ Server-side scripting can solve browser compatibility problems in that the data they send back to the client browsers is formatted as standard HTML.

✦ HTTP gateways are applications that reside at the server and provide access to external services from the Web applications.

✦ HTTP gateways are often implemented via Common Gateway Interface (CGI).

✦ CGI is a simple, mature method of deploying HTTP gateways that has wide support in the development community and makes use of scripts written in languages such as Perl, Python, and C++.

✦ CGI traditionally runs out-of-process in regards to the Web server. This reduces performance and limits the number of simultaneous users that the system can support.

✦ CGI can be made to run in process by implementing the CGI interpreter through Dynamic Link Libraries (DLLs), which load in the same program space as the Web server.

✦ CGI applications are stateless. They can't track information between user sessions.

✦ Out-of-process CGI is a potential security risk because a hacker could upload and execute a malicious script.

✦ GCI scripts are generally located in a directory called CGI-BIN.

✦ HTML form processing allows information to be entered at the Web browser, providing a front-end, or browser-based, data-entry environment.

✦ The HTML <FORM> tag delimits the content of the form in the Web page. All controls between the <FORM> opening tag and the </FORM> closing tag are processed as part of that form.

✦ The ACTION attribute of the `<FORM>` tag specifies the URL of the gateway process that will be used to process the form data. The METHOD attribute of the `<FORM>` tag specifies the method used to transmit the form content to the application.

✦ Two methods are available: GET and POST.

✦ GET causes the form field names, and the data that the fields contain, to be appended to the URL defined in the ACTION attribute. The data is then passed to the process at that URL as part of the call.

✦ The POST method transmits the form data separately from the URL call. This makes POST more secure because it can make use of encrypted transmission after the connection is established with the process at the URL indicated by the ACTION attribute.

✦ Server Application Programming Interfaces (SAPIs) are code libraries that extend Web server capabilities and address the performance and security limitations of traditional CGI implementations.

✦ Internet Server Application Programming Interface (ISAPI) is a Microsoft proprietary API that runs on IIS versions 4.0 and later, as well as on some proprietary third-party gateways.

✦ ISAPI supports both server-side and client-side scripting and is programmable from both VBScript and JScript (Microsoft's version of JavaScript).

✦ NSAPI is an API that runs on Netscape Enterprise Server.

✦ The main difference between ISAPI and NSAPI is the preference of programming language. ISAPI favors VBScript whereas NSAPI favors JavaScript.

✦ SAPIs are implemented as Dynamic Link Libraries (DLLs). The .dll file locations are dictated by the operating system.

✦ Active Server Pages (ASP), a Microsoft server-side scripting technology, defines six objects by which the developer can interact with the Web application.

✦ ASP favors the use of VBScript for coding, although it can make use of JavaScript and JScript.

✦ ASP script is embedded in HTML documents and interpreted by the Web server prior to the document being sent to the client.

✦ ASP files have an .asp extension. Other than this, and the fact that they have embedded code, they are identical to HTML documents and are treated as such by the Web server.

✦ Server-Side JavaScript (SSJS) is Netscape's server-side scripting technology.

✦ SSJS also defines objects that the developer may access to interact with the Web application, but SSJS only supports JavaScript as a development language.

✦ SSJS is supported on Netscape Enterprise Server, as well as on the full installation of the Netscape SuiteSpot server that includes Enterprise Server.

✦ SSJS is also embedded in standard HTML documents. The SSJS documents use a .js extension.

✦ Personal Home Page (PHP) is similar to both ASP and SSJS.

✦ PHP documents use a .php extension.

✦ PHP is free and is developed under open source, which encourages users of the software to report bugs and develop extensions for the community's benefit.

✦ Java Server Pages (JSP) use a Java servlet called the JSP engine to interpret JSP code.

✦ JSP engines are available for most Web servers running on Windows, Novell, and UNIX.

✦ JSP files have a .jsp extension.

✦ JSP offers greater capabilities than the other scripting languages in dealing with extended document tags, such as found in XML-derived pages.

✦ JSP is vendor-neutral and free.

✦ Java servlets are small java programs, written and compiled in Java, that extend Web server capabilities.

✦ Java is a powerful programming language designed for platform-independent application development.

✦ Java is supported by a run-time environment called the Java Virtual Machine. It is the JVM that executes the Java code.

✦ Java can be used to create applications, applets, and servlets.

✦ JVMs are available for and supported on Windows, Novell, Macintosh, and UNIX platforms.

✦ Servlets can be chained. In other words, one servlet can call another to access its functionality.

✦ Servlets have the ability to maintain states across sessions.

✦ Java (and as a result, Java servlets) provides support for the Common Object Request Broker Architecture (CORBA) that defines a common interface by which programs written in different languages may communicate.

✦ Databases are storage locations for information. They are made up of individual standalone files or files that contain related data structures.

✦ Databases are the primary storage mechanism for most online systems and are essential in e-commerce applications.

✦ Transaction processing involves recording transaction information in a database. Online transaction processing implies that the transaction information is recorded into the database in real-time, while the transaction is being performed.

✦ the three types of databases are non-relational, relational, and object-oriented.

✦ Object-oriented databases are the newest of the three and work well with object-oriented languages, such as Java and C++.

✦ Databases are controlled by DataBase Management Systems (DBMS), which is software that controls how data is accessed and maintained on the data server.

✦ Relational DataBase Management Systems (RDBMSs) control relational databases.

✦ Object DataBase Management Systems (ODBMSs) control object-oriented databases.

✦ DBMSs are generally distributed with certain responsibilities for database management residing on different systems.

✦ All DBMSs are responsible for securing the data, maintaining the data, and ensuring that the data is accessible and accurate.

✦ Hierarchical databases are older databases in which records are physically linked to one another and only one user can access the records at a time.

✦ Network databases also allow record linking, but allow simultaneous access of records by multiple users.

✦ Relational databases work by storing data in tables and then relating the tables together via common fields.

✦ Relational databases are often distributed with components residing on servers other than the database server.

✦ Services that reside outside of the database server are known as middleware because they are positioned between the client and the data.

✦ RDBMSs make use of the Structured Query Language (SQL), which a client or client service will use to instruct the database to store, retrieve, or manipulate data.

✦ Object Database Management Systems (ODBMS) arrange data in structures that mimic real-world structures, rather than the table structure employed by other databases.

✦ Benefits of ODBMS include increased performance and robustness.

✦ ODBMSs make use of the Object Query Language (OQL) as opposed to SQL in RDBMSs.

✦ ODBMSs can be used as a bridge between older DBMS systems and RDBMS systems.

✦ In accessing data services, three elements are addressed in designing the system: User Interface, Process or Business Logic, and Data Storage.

✦ The User Interface is responsible for providing a method for the user to initiate a request for data, and a method for formatting the data display.

✦ Process or Business rules dictate how the data will be accessed in response to a data request.

✦ Data Storage represents the data and the services that manage and control access to the physical data.

✦ In multi-tier systems, these three elements are distributed throughout the computing environment:

✦ One-tier systems put the User Interface and Business Logic elements on a single system. This system also provides the methods for accessing and manipulating the data and is quite often the same system that the data is physically stored on.

✦ The two-tier model separates the data management software from the User Interface and Business Logic by moving it to a separate system.

✦ Three-tier computing moves all three elements to separate systems.

✦ N-tier computing is the same as three-tier computing with the exception that multiple tier-two or middleware systems exist for increased performance and fault tolerance.

✦ "Thin client" solutions use a Web browser for the user interface, and components called upon by the Web server as the middleware and database servers for the third-tier.

✦ Database connectivity defines how systems physically connect to data services.

✦ Two standards exist for database connectivity: Open DataBase Connectivity (ODBC) and Java DataBase Connectivity (JDBC). Both implement drivers to define the database connection parameters.

✦ ODBC is Microsoft proprietary and is based on the X-Open standard.

✦ ODBC makes use of a system dependent Data Source Name (DSN) to define the database location, connection parameters, and the driver to be used.

✦ JDBC is platform-independent and can use four different driver types.

  • Type 1 drivers are bridging drivers.

  • Type 2 are native drivers provided by the database vendor.

  • Type 3 are drivers that use generic network calls to access the data server.

  • Type 4 communicate directly with supporting data servers.

✦ LiveWire and Server-Side JavaScript, which are used in Netscape Enterprise Server, were once considered to be synonymous. Recent releases have since defined LiveWire as the data access component, separate from SSJS.

✦ ColdFusion is a proprietary database access technology that uses the ColdFusion Markup Language (CML) to formulate data requests.

✦ CML is similar to HTML in that it uses tags, all of which start with the letters *CF*, as data access directives. CML files are known as *templates* and use a `.cmf` extension.

✦ ColdFusion can operate in conjunction with ISAPI, NSAPI or CGI. CGI is not recommended because ColdFusion is not stable in this environment.

✦ ActiveX Data Objects (ADO) is Microsoft's proprietary technology for accessing data sources.

✦ ADO is based on the Microsoft Object Linking and Embedding DataBase (OLE DB) model and is part of the Microsoft Component Object Model (COM) that defines how programs can communicate with other programs written in different languages.

✦ ADO is often implemented by embedding ADO objects in ASP pages. It can also be implemented client-side via ActiveX controls.

✦ Using ActiveX controls on the client limits the Web page to being used in Internet Explorer.

✦ Common Object Request Broker Architecture (CORBA) is a vendor-neutral alternative to ADO.

✦ Save as HTML works by creating either static or Dynamic HTML pages. Static pages use HTML table cell tags to format the data into static HTML tables. Dynamic solutions generally require a product such as IBM Net.Data.

✦   ✦   ✦

STUDY GUIDE

Assessment Questions

1. The software that acts as a bridge between the Web browser and the data server is called what?

    A. An HTML Bridge

    B. An HTTP Gateway

    C. A Redirector

    D. An HTML Gateway

2. Client-side scripting is useful for (Choose all that apply)

    A. Automating simple client functions such as pop-up menus.

    B. Creating connections to data servers.

    C. Retrieving server-side information such as the time at the Web server.

    D. Retrieving client-side information such as the Web browser type.

3. A developer is hired to create a Web application that will use an RDBMS as a data back end, and a Web browser as the client front end. The Web application will be hosted on an IIS 4.0 Server and will be written in ASP. The application will be deployed live on the Internet. How should the developer approach the task of scripting this application? Select the best answer.

    A. Use server-side script exclusively because there is too much difference between browser types to risk using client-script.

    B. Use client-side script exclusively to reduce, as much as possible, the load on the Web server.

    C. Use VBScript as both the client-side and server-side scripting language.

    D. Use JavaScript for client-side scripts and VBScript for server-side scripts.

4. When deploying an HTML Gateway solution, which statement is the most accurate?

    A. HTML Gateways are always implemented as CGI scripts.

    B. HTML Gateways are always implemented as SAPI processes.

    C. HTML Gateways may be implemented as CGI scripts, SAPI processes, or both.

    D. There is no such thing as an HTML gateway.

5. What are some features of CGI? (Choose all that apply)

    A. CGI is a mature technology.

    B. CGI is supported by the majority of Web servers now available.

    C. CGI script never runs out of process in relation to the Web server.

    D. CGI can make use of only one scripting language—Perl.

6. Which of the following are server-side scripting languages? (Choose all that apply)

    A. Server-Side JavaScript

    B. Active Server Pages

    C. PHP

    D. JSP

    E. All of the above

7. Match the following Web file types with their file extension.

    A. Personal home pages   ___ .jsp

    B. Java server pages   ___ .html

    C. Active server pages   ___ .php

    D. Normal Web pages   ___ .asp

8. Using the HTML `#include` tag to join an external file to an HTML document is called a what?

    A. Server-side join.

    B. Server side include.

    C. Server side lookup

    D. Page import.

9. What two features of Java servlets differentiate them from other server-side scripting technologies?

    A. Java servlets are compiled.

    B. Java servlets are run by the JVM.

    C. Java servlets won't run on servers that are not based on the Intel platform.

    D. Java servlets can be created with any scripting language.

10. What is the vendor-neutral standard for how programs that are written in different programming languages can communicate with one another?

   A. SSJS

   B. CORBA

   C. HTML Gateway

   D. CGI

11. Online transaction processing is characterized by which of the following statements? (Choose all that apply).

   A. Transaction information is recorded, while the transaction is taking place, in the data server.

   B. Transaction information is recorded at the client through the use of cookies.

   C. Online transaction processing is only done between the online business and financial institutions, not in regards to customer transactions.

   D. Online transaction processing is not relevant except in the case of very large business.

12. Which of the following three terms describe the three categories of database management systems?

   A. Relational Database Management Systems (RDBMS).

   B. Non-relational Database Management Systems (DBMS)

   C. Object Database Management Systems (ODBMS)

   D. Java Database Management Systems(JDBMS)

13. RDBMS systems use what method for tying related data tables together?

   A. Key fields

   B. Server-side includes

   C. Relationships

   D. Tables can't be related in an RDBMS, only data files.

14. Which of the following are benefits of Object DataBase Management Systems? (Choose all that apply)

   A. They are more robust than traditional DBMSs.

   B. They work well with object-oriented languages, such as Java and C++.

   C. They can't be used for business services — only for storage and management of objects in a software development process.

   D. They can be used as a bridge between older DBMSs and RDBMSs.

15. Object DataBase Management Systems use what language to formulate queries?

    A. Structured Query Language (SQL)

    B. Server Side Java Script

    C. Java

    D. Object Query Language (OQL)

16. What three statements characterize the n-tier computing model?

    A. Tier 1 represents the user interface.

    B. Tier 3 is the data.

    C. Tier n is the network infrastructure.

    D. Tier 2 represents services that provide process and business logic or rules.

17. What two standards have emerged to provide standard methods for connecting to databases and other data-related services?

    A. The Open Source movement.

    B. Open DataBase Connectivity (ODBC).

    C. There are no standards for database connectivity.

    D. Java DataBase Connectivity (JDBC).

18. Which of the following represent other methods of achieving database connectivity? (Choose all that apply).

    A. LiveWire.

    B. ColdFusion.

    C. NetObjects Fusion.

    D. ActiveX Data Objects.

    E. Save as HTML.

19. Which one of the following JDBC drivers provide a bridge between JDBC API calls and other API functions?

    A. Tier 1.

    B. Tier 2.

    C. Tier 3.

    D. Tier 4.

20. In HTML form processing, which statement is true concerning the attributes used in the HTML <FORM> tag?

A. The TARGET attribute is used to specify the URL of the target application. The METHOD tag specifies how the data is sent.

B. The METHOD tag specifies the name of the function to send the data to. The CODE tag specifies the location of the object that contains the function.

C. The ACTION attribute specifies the URL of the process that the form data will be sent to. The METHOD tag specifies how the data will be sent.

D. The ACTION attribute specifies the location to send the data to. The POST attribute specifies the method to use in sending the data.

Scenarios

Scenario 1

You are a consultant that has been hired to assist in the evaluation of a proposed online order tracking system for a door-to-door sales organization. The company employs 10 salespeople who make customer calls during the day. Any sales taken during the day are to be faxed or phoned into the office in the evening so that orders can be placed with the suppliers the next day.

The business owner wants to automate this process so evening staff won't be required to take the day's orders by phone. Also, some salespeople don't want to take the time in the evening to phone in their orders. They also want an automated system.

The salespeople all have laptops that the company has reimbursed them for. Some salespeople chose Compaq or IBM laptops, while some chose Apple PowerBooks. The company has a small network consisting of a Windows NT 4.0 server, a laser printer, and a desktop PC running Windows 98 for the manager, receptionist, book-keeper, and warehouse clerk. The company uses an off-the-shelf accounting package and is currently keeping track of customer orders in a Microsoft Access database. The company currently has an arrangement with an ISP for e-mail access for the organization.

A local software development company is proposing an n-tier solution, which will implement an additional NT 4.0 server as a database server running Microsoft SQL Server 7.0. IIS 4.0 will be installed on the existing NT 4.0 server, which currently has the accounting application and Access program on it. The Access system will be enhanced by moving the data structure to the SQL server, but will keep the Access front-end for the office staff to use in generating sales reports. A front-end system developed in C++ is proposed for the salespeople to use on their laptops. The sales-people will use this application to dial into the IIS server, where a custom ASP application will receive the day's orders and update the SQL database.

Do you perceive any problems in the design of this proposed system? What alternatives would you recommend, if any, in the design of the front-end systems for the salespeople and office staff? What alternatives, if any, would you recommend for the middle-tier and back-end solutions?

Scenario 2

You are working on a design project that will implement a Web-based odd-job registry. Subscribers to the service will be able to post ads via the Internet for odd jobs that they want done, such as yard cleanup and home repairs. Laborers and craftspeople interested in such work can browse for potential work. All users of the system will be private individuals. The system will make no attempt to provide them with Internet access.

Your colleague suggests that you create a Web-based application using a Windows 2000 server with IIS 5.0., an additional Windows 2000 server with SQL Server 2000, and a browser-based front end which will use ActiveX controls at the browser to connect to the Web application.

What implication does this have for browser compatibility? Is there a solution that will be more browser generic, while still making use of the IIS 5.0 Web server?

Answers to Chapter Questions

Chapter Pre-test

1. Tasks typically associated with server-side scripting include any function that accesses server-based information, either on the Web server itself, or through the use of connectivity processes on external servers.

2. CGI scripts are most often called from HTML forms. When a user fills in an HTML form and clicks the SUBMIT button, the HTML <FORM> tag uses its ACTION and METHOD attributes to define where and how the data in the form will be sent for processing.

3. ISAPI and NSAPI are both forms of Server Programming Interfaces (SAPIs). SAPIs are libraries of functions that extend Web server capabilities and are generally incorporated into Web servers as Dynamic Link Libraries (DLLs). Refer to the section "Server Programming Interfaces" in this chapter for additional explanation.

4. DBMSs are responsible for the integrity, security, and availability of the data that they manage. In other words, the data must be error-free, secure against intrusion, and available when needed by authorized users.

5. **ODBC** is a Microsoft proprietary database connectivity standard, whereas **JDBC** is developed by Javasoft. See the section "Database Connectivity" for additional information on both standards.

6. Java servlets are compiled Java programs as opposed to interpreted script embedded in Web documents. A Java servlet is processed by a Java Virtual Machine in a special run-time environment, that is available on a wide number of operating system platforms.

Assessment Questions

1. **D.** The HTML gateway software forwards a client request to a server or service, formats the response as an HTML document, and then sends it back to the client.

2. **A, D.** Client-side scripting should only access information or manipulate objects that reside on the client. Connections to data servers and retrieval of server information should be done with server-side processes.

3. **D.** When deciding which scripting language to employ, consider the environments. In this scenario, JavaScript is best as the scripting language because it is the most widely supported by various browser types. VBScript is the right choice for the ASP application because the ASP environment favors the use of VBScript.

4. **C.** HTML Gateways may be implemented via CGI or SAPI, depending on what the Web server supports. Although most support CGI, however, many are offering support for SAPI technologies as well.

5. **A, B.** CGI is a mature technology, supported by many developers and Web server environments. CGI script often runs out of process, which is one of the drawbacks of the environment. CGI can use many languages, such as Perl, Python or C++.

6. **E.** All of these examples are server-side scripting languages.

7. **A = .php, B = .jsp, C = .asp, D = .html**

8. **B.** Server-side include is the correct term when using the HTML #include tag. The other answers are all invalid terms.

9. **A, B.** Servlets are compiled Java programs. However, a compiled Java program can't run as an executable because it is compiled to object code as opposed to machine code. This is what gives Java its portability. The compiled Java programs are run by the Java Virtual Machine (JVM), which translates the object-code to machine code.

10. **B.** The Common Object Resource Architecture (CORBA) is vendor-neutral, platform-independent standard for implementing inter-process communication and operation. Any CORBA-compliant service or program can communicate with any other CORBA-compliant service or application, either locally or across a network; regardless of the programming language or platform it was developed in or is running on.

11. **A.** Online Transaction Processing (OLTP) implies the storage of transaction details as they are happening. This leads to challenges in terms of deploying a data solution that is robust enough to handle many simultaneous transactions, and stable enough to permit real-time processing of transaction information. OLTP is not just for large business, or just for use in bank-to-business transactions. OLTP is found at all levels of e-commerce applications where transactions are carried out.

12. **A, B, C.** DBMS, RDBMS, and ODBMS are the three categories of database management system in common use today. There is no such thing as a JDBMS.

13. **C.** An RDBMS uses relationships to connect the data in one table to the data in another. The relationships use common fields between the tables, such as a CustomerID field to relate the Customer table to the table containing Orders. Key fields are generally used in the parent side of the relationship to ensure that data duplication does not occur.

14. **A, B, D.** ODBMSs tend to recover from data errors or inconsistencies better than other DBMSs due to the way the data is structured. This makes them more robust. The data structures are object-oriented, so integration with object-oriented languages is made simpler because the languages have been optimized to deal with objects and their relationships. Given the flexibility with which ODBMs systems can deal with various data, they are ideal for implementing bridges between older, more structured, DBMS systems.

15. **D.** The Object Query Language (OQL) is optimized for requesting information in a format that is more suited to OBDMS storage and retrieval. Java and JavaScript may be used to create the OQL request, but it is OQL that the server understands and responds to. SQL is used in RDBMS systems.

16. **A, B, D.** The n-tier computing model describes the function and relative location of the components that make up a system. Tier 1 represents the user interface, Tier 2 the business or process logic, and Tier 3 the data storage. N-tier computing is simply Tier 3 computing with more Tier 2, or middleware, systems utilized for fault tolerance and load distribution. The network infrastructure is not mentioned at all in the n-tier model because it is assumed that the systems will be connected by some means, the physical nature of which is irrelevant to the tier design.

17. **B, D.** ODBC and JDBC are the two standards most widely supported for database connectivity. ODBC is a Microsoft proprietary standard, based on the X-Open industry standard. JDBC is a non-proprietary, platform-independent solution, developed by Sun Microsystems subsidiary, Javasoft.

18. **A, B, D, E.** NetObjects Fusion is a Web page development tool. Each of the other technologies is a proprietary data connectivity scheme.

19. **A.** JDBC Tier 1 drivers are bridging drivers that provide a link between JDBC API calls and another set of API calls such as ODBC. Tier 2 drivers are provided by the database manufacturer for translating JDBC calls to native calls of the database. Tier 3 drivers make use of standard network calls for sending messages to the data server and receiving responses back, and Tier 4 drivers rely on the database manufacturer embedding support for JDBC directly into their database product. Tier 1 drivers are most common, with some Tier 2, 3, and 4 drivers becoming available. Tier 4 is considered the most desirable due to enhanced performance.

20. **C.** The HTML <FORM> tag uses the ACTION attribute to specify the URL of the process to which the form information will be submitted. The METHOD attribute specifies the method that will be used to transmit the form data.

Scenarios

1. In this scenario, the front end for the sales people is being developed in C++. This will require separate coding for the Apple laptops from the Compaq and IBM systems. In effect, two separate applications will need to be developed and maintained. An alternative would be to take a "thin client" approach, in which an application is created at the Web site. ASP is an alternative because the Web server being proposed is IIS 4.0. This way, the application is available to both types of laptops because all that the users require for access is a Web browser.

   If an ASP application is to be developed for the salespeople, functionality for office staff can be built in as well. This is not required, however, because the Access front-end solution will work, and will give the office staff the ability to do their own reporting if desired.

   The back-end system running SQL Server should be capable of supporting the data requirements and will interface well with ASP.

2. Using ActiveX controls at the browser will force clients to use Internet Explorer because other browsers don't support ActiveX. In addition, the ActiveX controls will need to be downloaded to the client's browser upon their first use. Many people won't permit ActiveX controls to be installed on their systems for fear of hackers accessing their system. A more generic approach is to develop the application with ASP. No client controls are necessary because the ASP application can easily connect to the SQL server. Any client scripting for menu automation, or other client element manipulation can be done with JavaScript, and then embedded in the Web pages as client-side script because JavaScript is the most universally accepted client scripting language.

Introduction to Network Security

1. Identify network security concepts.
2. Employ auditing and a security policy.
3. Identify security threats and attacks.
4. Implement intrusion detection.
5. Explore virtual private networks.

CHAPTER PRE-TEST

1. What type of device or service provides a way to monitor misuse and intrusion of your systems?

2. If you want to connect your business partners to your personal intranet, what technology can you use?

3. When you trick someone into giving you his or her password through intimidation, what type of attack are you perpetrating?

4. A buffer overflow attack is a _____ attack.

5. True or False? For the strongest security, you should employ a multi-layered infrastructure.

6. What type of hacker has the knowledge to get hacking tools off the Internet but does not have a deep understanding of what he or she is doing?

7. Which two main ports does FTP use to communicate with other systems?

8. A VPN uses _____ to create a tunnel over the public Internet.

9. _____ can be used to view listening ports on a Windows work-station.

10. Which port does POP3 use to communicate?

✦ Answers to these questions can be found at the end of the chapter. ✦

People have been attacking, hacking, cracking, and exploiting networks for as long as networks have existed. This chapter discusses the importance of network security and provides you with information necessary to pass the CIW Foundations examination. Due to the wealth of information available the types of attacks on networks, the prevention of these attacks, and the mechanics of maintaining network security. an introduction to network security can easily span the entire length of this book. This chapter covers the following network security concepts:

✦ Auditing and policy usage

✦ Threats and attacks

✦ Intrusion detection

✦ Network protocol security

Concepts of Network Security

 Identify network security concepts.

Network security is concerned with ensuring that your network, system, and the data that traverses it is safe and secure from attack or theft. Network security involves a group or team of individuals with network and/or system security expertise preventing systems, and their data, from being damaged, stolen, or overheard through attack. Firewalls and intrusion detection systems also play a large roll in stopping, finding, or logging attacks and breaches on your system. As part of your network security, remember to keep management involved to help you implement and maintain a strong security policy.

A single firewall is not the answer to all of your security-related concerns. You need to address at least the following issues:

✦ Disaster recovery

✦ Backups

✦ Anti-virus software

✦ Intrusion detection

✦ System and log auditing

✦ Security policy testing

You need an in-depth, multi-layer security system to ensure adequate network security for your company.

Scanners and IDs in Practice

In a former workplace, I had to have my hand scanned to get into the data center. As it was unlikely that my arm would be separated from my body and pass through the data center door without me, this was an effective security measure. A video camera was also positioned right by the clear doors leading into the data center. This ensured that if someone snuck in behind you it was likely that he or she was taped doing so.

I worked in another environment that required an ID badge-based swipe card to get into the building and had a push button number-based code system on the door to the data center. This system had several drawbacks. A badge can be lost or stolen. The absence of video cameras internally provided no proof of any wrongdoing. The numeric code had not been changed in over seven years, so every disgruntled employee that had ever left the company still had access to the data center. These are all things to consider when analyzing your internal security system.

External security

Many attacks come from troublemakers lurking outside your network. Think of *external* as anything outside the boundaries of your protected private and internal network. Provide protection from external threats by implementing a firewall and Intrusion detection systems.

Internal security

Internal security is your biggest challenge as a network and systems security analyst. For example, you may set up a series of redundant firewalls and intrusion detection systems and then discover that the kid in the mailroom logged into one of your routers. Why did this happen? Most network administrators think that attacks come from outside predators, but limiting your attention to external threats can leave you completely vulnerable to internal attacks.

Many tools that can wreak havoc on your network are freely available on the Internet and can be downloaded and used to attack your systems from the inside. The people that commit these abuses can range from the stereotypical disgruntled employee to the computer student that is nosing around the systems while at work. Problems can also be caused accidentally without anyone's knowledge if proper security is not implemented.

In addition to firewalls and intrusion detection systems, biometrics, hand scanners, smart cards, video cameras and ID badges can also be used to increase security on your internal network and systems.

Operating System Security

Operating system security is the lock down, protection, auditing, and monitoring of all the clients and servers in your infrastructure. You can set up user or group-based security. Refer to Figure 18-1.

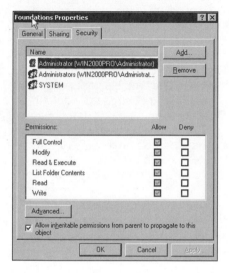

Figure 18-1: Windows 2000 folder properties and permissions security

With the type of security displayed in Figure 18-1, you can control access to a folder by adding or removing a user or a group of users who can access this folder. For example, remove the lax default administrative permissions on a Windows-based system for better operating system security.

You can monitor security on your operating systems by auditing them. Auditing is covered in the Auditing Fundamentals section of this chapter.

Network-Based Security

Lock down your routers, switches, and any other device that moves data through your network. Remember that a hacker can put a sniffer (a packet capture device used to "sniff" network traffic and display it for analysis purposes) on your network and eavesdrop for passwords. Use fiber optics so that you have immunity to this type of attack. Fiber-optical cable is usually made of a glass core that uses light or laser to send data across the media and can't be picked up by protocol analyzers that capture data packets and decode them to reveal sensitive data. To disallow certain data from passing from one location to another, you can also apply ACLs (access lists) to a router, firewall, or a server acting as a firewall, which permit or drop certain packets as they pass through your network devices. You can also set up a router or a firewall to disallow traffic to certain ports.

Exam Tip   For this exam and most exams that deals with security issues, know your basic ports. A port is what allows two TCP/IP-based machines to communicate and create a socket connection. For example, a Web client trying to connect to a Web server to view a Web page uses port 80 (by default).

You can change the ports, but if you do, specifically state which port you are trying to access. For example, to connect to a Web server at URL www.hungryminds.com you would simply type the URL into your browser. The Web server is expecting your connection via port 80, the predefined port. If you changed the default port to 8080, you would have to specify it in your Web browser, which is done by typing in the following URL: www.hungryminds.com:8080. This allows you to now connect to the Web server that is listening for your connection on port 8080. Placing a colon and the port number directly after the URL tells the web browser to try to make the connection to the web server by using a particular port (and not to try the default port value). Port numbers range from 0 to 65536. Ports 0 to 1023 are reserved for use by specific privileged services and are considered "well known." A list of the most popular services and their associated ports follows:

✦ FTP uses 20 and 21

✦ TELNET uses 23

✦ SMTP uses 25

✦ POP3 uses 110

✦ DNS uses 53

✦ HTTP uses 80

✦ NNTP uses 119

✦ NTP uses 123

Refer to www.IANA.org for a complete listing of existing ports. By typing the command NETSTAT -NA at a Windows command prompt, you can view all the listening ports open on your machine. This information is important in network security because you want a firewall or router to disallow traffic over certain ports. For example, you could block port 666 and disallow anyone in your organization from connecting to another machine over the Internet using that port. Figure 18-2 shows the command prompt using NETSTAT -NA to view listening ports:

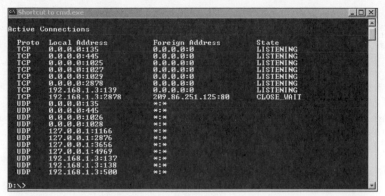

Figure 18-2: Command prompt window using NETSTAT command

Hackers and hacking

The industry's definition of a hacker is someone who is heavily involved with the use and exploiting of systems. Attackers and crackers are the "bad guys" and cause network security administrators and analysts a great deal of work in the areas of virus protection, backup, and data restoration. Most attacks are nothing but mischief, but some attackers have a deep understanding of computer-based technology.

Crackers have different rankings or levels. Which type of cracker is the most prevalent is debated, but the following outlines the basic groupings:

✦ **The Elite** are faceless, well-hidden individuals who know a great deal about exploiting systems. They are usually the creators of the freely available hacking tools on the Internet today.

✦ **A Black Hat** is a level down from the Elite. A Black Hat is dangerous and knows enough to create sophisticated tools and to cause mischief or harm.

✦ **A White Hat** has the same level of knowledge as a Black Hat, but protects against the crackers and attackers. You should strive to become a White Hat.

✦ **Script Kiddies** are the lowest level of attacker and the most numerous. It seems that everyone these days wants to be labeled a hacker. Everyone that knows how to get past the Windows screen saver password has "hacked" a system. Script Kiddies download free tools from the Internet and practice with them on your network. They include the 16-year-old kids that bump people out of chat rooms on the Internet and so on. Script Kiddies are generally easily caught.

Common problems and issues with security

Imagine you are a network manager and you just approved and oversaw the purchase and installation of a million dollars worth of equipment. You interviewed, hired, and trained three security analysts and administrators to run your network. Your network consists of four firewalls in redundant failover setups, two intrusion detection systems to proactively find intruders prowling at your gates. You wrote and implemented a 25-page security policy and set up biometrics at every door into the server room. You're secure and you feel good about your solid defense. So what do you have to worry about?

The modem

Suppose that an employee decides to dial into work without running the installation of the modem past the security department. This employee also sets up remote access software called PCAnywhere so that he can get files that he needs in order to do extra work at home. This is done with good intentions, but while this employee is accessing the network remotely, an attacker with a war dialer tool (found readily on the Internet) decides to target your network. A visit to your company's Web site has probably given this attacker the first set of numbers in your phone exchange through a help line or contact number. The exchange is put in the war dialer and your phone numbers are scanned one by one until the machine with the modem and the remote access software answers the war dialer's call. The attacker is now halfway to the intended destination inside your network.

 Note   If the remote access software is password protected (it usually isn't), other tools are readily available to perform brute-force attacks on your software to find the password. These tools use a loaded dictionary file, which has all the standard words found in a dictionary as well as nonstandard words, such as pet names. If you have a simple password, the attacker can penetrate your network without you or your intrusion detection systems knowing.

The help desk call

"Hello, this is the CEO, and I just walked into a meeting with my laptop and I can't log in. I need a file from my computer for my presentation. Could you please expedite a solution and change my password? Thanks!" You have just been exposed to an attack called Social Engineering, which is the simple use of trickery to discover the credentials needed to penetrate a security system.

This is the easiest attack because most help desk personnel are in a stressful "learning" environment and may not be highly trained in security attacks of this kind. Social engineering was a term that meant nothing to me when I started working in information technology. As a CIW Foundations candidate, being aware of social engineering is fundamental to maintaining network security. Be aware that critical systems can be easily accessed through intimidation or trickery.

The sticky pad

A note taped to the monitor can undermine the 10 million dollars you spent on the entire security infrastructure. Forget the social engineering attack perpetrated on an unsuspecting technician. What about walking into a cubicle and finding the user-name and password to the accounting program in plain sight? This is very common and requires a walk through by security personnel with a copy of the company security policy in hand.

Note   User education is the key to preventing potential security breaches from becoming realities.

The binoculars

Although it may be folklore or urban legend, a story exists that must be mentioned here to drive this topic home. Security was at such a premium in the Pentagon that they decided to run fiber optics throughout the building so that no data transmission could be intercepted or overheard by eavesdropping. Security was placed in every crevasse of the network to safeguard national security. Experts were hired to oversee, test, and update security.

One day a security guard received a call from another guard asking what to do about a suspicious individual outside the property of the Pentagon with a set of binoculars. A security team soon apprehended the individual for questioning. This person was using the high–powered binoculars to read information on PC monitor screens in officials' offices.

As a security guru, you have a lot to think about and security concepts run wide and deep. The million-dollar infrastructure is useless if penetrated by a simple modem or intimidating phone call.

Security Policies

Objective   Employ auditing and security policy.

All the concepts discussed in the previous sections are useless without a policy to enforce them. Many organizations overlook a security policy in their overall security strategy. The following two scenarios demonstrate instances in which a security policy should have been in place:

✦ **Scenario one:** An employee spends about 20 minutes a week surfing border-line pornography sites. One day, a passerby is offended by the nudity visible on his computer screen. The employee is confronted about the incident and reprimanded accordingly. The employee states that the reprimand is unfair because he was never told he could not download and view such material.

✦ **Scenario two:** An employee downloads little programs and screensavers off the Internet all day and infects her machine (as well as your network) with a nasty virus. Although you have an anti-virus solution, some data was damaged and lost in quarantine.

Having a security policy in place may have prevented both situations. If they were not prevented, a security policy would at least ensure that the individuals involved were aware of the consequences of their actions. In the policy, state that company machines are the property of the business and can only be used under specific guidelines outlining proper usage. You can add clauses stating that no pornography is to be viewed and software is not to be downloaded or installed without permission. Both incidents can be punishable by termination. With a security policy in place, you give yourself power to control system usage, and provide a set of clear guidelines that employees can follow. The policy also provides an element of fear that may deter some employees from trying inappropriate things.

Review the policy regularly and update it as necessary. Outdated policies that do not correctly define the business mission or your security guidelines are useless.

System policies

You can set up operating system policies. Operating system polices are little lock downs that you can apply within the operating system to restrict commands, disallow the user to make changes that remain upon reboot, and keep the system's Registry in the state agreed upon in the policy. A system policy restricts what a user can do by removing commands (or features) from the computer or disabling specific programs. Refer to Figure 18-3 for an example of this type of policy. Windows 2000 Server and Active Directory provide the option of using Group Policy, which is more powerful and more encompassing than local policy.

Note   You don't need Windows 2000 Server or Active Directory to lock down a local computer. All Microsoft operating systems (Windows 95 and later) support system policies.

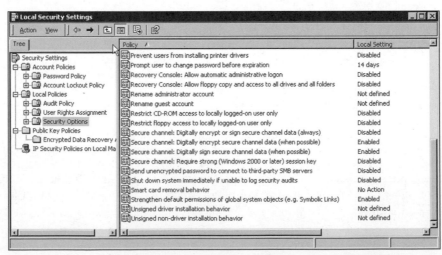

Figure 18-3: Implementing a security policy on a Windows 2000 client

Disaster recovery policy

Every network should have a disaster recovery policy that states what to do when danger and disaster strikes. A disaster could be an attacker penetrating your systems and deleting critical information. A disaster recovery policy outlines step-by-step procedures that are used to recover from the deletion of the critical information. Backup solutions, hot sites, cold sites, and a set of instructions can all be part of the disaster recovery policy.

A Hot site is a disaster recovery solution that has immediate failover to another system. This can provide near 100 percent uptime in case of a disaster that incapacitates your system. There is no backup to restore because the data is copied to another machine at the same time the original is written to the main system. When disaster hits, the second machine picks up where the primary machine failed and resumes normal operations. The failure is transparent to the user. In a cold site solution, the failed system must be rebuilt and then restored from a backup. There are pros and cons to both. In a hot site solution, the cost of the extra hardware is higher than a cold site, but your downtime is almost non-existent. A cold site solution is cheaper, but requires more down time in the event of a failure, and if the backup tapes don't work, then you may be done for good.

Auditing Fundamentals

What does it mean to audit a system? Audit is an accounting term that means to follow a paper trail in order to validate account book entries. How does this apply to network and systems security? A system audit follows electronic logs to track and validate or invalidate activity. If there is unauthorized access to files or systems, it can be picked up, recorded, and audited. Auditing usually needs to be configured on systems, so be aware that you may not automatically have auditing capabilities.

To audit your systems, configure auditing on the system on which you want to track activity. When users perform unauthorized actions, the security system picks up the activity and logs it. Review the logs for the specific actions you're interested in, such as unauthorized access. In Windows 2000, you can configure auditing within the local security policy management console within the administrative Tools folder. Drill down through the console to enable auditing on things such as object access failure or logon failures. This is crucial in setting up auditing to catch wrongdoing. Logon failures are enabled in Figure 18-4.

You can see and analyze failed logins in the system's Event Viewer. The Event Viewer is located within the Computer Management console in the Administrative Tools folder. The security portion of the Event Viewer allows you to verify failed logons or other actions that you configured to be audited.

Figure 18-4: Configuring Windows auditing

Types of Attacks

 Identify security threats and attacks.

A partial list of attacks follows:

Social engineering

Social engineering is a way for attackers to trick users, technicians, or just about anyone into revealing their username and password or accidentally giving attackers access to critical resources.

Dumpster diving

Have you ever written a password down that you wanted to remember, memorized it, and then thrown it away? If you are a security administrator, supervisor, or other individual that holds critical information, you had better believe someone is digging through your trash. Many systems have been broken into using this method.

War dialing

A war dialer is a unique tool used to dial numbers in sequence and wait for one to answer that allows access into your network. Security assessment teams, as well as attackers trying to penetrate your systems, frequently use this tool.

Denial of Service

A denial-of-service (DoS) attack denies a user or an organization access to resources they would normally have. The loss of service can affect your e-mail, your Web site, or any other service available on a network. Suppose that your company has a Web site that millions of people come to each day. What if they could not access your site? They might visit another site instead. If perpetrated with enough force and consistency, a denial-of-service attack can corrupt applications and files, requiring them to be reinstalled. DoS attacks are usually intentional, malicious, and intended to shut down your business. They can come from internal or external sources. Be careful not to cause an unintentional DoS attack on your own organization by blocking access to needed ports.

Refer to Figure 18-5 for an example of a denial-of-service attack.

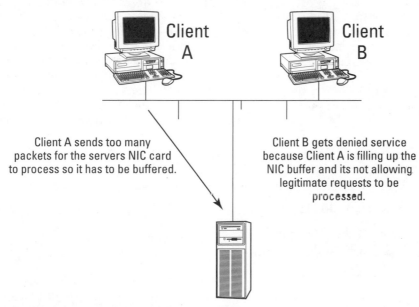

Client A

Client B

Client A sends too many packets for the servers NIC card to process so it has to be buffered.

Client B gets denied service because Client A is filling up the NIC buffer and its not allowing legitimate requests to be processed.

Figure 18-5: Typical denial-of-service attack

Denial-of-service attacks are generally caused by exploiting a machine's buffer over-flow mechanism. Most devices have a memory buffer where information coming in too fast can be "cached" until it can be addressed by the device. The buffer over-flow is now repairable with service packs and hot fixes (small repair packs to oper-ating systems and applications to fix known problems). The attacker can send a flood of packets to the recipient (your Web server) to fill the buffer. If this contin-ues, the buffer becomes full and legitimate requests (from your customers) are dropped outside the buffer, and they are denied service to your site. Keep up with the platform and operating system you are using and see what hot fixes or service packs can help patch this design flaw.

Exam Tip   For the CIW Foundations exam, you should also be familiar with spoofing, man-in-the-middle attacks, trapdoor attacks, and replay attacks.

Intrusion Detection

Objective   Implement intrusion detection.

To be intruded on is to have an entity occupy space that you have deemed to be your own. At times you may have so much personal space that you are unaware when someone else is in it. An intrusion detection system (IDS) can increase this awareness by allowing you to monitor unauthorized access to your network for analysis purposes. This technology is very handy for security analysts. The IDS box can gather and analyze information from various areas within a computer or a network. This information is used to identify possible internal or external security attacks. IDS systems can also scan your systems to assess their vulnerabilities; this technology is sometimes referred to as a vulnerability scanner. This tool can help confirm that you have patched all the holes in your network or point out open holes and potential problems. Always remember to get permission from your network administrator or management before you scan a network for vulnerabilities. A scan can actually take systems down and create further problems if not used correctly. Intrusion detection system functionality can accomplish the following tasks:

✦ Monitor and analyze both user and system activities

✦ Analyze system configurations and vulnerabilities

✦ Assess system and file integrity

✦ Recognize typical attack patterns

✦ Analyze abnormal activity patterns

✦ Track user policy violations

Refer to Figure 18-6 to view where an intrusion detection system may be placed within your organization.

Intrusion detection has been given much more attention in the last few years because of break-ins at Microsoft and other major companies around the world. ICSA.net is a huge organization that formed an intrusion detection consortium (IDSC). This consortium has been established to assist in the development of IDS systems and to establish standards that should be followed in regard to IDS systems.

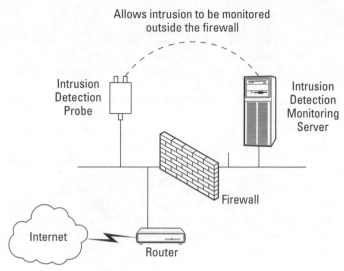

Figure 18-6: Intrusion detection system setup

Virtual Private Networks

 Explore virtual private networks.

What is a virtual private network (VPN)? Why would you consider a VPN as part of your infrastructure? What are the pros and cons of having a VPN?

A VPN is a network designed to ensure that the data that flows through the network is private and only visible to your organization. Your VPN is an extension of your infrastructure that flows over a public Internet-based connection. How does the data in a VPN remain private? The data is hidden using encryption and "tunneled" through the public Internet away from prying eyes.

Consider using a VPN if you want to save money on the purchase and maintenance of private dedicated lines. An Internet connection is a public connection to the rest of the world; you pay only for the access to it. The Internet is a viable solution to connect to your remote business sites.

Pros and cons of using a VPN

The biggest advantage to a VPN is that it makes use of the public telecommunication infrastructure. Using public lines is cost effective because the lines are maintained and not your responsibility. If you are not concerned about guaranteed bandwidth, this is the solution for you. If the Internet fails, however, you can't really get a level of service for repair that you could if you had owned those lines.

Another major con is that you cannot control the bandwidth. If you order a leased line from your telecommunications provider, it is their responsibility to provide you with the exact amount of bandwidth and service to which you are entitled based on your contract. In other words, if you analyze your application flow and know that you send about 150K of FTP traffic over your lines 75% of the active workday, you can lease a 256K line to make sure that the FTP traffic is able to travel through and still leave you enough bandwidth available for e-mail and other necessary traffic. With the VPN, you do not get a guaranteed amount of bandwidth at all times, which can seriously impact your business.

VPN encryption

Encryption is the lifeblood of the VPN. Without it, the VPN is not private at all. One device encrypts the data on the way out, and the receiving device decrypts the data when it arrives. You can increase security by not only encrypting the data, but also encrypting the sending and receiving network addresses as well. Point-to-Point Tunneling Protocol (PPTP), developed by Microsoft, 3Com, and several other companies, extends the use of VPN encryption over Windows Remote Access Service (RAS) features. VPN software is typically installed as part of a company's firewall server or appliance. Other forms of VPN encryption include a form of PPTP called Layer 2 Tunneling Protocol (L2TP).

Types of VPNs

You can choose from several types of VPNs depending on your business needs. They are all good solutions; you only need to find what works for your company.

Internet VPN

The Internet VPN connection is from one business unit to another via the public Internet. Remote users, such as a roving sales team, can also utilize an Internet VPN to connect remotely and access files securely over the Internet. The Internet VPN can be seen in Figure 18-7.

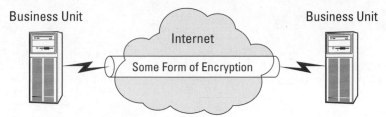

Figure 18-7: Typical Internet VPN Diagram

Intranet VPN

The intranet VPN handles traffic that may not involve data going over a wide area network and focuses on Local Area Network traffic. It is scaled down version of the Internet VPN, and users connect directly to your corporate intranet. The intranet VPN can be seen in Figure 18-8.

Figure 18-8: Typical intranet VPN

Extranet VPN

The extranet VPN is very similar to the intranet VPN. The biggest difference is that the extranet VPN allows companies that you do business with to connect to your intranet directly and share database information for enterprise resource planning (ERP) directly over the Internet. The extranet VPN can be seen in Figure 18-9.

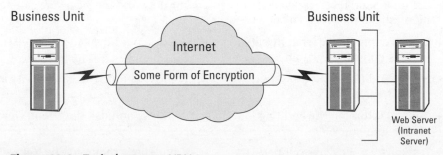

Figure 18-9: Typical extranet VPN

Tying it All Together

As a CIW Foundations candidate or a network security analyst preparing for the CIW Foundations exam, you need to understand the basic concepts of network and system security so that you can make educated decisions about how and why to protect your systems.

Figure 18-10 depicts the use of firewalls, proxies, IDS systems, and VPNs to protect data. Remember that all these tools should be considered when planning your network security infrastructure.

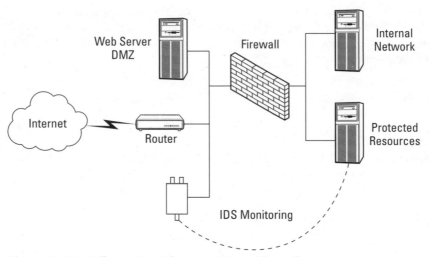

Figure 18-10: Full security with proxy, IDS and firewall systems

Key Point Summary

A summary of the important points covered in this chapter follows:

✦ Set up a multi-layered defense to secure your network, but be aware of common pitfalls that weaken such security.

✦ Pay attention to external threats to your network, but be aware that most attacks come from within.

✦ Set up auditing on your systems and review the logs for irregular activity and possible break-ins.

✦ You must turn on the auditing function in Windows and use the Event Viewer to see audited events.

✦ A security policy lays out network security guidelines that must be followed in order to keep your systems secure.

✦ Make sure you have the management's support to enforce your security policy.

✦ A virtual private network (VPN) transmits private data over a public network.

✦ A VPN uses encryption to protect data in transit.

✦ The three types of VPNs are Internet, intranet, and extranet.

✦ Denial-of-Service (DoS) attacks stop legitimate requests from reaching their intended destination.

✦ The most common DoS attack is the buffer overflow attack that fills up a system's buffers so it can't service legitimate requests.

✦ Social engineering is method used by attackers to trick users into giving them important credentials to access critical systems.

✦ An intrusion detection system (IDS) is a device that monitors and prevents intrusion into your protected systems.

✦ IDS systems should work in conjunction with the security policy so misuse of business systems can be met with disciplinary action immediately.

✦   ✦   ✦

STUDY GUIDE

Assessment Questions

1. Which system allows you to monitor system intrusion?

    A. VPN

    B. PIM

    C. IDS

    D. DME

2. A VPN is an acronym that stands for which of the following?

    A. Virtual private network

    B. Virtual public network

    C. Value add private network

    D. Valid public network

3. What type of attack is a buffer overflow attack?

    A. IDS

    B. Social engineering

    C. Denial engineering

    D. DoS

4. A security policy is something that needs what important piece from the following choices? (Choose the best choice)

    A. Upper management support and backing

    B. Hacker Support

    C. An Intranet Web page dedicated to it

    D. A hacker alliance to back it

5. If you acquire a set of credentials from a help desk technician by intimidating him or tricking him, what attack have you performed?

    A. DoS

    B. Dumpster diving

C. Social engineering

D. IDT

6. What security method is used to secure data and keep it from passing based on meeting criteria on a list?

    A. SEP

    B. STE

    C. ACL

    D. SMB

7. A VPN protects data by using _____ to provide a tunnel through which the data is sent.

    A. Encryption

    B. IDS

    C. SSL

    D. IPSENT

8. Auditing a Windows Operating System will result in entries within which of the Event Viewer logs?

    A. Application

    B. Security

    C. System

    D. All of the above

9. Most attacks on your network come from which of the following?

    A. The mailroom

    B. The CEO

    C. External sources

    D. Internal sources

10. The best system security infrastructure approach is to prepare a:

    A. Multi-layered defense

    B. VPN

    C. IPSNT protocol

    D. SSL

Lab Exercises

Lab 18-1 Removing administrative permissions from a folder

Note   To perform this lab correctly, you will need to be running Windows NT/2000 with a drive formatted with the NTFS files system.

1. Select a folder from your C:\ Drive or make a brand new one if you don't want to change permissions on an existing folder.

2. Right click the folder and go to properties.

3. Select the Security tab.

4. Remove the administrator account (remember, only do this as a test).

Note   Another way to disable the administrator account is to select it and deny write permissions to the administrator.

5. Unless you want to keep these settings, select cancel. Select OK to choose these new settings.

Lab 18-2 Setting auditing on a Windows 2000 machine for login logging

1. Go to Start ⇨ Settings ⇨ Control Panel ⇨ Administrative Tools.

2. Select the Local Security Policy MMC from the menu.

3. Open the MMC (Microsoft Management Console) and expand down to the `Local Policies` folder. Open it to reveal the `Audit Policy` folder.

4. Inside the `Audit Policy` folder, locate `Audit policies` in the right hand pane of the console. Find the first one that says audit account logon events.

5. Double-click the policy and select failure

6. Upon logging on and failing to apply the right credentials, the event will be logged to the security log in Event Viewer.

Lab 18-3 Viewing the Windows 2000 Security Log

Note   To get this lab to work correctly, log off the workstation you are working at and try to log in a few times incorrectly; this will generate some events for you to view.

1. Go to Start ⇨ Settings ⇨ Control Panel ⇨ Administrative Tools.

2. Select the Computer Management MMC from the menu.

3. Open the MMC. Expand down to the System Tools and expand the Event Viewer.

4. Select the Security Log.

In the right-hand pane you will find entries for failed logons that occurred after you set the system up to be audited. This can be viewed regardless of what you configured, but entries will only be seen if you configure auditing on such objects.

Lab 18-4 Performing eavesdropping with Sniffer Pro

1. Install Sniffer Pro. You can use Network Monitor if you do not have Sniffer Pro.

2. Collect data by going to the Capture menu and selecting Start.

3. After a few minutes of collecting data go back to the capture menu and select Stop and Display.

4. Click on the Decode tab of the Capture dialog box to view the traffic that was collected (you can find URL's, TCP/IP addresses, and so on).

Attackers will do this to capture data for eavesdropping.

Lab 18-5 Collecting data and a password with Sniffer Pro

1. Set up Sniffer Pro as in Lab 18-4.

2. Open the program and start collecting data as in Lab 18-4.

3. Log in to the Exchange server via the Outlook Express Client and make sure you don't select to encrypt any of the password information.

4. Select Stop and Display from the Capture menu within Sniffer. Scroll down to where you can find your Log in and you will see your password in clear text

This is a true test of password hacking with an analysis tool.

Chapter Pre-Test Answers

1. IDS

2. Extranet VPN

3. Social Engineering

4. Denial of Service

5. True

6. Script Kiddie

7. 20 and 21

8. Encryption

9. Netstat

10. 110

Answers to Assessment Questions

1. C. IDS allows you to monitor system intrusion.

2. A. VPN stands for virtual private network.

3. D. A buffer overflow is a denial-of-service attack.

4. A. A security policy must be supported by upper management.

5. C. Acquiring credentials through trickery or intimidation is an example of social engineering.

6. C. ACL secures data and keeps it from passing based on meeting criteria on a list.

7. A. A VPN protects data by using encryption to provide a tunnel through which the data is sent.

8. B. Auditing a Windows Operating System will result in entries in the Security logs.

9. D. Most attacks on your network come from internal sources.

10. A. The best system security infrastructure approach is to prepare a multi-layered defense.

Resources

www.cert.org

www.sans.org

www.securityportal.com

What's on the CD-ROM?

The CD-ROM that accompanies this book has been prepared to assist you in studying for the CIW Foundations exam. The following is a list of the resources and trial software provided:

- ◆ **Adobe Acrobat Reader 4.0** — Required software to access the PDF files provided.

- ◆ **Complete Electronic version of the CIW Certification Bible** — in Adobe PDF format.

- ◆ **Custom Designed Test Engine** — Complete with CIW Foundations test questions.

- ◆ **Lab Files** — All files necessary to complete the chapter Lab exercises.

- ◆ **Resource Links** — Quick link page to all of the Web site resources mentioned in the book.

- ◆ **Relevant RFC documents** — Complete set of Request for Comment (RFC) documents referenced in the book.

- ◆ **HotMetal Pro 5.0** — A powerful GUI-based Web site development tool from SoftQuad Software, Inc.

- ◆ **TextPad 4.5** — An excellent text editor from Helios Software Solutions. This tool is ideal for creating HTML Web pages.

- ◆ **DataSAFE Encryption** — Strong encryption software from NOVaSTOR Corporation to help you secure sensitive data.

- ◆ **WS_Ping ProPack 2.3** — An excellent network information tool from Ipswitch, Inc.

- ◆ **WS_FTP Pro** — Also from Ipswitch, this is an easy-to-use but powerful FTP client application for transfering data files between your PC and a remote FTP server.

- ◆ **VisualRoute 5, version 5.4a** — VisualRoute, from Visualware Inc., is an integrated ping, whois, and traceroute program that can be used to visually analyze Internet connectivity displaying the results on a world map.

Installing and Using the CD-ROM

The CD-ROM has been configured to auto-start the installation program as soon as it has been placed into your CD-ROM tray. If your computer or CD-ROM does not support auto-start, then you may perform the following steps to begin the installation:

1. Insert the CD-ROM into your computer's CD-ROM tray.

2. Click the Windows Start menu and choose the Run option.

3. Type the following into the Open field of the Run dialog box: (Replace the letter *d* with whichever letter represents your CD-ROM drive)

   ```
   d:\setup.exe
   ```

The following is an explanation of the options presented by the CD-ROM setup program:

✦ **Install** — Choosing this option will begin the installation of the necessary files onto your computer. Follow the prompts.

✦ **Explorer** — This option opens a Windows Explorer window that allows you to manually browse the contents of the CD-ROM.

✦ **Exit** — Exits the CD-ROM setup program without installing anything.

After this has been installed, you may access the CD-ROM's information by choosing the CIW Foundations Bible option from within the programs option in your Windows Start menu.

System Requirements

Make sure that your computer meets the minimum system requirements listed in this section. If your computer doesn't match up to most of these requirements, you may have a problem using the contents of the CD.

For Windows 9*x*, 2000, NT4 (with SP 4 or later), Me, or XP, and Linux:

✦ PC with a Pentium processor running at 120 Mhz or faster and a CD-ROM drive

✦ At least 32 MB of total RAM installed on your computer; for best performance, at least 64 MB is recommended.

✦ Ethernet network interface card (NIC) or modem with a speed of at least 28,800 bps

For Macintosh, you'll need a MAC OS computer with a 68040 or faster processor running OS 7.6 or later and the same RAM previously listed.

✦   ✦   ✦

Objective Mapping Matrix

T he following table is a comprehensive listing of the CIW Foundations exam objectives and the locations in the book where they are covered.

Table B-1
CIW Foundations Exam Objectives

Exam Objective	Section	Chapter
Trace the evolution of the Internet.	1	1
Explain the elements required to connect an Internet Client to the Internet.	1	1
Describe how the client/server model functions on the Internet.	1	1
Describe push and pull technology.	1	1
Define TCP/IP and state how the internet uses it.	1	1
Identify and describe major Internet protocols such as Hypertext Transfer Protocol (HTTP), e-mail, File Transfer Protocol, and newsgroups.	1	1
List several criteria for selecting an ISP.	1	1
Explain domain names and virtual domains.	1	1
Describe the functions of the ICANN and the InterNIC.	1	1
Identify the purpose and function of Uniform Resource Locators (URLs).	1	1
Describe the difference between the Internet, Intranets, and Extranets.	1	1
Define the origins of the World Wide Web, and explain the difference between the Web and the Internet.	1	2
Define Legacy Application.	1	2
Access, view and navigate Web pages using various Web browsers.	1	2
Enter Uniform Resource Locators (URLs).	1	2
View Web page source code.	1	2
Set preferences to customize a Web browser.	1	2
Configure browser home pages and manage history folders.	1	2
Configure and empty browser caches.	1	2
Save and organize frequently used Web Page addresses in the Favorites and Bookmarks folders.	1	2
Control browser image loading.	1	2
Explain the function of Wireless Application Protocol (WAP).	1	2

Exam Objective	Section	Chapter
Configure your browser to send e-mail.	1	3
Send and receive e-mail messages using various e-mail client programs.	1	3
Define and practice "netiquette:"	1	3
Create e-mail signatures to e-mail messages.	1	3
Attach a file to e-mail messages.	1	3
Describe the purpose of mailing lists.	1	3
Access and Download files using File Transfer Protocol (FTP).	1	3
Describe the FTP get and put commands.	1	3
Read and post messages to newsgroups.	1	3
Access resources using telnet.	1	3
Explain the function of search engines and their use of keywords.	1	4
Promote a Web site with enhanced search engine positioning.	1	4
Explain the functions of static, keyword and full-text search indexes.	1	4
Use search engines to seek information.	1	4
Search for Internet data using AND, OR, AND NOT, NOT, NEAR, wildcards, and plus and minus signs.	1	4
Use Boolean operators in an advanced Web search.	1	4
Search for graphics, people and mailing lists on the Internet.	1	4
Describe the purposes of Archie, Gopher and Veronica.	1	4
Define objects and their relationships to multimedia.	1	5
Explain the basics of C, C++, Java, JavaScript, ActiveX, JScript, and VBScript, and describe how they are related to each other.	1	5
Describe the purpose of plug-ins.	1	5
Identify plug-ins and viewers, including RealNetworks RealPlayer, Macromedia Shockwave and Flash Players, Apple QuickTime, and Adobe Acrobat Reader.	1	5

Continued

Table B-1 *(continued)*

Exam Objective	Section	Chapter
Listen to and view multimedia objects within your browser.	1	5
Identify various file formats, such as MPEG, MP3, MOV, AIFF, AU, WAV, AVI, EPS, TIFF, and RTF.	1	5
Describe cookies and their purpose.	1	6
Control Web server access to cookie files on your computer.	1	6
Configure browser security preferences.	1	6
Identify security risks when sending information over the Web.	1	6
Describe the importance of Hypertext Transfer Protocol Secure (HTTPS).	1	6
Explain how authentication, digital certificates and encryption provide Web security.	1	6
Describe a computer virus and explain how to protect your computer from virus attacks.	1	6
Identify the purpose of proxy severs and firewalls.	1	6
Define electronic commerce and compare it to traditional commerce.	1	7
Identify the principal features of Electronic Data Interchange (EDI) and Secure Electronic Transactions (SET).	1	7
Discuss the advantages and key issues of e-commerce.	1	7
Describe the functions and advantages of smart cards.	1	7
Explain the issues involved with copyrights, licensing, and trademarks.	1	7
Describe the fundamentals of project management, including the major stages of a design/development project cycle.	1	7
Distinguish between creating Web Pages using an HTML text editor and a GUI HTML editor.	2	8
Identify different types of GUI HTML editors that create HTML automatically.	2	8
Define HTML.	2	8
Describe the origins of HTML.	2	8

Exam Objective	Section	Chapter
Identify strategies for developing accessible Web pages.	2	8
Describe the standards organization that controls the various versions of HTML.	2	8
Identify the HTML 4.01 flavors.	2	8
List the benefits of Extensible HTML (XHTML).	2	8
List the benefits of Extensible HTML (XHTML) and how it relates to HTML and the Extensible Markup Language (XML).	2	8
Explain how HTML is related to XHTML.	2	8
Determine which browsers support which versions of HTML.	2	8
Identify strategies for developing accessible Web pages.	2	8
Identify front-end Web page design issues, such as the interface.	2	8
Define the concepts of creative design and branding standards, and illustrate their importance to business.	2	8
Identify back-end Web design issues, such as bandwidth and page names.	2	8
Explain Web document naming conventions.	2	8
Identify the issues that affect Internet site functionality.	2	8
Identify HTML document structure tags.	2	9
Explain the <META>tag and the Document Type Declaration (DTD).	2	9
Apply proper HTML tag usage.	2	9
Create simple HTML pages.	2	9
Format paragraphs and text with HTML tags.	2	9
Add horizontal rules to your Web pages and work with horizontal rule attributes.	2	9
Incorporate image files as stand-alone graphics.	2	9
Use the Web-safe color palette.	2	9
Change the page background color.	2	9
Use a tiled image across the page background.	2	9
Reference full and partial URL's.	2	10

Continued

Table B-1 *(continued)*

Exam Objective	Section	Chapter
Create hyperlinks for text.	2	10
Create hyperlinks for images.	2	10
Link to local files.	2	10
Link to remote sites.	2	10
Create an internal anchor and link to that anchor within the same file.	2	10
Create simple and complex HTML tables.	2	10
Add or remove table border lines.	2	10
Format table rows and cells using attributes.	2	10
Identify HTML form elements.	2	10
Construct a Web form using all the HTML form elements.	2	10
Test your Web form using a public test engine.	2	10
Create client-side image maps.	2	11
Define rectangle, circle, and polygon areas in an image.	2	11
Link defined areas to URLs.	2	11
Define image transparency.	2	11
Describe image interlacing.	2	11
Identify animated GIFs	2	11
Define frames and the purpose of the frameset document.	2	11
Use the <FRAMESET> and <FRAME> tags, and list several attributes of each.	2	11
Identify the purpose of the <NOFRAMES> tag.	2	11
Target links from one frame to another.	2	11
Specify default targets using the <BASE> tag.	2	11
Create borderless frames.	2	11
Describe the effects of Cascading Style Sheets (CSS) on design.	2	11
Identify the purpose and uses of JavaScript.	2	11
Describe the Benefits of Dynamic HTML (DHTML).	2	11

Exam Objective	Section	Chapter
Explain the function of the Document Object Model (DCOM) ad how it relates to browsers.	2	11
List the benefits of Extensible HTML (XHTML) and explain how it relates the HTML and the Extensible Markup Language.	2	11
Define "networking" and explain this concept's importance in today's data communications marketplace.	3	12
Identify and describe the functions of servers, workstations and hosts.	3	12
Define the term Internetwork, and define its role and usage as related to the Internet.	3	12
Relate Internetworks to the concept of the corporate enterprise network.	3	12
Identify networking architectures and provide at least two defining characteristics of each.	3	12
Describe the basic network topology characteristics.	3	12
Identify the major network operating systems-Microsoft Windows NT/2000, Unix, and Novell Netware-and their respective clients.	3	12
Discuss the Open Systems Interconnection Reference Model (OSI/RM), Including the layers and functions at each layer.	3	13
Explain Packets and describe packct creation.	3	13
Differentiate between protocols that reside at the network, transport and application layers of the OSI/RM.	3	13
Identify key internetworking protocols and explain the need for multi-protocol networks.	3	13
Define the nature, purpose and operational essentials of TCP/IP.	3	13
Compare, contrast and discuss the functions of networking protocols.	3	13
Bind protocols to a Network Interface Card.	3	13
Describe the basics of a local area network and a wide area network.	3	14
Identify and described the function of network access points.	3	14

Continued

Table B-1 *(continued)*

Exam Objective	Section	Chapter
Explain how the various LAN/WAN devices work together, including NICs, repeaters, hubs, bridges, routers, brouters, switches, gateways, CSU/DSUs, modems and patch panels.	3	14
Identify the differences among common transmission media used in networking, such as twisted-pair, coaxial, fiber optic cable and wireless media.	3	14
Describe transmission types including asynchronous and synchronous, simplex, half duplex, full duplex, baseband and broadband.	3	14
Explain the differences between logical and physical topologies.	3	14
Identify LAN standards, including the institute of electrical and electronics Engineers LAN standards, Apple LocalTalk, and Fiber Distributed Data Interface.	3	14
Identifier WAN standards, including X. 25 frame relay and asynchronous transfer mode.	3	14
Explain the function and types of T carrier E carrier systems.	3	14
Describe the purpose of Request for Comments (RFC).	3	15
Define and describe the Internet architecture model and various Internet protocols.	3	15
Describe port numbers and their functions, including well-known and registered port numbers.	3	15
Explain IP addressing, address classes and the concept of uniqueness.	3	15
Explain the use of private addresses.	3	15
Identify default subnet masks and explain their function.	3	15
Explain the routing process, including static versus dynamic routing, and interior versus exterior routing protocols.	3	15
Compare and contrast Routing Information Protocol (RIP) with Open Shortest Path First (OSPF).	3	15
Define the TCP/IP properties needed to configure a typical workstation.	3	15

Exam Objective	Section	Chapter
Describe various diagnostic tools for troubleshooting TCP/IP networks.	3	15
Identify and describe the functions and features of file and print, HTTP, proxy, caching, mail, mailing list, media, DNS, FTP, news, certificate, directory, catalog and transaction servers.	3	16
Describe how each type of networking server uses the TCP/IP suite protocols.	3	16
Describe access-security features of an HTTP server, including user names, passwords, and file-level access.	3	16
Define MIME, and explain how MIME types are used by HTTP and mail servers.	3	16
Describe the function of DNS, including the DNS hierarchy, root domain servers, top level domains and DNS record types.	3	16
Define daemon and identify the functions of the internet-related daemons named, inetd and telnetd.	3	16
Explain the uses of server-side scripting and define gateways.	3	17
Define the Common Gateway Interface (CGI).	3	17
Differentiate between client-side and server-side scripting.	3	17
Describe server programming interface alternatives to CGI, such as Java gateways, ActiveX Data Objects (ADO) and Server Application Programming Interfaces (SAPIs).	3	17
Explain server-side scripting applications, including JavaServer Pages (JSP), Personal Home Page (PHP), Active Server Pages (ASP) and Server-Side JavaScript (SSJS).	3	17
Explain the functions of Java servlets and how they differ from scripting languages.	3	17
List the different types of databases and database management systems, including DBMS and RDBMS.	3	17
Differentiate between Open Database Connectivity (ODBC) and Java Database Connectivity (JDBC).	3	17
Explain the need for network security and identify resources that need security.	3	18

Continued

Table B-1 *(continued)*		
Exam Objective	*Section*	*Chapter*
List the two major categories of security threats.	3	18
Identify various types of hacker attacks.	3	18
Describe a computer virus and explain how to protect your computer from virus attacks.	3	18
Explain the audit process.	3	18
Define authentication principles.	3	18
Explain the three major types of encryption	3	18
Describe enterprise-level security protocols, including virtual private networks (VPNs), Secure Socket Layer (SSL), and digital certificates.	3	18
List and discuss the four major types of firewalls.	3	18

✦   ✦   ✦

Sample Exam

With the following sample exam, you can test your readiness for the real thing. It has been designed to closely simulate the length, scope, and format of the real exam. However, please note that this is merely an example of the types of questions that you will be asked; they are not the actual questions.

Good luck!

Begin Test

1. Which of the following organizations is responsible for managing domain names on the Internet?

   a. ICANN

   b. ISP

   c. United States Department of Defense

   d. W3C type

2. Which of the following FQDNs contains a top-level domain that indicates it belongs to an educational institution?

   a. edu.purdue.com

   b. www.purdue.org

   c. www.harvard.com

   d. learn.yale.edu

3. Which of the following is not a valid URL?

   a. http//www.microsoft.com/support/service.htm

   b. mailto:cliff@golf.com

   c. news://news.tiger.com

   d. https://www.someplace.com/canada/regina/test.htm

4. Which of the following protocols are typically used to transmit data over a dial-up connection? (Choose all that apply)

   a. SLIP

   b. SET

   c. PPP

   d. PPTP

5. Which organization controls standards for HTML?

   a. CPAC

   b. WWW

   c. W3C

   d. ICANN

6. Which of the following are used to display HTML documents?

    a. Real Player

    b. Web browsers

    c. Text editors

    d. News client

7. Which of the following is not a valid e-mail address?

    a. `chuck@windsor.org`

    b. `big_cheese@provolone.net`

    c. `123@home.edu`

    d. `bbruin@hockey_net`

8. Which of the following protocols is used to send e-mail?

    a. SMTP

    b. POP

    c. FTP

    d. HTTP

9. What is the name given to the text that can be automatically added to the bottom of all outgoing e-mails?

    a. Certificate

    b. Caption

    c. Signature

    d. Trailer

10. Which of the following is an example of proper Netiquette?

    a. Never using any capital letters in electronic correspondence

    b. Pressing the send button after composing a message

    c. Running spell check prior to sending any message

    d. Never responding to an e-mail unless requested

11. Which of the following is associated with USENET?

    a. Mailing Lists

    b. NNTP

    c. Gopher

    d. SNMP

12. Which extension is typically associated with compressed files? (Choose all that apply)

    a. .zip

    b. .tar

    c. .com

    d. .sea

13. Alexander is using an FTP text-based client and wants to download a file called `game.zip` from the FTP server to which he is currently connected. Assuming Alexander has the rights to do so, which of the following commands should he use?

    a. ftp game.zip

    b. put game.zip

    c. get game.zip

    d. cd game.zip

14. Which of the following technologies are used to support multimedia on the Internet? (Choose all that apply)

    a. Java Applets

    b. ActiveX

    c. Browser Plug-ins

    d. VRML

15. Which of the following extensions is associated with Adobe Acrobat?

    a. .adb

    b. .pdf

    c. .tiff

    d. .acr

16. Which of the following is an HTML tag used to assist search engines in cross-referencing a Web site with key words?

    a. <META>

    b. <KEY>

    c. <SEARCHSPEC>

    d. <MAP>

17. Which of the following is an example of Boolean operators?

    a. AND

    b. NOT

    c. OR

    d. All of the above

18. Which of the following search strings, when entered in AltaVista, will result in a list of Web sites concerning professional hockey in Boston? (Choose the best answer)

    a. "pro hockey" near boston

    b. "Boston – Hockey"

    c. "Pro Hockey"+ Boston

    d. "Pro Hockey" – Boston

19. What is the name for the small text files placed on a Web site visitor's computer so that Web site administrators can gain marketing information about their visitors?

    a. Cache

    b. Cookies

    c. History

    d. Signatures

20. Which of the following are used to prove the identity of a company when using a Web browser?

    a. Cache

    b. Certificates

    c. Cookies

    d. Encryption signature

21. What are the usual key lengths in a typical commercial encryption?

    a. Either 40 byte or 128 byte

    b. Either 40 bit or 128 bit

    c. Either 32 byte or 1024 byte

    d. Either 32 bit or 1024 bit

22. Anonymous, basic, secure, and digital certificates are all forms of what?

    a. Authentication

    b. Encryption

    c. Synchronization

    d. Authorization

23. What are the three main elements of electronic commerce? (Choose three)

    a. Communication

    b. Data Management

    c. Security

    d. Certification

24. Which of the following is a standard method for transferring electronic commerce information between computers and companies?

    a. SETI

    b. EDI

    c. RIAA

    d. ISO 9001

25. Which of the following is considered a drawback to using a GUI-based HTML editor?

    a. With GUI-based HTML editors, you really can't see what your finished Web page will look like until you open it in a browser.

    b. GUI-based HTML editors are only available for Microsoft Windows based computers.

    c. GUI editors often don't keep up with changes to HTML.

    d. GUI editors require an extensive knowledge of HTML tags and syntax.

26. Which of the following are considered to be varieties of HTML?

    a. Strict

    b. Structured

    c. Frameset

    d. Transitional

27. Tags may consist of: (Choose all that apply)

    a. A value

    b. A markup

    c. An element

    d. An attribute

    e. A function

28. Which of the following represents the correct order in which the document structure tags should appear in an HTML document?

    a. <HEAD> <TITLE> <HTML> <BODY>

    b. <TITLE> <HTML> <HEAD> <BODY>

    c. <HTML> <HEAD> <TITLE> <BODY>

    d. <TITLE> <HEAD> <BODY> <HTML>

29. What is the purpose of a DTD tag?

    a. Used to state the version of the HTML editor used when creating a Web page

    b. Used to describe the version of HTML used in a Web page, as well as its primary language

    c. Centers all descriptive text on a central point

    d. Used to describe the contents of a Web page so they may be located by search engine queries

30. Elements that affect an entire paragraph or multiple paragraphs are referred to as:

    a. Block-level elements

    b. Paragraph-level elements

    c. Text-level elements

    d. Container elements

31. Which of the following tags are considered to be container tags?

    a. <P>

    b.

    c. <BODY>

    d. <H1>

32. What is the proper HTML syntax to bold the word *Holiday*?

    a. </B>Holiday</B>

    b. <B>Holiday</B>

    c. <B>Holiday

    d. <B>Holiday<\B>

33. Wendy wants to align an image file called "`farm.jpg`" to the left of a paragraph of text that follows. Which of the following HTML code segments will accomplish this?

    a. <IMG ALIGN="left"> <SRC=farm.jpg> Paragraph of text.....

    b. <IMG SRC="farm.jpg ALIGN="left"> Paragraph of text....

    c. <IMG SRC=farm.jpg> <ALIGN="right" Paragraph of text....>

    d. <IMG SRC=farm.jpg ALIGN="right"> Paragraph of text....

34. Which of the following elements are required in an HTML table?

    a. Table

    b. Table caption

    c. Table row

    d. Table header

35. You want to design a form element asking the user if they have ever used your product before. You decide to create this form element by using radio buttons on which the "No" option is selected by default. Which of the following HTML code segments is appropriate for this task?

    a.

```
Have you used our product in the past?
<INPUT TYPE="Radio" NAME=UsePrdct Value="yes" YES>
<INPUT TYPE="Radio" NAME=UsePrdct Value="no" no
CHECKED=NO>
```

    b.

```
Have you used our product in the past?
<INPUT TYPE="Radio" NAME=UsePrdct Value="yes"> Yes
<INPUT TYPE="Radio" NAME=UsePrdct Value="no"> No
```

c.

```
Have you used our product in the past?
<INPUT TYPE="Radio" NAME=UsePrdct Value="yes"> Yes
<INPUT TYPE="Radio" NAME=UsePrdct Value="no" CHECKED=YES>
No
```

d.

```
Have you used our product in the past?
<INPUT TYPE="Radio" NAME=UsePrdct Value="yes"> Yes
<INPUT TYPE="Radio" NAME=UsePrdct Value="no" CHECKED> No
```

36. Which of the following are valid uses of the <FRAMESET> tag? (Choose all that apply)

    a. <FRAMESET COLS="35%, 10%, 70%">

    b. <FRAMESET COLS="50%, 50%">

    c. <FRAMESET ROWS="*.*">

    d. <FRAMESET ROWS="185,*">

37. What are the three basic elements of a network? (Choose three)

    a. Transmission Media

    b. Clients

    c. Protocols

    d. Operating Systems

    e. Network Services

38. Which network model features the use of "dumb terminals"?

    a. Peer-to-Peer

    b. Client/Server

    c. Mainframe

    d. Token Ring

39. What type of computer typically acts as the second tier in three-tier computing?

    a. The client

    b. The Web server

    c. A database server

    d. A proxy server

40. Which of the following are disadvantages of a physical bus topology?

    a. The components required to construct a bus network are expensive

    b. Difficult to install

    c. A break in the cable will stop all network traffic

    d. All of the above

41. What type of topology is formed when two or more star networks are joined together through the use of FDDI technology?

    a. Star-Bus

    b. Star-Ring

    c. Mesh

    d. Ring

42. Place the following OSI layers in the proper order, starting from the bottom:

    a. Physical, Data Link, Network, Transport, Session, Presentation, Application

    b. Physical, Data Link, Transport, Network, Presentation, Session, Application

    c. Data Link, Physical, Network, Transport, Presentation, Session, Application

    d. Physical, Data Link, Network, Transport, Presentation, Session, Application

43. Which of the following comprises a packet? (Choose all that apply)

    a. Header

    b. Segment

    c. Trailer

    d. Data

44. Which of the following are application-level protocols? (Choose all that apply)

    a. FTP

    b. HTTP

    c. POP

    d. TCP

45. The order in which an operating system will try protocols when attempting to communicate across a network is referred to as its _____.

    a. Link service order

    b. Order of presentation

    c. Binding order

    d. Presentation sequence

46. At what layer of the OSI do repeaters work?

    a. Physical

    b. Data Link

    c. Network

    d. Transport

47. What type of address does a bridge look at in order to determine whether or not to pass a packet?

    a. IP Address

    b. Network Address

    c. Host Address

    d. MAC Address

48. Which of the following is true?

    a. Baseband transmission uses digital signaling.

    b. Broadband transmission is most commonly used in LANs.

    c. Cable TV is a good example of baseband transmission.

    d. Baseband transmission divides a transmission media into several channels by using a process called multiplexing.

49. Which IEEE 802 standard defines Ethernet?

    a. 802.2

    b. 802.3

    c. 802.5

    d. 802.10

50. The series of documents maintained by the IETF that lays out specifications and standards for protocols and services on the Internet is the
_____.

    a. IEEE 802 Standards

    b. ISO 9001 Standards

    c. RFCs

    d. OSI Standards

51. Well-known port numbers lie between _____ and _____.

    a. 0 and 65535

    b. 0 and 1023

    c. 1024 and 65535

    d. 1024 and 49152

52. What class of address is 125.23.22.1?

    a. Class A

    b. Class B

    c. Class C

    d. Class D

53. Which of the following is a loopback address?

    a. 0.0.0.0

    b. 255.255.255.255

    c. 127.0.0.1

    d. 192.168.0.0

54. Which of the following devices allows increased network security, IP address conservation, client transaction filtering, and increased Internet access performance?

    a. Proxy server

    b. Caching server

    c. Directory server

    d. Domain Name server

55. What type of server resolves IP addresses from host names?

    a. DNS server

    b. Proxy server

      c. Directory server

      d. Apache server

56. Which of the following is an encoding mechanism for e-mail attachments?

      a. MIME

      b. UUCoding

      c. BinHex

      d. All of the above

57. Which of the following mechanisms allows the processing of HTML form information?

      a. ActiveX

      b. Java Applets

      c. CGI Scripts

      d. Web Browser plug-ins

58. A hacker is attempting to break into a computer system by conducting a brute force password attack. The hacker is in what stage of the hacker process?

      a. Discovery

      b. Penetration

      c. Control

      d. Capture

59. What are the three main forms of encryption? (Choose three)

      a. Symmetric

      b. Asymmetric

      c. Simple

      d. Complex

      e. Hash

60. What button must a form contain so that it can be processed?

      a. Align

      b. Send

      c. Form

      d. Submit

      e. Create

Exam Answers

The following are the correct answers for the preceding sample questions. Additional explanations are given when required.

1. Which of the following organizations is responsible for managing domain names on the Internet?

    a. ICANN

    This acronym refers to the Internet Corporation for Assigned Names and Numbers.

2. Which of the following FQDNs contains a top-level domain that indicates it belongs to an educational institution?

    d. `learn.yale.edu`

    Top-level domains are the last portion of a Fully Qualified Domain Name; .edu has been set aside to represent educational institutions.

3. Which of the following is not a valid URL?

    a. `http//www.microsoft.com/support/service.htm`

    This URL is not valid because it doesn't have a colon ":" between the protocol and the forward slashes "//".

4. Which of the following protocols are typically used to transmit data over a dial-up connection? (Choose all that apply)

    a. SLIP

    c. PPP

    Serial Line Internet Protocol (SLIP) and Point-to-Point Protocol (PPP) are correct. SET is the acronym for Secure Electronic Transaction, which is a standard for electronic commerce over the Internet. PPTP is an acronym for Point-to-Point Tunneling Protocol, which is used for Virtual Private Networking.

5. Which organization controls standards for HTML?

    c. W3C

    The World Wide Web Consortium (W3C).

6. Which of the following are used to display HTML documents?

    b. Web browsers

    Web browsers, such as Microsoft's Internet Explorer and Netscape Navigator, are used to view HTML documents.

7. Which of the following is not a valid e-mail address?

d. bbruin@hockey_net

This address is not valid because it doesn't include a properly formatted domain name, such as hockey_net.org or hockey_net.com.

8. Which of the following protocols is used to send e-mail?

a. SMTP

Simple Mail Transport Protocol is used to send e-mails.

9. What is the name given to the text that can be automatically added to the bottom of all outgoing e-mails?

c. Signature

A signature is commonly used to place a sender's contact information at the bottom of all outgoing e-mails.

10. Which of the following is an example of proper Netiquette?

c. Running spell check prior to sending any message

Netiquette is a set of common-sense rules and practices that encourage politeness and respect. Making sure that a message is properly spelled and grammatically correct is one of these basic rules. Another rule is to avoid typing the entire message in capital letters because this denotes shouting. The use of some capital letters — at the beginning of sentences, for example — is perfectly acceptable.

11. Which of the following is associated with USENET?

b. NNTP

USENET is the collection of publicly accessible newsgroups. Newsgroup access is accomplished using the Network News Transfer Protocol.

12. Which of these extensions are typically associated with compressed files? (Choose all that apply)

a. .zip

b. .tar

d. .sea

The extension .zip is a common extension associated with compression applications, such as WinZip and PKZIP. The extension .tar is a compression extension found in the UNIX world. The extension .sea is the extension used for self-extracting Macintosh compressed Stuffit files.

13. Alexander is using an FTP text-based client and wants to download a file called `game.zip` from the FTP server to which he is currently connected. Assuming that Alexander has the rights to do so, which of the following commands should he use?

c. `get game.zip`

The `get` command is used to download files; `put` is for uploading; `ftp` is used for starting the client; and `cd` is used for changing directory.

14. Select from the following all of the technologies used to support multimedia on the Internet:

a. Java Applets

b. ActiveX

c. Browser Plug-ins

d. VRML

15. Which of the following extensions is associated with Adobe Acrobat?

b. .pdf

Adobe Acrobat uses the Portable Document Format.

16. Which of the following is an HTML tag used to assist search engines in cross-referencing a Web site with key words?

a. <META>

The <META> tag allows you to describe the contents of a Web page by using keywords. This allows search engines to index the page so that searches on these keywords will list the page.

17. Which of the following is an example of Boolean operators?

d. All of the above

AND, OR, and NOT are the standard Boolean operators.

18. Which of the following search strings, when entered in AltaVista, will result in a list of Web sites concerning professional hockey in Boston? (Choose the best answer)

c. "Pro Hockey" + Boston

This search tells AltaVista to return any page that has the phrase "Pro Hockey" as well as the word "Boston."

19. What is the name for the small text files placed on a Web site visitor's computer so that Web site administrators can gain marketing information about their visitors?

b. Cookies

A cookie is information that a Web site puts on your hard drive so that it can remember something about you at a later time. This can be used to customize information presented the next time you visit the site.

20. Which of the following are used to prove the identity of a company when using a Web browser?

> **b. Certificates**
>
> Certificates are used to establish an organization's credentials. They are typically obtained from a trusted certificate authority that vouches for the organization's identity.

21. What are the usual key lengths in a typical commercial encryption?

> **b. Either 40 bit or 128 bit**
>
> Key lengths are always listed as a bit length; 40 bit is the standard length used on the Internet, and 128 bit is considered to be strong encryption.

22. Anonymous, basic, secure, and digital certificates are all forms of what?

> **a. Authentication**
>
> These are all methods of proving a person's identity.

23. What are the three main elements of electronic commerce? (Choose 3)

> **a. Communication**
>
> **b. Data Management**
>
> **c. Security**

24. Which of the following is a standard method of transferring electronic commerce information between computers and companies?

> **b. EDI**
>
> Electronic Data Interchange

25. Which of the following is considered to be a drawback to using a GUI-based HTML editor?

> **c. GUI editors often don't keep up with changes to HTML**
>
> C is the only drawback because GUI editors allow you to see your Web page as you work on it; they are available for a variety of platforms — not just Windows; and they allow a user to create a Web page with little or no knowledge of HTML.

26. Which of these are considered varieties of HTML?

> **a. Strict**
>
> **c. Frameset**
>
> **d. Transitional**
>
> The flavor of an HTML page defines its ability to use the latest HTML features, yet remain backwards-compatible with older browsers.

27. Tags may consist of: (Choose all that apply)

a. A value

c. An element

d. An attribute

An element describes the function of a tag; an attribute defines an aspect of the element (such as color); and a value describes the attribute setting used. For example, in the tag <BODY BGCOLOR="red">, BODY is the element, BGCOLOR is an attribute, and "red" is the value.

28. Which of the following represents the correct order that the document structure tags should appear in a HTML document?

c. <HTML> <HEAD> <TITLE> <BODY>

<HTML> defines the document as HTML; <HEAD>specifies the header of the document and contains the <TITLE> tag, which is used to define the text that will appear in the title bar of the browser. Of the four, <BODY> always appears last and is used to signify the start of the main portion of the Web page.

29. What is the purpose of a DTD tag?

b. Used to describe the version of HTML used in a Web page, as well as its primary language.

30. Elements that affect an entire paragraph or multiple paragraphs are referred to as:

a. Block-level elements

Paragraphs are considered blocks of text; therefore, these types of elements are referred to as block-level attributes.

31. Which of the following tags are considered to be container tags?

c. <BODY>

d. <H1>

These are considered to be container tags because they require closing tags, </body> and </H1>, respectively.

32. What is the proper HTML syntax to bold the word *Holiday*:

b. <B>Holiday</B>

The <B> tag is considered to be a container tag; thus, it requires a closing tag. All closing tags use the forward slash "/."

33. Wendy wants to align an image file called "farm.jpg" so that it is aligned to the left of a paragraph of text that is to follow. Which of the following HTML code segments will accomplish this?

b. <IMG SRC="farm.jpg ALIGN="left"> Paragraph of text....

This answer uses the correct syntax for the IMG tag, which accomplishes Wendy's requirement.

34. Which of the following elements are required in an HTML table?

a. Table

c. Table Row

35. You want to design a form element asking the user if they have ever used your product before. You decide to create this form element by using radio buttons on which the "No" option is selected by default. Which of the following HTML code segments is appropriate?

d.

```
Have you used our product in the past?
<INPUT TYPE="Radio" NAME=UsePrdct Value="yes"> Yes
<INPUT TYPE="Radio" NAME=UsePrdct Value="no" CHECKED> No
```

Only D is syntactically correct *and* enables the "No" option by default.

36. Which of the following are valid uses of the <FRAMESET> Tag? (Choose all that apply)

b. <FRAMESET COLS="50%, 50%">

d. <FRAMESET ROWS="185,*">

Answer B instructs the browser to create two vertical frames — each of which is given half of the total screen width. Answer D creates two horizontal frames; the first is 185 pixels in height, and the second uses the remainder of the screen.

37. What are the three basic elements of a network? (Choose three)

a. Transmission Media

c. Protocols

e. Network Services

Although the other two choices are found on networks, the CIW courseware does not consider them to be basic elements.

38. Which network model features the use of "dumb terminals?"

c. Mainframe

39. What type of computer typically acts as the second tier in three-tier computing?

b. The Web server

In three-tier computing, the client is typically the first tier, the Web server is the second tier, and a database server is typically the third tier.

40. Which of the following are disadvantages of a physical bus topology?

c. A break in the cable will stop all network traffic.

Bus networks are simple to install and typically inexpensive; however, a break in the cable will stop all network traffic.

41. What type of topology is formed when two or more star networks are joined together through the use of FDDI technology?

> **b. Star-Ring**
>
> FDDI is a technology based on a physical ring topology; joining star networks with a ring results in a Star-Ring topology.

42. Place the following OSI layers in the proper order, starting at the bottom:

> **a. Physical, Data Link, Network, Transport, Session, Presentation, Application**

43. Which of the following comprises a packet? (Choose all that apply)

> **a. Header**
>
> **c. Trailer**
>
> **d. Data**

44. Which of the following are application-level protocols? (Choose all that apply)

> **a. FTP**
>
> **b. HTTP**
>
> **c. POP**
>
> These are all considered to be application-level protocols because they are found in the Application Layer of the Internet architecture model.

45. The order in which an operating system will try protocols when attempting to communicate across a network is referred to as its _____.

> **c. Binding order**

46. At what layer of the OSI do repeaters work?

> **a. Physical**
>
> Repeaters merely boost a signal so it can travel longer distances; they do not perform any level of filtering or routing — therefore, it is not required to operate beyond the Physical Layer.

47. What type of address does a bridge examine in order to determine whether or not to pass a packet?

> **d. MAC Address**
>
> A bridge is protocol-independent and is only required to look at MAC addresses.

48. Which of the following is true?

> **a. Baseband transmission uses digital signaling.**
>
> Baseband transmission uses digital signaling and only allows a single message to travel at any one time. Baseband is commonly found in LANs.

49. Which IEEE 802 standard defines Ethernet?

b. 802.3

50. The series of documents maintained by the IETF that lays out specifications and standards for protocols and services on the Internet are _____.

c. RFCs

Request for Comment documents

51. Well-known port numbers lie between _____ and _____.

b. 0 and 1023

Port numbers fall between 0 and 65535; numbers between 0 and 1023 are used to identify common Internet services.

52. What class of address is 125.23.22.1?

a. Class A

The first octet of a Class A address falls between 1 and 127 (127 is reserved for Loopback); Class B falls between 128 and 191; Class C falls between 192 and 223; Class D falls between 224 and 239; and Class E falls between 240 and 247.

53. Which of the following is a Loopback address?

c. 127.0.0.1

This address allows a client and a server on the same computer to communicate with each other.

54. Which of the following devices allows increased network security, IP address conservation, client transaction filtering, and increased Internet access performance?

a. Proxy Server

55. What type of server resolves IP addresses from host names?

a. DNS server

The role of a domain name server is to accept host names, or — more specifically — FQDNs, and to translate them to IP addresses for name resolvers.

56. Which of the following is an encoding mechanism for e-mail attachments?

d. All of the above

UUCoding was one of the first methods used to transmit attachments found commonly in UNIX; BinHex was developed for the Macintosh platform to send e-mail attachments. MIME is the most common method now used.

57. Which of the following mechanisms allows the processing of HTML form information?

c. CGI Scripts

Common Gateway Interface scripts are the common way of processing information supplied through an HTML form.

58. A hacker is attempting to break into a computer system by conducting a brute force password attack. In what stage of the hacker process is the hacker?

b. Penetration

The penetration phase is characterized as a hacker actively trying to gain entry into a system, such as in this scenario.

59. What are the three main forms of encryption?

a. Symmetric

b. Asymmetric

e. Hash

Symmetric occurs when data is encrypted and decrypted using the same algorithm; asymmetric occurs when data is encrypted using one key and then decrypted using a second key (these two keys are referred to as a key pair). Hash, or one-way, encryption occurs when data is encrypted to form a unique hash; this hash can't be unencrypted to obtain the original data.

60. What button must a form contain so that it can be processed?

d. Submit

Your form must contain a submit button in order to process the information entered in the form.

✦   ✦   ✦

Exam-Taking Tips

Any exam, whether you're first or twentieth, can be a stressful experience. Knowing what to expect and being properly prepared can help relieve some of that stress. The following appendix provides some background on the exam and some tips to make your exam experience as stress free as possible.

CIW Foundations Exam Information

Here is some key information regarding the CIW Foundations Exam:

- **Exam number:** 1D0-410

- **Exam publication date:** June 2001

- **Exam length:** 90 Minutes, 70 Questions (ten not scored)

- **Exam passing score:** 45 correct of the 60 scored questions (75 percent)

- **Exam type:** Computer based, multiple choice

The questions presented on the exam will test you on your understanding of the concepts addressed by the CIW Foundations exam objectives (see Appendix B for a complete listing). Table D-1 shows the distribution of the exam questions.

The remaining 10 questions are considered beta questions and are not scored. The beta questions presented can be based on any CIW Foundations exam objective.

All questions are taken from a substantial pool of questions so that virtually no two exams will be identical. Therefore, if you are unfortunate and have to retake an exam, it is possible that you will not get any of the same questions seen on any previous attempts.

Table D-1 CIW Foundations Exam Scored Question Distribution		
CIW Foundations Module	*Number of Exam Questions*	*CIW Exam Certification Bible Part Number*
Internet Fundamentals	24	I
Web Page Authoring Fundamentals	12	II
Network Fundamentals	24	III

Registering for the Exam

The CIW Foundations exam is offered by VUE Testing Services and Prometric Testing Centers. Both of these test providers have a substantial number of testing centers located in major cities and towns throughout the world.

There is no difference in the exam regardless of which testing organization you decide to register with, either in price or test content. Choose the organization most convenient for you.

At the time of your exam registration be prepared with the following information:

✦ **Testing partner name:** CIW

✦ **Exam title:** CIW Foundations

✦ **Exam code:** 1D0-410

✦ **Date and time at which you would like to take the exam (subject to availability):** Try to schedule your exam for the time of day when you are at your peak. For many, the hours between ten in the morning and two in the afternoon tend to be the most productive.

✦ **Location where you would like to take the exam**

✦ **Method of payment:** The exam is 125 (U.S.) dollars, paid either by exam voucher, credit card, or check. If paying by check, you will not be able to book a time and date for the exam until your check has cleared.

✦ **Your contact information:** Including, mailing address, and phone number.

✦ **You employer's information:** Name, address, and phone number (optional)

✦ **If you have previously registered for an exam through Prometric, you will need your Prometric testing ID number (even if now registering at VUE).** This number is often your government ID number, such as Social Security Number in the U.S. or Social Insurance Number in Canada. If this is your first registration, one will be provided.

Registering with VUE Testing Services

If you wish to book your examination through VUE Testing Services, you can register in any of the following ways:

✦ In person at any VUE authorized testing centers

✦ Online at: `http://www.vue.com/ciw`

✦ Over the phone

- North America: 1-(877) 619-2096 (toll free)

- Europe: 00800-BOOK-TEST or 00800-2665-8378 (toll free)

- For other regions please see the previously listed Web site for numbers.

Registering with Prometric Testing Centers

If you wish to book your examination through Prometric Testing Centers you can do so in either of the following ways:

✦ Online at: `http://www.2test.com`

✦ Over the phone at 1-800-380-EXAM (3926) (U.S. and Canada only)

Exam Day

On the day of the Exam be prepared to arrive at least 15 minutes before the start of your exam. You will be required to show two forms of identification and at least one of them must include picture identification. A driver's license and a valid credit card in your name are sufficient. Other forms of identification may include passports, student cards, Social Security Card (or other government ID), and corporate ID cards. If you are unsure if your Identification will be accepted, call the testing center prior to your exam time.

You will be required to read and sign a non-disclosure agreement regarding the exam questions. You may not carry in any of the following:

✦ Books

✦ Calculators

✦ Laptop computers

✦ Notes

✦ Scratch paper

✦ Any reference materials

You may, however, be given a testing center-approved writing pad and pens for use during the exam (all of which will need to be returned after completion of the exam).

After all of the pretest requirements have been taken care of and the exam station becomes available, you will be led to the testing room. You will be signed on to the testing station and you may begin.

If this is your first exam you will be given an opportunity to take a tutorial exam. This tutorial is intended for those who are not familiar with computer testing. The questions are not related to the real exam and are only provided to make you comfortable with the computer-based testing environment. These questions will not be graded, and the time spent on this exam will not affect the amount of time allotted for the real exam.

You may also be presented with an opportunity to participate in an optional survey. Typically the questions asked during this survey relate to your background, your business or organization, your certification plans, and general questions regarding how you prepared for the exam. Time spent on this survey will not affect the amount of time allotted for the real exam.

After the survey is completed you will be prompted to start the real exam. Take a deep breath and begin.

During the Exam

Consider the following tips during the exam:

✦ **Read each question carefully.** Remember that you have 90 minutes to complete the entire exam. This is a little more than one minute and 15 seconds per question, and many questions will take you much less time than that to answer, so relax and read the questions at a comfortable pace.

✦ **Read each answer carefully.** Each question will have four possible answers, and you will be asked to choose the best possible answer from amongst them. Even if the correct answer is not immediately apparent, you can often eliminate one or two of the answer choices, making your final choice much easier.

✦ **Don't get hung up.** If you are stumped on a question don't feel you have to put down an answer right away. Questions can be marked and revisited later. A later question may even provide a clue or trigger a memory that will give you the right answer or help you eliminate some of the distracters.

✦ **Review your answers.** After you have finished answering all of the questions on the exam (if time permits), do a quick run through of each question and your answer to make sure you didn't make a wrong choice by mistake. However, try not to second-guess yourself on answers. Many will tell you that your first choice is most often the right answer.

The Results

After you have finished answering all of the questions on the exam or when time has expired, you will immediately be given your results on the testing station monitor as well as a printed copy. You will not be provided with any indication as to which questions you got right or wrong, or with any correct answers. The results will consist of a target passing score and your score. If your score is equal to or greater than the target score, then you pass. Along with your final score, the results will include a breakdown of your performance per section. This allows you to see the areas in which you may be weak on should you have to study for a retake.

The results of your exam will automatically be forwarded to Prosoft Training.

Your hard copy of your test results should be embossed with an official testing center seal. Do not lose this printout. It is official proof of your results and can be presented as such should any discrepancy arise between your actual results and Prosoft's records.

Retakes

If you fail, don't be discouraged. Many very bright people have done the same. You can retake the exam at any time. All that is required is that you register and pay the exam fee again.

If you fail by only a small margin, it is best to retake the exam as soon as possible (within two weeks). Examine your result sheet and study those areas where you were weak. Keep in mind, however, that the exam changes every time you take it, so some concepts may appear for the first time during retakes.

If you fail by a large margin, do not rush to retake the exam. Instead, go thoroughly review all the exam objectives. Do not register for the exam again until you are truly confident that you have mastered the material.

✦ ✦ ✦

HTML 4.01 Elements and Attributes

HTML 4.01 Elements

This appendix provides you with the W3C Elements and the Attributes Tables, which is used often by many Web developers. You can get the original documentation from the W3C site at www.w3.org/TR/html401/index/elements.html. This is a very handy reference to have and you will use it often as a quick reference. The following list explains the column headings used in Table E-1. Reading this text first will assist you in understanding the chart set up by the W3C:

- ✦ **Name.** This cell informs you of the name of the element.

- ✦ **Start Tag.** This cell informs you whether the start tag is optional. If a capital "O" is found in the list filed, then you know it is optional.

- ✦ **End Tag.** This cell informs you whether the end tag is optional or forbidden. "O" stands for Optional and "F" stands for Forbidden. Please note that it is an Empty element if it is Forbidden.

- ✦ **Empty.** This cell informs you whether the tag is an Empty element, denoted by an "E."

- ✦ **Depr.** This cell informs you whether the element is depreciated and is denoted with a "D." When XHTML becomes a fully accepted and widely used language, you may want to avoid this type of tag because it will be phased out.

- ✦ **DTD.** This cell informs you which DTD the element can be used with. If the field is empty, it is "Strict;" if it is "L," it is "Transitional;" and if it is "F," it is a Frameset.

- ✦ **Description.** This cell informs you what the element is or other important information.

Table E-1
Index of HTML 4.01 Elements

Name	Start Tag	End Tag	Empty	Depr.	DTD	Description
a						Anchor
abbr						Abbreviated form (e.g., WWW, HTTP, etc.)
acronym						
address						Information on author
applet				D	L	Java applet
area		F	E			Client-side image map area
b						Bold text style
base		F	E			Document base URI
basefont		F	E	D	L	Base font size
bdo						I18N BiDi over-ride
big						Large text style
blockquote						Long quotation
body	O	O				Document body
br		F	E			Forced line break
button						Push button
caption						Table caption
center				D	L	Shorthand for DIV align=center
cite						Citation
code						Computer code fragment
col		F	E			Table column
colgroup		O				Table column group
dd		O				Definition description
del						Deleted text
dfn						Instance definition
dir				D	L	Directory list
div						Generic language/style container

Name	Start Tag	End Tag	Empty	Depr.	DTD	Description
dl						Definition list
dt		O				Definition term
em						Emphasis
fieldset						Form control group
font				D	L	Local change to font
form						Interactive form
frame		F	E		F	Subwindow
frameset					F	Window subdivision
h1						Heading
h2						Heading
h3						Heading
h4						Heading
h5						Heading
h6						Heading
head	O	O				Document head
hr		F	E			Horizontal rule
html	O	O				Document root element
i						Italic text style
iframe					L	Inline subwindow
img		F	E			Embedded image
input		F	E			Form control
ins						Inserted text
isindex		F	E	D	L	Single line prompt
kbd						Text to be entered by the user
label						Form field label text
legend						Fieldset legend
li		O				List item
link		F	E			A media-independent link
map						Client-side image map
menu				D	L	Menu list

Continued

Table E-1 *(continued)*

Name	Start Tag	End Tag	Empty	Depr.	DTD	Description
meta		F	E			Generic meta information
noframes					F	Alternate content container for non frame-based rendering
noscript						Alternate content container for non script-based rendering
object						Generic embedded object
ol						Ordered list
optgroup						Option group
option		O				Selectable choice
p		O				Paragraph
param		F	E			Named property value
pre						Preformatted text
q						Short inline quotation
s				D	L	Strike-through text style
samp						Sample program output, scripts, etc.
script						Script statements
select						Option selector
small						Small text style
span						Generic language/style container
strike				D	L	Strike-through text
strong						Strong emphasis
style						Style info
sub						Subscript
sup						Superscript
table						
tbody	O	O				Table body

Name	Start Tag	End Tag	Empty	Depr.	DTD	Description
td		O				Table data cell
textarea						Multi-line text field
tfoot		O				Table footer
th		O				Table header cell
thead		O				Table header
title						Document title
tr		O				Table row
tt						Teletype or monospaced text style
u				D	L	Underlined text style
ul						Unordered list
var						Instance of a variable or program argument

Copyright (c)1997-1999 W3C(r) (MIT, INRIA, Keio), All Rights Reserved. W3C liability, trademark, document use and software licensing rules apply.

HTML 4.01 Attributes

The following list explains the column headings in Table E-2. Read this text first to understand how to read the chart set up by the W3C:

✦ **Name.** This field informs you of the name of the attribute.

✦ **Related Elements.** This field informs you of which elements you can use with the attribute listed.

✦ **Type.** This field informs you of the type of value.

✦ **Default.** This field informs you of the default value of the attribute—if one is applicable.

✦ **Depr.** This cell informs you whether the attribute is deprecated and is denoted with a "D."

✦ **DTD.** This cell informs you of which DTD the attribute can be used with. If the field is empty, it is "Strict;" if it is "L," it is "Transitional;" and if it is an "F," it is a Frameset.

✦ **Comment.** Any other applicable information.

Table E-2
Index of HTML 4.01 Attributes

Name	Related Elements	Type	Default	Depr.	DTD	Comment
abbr	td, th	Plain text	#IMPLIED			Abbreviation for header cell
accept-charset	form	A space-separated list of character encodings, as per RFC2045	#IMPLIED			List of supported charsets
accept	form, input	Comma-separated list of media types, as per RFC2045	#IMPLIED			List of MIME types for file upload
accesskey	a, area, button, input, label, legend, textarea	A single character from ISO10646	#IMPLIED			Accessibility key character
action	form	A Uniform Resource Identifier	#REQUIRED			Server-side form handler
align	caption	(top | bottom | left | right)	#IMPLIED	D	L	Relative to table
align	applet, iframe, img, input, object	(top | middle | bottom | left | right)	#IMPLIED	D	L	Vertical or horizontal alignment
align	legend	(top | bottom | left | right)	#IMPLIED	D	L	Relative to fieldset
align	table	(left | center | right)	#IMPLIED	D	L	Table position relative to window
align	hr	(left | center | right)	#IMPLIED	D	L	
align	div, h1, h2, h3, h4, h5, h6, p	(left | center | right | justify)	#IMPLIED	D	L	Align, text alignment
align	col, colgroup, tbody, td, tfoot, th, thead, tr	(left | center | right | justify | char)	#IMPLIED			
alink	body	A color using sRGB: #RRGGBB as Hex values	#IMPLIED	D	L	Color of selected links
alt	applet	Plain text	#IMPLIED	D	L	Short description

Name	Related Elements	Type	Default	Depr.	DTD	Comment
alt	area, img	Plain text	#REQUIRED			Short description
alt	input	CDATA	#IMPLIED			Short description
archive	applet	CDATA	#IMPLIED	D	L	Comma-separated archive list
archive	object	CDATA	#IMPLIED			Space-separated list of URIs
axis	td, th	CDATA	#IMPLIED			Comma-separated list of related headers
background	body	A Uniform Resource Identifier	#IMPLIED	D	L	Texture tile for document background
bgcolor	table	A color using sRGB: #RRGGBB as Hex values	#IMPLIED	D	L	Background color for cells
bgcolor	tr	A color using sRGB: #RRGGBB as Hex values	#IMPLIED	D	L	Background color for row
bgcolor	td, th	A color using sRGB: #RRGGBB as Hex values	#IMPLIED	D	L	Cell background color
bgcolor	body	A color using sRGB: # RRGGBB as Hex values	#IMPLIED	D	L	Document background color
border	table	Integer representing length in pixels	#IMPLIED around table			Controls frame width
border	img, object	Integer representing length in pixels	#IMPLIED	D	L	Link border width
cellpadding	table	nn for pixels or nn% for percentage length	#IMPLIED			Spacing within cells
cellspacing	table	nn for pixels or nn% for percentage length	#IMPLIED			Spacing between cells
char	col, colgroup, tbody, td, tfoot, th, thead, tr	A single character from ISO10646	#IMPLIED			Alignment char, e.g. char='.'
charoff	col, colgroup, tbody, td, tfoot, th, thead, tr	nn for pixels or nn% for percentage length	#IMPLIED			Offset for alignment char

Continued

Table E-2 *(continued)*

Name	Related Elements	Type	Default	Depr.	DTD	Comment
charset	a, link, script	A space-separated list of character encodings, as per RFC2045	#IMPLIED			Char encoding of linked resource
checked	input	(checked)	#IMPLIED			For radio buttons and check boxes
cite	blockquote, q	A Uniform Resource Identifier	#IMPLIED			URI for source document or msg
cite	del, ins	A Uniform Resource Identifier	#IMPLIED			Info on reason for change
class	all elements but base, basefont, head, html, meta, param, script, style, title	CDATA	#IMPLIED			Space-separated list of classes
classid	object	A Uniform Resource Identifier	#IMPLIED			Identifies an implementation
clear	br	(left | all | right | none)	none	D	L	Control of text flow
code	applet	CDATA	#IMPLIED	D	L	Applet class file
codebase	object	A Uniform Resource Identifier	#IMPLIED			Base URI for classid, data, archive
codebase	applet	A Uniform Resource Identifier	#IMPLIED	D	L	Optional base URI for applet
codetype	object	Media type, as per RFC2045	#IMPLIED			Content type for code
color	basefont, font	A color using sRGB: #RRGGBB as Hex values	#IMPLIED	D	L	Text color
cols	frameset	Comma-separated list of MultiLength	#IMPLIED		F	List of lengths, default: 100% (1 col)
cols	textarea	Number	#REQUIRED			

Name	Related Elements	Type	Default	Depr.	DTD	Comment
colspan	td, th	Number	1			Number of cols spanned by cell
compact	dir, dl, menu, ol, ul	(compact)	#IMPLIED	D	L	Reduced inherited spacing
content	meta	CDATA	#REQUIRED			Associated information
coords	area	Comma-separated list of lengths	#IMPLIED			Comma-separated list of lengths
coords	a	Comma-separated list of lengths	#IMPLIED			For use with client-side image maps
data	object	A Uniform Resource Identifier	#IMPLIED			Reference to object's data
datetime	del, ins	Date and time information. ISO date format	#IMPLIED			Date and time of change
declare	object	(declare)	#IMPLIED			Declare but don't instantiate flag
defer	script	(defer)	#IMPLIED			UA may defer execution of script
dir	all elements but applet, base, basefont, bdo, br, frame, frameset, iframe, param, script	(ltr | rtl)	#IMPLIED			Direction for weak/neutral text
dir	bdo	(ltr | rtl)	#REQUIRED			Directionality
disabled	button, input, optgroup, option, select, textarea	(disabled)	#IMPLIED			Unavailable in this context
enctype	form	Media type, as per RFC2045	"application/x-www-form-urlencoded"			
face	basefont, font	CDATA	#IMPLIED	D	L	Comma-separated list of font names

Continued

Table E-2 (continued)

Name	Related Elements	Type	Default	Depr.	DTD	Comment
for	label	IDREF	#IMPLIED			Matches field ID value
frame	table	(void | above | below | hsides | lhs | rhs | vsides | box | border)	#IMPLIED			Which parts of frame to render
frameborder	frame, iframe	(1 | 0)	1		F	Request frame borders
headers	td, th	IDREFS	#IMPLIED			List of id's for header cells
height	iframe	nn for pixels or nn% for percentage length	#IMPLIED		L	Frame height
height	td, th	nn for pixels or nn% for percentage length	#IMPLIED	D	L	Height for cell
height	img, object	nn for pixels or nn% for percentage length	#IMPLIED			Override height
height	applet	nn for pixels or nn% for percentage length	#REQUIRED	D	L	Initial height
href	a, area, link	A Uniform Resource Identifier	#IMPLIED			URI for linked resource
href	base	A Uniform Resource Identifier	#IMPLIED			URI that acts as base URI
hreflang	a, link	A language code, as per RFC1766	#IMPLIED			Language code
hspace	applet, img, object	Integer representing length in pixels	#IMPLIED	D	L	Horizontal gutter
http-equiv	meta	Name	#IMPLIED			HTTP response header name
id	all elements but base, head, html, meta, script, style, title	ID	#IMPLIED			Document-wide unique id

Name	Related Elements	Type	Default	Depr.	DTD	Comment
ismap	img, input	(ismap)	#IMPLIED			Use server-side image map
label	option	Plain text	#IMPLIED			For use in hierarchical menus
label	optgroup	Plain text	#REQUIRED			For use in hierarchical menus
lang	all elements but applet, base, basefont, br, frame, frameset, iframe, param, script	A language code, as per RFC1766	#IMPLIED			Language code
language	script	CDATA	#IMPLIED	D	L	Predefined script language name
link	body	A color using sRGB: #RRGGBB as Hex values	#IMPLIED	D	L	Color of links
longdesc	img	A Uniform Resource Identifier	#IMPLIED			Link to long description (complements alt)
longdesc	frame, iframe	A Uniform Resource Identifier	#IMPLIED		F	Link to long description (complements title)
marginheight	frame, iframe	Integer representing length in pixels	#IMPLIED		F	Margin height in pixels
marginwidth	frame, iframe	Integer representing length in pixels	#IMPLIED		F	Margin widths in pixels
maxlength	input	Number	#IMPLIED			Max chars for text fields
media	style	Single or comma-separated list of media descriptors	#IMPLIED			Designed for use with these media
media	link	Single or comma-separated list of media descriptors	#IMPLIED			For rendering on these media
method	form	(GET | POST)	GET			HTTP method used to submit the form

Continued

Table E-2 *(continued)*

Name	Related Elements	Type	Default	Depr.	DTD	Comment
multiple	select	(multiple)	#IMPLIED			Default is single selection
name	button, textarea	CDATA	#IMPLIED			
name	applet	CDATA	#IMPLIED	D	L	Allows applets to find each other
name	select	CDATA	#IMPLIED			Field name
name	form	CDATA	#IMPLIED			Name of form for scripting
name	frame, iframe	CDATA	#IMPLIED		F	Name of frame for targetting
name	img	CDATA	#IMPLIED			Name of image for scripting
name	a	CDATA	#IMPLIED			Named link end
name	input, object	CDATA	#IMPLIED			Submit as part of form
name	map	CDATA	#REQUIRED			For reference by usemap
name	param	CDATA	#REQUIRED			Property name
name	meta	NAME	#IMPLIED			Meta information name
nohref	area	(nohref)	#IMPLIED			This region has no action
noresize	frame	(noresize)	#IMPLIED		F	Allow users to resize frames?
noshade	hr	(noshade)	#IMPLIED	D	L	
nowrap	td, th	(nowrap)	#IMPLIED	D	L	Suppress word wrap
object	applet	CDATA	#IMPLIED	D	L	Serialized applet file
onblur	a, area, button, input, label, select, textarea	Script expression	#IMPLIED			The element lost the focus

Name	Related Elements	Type	Default	Depr.	DTD	Comment
onchange	input, select, textarea	Script expression	#IMPLIED			The element value was changed
onclick	all elements but applet, base, basefont, bdo, br, font, frame, frameset, head, html, iframe, isindex, meta, param, script, style, title	Script expression	#IMPLIED			A pointer button was clicked
ondblclick	all elements but applet, base, basefont, bdo, br, font, frame, frameset, head, html, iframe, isindex, meta, param, script, style, title	Script expression	#IMPLIED			A pointer button was double clicked
onfocus	a, area, button, input, label, select, textarea	Script expression	#IMPLIED			The element got the focus
onkeydown	all elements but applet, base, basefont, bdo, br, font, frame, frameset, head, html, iframe, isindex, meta, param, script, style, title	Script expression	#IMPLIED			A key was pressed down
onkeypress	all elements but applet, base, basefont, bdo, br, font, frame, frameset, head, html, iframe, isindex, meta, param, script, style, title	Script expression	#IMPLIED			A key was pressed and released

Continued

Table E-2 (continued)

Name	Related Elements	Type	Default	Depr.	DTD	Comment
onkeyup	all elements but applet, base, basefont, bdo, br, font, frame, frameset, head, html, iframe, isindex, meta, param, script, style, title	Script expression	#IMPLIED			A key was released
onload	frameset	Script expression	#IMPLIED		F	All the frames have been loaded
onload	body	Script expression	#IMPLIED			The document has been loaded
onmousedown	all elements but applet, base, basefont, bdo, br, font, frame, frameset, head, html, iframe, isindex, meta, param, script, style, title	Script expression	#IMPLIED			A pointer button was pressed down
onmousemove	all elements but applet, base, basefont, bdo, br, font, frame, frameset, head, html, iframe, isindex, meta, param, script, style, title	Script expression	#IMPLIED			A pointer was moved within
onmouseout	all elements but applet, base, basefont, bdo, br, font, frame, frameset, head, html, iframe, isindex, meta, param, script, style, title	Script expression	#IMPLIED			A pointer was moved away

Name	Related Elements	Type	Default	Depr.	DTD	Comment
onmouseover	all elements but applet, base, basefont, bdo, br, font, frame, frameset, head, html, iframe, isindex, meta, param, script, style, title	Script expression	#IMPLIED			A pointer was moved onto
onmouseup	all elements but applet, base, basefont, bdo, br, font, frame, frameset, head, html, iframe, isindex, meta, param, script, style, title	Script expression	#IMPLIED			A pointer button was released
onreset	form	Script expression	#IMPLIED			The form was reset
onselect	input, textarea	Script expression	#IMPLIED			Some text was selected
onsubmit	form	Script expression	#IMPLIED			The form was submitted
onunload	frameset	Script expression	#IMPLIED		F	All the frames have been removed
onunload	body	Script expression	#IMPLIED			The document has been removed
profile	head	A Uniform Resource Identifier	#IMPLIED			Named dictionary of meta info
prompt	isindex	Plain text	#IMPLIED	D	L	Prompt message
readonly	textarea	(readonly)	#IMPLIED			
readonly	input	(readonly)	#IMPLIED			For text and passwd
rel	a, link	Space-separated list of link types	#IMPLIED			Forward link types
rev	a, link	Space-separated list of link types	#IMPLIED			Reverse link types
rows	frameset	Comma-separated list of MultiLength	#IMPLIED		F	List of lengths, default: 100% (1 row)

Continued

Table E-2 (continued)

Name	Related Elements	Type	Default	Depr.	DTD	Comment
rows	textarea	Number	#REQUIRED			
rowspan	td, th	Number	1			Number of rows spanned by cell
rules	table	(none | groups | rows | cols | all)	#IMPLIED			Rulings between rows and cols
scheme	meta	CDATA	#IMPLIED			Select form of content
scope	td, th	(row | col | rowgroup | colgroup)	#IMPLIED			Scope covered by header cells
scrolling	frame, iframe	(yes | no | auto)	auto		F	Scrollbar or none
selected	option	(selected)	#IMPLIED			
shape	area	(rect | circle | poly | default)	rect			Controls interpretation of coords
shape	a	(rect | circle | poly | default)	rect			For use with client-side image maps
size	hr	Integer representing length in pixels	#IMPLIED	D	L	
size	font	CDATA	#IMPLIED	D	L	
size	input	CDATA	#IMPLIED			Specific to each type of field
size	basefont	CDATA	#REQUIRED	D	L	Base font size for FONT elements
size	select	Number	#IMPLIED			Rows visible
span	col	Number	1			COL attributes affect N columns
span	colgroup	Number	1			Default number of columns in group

Name	Related Elements	Type	Default	Depr.	DTD	Comment
src	script	A Uniform Resource Identifier	#IMPLIED			URI for an external script
src	input	A Uniform Resource Identifier	#IMPLIED			For fields with images
src	frame, iframe	A Uniform Resource Identifier	#IMPLIED		F	Source of frame content
src	img	A Uniform Resource Identifier	#REQUIRED			URI of image to embed
standby	object	Plain text	#IMPLIED			Message to show while loading
start	ol	Number	#IMPLIED	D	L	Starting sequence number
style	all elements but base, basefont, head, html, meta, param, script, style, title	Style sheet data	#IMPLIED			Associated style info
summary	table	Plain text	#IMPLIED			Purpose/structure for speech output
tabindex	a, area, button, input, object, select, textarea	Number	#IMPLIED			Position in tabbing order
target	a, area, base, form, link	Render in this frame	#IMPLIED		L	Render in this frame
text	body	A color using sRGB: #RRGGBB as Hex values	#IMPLIED	D	L	Document text color
title	all elements but base, basefont, head, html, meta, param, script, title	Plain text	#IMPLIED			Advisory title

Continued

Table E-2 (continued)

Name	Related Elements	Type	Default	Depr.	DTD	Comment
type	a, link	Media type, as per RFC2045	#IMPLIED			Advisory content type
type	object	Media type, as per RFC2045	#IMPLIED			Content type for data
type	param	Media type, as per RFC2045	#IMPLIED			Content type for value when valuetype=ref
type	script	Media type, as per RFC2045	#REQUIRED			Content type of script language
type	style	Media type, as per RFC2045	#REQUIRED			Content type of style language
type	input	(TEXT | PASSWORD | CHECKBOX | RADIO | SUBMIT | RESET | FILE | HIDDEN | IMAGE | BUTTON)	TEXT			What kind of widget is needed
type	li	DISC | SQUARE | CIRCLE or 1 | a | A | i | I	#IMPLIED	D	L	List item style
type	ol	1 | a | A | i | I	#IMPLIED	D	L	Numbering style
type	ul	DISC | SQUARE | CIRCLE	#IMPLIED	D	L	Bullet style
type	button	(button | submit | reset)	submit			For use as form button
usemap	img, input, object	A Uniform Resource Identifier	#IMPLIED			Use client-side image map
valign	col, colgroup, tbody, td, tfoot, th, thead, tr	(top | middle | bottom | baseline)	#IMPLIED			Vertical alignment in cells
value	input	CDATA	#IMPLIED			Specify for radio buttons and checkboxes
value	option	CDATA	#IMPLIED			Defaults to element content
value	param	CDATA	#IMPLIED			Property value

Name	Related Elements	Type	Default	Depr.	DTD	Comment
value	button	CDATA	#IMPLIED			Sent to server when submitted
value	li	Number	#IMPLIED	D	L	Reset sequence number
valuetype	param	(DATA | REF | OBJECT)	DATA			How to interpret value
version	html	CDATA	%HTML. Version;	D	L	Constant
vlink	body	A color using sRGB: #RRGGBB as Hex values	#IMPLIED	D	L	Color of visited links
vspace	applet, img, object	Integer representing length in pixels	#IMPLIED	D	L	Vertical gutter
width	hr	nn for pixels or nn% for percentage length	#IMPLIED	D	L	
width	iframe	nn for pixels or nn% for percentage length	#IMPLIED		L	Frame width
width	img, object	nn for pixels or nn% for percentage length	#IMPLIED			Override width
width	table	nn for pixels or nn% for percentage length	#IMPLIED			Table width
width	td, th	nn for pixels or nn% for percentage length	#IMPLIED	D	L	Width for cell
width	applet	nn for pixels or nn% for percentage length	#REQUIRED	D	L	Initial width
width	col	Pixel, percentage, or relative	#IMPLIED			Column width specification
width	colgroup	Pixel, percentage, or relative	#IMPLIED			Default width for enclosed COLs
width	pre	Number	#IMPLIED		L	

Reference

www.w3.org/TR/html4/index/elements.html

www.w3.org/TR/html4/index/attributes.html

◆   ◆   ◆

Overview of the CIW Certification Tracks

There are four Certified Internet Webmaster certifications:

✦ CIW Associate

✦ CIW Professional

✦ Master CIW

✦ CIW Certified Instructor

The following sections offer a description of each of the certifications and the requirements for obtaining them.

Note   This following information is provided as a reference only. These certifications and their associated requirements are subject to change at anytime at the discretion of ProsoftTraining Inc. Refer to their Web site at www.ciwcertified.com for up-to-date CIW certification information.

CIW Associate

The CIW Associate is the CIW entry-level certification. It is an acknowledgment that you have the fundamental knowledge that an Internet professional is expected to understand and use. This certification serves as a prerequisite to all other CIW certifications

To gain your CIW Associate Certification you must pass the CIW Foundations Exam (1D0-410) available through either Prometric, Inc. or VUE testing services. You must also fill out the online CIW Certification Agreement available at the following URL: http://www.ciwcertified.com/certifications/3steps.asp

Cross-Reference   See Appendix D for more information regarding this exam

This certification is also available for those who have passed CompTIA's i-Net+ (IKO-001) exam (also available through Prometric and VUE). To obtain your certification you must send the following to Prosoft Training:

✦ A copy of your CompTIA i-Net+ exam score report.

✦ A completed i-Net+ CIW Foundations Exam Credit Application Form. This form is available on the CIW certified website at the following URL: http://www.ciwcertified.com/certifications/3steps.asp

✦ A Processing Fee of $49 (US) (subject to change)

Send all of this information to the following address or fax number:

ProsoftTraining
Certification Programs
3001 Bee Caves Road
Suite 300
Austin, TX 78746 USA
ATTENTION: i-Net+ applications
Fax: 1-512-439-3938

Note   For those of you who wish to obtain your CIW Certified Instructor designation you will be required to pass the CIW Foundations Exam regardless of your iNet+ status.

CIW Professional

The second level of certification in the CIW certification group is CIW Professional. To earn this level of certification you must first qualify for your CIW Associate certification and pass at least one of the eight industry-recognized, job-role specific exams chosen from any one of the four Master CIW certification tracks. A complete listing of these job-role specific exams can be found under the Master CIW heading below.

Master CIW

You may gain your Master CIW status by completing any one of the four Master CIW tracks, including the following:

✦ Master CIW Administrator

✦ Master CIW Enterprise Developer

✦ Master CIW Designer

✦ Master CIW Web Site Administrator

Each one of these certification tracks focuses on one of the four main job-related fields of expertise found in today's corporate networks. A description of each of these Master CIW certifications follows.

Master CIW Administrator

The focus of this track is on obtaining the skills to be a functional and competent network administrator. To complete this track you must first pass the Foundations Certification Exam, and then complete three job-specific CIW exams.

Master CIW Enterprise Developer

The Master CIW Enterprise Developer track is a very compressive track focusing on giving you the skills necessary to develop multi-tier database and legacy connectivity solutions for Web-enabled applications. Along with the CIW Associate certification, this track requires the completion of three job-specific exams and four Web language exams.

Master CIW Designer

The Master CIW Designer Track is for those individuals who wish to obtain the skills to design and create functional, well-designed Web sites. To obtain this certification you must obtain the CIW Associate certification and complete two job-specific exams.

Master CIW Web Site Manager

The newest of the CIW Master series certifications, Master CIW Web Site Manager, is a certification for those wishing to understand and apply the skills required to administer and implement Web sites. This certification requires you to obtain the CIW Associate certification, pass two language exams, and two job-specific exams.

CIW Certified Instructor

The CIW Certified Instructor (CIW CI) certification is for those individuals who wish to deliver ProsoftTraining Certified Internet Webmaster official curriculum courses. The following are the requirements that you must complete in order to obtain your CIW CI certification:

✦ Obtain your CIW Associate certification.

Note All CIW CIs are required to pass the CIW Foundations Exam (1D0-410), regardless of their CompTIA's i-Net+ status.

✦ Complete and submit the online CIW CI Application. This form is available at http://www.ciwcertified.com/apps/CIProgramApplication

✦ Show proof of attendance in a CIW Foundations course that has been offered through a CIW Authorized Training Provider. This requires the faxing of your official course Attendance Certificate to the following number: 512-439-3938.

This requirement can be waived for those individuals who have obtained their CIW Professional certification or hold a valid Instructor Certification in any of the following:

- Certified Novell Instructor (CNI)
- Microsoft Certified Trainer (MCT)
- Certified Technical Trainer (CTT)
- Certified Lotus Instructor (CLI)
- Santa Cruz Operations Certified Instructor
- Cisco Certified Academic Instructor (CCAI)
- Sun Microsystems

An Instructor Waiver Form is available at the following address at http://www.ciwcertifed.com/faq/CIfaq.asp

✦ Show proof of instructional experience. This experience can include any of the following:

- Technical Instructor certificate or transcript from an industry-recognized certification track (Microsoft Certified Trainer certificate, for example)
- A Train-the-Trainer Certificate. Several organizations offer Train-the-Trainer courses for other organizations wishing to train their employees to deliver training either to customers or to other employees. You may wish to contact your Human Resources department to see if your organization currently has such an arrangement.
- An accredited teaching certificate (Bachelors of Education, for example)
- A T-Prep curse completion certificate. T-Preps are instructor readiness courses conducted by Prosoft Training, Inc. for instructor candidates.
- A current resume, two letters of recommendation, and ten student evaluations.

✦ You must also have passed the corresponding CIW exam for any of the CIW courses you wish to instruct.

Any questions regarding the CIW CI certification program can be directed to the following e-mail address: ciw.ci@ciwcertified.com

✦　✦　✦

Glossary

Access Control The power to limit the abilities of a user with respect to a resource.

Active Content Macros or embedded scripts that are created using technologies such as ActiveX or JavaScript, which allow dynamic or changing objects within Web pages.

AppleTalk A proprietary protocol suite that was designed by Apple Corporation for use by their Apple Macintosh computers to share files and printers in a networked environment.

Applets Java programs downloaded from Web pages and executed within a browser.

Application Layer The top layer in the Internet architecture model, it is responsible for providing network access to applications. Protocols at this level include: HTTP, FTP, TFTP, SMTP, NNTP, DNS, SNMP, BOOTP, and DHCP.

Application-Level Gateway This firewall component analyzes data packets at the Application Layer of the OSI/RM and can filter traffic on an application-by-application basis.

ARP Both a protocol and a command line utility, the Address Resolution Protocol is used by computers to identify a MAC address given its corresponding IP address. Successful resolution is stored in a computer's ARP table. The `arp` command line utility is used to view and manipulate a computer's ARP table.

Asset A resource held by an organization that is considered to be of value.

Asymmetric Encryption A form of encryption based on key pairs in which data encrypted with one of the two keys can only be decrypted by using the other key.

Attachment A file sent along with an e-mail message.

Attenuation Degradation of data signals as they flow through the transmission media.

Attribute Indicates or identifies a specific characteristic about the element. For example, "BGCOLOR" in the following tag is considered an attribute:

<BODY BGCOLOR="red">

Authentication The process of proving one's identity. User IDs and passwords are commonly used for authentication.

Back-end Another name for a server in the client/server network model.

Bandwidth The transmission capacity of a given medium.

Baseband A data transmission method in which the message takes all of the bandwidth of the cable, thus leaving no room to carry any other signals. Therefore, only one signal can travel on the transmission media at any one time. Baseband transmission is the most common transmission type used in local area networks (LANs).

Bastion Any device that performs firewall services.

Binary A number system in which only the numbers 0 and 1 are used to represent any value.

Binding See Protocol Binding.

BinHex An attachment encoding a mechanism developed for use in the Apple Macintosh environment. BinHex encoded files can be identified by their .hqx extensions.

Biometrics In computer science, this is a form of authentication based on human characteristics, such as fingerprints, retina scans, speech, etc.

Bit One binary digit, either a 0 or a 1.

Block-level Element Any HTML element designed to affect a block of text, such as a paragraph.

Boolean Operator A word or symbol, such as "+", "-", "AND", "OR", or "NOT", which may be used while specifying search criteria in a search engine. Boolean operators help you direct your search to better meet your needs by allowing you to include or exclude certain words or phrases in the results.

Bridge A device used to divide a network into multiple segments in an effort to increase network efficiency and performance. Bridges segment traffic based on MAC address information; as such, they operate at the Data Link Layer of the OSI/RM.

Broadband A data transmission method in which several signals may be transmitted at any one time.

Broadcast A network packet sent to all hosts on a network.

Brouter Brouters operate at both the Data Link Layer and Network Layer of the OSI/RM; as such, they combine the strength of both Bridges and Routers.

Byte The amount of storage required to store a single character (such as the letter "A"); 1 byte is equivalent to 8 bits.

Caching Server Typically associated with Web servers and clients, a caching server is a service that is dedicated to storing data retrieved by users. Subsequent requests for the same information can then be retrieved directly from the caching server as opposed to requiring clients to retrieve the data from the originating server.

Cascading Style Sheets (CSS) Style sheets that allow Web site designers to define how page elements, such as headings, links, and text, appear on all pages following the style sheet.

Catalog Server A server that performs indexing of information distributed across a network. It allows users to look for information in one central location. Locating information is further simplified because catalog servers typically allow the searches based on a variety of different criteria, such as document creation dates, author name, key words contained in the document, and so on.

Certificate Server Distributes and verifies digital certificates or electronic keys. These digital certificates can be used to verify the identities of parties involved in electronic data exchange.

Circuit Level Gateway A device that operates at the Transport Layer of the OSI/RM. These devices accept packets from clients, and they perform a check of the packets against a set of predefined rules. If the packets are deemed acceptable, the Circuit Level Gateway then forwards them to the appropriate destination having modified the packet in such a way that the packet appears to have originated at the Circuit Level Gateway.

Client Any system or application that requests access to resources or services from a server.

Client/Server Network Model A decentralized network architecture in which the processing of information is split between both a client computer and a server computer.

Container Tags Tags that work in pairs — one tag at the start of an element and another at the end of an element.

Cookie A small text file given by a Web server to a Web browser to be saved on the Web browser's hard drive. The contents of this file can be derived from your actions while visiting the Web site, or by your responses from filling out a form at the Web site. The Web server can reference this file later during subsequent visits to the Web site in many cases to present you with custom Web pages.

CSMA/CD Carrier Sense Multiple Access with Collision Detection is a transmission media access method used in Ethernet networks to control when a network node can send data. See also Token passing.

CSU/DSU Used to format and send data over a variety of different WAN connection media, a CSU/DSU is a device that combines a Channel Service Unit (CSU) and a Data Service Unit (DSU). The CSU component is responsible for performing error reporting and diagnostics testing for a telecommunications line. The DSU component converts digital data signals used in a LANs to and from bipolar signals used over WAN transmission media, such as T1 or T3 lines.

Daemon A process on a UNIX-based computer that operates in the background and reacts to specific events. For example, the Line Printer Daemon is a print server service that typically runs in a UNIX/LINUX environment; its main duty is to react to print requests by forwarding them on to managed print devices.

Demultiplexing A term used to describe the method that a receiving computer processes an incoming data packet.

Direct Routing When the source and destination of a packet is on the same physical network segment. See indirect routing

Directory Server A server whose job is to provide a database of network resources.

Disk Cache A storage area on your computer for storing accessed data to speed up subsequent requests for the same data. Web browsers keep a copy of Web pages visited in a disk cache, thus future visits to these sites can use the local copy of these Web pages rather then requiring the Web page to be downloaded again.

Dithering The process a computer uses to estimate color by mixing a combination of RGB.

Document Type Declaration (DTD) A definition placed into an HTML, SGML, or XML document that defines how the document should be interpreted by a client application.

Domain Name Server (DNS Server) A server that provides host name-to-IP address resolution services via the domain name system.

Domain Name System A hierarchical system developed for the Internet that maps Fully Qualified Domain Names to IP addresses.

Domain Name A name used to identify an entity on the Internet, such as a company or other organization. For example, `ibm.com` is a domain name that identifies IBM on the Internet.

Dynamic Host Configuration Protocol (DHCP) DHCP is a protocol that supports the automatic assignment of TCP/IP configuration information to network hosts.

Dynamic Host Configuration A method used to automate the task of assignment of TCP/IP configuration information requiring the use of a Dynamic host configuration (DHCP) protocol server.

Dynamic Link Library (DLL) A program subroutine that can be shared among several applications.

Dynamic Router A router that shares routing information with other routers by using some form of routing protocol, such as RIP or OSPF.

Dynamic Web Page A complex Web document that may consist of data drawn from several sources compiled together at the time the page is requested.

Electronic Data Interchange (EDI) A standard format developed for exchanging electronic data between organizations using a network such as the Internet.

E-Mail Server A server that has the ability to store retrieve and forward e-mail messages.

E-mail Signature A few lines of text that can be automatically added to the bottom of all outgoing messages. It is very common to use a signature to place the sender's name, address, and other contact information onto a message.

Empty Tags Tags that don't have corresponding closing tags.

Encryption The process of scrambling data to protect data.

Event Handler A process that reacts to user input, such as moving or clicking of the mouse.

Exterior Routing Protocols Protocols used to share routing information with routers external to an organization. The two most common exterior routing protocols are Exterior Gateway Protocol (EGP) and Border Gateway protocol (BGP).

Extranet An Internet-accessible Web site that restricts access to its users. For example, an organization may create an extranet by opening up portions of their intranet for customers or business partners.

File Transfer Protocol (FTP) A protocol used to transfer files between client and server FTP applications. FTP requires TCP as a transport protocol to provide connection-oriented file transfers.

Firewall A system made up of one or more devices, such as computers, which is designed to prevent and control unauthorized access to a private network. Firewalls may also be used to limit internal user's access beyond the private network.

Front-end Another name for a client in a client/server network model.

FTP Server A server that allows the transfer of files between a client and server by using the FTP protocol.

Full-Duplex Transmission Two-way communication between devices in which both can send and receive at the same time (a phone call, for example). See also Simplex Data Transmission and Half-Duplex Transmission.

Fully Qualified Domain Names — FQDN The names used to contact computers on the Internet are referred to as fully qualified domain names or FQDNs. FQDNs are written as three or more labels, consisting of letters and numbers, and separated by periods. An example of a FQDN is `www.somedomain.com`.

Gateway A device or service that provides translation services from one protocol to another.

Gigabyte 1,024 Megabytes.

Half-Duplex Transmission Two-way communication between devices where only one device can transmit at a time (a CB radio or Walkie-Talkie, for example). See also Simplex Data Transmission and Full-Duplex Transmission.

Hexadecimal The base 16 number system that uses 16 unique symbols to represent values. As with the base 10 system, hexadecimal uses the numbers 0 to 9 but also includes the letters A through F to represent the digits 10, 11, 12, 13, 14, and 15, respectively. This system allows the representation of very large numbers with relatively few digits.

Home Page The default Web page that the Web server hands out when no specific file has been requested.

Hop A routing term referring to the number of routers that a packet must travel through to get to its destination.

Host ID The last portion of an IP address. The host ID is used to uniquely identify a particular host on a network segment.

Host Name A name given to a computer in a TCP/IP network. The host name is the first part of a Fully Qualified Domain Name; for example, the host name of the FQDN of `www.somedomain.com` is `www`.

Host A host is any computer that provides information to other computers through a network. It is, however, common to also to use the term "host" to refer to any computer attached to a network, including a client or a workstation.

HTTP Gateway A Web server process that acts as a gateway between a client and back-end service process, such as a database application.

Hub The central connection device in an Ethernet star-based network. Devices are plugged into ports on the hub; when one device sends data signals to the hub, they are regenerated and sent to all other devices connected to the hub. Due to the fact that they regenerate signals, they are often referred to as *multi-port repeaters*. Hubs work at the Physical Layer of the OSI/RM.

Hyperlink An element on a Web page that, when clicked, forces your browser to jump to a specific location, which may be on the same Web page or at some other location.

Hypertext Markup Language (HTML) The standard Web page authoring language.

Hypertext Transfer Protocol (HTTP) A protocol designed to transfer HTML Web pages. Web browsers typically act as the client making HTTP requests for documents from HTTP (Web) servers.

Image links Hyperlinks created from images, such that when a user clicks the image, they are taken to the hyperlink's destination.

Image Maps A specific location on an image that has been defined as a hyperlink. One image may have several image maps.

Indirect Routing The routing that must occur when the source and destination of a packet of data do not reside on the same physical network segment. In other words, indirect routing occurs when packets must pass through a router to reach their destination.

Interior Routing Protocols Protocols used to share routing information with routers that are within an organization's network. The two common interior routing protocols that you should be aware of: Routing Information Protocol (RIP) and Open Shortest Path First (OSPF).

Internal Links Hyperlinks that jump to a specific location on the same Web page where the hyperlink resides.

Internet Architecture Model Similar to and based upon the OSI/RM, this standards model breaks up the TCP/IP communication process into four layers: Network Access Layer, Internet Layer, Transport Layer, and Application Layer.

Internet Control Message Protocol (ICMP) Typically used by routers and hosts as an error reporting protocol. For example, if a router encounters problems when trying to determine the destination for a packet, it may issue an ICMP error packet informing the source of the problem.

Internet Group Management Protocol (IGMP) A protocol used to establish and maintain in multicast groups.

Internet Layer The second layer of the Internet architecture model, it is responsible for addressing and routing TCP/IP packets; protocols at this level include: IP, ARP, RARP, IGMP, and ICMP.

Internet Messaging Access Protocol (IMAP) A protocol that allows a user to access e-mails currently stored on a mail server. Unlike POP, however, IMAP allows a user to browse and manage e-mails remotely without requiring the e-mails to be downloaded to the client first.

Internet Protocol (IP) A TCP/IP protocol providing two primary functions—addressing and fragmentation. Regarding addressing, IP is responsible for placing the appropriate address information on all packets to be sent and for choosing the appropriate route through which to send the packets. Regarding fragmentation, IP determines the maximum packet size for the segment to which the computer is attached and to fragment data packets when required.

Internet Protocol Address A unique 32-bit number assigned to a host to identify the location of a host on a network.

Internet Service Providers (ISP) A company or organization that provides access to the Internet to either individuals, organizations, or both.

Intranet An intranet is an Internet-like Web site that an organization has set up for the exclusive use of its employees. An intranet typically contains links to organization-specific data.

Ipconfig A command line utility used to display current TCP/IP configuration information for a Windows NT/2000 host. (Similar to `winipcfg` for Windows 95,98 and ME.)

IPX/SPX A routable protocol suite commonly used in Novell Netware operating systems.

Java Servlet A server-based Java program that is used to extend the functionality of the server.

Java Virtual Machine An operating system that runs on another operating system to allow Java programs to execute.

Key A string of characters used along with an encryption or decryption algorithm to encode or decode encrypted data.

Kilobyte 1,024 Bytes.

Legacy browser Any older browser that may not be capable of dealing with the latest advancements in Web technology and therefore, may limit one's ability to view such content.

Local Area Network (LAN) A network in which all components are in the same small geographic area.

Loopback Address The address 127.0.0.1 is an IP address that has been reserved as the Loopback address. Its purpose is to allow the testing of TCP/IP software regardless of the state of the physical connection to the network. If you ping 127.0.0.1, you will get a response if TCP/IP is bound to your network card.

MAC address A globally unique 48-bit address assigned to a network card. The MAC address is written as a 12-digit hexadecimal number.

Mailing Lists An electronic mailing list is a group of e-mail addresses belonging to individuals interested in a particular subject. E-mails sent to the mailing list are passed on to all those who belong to or subscribe to the list.

Mainframe Network Model A centralized network architecture in which all devices are controlled by a powerful central computer known as a *mainframe*. The mainframe is also responsible for all processing.

Markup Tag HTML elements enclosed in brackets that give instructions to browsers or other interpreters. Tags may consist of an element name, attributes, and values.

Media Server A server that provides streaming media over a network. Streaming media is either video or sound that is provided by the server in a continuous fashion.

Megabyte 1,024 Kilobytes.

Meta Tag A tag used to provide information about your Web site so it can be located by search engines.

Meta-Language A language such as SGML that is used to define other languages, such as HTML.

MIME Multi-purpose Internet Mail Extensions is a common method of encoding and decoding file attachments within e-mails and Web pages.

Modem Historically, this has been a device that allows a computer to send data to other computer over a standard telephone line. More recently, however, the term *modem* has been used to describe any device that translates the computer's digital format into a format that can be carried over a communication's network.

Multicast A network packet sent to a subset of computers on a network.

Multiplexing A term used to describe how the various layers of the Internet architecture model are combined to build a complete data packet.

Multi-Port Repeater See Hub.

Name Resolvers Client DNS software that has been configured with at least one address of a name server, which will be used to resolve IP addresses from names unknown to the client.

Name Server Servers that can be called upon for name-to-IP address resolution.

NetBEUI A small, fast, and efficient Transport and Network Layer non-routable protocol developed by IBM and often found in Microsoft-based networks.

Netiquette A set of rules and practices that encourage politeness and respect, which should be followed when communicating with others on the Internet.

Netstat A command line utility that is used to display protocol statistics and current TCP/IP network connection information.

Network Access Layer The lowest layer of the Internet architecture model, it provides the same services as those found in the Physical and Data Link Layers of the OSI/RM. Dependant on the underlying architecture of the network, such as Ethernet, Token Ring, etc.

Network Access Point (NAP) A point at which two or more major ISPs high speed networks interconnect.

Network Analyzer Often referred to as *packet sniffers*, network analyzers allow administrators to capture and analyze data crossing a network. The analysis can include network usage statistics protocol analysis, as well as individual packet analysis.

Network ID The first part of any host's IP address is its network ID. The network ID identifies what network—or more specifically—what network segment to which a particular host belongs. All computers in the same network segment must have the same network ID.

Network Interface Card (NIC) A device installed into a network node, such as a computer, to allow the node to connect to the network.

Network News Transfer Protocol (NNTP) A protocol used to exchange newsgroup articles, such USENET postings.

Network Operating System (NOS) Computer software responsible for managing and providing access to resources and services on the network.

Network Topology A physical topology describes the shape or layout of a network; common network topologies include: Bus, Star, Ring, Mesh, and Hybrid.

Network Two or more computers connected together for the purpose of sharing resources.

Newsgroups Electronic bulletin-board type discussion forums that interested parties can access to read messages (referred to as *postings*), share ideas, ask questions, submit answers, and generally discuss topics of common interest — all in a text-based format.

Node Any device on a TCP/IP network capable of sending and receiving TCP/IP data packets.

Nonrepudiation The inability of either party involved in a transaction to deny that the transaction occurred.

One-Way Encryption A form of encryption in which data is put through an algorithm to form a unique hash value that can't be unencrypted. Hash values are often generated to confirm that data has not been tampered with.

Open Shortest Path First (OSPF) A common interior routing protocol often used by dynamic routers to exchange routing table information. Routers are configured to support OSPF. Unlike RIP, OSPF only sends routing table update messages when changes actually occur and even then, it only sends the changes themselves — not its entire routing table. OSPF uses variable route selection, which allows for load balancing and selection of the best route — not necessarily the shortest route.

Open System Interconnection Reference Model (OSI/RM) A set of standards that outline the process of preparing data for transmission across a network.

Packet Filter A device that examines each packet as it is sent through a series of rules (the rules dictate whether the packet can be forwarded on or not). The packet filter may be used to ensure that only data packets coming from acceptable sources are allowed to pass into a secure network.

Packet A discrete unit of data transmitted across a network. Packets consist of three parts: Header, Data, and Trailer.

Patch Panels A collection of sockets mounted together for organizing network cables, typically found in network wiring closets.

Peer-to-Peer Networks A network in which all computers can act as both clients and servers.

PING A utility used to test connectivity between systems in a TCP/IP environment.

Plug-in An application that is installed into a browser to increase its abilities. For example, a plug-in may give a Web browser the ability to display video.

Port Numbers Numbers ranging from 0 to 65535 that are used by both UDP and TCP to distinguish their various services.

Post Office Protocol (POP) A protocol used to retrieve mail stored on an e-mail server. The current version is POP3.

Private IP Addresses Ranges of IP addresses that have been deemed non-routable on the Internet. Internet backbone routers are configured to drop any data packet with a destination address that falls within these ranges. The ranges include: 192.168.0.0 to 192.168.255.255, 172.16.0.0 to 172.32.255.255, and 10.0.0.0 to 10.255.255.255

Protocol Binding The assigning of a protocol to a network interface card (NIC).

Protocol A set of rules that a device or service follows in order to communicate with others.

Proxy Server Used for increasing both security and performance of a network. It acts as an intermediary between clients and servers, thus preventing direct communication between them. Proxy servers can support the caching of server responses for future requests for the same data, thus improving the response time to the client.

Pull Technology An interaction where data is sent to a client only after it has been requested by that client.

Push Technology An interaction in which a server sends data to a client without the client making a specific request for it.

Registrar An organization that may register domain names for others to allow them to have a presence on the Internet.

Repeater A device installed onto a network to regenerate data signals to prevent data loss due to attenuation. Repeaters operate at the Physical Layer of the OSI/RM.

Request for Comments (RFC) Published standards documents that are maintained by the Internet Engineering Task Force (IETF). The purpose of these documents is to lay out specifications and standards for the various protocols and services currently used on the Internet.

Reverse Address Resolution (RARP) A protocol used to find an IP address based on a particular MAC address. Diskless workstations, for example, will issue a RARP when they first start up so they can obtain an IP address for themselves.

Root Level Domain Denoted simply by a period (.). Serves as the top of the DNS name space.

Router A protocol-specific device that is used to either link networks together or to break a large network into smaller networks (often referred to as *subnets*). Routers operate at the Network Layer.

Routing Information Protocol (RIP) A common interior routing protocol often used by dynamic routers to exchange routing table information. Routers configured to support RIP will send their complete routing tables every thirty seconds across all network segments connected to the router. Routers sharing any of these segments receive the tables, update their own to reflect any new information, and then broadcast their tables across all network segments that they are connected to, thus propagating any changes across the network. Route selection is always based on least number of hops.

Routing Table When a router obtains a packet of data through indirect routing, it must determine where to send the packet in order for it to reach its intended destination. To do this, the router consults its routing table. A routing table is a list of known networks, the path to those networks, and an indication of where those networks are in relation to the router (often listed as a hop count or metric).

Search Engine A Web-based application that allows users to search the Internet for specific information. Lycos, Excite, Yahoo!, AltaVista, and Google are examples of some of the many search engines available.

Second Level Domain A domain directly below a top level domain in the domain name system. In most cases, the second level domain identifies an organization, such as `microsoft.com`, `ibm.com`, and `whitehouse.gov`.

Secure MIME (S/MIME) Secure Multi-purpose Internet Mail Extensions is a common method of securely encoding and decoding file attachments within e-mails and Web pages. S/MIME uses the Rivest-Shamir-Adleman (RSA) encryption system.

Server Any computer or application that provides services or resources to other computers.

Server-Based Networks A network in which computers act as either clients or servers, but not both.

Shell A term usually used in the UNIX environment that refers to the interface the user works with to interact with the operating system.

Simple Mail Transport Protocol (SMTP) SMTP is the mail transfer protocol for the TCP/IP suite. SMTP is used to send e-mail from a client to a server or from one e-mail server to another. SMTP is typically used in conjunction with Post Office Protocol Version 3 (POP3) or Internet Message Access Protocol Version 4 (IMAP4).

Simple Network Management Protocol (SNMP) A protocol often used for managing and monitoring TCP/IP-based network devices, such as routers, switches, and servers. Many hardware vendors produce devices that allow administrators to manage them remotely from a management utility by using SNMP.

Simplex Data Transmission A form of signal transmission in which the signals can travel in only one direction (a Public Address system, for example). See Half-Duplex and Full-Duplex Transmission.

Smart Card A small card similar in size, shape, and appearance to a credit card. It contains an embedded computer chip that can hold the data. These devices are often used for authentication purposes.

Social Engineering A non-technical form of security attack that typically features the hacker tricking employees or others into revealing information that may allow the hacker access to a network.

Spider A program used by a Web search engine designed to locate Web pages so they may be indexed and then later retrieved during future search requests.

Static Host Configuration The process of manually assigning TCP/IP configuration information to a network node.

Static Router A router that has been manually configured and does not participate in route sharing with other routers.

Sub-domain A division of a second level domain in the domain name system. The name *radio* is a sub-domain in the following: www.radio.cbc.ca.

Subnet Mask The role of the subnet mask is to tell the computer what part of its IP address is the network ID and what part is the host ID. For example, if a computer has an IP address of 141.11.22.1 and a subnet mask of 255.255.0.0, then the computer knows that it has a network address of 141.11.0.0 and a host address of 0.0.22.1 on that network.

Switch A device often used as the central connection point in a star topology network. These devices can direct signals from a source to a destination. Layer 2 switches work at the Data Link layer of the OSI/RM Layer 3 at the Network Layer and Layer 4 at the Transport Layer.

Symmetric Encryption Encryption in which the same key is used to both encrypt and decrypt the data.

TCP/IP The protocol suite of the Internet, it is an open standard routable protocol suite.

Telnet Telnet is a protocol used to support terminal emulation sessions from a client to a server.

Text Level Elements Any HTML element designed to affect a single unit of text such as a letter, a word, or a sentence.

The Hacker Process The three stages that a hacker will go through to compromise a network or system: Discovery, Penetration, and Control.

Threat Anyone who would take advantage of a vulnerability in a system.

Three-tier computing An extension of the client/server networking model in which a client computer acts as the first tier, an intermediary application server (usually a Web server) as the second tier, and usually a database server as the third tier.

Token Passing A media access technique in which access to the network transmission media is controlled through the use of a token. Only the network node with the token may send data. This is the access method of both Token ring and FDDI-based networks.

Top Level Domain A domain directly below the root in the domain name system. Examples of top level domains include: .com, .org, .edu, .ca, and .au.

Topology See Network Topology.

Trace Route Utility A TCP/IP diagnostic utility that displays the routing path that a packet of data takes from its source to its destination.

Transaction Server A server whose primary job is to coordinate all of the tasks involved in completing an online transaction.

Transmission Control Protocol (TCP) A connection-oriented TCP/IP transport layer protocol used to establish and maintain logical connections between computers to ensure error-free transmission of data.

Transmission Media The manner in which the various components of the network connect. There are many different types of transmission media, including network cable, microwave, and radio transmission.

Transport Layer The third layer in the Internet architecture model, it is responsible for providing communication sessions between computers. Protocols at this level include TCP and UDP.

Trivial File Transfer Protocol (TFTP) Similar to FTP, TFTP is a protocol used to transfer files between clients and servers. Unlike FTP, however, TFTP uses the UDP connectionless transport protocol and does not require nor support user authentication. These major differences make TFTP very small and simple. This protocol is often used by diskless workstations and some routers to obtain configuration information during their startup process.

Trojan horse A program that appears to act in one manner but contains code that can carry out additional unexpected and often malicious actions.

Two-tier computing Also known as Client/Server computing where the client acts as the first tier and the server as the second tier. (See also three-tier computing)

Unicast A network packet sent to a specific host on a network.

Universal Resource Locator (URL) A form of addressing in which not only a location of a resource is supplied but also the protocol or method that is used to access that resource.

USENET A publicly accessible collection of thousands of newsgroups and mailing lists on the Internet.

User Datagram Protocol (UDP) A connectionless TCP/IP transport layer protocol used to send data between two computers. Unlike TCP, UDP does not guarantee delivery. The sending computer simply sends the data; it will make a best effort to get it to the destination computer but it does not expect nor ask for any acknowledgement of the packets received by the client. It is up to the client machine to compensate for packets that do not arrive. Applications that use UDP typically transfer small amounts of data at a time.

UUcoding UNIX to UNIX encoding (UUCODE) is an older method of encoding and decoding e-mail attachments. Once extremely popular in the UNIX environment, this method has been largely replaced by MIME. (The common acronym is UUEN-CODE).

Viewer A small application that allows the viewing of the contents of a specific file type. For example, a Microsoft PowerPoint viewer allows you to view the contents of files saved in a PowerPoint format.

Virtual Directories A virtual directory is simply a Web path name given to a physical folder. This physical directory can be a subfolder within the Web root, a separate folder altogether on the server's file systems, or a file location on a different server.

Virtual Domain A domain name hosted on a third party ISP server. An organization may want an Internet presence but lack the expertise to manage a Web server; thus, they may rely on an ISP to do so.

Vulnerability A weakness in a system that can be exploited.

Web Server A Web server, or as it is also known, an HTTP server, is a computer that runs the HTTP server service. The main purpose of this service is to supply HTTP clients with documents referred to as Web pages.

WHOIS A TCP/IP utility that allows you to find information regarding the owner of second-level domain names on the Internet.

Wide Area Network (WAN) The interconnection of geographically separate LANs.

Winipcfg A graphical utility that displays TCP/IP configuration information for a Windows 95, 98, and ME based computer. (Similar to `ipconfig` in Windows NT and 2000.)

Wireless Application Protocol (WAP) A set of communication protocols that allow communication with wireless devices, such as cell phones.

Wireless Markup language (WML) A markup language used to create Web pages that can be displayed on wireless devices, such as cell phones.

Workstation The term once reserved for high end-desk top computers, it now generally means any computer at which a user sits to run applications.

World Wide Web Consortium (W3C) An international standards body dedicated to developing and promoting standards for the World Wide Web.

X.500 A directory access protocol that allows for the creation of distributed directory service. A single directory service database may be distributed and shared between many directory servers, thus forming a global directory.

Index

Continued

Continued

Hungry Minds, Inc.
End-User License Agreement

READ THIS. You should carefully read these terms and conditions before opening the software packet(s) included with this book ("Book"). This is a license agreement ("Agreement") between you and Hungry Minds, Inc. ("HMI"). By opening the accompanying software packet(s), you acknowledge that you have read and accept the following terms and conditions. If you do not agree and do not want to be bound by such terms and conditions, promptly return the Book and the unopened software packet(s) to the place you obtained them for a full refund.

1. **License Grant.** HMI grants to you (either an individual or entity) a nonexclusive license to use one copy of the enclosed software program(s) (collectively, the "Software") solely for your own personal or business purposes on a single computer (whether a standard computer or a workstation component of a multi-user network). The Software is in use on a computer when it is loaded into temporary memory (RAM) or installed into permanent memory (hard disk, CD-ROM, or other storage device). HMI reserves all rights not expressly granted herein.

2. **Ownership.** HMI is the owner of all right, title, and interest, including copyright, in and to the compilation of the Software recorded on the disk(s) or CD-ROM ("Software Media"). Copyright to the individual programs recorded on the Software Media is owned by the author or other authorized copyright owner of each program. Ownership of the Software and all proprietary rights relating thereto remain with HMI and its licensers.

3. **Restrictions On Use and Transfer.**

   (a) You may only (i) make one copy of the Software for backup or archival purposes, or (ii) transfer the Software to a single hard disk, provided that you keep the original for backup or archival purposes. You may not (i) rent or lease the Software, (ll) copy or reproduce the Software through a LAN or other network system or through any computer subscriber system or bulletin-board system, or (iii) modify, adapt, or create derivative works based on the Software.

   (b) You may not reverse engineer, decompile, or disassemble the Software. You may transfer the Software and user documentation on a permanent basis, provided that the transferee agrees to accept the terms and conditions of this Agreement and you retain no copies. If the Software is an update or has been updated, any transfer must include the most recent update and all prior versions.

4. **Restrictions on Use of Individual Programs.** You must follow the individual requirements and restrictions detailed for each individual program in Appendix A of this Book. These limitations are also contained in the individual license agreements recorded on the Software Media. These limitations may include a requirement that after using the program for a specified period of time, the user must pay a registration fee or discontinue use. By opening the Software packet(s), you will be agreeing to abide by the licenses and restrictions for these individual programs that are detailed in Appendix A and on the Software Media. None of the material on this Software Media or listed in this Book may ever be redistributed, in original or modified form, for commercial purposes.